AA007902

Natural Legal Language Processing Workshop (NLLP 2024)

Miami, Florida, USA
16 November 2024

ISBN: 979-8-3313-0849-0

Printed from e-media with permission by:

Curran Associates, Inc.
57 Morehouse Lane
Red Hook, NY 12571

Some format issues inherent in the e-media version may also appear in this print version.

Association for Computational Linguistics
209 N. Eighth Street
Stroudsburg, Pennsylvania 18360

Phone: 1-570-476-8006
Fax: 1-570-476-0860

acl@aclweb.org

Additional copies of this publication are available from:

Curran Associates, Inc.
57 Morehouse Lane
Red Hook, NY 12571 USA
Phone: 845-758-0400
Fax: 845-758-2633
Email: curran@proceedings.com
Web: www.proceedings.com

NLLP 2024

Natural Legal Language Processing Workshop 2024

Proceedings of the Workshop

November 16, 2024

The NLLP organizers gratefully acknowledge the support from the following sponsors.

Gold

Bloomberg Engineering

HUMAN ADS

Order copies of this and other ACL proceedings from:

Association for Computational Linguistics (ACL)
317 Sidney Baker St. S
Suite 400 - 134
Kerrville, TX 78028
USA
Tel: +1-855-225-1962
acl@aclweb.org

Introduction

Welcome to the sixth edition of the NLLP (Natural Legal Language Processing) Workshop, co-located with the 2024 Conference on Empirical Methods in Natural Language Processing.

Different industrial sectors have embraced natural language processing (NLP) technologies, which have altered services and products in healthcare, finance, education among others. The legal domain, in particular, stands as a promising frontier for the exploration of interesting research problems. Electronic tools have become increasingly integral in the practice of law, with their usage projected to undergo exponential growth. By its very nature, the practice of law necessarily involves the analysis and interpretation of language. The potential for NLP applications to provide benefit to practitioners of law and consumers of legal services around the world is enormous.

We organized this workshop to bring together researchers, practitioners, policy makers from around the world who develop NLP techniques within the legal domain. This is an exciting opportunity to expand the boundaries of our field by identifying new problems and exploring new data as it interacts with the full inventory of NLP and machine learning approaches. In this spirit, the Organizing and Program Committee was assembled to include researchers from both academia and industry, from NLP and legal backgrounds.

We were interested in the following types of papers: (1) applications of NLP methods to legal tasks; (2) experimental results using and adapting NLP methods in legal documents; (3) descriptions of new legal tasks for NLP; (4) creation of curated and/or annotated resources; (5) descriptions of systems which use NLP technologies for legal text; (6) industrial research in this area and (7) interdisciplinary position papers.

In addition, this year we introduced The LegalLens Shared Task, organized by Darrow.ai in collaboration with the NLLP2024 workshop including two shared sub-tasks: Sub-Task A. Legal Named Entity Recognition (L-NER): Given possible online media text (review), determine or extract legal entities such as violation,"violation by,"violation on,and law.Sub-Task B. Legal Natural Language Inference (L-NLI): Given a premise summarizing a class action complaint and a hypothesis from an online media text, determine if the relationship is entailed, contradicted, or neutral, indicating any association between the review and the complaint. A total of 87 individual users grouped in 38 teams participated in the shared task, out of which the seven highest-scoring teams were elected to write a system description paper. Most of the teams participated in both sub-tasks.

We once again received an exceptionally high number of submissions. In total, we received 68 submissions on our direct submission website, out of which we accepted 26 for an acceptance rate of 38%. We also received 5 ARR (ACL Rolling Review) commitments -papers that have received reviews and meta-review via the ARR system- of which we accepted 2 for publication. Overall, we accepted 28 papers out of 73 submissions (overall acceptance rate remains 38%) All papers were reviewed by at least 3 members of the Program Committee, one of whom was usually a legal scholar. In addition, we also offered a venue for presentation for 5 papers accepted to the Findings of EMNLP 2024 on the above topics. Finally, the proceedings feature 7 system description papers for the shared task as well as one paper that describes the shared task, for a total of 41 papers. All papers except shared task descriptions were invited to have an oral presentation, either in-person or remote and all papers were invited to participate in the poster session.

The papers cover a wide range of topics including new data sets for legal NLP, position papers on open legal NLP issues, legal perspectives on NLP topics, as well as applications of NLP tasks to legal documents including retrieval, information extraction, generation, legal judgement prediction and statutory reasoning. Again we saw a number of papers explore the use of Large Language Models (LLMs) in the legal domain spanning from fundamental questions to usage methods and applications such as prompting strategies, chain-of-thought applications in retrieval tasks or e-discovery. We note in particular a focus on language model evaluation this year and new legal corpora that we hope will lead to a synergy promoting better modeling and better testing on legal texts going forward.

We thank our invited speaker Omri Ben-Shahar, who is the Leo and Eileen Herzel Professor of Law, and

Kearney Director and founder of the Coase-Sandor Institute for Law and Economics at the University of Chicago Law School for accepting our invitation. In the tradition of past NLLP workshops, the invited speaker is a legal scholar with an interest in empirical methods for legal analysis including NLP methods. His talk is entitled Privacy Protection, At What Cost?which aims to challenge the adequacy of the data privacy protection paradigm and expose the harms to society that certain privacy-fueled protections may cause.

We thank everyone who expressed interest in the workshop, all authors of submitted papers, members of the Program Committee who did an excellent job at reviewing papers given a short turnaround time, everyone attending the workshop and the EMNLP 2024 conference for hosting us and the workshop. We thank our sponsors – Bloomberg and the European Research Council Starting Grant project HUMANads – for their contributions.

The NLLP Workshop organizers.

http://nllpw.org

Organizing Committee

Organizers

Nikolaos Aletras, The University of Sheffield
Ilias Chalkidis, University of Copenhagen
Leslie Barrett, Bloomberg Law
Cătălina Goanță, Utrecht University
Daniel Preoțiuc-Pietro, Bloomberg
Gerasimos Spanakis, Maastricht University

Program Committee

Reviewers

Sallam Abualhaisa, Tomaso Agnoloni, Ion Androutsopoulos, Elliott Ash, Tom Ault

Claire Barale, Thales Bertaglia, Andrew Blair-Stanek, Stephanie Brandl, Baldwin Breck

Rajarathnam Chandramouli, Jiahong Chen, Odysseas Spyridon Chlapanis, Ashish Chouhan

Marina Danilevsky, Tony Davis, Stefania Degaetano-Ortlieb, Arthur Dyevre

Nicolas Garneau, Piyush Ghai, Kimani Goddard

Ben Hagag, Nils Holzenberger

Karthik Kannapur, Daniel Katz, Ken Kawamura, Aykut Koc, Manolis Koubarakis

Ruta Liepina

Pauline McBride, Adam Meyers, Jelena Mitrović

Maria Navas-Loro, Joel Niklaus, Milda Norkute

Kartik Palani, Henrik Palmer Olsen

Georg Rehm

T.Y.S.S. Santosh, Vageesh Saxena, Madhavan Seshadri, Dan Simonson, Jerrold Soh, Alexandru Sotropa

Andrea Tagarelli, Dimitrios Tsarapatsanis

Josef Valvoda, Gijs Van Dijck, Jacob van de Kerkhof, Hellen van der Kroef

Jianqiang Wang, Hannes Westermann, Adam Wyner

Marcos Zampieri, Frederike Zufall

Keynote Talk

Privacy Protection, At What Cost?

Omri Ben-Shahar
University of Chicago Law School

Abstract: Data privacy protection is the dominant paradigm in the regulation of the digital economy. In this keynote lecture, University of Chicago Law Professor Omri Ben-Shahar challenges the adequacy of the data privacy paradigm. He argues that it fails to capture the most worrisome harms—what he calls 'data pollution'—which are inflicted against public rather than private interests. He further demonstrates that privacy-fueled restrictions on valuable data technologies impose a large, mostly unrecognized, harms on society.

Bio: Omri Ben-Shahar earned his PhD in Economics and SJD from Harvard in 1995 and his BA and LLB from the Hebrew University in 1990. Before coming to Chicago, he was the Kirkland & Ellis Professor of Law and Economics at the University of Michigan. Prior to that, he taught at Tel-Aviv University, was a member of Israel's Antitrust Court, and clerked at the Supreme Court of Israel. He teaches contracts, sales, trademark law, insurance law, consumer law, sales law, e-commerce, food law, law and economics, and game theory and the law. He writes primarily in the fields of contract law and consumer protection. He is the co-author of Personalized Law: Different Rules for Different People (Oxford 2021, with Ariel Porat) and More Than You Wanted to Know: The Failure of Mandated Disclosure (Princeton 2014, with Carl Schneider). Professor Ben-Shahar is the Kearney Director of the Coase-Sandor Institute for Law and Economics. He is also the Co-Reporter for the American Law Institute's Restatement of Consumer Contracts.

Table of Contents

LeGen: Complex Information Extraction from Legal sentences using Generative Models
Chaitra C R, Sankalp Kulkarni, Sai Rama Akash Varma Sagi, Shashank Pandey, Rohit Yalavarthy, Dipanjan Chakraborty and Prajna Devi Upadhyay 1

Summarizing Long Regulatory Documents with a Multi-Step Pipeline
Mika Sie, Ruby Beek, Michiel Bots, Sjaak Brinkkemper and Albert Gatt 18

Enhancing Legal Expertise in Large Language Models through Composite Model Integration: The Development and Evaluation of Law-Neo
Zhihao Liu, Yanzhen Zhu and Mengyuan Lu 33

uOttawa at LegalLens-2024: Transformer-based Classification Experiments
Nima Meghdadi and Diana Inkpen 42

Quebec Automobile Insurance Question-Answering With Retrieval-Augmented Generation
David Beauchemin, Richard Khoury and Zachary Gagnon 48

Rethinking Legal Judgement Prediction in a Realistic Scenario in the Era of Large Language Models
Shubham Kumar Nigam, Aniket Deroy, Subhankar Maity and Arnab Bhattacharya 61

The CLC UKET Dataset: Benchmarking Case Outcome Prediction for the UK Employment Tribunal
Huiyuan Xie, Felix Steffek, Joana De Faria, Christine Carter and Jonathan Rutherford 81

Information Extraction for Planning Court Cases
Drish Mali, Rubash Mali and Claire Barale 97

Automated Anonymization of Parole Hearing Transcripts
Abed Itani, Wassiliki Siskou and Annette Hautli-Janisz 115

Towards an Automated Pointwise Evaluation Metric for Generated Long-Form Legal Summaries
Shao Min Tan, Quentin Grail and Lee Quartey 129

Enhancing Contract Negotiations with LLM-Based Legal Document Comparison
Savinay Narendra, Kaushal Shetty and Adwait Ratnaparkhi 143

Attributed Question Answering for Preconditions in the Dutch Law
Felicia Redelaar, Romy Van Drie, Suzan Verberne and Maaike De Boer 154

Algorithm for Automatic Legislative Text Consolidation
Matias Etcheverry, Thibaud Real-del-Sarte and Pauline Chavallard 166

Measuring the Groundedness of Legal Question-Answering Systems
Dietrich Trautmann, Natalia Ostapuk, Quentin Grail, Adrian Pol, Guglielmo Bonifazi, Shang Gao and Martin Gajek 176

Transductive Legal Judgment Prediction Combining BERT Embeddings with Delaunay-Based GNNs
Hugo Attali and Nadi Tomeh 187

Cross Examine: An Ensemble-based approach to leverage Large Language Models for Legal Text Analytics
Saurav Chowdhury, Lipika Dey and Suyog Joshi 194

LLMs to the Rescue: Explaining DSA Statements of Reason with Platform's Terms of Services
Marco Aspromonte, Andrea Ferraris, Federico Galli and Giuseppe Contissa 205

BLT: Can Large Language Models Handle Basic Legal Text?
Andrew Blair-Stanek, Nils Holzenberger and Benjamin Van Durme 216

Multi-Property Multi-Label Documents Metadata Recommendation based on Encoder Embeddings
Nasredine Cheniki, Vidas Daudaravicius, Abdelfettah Feliachi, Didier Hardy and Marc Wilhelm Küster 233

Comparative Study of Explainability Methods for Legal Outcome Prediction
Ieva Staliunaite, Josef Valvoda and Ken Satoh 243

Bonafide at LegalLens 2024 Shared Task: Using Lightweight DeBERTa Based Encoder For Legal Violation Detection and Resolution
Shikha Bordia 259

LAR-ECHR: A New Legal Argument Reasoning Task and Dataset for Cases of the European Court of Human Rights
Odysseas Chlapanis, Dimitris Galanis and Ion Androutsopoulos 267

Gaps or Hallucinations? Scrutinizing Machine-Generated Legal Analysis for Fine-grained Text Evaluations
Abe Hou, William Jurayj, Nils Holzenberger, Andrew Blair-Stanek and Benjamin Van Durme 280

Classify First, and Then Extract: Prompt Chaining Technique for Information Extraction
Alice Kwak, Clayton Morrison, Derek Bambauer and Mihai Surdeanu 303

Augmenting Legal Decision Support Systems with LLM-based NLI for Analyzing Social Media Evidence
Ram Mohan Rao Kadiyala, Siddartha Pullakhandam, Kanwal Mehreen, Subhasya Tippareddy and Ashay Srivastava 318

Empowering Air Travelers: A Chatbot for Canadian Air Passenger Rights
Maksym Taranukhin, Sahithya Ravi, Gabor Lukacs, Evangelos Milios and Vered Shwartz . . . 326

Enhancing Legal Violation Identification with LLMs and Deep Learning Techniques: Achievements in the LegalLens 2024 Competition
Nguyen Tan Minh, Duy Ngoc Mai, Le Xuan Bach, Nguyen Huu Dung, Pham Cong Minh, Ha Thanh Nguyen and Thi Hai Yen Vuong 336

LegalLens 2024 Shared Task: Masala-chai Submission
Khalid Rajan and Royal Sequiera 346

Semantists at LegalLens-2024: Data-efficient Training of LLM's for Legal Violation Identification
Kanagasabai Rajaraman and Hariram Veeramani 355

LegalLens Shared Task 2024: Legal Violation Identification in Unstructured Text
Ben Hagag, Gil Gil Semo, Dor Bernsohn, Liav Harpaz, Pashootan Vaezipoor, Rohit Saha, Kyryl Truskovskyi and Gerasimos Spanakis 361

DeBERTa Beats Behemoths: A Comparative Analysis of Fine-Tuning, Prompting, and PEFT Approaches on LegalLensNER
Hanh Thi Hong Tran, Nishan Chatterjee, Senja Pollak and Antoine Doucet 371

LexSumm and LexT5: Benchmarking and Modeling Legal Summarization Tasks in English
Santosh T.Y.S.S, Cornelius Weiss and Matthias Grabmair 381

Towards Supporting Legal Argumentation with NLP: Is More Data Really All You Need?
Santosh T.Y.S.S, Kevin Ashley, Katie Atkinson and Matthias Grabmair 404

Program

Saturday, November 16, 2024

09:00 - 09:15 *Workshop Opening*

09:10 - 10:30 *Session 1*

Summarizing Long Regulatory Documents with a Multi-Step Pipeline
Mika Sie, Ruby Beek, Michiel Bots, Sjaak Brinkkemper and Albert Gatt

Towards an Automated Pointwise Evaluation Metric for Generated Long-Form Legal Summaries
Shao Min Tan, Quentin Grail and Lee Quartey

Cross Examine: An Ensemble-based approach to leverage Large Language Models for Legal Text Analytics
Saurav Chowdhury, Lipika Dey and Suyog Joshi

LexSumm and LexT5: Benchmarking and Modeling Legal Summarization Tasks in English
Santosh T.Y.S.S, Cornelius Weiss and Matthias Grabmair

Algorithm for Automatic Legislative Text Consolidation
Matias Etcheverry, Thibaud Real-del-Sarte and Pauline Chavallard

LeGen: Complex Information Extraction from Legal sentences using Generative Models
Chaitra C R, Sankalp Kulkarni, Sai Rama Akash Varma Sagi, Shashank Pandey, Rohit Yalavarthy, Dipanjan Chakraborty and Prajna Devi Upadhyay

Information Extraction for Planning Court Cases
Drish Mali, Rubash Mali and Claire Barale

Automated Anonymization of Parole Hearing Transcripts
Abed Itani, Wassiliki Siskou and Annette Hautli-Janisz

BLT: Can Large Language Models Handle Basic Legal Text?
Andrew Blair-Stanek, Nils Holzenberger and Benjamin Van Durme

Classify First, and Then Extract: Prompt Chaining Technique for Information Extraction
Alice Kwak, Clayton Morrison, Derek Bambauer and Mihai Surdeanu

Saturday, November 16, 2024 (continued)

HiCuLR: Hierarchical Curriculum Learning for Rhetorical Role Labeling of Legal Documents
Santosh T.Y.S.S, Apolline Isaia, Shiyu Hong and Matthias Grabmair

10:30 - 11:00 *Break*

11:00 - 12:10 *Session 2*

Rethinking Legal Judgement Prediction in a Realistic Scenario in the Era of Large Language Models
Shubham Kumar Nigam, Aniket Deroy, Subhankar Maity and Arnab Bhattacharya

The CLC-UKET Dataset: Benchmarking Case Outcome Prediction for the UK Employment Tribunal
Huiyuan Xie, Felix Steffek, Joana De Faria, Christine Carter and Jonathan Rutherford

Transductive Legal Judgment Prediction Combining BERT Embeddings with Delaunay-Based GNNs
Hugo Attali and Nadi Tomeh

Comparative Study of Explainability Methods for Legal Outcome Prediction
Ieva Staliunaite, Josef Valvoda and Ken Satoh

Incorporating Precedents for Legal Judgement Prediction on European Court of Human Rights Cases
Santosh T.Y.S.S, Mohamed Hesham Elganayni, Stanisław Sójka and Matthias Grabmair

The Craft of Selective Prediction: Towards Reliable Case Outcome Classification - An Empirical Study on European Court of Human Rights Cases
Santosh T.Y.S.S, Irtiza Chowdhury, Shanshan Xu and Matthias Grabmair

Quebec Automobile Insurance Question-Answering With Retrieval-Augmented Generation
David Beauchemin, Richard Khoury and Zachary Gagnon

Attributed Question Answering for Preconditions in the Dutch Law
Felicia Redelaar, Romy Van Drie, Suzan Verberne and Maaike De Boer

Measuring the Groundedness of Legal Question-Answering Systems
Dietrich Trautmann, Natalia Ostapuk, Quentin Grail, Adrian Pol, Guglielmo Bonifazi, Shang Gao and Martin Gajek

Saturday, November 16, 2024 (continued)

12:10 - 14:00 *Lunch and In-Person Poster Session*

uOttawa at LegalLens-2024: Transformer-based Classification Experiments
Nima Meghdadi and Diana Inkpen

Bonafide at LegalLens 2024 Shared Task: Using Lightweight DeBERTa Based Encoder For Legal Violation Detection and Resolution
Shikha Bordia

Augmenting Legal Decision Support Systems with LLM-based NLI for Analyzing Social Media Evidence
Ram Mohan Rao Kadiyala, Siddartha Pullakhandam, Kanwal Mehreen, Subhasya Tippareddy and Ashay Srivastava

Enhancing Legal Violation Identification with LLMs and Deep Learning Techniques: Achievements in the LegalLens 2024 Competition
Nguyen Tan Minh, Duy Ngoc Mai, Le Xuan Bach, Nguyen Huu Dung, Pham Cong Minh, Ha Thanh Nguyen and Thi Hai Yen Vuong

LegalLens 2024 Shared Task: Masala-chai Submission
Khalid Rajan and Royal Sequiera

Semantists at LegalLens-2024: Data-efficient Training of LLM's for Legal Violation Identification
Kanagasabai Rajaraman and Hariram Veeramani

DeBERTa Beats Behemoths: A Comparative Analysis of Fine-Tuning, Prompting, and PEFT Approaches on LegalLensNER
Hanh Thi Hong Tran, Nishan Chatterjee, Senja Pollak and Antoine Doucet

14:00 - 15:00 *Keynote - Privacy Protection, At What Cost? - Omri Ben-Shahar (University of Chicago Law School)*

15:00 - 15:30 *Shared Task*

LegalLens Shared Task 2024: Legal Violation Identification in Unstructured Text
Ben Hagag, Gil Gil Semo, Dor Bernsohn, Liav Harpaz, Pashootan Vaezipoor, Rohit Saha, Kyryl Truskovskyi and Gerasimos Spanakis

15:30 - 16:00 *Break*

16:00 - 17:30 *Session 4*

LLMs to the Rescue: Explaining DSA Statements of Reason with Platform's Terms of Services
Marco Aspromonte, Andrea Ferraris, Federico Galli and Giuseppe Contissa

Enhancing Contract Negotiations with LLM-Based Legal Document Comparison
Savinay Narendra, Kaushal Shetty and Adwait Ratnaparkhi

Multi-Property Multi-Label Documents Metadata Recommendation based on Encoder Embeddings
Nasredine Cheniki, Vidas Daudaravicius, Abdelfettah Feliachi, Didier Hardy and Marc Wilhelm Küster

CLERC: A Dataset for U. S. Legal Case Retrieval and Retrieval-Augmented Analysis Generation
Abe Hou, Orion Weller, Guanghui Qin, Eugene Yang, Dawn Lawrie, Nils Holzenberger, Andrew Blair-Stanek and Benjamin Van Durme

Empowering Air Travelers: A Chatbot for Canadian Air Passenger Rights
Maksym Taranukhin, Sahithya Ravi, Gabor Lukacs, Evangelos Milios and Vered Shwartz

The impact of formulaic language in the Court of Justice of the European Union on the performance of lexical and dense retrieval methods
Larissa Mori, Carlos Sousa De Oliveira, Yuehwern Yih and Mario Ventresca

Gaps or Hallucinations? Scrutinizing Machine-Generated Legal Analysis for Fine-grained Text Evaluations
Abe Hou, William Jurayj, Nils Holzenberger, Andrew Blair-Stanek and Benjamin Van Durme

How Many Van Goghs Does It Take to Van Gogh? Finding the Imitation Threshold
Sahil Verma, Royi Rassin, Arnav Mohanty Das, Gantavya Bhatt, Preethi Seshadri, Chirag Shah, Jeff Bilmes, Hannaneh Hajishirzi and Yanai Elazar

Towards Supporting Legal Argumentation with NLP: Is More Data Really All You Need?
Santosh T.Y.S.S, Kevin Ashley, Katie Atkinson and Matthias Grabmair

Misinformation with Legal Consequences (MisLC): A New Task Towards Harnessing Societal Harm of Misinformation
Chu Fei Luo, Radin Shayanfar, Rohan Bhambhoria, Samuel Dahan and Xiaodan Zhu

Saturday, November 16, 2024 (continued)

LAR-ECHR: A New Legal Argument Reasoning Task and Dataset for Cases of the European Court of Human Rights
Odysseas Chlapanis, Dimitris Galanis and Ion Androutsopoulos

Developing a Pragmatic Benchmark for Assessing Korean Legal Language Understanding in Large Language Models
Yeeun Kim, Young Rok Choi, Eun Kyung Choi, Jin Hwan Choi, Hai Jin Park and Wonseok Hwang

Enhancing Legal Expertise in Large Language Models through Composite Model Integration: The Development and Evaluation of Law-Neo
Zhihao Liu, Yanzhen Zhu and Mengyuan Lu

17:30 - 17:40 *Closing Remarks & Best Presentation Award*

LeGen: Complex Information Extraction from Legal sentences using Generative Models

Chaitra C R[1], Sankalp Kulkarni[2], Sai Rama Akash Varma Sagi[2], Shashank Pandey[2], Rohit Yalavarthy[1], Dipanjan Chakraborty[1], Prajna Upadhyay[1]

[1]BITS Pilani, Hyderabad

[2]Work done when affiliated to BITS Pilani Hyderabad

p20210024@hyderabad.bits-pilani.ac.in, sankalpkulkarni@gmail.com, ss24bc@fsu.edu

s.pandey@nyu.edu, {f20212294,dipanjan,prajna.u}@hyderabad.bits-pilani.ac.in

Abstract

Constructing legal knowledge graphs from unstructured legal texts is a complex challenge due to the intricate nature of legal language. While open information extraction (OIE) techniques can convert text into triples of the form ⟨subject, relation, object⟩, they often fall short of capturing the nuanced relationships within lengthy legal sentences, necessitating more sophisticated approaches known as complex information extraction. This paper proposes *LeGen* – an end-to-end approach leveraging pre-trained large language models (GPT-4o, T5, BART) to perform complex information extraction from legal sentences. *LeGen* learns and represents the discourse structure of legal sentences, capturing both their complexity and semantics. It minimizes error propagation typical in multi-step pipelines and achieves up to a 32.2% gain on the Indian Legal benchmark. Additionally, it demonstrates competitive performance on open information extraction benchmarks. A promising application of the resulting legal knowledge graphs is in developing question-answering systems for government schemes, tailored to the Next Billion Users who struggle with the complexity of legal language. Our code and data are available at https://github.com/prajnaupadhyay/LegalIE.

Sentence	Clauses	Relations	Relations among Clauses
If balance amount in the account of a deceased is higher than 150,000 then the nominee or legal heir has to prove the identity to claim the amount	1) Balance amount in the account of a deceased is higher than 150,000 then 2) The nominee has to prove the identity to claim the amount 3) Legal heir has to prove the identity to claim the amount	CONDITION, DISJUNCTION	$R_{CONDITION}$(Balance amount in the account of a deceased is higher than 150,000 then, $R_{DISJUNCTION}$(The nominee has to prove the identity to claim the amount, Legal heir has to prove the identity to claim the amount))

Table 1: Examples of clauses and relations CAUSE, CONDITION, CONTRAST, and DISJUNCTION among clauses

1 Introduction

The Next Billion Users, new adopters of digital technology, struggle to utilize digital devices effectively for accessing critical information such as rights, employment opportunities, health, and education (Google, 2023). This is partly due to the predominantly textual nature of available information, particularly in legal contexts, characterized by intricate and lengthy sentence structures (Abdallah et al., 2023). Processing and acting upon such information impose significant cognitive burdens on these users, who often lack the necessary education and skills to comprehend it (Joshi, 2013).

NLP techniques can assist in structuring and organizing legal data to enable automatic search and retrieval (Dale, 2019; Zhong et al., 2020). Open information extraction (OIE) techniques (Kolluru et al., 2020; Stanovsky et al., 2018; Etzioni et al., 2011) can be used to extract structured information such as triples of the form ⟨subject, relation, object⟩ from a sentence in a domain-independent manner. However, legal text poses unique challenges - Legal sentences and documents are lengthy with complex inter-clausal relationships between them (Chalkidis et al., 2020). Existing OIE techniques are not equipped to return the best results on legal sentences. For instance, the output of OpenIE6 (Kolluru et al., 2020) on *If over 50 percent of a company's workers take concerted casual leave, it will be treated as a strike* are two triples - i) ⟨it, will be treated, as a strike⟩, ii) ⟨over 50 percent of a company's workers, take concerted, casual leave⟩. The model cannot identify complex relationships between the two extractions, such as condition. Apart from condition, clauses can have relations such as contrast or disjunction, etc (Table 1) among them. Identifying such relations is important to design systems that empower users to interpret complex legal information.

The problem of extracting structure beyond triples is handled by a relatively new area of re-

Proceedings of the Natural Legal Language Processing Workshop 2024, pages 1–17
November 16, 2024 ©2024 Association for Computational Linguistics

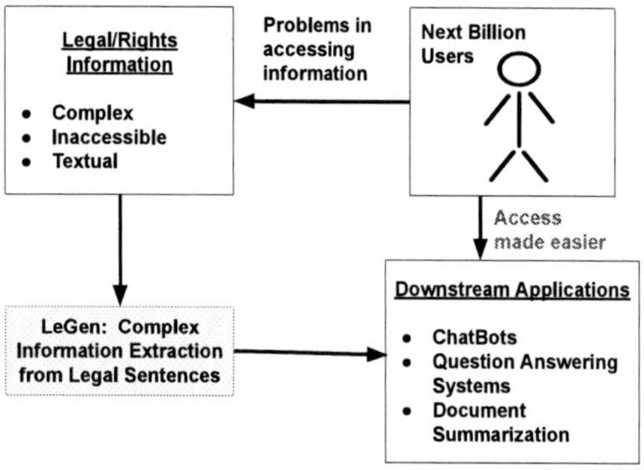

Figure 1: Next Billion Users often face challenges accessing legal text as it is complex and textual. LeGen can help these users understand the legal text better through downstream applications.

search known as complex information extraction (Mahouachi and Suchanek, 2020). Complex information extraction from legal sentences can support many downstream tasks, such as the automatic curation of legal knowledge bases (Correia et al., 2022) and analysis of court proceedings (Zadgaonkar and Agrawal, 2021). Existing techniques for complex information extraction (Niklaus et al., 2019; Prasojo et al., 2018) involve multiple-step pipelines for identifying clauses and relationships from sentences that propagate errors. They also lack language understanding and generalization skills.

This paper proposes $LeGen$, an end-to-end generative approach for complex information extraction from legal sentences (Figure 1). Generative architectures, such as T5 (Raffel et al., 2020), BART (Lewis et al., 2019), or GPT (Radford et al., 2018) have been very successful in understanding text and generalization. These architectures capture both the structure and semantics of a complex sentence more accurately. Such end-to-end modelling reduces the propagation of errors across multiple steps. In this work, we demonstrate how the discourse tree structure (Niklaus et al., 2019) (Section 3.1) of a legal sentence can be learnt using large language models such as BART, T5 and GPT. Our salient contributions are:

1. We propose $LeGen$, an end-to-end generative approach that learns accurate tree-based representations to encode the complex structure of any legal statement.

2. We report substantial gain over Graphene (Niklaus et al., 2019), a state-of-the-art complex information extraction technique on the Indian Legal benchmark.

3. We release the discourse tree structures for legal text curated from Indian Law statements.

4. We show $LeGen$'s flexibility by training it as a coordinate boundary detection task and conclude that it is competitive (Kolluru et al., 2020).

5. We propose new metrics for measuring the quality of discourse trees.

Our paper is organized as follows. We formally describe the problem in Section 2 and introduce $LeGen$ in Section 3. We discuss our experiments and results in Section 4 and 5. In Section 6, we discuss work related to legal, complex, and open information extraction and in Section 7, we discuss future work. The limitations of our approach are described in Section 9. Additional details and experiments are listed in the Appendix (Section A).

2 Problem Definition

We denote the sentences (example in Table 1) by $\mathcal{S}$. Our goal is to identify from $\mathcal{S}$:

1. A set C of all clauses in $\mathcal{S}$. A clause refers to an indivisible, atomic sentence in $\mathcal{S}$. C = {"`Balance amount in the account of a deceased is higher than 150,000 then`", "`The nominee has to prove the identity to claim the amount`", "`Legal heir has to prove the identity to claim the amount`"} for the example in Table 1.

2. A set $COMP$ of complex sentences that are obtained either by i) combining N clauses *which are subsets of clauses,* C, using an N-ary relation, or, ii) by combining subsets of C and $COMP$ using N-ary relation.

3. A set R of N-ary relations that relate N clauses or complex sentences and generate a new complex sentence. In other words, R_{r_i}: $\{C \cup COMP\}^N \longrightarrow COMP$, where $R_{r_i} \in R$. For $\mathcal{S}$, $R = \{R_{\texttt{condition}}, R_{\texttt{disjunction}}\}$. The output of $R_{\texttt{condition}}$("`Balance amount in the account of a deceased is higher than 150,000 then`", $R_{\texttt{disjunction}}$"`The nominee has to prove the identity to claim the amount`","`Legal heir has to prove the identity to claim the amount`")) is $\mathcal{S}$.

Three properties that should be satisfied by C, $COMP$ and R are:

Correct: Every $c \in C$, $c' \in COMP$ and $r \in R$ should convey the same meaning as expressed in $\mathcal{S}$

Non-redundant: C, R, and $COMP$ should not contain repeated information

Complete: All information conveyed in the sentence should be expressed by C, R, and $COMP$

3 LeGen

We propose $LeGen$, an end-to-end generative model to perform complex information extraction from legal sentences. $LeGen$ is based on the idea of discourse trees, which are defined in the next subsection. We model it as a generation task, that outputs discourse trees for a sentence.

3.1 Discourse Tree

The Discourse Tree (Cetto et al., 2018; Niklaus et al., 2019) originates from Rhetorical Structure Theory (RST) (Mann and Thompson, 1988), which identifies hierarchical text structures and rhetorical relations between text parts. These relations are categorized as coordination and subordination.

Coordinating sentences join independent clauses with coordinating conjunctions like `and`, `or`, and `but`. Subordination sentences combine main clauses with dependent clauses, using subordinating conjunctions like `while`, `because`, `if`, etc.

The Discourse Tree follows a top-down approach, breaking text into smaller parts, unlike the bottom-up approach of RST. Simplified sentences can vary and may require adjustments based on specific structures. Figure 2 (left) illustrates a Discourse Tree example, with leaf nodes representing clauses and non-leaf nodes representing complex sentences formed by combining clauses using relation labels. Relations in a discourse tree fall into co-ordinations and sub-ordinations categories.

Our goal is to learn accurate discourse trees for legal sentences (Section 3.2). We can model two types of discourse structures:

Discourse Trees for Identifying Subordinations and Coordinations In this case, we learn both subordination and coordination from the sentence. The sentence is parsed into multiple clauses, also referred to as EDUs (Elementary Discourse Units), by identifying logical connectives such as subordinates and coordinates. Both the clauses and the relationships between them are identified and structured as a linear discourse tree. We refer to this task as `Task 1` henceforth.

Discourse Trees for Coordination Boundary Detection The problem of coordinate boundary detection (Saha et al., 2018) can be expressed as a special case of learning discourse tree where all the non-leaf nodes represent the same relation, i.e. COORDINATION. We investigate this approach to learn discourse trees for the problem of coordinate boundary detection. We refer to this task as `Task 2`.

We build separate models for identifying coordinates and subordinates due to the distinct nature of each task. The coordination task focuses on recognizing coordination boundaries and forming independent clauses, involving only one type of relationship. In contrast, the subordination task involves identifying multiple inter-clausal relationships. Combining these tasks could increase the problem's complexity (Evans, 2011).

3.2 Generating Discourse Trees

Any existing rule-based approach can be used to generate the discourse trees for sentences. Currently, Graphene (Niklaus et al., 2019) generates discourse trees with good precision and recall. Graphene uses a set of 39 hand-crafted rules to identify 19 relations (Cetto et al., 2018). However, on analyzing these rules, we observed redundancies and inconsistencies. $i)$ For instance, it is very difficult to distinguish between BACKGROUND, ELABORATION, or EXPLANATION relations. $ii)$ the rules proposed for identifying TEMPORAL_BEFORE and TEMPORAL_AFTER relations from the text are not accurate. $iii)$ Does not identify the date and named entities correctly. To address $i)$ and $ii)$, we merged BACKGROUND, ELABORATION, and EXPLANATION into ELABORATION. We converted TEMPORAL_BEFORE and TEMPORAL_AFTER into a single TEMPORAL relation. We did not address $iii)$, but we show in Section 5 that $LeGen$ is robust to these issues. The final 10 relation set used in the training are SPATIAL, LIST, ATTRIBUTION, CONTRAST, DISJUNCTION, CAUSE, CONDITION, ELABORATION, TEMPORAL and PURPOSE. The above relations are explained in detail with the example in the Appendix (Section A).

3.3 Encoding of Discourse Tree

Figure 2 demonstrates the conversion of a discourse tree into a sequence encoding, simplifying complex information extraction. We treat this process as a generation task, where the input is the legal sentence and the output is the tree encoding. Our method converts original input sentences, including clauses and relationships, into explicit discourse

If balance amount in the account of a deceased is higher than ₹150,000 then the nominee or legal heir has to prove the identity to claim the amount.

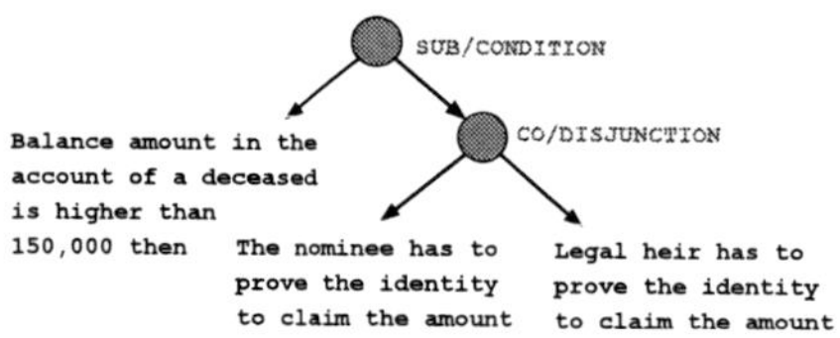


```
SUB/CONDITION('Balance amount in the account of a deceased is higher than 150,000 then .', CO/DISJUNCTION('The nominee has to prove the identity to claim the amount .','Legal heir has to prove the identity to claim the amount .'))
```

Figure 2: Discourse tree for an example law sentence (on the left). Corresponding linear encoding of the Discourse tree (on the right). `SUB` and `CO` refer to subordination and coordination, respectively.

trees. We encode the discourse tree by doing a pre-order traversal of the tree. Algorithm 1 discusses our steps.

Algorithm 1: Generating encoding $\mathcal{E}$ for a Discourse Tree T.

Input: Discourse Tree $\mathcal{T}$ with root *root*
Output: Encoding, $\mathcal{E}$
Append '*root.label*(' to $\mathcal{E}$
foreach *child of root in* $\mathcal{T}$ **do**
  if *child is a leaf* **then**
    Append '*child.label*,' to $\mathcal{E}$
  end
  else
    Generate encoding $\mathcal{E}'$ of Discourse SubTree with *child* as root
    Append $\mathcal{E}'$ to $\mathcal{E}$
  end
end
Append ')' to $\mathcal{E}$
return $\mathcal{E}$

3.4 Learning Discourse Tree with LLMs

The sequence generated using Algorithm 1 can be learnt by fine-tuning smaller LLMs such as T5 or BART or prompting larger LLMs such as GPT in a few-shot or zero-shot manner. We have prompted larger models (GPT) only as smaller models like T5 and BART lack the flexibility or capacity to interpret the complex prompts (Raffel et al., 2020). We propose using the following approaches for prompting GPT-4o:

Few shot Learning: We provided the model with a few examples, each illustrating different types of relationships and the clauses that might be present in the sentence. The prompts are in Section A.8 and A.9.

Zero-Shot Learning: In the absence of any examples, we provided explicit steps to construct a discourse tree to ensure a consistent output format, aligning these steps with the chain-of-thought (CoT) process (Feng et al., 2024). We tried two kinds of zero-shot learning.

1. Unrestricted: We did not supply any examples or specify any particular types of relationships. The model was expected to infer the relationships based on the presence of subordinates and coordinates within the sentences. This is illustrated in Section A.7.

2. Restricted: We provided the model with a predefined set of relationships as outlined in Section A.1, and the prompts used for the same can be found in Section A.6.

There are no restricted and unrestricted relations in `Task 2` as it has only one kind of relation, `COORDINATION`, and the prompts are in Section A.10.

3.5 Custom Loss Function for Handling Hallucinations

Any generative model is prone to hallucinations (Ji et al., 2023). Handling them is crucial in the context of generating trees for an accurate understanding of legal sentences. A common form of hallucination observed is repetition, i.e. more than 1 leaf node in the tree contains the same sentence. This form of hallucination is difficult to be penalized using regular cross entropy loss function since in most of the cases, all leaf node sentences only differ by a few words, so when the model generates the same sentences for multiple leaf nodes, regular loss would still be low. So, we propose a custom loss function to punish the model for this kind of output.

$$Custom\_Loss = Reg\_Loss \times \left(1 + \lambda\left(1 - \frac{u(T)}{n(T)}\right)\right)$$

where T denotes the discourse tree, Reg_Loss refers to regular cross-entropy loss, $n(T)$ denotes the number of leaf nodes in T, $u(T)$ denotes the number of unique leaf nodes, and λ is a hyperparameter which can take any real value greater than zero. If $n(t) = u(T)$, $Reg\_Loss = Custom\_Loss$. The loss increases linearly parameterized by λ as $u(t) << n(t)$.

4 Experiments

4.1 Datasets

4.1.1 Training

We trained $LeGen$ using 17k sentences from Penn Tree Bank (Marcus et al., 1993) dataset. We have used the same dataset for both `Task 1` and `Task 2` because we wanted to test the transfer learning capability of our approach on the legal domain. We performed our experiments on 32x2 cores AMD EPYC 7532, 1 TB of memory, and 8x A100 SXM4 80GB GPU systems. We trained the models using BART-base (139 M), BART-small (70.5 M), T5-base (246 M), and T5-small (77M) architectures. BART trained faster (2 hours on small and 2.5 hours on base). T5 took considerably longer time (3 hours for small and 4 hours for base). We train it separately for `Task 1` and `Task 2`.

For `Task 1`, we encoded every sentence into a discourse tree structure as described in Section 3.2. We trained BART (Lewis et al., 2019) and T5 (Abdallah et al., 2023) models for 30 epochs using cross-entropy loss with a learning rate of $e^{-}5$. Results are averaged over 3 seeds (Section 5). With GPT-4o models, we experimented with three kinds of prompting as outlined in Section 3.4. We selected 11 examples for few-shot learning, corresponding to the 10 identified types of relationships in the text, plus an additional example for cases where the sentence cannot be split (NONE) (Section A.8). For zero-shot learning, we applied Chain of Thought-style prompting with both restricted and unrestricted sets of relationships.

For `Task 2`, we kept the same hyperparameters that we used for the `Task1` and obtained the best results for batch size 3. Results are averaged over 3 seeds (Section 5). For both of them, we also trained the model with a custom loss function, setting $\lambda = 1$. With GPT-4o models, we provided the model with 11 examples for few-shot learning, with the prompt in Section A.9. These examples included sentences across hierarchical levels (0-5), showing how input sentences can be split into independent ones. For zero-shot learning, we provided steps to build a hierarchical representation of coordinating sentences, with prompts in Section A.10 . We only performed restricted prompting because it involves only one type of relation. The GPT-4o model parameters were set to: *temperature = 1* and *top_p = 1*

4.1.2 Test

1) ILDC Dataset (Used for Task 1). ILDC is a Indian Legal Dataset (Malik et al., 2021) comprising the transcripts of 35k Indian Supreme Court Cases. We sampled 50 sentences from this corpus. The dataset is fairly noisy with multiple spelling and structural inconsistencies.

2) Indian Legal Dataset (Used for Task 1). ILDC corpus is noisy, so we looked for cleaner legal sentences to test our model. We constructed a new dataset of 107 sentences from Wiki on Labour Law [1]. We used the Petscan tool to collect sentences belonging to the 'Labour Law' category from Wiki. These sentences contained multiple references, requiring pre-processing to remove mentions of other articles. The sentences were also presented as itemized lists, which had to be merged into single sentences. To understand the data, two authors of the paper spent time constructing the discourse tree structure for each sentence from scratch. We observed that there were multiple correct tree representations for one sentence, as evident from the example in Section A.3. The problem becomes more complex for trees with greater height.

3) Penn Tree Bank (Used for Task 2). Penn Tree Bank (Marcus et al., 1993) consists of 985 sentences from articles in the Wall Street Journal. It is annotated with coordinate boundaries (`and`, `or`, `but`, `comma-separated list`) and the text spans it connects. This test set was used to evaluate $LeGen$'s flexibility in identifying co-ordinations.

4.2 Metrics

4.2.1 Metrics for Task 1

Various metrics have been proposed in the literature to evaluate discourse trees (Vadlapudi et al., 2009; Yuan et al., 2021). A key disadvantage of these metrics is that they either focus on surface-level relations, or they completely ignore the relations (Mitocariu et al., 2013), without adequately addressing multiple discourse relations such as `ELABORATION`, `CAUSE`, or `RESULT`. The metric proposed in (Yuan et al., 2021) specifically focuses on dependency

[1]https://en.wikipedia.org/wiki/Indian_labour_law

distance and the complexity of constructing the discourse tree but does not account for inter-clausal relations. Additionally, discourse trees are often evaluated based on their performance in downstream tasks, such as question answering (Pyatkin et al., 2020; Sovrano et al., 2024) or machine translation (Yuan et al., 2021). We also noted that a single sentence could have multiple correct tree representations, particularly evident for taller trees as illustrated in Section A.3 (Appendix). Given these issues, we used human judgment to evaluate the trees based on i) structure of the tree and ii) content of the tree, i.e., the relation labels. We propose two metrics.

Tree Structure Evaluation (TSE). We employed a strict evaluation technique, i.e. it was marked as correct only if all the 3 requirements cited in Section 2 were satisfied – i) Every node in the tree was correctly split. ii) Tree does not contain multiple nodes with the same information, iii) All information in the sentence was conveyed in the tree. **TSE** reports the percentage of sentences that generated correct trees.

Tree Content Evaluation (TCE). To assess tree content, annotators were tasked with labeling each relation as correct or incorrect, informed about the relations present in the test set. A relation was marked incorrect if it was expressed differently or if it connected incorrect clauses. Inaccuracies in relations resulted in penalties applied to the entire tree structure post-clause verification.

4.2.2 Metrics for Task 2

We employed a **mapping-based approach** proposed in CalmIE (Saha et al., 2018) to compare the clauses generated by our technique with the gold set. For every conjunctive sentence, we evaluated it by matching its collection of system-generated clauses with the reference set. This involved establishing the most optimal one-to-one correspondence between the clauses in both sets. Subsequently, precision was determined for each mapping by calculating the ratio of shared words to the total words in the generated sentence, while recall was calculated as the ratio of shared words to the total words in the reference sentence.

Let $G = \{G_1, G_2, G_3 \ldots\}$ be gold/reference clauses each represented as a bag of words model, i.e. $G_i = \{G_i^{a1}, G_i^{a2}, G_i^{a3} \ldots\}$ where each G_i^{aj} denotes a token in a clause. Similarly let $T = \{T_1, T_2, T_3 \ldots\}$ be clauses generated by a model where $T_i = \{T_i^{a1}, T_i^{a2}, T_i^{a3} \ldots\}$. CalmIE performs matching in a greedy fashion, however, this type of matching is not optimal and might change based on the order in which greedy matching is performed. So, we performed matching to get the global maximum. This problem of finding the global optimum from a distance or similarity matrix can be treated as a linear sum assignment problem (Crouse, 2016). We matched clauses from Gold Set G and Predicted Set T to maximise the F1 score. The F1 score was computed using precision and recall metrics. All equations are presented in the Appendix in Section A.2 of appendix A.

4.3 Baselines

Graphene Default. We used the default Graphene (Niklaus et al., 2019) as the competing technique for `Task 1`. We observed that although it can split long complex sentences, it is unable to identify the relations correctly.

Graphene. We used modified Graphene (Refer Section 3.2) as the competing technique for `Task 1`.

OpenIE6_Coordinate-Boundary_Detection. We used the Coordination Boundary Detection Model released with OpenIE6 as our baseline for `Task 2`.

5 Results

5.1 Task 1

Table 2 presents the results for TSE and TCE scores and the number of clauses and relations generated in the discourse trees using three different techniques. The results demonstrate that the generative approach to discourse tree creation significantly outperforms Graphene on both datasets—the Indian Legal Dataset and ILDC. The GPT-4o model performs the best, achieving a TSE score of 82% on the Indian Legal Dataset and 90% on the ILDC Dataset. T5 and BART-Base hallucinates more and the reason for its underperformance is the generation of terms not present in the original sentence. Graphene Default performs worse than modified Graphene. While it splits clauses correctly, it's TCE is much lower because of our observations reported in Section 3.2.

Graphene also underperforms in sentences where domain-specific named entities such as statutes, laws, or case names are present, e.g. *Shops and Establishment Act 1960* or *The Factories Act 1948* (Indian Legal Dataset of Table 3).

Dataset	Models	TSE	TCE	#(Relations, Clauses)
ILDC	Graphene Default	0.54	0.74	(174,125)
	Graphene	0.54	0.77	(174,125)
	T5	0.56	**1**	(137,88)
	T5 Custom Loss	0.56	1	(137,88)
	BART	0.48	1	(111,62)
	BART Custom Loss	0.48	0.83	(127,76)
	GPT-4o (11 Shot)	**0.90**	<u>0.89</u>	(100,50)
	GPT-4o(Zero shot CoT U)	<u>0.70</u>	0.88	(152,96)
	GPT-4o (Zero shot CoT R)	0.64	<u>0.90</u>	(156,92)
Indian Legal Dataset	Graphene Default	0.62	0.54	(247, 347)
	Graphene	0.62	0.92	(247, 347)
	T5	0.71	<u>0.96</u>	(191, 349)
	T5 Custom Loss	0.56	**1**	(404,238)
	BART	0.70	0.92	(183, 281)
	BART Custom Loss	0.61	0.95	(289,185)
	GPT-4o (11 Shot)	**0.82**	0.87	(236,134)
	GPT-4o (Zero shot CoT U)	0.76	0.79	(319,248)
	GPT-4o (Zero shot CoT R)	<u>0.79</u>	0.90	(317,187)

Table 2: Results for Task 1: TSE and TCE results of Graphene, GPT-4o, T5, and BART with regular and custom loss function on 2 datasets averaged over 3 seeds. The best values are in bold. The second best is underlined. U stands for Unrestricted and R stands for Restricted.

Graphene also cannot identify non distributive coordination like 'between' and splits sentences on them. All these issues are handled very well by generative models even though they were trained on Graphene's output. The error analysis of the T5 and BART models is presented in Section A.4.

GPT-4o models perform auto-correction of words as observed in the ILDC dataset in Table 3, which is a further improvement on T5 and BART. The input sentence of the ILDC data set has many words which are misspelt, like `companytained`, `companydition` and `companytract`, which was auto-corrected by the GPT-4o model to `contained`,`condition` and `contract`.

While evaluating for **TCE**, we took into consideration the fact that there could be multiple ways of representing sentences with different relations. There are situations where models can split the sentences but are unable to identify the relations, and BART has made spelling mistakes in identifying the relation. Although such scenarios were rare in T5, we came across them in Graphene and BART.

Inter-annotator Agreement. We sampled 50% of the sentences annotated by Annotator 1 and asked Annotator 2 to evaluate them. We obtained a Cohen's Kappa agreement value of 0.73 for TSE and 0.71 for TCE, indicating substantial agreement (Blackman and Koval, 2000).

5.2 Task 2

Table 4 shows our results. We obtained competent results from the T5-base against OpenIE6_Coordinate-Boundary_Detection. The slight drop in the performance of T5-Base could be attributed to ambiguous labels in the Penn Tree Bank dataset. For instance, one split in the gold for "*He retired as senior vice president, finance and administration, and chief financial officer of the company Oct. 1*" is "*He retired as senior vice president, finance Oct. 1*", while T5 generates "*He retired as senior vice president, finance, of the company Oct. 1*". T5 generates a better split but it gets penalised because this is not captured in gold.

BART did not perform well as it hallucinated while generating the output where it used words that are not in the input. BART was also unable to split all elements of comma-separated lists. The same problem was observed for T5-small which improved with T5-base.

The results obtained for `Task 2` with few-shot and zero-shot learning did not match those achieved with T5 and BART. The GPT-4o model did not perform well mainly because of two reasons: difficulty in correctly splitting sentences into multiple hierarchical levels and the loss of contextual information. The model could correctly identify the conjunctions in the sentence but failed to form independent clauses. We are working towards fixing this issue with GPT models by refining the prompts to include context information and also improving hierarchical levels wherever needed.

5.3 Effect of Custom Loss Function

On `Task 2`, using the custom loss function improved the results for T5-small, T5-Base, and BART-Base (Table 4, example in Appendix, Figure **??**). BART hallucinates by inventing new relations in the discourse tree which is not handled by our custom loss function. This could be the reason for low performance of BART-small with custom loss.

On `Task 1`, using the custom loss function gave mixed results. Results are shown in Table 2. On the ILDC corpus, it didn't lead to any improvement for TSE while TCE reduced for BART. This is similar to what we observed for BART on `Task 2`. On the Indian Legal Dataset, enforcing custom loss made the model split a sentence into more number of clauses, however, this does not necessarily mean it is a correct splitting. This led to a reduction in the TSE scores. The total number of relations gen-

Dataset	Input	Clauses generated by Graphene	Clauses generated by T5 BASE	Clauses generated by GPT-4o model
Indian Legal Dataset	The Factories Act 1948 and the Shops and Establishment Act 1960 mandate 15 working days of fully paid vacation leave each year to each employee with an additional 7 fully paid sick days.	1) This was with an additional 7 fully paid 2) This was to each employee 3) The Factories leave each year sick days 4) Act 1948 mandate 15 working days of fully paid vacation The Factories 5) The Shops and Establishment Act 1960 mandate 15 working days of fully paid vacation The Factories	1) This was to each employee with an additional 7 fully paid sick days 2) The Factories Act 1948 mandate 15 working days of fully paid vacation leave each year 3) The Shops and Establishment Act 1960 mandate 15 working days of fully paid vacation leave each year.	1) The Factories Act 1948 and the Shops and Establishment Act 1960 mandate 15 working days of fully paid vacation leave each year to each employee. 2) This was in addition to 7 fully paid sick days.
ILDC	Learned companynsel appearing on behalf of the appellant has argued that the arbitration clause companytained in the tender companydition amounts to a companytract of adhesion, and since there is unfair bargaining strength between respondent No.2 and the appellant, this clause ought to be struck down following the judgment in Central Inland Water Transport Corpn.v. Brojo Nath Ganguly, 1986 3 SCC 156.	1) This was what learned companynsel appearing on behalf of the appellant has argued . 2) The arbitration clause companytained in the tender companydition amounts to a companytract of adhesion. 3) Central Inland Water Transport Corpn.v. Brojo Nath Ganguly was 1986 3 SCC 156. 4) There is unfair bargaining strength between respondent No. 2. 5) There is the appellant. 6) This clause ought to be struck down following the judgment in Central Inland Water Transport Corpn.v . Brojo Nath Ganguly .	1) Brojo Nath Ganguly was the judgment in Central Inland Water Transport Corpn.v . Brojo Nath Ganguly , 1986 3 SCC 156. 2) This was what learned companynsel appearing on behalf of the appellant has argued. 3) The arbitration clause companytained in the tender companydition amounts to a companytract of adhesion , and since there is unfair bargaining strength between respondent No.2 and the appellant , this clause ought to be struck down following Brojo Nath Ganguly , 1986 3 SCC 156.	1) Learned counsel appearing on behalf of the appellant has argued. 2) That the arbitration clause contained in the tender condition amounts to a contract of adhesion. 3) And since there is unfair bargaining strength between respondent No.2 and the appellant. 4) This clause ought to be struck down following the judgment in Central Inland Water Transport Corpn.v. Brojo Nath Ganguly, 1986 3 SCC 156.

Table 3: Examples showing the superiority of generative architectures in identifying correct clauses. Their strength also lies in the accurate detection of named entities and auto-correction.

erated by both BART and T5 reduced which may have led to an increase in TCE scores. Overall, we can conclude that subordination is a more complex task than coordination which needs more nuanced handling of hallucinations.

Models	Mapping Based Approach			
	Loss function	Precision	Recall	F1 Score
OpenIE6_Coordinate -Boundary_Detection	Regular	**0.9803**	**0.9845**	**0.9816**
T5 Small	Custom	0.9671	0.9538	0.9578
	Regular	0.9647	0.9544	0.9571
T5 Base	Custom	0.9756	0.974	0.9739
	Regular	0.9747	0.973	0.9726
BART Small	Custom	0.8273	0.7334	0.7672
	Regular	0.8215	0.7391	0.7682
BART Base	Custom	0.8418	0.7613	0.7903
	Regular	0.8369	0.7574	0.7903
GPT-4o (11 Shot)	-	0.4124	0.2816	0.3198
GPT-4o (Zero Shot CoT)	-	0.6024	0.3823	0.4503

Table 4: Results on Task 2: Mapping-based approach is used to calculate precision, recall and f1 score using cross-entropy loss function and custom loss function. The best values are in bold. The second best is underlined.

6 Related Work

6.1 Legal Information Extraction

Legal Information Extraction has advanced with NLP techniques aiding legal professionals (Chalkidis et al., 2017; Leivaditi et al., 2020; Cardellino et al., 2017). Although open information extraction methods attempt structured triple extraction from legal statements (Zadgaonkar and Agrawal, 2021), challenges remain (see Section 1). Core tasks include NER, document summarization, and judgment prediction (LJP), facilitated by systems like Eunomos (Boella et al., 2016; Abood and Feltenberger, 2018; Nguyen et al., 2018) and enhanced by legal ontologies like YAGO (Cardellino et al., 2017).

Early judgment prediction relied on rule-based models (HYPO, CATO) (Rissland and Ashley, 1987; Aleven and Ashley, 1995) and ML approaches like SVMs (Aletras et al., 2016), which achieved 79% accuracy. Recent studies continued this with neural models (Medvedeva et al., 2020;

Chalkidis et al., 2019a) and semi-supervised techniques (Branting et al., 2021). Adapted pre-trained models such as LegalBERT (Chalkidis et al., 2020) and datasets in multiple languages have enriched the field (Chalkidis et al., 2021, 2019b).

In the Indian context, works like InLegalBERT (Paul et al., 2023) and corpora like ILDC (Malik et al., 2021) advance NLP on Indian legal data. Legal tasks in ILDC include NER, rhetorical role prediction (Kalamkar et al., 2022), and court judgment prediction (Modi et al., 2023). Other Indian resources include HLDC for bail prediction (Kapoor et al., 2022), LJP (Cui et al., 2023) and NLP benchmarks (Kalamkar et al., 2021).

6.2 Open Information Extraction

Open Information Extraction uses an independent paradigm to extract the information as a triple, ⟨subject, relation, object⟩. (Yates et al., 2007) introduced the concept of Open Information Extraction and proposed Text Runner. Following this, many rule-based systems were developed, like REVERB (Etzioni et al., 2011) and OpenIE5 (Saha et al., 2018). RNNOIE (Stanovsky et al., 2018) which uses a neural-based approach to open information extraction and is trained by the data extracted from non-neural systems. The state-of-the-art in Open Information Extraction, OpenIE6 (Kolluru et al., 2020) uses iterative grid labeling with BERT architecture to generate triples from input.

6.3 Complex Information Extraction

Several OIE systems address complex sentence extraction (Mahouachi and Suchanek, 2020), including OLLIE (Schmitz et al., 2012), MinIE (Gashteovski et al., 2017), and Graphene (Cetto et al., 2018). Methods vary from rule-based (ClausIE, MinIE) to syntactical (StuffIE (Prasojo et al., 2018)) and structured approaches (Graphene (Niklaus et al., 2019)). Our work uniquely explores generative neural architectures for complex information extraction.

6.4 Discourse Tree and its Applications

Discourse trees (DT) originated from Rhetorical Structure Theory (RST), which organizes text through relations within parts to create hierarchical structures. DTs can be generated by various methods, including data-driven approaches assessing topicality (Schilder, 2002), learning-based techniques for sentence and cross-sentence relations (Soricut and Marcu, 2003; Baldridge and Lascarides, 2005), shift-reduce parsing (Ji and Eisenstein, 2014), and handcrafted rules (Cetto et al., 2018). Recent advances leverage NLP and computer vision for constructing DTs from heterogeneous data (Schneider et al., 2023). Different DT representations, like SDRT and EDU theory, approach discourse as either structured graphs or without assuming tree structures. DTs are applied in tasks such as Question Answering (Sovrano et al., 2024), answer indexing (Galitsky and Ilvovsky, 2019), and summarization (Yoshida et al., 2014; Pu and Demberg, 2024). Our work, however, focuses on constructing DTs at the sentence level rather than the document level as in previous studies.

7 Conclusion

We developed an end-to-end generative model for legal information extraction that improves legal sentence comprehension. Using T5, BART, and GPT-4o models, we learned sentence discourse trees, which outperformed Graphene on an Indian Legal and ILDC Dataset and achieved competitive performance in coordinate boundary detection. In the future, we will use the discourse trees generated from Indian Law to populate a legal knowledge graph which can be used to develop a question-answering system to support low-literate users.

8 Acknowledgements

We would like to thank the HPC facility at BITS Pilani Hyderabad Campus for extending their support to conduct experiments. The last 2 authors are supported by OpenAI Researcher Access and API Award and BITS Pilani Sparkle Grant. The last author is also supported by BITS Pilani New Faculty Seed Grant in executing this project.

9 Limitations

∗ Our dataset could be biased due to unequal training instances for each kind of relation.
∗ GPT models generate a varied number of clauses and relations for the same input sentence. This randomness of GPT models is propagated to our models as well. Due to this, our models generate a varied number of clauses and relations for the same input sentence.
∗ Due to the presence of multiple correct discourse trees for subordination tasks, it is difficult to create a benchmark to automatically evaluate the models. They require expensive human annotations.

References

Abdelrahman Abdallah, Bhawna Piryani, and Adam Jatowt. 2023. Exploring the state of the art in legal qa systems. *arXiv preprint arXiv:2304.06623*.

Aaron Abood and Dave Feltenberger. 2018. Automated patent landscaping. *Artificial Intelligence and Law*, 26(2):103–125.

Nikolaos Aletras, Dimitrios Tsarapatsanis, Daniel Preoţiuc-Pietro, and Vasileios Lampos. 2016. Predicting judicial decisions of the european court of human rights: A natural language processing perspective. *PeerJ computer science*, 2:e93.

Vincent Aleven and Kevin D Ashley. 1995. Doing things with factors. In *Proceedings of the 5th international conference on artificial intelligence and law*, pages 31–41.

Jason Baldridge and Alex Lascarides. 2005. Probabilistic head-driven parsing for discourse structure. In *Proceedings of the Ninth Conference on Computational Natural Language Learning (CoNLL-2005)*, pages 96–103.

Nicole J-M Blackman and John J Koval. 2000. Interval estimation for cohen's kappa as a measure of agreement. *Statistics in medicine*, 19(5):723–741.

Guido Boella, Luigi Di Caro, Llio Humphreys, Livio Robaldo, Piercarlo Rossi, and Leendert van der Torre. 2016. Eunomos, a legal document and knowledge management system for the web to provide relevant, reliable and up-to-date information on the law. *Artificial Intelligence and Law*, 24:245–283.

L Karl Branting, Craig Pfeifer, Bradford Brown, Lisa Ferro, John Aberdeen, Brandy Weiss, Mark Pfaff, and Bill Liao. 2021. Scalable and explainable legal prediction. *Artificial Intelligence and Law*, 29:213–238.

Cristian Cardellino, Milagro Teruel, Laura Alonso Alemany, and Serena Villata. 2017. Legal nerc with ontologies, wikipedia and curriculum learning. In *15th European Chapter of the Association for Computational Linguistics (EACL 2017)*, pages 254–259.

Matthias Cetto, Christina Niklaus, André Freitas, and Siegfried Handschuh. 2018. Graphene: Semantically-linked propositions in open information extraction. *arXiv preprint arXiv:1807.11276*.

Ilias Chalkidis, Ion Androutsopoulos, and Nikolaos Aletras. 2019a. Neural legal judgment prediction in english. *arXiv preprint arXiv:1906.02059*.

Ilias Chalkidis, Ion Androutsopoulos, and Achilleas Michos. 2017. Extracting contract elements. In *Proceedings of the 16th edition of the International Conference on Articial Intelligence and Law*, pages 19–28.

Ilias Chalkidis, Manos Fergadiotis, Prodromos Malakasiotis, Nikolaos Aletras, and Ion Androutsopoulos. 2020. Legal-bert: The muppets straight out of law school. *arXiv preprint arXiv:2010.02559*.

Ilias Chalkidis, Manos Fergadiotis, Prodromos Malakasiotis, and Ion Androutsopoulos. 2019b. Large-scale multi-label text classification on eu legislation. *arXiv preprint arXiv:1906.02192*.

Ilias Chalkidis, Manos Fergadiotis, Dimitrios Tsarapatsanis, Nikolaos Aletras, Ion Androutsopoulos, and Prodromos Malakasiotis. 2021. Paragraph-level rationale extraction through regularization: A case study on european court of human rights cases. *arXiv preprint arXiv:2103.13084*.

Fernando A Correia, Alexandre AA Almeida, José Luiz Nunes, Kaline G Santos, Ivar A Hartmann, Felipe A Silva, and Hélio Lopes. 2022. Fine-grained legal entity annotation: A case study on the brazilian supreme court. *Information Processing & Management*, 59(1):102794.

David F Crouse. 2016. On implementing 2d rectangular assignment algorithms. *IEEE Transactions on Aerospace and Electronic Systems*, 52(4):1679–1696.

Junyun Cui, Xiaoyu Shen, and Shaochun Wen. 2023. A survey on legal judgment prediction: Datasets, metrics, models and challenges. *IEEE Access*.

Robert Dale. 2019. Law and word order: Nlp in legal tech. *Natural Language Engineering*, 25(1):211–217.

Oren Etzioni, Anthony Fader, Janara Christensen, Stephen Soderland, et al. 2011. Open information extraction: The second generation. In *Twenty-Second International Joint Conference on Artificial Intelligence*. Citeseer.

Richard J Evans. 2011. Comparing methods for the syntactic simplification of sentences in information extraction. *Literary and linguistic computing*, 26(4):371–388.

Guhao Feng, Bohang Zhang, Yuntian Gu, Haotian Ye, Di He, and Liwei Wang. 2024. Towards revealing the mystery behind chain of thought: a theoretical perspective. *Advances in Neural Information Processing Systems*, 36.

Boris Galitsky and Dmitry Ilvovsky. 2019. Two discourse tree-based approaches to indexing answers. In *Proceedings of the International Conference on Recent Advances in Natural Language Processing (RANLP 2019)*, pages 367–372.

Kiril Gashteovski, Rainer Gemulla, and Luciano del Corro. 2017. Minie: minimizing facts in open information extraction. Association for Computational Linguistics.

Google. 2023. Next billion users. `https://blog.google/technology/next-billion-users/`.

Yangfeng Ji and Jacob Eisenstein. 2014. Representation learning for text-level discourse parsing. In *Proceedings of the 52nd annual meeting of the association for computational linguistics (volume 1: Long papers)*, pages 13–24.

Ziwei Ji, Nayeon Lee, Rita Frieske, Tiezheng Yu, Dan Su, Yan Xu, Etsuko Ishii, Ye Jin Bang, Andrea Madotto, and Pascale Fung. 2023. Survey of hallucination in natural language generation. *ACM Computing Surveys*, 55(12):1–38.

Anirudha Joshi. 2013. Technology adoption by'emergent'users: the user-usage model. In *Proceedings of the 11th Asia Pacific conference on computer human interaction*, pages 28–38.

Prathamesh Kalamkar, Astha Agarwal, Aman Tiwari, Smita Gupta, Saurabh Karn, and Vivek Raghavan. 2022. Named entity recognition in indian court judgments. *Preprint*, arXiv:2211.03442.

Prathamesh Kalamkar, Janani Venugopalan, and Vivek Raghavan. 2021. Benchmarks for indian legal nlp: a survey. In *JSAI International Symposium on Artificial Intelligence*, pages 33–48. Springer.

Arnav Kapoor, Mudit Dhawan, Anmol Goel, TH Arjun, Akshala Bhatnagar, Vibhu Agrawal, Amul Agrawal, Arnab Bhattacharya, Ponnurangam Kumaraguru, and Ashutosh Modi. 2022. Hldc: Hindi legal documents corpus. *arXiv preprint arXiv:2204.00806*.

Keshav Kolluru, Vaibhav Adlakha, Samarth Aggarwal, Soumen Chakrabarti, et al. 2020. Openie6: Iterative grid labeling and coordination analysis for open information extraction. *arXiv preprint arXiv:2010.03147*.

Spyretta Leivaditi, Julien Rossi, and Evangelos Kanoulas. 2020. A benchmark for lease contract review. *arXiv preprint arXiv:2010.10386*.

Mike Lewis, Yinhan Liu, Naman Goyal, Marjan Ghazvininejad, Abdelrahman Mohamed, Omer Levy, Ves Stoyanov, and Luke Zettlemoyer. 2019. Bart: Denoising sequence-to-sequence pre-training for natural language generation, translation, and comprehension. *arXiv preprint arXiv:1910.13461*.

Mechket Emna Mahouachi and Fabian M Suchanek. 2020. Extracting complex information from natural language text: A survey. In *CIKM (Workshops)*.

Vijit Malik, Rishabh Sanjay, Shubham Kumar Nigam, Kripa Ghosh, Shouvik Kumar Guha, Arnab Bhattacharya, and Ashutosh Modi. 2021. Ildc for cjpe: Indian legal documents corpus for court judgment prediction and explanation. *arXiv preprint arXiv:2105.13562*.

William C Mann and Sandra A Thompson. 1988. Rhetorical structure theory: Toward a functional theory of text organization. *Text-interdisciplinary Journal for the Study of Discourse*, 8(3):243–281.

Mitchell Marcus, Beatrice Santorini, and Mary Ann Marcinkiewicz. 1993. Building a large annotated corpus of english: The penn treebank.

Masha Medvedeva, Michel Vols, and Martijn Wieling. 2020. Using machine learning to predict decisions of the european court of human rights. *Artificial Intelligence and Law*, 28:237–266.

Elena Mitocariu, Daniel Alexandru Anechitei, and Dan Cristea. 2013. Comparing discourse tree structures. In *Computational Linguistics and Intelligent Text Processing: 14th International Conference, CICLing 2013, Samos, Greece, March 24-30, 2013, Proceedings, Part I 14*, pages 513–522. Springer.

Ashutosh Modi, Prathamesh Kalamkar, Saurabh Karn, Aman Tiwari, Abhinav Joshi, Sai Kiran Tanikella, Shouvik Kumar Guha, Sachin Malhan, and Vivek Raghavan. 2023. Semeval 2023 task 6: Legaleval - understanding legal texts. *Preprint*, arXiv:2304.09548.

Truong-Son Nguyen, Le-Minh Nguyen, Satoshi Tojo, Ken Satoh, and Akira Shimazu. 2018. Recurrent neural network-based models for recognizing requisite and effectuation parts in legal texts. *Artificial Intelligence and Law*, 26:169–199.

Christina Niklaus, Matthias Cetto, André Freitas, and Siegfried Handschuh. 2019. Transforming complex sentences into a semantic hierarchy. *arXiv preprint arXiv:1906.01038*.

Shounak Paul, Arpan Mandal, Pawan Goyal, and Saptarshi Ghosh. 2023. Pre-trained language models for the legal domain: a case study on indian law. In *Proceedings of the Nineteenth International Conference on Artificial Intelligence and Law*, pages 187–196.

Radityo Eko Prasojo, Mouna Kacimi, and Werner Nutt. 2018. Stuffie: Semantic tagging of unlabeled facets using fine-grained information extraction. In *Proceedings of the 27th ACM International Conference on Information and Knowledge Management*, pages 467–476.

Dongqi Pu and Vera Demberg. 2024. Rst-lora: A discourse-aware low-rank adaptation for long document abstractive summarization. *arXiv preprint arXiv:2405.00657*.

Valentina Pyatkin, Ayal Klein, Reut Tsarfaty, and Ido Dagan. 2020. Qadiscourse–discourse relations as qa pairs: Representation, crowdsourcing and baselines. *arXiv preprint arXiv:2010.02815*.

Alec Radford, Karthik Narasimhan, Tim Salimans, Ilya Sutskever, et al. 2018. Improving language understanding by generative pre-training.

Colin Raffel, Noam Shazeer, Adam Roberts, Katherine Lee, Sharan Narang, Michael Matena, Yanqi Zhou, Wei Li, and Peter J Liu. 2020. Exploring the limits of transfer learning with a unified text-to-text transformer. *The Journal of Machine Learning Research*, 21(1):5485–5551.

Edwina L Rissland and Kevin D Ashley. 1987. A case-based system for trade secrets law. In *Proceedings of the 1st international conference on Artificial intelligence and law*, pages 60–66.

Swarnadeep Saha et al. 2018. Open information extraction from conjunctive sentences. In *Proceedings of the 27th International Conference on Computational Linguistics*, pages 2288–2299.

Frank Schilder. 2002. Robust discourse parsing via discourse markers, topicality and position. *Natural Language Engineering*, 8(2-3):235–255.

Michael Schmitz, Stephen Soderland, Robert Bart, Oren Etzioni, et al. 2012. Open language learning for information extraction. In *Proceedings of the 2012 joint conference on empirical methods in natural language processing and computational natural language learning*, pages 523–534.

Florian Schneider, Tim Fischer, Fynn Petersen-Frey, Isabel Eiser, Gertraud Koch, and Chris Biemann. 2023. The D-WISE tool suite: Multi-modal machine-learning-powered tools supporting and enhancing digital discourse analysis. In *Proceedings of the 61st Annual Meeting of the Association for Computational Linguistics (Volume 3: System Demonstrations)*, pages 328–335, Toronto, Canada. Association for Computational Linguistics.

Radu Soricut and Daniel Marcu. 2003. Sentence level discourse parsing using syntactic and lexical information. In *Proceedings of the 2003 Human Language Technology Conference of the North American Chapter of the Association for Computational Linguistics*, pages 228–235.

Francesco Sovrano, Monica Palmirani, Salvatore Sapienza, and Vittoria Pistone. 2024. Discolqa: zero-shot discourse-based legal question answering on european legislation. *Artificial Intelligence and Law*, pages 1–37.

Gabriel Stanovsky, Julian Michael, Luke Zettlemoyer, and Ido Dagan. 2018. Supervised open information extraction. In *Proceedings of the 2018 Conference of the North American Chapter of the Association for Computational Linguistics: Human Language Technologies, Volume 1 (Long Papers)*, pages 885–895.

Ravikiran Vadlapudi, Poornima Malepati, and Suman Yelati. 2009. Hierarchical discourse parsing based on similarity metrics. In *Proceedings of the Student Research Workshop*, pages 89–93.

Alexander Yates, Michele Banko, Matthew Broadhead, Michael J Cafarella, Oren Etzioni, and Stephen Soderland. 2007. Textrunner: open information extraction on the web. In *Proceedings of Human Language Technologies: The Annual Conference of the North American Chapter of the Association for Computational Linguistics (NAACL-HLT)*, pages 25–26.

Yasuhisa Yoshida, Jun Suzuki, Tsutomu Hirao, and Masaaki Nagata. 2014. Dependency-based discourse parser for single-document summarization. In *Proceedings of the 2014 Conference on Empirical Methods in Natural Language Processing (EMNLP)*, pages 1834–1839.

Jingting Yuan, Qiuhan Lin, and John SY Lee. 2021. Discourse tree structure and dependency distance in efl writing. In *20th International Workshop on Treebanks and Linguistic Theories (TLT 2021)*, pages 105–115. Association for Computational Linguistics (ACL).

Ashwini V Zadgaonkar and Avinash J Agrawal. 2021. An overview of information extraction techniques for legal document analysis and processing. *International Journal of Electrical & Computer Engineering (2088-8708)*, 11(6).

Haoxi Zhong, Chaojun Xiao, Cunchao Tu, Tianyang Zhang, Zhiyuan Liu, and Maosong Sun. 2020. How does nlp benefit legal system: A summary of legal artificial intelligence. *arXiv preprint arXiv:2004.12158*.

A Appendix

A.1 Graphene Relations used for LeGen training

1. **SPATIAL**: This relation is used to denote the place of occurrence of an event.

   E.g., The Interstate Migrant Workmen Act 's purpose was to protect workers whose services were requisitioned outside their native states in India .

   ```
   SUB/ELABORATION('The Inter-state Migrant Workmen Act 's purpose was to protect workers .', SUB/SPATIAL('This is in India .','Workers 's services are requisitioned outside their native states .'))
   ```

2. **ATTRIBUTION**: This relation is used when a statement is being made by some person or institution.

   Eg: But some militant SCI TV junk-holders say that 's not enough .

   ```
   SUB/ATTRIBUTION('This is what some militant SCI TV junk-holders say .',"s not enough .')
   ```

3. **CONTRAST**: This relation is indicated by the words 'although' , 'but' , 'but now', 'despite' , 'even though' , 'even when', 'except when' , 'however', 'instead' , 'rather', 'still' ,

'though' , 'thus', 'until recently', 'while' and 'yet'.

Eg: This can have its purposes at times , but there 's no reason to cloud the importance and allure of Western concepts of freedom and justice .

```
CO/CONTRAST(SUB/ELABORATION('This is at times .','This can have its purposes .' ), 'There 's no reason to cloud the importance and allure of Western concepts of freedom and justice .')
```

Eg2: No one has worked out the players ' average age , but most appear to be in their late 30s .

```
CO/CONTRAST('No one has worked out the players ' average age .',' most appear to be in their late 30s . ')
```

4. **LIST**: This is used to indicate conjunctions ('and' or comma seperated words) between the sentences

   Eg: He believes in what he plays , **and** he plays superbly .

   ```
   CO/LIST('He believes in what he plays .','He plays superbly .')
   ```

5. **DISJUNCTION**: This is used to show the presence of 'OR' in the sentences.

   Eg: The carpet division had 1988 sales of $ 368.3 million, or almost 14 % of Armstrong 's $ 2.68 billion total revenue .

   ```
   CO/DISJUNCTION('The carpet division had 1988 sales of $ 368.3 million .','The carpet division had 1988 sales of almost 14 % of Armstrong 's $ 2.68 billion total revenue .')
   ```

6. **CAUSE**: Indicates the presence of the word - 'because' or 'since'.

   Eg: Jaguar 's own defenses against a hostile bid are weakened , analysts add , because fewer than 3 % of its shares are owned by employees and management .

   ```
   SUB/CAUSE('Jaguar 's own defenses against a hostile bid are weakened , analysts add .','Fewer than 3 % of its shares are owned by employees and management .')
   ```

7. **CONDITION**: When multiple sentences are connected by phrase 'if' 'in case','unless' and 'until', CONDITION relationship phrase is used to denote the connection between the sentences.

   Eg: Unless he closes the gap , Republicans risk losing not only the governorship but also the assembly next month .

   ```
   SUB/CONDITION('He closes the gap .','Republicans risk losing not only the governorship but also the assembly next month .')
   ```

8. **ELABORATION**: Identified by the presence of words such as 'more provocatively','even before' ,' for example','recently',' so' ,'so far' ,' where' ,'whereby' and 'whether' .

   REGEX:

   ```
   `since(\\W(.*?\\W)?)now"
   ```

   Eg: Not one thing in the house is **where** it is supposed to be, but the structure is fine.

   ```
   CO/CONTRAST(SUB/ELABORATION('Not one thing in the house is .','It is supposed to be .' ), 'The structure is fine .')
   ```

9. **TEMPORAL**: Denotes the time or date of occurrence of the event.

   Eg: These days he hustles to house-painting jobs in his Chevy pickup before and after training with the Tropics .

   ```
   SUB/TEMPORAL('These days he hustles to house-painting jobs in his Chevy pickup before and after .','These days he is training with the Tropics .')
   ```

10. **PURPOSE**: This kind of relation is identified by the presence of words such as 'for' or 'to'.

    Eg: But we can think of many reasons to stay out for the foreseeable future and well beyond .

    ```
    SUB/PURPOSE('But we can think of many reasons .','This is to stay out for the foreseeable future and well beyond .')
    ```

A.2 Precision, Recall, and F1 score computation

$$p = precision(G_i, T_j) = \frac{|G_i \cap T_i|}{|T_i|} \quad (1)$$

$$r = recall(G_i, T_j) = \frac{|G_i \cap T_i|}{|G_i|} \quad (2)$$

$$f1(G_i, T_j) = \frac{2pr}{p + r} \quad (3)$$

Let $m(.)$ be matching function such that G_i matches with $T_{m(i)}$ and conversely $G_{m(j)}$ matches with T_j. If $|G| \neq |T|$, then only $k = min(|G|, |T|)$ matches are possible. Thus in such cases, $m(i)$ will not return valid value for all i and $precision(G_i, T_{m(i)})$ and $recall(G_i, T_{m(i)})$ will be zero.

$$\begin{aligned} p_{example} &= precision(G, T) \\ &= \frac{1}{|T|}\sum_{i=1}^{|T|} precision(G_{m(i)}, T_i) \end{aligned} \quad (4)$$

$$\begin{aligned} r_{example} &= recall(G, T) \\ &= \frac{1}{|G|}\sum_{i=1}^{|G|} precision(G_i, T_{m(i)}) \end{aligned} \quad (5)$$

$$f1_{example} = (G, T) = \frac{2p_{example}r_{example}}{p_{example} + r_{example}} \quad (6)$$

Please note that (4) to (6) represent scores for only one example in the test set.

A.3 Multiple correct trees for same sentence

Eg: The Code on Wages Bill was introduced in the Lok Sabha on 10 August 2017 by the Minister of State for Labour and Employment (Independent Charge), Santosh Gangwar.

Tree1: `SUB/ELABORATION('This was by the Minister of State for Labour and Employment ( Independent Charge ), Santosh Gangwar', SUB/TEMPORAL('The Code on Wages Bill was introduced in the Lok Sabha', 'This was on 10th August 2017'))`

Tree2: `SUB/TEMPORAL( 'This was on 10th August 2017', SUB/ELABORATION('This was by the Minister of State for Labour and Employment ( Independent Charge ), Santosh Gangwar', 'The Code on Wages Bill was introduced in the Lok Sabha', 'This was on 10th August 2017'))`

A.4 Error Analysis

We manually analyzed the outcomes of subordination as predicted by the T5 Base and BART Base models. The primary causes of errors are identified as follows:

1. Clauses not correctly identified by model: We observed that the T5 model failed to correctly identify clauses 16% of the time, and the BART model, experiencing similar challenges, had a 17% failure rate. Moreover, BART occasionally not only failed to recognize clauses but also exhibited hallucinations during these instances.

2. Wrong Relation or relation not identified at all: We observed that the T5 model fails to identify the correct relation, defaulting to `ELABORATION`, 0.018% of the time. We found one example in T5 where the model exhibited hallucination as well as generated wrong clauses. Similarly, BART also struggles to identify the relation in 0.04% of cases and tends to exhibit more instances of hallucination compared to the T5 model.

3. Both Clauses and Relation are wrong: T5 encountered challenges in identifying both relations and clauses in 0.018% of cases, whereas BART faced failures 0.03% of the time and demonstrated a higher frequency of hallucinations.

4. Not split the sentences: T5 and BART experienced difficulty in sentence splitting in 0.07% of instances.

5. Model repeats the original input sentence in the split and Hallucination: T5 encountered challenges in both sentence splitting and hallucination 0.06% times, whereas BART exhibited a higher rate of hallucination and failed to split 0.14% of the time.

6. Grammatical error: We found minimal grammatical errors in the hierarchical sentence structure, such as bracket mismatches and misspellings. T5 made a grammatical mistake only once, while BART made two grammatical errors.

In summary, we noticed that BART exhibited a higher frequency of hallucinations compared to T5. This occurred particularly when BART struggled to identify both clauses and relations within the input sentence.

A.5 Relation count in Indian Legal Dataset

Table 5 shows relation distribution in the test dataset and the accuracy of prediction by T5.

Relation	Count	T5 BASE ACCURACY OF RELATION PREDICTION
SPATIAL	10	0.2
ATTRIBUTION	18	0.44
ELABORATION	446	0.18
TEMPORAL	3	0.67
CONTRAST	23	0.69
LIST	112	0.3
DISJUNCTION	26	0.15
CAUSE	5	0.08
CONDITION	18	0.72
PURPOSE	18	0.27

Table 5: Relation distribution in Indian Legal Test data

A.6 Zero Shot Restricted CoT Prompt for Subordination Task

To construct the discourse Tree, follow the below steps:

Step 1: Identify the subordinating phrases like for, while, however, because, as, etc., in the input sentence and then divide it into two sentences (clauses) by identifying the relation between them. If there are no subordinating phrases, identify coordinating phrases and create two independent clauses by identifying the relation between them. Make sure clauses are complete by adding terms like 'This was' at the beginning of the clauses for incomplete clauses. Relation includes ELABORATION, SPATIAL, CONTRAST, CONDITION, SPATIAL, ATTRIBUTION, DISJUNCTION, LIST, CAUSE, TEMPORAL and PURPOSE. Use only the above relations.

Step 2: For each of the clauses identified in Step 1, identify a subordinating phrase in each of the clauses and repeat Step 1.

Step 3: If there are no subordinating phrases in clauses identified in step 1, identify coordinating phrases like and, or, and but and repeat step 1

Step 4: Repeat steps 1 to 3 till all the subordinating and coordinating phrases in the individual clauses are identified.

Step 5: If there are no subordinating or coordinating phrases in the input sentence, then the output will be the same as the input sentence. Else, output the discourse tree in the format: The Discourse Tree: "Relation('Clause1', Relation ('Clause.', 'Clause.') 'Clause2' ...)"

A.7 Zero Shot Unrestricted CoT Prompt for Subordination Task

To construct the discourse Tree, follow the below steps:

Step 1: Identify the subordinating phrases like 'for', 'while', however, because, as, etc., in the input sentence and then divide it into two sentences (clauses) by identifying the relation between them. If there are no subordinating phrases, identify coordinating phrases and create two independent clauses by identifying the relation between them. Make sure clauses are complete by adding terms like 'This was' at the beginning of the clauses for incomplete clauses.

Step 2: For each of the clauses identified in Step 1, identify a subordinating phrase in each of the clauses and repeat Step 1.

Step 3: If there are no subordinating phrases in clauses identified in step 1, identify coordinating phrases like and, or, and but and repeat step 1

Step 4: Repeat steps 1 to 3 till all the subordinating and coordinating phrases in the individual clauses are identified.

Step 5: If there are no subordinating or coordinating phrases in the input sentence, then the output will be the same as the input sentence. Else, output the discourse tree in the format: The Discourse Tree: "Relation ('Clause1', Relation ('Clause', 'Clause') 'Clause2' ...)"

A.8 11 Shot Prompt used for Subordination Task

Following are a few examples of legal input sentences under 'Input' that have been converted into discourse trees, which are shown under 'Output'. using the following examples as a format, convert new legal sentences into trees. Create a discourse tree from the provided sentence without introducing new words or explanations. A discourse tree identifies hierarchical text structures and rhetorical relations between text parts. These relations are categorized as coordination and subordination. below are some examples of how the discourse tree should be generated -

1. ***SPATIAL:*** *This relation is used to denote the place of occurrence of an event .*
   Eg: The Interstate Migrant Workmen Act 's purpose was to protect workers whose services are requisitioned outside their native states in India .

SUB/ELABORATION('The Inter-state Migrant Workmen Act 's purpose was to protect workers .', **SUB/SPATIAL**('This is in India .','Workers 's services are requisitioned outside their native states .'))

2. ***ATTRIBUTION**: This relation is used when a statement is being made by some person or institution.*
   Eg: But some militant SCI TV junk-holders say that 's not enough .
   SUB/ATTRIBUTION('This is what some militant SCI TV junk-holders say .',"s not enough .')

3. ***CONTRAST**: This relation is indicated by the words 'although' , 'but' , 'but now', 'despite' , 'even though' , 'even when', 'except when' , 'however', 'instead' , 'rather", 'still' , 'though' , 'thus', 'until recently', 'while' and 'yet'.*
   Eg: This can have its purposes at times , but there 's no reason to cloud the importance and allure of Western concepts of freedom and justice.
   CO/CONTRAST(SUB/ELABORATION('This is at times .','This can have its purposes .'), 'There 's no reason to cloud the importance and allure of Western concepts of freedom and justice .')

4. ***LIST** : This is used to indicate conjunctions ('and' or comma seperated words) between the sentences*
   *Eg: He believes in what he plays , **and** he plays superbly .*
   CO/LIST('He believes in what he plays .','He plays superbly .')

5. ***DISJUNCTION**: This is used to show the presence of 'OR' in the sentences.*
   Eg: The carpet division had 1988 sales of $ 368.3 million , or almost 14 % of Armstrong 's $ 2.68 billion total revenue .

   CO/DISJUNCTION('The carpet division had 1988 sales of $ 368.3 million .','The carpet division had 1988 sales of almost 14 % of Armstrong 's $ 2.68 billion total revenue .')

6. ***CAUSE**: Indicates the presence of the word - 'because' or 'since'.*
   Eg: Jaguar 's own defenses against a hostile bid are weakened , analysts add , because fewer than 3 % of its shares are owned by employees and management .

   SUB/CAUSE('Jaguar 's own defenses against a hostile bid are weakened , analysts add .','Fewer than 3 % of its shares are owned by employees and management .')

7. ***CONDITION**: When multiple sentences are connected by phrase 'if' 'in case', 'unless' and 'until', CONDITION relationship phrase is used to denote the connection between the sentences.*
   Eg: Unless he closes the gap , Republicans risk losing not only the governorship but also the assembly next month .
   SUB/CONDITION('He closes the gap .','Republicans risk losing not only the governorship but also the assembly next month .')

8. ***ELABORATION**: Identified by the presence of words such as 'more provocatively', 'even before' , 'for example', 'recently' , 'so' , 'so far' , ' where' , 'whereby' and 'whether' .*

   REGEX:

   ```
   `since(\\W(.*?\\W)?)now"
   ```

   *Eg: Not one thing in the house is **where** it is supposed to be , but the structure is fine .*
   CO/CONTRAST(SUB/ELABORATION('Not one thing in the house is .','It is supposed to be .'), 'The structure is fine .')

9. ***TEMPORAL** : Denotes the time or date of occurrence of the event.*
   Eg: These days he hustles to house-painting jobs in his Chevy pickup before and after training with the Tropics .
   SUB/TEMPORAL('These days he hustles to house-painting jobs in his Chevy pickup before and after .','These days he is training with the Tropics .')

10. ***PURPOSE**: This kind of relation is identified by the presence of words such as 'for' or 'to'.*
    Eg: But we can think of many reasons to stay

out for the foreseeable future and well beyond .

`SUB/PURPOSE('But we can think of many reasons .','This is to stay out for the foreseeable future and well beyond .')`

11. ***NONE**: This kind of relation is given if the sentence does not contain any subordinates or coordinates.*
    Eg: Or was it because Ms. Collins had gone?
    NONE

A.9 11 Shot Prompt used for Co-ordination Task

Coordination is a frequently occurring syntactic structure along with several phrases, known as conjuncts. The task of coordination disambiguation is identifying the boundaries of each conjunct with a single coordinator word as one coordinate structure instance. Given a coordinator word (e.g., 'and', 'or' or 'but'), a system must return each conjunct span if the word actually plays the role of a coordinator; otherwise, NONE is output for the absence of coordination. Following this, 11 examples are provided.

A.10 Zero Shot CoT Prompt for Coordination Task

Coordinating sentences join independent clauses with coordinating conjunctions like 'and', 'or', and 'but', enhancing sentence complexity. Your task is to form independent clauses by identifying the coordinating phrases. To construct the hierarchical tree, follow the below steps:

Step 1: Identify the coordinating phrase like and, or and but. Sometimes a sentence can have comma as well to distinguish between different words. Consider that as well while forming independent sentences.
Step 2: Join all the dependent phrases of the coordinating phrase to make an independent sentence. Independant phrases should contains subject, object and a verb.
Step 3: Loop over all the clauses from step 2, and if there are still coordinating phrases present, repeat steps 1 and step 2 till all the coordinating phrases are identified in the input sentence. The clauses should be completely independent.
Step 4: Repeat steps 1 to 3 till all the subordinating and coordinating phrases in the individual clauses are identified.
Step 5: Do not print the results of intermediate steps; print only the final output. If there are no coordinating phrases in the input sentence, the output will be NONE. Else, the output of the hierarchical tree in the format : "COORDINATION('Clause1', Clause2', COORDINATION('clause', 'clause2').......)"

Summarizing Long Regulatory Documents with a Multi-Step Pipeline

Mika Sie
Utrecht University
mikasie6@gmail.com

Ruby Beek
Power2X
ruby.beek@power2x.com

Michiel Bots
Power2X
michiel.bots@power2x.com

Sjaak Brinkkemper
Utrecht University
s.brinkkemper@uu.nl

Albert Gatt
Utrecht University
a.gatt@uu.nl

Abstract

Due to their length and complexity, long regulatory texts are challenging to summarize. To address this, a multi-step extractive-abstractive architecture is proposed to handle lengthy regulatory documents more effectively. In this paper, we show that the effectiveness of a two-step architecture for summarizing long regulatory texts varies significantly depending on the model used. Specifically, the two-step architecture improves the performance of decoder-only models. For abstractive encoder-decoder models with short context lengths, the effectiveness of an extractive step varies, whereas for long-context encoder-decoder models, the extractive step worsens their performance. This research also highlights the challenges of evaluating generated texts, as evidenced by the differing results from human and automated evaluations. Most notably, human evaluations favoured language models pretrained on legal text, while automated metrics rank general-purpose language models higher. The results underscore the importance of selecting the appropriate summarization strategy based on model architecture and context length.

1 Introduction

Automatic text summarisation (ATS) involves generating a compressed, concise, and fluent version of an input text while preserving its main key points. A summary proves useful because it helps people process and understand texts faster and better. Summarizing regulatory texts is important for making complex legal language more accessible and ensuring compliance by condensing information into a concise, understandable format. [1]

Current ATS methods use either extractive or abstractive summarization. An advantage of extractive summarization is that it captures sentences and information literally, resulting in a factually consistent summary. However, the summary is harder to read and less intuitive as sentences are copied and combined. Abstractive summaries are more coherent and fluent as they summarize texts in a human-like fashion. But it also has disadvantages because an intricate understanding of the original text is required and the summary can be factually inconsistent. In this paper, our aim is to explore the advantages of both strategies, as we leverage them for the summarisation of very lengthy, regulatory documents.

A regulatory text is a formal document issued by a government or regulatory body that outlines rules, guidelines, or standards to govern the conduct, practices, or operations within a specific industry, sector, or jurisdiction. Regulatory documents are difficult to process due to their extensive size, unique structure, numerous citations and references, ambiguity, and domain-specific vocabulary. Current automatic summarization tools face challenges with regulatory texts, either because their length exceeds the context length of LLMs, or because the length and structure of the input document raise the risk of omissions in the summary. Leaving out important information could have major negative effects.

This paper compares two-step and multi-step summarisation methods for regulatory documents, comparing the effectiveness of different neural model architectures and combinations. Our approach consists of the following steps, illustrated in Figure 1. First, the document is segmented into smaller units or 'chunks'. Each chunk is then processed by an extractive summarization model, and all resulting summaries are concatenated. This extractive step may need to be conducted iteratively. The outcome of extraction is then summarized in an abstractive manner, creating a final summary. Combining these two summarization steps could prove useful in handling the large size of the original text. It uses extracted salient sentences to de-

[1] Code and models are available on GitHub and HuggingFace.

Proceedings of the Natural Legal Language Processing Workshop 2024, pages 18–32
November 16, 2024 ©2024 Association for Computational Linguistics

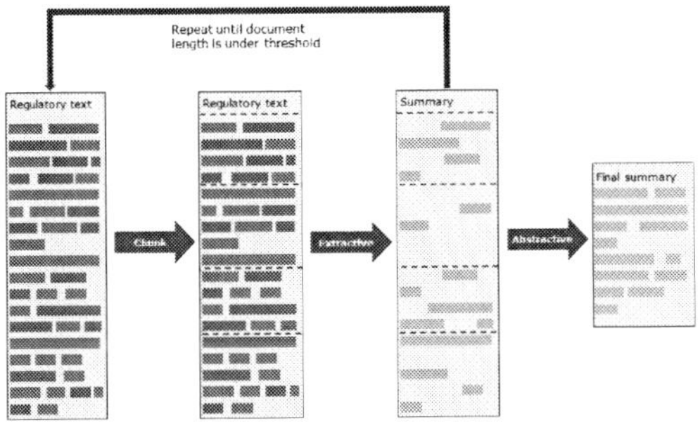

Figure 1: Summarization process proposed by this research. Dotted lines indicate the borders of the chunks.

velop a coherent, fluent summary. Similar architectures have been used on different types of texts and have shown promising results (Pilault et al., 2020; Zhang et al., 2022; Klaus et al., 2022; Bleiweiss, 2023). However, summarizing long regulatory documents using this architecture has been researched less extensively. In particular, our goal is to evaluate various models used for each step to identify the most effective combination of models for the summarization task, paying particular attention to whether preliminary extraction is more beneficial if performed with domain-specific (legal) rather than domain-general models. A second important goal is to compare the effect of context length on the quality of the generated summaries: models allowing longer context lengths need less extraction. Given the growing trend for large language models to allow longer document lengths, it is increasingly important to understand whether such models are able to acquire a comprehensive understanding of a full document, or whether preliminary distillation of information is helpful (Li et al., 2024).

2 Related work

Long document summarisation Pretrained language models (LMs) struggle with long texts due to limitations on input context length. For example, BERT (Devlin et al., 2019) and T5 (Raffel et al., 2020) have a context length of 512 tokens while PEGASUS's (Zhang et al., 2020a) and BART's (Lewis et al., 2020) context length is 1024 tokens.

To counter this limitation, some long document architectures incorporate a different self-attention mechanism, calculating attention between specific parts of the sequence instead of calculating the attention for every possible combination of the sequence. This enables them to process long sequences because the computation requirements will not grow quadratically. Longformer (Beltagy et al., 2020) is an encoder-only architecture based on RoBERTa (Liu et al., 2019), designed to handle long-range dependencies more efficiently than standard transformers, and accepting inputs of up to 4096 tokens. It employs a combination of global attention and sliding window attention instead of full attention, which scales linearly with the input sequence. LED (Beltagy et al., 2020) adds a decoder to the Longformer architecture, turning it into the Longformer Encoder-Decoder model. The decoder does use the full attention mechanism but LED retains its linear computation capability. Similar examples of LMs designed for longer documents include BigBird (which accepts a context length of 4096 tokens; Zaheer et al., 2020), LongT5 (Guo et al., 2022) and PegasusX (Phang et al., 2023), both of which accept contexts of 16,384 tokens.

Extending context length is often a goal in recent releases of decoder-only LLMs, such as the GPT family of models. Other examples include LLaMA-2-7B-32k (Tog), which is an LLM based on LLaMA-2 (Touvron et al., 2023) with a context length of 32768.

Multi-step summarisation The idea of multi-step methods is to leverage both extractive and abstractive techniques to alleviate the burden of summarising very long documents. Pilault et al. (Pilault et al., 2020) add one extractive step before generating the abstractive summary. The extractive parts are then used beside the original text as input for the transformer. A related approach is taken in CreativeSumm (Kim et al., 2022) for the summarisation of lengthy movie scripts. Liu et al. (2018) summarise Wikipedia articles by first performing an extractive step, using the extracted sentences as additional input to the summariser. Bleiweiss (2023) propose a two-step method for long biographical novels. Klaus et al. (2022) make use of a two-step method to summarize legal regulatory documents. Klaus et al. use TextRank (Mihalcea and Tarau, 2004), a graph-based extractive summarization approach, for the first extractive step and BERT (Devlin et al., 2019) or RoBERTa (Liu et al., 2019) for a second extractive step.

A generalisation of the two-step strategy was proposed in the form of Summ^N (Zhang et al., 2022). Summ^N splits the data samples and generates coarse summaries, possibly over multiple stages (N), before producing a final fine-grained abstractive summary. This method outperformed previous state-of-the-art methods on different datasets. Different from our work, Summ^N makes use of abstractive summarisation for both the coarse-grained and the final, more fine-grained summarisation steps. Instead, we use extractive summarisation for the first stage.

Inspired by multi-step methods, we experiment in this paper with various combinations of extractive and abstractive steps, in an effort to identify the best architecture for summarisation of long, regulatory documents.

Divide-and-conquer (chunking) strategies An interesting class of approaches to long document summarisation involves a 'divide-and-conquer' strategy. Briefly, the idea is to chunk the document into sub-parts before summarisation, where sub-part identification may also exploit the document structure. Examples of this are the context-aware chunking strategy for academic articles used in DANCER (Gidiotis and Tsoumakas, 2020) and the work of Shen and Lam (2022), whose model directly learns the correspondence between document sections and summary parts. In our work, we also explore the role of chunking strategies and their effectiveness in producing coherent summaries.

Domain-specific Legal Language Models An important question in the processing of texts in specialised domains is whether in-domain pretraining is beneficial, given that specialised domains have stylistic and other peculiarities. Relevant to the present paper is the case of legal text (of which regulatory texts are a subset), which has well-studied distinctive stylistic characteristics (Turtle, 1995; Kanapala et al., 2019; Jain et al., 2021). Studies have shown that in-domain pretraining can be beneficial in downstream NLP tasks (Gururangan et al., 2020) and domain-specific LMs have been developed for healthcare (Huang et al., 2020; Lee et al., 2020), science (Beltagy et al., 2019) and finance (Yang et al., 2020; Wu et al., 2023), among many others. Pre-trained LMs for law include Lawyer LLaMA(Huang et al., 2023), Lawformer (Xiao et al., 2021), LegalLongformer (Mamakas et al., 2022), PEGASUS-Billsum (Zhang et al., 2020a), LegalBERT (Chalkidis et al., 2020b), CaseLawBERT (Zheng et al., 2021), PoL-BERT (Henderson et al., 2022) and LexLM (Chalkidis et al., 2023). In an early study, Chalkidis et al. (2020b) showed that LegalBERT consistently outperformed BERT-based models on a variety of NLP tasks, including EURLEX57K (Chalkidis et al., 2020c), ECHR-CASES (Chalkidis et al., 2020a), and CONTRACTS-NER (Chalkidis et al., 2017). Building on this work, Mamakas et al. (2022) introduced LegalLongformer, initialised with LegalBERT's parameters, to handle long legal texts. Chalkidis et al. (2023) introduced LexLM, a model pre-trained on a multinational English legal data. Additionally, they introduced a version of LexLM utilizing the Longformer (Beltagy et al., 2020) attention mechanism, enhancing the capability to handle long legal documents. In comparative evaluations, LexLM models outperformed other legal LMs, such as CaseLawBERT and PoL-BERT, particularly in prior knowledge assessment and downstream task performance. Notably, RoBERTa (Liu et al., 2019) also showed strong performance, occasionally surpassing some specialized legal models.

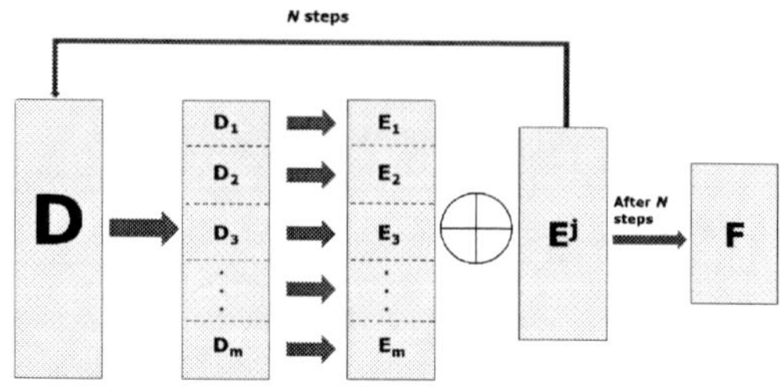

Figure 2: Visualisation of the summarisation process. N represents the amount of extractive steps and the $\oplus$ symbol represents the concatenation process.

Building on these observations, in our experiments we also compare general-purpose models with a representative subset of legal LMs, particularly for the extractive summarisation step.

3 Method

Our approach to the summarisation of long regulatory documents is a multi-step process consisting of extraction followed by abstraction, where extraction is intended to alleviate the problem of limited context length accepted by a model. In particular, if the length of a source document $|D|$ exceeds the context length K of an abstractive model, creating an intermediate extractive summary could help identify essential information across the document span, a more informed strategy than truncating the document to fit within K.

The overall process is visualised in Figure 2. We view a source document $D = \{D_1, D_2, D_3, ...D_m\}$ as a sequence of chunks D_i.

A chunk is summarised by an extractive summarisation model, which produces an intermediary summary $E^j = E_1^j \oplus E_2^j \oplus E_3^j \oplus, ..., \oplus E_M^j$, where E_i^j represents an intermediate summary of chunk D_i at extractive step j. Thus, the intermediate summary E^j comprises the summaries of all the chunks concatenated in the same order as in the original text. The extractive summarisation model has a compression ratio $R \in [0, 1]$. One way to define R is in terms of the ration of the length of an article and that of its summary (Grusky et al., 2018); below, we also explore other possible definitions for R. Before the summarisation is performed, the number of extractive steps N taken is determined, such that the extractive summary produced at step $n \leq N$ is the input to the extractive step $n + 1 \leq N$. The extractive summary after N steps is the input to the abstractive summarisation model, which yields the final summary F.

3.1 Dataset

The dataset used to fine-tune the abstractive model is EUR-Lex-Sum (Aumiller et al., 2022). This dataset consists of documents from the European Union law platform with corresponding manually curated summaries. Only the English part of the dataset, composed of 1504 document -summary pairs, was used for this task. It has been divided into training, validation, and test sets, containing 1129 pairs, 187 and 188 pairs, respectively. The dataset is characterised by a small number of documents whose length far exceeds that of the others. To ensure consistency in our evaluation, we define any document whose word count is more than two standard deviations above the mean as an outlier and remove it from the training, validation and test subsets originally provided by Aumiller et al. (2022). In total, 62 instances were removed by this criterion. The final dataset consists of 1091 training, 172 validation and 179 test samples.

3.2 Architecture

Extractive step(s) As described above, documents are first summarised over N extractive steps. Note that the extractive step is only performed if the length of the document exceeds the context length K of the abstractive model. The number of extractive steps needed ultimately depends on the compression ratio R that we require for the summarisation, corresponding to two-step (one extraction step followed by abstraction) and multi-step approaches. We experiment with three different strategies for computing R for an abstractive model with context length $K$and a document of length $|D|$. Note that K and $|D|$ are fixed in advance for a given model and document.

Our first strategy is to use a **fixed compression ratio**, empirically setting $R = 0.4$. In this case, $N \geq 1$ and is estimated as follows (see Appendix A.1 for details of how this is derived):

$$N = \left\lceil \frac{\log\left(\frac{K}{|D|}\right)}{\log(R)} \right\rceil \tag{1}$$

The second strategy is to use a **dependent compression ratio**, which depends on the document's size and the abstractive model's context length, resulting in $N = 1$:

$$R = \frac{K}{|D|} \tag{2}$$

The final strategy is a **hybrid ratio**, where we perform $N - 1$ extractive steps with a fixed ratio, with a final extractive step N using a dependent ratio. The hybrid ratio could be more effective than the fixed ratio because it is focused on ensuring that the final intermediate summary optimally fits the context length of the abstractive model. We define the hybrid ratio as follows:

$$R = \begin{cases} 0.4 & \text{for steps } 1, 2, \ldots, N-1 \\ \frac{K}{|D|} & \text{for step } N \end{cases} \tag{3}$$

Extractive models One of our goals is to compare the impact of domain-specific LMs and general-purpose LMs. In what follows, non-domain specific LMs will be referred to as 'general' LMs, and domain-specific legal LMs will be referred to as 'legal' LMs. The top panel of Table 1 lists all the extractive summarisation models used. Based on this comparison, we aim to identify the optimal extractive model.

We compare all the extractive models with the three ratio types described above, with a view to determining the optimal extractive strategy to support abstractive summarisation. To identify the optimal extractive model, we compare the impact of different extractive models and compression ratios on downstream abstractive summarisation with BART (Lewis et al., 2020). Specifically, we compare the output of a BART summariser, finetuned on using input from different extractive models. We compare this to a baseline BART model with

Model	Context length	Legal LM	Type	Architecture
RoBERTa (Liu et al., 2019)	512	✗	Extractive	Encoder
Longformer (Beltagy et al., 2020)	4096	✗	Extractive	Encoder
LegalBERT-SC (Chalkidis et al., 2020b)	512	✓	Extractive	Encoder
LexLM (Chalkidis et al., 2023)	512	✓	Extractive	Encoder
LexLM - Longformer (Chalkidis et al., 2023)	4096	✓	Extractive	Encoder
BART (Lewis et al., 2020)	1024	✗	Abstractive	Encoder-Decoder
T5 (Raffel et al., 2020)	512	✗	Abstractive	Encoder-Decoder
LongT5 (Guo et al., 2022)	16384	✗	Abstractive	Encoder-Decoder
Pegasus (Zhang et al., 2020b)	1024	✗	Abstractive	Encoder-Decoder
PegasusX (Phang et al., 2022)	16384	✗	Abstractive	Encoder-Decoder
Llama3 (AI, 2024)	8192	✗	Abstractive	Decoder

Table 1: Summarisation models used. The context length is expressed in number of tokens. Top: models used for extractive summarisation; bottom: models used for abstractive summarisation.

no extractive steps. In total, we compare sixteen model configurations. The optimal extractive strategy under this experimental setting was then used to fine-tune subsequent abstractive models.

Abstractive step The abstractive step was only performed once the length of the intermediate summary $|E^j|$ is within the context length K of an abstractive summarisation model. The abstractive step involves creating the final summary F by an abstractive summarisation model fine-tuned on the intermediate summary E^j.

We compare a variety of abstractive models, listed in the bottom panel of Table 1. The context length of the abstractive summarisation model is an important consideration as it affects the number of extractive steps. A longer context length implies that fewer extractive steps need to be taken. By hypothesis, the quality of the final summary should be higher the fewer the extractive steps, since there is less potential in this case for information loss. To quantify this, we chose models that permit a direct comparison of context length effects, while keeping architecture largely constant. We compare T5 (Raffel et al., 2020) against LongT5 (Guo et al., 2022), and Pegasus (Zhang et al., 2020b) against PegasusX (Phang et al., 2022) to determine the effect of a long context length in the abstractive summarization model. Finally, we include Llama3 (AI, 2024), as an example of a SOTA large language model based on a decoder architecture (T5 and Pegasus are encoder-decoder models).

Full parameter fine-tuning was performed for all abstractive models except Llama3, which was fine-tuned using QLoRA (Dettmers et al., 2023) as full parameter fine-tuning was not feasible due to its size. Data had to be prepared in a different way for Llama3 as it is the sole decoder-only model used in our experiments. A single combined sequence is used instead of separate input and output sequences. To accommodate a summary of 1500 tokens, 1500 tokens are subtracted from the model's context length, resulting in an effective context length of 6692 tokens for Llama3. The extractive summarisation process was adjusted to summarise the reference text to fit within this 6692-token limit, ensuring minimal truncation. See Appendix A.2 and A.3 for more details on model finetuning, including hyperparameters.

3.3 Evaluation

Evaluation metrics Multiple evaluation metrics were used to assess the proposed architecture from different aspects. This research employed ROUGE-1, ROUGE-2, ROUGE-L (Lin, 2004), BERTScore (Zhang et al., 2020b), BARTScore (Yuan et al., 2021), and BLANC (Vasilyev et al., 2020a). Details of the implementations used for the evaluation metrics are in Appendix A.4.

Expert evaluation Besides automated metrics, we also performed a small-scale qualitative human evaluation involving expert readers. The human evaluation provides insights into the quality of the summaries, complementing the quantitative data from automated metrics with qualitative feedback. After selecting the optimal extractive model and training the abstractive models, we generate summaries of a new text which is not in the training dataset.[2] Summaries generated with the different abstractive models were compared by the expert readers. This document was chosen specifically because the expert readers were already familiar with the contents and, hence, were able to judge summary quality more reliably.

The evaluators were two experts from the com-

[2]The text in question is the Carbon Border Adjust Mechanism document (European Union, 2023).

Criterion	Description
Factual Correctness	Evaluation of how factually correct the summary is relative to the source document.
Usability	Assessment of how practical and user-friendly the summary is.
Accuracy	Assessment of the precision and correctness of the information in the summary.
Fluency	Assessment of the summary's smoothness and ease of reading in terms of form, content, and grammar.
Coherence	Measure of how logical the summary is to it is linguistic context.

Table 2: Criteria for human evaluation.

pany ANON, a collaborator on this project whose personnel have extensive experience with regulatory documents issued by the European Union. The experts were asked to read summaries generated by different summarization architectures and evaluate them based on a set of criteria. The criteria included *Factual Correctness*, *Usability*, *Accuracy*, *Fluency*, and *Coherence*. Each criterion was rated on a scale from 1 to 5. Detailed descriptions of these criteria can be found in Table 2 and are based on the findings of Howcroft et al. (2020)'s meta-review of constructs used in human evaluation of Natural Language Generation systems. In addition to scoring the summaries, experts were also asked to comment on the quality of summaries.

Due to resource and time constraints, we selected specific architectures to be included in the qualitative evaluation. To analyse the impact of different extractive models, we compare different versions of BART, using (1) the best extractive model; (2) no extractive step; (3) the best legal LM for extraction; and (4) the best long-context extractive model. To analyse the impact of different abstractive strategies, we also include (5) the best long-context abstractive model; and (6) the best decoder-only model.

4 Results

4.1 Comparison of extractive models

Table 3 contains the results on different metrics for abstractive summarisation using BART, in combination with different extractive strategies. It can be seen that RoBERTa with a dependent ratio scores the highest on ROUGE-1, ROUGE-2, ROUGE-L, and BERTScore. RoBERTa with a hybrid ratio achieves the highest score on BLANC. On the other hand, the best BARTScore is obtained when we do not combine any extractive summarisation to compress the input to BART.

In the rest of this section, we discuss these results in light of the different experimental conditions.

4.1.1 Effect of number of extractive stages

The results indicate that models using the dependent ratio type generally achieve higher performance across most metrics. Notably, the RoBERTa model with the dependent ratio type attains the highest scores in ROUGE-1 (0.4873), ROUGE-2 (0.1974), ROUGE-L (0.2247), and BERTScore (0.8721), suggesting superior performance in these areas. However, the BART model without any extractive steps achieves the best scores in BARTScore (-3.4154) and BLANC (0.1700), indicating a stronger performance in these specific metrics despite not utilizing extraction.

Using a multi-step architecture, that is, one that performs multiple extractive iterations (up to N; see Section 3), sentences from differnt document chunks get combined during the summarization process. This could introduce noise and consequently fail to capture the most relevant and coherent information, resulting in lower performance. It seems that using a single extractive step is more effective at capturing the most important sentences out of a chunk relative to the context of the global document. We hypothesise that this explains the superiority of the dependent ratio (where $N = 1$) on most metrics.

Effect of Legal Language Models General-purpose LMs such as RoBERTa achieve slightly higher scores across all metrics except BARTScore, compared to legal LMs. For this comparison, RoBERTa was compared against LegalBERT and LexLM, and Longformer was compared against LexLM-Longformer to accommodate for the context lengths.

These results indicate that, when used as extractors for preliminary document compression, the broad range of training data types that general-purpose LMs are exposed to gives them an advantage in locating important information in the document. In contrast, legal LMs can suffer from a 'narrow' focus, resulting in less coherent and com-

Extractive model	Ratio type	R1	R2	RL	BERTScore	BARTScore	BLANC
N/A	No extraction	0.4590	0.1954	0.2174	0.8702	**-3.4154**	0.1029
RoBERTa	Fixed	0.4670	0.1798	0.2171	0.8692	-3.5654	0.1040
RoBERTa	Dependent	**0.4873**	**0.1974**	**0.2247**	**0.8721**	-3.5590	0.1272
RoBERTa	Hybrid	0.4809	0.1889	0.2193	0.8700	-3.5781	**0.1296**
LegalBERT	Fixed	0.4390	0.1766	0.2158	0.8700	-3.4893	0.1099
LegalBERT	Dependent	0.4619	0.1854	0.2174	0.8713	-3.5143	0.1117
LegalBERT	Hybrid	0.4469	0.1774	0.2137	0.8665	-3.5714	0.1098
LexLM	Fixed	0.4571	0.1745	0.2123	0.8692	-3.6130	0.1154
LexLM	Dependent	0.4859	0.1954	0.2227	0.8713	-3.5441	0.1277
LexLM	Hybrid	0.4582	0.1792	0.2135	0.8665	-3.5639	0.1102
Longformer	Fixed	0.4436	0.1686	0.2103	0.8684	-3.5901	0.1029
Longformer	Dependent	0.4613	0.1874	0.2194	0.8712	-3.5835	0.1238
Longformer	Hybrid	0.4778	0.1862	0.2181	0.8703	-3.5697	0.1256
LexLM-Longformer	Fixed	0.4250	0.1584	0.2041	0.8659	-3.6141	0.0959
LexLM-Longformer	Dependent	0.4751	0.1852	0.2164	0.8689	-3.5344	0.1272
LexLM-Longformer	Hybrid	0.4619	0.1819	0.2189	0.8692	-3.5833	0.1199

Table 3: Results for all extractive summarization models in combination with BART.

Abstractive model	Ratio type	R1	R2	RL	BERTScore	BARTScore	BLANC
BART	No extraction	0.4590	0.1954	0.2174	0.8702	-3.4154	0.1029
BART	Dependent	**0.4873**	**0.1974**	0.2247	**0.8721**	-3.5590	0.1272
T5	No extraction	0.3033	0.1241	0.1994	0.8443	-2.1585	0.0760
T5	Dependent	0.2934	0.0926	0.1857	0.8404	-2.2234	0.0812
LongT5	No extraction	0.3261	0.1309	0.2192	0.8497	-2.2195	0.1128
LongT5	Dependent	0.2854	0.0969	0.0969	0.8444	-2.0423	0.1051
Pegasus	No extraction	0.3305	0.1293	0.2260	0.8499	**-1.8067**	0.0923
Pegasus	Dependent	0.3067	0.0911	0.2021	0.8435	-1.8940	0.0952
PegasusX	No extraction	0.3673	0.1622	**0.2304**	0.8523	-2.4528	0.1086
PegasusX	Dependent	0.3052	0.1162	0.1960	0.8413	-2.4305	0.0999
Llama3	No extraction	0.4088	0.1816	0.2107	0.7854	-3.3424	0.1177
Llama3	Dependent	0.4474	0.1885	0.2284	0.8687	-3.1268	0.1231

Table 4: Evaluation results of all abstractive models with and without an extractive step.

	Extr. model	Ratio	Abstr. model	FC	U	Acc	Fl	Coh
1	RoBERTa	Dep.	BART	2.0	2.0	1.5	1.5	2.0
2	-	NE	BART	3.5	1.0	2.0	**3.0**	1.5
3	LexLM	Dep.	BART	**4.0**	**3.5**	**3.0**	**3.0**	**3.0**
4	Longformer	Dep.	BART	2.0	2.0	2.5	1.5	2.0
5	-	NE	PegasusX	3.5	1.0	2.5	**3.0**	1.0
6	RoBERTa	Dep.	Llama3	3.0	2.5	2.5	2.5	2.0

Table 5: Average human evaluation results. Dep: Dependent ratio; NE: No extraction; FC: Factual Correctness; U: Usability; Acc: Accuracy; Fl: Fluency; Coh: Coherence

prehensive extractive summaries. This insight suggests that general LMs can be effective for domain-specific tasks, at least for preparatory steps such as the one considered here.

Effect of context length for the extractive step Models with shorter context lengths for the extractive step achieve higher scores across all metrics. RoBERTa was compared against Longformer for general LMs and LegalBERT and LexLM against LexLM-Longformer for legal LMs. This approach ensures a fair comparison by accommodating general and legal language model differences.

This finding is surprising, since one would assume that longer-context models would perform better by capturing more global context. However, when sequences are excessively long, the models might struggle to maintain and encode all relevant information, leading to reduced sensitivity to portions of the input, in line with findings such as those reported by Fu et al. (2023), among others.

This could explain why shorter context models, which deal with more manageable chunks of information, consistently perform better in the extraction task.

Optimal extractive model Based on Table 3, RoBERTa with a dependent ratio will be chosen as the optimal extractive model and is used in the remainder of the experiments reported below.

4.2 Comparison of abstractive models

For every abstractive model, two versions are compared: one leveraging RoBERTa with a dependent ratio and one without using any extractive step at all. The results for all abstractive models and their variants can be seen in Table 4. For clarity, models that incorporate an extractive step will be referred to by the name of the abstractive model. Models that do not use an extractive step will be denoted by appending "-NE" to the name of the abstractive model, where "NE" signifies "No Extraction".

Effect of extractive step The performance of encoder-decoder abstractive summarization models generally worsens when using one extractive step, though this differs per model. This is evident in the results for T5, LongT5, Pegasus, and PegasusX, where the versions without extraction tend to outperform their counterparts with an extractive step. BART presents a more varied picture as it differs per metric in which variant scores higher. Since encoder-decoder models generate a condensed representation of the text, one explanation for these results is that by introducing an intermediate extractive summary we compromise the performance of the encoder. This could happen because the intermediate summary is less coherent than the input document as a whole.

LLama3, the decoder-only model seems to benefit from an additional extractive step, obtaining better results on all metrics when compared to the version with no extraction. The beneficial effect of extraction here is likely due to the limited context of Llama3 and the risk of loss of sensitivity to longer inputs, as decodig proceeds (Fu et al., 2023). These shortcomings could be mitigated by performing some preliminary input compression and identification of core information.

Effect of context length for the abstractive step Long context models generally outperform their short context counterparts, with some exceptions. Long context models without an extractive step outperform short context models without an extractive step on all metrics, except BARTScore. When an extractive step is used, results vary as short context models show advantages on specific metrics. In other words, models with shorter input contexts benefit from input compression, as expected. Long context models without an extractive step generally outperform short context models with an extractive step across all metrics.

4.3 Human evaluation

Human evaluation scores are in Table 5. Experts' individual scores and comments are in Appendix B. Recall that the human evaluation was performed after selecting the optimal extractive model and fine-tuning all abstractive models. Overall, the expert evaluators preferred architectures that relied on a legal LM or a long context model in the extractive step. Indeed, the model that was preferred across all criteria was BART coupled with a LexLM extractor with a dependent compression ratio. The experts' comments suggested that this architecture did have shortcomings, but these were counterbalanced by other factors. For example, one expert noted that the summary correctly grasps the key points of the regulation, making it quite useful, despite the fact that is it incomplete and has shortcomings on fluency and coherence.

Common criticisms of the summaries by the experts included excessive repetition in the case of some architectures, which severely decrease the quality of the produced summary. Furthermore, while some summaries may appear well-structured and readable, they fail to capture the essential points of the regulation or contain factual errors.

A somewhat surprising outcome is that LLaMA-3 scores relatively poorly on coherence and fluency, compared to the best-performing model. It should be noted that the two evaluators diverged significantly in their scores for this model on these criteria (compare Tables 8 and 9 in Appendix B). Furthermore, as noted above, LLaMA was treated somewhat differently since it is the only decoder-only model. In particular, we subtracted 1500 tokens from the model's context length to accommodate the extractive summary; this too could have impacted results, though we adjusted the extractive summarisation process to ensure minimal truncation.

Despite the fact that this is a small-scale evaluation (a point we return to in Section 5), there are interesting divergences between expert judgments and the conclusions drawn based on the automatic metrics, an observation which is quite common in the NLG and summarisation literature (cf. Belz and Reiter, 2006; Reiter, 2018; Celikyilmaz et al., 2021).

In particular, experts suggest that legal LMs help achieve more satisfactory summaries if used in the extractive step. On the other hand, both automatic and human evaluation suggest that BART is a competitive model for summarisation, especially if preceded by an extractive step.

5 Conclusion

In this paper, we focused on summarisation of long regulatory documents. Our findings indicate that while models with a longer context length do not benefit from extraction, an extractive step renders BART, an encoder-decoder architecture, highly competitive. A small-scaled evaluation with human experts confirms this finding. However, experts also indicate a preference for summaries relying on extraction with a domain-specific, legal language model.

Future work should consider whether these findings are generalisable to other domains. Furthermore, a more extensive human evaluation is required to ensure that our findings are reliable. This is particularly crucial given that human expert judgments are not perfectly aligned with the outcomes of our metric-based evaluation, which echoes findings from other studies. A further possible research direction is to use a state-of-the-art LLM as an evaluator or 'judge' for generated texts, a strategy which recent research suggests is increasingly viable (Liu et al., 2023; Zheng et al., 2023), though also one that requires some caution in view of results suggesting self-bias on the part of LLMs (Panickssery et al., 2024), as well as lower reliability in comparison with expert judgment (Bavaresco et al., 2024).

References

Llama-2-7B-32K-Instruct — and fine-tuning for Llama-2 models with Together API.

Meta AI. 2024. Introducing meta llama 3: The most capable openly available llm to date. Accessed: 2024-06-04.

Dennis Aumiller, Ashish Chouhan, and Michael Gertz. 2022. Eur-lex-sum: A multi- and cross-lingual dataset for long-form summarization in the legal domain. In *Proceedings of the 2022 Conference on Empirical Methods in Natural Language Processing, EMNLP 2022*.

Anna Bavaresco, Raffaella Bernardi, Leonardo Bertolazzi, Desmond Elliott, Raquel Fernández, Albert Gatt, Esam Ghaleb, Mario Giulianelli, Michael Hanna, Alexander Koller, André F. T. Martins, Philipp Mondorf, Vera Neplenbroek, Sandro Pezzelle, Barbara Plank, David Schlangen, Alessandro Suglia, Aditya K. Surikuchi, Ece Takmaz, and Alberto Testoni. 2024. LLMs instead of Human Judges? A Large Scale Empirical Study across 20 NLP Evaluation Tasks. *arXiv preprint*.

Iz Beltagy, Kyle Lo, and Arman Cohan. 2019. Scibert: A pretrained language model for scientific text. In *Proceedings of the 2019 Conference on Empirical Methods in Natural Language Processing and 9th International Joint Conference on Natural Language Processing*.

Iz Beltagy, Matthew E. Peters, and Arman Cohan. 2020. Longformer: The long-document transformer. *Preprint*, arXiv:2004.05150.

Anja Belz and E Reiter. 2006. Comparing Automatic and Human Evaluation of NLG Systems. In *Proceedings of the 11th Conference of the European Chapter of the Association for Computational Linguistics (EACL'06)*, pages 313–320.

Avi Bleiweiss. 2023. Two-step text summarization for long-form biographical narrative genre. In *Proceedings of the 4th Workshop on Computational Approaches to Discourse (CODI 2023)*, pages 145–155, Toronto, Canada. Association for Computational Linguistics.

Asli Celikyilmaz, Elizabeth Clark, and Jianfeng Gao. 2021. Evaluation of Text Generation: A Survey. *arXiv preprint*. ArXiv:2006.14799 [cs].

Ilias Chalkidis, Ion Androutsopoulos, and Nikolaos Aletras. 2020a. Neural legal judgment prediction in english. In *Proceedings of the 57th Annual Meeting of the Association for Computational Linguistics*.

Ilias Chalkidis, Ion Androutsopoulos, and Achilleas Michos. 2017. Extracting contract elements. In *Proceedings of the International Conference on Artificial Intelligence and Law*.

Ilias Chalkidis, Manos Fergadiotis, Prodromos Malakasiotis, Nikolaos Aletras, and Ion Androutsopoulos. 2020b. Legal-bert: The muppets straight out of law school. In *Findings of the Association for Computational Linguistics Findings of ACL: EMNLP 2020*.

Ilias Chalkidis, Manos Fergadiotis, Prodromos Malakasiotis, and Ion Androutsopoulos. 2020c. Large-scale multi-label text classification on eu legislation. In *Proceedings of the 57th Annual Meeting of the Association for Computational Linguistics*.

Ilias Chalkidis, Nicolas Garneau, Anders Søgaard, Cătălină Goantă, and Daniel Martin Katz. 2023. Lexfiles and legallama: Facilitating english multinational legal language model development. In *Proceedings of the Annual Meeting of the Association for Computational Linguistics*.

Tim Dettmers, Artidoro Pagnoni, Ari Holtzman, and Luke Zettlemoyer. 2023. Qlora: Efficient finetuning of quantized llms. *Preprint*, arXiv:2305.14314.

Jacob Devlin, Ming Wei Chang, Kenton Lee, and Kristina Toutanova. 2019. Bert: Pre-training of deep bidirectional transformers for language understanding. In *Proceedings of the 2019 Conference of the North American Chapter of the Association for Computational Linguistics: Human Language Technologies*, volume 1.

European Union. 2023. Regulation (eu) 2023/0956 of the european parliament and of the council of 10 may 2023 on machinery. Accessed: 2024-06-28.

Zihao Fu, Wai Lam, Qian Yu, Anthony Man-Cho So, Shengding Hu, Zhiyuan Liu, and Nigel Collier. 2023. Decoder-Only or Encoder-Decoder? Interpreting Language Model as a Regularized Encoder-Decoder. *arXiv preprint*. ArXiv:2304.04052 [cs].

Alexios Gidiotis and Grigorios Tsoumakas. 2020. A divide-and-conquer approach to the summarization of long documents. *IEEE/ACM Transactions on Audio Speech and Language Processing*, 28.

Max Grusky, Mor Naaman, and Yoav Artzi. 2018. Newsroom: A dataset of 1.3 million summaries with diverse extractive strategies. In *Proceedings of the 2018 Conference of the North American Chapter of the Association for Computational Linguistics: Human Language Technologies*, volume 1.

Mandy Guo, Joshua Ainslie, David Uthus, Santiago Ontañón, Jianmo Ni, Yun Hsuan Sung, and Yinfei Yang. 2022. Longt5: Efficient text-to-text transformer for long sequences. In *Findings of the Association for Computational Linguistics: NAACL 2022*.

Suchin Gururangan, Ana Marasovic, Swabha Swayamdipta, Kyle Lo, Iz Beltagy, Doug Downey, and Noah A. Smith. 2020. Don't stop pretraining: Adapt language models to domains and tasks. In *Proceedings of the Annual Meeting of the Association for Computational Linguistics*.

Peter Henderson, Mark S. Krass, Lucia Zheng, Neel Guha Christopher D. Manning, Dan Jurafsky, and Daniel E. Ho. 2022. Pile of law: Learning responsible data filtering from the law and a 256gb open-source legal dataset. In *Advances in Neural Information Processing Systems*, volume 35.

David M. Howcroft, Anya Belz, Miruna Clinciu, Dimitra Gkatzia, Sadid A. Hasan, Saad Mahamood, Simon Mille, Emiel van Miltenburg, Sashank Santhanam, and Verena Rieser. 2020. Twenty years of confusion in human evaluation: Nlg needs evaluation sheets and standardised definitions. In *Proceedings of the 13th International Conference on Natural Language Generation*.

Edward J. Hu, Yelong Shen, Phillip Wallis, Zeyuan Allen-Zhu, Yuanzhi Li, Shean Wang, Lu Wang, and Weizhu Chen. 2021. Lora: Low-rank adaptation of large language models. *Preprint*, arXiv:2106.09685.

Kexin Huang, Jaan Altosaar, and Rajesh Ranganath. 2020. Clinicalbert: Modeling clinical notes and predicting hospital readmission. *Preprint*, arXiv:1904.05342.

Quzhe Huang, Mingxu Tao, Chen Zhang, Zhenwei An, Cong Jiang, Zhibin Chen, Zirui Wu, and Yansong Feng. 2023. Lawyer llama technical report. *Preprint*, arXiv:2305.15062.

Deepali Jain, Malaya Dutta Borah, and Anupam Biswas. 2021. Summarization of legal documents: Where are we now and the way forward. *Computer Science Review*, 40.

Ambedkar Kanapala, Sukomal Pal, and Rajendra Pamula. 2019. Text summarization from legal documents: a survey. *Artificial Intelligence Review*, 51.

Eunchong Kim, Taewoo Yoo, Gunhee Cho, Suyoung Bae, and Yun-Gyung Cheong. 2022. The creativesumm 2022 shared task: A two-stage summarization model using scene attributesutterances. In *Proceedings of The Workshop on Automatic Summarization for Creative Writing*.

Svea Klaus, Ria Van Hecke, Kaweh Djafari Naini, Ismail Sengor Altingovde, Juan Bernabé-Moreno, and Enrique Herrera-Viedma. 2022. Summarizing legal regulatory documents using transformers. In *=Proceedings of the 45th International ACM SIGIR Conference on Research and Development in Information Retrieval*.

Jinhyuk Lee, Wonjin Yoon, Sungdong Kim, Donghyeon Kim, Sunkyu Kim, Chan Ho So, and Jaewoo Kang. 2020. Biobert: A pre-trained biomedical language representation model for biomedical text mining. *Bioinformatics*, 36.

Mike Lewis, Yinhan Liu, Naman Goyal, Marjan Ghazvininejad, Abdelrahman Mohamed, Omer Levy, Ves Stoyanov, and Luke Zettlemoyer. 2020. Bart: Denoising sequence-to-sequence pre-training for natural language generation, translation, and comprehension. In *Proceedings of the Annual Meeting of the Association for Computational Linguistics*.

Jiaqi Li, Mengmeng Wang, Zilong Zheng, and Muhan Zhang. 2024. LooGLE: Can Long-Context Language Models Understand Long Contexts? *arXiv preprint*. ArXiv:2311.04939 [cs].

C Y Lin. 2004. Rouge: A package for automatic evaluation of summaries. *Proceedings of the workshop on text summarization branches out (WAS 2004)*.

Peter J. Liu, Mohammad Saleh, Etienne Pot, Ben Goodrich, Ryan Sepassi, Łukasz Kaiser, and Noam Shazeer. 2018. Generating wikipedia by summarizing long sequences. In *Proceedings of the 6th International Conference on Learning Representations, ICLR 2018*.

Yang Liu, Dan Iter, Yichong Xu, Shuohang Wang, Ruochen Xu, and Chenguang Zhu. 2023. G-Eval: NLG Evaluation using Gpt-4 with Better Human Alignment. In *Proceedings of the 2023 Conference on Empirical Methods in Natural Language Processing*, pages 2511–2522, Singapore. Association for Computational Linguistics.

Yinhan Liu, Myle Ott, Naman Goyal, Jingfei Du, Mandar Joshi, Danqi Chen, Omer Levy, Mike Lewis, Luke Zettlemoyer, and Veselin Stoyanov. 2019. Roberta: A robustly optimized bert pretraining approach. *Preprint*, arXiv:1907.11692.

Dimitris Mamakas, Petros Tsotsi, Ion Androutsopoulos, and Ilias Chalkidis. 2022. Processing long legal documents with pre-trained transformers: Modding legalbert and longformer. In *Proceedings of the Natural Legal Language Processing Workshop 2022*.

Rada Mihalcea and Paul Tarau. 2004. Textrank: Bringing order into texts. In *Proceedings of the 2004 Conference on Empirical Methods in Natural Language Processing*.

Ramesh Nallapati, Bowen Zhou, Cicero dos Santos, Çaglar Gulçehre, and Bing Xiang. 2016. Abstractive text summarization using sequence-to-sequence rnns and beyond. In *Proceedings of the 20th SIGNLL Conference on Computational Natural Language Learning*.

Arjun Panickssery, Samuel R. Bowman, and Shi Feng. 2024. LLM Evaluators Recognize and Favor Their Own Generations. *arXiv preprint*. ArXiv:2404.13076 [cs].

Jason Phang, Yao Zhao, and Peter Liu. 2023. Investigating efficiently extending transformers for long input summarization. In *Proceedings of the 2023 Conference on Empirical Methods in Natural Language Processing*, pages 3946–3961, Singapore. Association for Computational Linguistics.

Jason Phang, Yao Zhao, and Peter J. Liu. 2022. Investigating efficiently extending transformers for long input summarization. *Preprint*, arXiv:2208.04347.

Jonathan Pilault, Raymond Li, Sandeep Subramanian, and Christopher Pal. 2020. On extractive and abstractive neural document summarization with transformer language models. In *Proceedings of the 2020 Conference on Empirical Methods in Natural Language Processing*.

Colin Raffel, Noam Shazeer, Adam Roberts, Katherine Lee, Sharan Narang, Michael Matena, Yanqi Zhou, Wei Li, and Peter J. Liu. 2020. Exploring the limits of transfer learning with a unified text-to-text transformer. *Journal of Machine Learning Research*, 21.

Sebastian Raschka. 2023. Practical tips for finetuning llms using lora (low-rank adaptation). Accessed: 2024-06-10.

Ehud Reiter. 2018. A Structured Review of the Validity of BLEU. *Computational Linguistics*, 44(3).

Xin Shen and Wai Lam. 2022. Improved divide-and-conquer approach to abstractive summarization of scientific papers. In *Proceedings of the 4th International Conference on Natural Language Processing, ICNLP 2022*.

Hugo Touvron, Louis Martin, Kevin Stone, Peter Albert, Amjad Almahairi, Yasmine Babaei, Nikolay Bashlykov, Soumya Batra, Prajjwal Bhargava, Shruti Bhosale, Dan Bikel, Lukas Blecher, Cristian Canton Ferrer, Moya Chen, Guillem Cucurull, David Esiobu, Jude Fernandes, Jeremy Fu, Wenyin Fu, Brian Fuller, Cynthia Gao, Vedanuj Goswami, Naman Goyal, Anthony Hartshorn, Saghar Hosseini, Rui Hou, Hakan Inan, Marcin Kardas, Viktor Kerkez, Madian Khabsa, Isabel Kloumann, Artem Korenev, Punit Singh Koura, Marie-Anne Lachaux, Thibaut Lavril, Jenya Lee, Diana Liskovich, Yinghai Lu, Yuning Mao, Xavier Martinet, Todor Mihaylov, Pushkar Mishra, Igor Molybog, Yixin Nie, Andrew Poulton, Jeremy Reizenstein, Rashi Rungta, Kalyan Saladi, Alan Schelten, Ruan Silva, Eric Michael Smith, Ranjan Subramanian, Xiaoqing Ellen Tan, Binh Tang, Ross Taylor, Adina Williams, Jian Xiang Kuan, Puxin Xu, Zheng Yan, Iliyan Zarov, Yuchen Zhang, Angela Fan, Melanie Kambadur, Sharan Narang, Aurelien Rodriguez, Robert Stojnic, Sergey Edunov, and Thomas Scialom. 2023. Llama 2: Open foundation and fine-tuned chat models. *Preprint*, arXiv:2307.09288.

Howard Turtle. 1995. Text retrieval in the legal world. *Artificial Intelligence and Law*, 3.

Oleg Vasilyev, Vedant Dharnidharka, and John Bohannon. 2020a. Fill in the BLANC: Human-free quality estimation of document summaries. In *Proceedings of the First Workshop on Evaluation and Comparison of NLP Systems*, pages 11–20, Online. Association for Computational Linguistics.

Oleg V. Vasilyev, Vedant Dharnidharka, Nicholas Egan, Charlene Chambliss, and John Bohannon. 2020b. Sensitivity of BLANC to human-scored qualities of text summaries. *CoRR*, abs/2010.06716.

Shijie Wu, Ozan Irsoy, Steven Lu, Vadim Dabravolski, Mark Dredze, Sebastian Gehrmann, Prabhanjan Kambadur, David Rosenberg, and Gideon Mann. 2023. Bloomberggpt: A large language model for finance. *Preprint*, arXiv:2303.17564.

Chaojun Xiao, Xueyu Hu, Zhiyuan Liu, Cunchao Tu, and Maosong Sun. 2021. Lawformer: A pre-trained language model for chinese legal long documents. *AI Open*, 2.

Yi Yang, Mark Christopher Siy UY, and Allen Huang. 2020. Finbert: A pretrained language model for financial communications. *Preprint*, arXiv:2006.08097.

Weizhe Yuan, Graham Neubig, and Pengfei Liu. 2021. Bartscore: Evaluating generated text as text generation. In *Advances in Neural Information Processing Systems*, volume 33.

Manzil Zaheer, Guru Guruganesh, Avinava Dubey, Joshua Ainslie, Chris Alberti, Santiago Ontanon, Philip Pham, Anirudh Ravula, Qifan Wang, Li Yang, and Amr Ahmed. 2020. Big bird: Transformers for longer sequences. In *Advances in Neural Information Processing Systems*, volume 2020-December.

Jingqing Zhang, Yao Zhao, Mohammad Saleh, and Peter J. Liu. 2020a. Pegasus: Pre-training with extracted gap-sentences for abstractive summarization. In *Proceedings of the 37th International Conference on Machine Learning, ICML 2020*, volume PartF168147-15.

Tianyi Zhang, Varsha Kishore, Felix Wu, Kilian Q. Weinberger, and Yoav Artzi. 2020b. Bertscore: Evaluating text generation with bert. In *Proceedings of the 8th International Conference on Learning Representations, ICLR 2020.*

Yusen Zhang, Ansong Ni, Ziming Mao, Chen Henry Wu, Chenguang Zhu, Budhaditya Deb, Ahmed H. Awadallah, Dragomir Radev, and Rui Zhang. 2022. Summn: A multi-stage summarization framework for long input dialogues and documents. In *Proceedings of the Annual Meeting of the Association for Computational Linguistics*, volume 1.

Yanli Zhao, Andrew Gu, Rohan Varma, Liang Luo, Chien-Chin Huang, Min Xu, Less Wright, Hamid Shojanazeri, Myle Ott, Sam Shleifer, Alban Desmaison, Can Balioglu, Pritam Damania, Bernard Nguyen, Geeta Chauhan, Yuchen Hao, Ajit Mathews, and Shen Li. 2023. Pytorch fsdp: Experiences on scaling fully sharded data parallel. *Preprint*, arXiv:2304.11277.

Lianmin Zheng, Wei-Lin Chiang, Ying Sheng, Siyuan Zhuang, Zhanghao Wu, Yonghao Zhuang, Zi Lin, Zhuohan Li, Dacheng Li, Eric Xing, Hao Zhang, Joseph E. Gonzalez, and Ion Stoica. 2023. Judging LLM-as-a-Judge with MT-Bench and Chatbot Arena. In *Proceedings of the NeurIPS 2023 Datasets and Benchmarks Track.*

Lucia Zheng, Neel Guha, Brandon R. Anderson, Peter Henderson, and Daniel E. Ho. 2021. When does pretraining help?: Assessing self-supervised learning for law and the casehold dataset of 53,000+ legal holdings. In *Proceedings of the 18th International Conference on Artificial Intelligence and Law, ICAIL 2021.*

A Further details on the method

A.1 Derivation of N

The following is the derivation of Equation 1:

1. The length of the intermediary summary $|E^j|$ after the first step is $R \cdot |D|$. After the second step, it is $R^2 \cdot |D|$ and so on. This implies that the length of the intermediary summary after N steps is:

$$|E^N| = R^N \cdot |D|$$

2. Extractive steps are performed until the length of the intermediary summary is within the context length of the abstractive summarisation model, K:

$$R^N \cdot |D| \leq K$$

3. To estimate N, take the logarithm on both sides:

$$N \cdot \log(R) \leq \log\left(\frac{K}{|D|}\right)$$

4. Then, solve for N:

$$N \leq \frac{\log\left(\frac{K}{|D|}\right)}{\log(R)}$$

5. N is then rounded up to the highest integer. So, the formula for estimating the number of extractive steps N needed before the final abstractive step can be taken is:

$$N = \left\lceil \frac{\log\left(\frac{K}{|D|}\right)}{\log(R)} \right\rceil \tag{4}$$

A.2 Hyperparameter settings

Table 6 summarises the hyperparameters used to finetune BART, T5, LongT5, Pegasus and PegasusX.

Hyperparameter	Setting
Learning rate	$5e^{-05}$
Epochs	40
Effective batch size	16
Warmup ratio	0.1
Weight decay	0.01
Early stopping patience	5
Metric for best model	Validation loss
Maximum generation length	1500

Table 6: Hyperparameter settings for BART, T5, LongT5, Pegasus and PegasusX.

A.3 Llama3 hyperparameter settings and training procedure

Table 7 shows the hyperparameters used to fine-tuned Llama3 on the abstractive evaluation task.

Hyperparameter	Setting
Learning rate	$5e^{-05}$
Epochs	10
Effective batch size	16
Warmup ratio	0.1
Weight decay	0.01
Early stopping patience	-
Metric for best model	-
LoRA rank (r)	8
LoRA alpha	16
LoRA dropout	0.1
Precision for frozen model weights	4-bit NF
Precision for low-rank matrices	bfloat16
Precision for calculations	bfloat16
Double Quantization	True

Table 7: Llama3 settings.

Fully Sharded Data Parallel (FSDP) (Zhao et al., 2023) was used to fine-tune Llama3 with the Hugging Face implementation. Due to issues when combining FSDP and QLoRA, the best-performing model could not be loaded, and early stopping patience and best model metric were not set. To mitigate overfitting, we used 10 epochs instead of 40, based on preliminary results indicating convergence between 4-20 epochs. For QLoRA, low-rank matrices were injected into the query, key, value matrices, and linear layers of Llama3, following settings from prior research (Raschka, 2023) (Hu et al., 2021). To fine-tune Llama3, we combined the reference text and golden reference summary into a single sequence, providing Llama3 with the following input sequence:

```
Summarise the following text.
### Text:
{reference text}
### Summary:
{golden reference summary}
```

During prediction, no exemplary summary was given, allowing Llama3 to create a new summary.

A.4 Evaluation metrics details

We implemented ROUGE (Lin, 2004) and BERTScore (Zhang et al., 2020b) using the HuggingFace evaluate library, comparing predictions against reference summaries using F-scores. For BERTScore, we employed the Longformer (Beltagy et al., 2020) architecture for its long context length. BARTScore (Yuan et al., 2021) was implemented with Stanford's string2string library, using BART(Lewis et al., 2020) fine-tuned on the CNN/Daily Mail dataset (Nallapati et al., 2016). BARTScore calculates precision and recall based on log-likelihood, combined into an F-score, and is limited by BART's 1024-token context length. We used BLANC-help (Vasilyev et al., 2020a) from the BLANC package, with a gap of two as this best correlates with human evaluation (Vasilyev et al., 2020b). BLANC, using BERT base (Devlin et al., 2019), is limited by its 512-token context.

B Human evaluation results

Individual results for the two expert evaluations on each criterion are shown in Tables 8 and 9. These results are the basis for the averaged results in Section 4.3 in the main paper. Below, we also summarise the main observations from the evaluators' comments on the summary outputs, for each architecture (architectures are numbered according to the order in the tables).

Architecture 1 The evaluators indicated that the summary is not usable for readers without prior knowledge of the topic due to its incompleteness, factual mistakes, and inaccuracies. While it does touch upon the main principle of CBAM, some of the procedures and rules are described incorrectly.

Architecture 2 The evaluators indicated that the summary is not usable for readers as it places information in the wrong place, describing background details in the 'key points' section instead of the main content of the regulation. Additionally, one evaluator mentions that the summary completely misses the main point of what CBAM is, despite the state information being mostly correct with only a few mistakes.

Architecture 3 One evaluator indicates that the summary correctly grasps the key points of the regulation, making it quite useful. However, the evaluator noted that it is not fully complete and that the fluency and coherence of the sentences could be improved. Despite these shortcomings, the summary is considered a good starting point.

Architecture 4 One evaluator noted that this summary is less flawed than that generated by Architecture 1 but is still unusable due to containing a significant amount of false information and incorrect words.

Architecture 5 Both mentioned that the summary contains excessive repetitions. Although the summary starts well, its usability degrades as more repetitions are encountered.

Architecture 6 One evaluator states that the summary contains quite some useful information. However because the summary contains a lot of repetition, it becomes unusable.

Architecture #	Extr. model	Ratio	Abstr. model	FC	U	Acc	Fl	Coh
1	RoBERTa	Dep.	BART	1	1	1	1	1
2	-	NE	BART	3	1	1	**2**	1
3	LexLM	Dep.	BART	**4**	**3**	**3**	**2**	**2**
4	Longformer	Dep.	BART	1	1	1	1	1
5	-	NE	PegasusX	**4**	1	2	1	1
6	RoBERTa	Dep.	Llama3	3	1	2	1	1

Table 8: Human evaluation results participant 1. Dep: Dependent ration; NE: No extraction; FC: Factual Correctness; U: Usability; Acc: Accuracy; Fl: Fluency; Coh: Coherence

Architecture #	Extr. model	Ratio	Abstr. model	FC	U	Acc	Fl	Coh
1	RoBERTa	Dep.	BART	3	3	2	2	3
2	-	NE	BART	**4**	1	3	4	2
3	LexLM	Dep.	BART	**4**	**4**	3	4	**4**
4	Longformer	Dep.	BART	3	3	**4**	2	3
5	-	NE	PegasusX	3	1	3	**5**	1
6	RoBERTa	Dep.	Llama3	3	4	3	4	3

Table 9: Human evaluation results participant 2. Dep: Dependent ration; NE: No extraction; FC: Factual Correctness; U: Usability; Acc: Accuracy; Fl: Fluency; Coh: Coherence

Enhancing Legal Expertise in Large Language Models through Composite Model Integration: The Development and Evaluation of Law-Neo

Zhihao Liu[1], Yanzhen Zhu[1], Mengyuan Lu[1],

[1]Shandong University of Finance and Economics,
Correspondence: 202116440220@mail.sdufe.edu.cn

Abstract

Although large language models (LLMs) like ChatGPT (OpenAI et al., 2024) have demonstrated considerable capabilities in general domains, they often lack proficiency in specialized fields. Enhancing a model's performance in a specific domain, such as law, while maintaining low costs, has been a significant challenge. Existing methods, such as fine-tuning or building mixture of experts (MoE) models, often struggle to balance model parameters, training costs, and domain-specific performance. Inspired by composition to augment language models (Bansal et al., 2024), we have developed Law-Neo, a novel model designed to enhance legal LLMs. This model significantly improves the model's legal domain expertise at minimal training costs, while retaining the logical capabilities of a large-scale anchor model. Our Law-Neo model outperformed other models in comprehensive experiments on multiple legal task benchmarks, demonstrating the effectiveness of this approach.

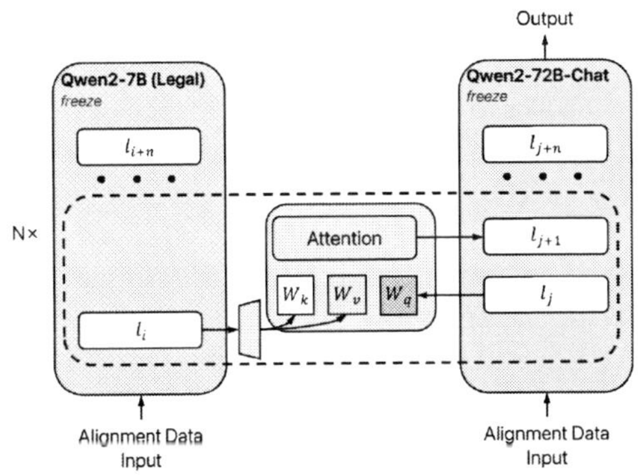

Figure 1: Architecture of Law-Neo. The Qwen2-72B-Chat model is enhanced with legal domain knowledge from Qwen2-7B (Legal) by sharing layer parameters. Both models remain unchanged during the composite training process, with a few additional parameters learned over their layer representations.

1 Introduction

Large Language Models (LLMs) have shown significant capabilities, including commonsense and factual reasoning, world knowledge, and language generation. These abilities have been validated across various scientific fields such as finance, biochemistry, and medicine (Chen et al., 2023; Ren et al., 2023; Ferruz et al., 2022; Thirunavukarasu et al., 2023; Fan et al., 2024). However, the training cost escalates as the number of parameters in LLM increases when enhancing model's domain-specific capabilities. This cost barrier is a significant challenge in developing domain-specific LLMs, such as those for the legal field.

To address these challenges, we propose the development of a comprehensive LLM-based legal assistance system.

Main Contributions In this paper, we present Law-Neo, a legal domain model trained at a relatively low cost while achieving satisfactory performance. This was accomplished by augmenting the Qwen2-72B-Chat model with a legal domain-specific model based on Qwen2-7B. We describe the training process of this composite model, which integrates multiple sub-models, each requiring different capability enhancements.

Our results on the Unified Qualification Exam for Legal Professionals and various downstream task benchmarks indicate that Law-Neo outperforms existing methods in several aspects. Qualitative analysis demonstrates that Law-Neo surpasses GPT-4 by 23 points in scoring on the Unified Qualification Exam for Legal Professionals, showcasing its robust legal consultation capabilities.

The data and training code used in this work are publicly available at `https://github.com/SkyFlap/Law-Neo`.

2 Related Work

Since the development of BERT (Devlin et al., 2019), significant efforts have been made to create

Proceedings of the Natural Legal Language Processing Workshop 2024, pages 33–41
November 16, 2024 ©2024 Association for Computational Linguistics

language models (LMs) specifically tailored for the legal domain. Initially, these models were small and followed the paradigm of pre-training followed by downstream task fine-tuning. Recent advancements have seen an increase in model size and the introduction of instruction fine-tuning, with evaluations extending across a broader spectrum of legal tasks. Most existing legal LLMs are text-based, with a focus on Chinese, English, or multi-language support (Chen et al., 2024).

2.1 Pre-Trained and Fine-Tuned PLMs

LegalBERT (Chalkidis, 2023) represents an early endeavor to develop pre-trained language models (PLMs) for legal tasks such as legal text classification (LTC). This model underwent additional pre-training on legal corpora and was subsequently fine-tuned with task-specific data. Lawformer (Xiao et al., 2021) is a Transformer-based model specifically pre-trained to manage lengthy legal texts, and it has been employed for tasks such as legal judgment prediction (LJP), legal reading comprehension (LRC), and legal question answering (LQA).

2.2 Pre-Trained and Fine-Tuned LLMs

In the realm of large language models (LLMs), models are pre-trained and fine-tuned specifically for legal tasks or datasets. These legal-specific LLMs often incorporate external knowledge bases and undergo extensive initial training to handle a wide range of legal data. Notable models include LexiLaw (Haitao, 2024), a fine-tuned Chinese legal model based on ChatGLM-6B (Zeng et al., 2024a), and Fuzi.mingcha (Deng et al., 2023), which is also based on ChatGLM-6B and fine-tuned on the CAIL2018 dataset (Xiao et al., 2018). Wisdom-Interrogatory (Wu et al.) builds upon Baichuan2-7B (Baichuan, 2023), and LawGPT-7B-beta1.0 (Nguyen, 2023) is pre-trained on 500,000 Chinese judgment documents, based on Chinese-LLaMA-7B (Cui et al., 2023). Additionally, HanFei (He et al., 2023) is a fully pre-trained and fine-tuned LLM with 7 billion parameters.

Further advancements in large-scale LLMs include LawyerLLaM (Huang et al., 2023), based on Chinese-LLaMA-13B (Cui et al., 2023) and fine-tuned with general and legal instructions, as well as ChatLaw-13B (Cui et al., 2024b), fine-tuned on Ziya-LLaMA-13B-v1 (Wang et al., 2022), and ChatLaw-33B (Cui et al., 2024b), fine-tuned on Anima-33B (Ogavinee and et al., 2022). Models in other languages have also emerged, such

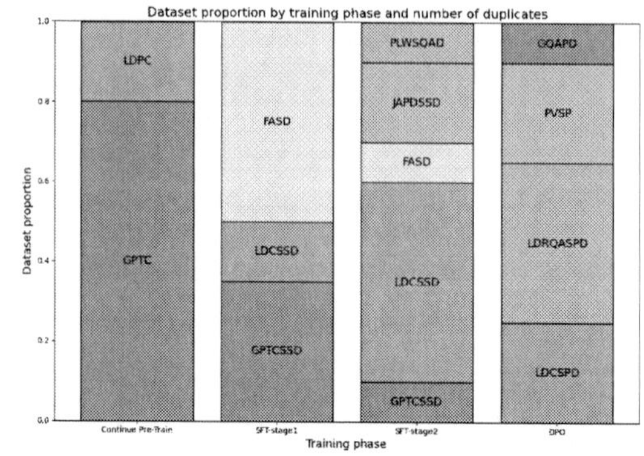

Figure 2: Proportions of Dataset Types Used at Each Step in Training Qwen2-7B (Legal). General Pre-training Corpus (GPTC), Legal Domain Pre-training Corpus (LDPTC), Foundational Abilities Supervised Data (FASD), Legal Domain Corpus Synthetic Supervised Data (LDCSSD), General Pre-training Corpus Synthetic Supervised Data (GPTCSSD), Public Legal Website Search and QA Data (PLWSQAD), Legal Domain Real QA Synthetic Preference Data (LDRQASPD), Public Video Case Synthetic Preference Data (PVSP), Legal Domain Corpus Synthetic Preference Data (LDCSPD), General QA Preference Data (GQAPD), and Judgment, Arbitration, and Prosecutorial Documents Synthetic Supervised Data (JAPDSSD). Homogeneous variant corpora were used at different stages to prevent catastrophic forgetting and capability degradation.

as SaulLM-7B (Colombo et al., 2024), based on Mistral-7B (Jiang et al., 2023), and JURU (Junior et al., 2024), the first LLM pre-trained for the Brazilian legal domain.

A recent innovation in this field is the introduction of ChatLaw-4x7B (Cui et al., 2024a), a mixture of experts model (MoE) designed to address hallucinations and insufficient domain expertise in LLMs. However, training MoE architectures presents significant challenges, particularly in balancing the training of expert models and sample load distribution (Zeng et al., 2024b; Pan et al., 2024).

These legal-specific LLMs, typically following an initial pre-training phase, are tailored to specific legal datasets and tasks. This tailoring enhances both the precision and practical applicability of legal NLP technologies.

3 Method

This section focuses on Law-Neo as illustrated in Fig.1. While our model comprises three main components—the **domain knowledge model** (Qwen2-

7B-Legal), the **anchor model** (Qwen2-72B-Chat Yang et al., 2024), and the **parameter-merging block**—this section will specifically discuss the **domain knowledge model** and the **parameter-merging block** in detail.

Our approach assumes: (i) **The model weights are fixed and unmodifiable**, reflecting the high computational cost of training or fine-tuning large LLMs from scratch in production environments. Pre-trained models are treated as fixed assets to ensure cost efficiency and stability. (ii) **We can access model weights, perform forward and backward passes, and retrieve intermediate representations**. This is feasible with many open-source LLMs, allowing us to use their parameters for inference and further training. (iii) **We lack access to the original training data, hyperparameters, or training states**, as open-source LLMs typically do not provide such information.

3.1 Legal Domain Model Qwen2-7B (Legal)

Here, we introduce the base model selection and provide more details about it. We've chosen Qwen2-7B-Base, which was released by the Qwen Team (Yang et al., 2024), is selected as the base model. We performed specified **Data Preparation** and **Model Training** upon the base model to better fit legal domain.

In June 2024, the Qwen Team open-sourced their Qwen2 series models. We used Qwen2-7B-Base as the base model. Fig.2 illustrates the processes applied to this base model, which involve two main steps: data preparation and model training.

Data Preparation: Following the data processing pipeline from the MAP-Neo (Zhang et al., 2024) technical report, we filtered legal-related training corpora from publicly available pre-training datasets (FinWeb, Penedo et al., 2024; Matrix, Zhang et al., 2024; etc.). We collected extensive current Chinese laws and regulations, including local and central regulations, multilateral and bilateral treaties involving China, and specific industry norms. The continued pre-training included over 10,000 manually collected books and papers, processed using methods from MAP-Neo. For post-training data preparation, we collected Chinese case law and synthesized supervised data using GLM4 (Zeng et al., 2024a). Inspired by CQIA (Bai et al., 2024), we gathered online case explanation videos, converted their audio to text, and generated preference data using GLM4. For specific details, please refer to the appendix A.

Model Training: We first performed full-parameter continued pre-training on the Qwen2-7B-Base model, utilizing both general pre-training corpora and the collected legal domain corpora. To ensure the LLM makes human-consistent judgments in the legal domain, we conducted supervised fine-tuning (SFT) in two phases. The first phase enhanced the model's foundational abilities (e.g., code and math skills) using over 2 million instructional data points. The second phase focused on improving the model's conversational abilities and legal judgment capabilities while retaining the foundational skills acquired in the first phase. We used the prepared legal domain SFT data and collected over 100,000 multi-turn conversation data from real user interactions. We then aligned the LLM using DPO.

3.2 Model Parameter-Merging Block

As illustrated in Fig.1, our approach involves concurrent operations on selected layers from two large language models (LLMs). Specifically, we introduce two sets of additional parameters over these layers: (1) a straightforward set of linear transformations, $f_{\text{proj}}(.)$, which project an ith layer representation from Qwen2-7B (Legal) to the dimensionality of representations from Qwen2-72B; and (2) a series of cross-attention layers, $f_{\text{cross}}(.,.)$, which perform cross-attention between this transformed layer representation and a jth layer representation from Qwen2-72B. The output of the cross-attention is then added as a residual connection to the layer representations of Qwen2-72B. For specific details, please refer to the appendix D.

4 Experiments

We evaluated the performance of LawBench (Fei et al., 2023) and the Unified Qualification Exam for Legal Professionals. Additionally, we conducted benchmark testing for the LJP(Legal Judgment Prediction) task. Our primary focus, lies in LJP tasks utilizing fact-based articles from the CAIL2018 (Xiao et al., 2018) dataset.

4.1 Performance on LawBench

We evaluated our model on LawBench (Fei et al., 2023), a benchmark for the Chinese legal system assessing three cognitive levels: (1) Legal Knowledge Memory, (2) Legal Knowledge Understanding, and (3) Legal Knowledge Application.

As shown in Table 1, our **Law-Neo** model achieves an average score of 64.38, posi-

Model	LawBench Average Score	UQELP Average Score	CAIL2018 F-1
GPT Series			
GPT-3.5 (Brown et al., 2020)	42.15	78	0.29
GPT-4 (OpenAI et al., 2024)	52.35	103	**0.52**
General LLMs			
Baichuan2-7B (Baichuan, 2023)	38.08	61	–
ChatGLM2-6B (Zeng et al., 2024a)	29.88	34	–
InternLM2-7B (Cai et al., 2024)	43.78	41	–
Qwen2-72B-Chat (Yang et al., 2024)	56.26	–	–
Legal LLMs			
Fuzi-Mingcha-6B (Wang et al., 2022)	32.08	34	0.25
ChatLaw-13B (Cui et al., 2024b)	32.76	–	0.33
Wisdom-Interrogatory-7B (Wu et al.)	31.41	–	0.33
Chatlaw-MoE-4×7B (Cui et al., 2024a)	60.08	115	–
Qwen2-7B-Legal (ours)	51.25	84	0.39
Law-Neo (ours)	**64.38**	**126**	0.46

Table 1: Summary of LLM's performance comparisons on benchmarks: We conducted experiments using three benchmark tests, namely LawBench, Unified Qualification Exam for Legal Professionals (UQELP), and CAIL2018.

tioned competitively between GPT-3.5 and GPT-4, which score 42.15 and 52.35, respectively. While Chatlaw-MoE scores higher at 60.08, our model significantly outperforms Legal LLMs like Fuzi-Mingcha (32.08) and General LLMs like InternLM2-7B (43.78), and also shows a marked improvement over models like Qwen2-7B-Legal (51.25). This demonstrates that our model parameter-merging training strategy is effective in achieving superior performance.

4.2 Performance on Unified Qualification Exam for Legal Professionals

We also assessed our model using China's Unified Qualification Exam for Legal Professionals, which includes single-choice, multiple-choice, and uncertain-choice questions across various legal fields.

As indicated in Table 1, our **Law-Neo** model achieved an average score of 126, positioning it ahead of most models, including Chatlaw-MoE (115) and GPT-4 (103). Our model surpasses General LLMs such as Baichuan2-7B (61) and ChatGLM2-6B (34), as well as Legal LLMs like Fuzi-Mingcha (34). It also shows a significant improvement over Qwen2-7B-Legal (84), which further emphasizes the strength of our approach.

4.3 Performance on CAIL2018 Task

CAIL2018 (Xiao et al., 2018), a large-scale LJP task, includes over 2.6 million criminal cases from the Supreme People's Court of China, annotated with applicable law articles, charges, and prison terms.

In Table 1, our **Law-Neo** model achieves an F-1 score of 0.46, showing strong performance. While GPT-4 scores higher at 0.52, our model outperforms GPT-3.5 (0.29) and General LLMs like Qwen2-7B-Chat (0.37). It also surpasses Legal LLMs such as Chatlaw-13B and Wisdom-Interrogatory (both 0.33). These results highlight **Law-Neo**'s robustness in legal language processing and its competitive edge in legal tasks, especially considering that it did not leverage a mixed expert model during training, unlike Chatlaw-MoE.

5 Training Overhead

Our training procedure was conducted on a GPU server equipped with eight 80GB A800 GPUs and an Intel Xeon 8470 processor. The entire training process took approximately 19.24 hours.

The comparative training regimen for ChatLaw was conducted on a GPU server equipped with eight 80GB A100 GPUs and two Intel Xeon 8358P processors. The entire training process was completed in approximately 23.14 hours, which exceeds our training duration by 3.9 hours.

6 Conclusion

In this paper, we introduced Law-Neo, an innovative approach to enhancing large language models (LLMs) for the legal domain by leveraging the concept of composition to augment existing models. Our methodology focused on integrating Qwen2-72B-Chat with a legal domain-specific model based on Qwen2-7B. Our comprehensive experiments, conducted on multiple legal benchmarks including LawBench, the Unified Qualification Exam for Legal Professionals (UQELP), and CAIL2018, demonstrate the efficacy of our approach. The Law-Neo model outperformed several existing models, including general-purpose LLMs and specialized legal LLMs. Our results indicate that integrating models through shared parameters can effectively enhance their specialized knowledge without sacrificing the foundational abilities of the base models.

7 Ethics Statement

The development and application of Law-Neo, an advanced legal large language model (LLM), bring forth significant ethical considerations, particularly regarding bias amplification, interpretability, accountability, and oversight. Law-Neo, like other LLMs, has been trained on extensive legal corpora, including laws, regulations, and judicial decisions. Despite efforts to ensure a balanced dataset, the model may still reflect and perpetuate biases found in the source material. This risk is especially concerning in the legal field, where unbiased and fair decision-making is crucial. Additionally, the complex decision-making process of these models is not easily transparent, making it difficult to scrutinize and understand their outputs fully, which can undermine trust in automated legal tools. Establishing clear guidelines and frameworks for the accountability and oversight of AI systems like Law-Neo is crucial. This includes defining the roles and responsibilities of developers, users, and regulatory bodies in monitoring the deployment and impact of these models. Regular audits, bias assessments, and updates should be conducted to ensure the model remains fair, transparent, and aligned with ethical standards.

References

Yuelin Bai, Xinrun Du, Yiming Liang, Yonggang Jin, Ziqiang Liu, Junting Zhou, Tianyu Zheng, Xincheng Zhang, Nuo Ma, Zekun Wang, et al. 2024. Coig-cqia: Quality is all you need for chinese instruction fine-tuning. *Preprint*, arXiv:2403.18058.

Baichuan. 2023. Baichuan 2: Open large-scale language models. *arXiv preprint arXiv:2309.10305*.

Rachit Bansal, Bidisha Samanta, Siddharth Dalmia, Nitish Gupta, Shikhar Vashishth, Sriram Ganapathy, Abhishek Bapna, Prateek Jain, and Partha Talukdar. 2024. Llm augmented llms: Expanding capabilities through composition. *Preprint*, arXiv:2401.02412.

Tom B. Brown, Benjamin Mann, Nick Ryder, Melanie Subbiah, Jared Kaplan, Prafulla Dhariwal, Arvind Neelakantan, Pranav Shyam, Girish Sastry, Amanda Askell, et al. 2020. Language models are few-shot learners. *Preprint*, arXiv:2005.14165.

Zheng Cai, Maosong Cao, Haojiong Chen, Kai Chen, Keyu Chen, Xin Chen, Xun Chen, Zehui Chen, Zhi Chen, Pei Chu, et al. 2024. Internlm2 technical report. *Preprint*, arXiv:2403.17297.

Ilias Chalkidis. 2023. Chatgpt may pass the bar exam soon, but has a long way to go for the lexglue benchmark. *Preprint*, arXiv:2304.12202.

Wei Chen, Qiushi Wang, Zefei Long, Xianyin Zhang, Zhongtian Lu, Bingxuan Li, Siyuan Wang, Jiarong Xu, Xiang Bai, Xuanjing Huang, et al. 2023. Discfinllm: A chinese financial large language model based on multiple experts fine-tuning. *Preprint*, arXiv:2310.15205.

Zhiyu Zoey Chen, Jing Ma, Xinlu Zhang, Nan Hao, An Yan, Armineh Nourbakhsh, Xianjun Yang, Julian McAuley, Linda Petzold, and William Yang Wang. 2024. A survey on large language models for critical societal domains: Finance, healthcare, and law. *Preprint*, arXiv:2405.01769.

Pierre Colombo, Telmo Pessoa Pires, Malik Boudiaf, Dominic Culver, Rui Melo, Caio Corro, Andre F. T. Martins, Fabrizio Esposito, Vera Lúcia Raposo, Sofia Morgado, et al. 2024. Saullm-7b: A pioneering large language model for law. *Preprint*, arXiv:2403.03883.

Jiaxi Cui, Munan Ning, Zongjian Li, Bohua Chen, Yang Yan, Hao Li, Bin Ling, Yonghong Tian, and Li Yuan. 2024a. Chatlaw: A multi-agent collaborative legal assistant with knowledge graph enhanced mixture-of-experts large language model. *Preprint*, arXiv:2306.16092.

Jiaxi Cui, Munan Ning, Zongjian Li, Bohua Chen, Yang Yan, Hao Li, Bin Ling, Yonghong Tian, and Li Yuan. 2024b. Chatlaw: Open-source legal large language model with integrated external knowledge bases. *Preprint*, arXiv:2306.16092.

Yiming Cui, Ziqing Yang, and Xin Yao. 2023. Efficient and effective text encoding for chinese llama and alpaca. *arXiv preprint arXiv:2304.08177*.

Wentao Deng, Jiahuan Pei, Keyi Kong, Zhe Chen, Furu Wei, Yujun Li, Zhaochun Ren, Zhumin Chen, and Pengjie Ren. 2023. Syllogistic reasoning for legal judgment analysis. In *Proceedings of the 2023 Conference on Empirical Methods in Natural Language Processing*, pages 13997–14009, Singapore. Association for Computational Linguistics.

Jacob Devlin, Ming-Wei Chang, Kenton Lee, and Kristina Toutanova. 2019. BERT: Pre-training of deep bidirectional transformers for language understanding. In *Proceedings of the 2019 Conference of the North American Chapter of the Association for Computational Linguistics: Human Language Technologies, Volume 1 (Long and Short Papers)*, pages 4171–4186, Minneapolis, Minnesota. Association for Computational Linguistics.

Weijie Fan, Yi Yang, Jing Qi, Qichuan Zhang, Cuiwei Liao, Li Wen, Shuang Wang, Guangxian Wang, Yu Xia, Qihua Wu, et al. 2024. A deep-learning-based framework for identifying and localizing multiple abnormalities and assessing cardiomegaly in chest x-ray. *Nature Communications*, 15(1):1347.

Zhiwei Fei, Xiaoyu Shen, Dawei Zhu, Fengzhe Zhou, Zhuo Han, Songyang Zhang, Kai Chen, Zongwen Shen, and Jidong Ge. 2023. Lawbench: Benchmarking legal knowledge of large language models. *Preprint*, arXiv:2309.16289.

Noelia Ferruz, Steffen Schmidt, and Birte Höcker. 2022. Protgpt2 is a deep unsupervised language model for protein design. *Nature Communications*, 13(1):4348.

C. Haitao. 2024. LexiLaw: A legal text processing toolkit. `https://github.com/CSHaitao/LexiLaw`. Accessed: 2024-04-29.

Wanwei He, Jiabao Wen, Lei Zhang, Hao Cheng, Bowen Qin, Yunshui Li, Feng Jiang, Junying Chen, Benyou Wang, and Min Yang. 2023. Hanfei-1.0.

Quzhe Huang, Mingxu Tao, Chen Zhang, Zhenwei An, Cong Jiang, Zhibin Chen, Zirui Wu, and Yansong Feng. 2023. Lawyer llama technical report. *Preprint*, arXiv:2305.15062.

Albert Q. Jiang, Alexandre Sablayrolles, Arthur Mensch, Chris Bamford, Devendra Singh Chaplot, Diego de las Casas, Florian Bressand, Gianna Lengyel, Guillaume Lample, Lucile Saulnier, et al. 2023. Mistral 7b. *Preprint*, arXiv:2310.06825.

Roseval Malaquias Junior, Ramon Pires, Roseli Romero, and Rodrigo Nogueira. 2024. Juru: Legal brazilian large language model from reputable sources. *Preprint*, arXiv:2403.18140.

Ha-Thanh Nguyen. 2023. A brief report on lawgpt 1.0: A virtual legal assistant based on gpt-3. *Preprint*, arXiv:2302.05729.

Vinayak Yogesh Ogavinee and et al. 2022. Anima: A comprehensive toolkit for medical image analysis. `https://github.com/lyogavin/Anima`. Accessed: 2024-07-12.

OpenAI, Josh Achiam, Steven Adler, Sandhini Agarwal, Lama Ahmad, Ilge Akkaya, Florencia Leoni Aleman, Diogo Almeida, Janko Altenschmidt, Sam Altman, et al. 2024. Gpt-4 technical report. *Preprint*, arXiv:2303.08774.

Bowen Pan, Yikang Shen, Haokun Liu, Mayank Mishra, Gaoyuan Zhang, Aude Oliva, Colin Raffel, and Rameswar Panda. 2024. Dense training, sparse inference: Rethinking training of mixture-of-experts language models. *Preprint*, arXiv:2404.05567.

Guilherme Penedo, Hynek Kydlíček, Loubna Ben allal, Anton Lozhkov, Margaret Mitchell, Colin Raffel, Leandro Von Werra, and Thomas Wolf. 2024. The fineweb datasets: Decanting the web for the finest text data at scale. *Preprint*, arXiv:2406.17557.

Colin Raffel, Noam Shazeer, Adam Roberts, Katherine Lee, Sharan Narang, Michael Matena, Yanqi Zhou, Wei Li, and Peter J. Liu. 2020. Exploring the limits of transfer learning with a unified text-to-text transformer. *J. Mach. Learn. Res.*, 21:140:1–140:67.

Ren Ren, Shenglin Cai, Xiaona Fang, Xiaoyi Wang, Zheng Zhang, Micol Damiani, Charlotte Hudlerova, Annachiara Rosa, Joshua Hope, Nicola J. Cook, et al. 2023. Multiplexed detection of viral antigen and rna using nanopore sensing and encoded molecular probes. *Nature Communications*, 14(1):7362.

Arun James Thirunavukarasu, Darren Shu Jeng Ting, Kabilan Elangovan, Laura Gutierrez, Ting Fang Tan, and Daniel Shu Wei Ting. 2023. Large language models in medicine. *Nature Medicine*, 29(8):1930–1940.

Ashish Vaswani, Noam Shazeer, Niki Parmar, Jakob Uszkoreit, Llion Jones, Aidan N. Gomez, Lukasz Kaiser, and Illia Polosukhin. 2017. Attention is all you need. In *Advances in Neural Information Processing Systems 30: Annual Conference on Neural Information Processing Systems 2017, December 4-9, 2017, Long Beach, CA, USA*, pages 5998–6008.

Junjie Wang, Yuxiang Zhang, Lin Zhang, Ping Yang, Xinyu Gao, Ziwei Wu, Xiaoqun Dong, Junqing He, Jianheng Zhuo, Qi Yang, et al. 2022. Fengshenbang 1.0: Being the foundation of chinese cognitive intelligence. *CoRR*, abs/2209.02970.

Yiquan Wu, Yuhang Liu, Yifei Liu, Ang Li, Siying Zhou, and Kun Kuang. wisdominterrogatory. Available at GitHub.

Chaojun Xiao, Xueyu Hu, Zhiyuan Liu, Cunchao Tu, and Maosong Sun. 2021. Lawformer: A pre-trained language model for chinese legal long documents. *Preprint*, arXiv:2105.03887.

Chaojun Xiao, Haoxi Zhong, Zhipeng Guo, Cunchao Tu, Zhiyuan Liu, Maosong Sun, Yansong Feng, Xianpei Han, Zhen Hu, Heng Wang, et al. 2018. Cail2018: A large-scale legal dataset for judgment prediction. *Preprint*, arXiv:1807.02478.

An Yang, Baosong Yang, Binyuan Hui, Bo Zheng, Bowen Yu, Chang Zhou, Chengpeng Li, Chengyuan Li, Dayiheng Liu, Fei Huang, et al. 2024. Qwen2 technical report. *arXiv preprint arXiv:2407.10671*.

Aohan Zeng, Bin Xu, Bowen Wang, Chenhui Zhang, Da Yin, Dan Zhang, Diego Rojas, Guanyu Feng, Hanlin Zhao, Hanyu Lai, Hao Yu, Hongning Wang, Jiadai Sun, Jiajie Zhang, Jiale Cheng, Jiayi Gui, Jie Tang, Jing Zhang, Jingyu Sun, Juanzi Li, Lei Zhao, Lindong Wu, Lucen Zhong, Mingdao Liu, Minlie Huang, Peng Zhang, Qinkai Zheng, Rui Lu, Shuaiqi Duan, Shudan Zhang, Shulin Cao, Shuxun Yang, Weng Lam Tam, Wenyi Zhao, Xiao Liu, Xiao Xia, Xiaohan Zhang, Xiaotao Gu, Xin Lv, Xinghan Liu, Xinyi Liu, Xinyue Yang, Xixuan Song, Xunkai Zhang, Yifan An, Yifan Xu, Yilin Niu, Yuantao Yang, Yueyan Li, Yushi Bai, Yuxiao Dong, Zehan Qi, Zhaoyu Wang, Zhen Yang, Zhengxiao Du, Zhenyu Hou, and Zihan Wang. 2024a. Chatglm: A family of large language models from glm-130b to glm-4 all tools. *Preprint*, arXiv:2406.12793.

Zihao Zeng, Yibo Miao, Hongcheng Gao, Hao Zhang, and Zhijie Deng. 2024b. Adamoe: Token-adaptive routing with null experts for mixture-of-experts language models. *Preprint*, arXiv:2406.13233.

Ge Zhang, Scott Qu, Jiaheng Liu, Chenchen Zhang, Chenghua Lin, Chou Leuang Yu, Danny Pan, Esther Cheng, Jie Liu, Qunshu Lin, et al. 2024. Map-neo: Highly capable and transparent bilingual large language model series. *Preprint*, arXiv:2405.19327.

Yaowei Zheng, Richong Zhang, Junhao Zhang, Yanhan Ye, Zheyan Luo, Zhangchi Feng, and Yongqiang Ma. 2024. Llamafactory: Unified efficient fine-tuning of 100+ language models. In *Proceedings of the 62nd Annual Meeting of the Association for Computational Linguistics (Volume 3: System Demonstrations)*, Bangkok, Thailand. Association for Computational Linguistics.

A Synthesized Prompt Templates

To create an effective training dataset, it is essential to ensure that the data are diverse and cover a wide range of types and tasks. Table 2 provides a detailed overview of the data sources.

During the various stages of training, we utilized homologous variant data, a significant portion of which was synthesized using GLM4. The detailed process, including the prompt templates and their effects, is illustrated in Table 3.

B Pre-Training

In order to continued pre-train the Qwen2-7B model, we adhere to the strategy it followed during the continued pre-training phase, which involves predicting the subsequent token based on the context provided by the preceding token. The context length for our continued pre-training is set to 8192. For the creation of data batches, we shuffle and amalgamate the documents, subsequently truncating them to the aforementioned context lengths. To enhance computational efficiency and curtail memory consumption, we incorporate Flash Attention within the attention modules. The standard optimization algorithm employed for pretraining is AdamW. The hyperparameters are configured with $\beta_1 = 0.9$, $\beta_2 = 0.95$, and $\epsilon = 10^{-8}$. We utilize a `cosine_with_warmup` learning rate schedule, with a designated peak learning rate for each model size; the warmup steps are set to 3500. The learning rate is tapered down to a minimum of 10% of the peak learning rate, with the maximum learning rate established at 3×10^{-4}. The models are trained using BFloat16 mixed precision to ensure training stability.

C Post-Training

Consistent with pretraining, we also apply next-token prediction as the training task for SFT. We apply the loss masks for the system and user inputs.The model's training process utilizes the AdamW optimizer, with the following hyperparameters: β_1 set to 0.9, β_2 set to 0.95 and ϵ set to 10^{-8}. The sequence length is limited to 8192, and the batch size is 64. The model undergoes a total of 10000steps, with the learning rate gradually increased over 4096 steps, reaching a peak of 9×10^{-6}. To prevent over fitting, weight decay is applied with a value of 0.1, dropout is set to 0.1, and gradient clipping is enforced with a limit of 1.0

During the DPO training phase, we employed the LLaMa-Fatory (Zheng et al., 2024) as an auxiliary tool, conducting a total of 5,000 training steps. The `warmup_with_cosine` strategy was utilized, wherein the learning rate gradually increased to reach its maximum value of 1.5×10^{-5} over the initial 2,237 steps, followed by a gradual decrease.

D Parameter-Merging

Compositional Layers: According to the technical report on the Qwen2 series models (Yang et al., 2024), Qwen2-7B (m_A) and Qwen2-72B (m_B) consist of 28 layers (N_A) and 80 layers (N_B), respectively. The hidden size of the two models is noted as $3,584$ (D_A) for Qwen2-7B and $8,192$ (D_B) for Qwen2-72B. Due to the significant difference in the number of layers between the two models, when selecting the combined layers $\mathbb{L}_A$ and

Type	Description	Token
Legal Regulations	This category encompasses the Constitution, central-level regulations, local regulations at various levels, departmental rules and regulations, as well as bilateral and multilateral treaties, agreements, and other documents with the nature of treaties or agreements concluded by the People's Republic of China with foreign countries.	7.5B
Case Documents	This includes judicial decisions from the courts, arbitration awards from arbitration institutions, and prosecutorial documents from the procuratorates.	1.33B
Legal Manuscripts	These are core journals indexed by CNKI (China National Knowledge Infrastructure), select theses and dissertations, and certain publications from legal publishing houses.	5.7B
Legal Q&A Data	Rich in legal Q&A data, including common legal questions and their corresponding answers. It covers multiple legal fields such as contract law, labor law, intellectual property, etc.	5.47B

Table 2: List of datasets used during training.

$\mathbb{L}_B$, we opted to include all layers from Qwen2-7B and a subset of layers from Qwen2-72B. The relationship between them is as follows:

$$N_A = |\mathbb{L}_A| = |\mathbb{L}_B|$$
$$l_{A,i} = l_{B,i} = n_{B,i+24}$$

where $l_{A,i}$ represents the i-th selected layer in the set of selected combined layers for the Qwen2-7B model, and $n_{B,i}$ represents the i-th model layer among all layers of the Qwen2-72B model. Further, $\mathbb{H}_A \in \{H_{A,1}, H_{A,2}, \ldots, H_{A,28}\}$ denote the layer representations for the given input after each layer in $\mathbb{L}_A$.

Learned Projections: Next we map representations from Qwen2-7B to that of Qwen2-72B via a projection layer. In particular, for each layer in $\mathbb{L}_A$, we learn a projection function $f_{\text{proj}} : \mathbb{R}^{D_A} \to \mathbb{R}^{D_B}$, that projects representations from these layers to the desired representation size of Qwen2-72B. Let,

$$f_{\text{proj}}(\mathbb{H}_A) \leftarrow \{f_{\text{proj}}(H_{A,1}), \ldots, f_{\text{proj}}(H_{A,28})\}$$

This transformation enables cross-attention across models, and also performs an alignment of representations from Qwen2-7B and Qwen2-72B despite frozen weights of the base models.

Cross-attention Layers: Similar to the multi-headed cross-attention in encoder-decoder models (for example Vaswani et al., 2017 and Raffel et al., 2020)– we introduce cross-attention between representations of the Qwen2-72B and the Qwen2-7B model. In particular, we use $f_{proj}(H_{A,i})$ from the Qwen2-7B model as the *key* and *value* vectors for each head in cross-attention. We use the vector $H_{B,j}$ from the Qwen2-72B model as the *query* vector.

<table>
<tr><td colspan="2">↪Prompt Templates</td></tr>
<tr><th>SFT Prompt for English Contents</th><th>DPO Prompt for English Contents</th></tr>
<tr><td># Legal Consultation Simulator
You need to construct a pair of Q&A legal consultation data based on the legal regulations provided by the user. The questions should not directly ask about the content of the legal regulations but should conform to the user's normal questioning habits. The legal regulations provided by the user are: {Contents}</td><td># Legal Consultation Simulator
You are an AI assistant proficient in law, and you need to use your legal knowledge to answer the questions posed by users. The user's question is:{Contents}</td></tr>
<tr><td colspan="2">↪Demonstrations</td></tr>
<tr><th>Before Synthesized</th><th>After Synthesized</th></tr>
<tr><td>Article 37: An applicant for a degree or a degree holder, who has one of the following circumstances during the process of pursuing the degree, may have the degree not conferred or revoked by the degree-granting institution upon the resolution of the Degree Evaluation Committee: (1) The thesis or practical results are identified as having academic misconduct such as ghostwriting, plagiarism, or forgery; (2) Misappropriating or impersonating someone else's identity to obtain admission qualifications, or obtaining admission qualifications or graduation certificates through other illegal means; (3) There are other serious illegal acts during the period of study that should not be granted a degree according to the law.</td><td>Question: What are the consequences if my thesis is found to be plagiarized during the period of pursuing a degree? Answer: According to the provisions of Article 37 of the relevant laws and regulations, if your thesis or practical results are identified as having academic misconduct such as ghostwriting, plagiarism, or forgery during the period of pursuing a degree, the Degree Evaluation Committee may decide not to confer the degree upon you or revoke the degree already granted. Please pay close attention to academic integrity and comply with the laws and regulations.</td></tr>
<tr><th>Chosen</th><th>Rejected</th></tr>
<tr><td>According to existing laws and regulations, an individual who maliciously attacks a public transport driver in the process of driving, or attempts to seize control, thereby disrupting the normal operation of the public transport vehicle and threatening public safety, may be sentenced to fixed-term imprisonment of not more than one year, detention, or control, and must also bear the responsibility of a fine. If the perpetrator's actions also violate other related criminal charges, such as seriously obstructing safe driving and causing significant personal injury and property damage, they should still be convicted and punished according to the more severe provisions. For example, they may be determined to have committed the crime of "endangering public safety by dangerous means." The minimum sentence for intentional crimes of this category starts at three years, and the maximum penalty can be the death penalty.</td><td>In China, criminal acts that obstruct safe driving, such as drunk driving, speeding, fatigue driving, and using a mobile phone, may be sentenced to detention, fines, or even traffic accident crimes according to the relevant provisions of the "Criminal Law of the People's Republic of China," based on the severity and consequences of the act. In serious cases, imprisonment may result. The specific judgment will also take into account factors such as the perpetrator's subjective malice, the dangerousness of the act, and the consequences caused. For more detailed legal advice or case analysis, it is recommended to consult a professional legal person.</td></tr>
</table>

Table 3: The synthesized prompt templates with Demonstrations in English.

uOttawa at LegalLens-2024: Transformer-based Classification Experiments

Nima Meghdadi and Diana Inkpen

School of Electrical Engineering and Computer Science
University of Ottawa,
Ottawa, ON, K1N 6N5
nmegh082@uottawa.ca diana.inkpen@uottawa.ca

Abstract

This paper presents the methods used for LegalLens-2024 shared task, which focused on detecting legal violations within unstructured textual data and associating these violations with potentially affected individuals. The shared task included two subtasks: A) Legal Named Entity Recognition (L-NER) and B) Legal Natural Language Inference (L-NLI). For subtask A, we utilized the spaCy library, while for subtask B, we employed a combined model incorporating RoBERTa and CNN. Our results were 86.3% in the L-NER subtask and 88.25% in the L-NLI subtask. Overall, our paper demonstrates the effectiveness of transformer models in addressing complex tasks in the legal domain. The source code for our implementation is publicly available at https://github.com/NimaMeghdadi/uOttawa-at-LegalLens-2024-Transformer-based-Classification

1 Introduction

The huge amount of information and massive use of the internet has propelled to ignore legal violations, individual rights, cultural values and societal norms. These hidden violations demand serious attention and urgent solution due to serious effects on rights and justice and it requires advanced tools for professionals to effectively manage large amount of paperwork.

Legal violation identification seeks to automatically detect legal violations within unstructured text and link these violations to potential victims. The LegalLens 2024 shared task (Bernsohn et al., 2024) aims to foster a legal research community by tackling two key challenges in the legal domain. Subtask A focuses on identifying legal violations (a.k.a Identification Setup) using Named Entity Recognition (NER). Subtask B focuses on linking these violations to potentially affected individuals (a.k.a Identification Setup) using Natural Language Inference (NLI).

Our team participated in both subtasks of the shared task. In subtask A, we used the spaCy library and a DeBERTa-based model. In subtask B, we developed a RoBERTa-based model combined with a CNN-based model.

2 Related Work

There has been extensive research on Legal Named Entity Recognition (NER) for German legal documents. Leitner et al. (2019) developed NER models using CRF and BiLSTM, while Darji et al. (2023) used a BERT-based model. Many languages are using NER to expedite the process of judicial decision-making. For the Turkish language, Çetindağ et al. (2023) developed an NER model using BiLSTM and several word embeddings like GloVe, Morph2Vec, and neural network-based character feature extraction techniques. In Portuguese, Bonifacio et al. (2020) and Albuquerque et al. (2023) focused on NER models specific to the legal domain. The former developed a model using ELMo and BERT with the LeNER-Br dataset (Luz de Araujo et al., 2018), while the latter evaluated BiLSTM+CRF and fine-tuned BERT models on legal and legislative domains to automate and accelerate tasks such as analysis, categorization, search, and summarization. In Italian, Pozzi et al. (2023) created a model that combines transformer-based Named Entity Recognition (NER), transformer-based Named Entity Linking (NEL), and NIL prediction. In Chinese, Zhang et al. (2023) proposed a NER method for the legal domain named RoBERTa-GlobalPointer, combining character-level and word-level feature representations using RoBERTa and Skip-Gram, which were then concatenated and scored with the GlobalPointer method. Lee et al. (2023) also developed a legal domain NER model called LeArNER, which employs Bouma's unsupervised learning for feature extraction and utilizes the LERT and LSTM

Proceedings of the Natural Legal Language Processing Workshop 2024, pages 42–47
November 16, 2024 ©2024 Association for Computational Linguistics

models for sequence annotation.

Kim et al. (2024) described methods for the COLIEE 2023 competition, using a sentence transformer model for case law retrieval and a fine-tuned DeBERTa model for legal entailment that used SNLI (Bowman et al., 2015) and MultiNLI (Williams et al., 2018) datasets for training. Tang (2023) explored improving legal Natural Language Inference (NLI) by employing general NLI datasets with supervised fine-tuning and examining the impact of transfer learning from Adversarial NLI to ContractNLI. The objective of Valentino and Freitas (2024) is to offer a theoretically grounded characterization of explanation-based Natural Language Inference (NLI) by integrating contemporary philosophical accounts of scientific explanation with an analysis of natural language explanation corpora. Gubelmann et al. (2023) investigated how large language models (LLMs) handle different pragmatic sentence types, like questions and commands, in natural language inference (NLI), highlighting the insensitivity of MNLI and its fine-tuned models to these sentence types. It developed and publicly released fine-tuning datasets to address this issue and explored ChatGPT's approach to entailment.

3 Subtask A: Legal Named Entity Recognition(L-NER)

Subtask A, which involves finding named entities for specific types that may appear in legal texts, is explained in this section.

We developed a BERT-based model for this subtask as part of the LegalLens task, achieving an F1-score(Macro F1-score) of 86.3%.

3.1 Dataset Details

We used the dataset provided by the organizers of the shared task. The provided data was split into training and test sets, with each set consisting of tokenized text and the corresponding entities for those tokens. It is important to note that the provided test set includes labeled data, which is different from the separate test data that the organizers will use to evaluate the model. The split dataset used for validation in this research consists of 20% of training data and is shown in Table 1.

The entity types are fully described in (Bernsohn et al., 2024). The labels include four entity types: violation, violation by, violation on, and law, with detailed counts for each entity available in (Bernsohn et al., 2024).

Type	Number of documents
Training	568
Validation	142
Test	617

Table 1: The number of documents used to train the model is detailed

Hyperparameter	Value
Learning Rate	5e-5
Batch Size	16
Maximum Steps	20,000
Dropout Rate	0.1
Optimizer	Adam

Table 2: Hyperparameters of the fine-tuned model for subtask A (L-NER)

3.2 Preprocessing

For this subtask, we configure the spaCy pipeline with an emphasis on tokenization and vector initialization. The tokenizer used is the standard spaCy tokenizer, which splits the text into tokens for downstream tasks. We utilize the spacy.Tokenizer.v1 configuration, which efficiently handles tokenization according to spaCy's standards.

Next, we handle vector initialization. In this setup, vectors map tokens to high-dimensional representations, which helps capture semantic meaning during training. The data by converting the text and its annotations into a format compatible with spaCy.

3.3 Model Training

Our training utilizes the SpaCy pipeline configured with a transformer model and a transition-based parser for NER tasks. The deberta-v3-base model has been selected for the main transformer architecture, offering robust contextual embeddings for token-level classification (He et al., 2021).

Hyperparameters for the training are optimized based on performance on the development set. The key hyperparameters can be seen in Table 2.

3.4 Results and Discussion

We found that models utilizing spaCy achieved better results compared to those without it. Additionally, BERT base models outperformed other models in our experiments. However, we discov-

Model	F1-score
roberta-base	52.55
nlpaueb/legal-bert-base-uncased	53.29
lexlms/legal-roberta-base	54.80
lexlms/legal-roberta-base (Alibaba-NLP/gte-large-en-v1.5)	62.69
roberta-base with spacy	80.49
deberta-v3-base with spacy	**86.37**

Table 3: Comparison of F1-score in various models for the NER subtask

Model	F1-score
Nowj	**0.416**
Flawless Lawgic	0.402
UOttawa	***0.402***
Baseline	0.381
Masala-chai	0.380
UMLaw&TechLab	0.321
Bonafide	0.305

Table 4: Comparison of top 5 teams results on the hidden test set for the NER subtask, measured by F1-score (Hagag et al., 2024).

ered that initializing embeddings from Hugging Face leaderboard embeddings did not lead to improved results. Table 3 compares the F1-scores of various models on the labelled test data.

3.5 Direct Comparison to Related Work

The organizers of the shared task provided a hidden test set, on which our model achieved an F1-score of 0.402, securing third place in the competition. The performance of the top five teams is presented in Table 4.

4 Subtask B: Legal Natural Language Inference (L-NLI)

The goal of this subtask is to automatically classify the relationships between different legal texts. Specifically, we aim to determine whether a legal premise, such as a summary of a legal complaint, entails, contradicts, or remains neutral with respect to a given hypothesis, like an online review. This task, termed Legal Natural Language Inference (L-NLI), involves sentence-pair classification to assess these relationships. By creating an NLI corpus tailored for legal documents, we facilitate applications like legal case matching and automated legal reasoning. Detailed task definitions and datasets are provided in (Bernsohn et al., 2024) and related resources.

4.1 Dataset Details

The LegalLensNLI dataset, provided by the organizers of the shared task, is specifically designed to explore the connections between legal cases and the individuals affected by them, with a particular focus on class action complaints. This dataset contains 312 entries. A comprehensive description of the dataset collection process can be found in (Bernsohn et al., 2024). For this subtask, only the training set is included, and the validation set is separated into four specific domains, as outlined in Table 6.

4.2 Preprocessing

This subtask has a different objective compared to Subtask A, so SpaCy may not perform well for this task. In this subtask, we began by loading the ynie/roberta-large-snli_mnli_fever_anli_R1_R2_R3-nli model (Nie et al., 2020) using the AutoTokenizer and AutoModel classes from the transformers library. The AutoTokenizer class was employed to tokenize the input sentences, converting them into a format suitable for the roberta-large model. The tokenization process involved splitting the text into tokens and converting them into numerical representations, which are then padded and truncated to a consistent length. This ensures that the input sequences are properly aligned when fed into the model.

Following tokenization, we implemented a method to encode the combined premise and hypothesis sentences for both the Roberta model and a CNN model. The CNN model required a different form of input preparation, where the combined texts were tokenized and encoded to maintain the sequence's structure for CNN processing. These tokenized datasets were then converted into PyTorch tensors and mapped accordingly, enabling their use in a combined model that integrates both the Roberta model and the CNN. Subtask B involves finding the similarity between the hypothesis and premises. By using a CNN model to highlight the keywords in sentences, the combined model may perform better.

4.3 Model Training

Our combined model architecture integrates the ynie/roberta-large-snli_mnli_fever_anli_R1_R2_R3-nli model

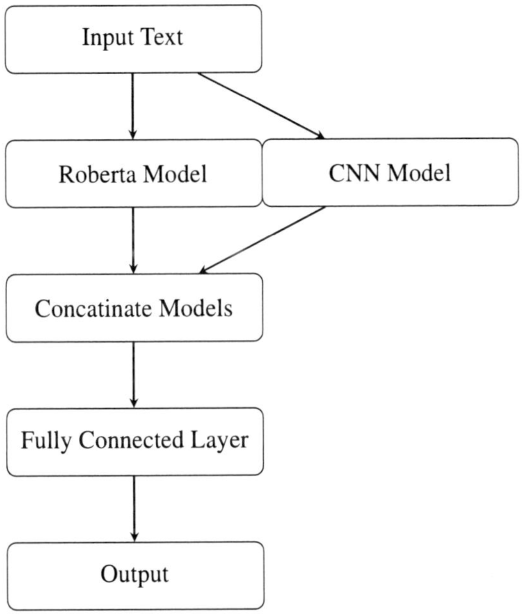

Figure 1: Diagram of combined model (Roberta and CNN)

with a custom-built CNN model for keyword detection. The Roberta model is responsible for capturing contextual information from the text, while the CNN model detects important keyword patterns within the input text. The outputs from both models are concatenated and passed through a fully connected layer (softmax) to produce the final classification decision, the architecture of the model can be seen in Figure1. In more detail, the RoBERTa model consists of one embedding layer and 24 Transformer encoder layers, while the CNN model includes one embedding layer and three convolutional layers, each with a different filter size (2, 3, 4), followed by a fully connected layer. In total, we have 31 layers Training was conducted using the Trainer class from the transformers library, which facilitated the fine-tuning of the model. We defined specific hyperparameters, that can be seen Table 5. The model was evaluated at the end of each epoch, with the best model being saved based on the F1-score. The training process also included strategies for early stopping and warmup steps to optimize performance.

This approach combines the strengths of both the Roberta model and CNN, allowing for a more comprehensive analysis of the text data. The fine-tuning process ensures that the model is well-suited for the specific task of classifying legal text as 'Entailed', 'Neutral', or 'Contradict'.

Hyperparameter	**Value**
Learning Rate	2e-5
Batch Size (train and Eval)	4
Number of Epochs	20
Weight Decay:	0.01

Table 5: Hyperparameters of the fine-tuned model for subtask A (L-NLI)

Model	CP	Privacy	TCPA	Wage	**Avg**
Falcon 7B	**87.2**	84.5	83.9	68.5	81.02
without cnn	87.23	85.48	83.88	90.6	86.77
roberta-base	82.9	62.0	69.5	69.7	71.02
Our model	84.4	**90**	**84**	**96**	**88.6**

Table 6: Comparison of F1-score on the validation set for various models for the NLI task for specific-domain (Consumer Protection, Privacy,TCPA and Wage)

4.4 Results and Discussion

We found that pre-trained NLI models can perform significantly better than vanilla models and LLMs. Falcon 7B and RoBERTa base are the best performing models for LLMs and vanilla models, respectively, as shown in Table 6. The validation set has been selected to be domain-specific, based on legal_act.

4.5 Direct Comparison to Related Work

The shared task organizers evaluated the models using a hidden test set, where our model attained an F1-score of 0.724, placing fifth in the competition. The results of the top five teams are detailed in Table 7.

5 Conclusion and Future Work

Our experiments demonstrated the success of transformer models, such as RoBERTa and DeBERTa, in handling complex legal tasks, including violation detection and inference. In Subtask A (L-NER), incorporating DeBERTa into the spaCy pipeline

Model	**F1-score**
1-800-Shared-Tasks	**0.853**
Baseline	0.807
Semantists	0.785
Nowj	0.746
UOttawa	***0.724***

Table 7: Performance of the leading 5 teams on the hidden test set in the NLI subtask, measured by F1-score (Hagag et al., 2024).

yielded strong results for legal named entity recognition. In Subtask B (L-NLI), combining RoBERTa with CNN for keyword detection boosted classification accuracy.

However, despite using robust models, generalizing to unseen cases proved challenging, particularly with nuanced legal language. While the CNN improved phrase detection, more advanced methods, like attention mechanisms, may further enhance performance.

Future work should explore architectures finetuned on legal texts or combine transformers with graph models to capture legal relationships. Additionally, leveraging LLMs like GPT-4 could improve legal reasoning.

References

Hidelberg O Albuquerque, Ellen Souza, Adriano LI Oliveira, David Macêdo, Cleber Zanchettin, Douglas Vitório, Nádia FF da Silva, and André CPLF de Carvalho. 2023. On the assessment of deep learning models for named entity recognition of brazilian legal documents. In *EPIA Conference on Artificial Intelligence*, pages 93–104. Springer.

Dor Bernsohn, Gil Semo, Yaron Vazana, Gila Hayat, Ben Hagag, Joel Niklaus, Rohit Saha, and Kyryl Truskovskyi. 2024. LegalLens: Leveraging LLMs for legal violation identification in unstructured text. In *Proceedings of the 18th Conference of the European Chapter of the Association for Computational Linguistics (Volume 1: Long Papers)*, pages 2129–2145, St. Julian's, Malta. Association for Computational Linguistics.

Luiz Henrique Bonifacio, Paulo Arantes Vilela, Gustavo Rocha Lobato, and Eraldo Rezende Fernandes. 2020. A study on the impact of intradomain finetuning of deep language models for legal named entity recognition in portuguese. In *Intelligent Systems: 9th Brazilian Conference, BRACIS 2020, Rio Grande, Brazil, October 20–23, 2020, Proceedings, Part I 9*, pages 648–662. Springer.

Samuel R. Bowman, Gabor Angeli, Christopher Potts, and Christopher D. Manning. 2015. A large annotated corpus for learning natural language inference. In *Proceedings of the 2015 Conference on Empirical Methods in Natural Language Processing*, pages 632–642, Lisbon, Portugal. Association for Computational Linguistics.

Can Çetindağ, Berkay Yazıcıoğlu, and Aykut Koç. 2023. Named-entity recognition in turkish legal texts. *Natural Language Engineering*, 29(3):615–642.

Harshil Darji, Jelena Mitrović, and Michael Granitzer. 2023. German bert model for legal named entity recognition. *arXiv preprint arXiv:2303.05388*.

Reto Gubelmann, Aikaterini-Lida Kalouli, Christina Niklaus, and Siegfried Handschuh. 2023. When truth matters-addressing pragmatic categories in natural language inference (nli) by large language models (llms). In *Proceedings of the 12th Joint Conference on Lexical and Computational Semantics (* SEM 2023)*, pages 24–39.

Ben Hagag, Liav Harpaz, Gil Semo, Dor Bernsohn, Rohit Saha, Pashootan Vaezipoor, Kyryl Truskovskyi, and Gerasimos Spanakis. 2024. Legallens shared task 2024: Legal violation identification in unstructured text. *Preprint*, arXiv:2410.12064.

Pengcheng He, Jianfeng Gao, and Weizhu Chen. 2021. Debertav3: Improving deberta using electra-style pretraining with gradient-disentangled embedding sharing. *Preprint*, arXiv:2111.09543.

Mi-Young Kim, Juliano Rabelo, Housam Khalifa Bashier Babiker, Md Abed Rahman, and Randy Goebel. 2024. Legal information retrieval and entailment using transformer-based approaches. *The Review of Socionetwork Strategies*, 18(1):101–121.

Shao-Man Lee, Yu-Hsiang Tan, and Han-Ting Yu. 2023. Learner: few-shot legal argument named entity recognition. In *Proceedings of the Nineteenth International Conference on Artificial Intelligence and Law*, pages 422–426.

Elena Leitner, Georg Rehm, and Julian Moreno-Schneider. 2019. Fine-grained named entity recognition in legal documents. In *International conference on semantic systems*, pages 272–287. Springer.

Pedro Henrique Luz de Araujo, Teófilo E de Campos, Renato RR de Oliveira, Matheus Stauffer, Samuel Couto, and Paulo Bermejo. 2018. Lener-br: a dataset for named entity recognition in brazilian legal text. In *Computational Processing of the Portuguese Language: 13th International Conference, PROPOR 2018, Canela, Brazil, September 24–26, 2018, Proceedings 13*, pages 313–323. Springer.

Yixin Nie, Adina Williams, Emily Dinan, Mohit Bansal, Jason Weston, and Douwe Kiela. 2020. Adversarial NLI: A new benchmark for natural language understanding. In *Proceedings of the 58th Annual Meeting of the Association for Computational Linguistics*. Association for Computational Linguistics.

Riccardo Pozzi, Riccardo Rubini, Christian Bernasconi, and Matteo Palmonari. 2023. Named entity recognition and linking for entity extraction from italian civil judgements. In *International Conference of the Italian Association for Artificial Intelligence*, pages 187–201. Springer.

Yiu Kei Tang. 2023. Natural language inference transfer learning in a multi-task contract dataset: In the case of contractnli: a document information extraction system.

Marco Valentino and André Freitas. 2024. On the nature of explanation: An epistemological-linguistic perspective for explanation-based natural language inference. *Philosophy & Technology*, 37(3):88.

Adina Williams, Nikita Nangia, and Samuel Bowman. 2018. A broad-coverage challenge corpus for sentence understanding through inference. In *Proceedings of the 2018 Conference of the North American Chapter of the Association for Computational Linguistics: Human Language Technologies, Volume 1 (Long Papers)*, pages 1112–1122. Association for Computational Linguistics.

Xinrui Zhang, Xudong Luo, and Jiaye Wu. 2023. A roberta-globalpointer-based method for named entity recognition of legal documents. In *2023 International Joint Conference on Neural Networks (IJCNN)*, pages 1–8. IEEE.

Quebec Automobile Insurance Question-Answering With Retrieval-Augmented Generation

David Beauchemin[*†], **Zachary Gagnon**[*‡], and **Richard Khoury**[†]
Université Laval, Québec, Canada
Computer Science Department[†]
[†]{david.beauchemin, richard.khoury}@ift.ulaval.ca,
[‡]zachary.gagnon.1@ulaval.ca

Abstract

Large Language Models (LLMs) perform outstandingly in various downstream tasks, and the use of the Retrieval-Augmented Generation (RAG) architecture has been shown to improve performance for legal question answering (Nuruzzaman and Hussain, 2020; Louis et al., 2024). However, there are limited applications in insurance questions-answering, a specific type of legal document. This paper introduces two corpora: the Quebec Automobile Insurance Expertise Reference Corpus and a set of 82 Expert Answers to Layperson Automobile Insurance Questions. Our study leverages both corpora to automatically and manually assess a GPT4-o, a state-of-the-art LLM, to answer Quebec automobile insurance questions. Our results demonstrate that, on average, using our expertise reference corpus generates better responses on both automatic and manual evaluation metrics. However, they also highlight that LLM QA is unreliable enough for mass utilization in critical areas. Indeed, our results show that between 5% to 13% of answered questions include a false statement that could lead to customer misunderstanding.

1 Introduction

To protect their financial situation and property, vehicle owners and homeowners need to buy property damage insurance. However, most people have little to no proper knowledge of insurance products, and rely on insurance representatives to help them properly select and comprehend these products (RLRQ, 2004; AMF, 2019). As a result, in order to protect the public, insurance regulators, such as the "Autorité des marchés financiers" (AMF) in Quebec, make sure that insurance representatives are well-trained and educated, and that insurers properly inform their customers (AMF, 2024a).

However, customers are increasingly interested in buying insurance products online (Claire et al., 2018). This change impacts how an insurer can adequately inform their customer. Traditionally, customers buy products in person or through phone insurance representatives, which allows an insurance expert to help the customer understand the different products and buy the correct one. With an online sale, customers are left to gather information by themselves (AMF, 2018; Johnson, 2018). Moreover, insurance is regulated locally, which means that insurance products, coverages and laws are different from one jurisdiction to the next. Consequently, while many resources are available online, such as "infoassurance" (IBC and GAA, 2024), only the limited set of resources from one's own locality are applicable, and customers must take care not to get information from elsewhere.

The rapid progress in natural language processing and the growing availability of insurance data present unprecedented opportunities to bridge the gap between people and insurance knowledge. For instance, legal text summarization (Shukla et al., 2022) holds the potential to simplify complex legal documents for laypeople. Similarly, insurance question-answering (QA) could offer affordable, expert-like assistance to non-expert customers.

To this end, we present an end-to-end approach aimed at generating high-quality answers to Quebec automobile insurance questions. Our methodology harnesses the popular "Retrieval-Augmented Generation" (RAG) approach. The main contributions of this work are therefore:

1. The creation and release of a Quebec Automobile Insurance Expertise References Corpus[1];
2. The creation and release of a corpus of 82 Expert Answers to Laypeople Automobile Insurance Questions[2];

[*]Contributed equally to this work.

[1]https://github.com/GRAAL-Research/quebec-insurance-rag-corpora

[2]https://github.com/GRAAL-Research/quebec-insurance-rag-corpora

Proceedings of the Natural Legal Language Processing Workshop 2024, pages 48–60
November 16, 2024 ©2024 Association for Computational Linguistics

3. A set of experiments to assess the performance of GPT-4o, a state-of-the-art LLM, on our QA corpus, including a manual evaluation of the generated answers.

This paper is outlined as follows: first, we study the relevant questions-answering legal RAG research and its related corpora in Section 2. Then, we propose our corpora in Section 3, and in Section 4, Section 5 and Section 6 we present a set of experiments aimed at evaluating the performances of GPT-4o at answering Quebec automobile insurance questions. Finally, in Section 7, we conclude and discuss our future work.

2 Related Work

Legal-Domain QA RAG The advent of large language models (LLMs) has led to advances in many previously arduous tasks, such as in the application of the RAG concept in QA tasks, which has attracted a great deal of research interest in recent years (Pipitone and Alami, 2024). Answering legal questions has always been more complex due to the inherent difficulties of exploiting specialized texts that stem from handing specialized terminology (Wiratunga and Ram, 2011) and intricate sentence structures (Katz et al., 2023). Recently, Louis et al. (2024) has presented an end-to-end methodology to generate answers to any statutory law question leveraging a RAG architecture, along with a long-form legal question answering dataset comprising 1,868 expert-annotated legal questions in French. Likewise, the insurance sector, with its complex documents and nuanced information, could benefit from these advancements. Consequently, although research is mainly focused on the legal field, there is also a growing interest in the insurance sector, including for insurance RAG. Nuruzzaman and Hussain (2020) have presented a chatbot that generates accurate and contextual responses by identifying intentions and entities while ensuring semantic relevance and meaning of responses. It is trained on domain-specific datasets to understand insurance-specific terms and information. It notably uses RAG strategies to generate responses. Likewise, Na et al. (2022) focuses on a single-turn dialogue covering insurance QA on a Korean dataset to respond to insurance customers.

Legal and Insurance Corpora The number of datasets available in the legal and insurance domains has increased in recent years (Martinez-Gil, 2023; Cui et al., 2023). One example is CUAD (Hendrycks et al.), a dataset for legal contract review that includes 13,000 human annotations. The first insurance QA dataset was proposed by Feng et al. (2015), and consists in 16,889 question-answer pairs; they also conducted experiments to assess different approaches at answering insurance questions. More recently, Butler (2023) have proposed a corpus of 2,124 synthetic question-answer pairs concerning Australian law. The corpus was generated using GPT-4 and the Open Australian Legal Corpus, but the answers were not reviewed by an insurance expert. However, as of yet, no such corpus exists for automobile insurance questions.

3 Corpora

This section describes the two corpora we created for our work: our French corpus of automobile insurance expertise references documentation for the Province of Quebec (Canada), and our French corpus of 82 layperson questions about Quebec automotive insurance and their expert answers and annotations. First, we will describe our process for creating each corpus[3] and then present some key statistics.

3.1 Corpus Creation

3.1.1 Quebec Automobile Insurance Expertise Reference Corpus

This corpus is composed of a set of documents extracted from seven official and reliable online sources about automobile insurance in Quebec. These sources have been selected in partnership with a Canadian insurance company. They have been divided into the following four categories:

- The **Laws** category includes two pieces of provincial legislation related to Quebec automobile insurance. The first one is the *Loi sur l'assurance automobile* (Quebec, 2024), which establishes the regulations governing insurers and insureds in Quebec. The second one is the *Code de sécurité routière* (Quebec, 2016), and it governs the use of all motorized vehicles and pedestrians on public roads to ensure safety.
- The **F.P.Q. 1** category includes the manually extracted Quebec mandatory-approved automobile insurance contracts (AMF; Beauchemin and Khoury, 2023). The F.P.Q. 1 is divided into civil

[3]We also discuss the risk of data leakage in our Limitations section.

liability and property damage. Optional coverages are described in endorsements. We have included one realistic synthetic contract that includes all available endorsements.

- The **Insurance Regulator Educative Resources** category includes informative resources from the AMF, Quebec's regulatory body for financial and insurance products and services (AMF, 2024a). We included its educational information related to automobile insurance for customers.
- The **Domain-Specific Educative Resources** category includes educative resources from four insurance domain organizations. They all propose various educational resources to the public through their online blog. The first, the *Chambre de l'Assurance de Dommages*, is the regulatory body that oversees the training and ethics of insurance agents, brokers and claims adjusters (ChAD, 2024). The second, the *Groupement des Assureurs Automobiles*, is the association of all home and car insurance insurers in Quebec. It oversees and develops various mechanisms to improve the property damage system (GAA, 2024). The third, *Éducaloi*, is a non-profit organization created by the Quebec Ministry of Justice that informs the public on legal matters, such as insurance products (Éducaloi, 2024). Lastly, *Infoassurances* is an insurance information website created by the Insurance Bureau of Canada and the *Groupement des Assureurs Automobiles* for the purpose of "properly informing customers about property insurance" (IBC and GAA, 2024).

We have selected 21 online documents from these sources that focus on the subject of "automobile insurance". The documents can be pieces of legislation, legal insurance documents, informative resources, or informative blog articles. The content of each document has been manually extracted and cleaned to remove trailing whitespace, along with paragraphs that are either "replaced" or "repealed" in a piece of legislature.

3.1.2 Corpus of Expert Answers to Laypeople's Automobile Insurance Questions

This corpus comprises a set of French questions and answers related to automotive insurance in Quebec. They were manually extracted from highly-reliable sources that were selected in partnership with a Canadian insurance company, like for the previous references corpus. Our selected sources are divided into the following four categories:

- The **Quebec Insurance Company FAQ** category includes question-answer pairs taken from the FAQ web pages of four insurers', namely, Beneva (Beneva, 2024), Desjardins Assurances (Desjardins Assurances, 2024), Belairdirect (Belairdirect, 2024) and Sonnet (Sonnet, 2024). These insurers have been selected based on two selection criteria. First, they must sell automotive insurance in Quebec. Second, the questions in their FAQ must not overlap with those of other selected insurers. For example, Intact Assurance's (Intact Insurance, 2024) FAQ is identical to Belairdirect's, since both companies belong to the same corporation[4], and therefore that insurer was excluded.
- The **Regulator** category includes insurance professional practice examination questions and answers from the regulator (AMF, 2024b).
- The **Domain-Specific Educative Resources** category includes question-answer pairs available through two educative resources and blogs from insurance sector organizations, namely the *Chambre de l'Assurance de Dommages* and *Infoassurances*. These two sources are also used as reference sources. We have carefully ensured no overlap between the extracted questions and the extracted reference content from these sources.
- The **Quebec Public Automobile Insurance Plan** category includes question-answer pairs from the Quebec government agency responsible for the automobile insurance plan that covers all bodily injuries (SAAQ, 2024).

We extracted 82 question-answer pairs from these sources, along with a category for each pair. Seven categories were extracted from the sources; each question is related to one of the following categories:

- **Legal Obligations** are questions related to the insuree's and insurer's legal obligation. For example, it could be a question about the minimum amount of civil liability insurance required.
- **Civil Liability Coverage** are questions related to civil liability coverage. This could be for example a question about how a civil liability claim works.
- **Property Coverage** are questions related to at-fault accidents and the scope of property damage

[4]https://www.intactfc.com/en

protection. For example, there could be a question about how to file an at-fault claim.

- **Endorsement** are questions related to any endorsements in insurance contracts. For example, it could be a question about the protections found in an endorsement.
- **Terms and Conditions** are questions related to an insurance contract's general terms and conditions. It could be a question about the consequence of a customer not paying their premium for instance.
- **General** are questions related to the general elements of the insurance sector. One example could be a question about why insurance companies use credit scores during the insurance proposal.
- **Public Automobile Insurance Plan** are questions related to bodily injury coverage offered by the public automobile insurance plan in Quebec. This for example could be a question about the program coverage and exclusions.

3.2 Corpora Analysis

Table 1 presents some key statistics of our French corpora and similar English insurance QA corpora introduced in Section 2. For the English insurance QA corpora, we have used their latest official version[5]. All statistics were computed using SpaCy's latest language-specific tokenizer (Honnibal et al., 2020). They exclude new lines (`\n`), whitespaces, punctuations and some special characters (<, >, | and $). Moreover, to evaluate the reading complexity level of the contracts, we compute readability scores using the frequently used Flesch-Kincaid formula (Flesch, 1948). It computes a score using a scale from 0 (hardest) to 100 (easier) to assess the readability level. We will first analyze our reference corpus and then compare our QA corpus with similar corpora using Table 1.

3.2.1 Our References Corpus Analysis

In Table 1 (left side), we see that all four sources share relatively similar statistics. Indeed, the average number of lexical words (LW), average sentence lengths (both), and average number of sentences are relatively similar. Moreover, since legal documents are known to be complex and lengthy and to use specialized vocabulary (Katz et al., 2023), we can see that the average number of tokens, lexical richness and average Flesch-Kincaid score are lower than the two other types of documents.

3.2.2 Question-Answering Corpora Comparison

We can see in Table 1 (right side) that our QA corpus shares similar patterns to the other corpora. Indeed, for all corpora, the questions use less than half the vocabulary size as the answers and are half as long in terms of tokens, LW, number of sentences, and average sentence length as the answers. They are also easier to read than the answers based on the Flesch-Kincaid score. However, ours is significantly smaller compared to other similar corpora due to its nature. Indeed, the other two similar corpora focus on the broader insurance domain. For example, Insurance QA includes questions about all types of insurance (property, life, and health) throughout the USA. In contrast, our corpus focuses on a single insurance product for a single province in Canada.

4 QA Methodology

This section details our methodology for leveraging a large language model (LLM) to answer insurance questions. Our choice of architecture is similar to Louis et al. (2024), Ajmi (2024), and Wiratunga et al. (2024). We use a RAG architecture to inject domain expertise into an LLM generation for QA. Like the previous authors, our RAG architecture is inspired by the concept of "advanced RAG" (Gao et al., 2023), an architecture that adds a pre- and post-retrieval steps to the traditional processing. Our architecture was built using `LangChain` (Chase, 2022), a Python framework that consolidates the various components of the RAG architecture. As illustrated in Figure 1, first, a retriever selects a small subset of insurance documents from our reference corpus (red), some relevant to the question and some not. Then, a generator conditions its answer on the subset of articles returned by the retriever (blue). We describe these two components in details in the following subsections.

4.1 Retriever

The function of our retriever component is to extract from our reference corpus portions of texts, such as sentences or paragraphs, that are relevant to a question and to present them at the forefront of the returned results. It is a two-step operation consisting of pre-processing and retrieval steps.

[5] https://github.com/shuzi/insuranceQA, https://huggingface.co/datasets/umarbutler/open-australian-legal-qa

	References Corpus					Our QA Corpus		Australian Legal QA		Insurance QA	
	Laws	F.P.Q. 1	Regulator	Sector	Avg	Questions	Answers	Questions	Answers	Questions	Answers
Number of QA pair	N/A	N/A	N/A	N/A	N/A	82		2,124		16,889	
Vocabulary size	4,638	1,751	1,038	1,029	6,201	367	950	6,657	13,583	3,658	19,355
Avg number of tokens	89.41	87.43	115.52	109.83	90.60	14.45	57.98	26.03	85.99	7.36	99.98
Avg number of LW	38.95	42.14	51.2	49.71	40.20	6.68	25.67	14.57	44.6	4.03	45.91
Avg number of sentence	4.13	8.12	7.33	7.12	4.96	1.24	3.00	1.41	3.12	1.00	5.42
Avg sentence length (tokens)	21.37	11.81	17.05	16.67	19.56	12.22	20.86	21.09	31.22	7.32	19.57
Avg sentence length (LW)	9.25	5.89	7.61	7.51	8.61	5.59	9.34	11.74	16.52	4.02	9.12
Lexical richness	0.11	0.18	0.37	0.36	0.10	0.48	0.37	0.21	0.14	0.05	0.02
Avg Flesch-Kincaid score	46.67	56.45	61.41	65.6	49.31	73.66	60.19	55.8	46.1	71.25	66.78

Table 1: Aggregate statistics of our French corpora and similar English insurance QA corpora introduced in Section 2. "Avg" stands for average, "LW" for lexical words.

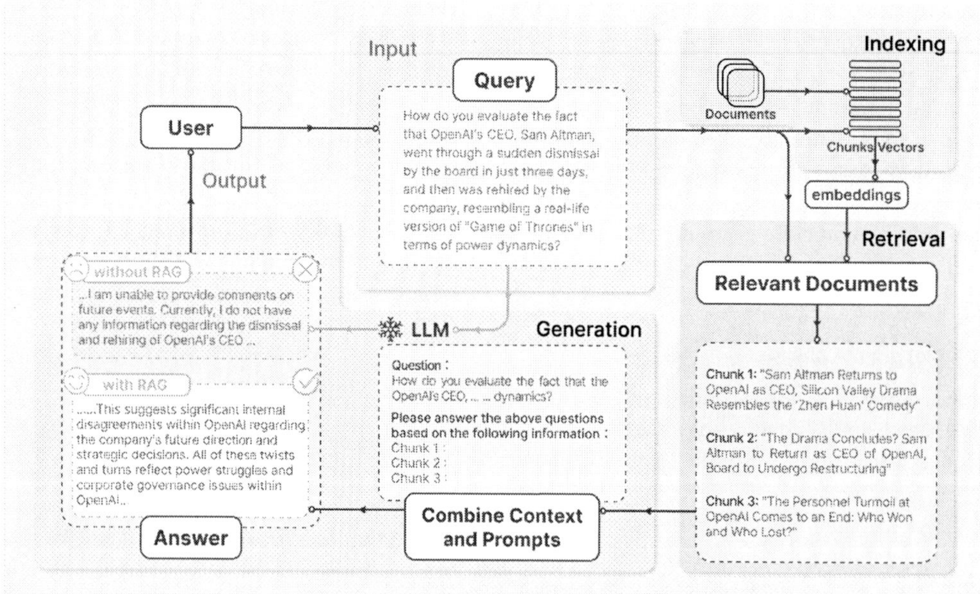

Figure 1: A representative instance of the 3-steps RAG process applied to question answering. 1) Indexing: Documents are split into chunks, and encoded into vectors in a vector database. 2) Retrieval: Retrieve the Top k chunks most relevant to the question based on semantic similarity. 3) Generation: Input the original question and the retrieved chunks together into LLM to generate the final answer. The illustration is taken from Gao et al. (2023).

4.1.1 Pre-Processing

During the pre-processing step, all our documents in the reference corpus go through a two-step pre-processing stage to prepare our document for our retrieval algorithm. The first step is to split the document into smaller chunks of text (i.e. chunking). Based on the best practices for RAG in Wang et al. (2024), we use a fixed chunk size of 500 characters which gives optimal performance for document search since it standardizes their size for better similarity search results. Moreover, legal documents are similar to the financial reports of Yepes et al. (2024) because they use a standard structure to present their content. For example, laws are divided in chapters composed of articles relevant to their subject, which are in turn composed of sub-articles related to the main article. We thus process the documents using a parent-child split function to capture this structure. However, the complete chunk is also supplied for generation when the similarity function is performed during retrieval on the child-split. Namely, if a sub-article is extracted as a relevant text, the main article's text chunk will be provided, not only the sub-article.

The second step is to encode all chunks into dense embedding representation for retrieval. To do so, we use `text-embedding-ada-002` (Greene et al., 2022), a 1,536 dimension multilingual all-purpose embeddings model proposed by OpenAI. This embedding model has proven successful in the insurance field (Mohanan, 2024).

4.1.2 Retrieval

The retrieval step seeks to retrieve a subset of articles using an algorithm that leverages dense word embeddings (i.e. `text-embedding-ada-002`) for retrieval. Our retrieval process is a 3-step process that uses the question as a query. First, the question is encoded using the retriever embedding model. Second, using our dense retriever, we retrieve the `top-5` relevant documents from the reference corpus using cosine similarity to measure the semantic similarity between the query and each document. Third, we merge all relevant reference documents using a context compressor (Cheng et al., 2024). This compressor calls an LLM for each reference using the extracted document (context), the user query, and a formatted prompt that specifies the compressor's task. With this prompt, the LLM is asked to return only the relevant part of the context given the query and, if needed, reformulate the context in certain difficult-to-understand cases, as is sometimes the case with technical legal texts. The compressor reduces the context size, thus keeping the prompt size within an acceptable range, in order to prevent certain issues. Indeed, it is known that excessively large prompts can degrade the quality of answer generation (Levy et al., 2024). Moreover, a lost-in-the-middle effect can cause a language model to omit information contained in the middle portion of the prompt (Liu et al., 2024). This approach helps merge content from different sources to create a better-contextualized reference document for an LLM to generate an answer (Wang et al., 2024).

4.2 Generation

Our generator's goal is to formulate an exhaustive and concise answer to an automotive insurance question based on the information provided by the retrieval process. Our generator uses `GPT-4o`, the latest OpenAI LLM model. The prompt is constructed using the question and the context obtained from the retrieved reference documents, along with specific task instructions designed to guide the LLM in formulating a comprehensive and accurate answer.

As shown in Figure 2 and Figure 3, we have used two prompts for our experiment. The first (Figure 2) is a zero-shot prompt where the LLM is simply asked to answer the question. The second (Figure 3 is a domain-specific prompt that gives additional information to support the LLM. In each prompt, `{input}` corresponds to the question, and `{context}` to the retrieved references.

> Répondez à la question suivante EN FRANÇAIS.

> Voici la question: {input}.

(a) Basic zero-shot prompt adapted from Kew et al. (2023) followed by the input question to respond to.

> Answer the following question IN FRENCH.

> Here's the question: {input}.

(b) Translation of the prompt presented in Figure 2a.

Figure 2: Zero-shot prompt used for text generation. Blue boxes contain the task instructions. Yellow boxes contain the prefix for the model to continue.

> Vous êtes un expert en assurances automobile dans le domaine de l'assurance de dommages. Vous répondez à des questions EN FRANÇAIS liés à l'assurance automobile AU QUÉBEC. Vous utilisez le contexte fourni ci-bas. Répondez EN PHRASES COMPLÈTES et soyez concis.

> Voici la question: {input};
> Voici le contexte : {contexte}.

(a) Domain-specific prompt with prompt engineering (i.e. role, task, domain of application) adapted from Kew et al. (2023) followed by the input question to respond to.

> You are an automobile insurance expert in the property and casualty insurance field. You are answering questions in FRENCH related to automobile insurance in QUEBEC. Use the context provided below. Answer in FULL PHRASES and be concise.

> Here's the question: {input};
> Here's the context: {context}.

(b) Translation of the prompt presented in Figure 3a.

Figure 3: Prompt used for text generation. Blue boxes contain the task instructions. Yellow boxes contain the prefix for the model to continue.

5 Experiments

The goal of our experiments is to assess whether an LLM can adequately answer technical questions with complex answers, namely Quebec insurance questions, with or without a RAG architecture. To achieve this, we conduct experiments to automatically and manually evaluate six approaches.

5.1 Experimentation Setup

Baseline For our baseline, we use our zero-shot prompt to assess GPT-4o out-of-the-box capabilities to answer Quebec insurance questions. We label it `Zero-shot` in our result tables.

RAG Architecture Approaches For our other five experiments, we use our RAG architecture described in Section 4 and the domain-specific prompt, with an increasing number of reference sources. Namely, we start with an approach that uses no references. The difference between this approach and the baseline is only prompt engineering. Then, we incrementally add in reference sources. The next approach only uses the **Laws** source, the following adds the **F.P.Q. 1**, then we add the AMF reference, and finally we add the educative resources to use all four references. We label these five approaches, `No references`, `Laws`, `Laws, F.P.Q. 1`, `Laws, F.P.Q. 1, AMF` and `All references` respectively.

5.2 Evaluation

5.2.1 Automatic Evaluation

Following Chen et al. (2019), we evaluate the accuracy of machine-generated answers compare to reference answers using three N-grams based metrics: BLEU-{1, 4, AVG} (Papineni et al., 2002), ROUGE-{1, 2, L} (F1-Score) (Lin and Och, 2004) and METEOR (Banerjee and Lavie, 2005) scores. We also use two deep similarity metrics that measure the similarity between a machine-generated text and a reference document to compute "how semantically related are those two documents" using words embedding: BERTScore (Zhang et al., 2019), and MeaningBERT (Beauchemin et al., 2023). Each metric uses a slightly different approach to compute this similarity. The first feeds the machine- and human-generated documents separately through a BERT model, then computes a token-by-token alignment between the documents using pairwise cosine similarity. The second, MeaningBERT, uses a fine-tuned pre-trained BERT model train to predict how similar two documents are; the model aims to maximize its correlation with human evaluation. We report the results averaged over five restarts from different random seeds.

5.2.2 Manual Evaluation

To discern the strengths and shortcomings of our generator with or without using an RAG architecture, we conduct a detailed manual analysis of all question-answer pairs. Inspired by Chartier et al. (2024) and Baray et al. (2024), we, in partnership with our insurance partner, have developed an evaluation guide with an exam-like setup to evaluate each pair.Based on the expert answers, we defined a set of criteria, or key elements that a machine-generated answer must include. To evaluate each criterion, we developed a grading scale inspired by the one used by Chartier et al. (2024) and Baray et al. (2024); this scale is presented in Table 2. In

Grade	Description
-1	The system gives a false answer for the criterion i. For example, an answer states that civil liability covers property damage on the insured car if the owner is responsible, which is false.
0	The system does not give a proper answer to the criterion i or give an answer at all.
1	The system gives an incomplete answer to the criterion i.
2	The system gives a complete answer to the criterion i.

Table 2: Our evaluation grading scale to evaluates a machine-generated answer using a set of criteria.

case of a false answer to a criterion, we penalize the score with a negative point since an erroneous answer could mislead the customer or hinder their understanding of an insurance product. On the other hand, a complete answer to a criterion results in the maximum score of 2 points. In total, 288 criteria have been extracted from the human answers. On average, each question has 3.51 criteria with a standard deviation of 1.75. The maximum grade a system can receive is $288 \times 2 = 576$ points, and the lowest is -288 points when a system always gives a false answer.

Since we ran 5 runs of each setup with random restarts, we randomly select one of the five for our manual evaluation. One of the authors, with ten years of experience in Quebec Insurance, conducted the evaluation. Appendix A presents the evaluation interface used for our evaluation (in French). During the evaluation, the evaluator is randomly presented with a randomly-selected generated answer from one of the six experimental setups, and he does not know which approach he evaluate.

6 Results

In this section, we present and discuss both our quantitative and qualitative results. We also have conducted an ablation study that also use each source individually in Appendix B.

6.1 Quantitative Results

The left-hand side of Table 3 presents the results of the automatic metrics averaged over the five random restarts, with **bolded** value indicating the best score. First, we observe that, for all automatic metrics, on average, the `All references` approach outperforms other methods. Moreover, this method's BLEU, ROUGE, and METEOR scores indicate that it gives answers using a vocabulary similar to that of humans in the ground truth. These scores are 40% to 300% higher than the zero-shot baseline approach. It shows that using all our references greatly improves the LLM's ability to answer questions properly. However, surprisingly, the second best approach is the `No reference` approach, which outperforms approaches using the same prompt along with a subset of our references. We hypothesize that using Laws and other juridical documents confuses the LLM and generates longer text that are penalized by automatic N-grams metrics. We will explore and discuss this in the following section.

A second observation is that the approach with the highest variation in performance over the five restarts is `All references`. Indeed, this approach's standard deviation is the highest of all setups, and is nearly three times higher than the lowest one. It indicates that using this approach can also yield suboptimal generations.

Finally, to further assess our approaches' performance, we report the two best approaches z-test significance test in Table 4. Our null hypothesis is that the pair of approaches have equal performances, meaning that values smaller or greater than $|1.96|$ allow us to reject the null hypothesis with $\alpha = 0.05$. A positive value means that the `No references` model (left) performs significantly better than the `All references` (right), and a negative value means the opposite. We can see that for most metrics, `All references` has a significantly better performance compared to `No references`; we can conclude that `All references` is better than `No references`.

6.2 Qualitative Results

The right-hand side of Table 3 also presents the manual grading obtained using our evaluation guide, with **bolded** value indicating the best score. Once again, we observe that `All references` approach outperforms other methods, achieving a score nearly double that of the baseline method.

Moreover, `No references` scores are higher than approaches that use a portion of the references corpus.This seems to indicate that responses from partial references are not just longer but are also incomplete. Indeed, we observed that using legal documents generates longer responses, but the generated answers tend to be of lower quality. For example, to the question "What is the recommended amount of civil liability insurance I should carry when driving outside Quebec?" (translated), the `Laws` model answers with the definition of civil liability instead of responding with the recommended amount of 2 million dollars. In contrast, the `No references` approach answers with the correct amount. It is likely due to data leakage: GPT-4o might have been trained using some of our references and memorized the correct answer. By forcing a different context from incomplete references, the LLM seems to forget or overwite that information.

An interesting situation occurred with the question "I was injured in a car accident. What should I do?" (translated). All evaluated generations take the questions literally and assume the driver has just been injured, and thus propose steps to secure the insuree such as "call an ambulance". In contrast, the ground truth specified the administrative steps to proceed with a bodily injury claim. It shows that, in this case, LLM cannot infer the actual context of the question.

Another interesting situation is whether or not the model abstains from answering in cases where the context is unknown or the information to respond to the question is unavailable for the model. In none of the cases we examined, the model abstained from answering the question. It always strived to be as helpful as possible. However, while sufficient, our prompt could be enhanced to further boost performance. By adapting it to generate better responses and prevent the model from responding when uncertain, we hypothesize that we could improve its performance by improving the prompt.

Moreover, in many cases, without specific references to Quebec insurance specifications, the response contained French insurance information. For example, the `No References` model responded to many questions with specific details of automobile insurance with France-based examples such as civil liability coverage. This pattern disappeared with the addition of the references.

Finally, we can see that the zero-shot approach generates the lowest grade and the highest number of false answers. This highlights the risk of using an out-of-the-box LLM to generate technical answers with precise answer elements, as in our situation. It also highlights that using our RAG approach with our references corpus can lower this risk substantially.While the risk of false answers

	ROUGE			BERTScore	MeaningBERT	BLEU			METEOR	Exam Score (%)	False Statement
	1	2	L			Average	1	4			
Zero-shot	0.27±0.10	0.09±0.06	0.16±0.06	66.93±4.33	71.42±11.21	4.10±4.25	21.28±10.63	1.39±2.63	24.23±7.61	27.43	34
No references	0.35±0.09	0.14±0.08	0.22±0.07	71.40±4.43	78.17±10.62	7.06±6.16	33.63±14.63	3.05±5.00	27.02±9.68	32.29	20
Laws	0.32±0.1	0.12±0.08	0.20±0.07	70.743±4.54	77.05±11.11	6.177±5.76	31.276±15.05	2.76±5.49	26.29±9.68	27.78	20
Laws, F.P.Q. 1	0.32±0.11	0.13±0.11	0.21±0.1	70.29±5.1	75.44±11.0	6.73±7.47	30.40±15.02	3.30±6.26	27.05±10.42	29.51	19
Laws, F.P.Q. 1, AMF	0.33±0.11	0.14±0.11	0.21±0.1	70.89±5.59	76.91±10.63	7.62±8.02	31.76±16.0	3.93±7.12	27.76±10.78	34.20	18
All references	**0.375±0.14**	**0.18±0.15**	**0.25±0.14**	**71.99±5.9**	**78.87±10.17**	**10.68±11.71**	**33.77±16.66**	**5.98±9.91**	**33.61±14.69**	**51.74**	14

Table 3: Automatic metrics (left) average and one standard deviation over the five restarts on our questions-answering corpus and manual (right) evaluation using our evaluation guide. The best score is **bolded**.

	ROUGE			BERTScore	MeaningBERT	BLEU			METEOR	Exam Score (%)
	1	2	L			AVG	1	4		
No references/All references	**-3.25**	**-3.94**	**-3.28**	-1.57	**-2.47**	**-3.60**	**-4.00**	**-3.49**	**-2.96**	**-2.52**

Table 4: Z-test significance test of our two bests approaches (**bold** value are rejected null hypothesis with $\alpha = 0.05$).

remain present, it is a better way for consumers get easier access to insurance expertise.

No analysis was done as to how the system performs when the question is out of the context of references – does it hallucinate an answer, does it abstain from answering? Would be important to classify what kinds of questions can be answered by the system in order to put guard-rails on it.

6.3 Discussions

Evaluation of RAG systems typically relies on automatic generation N-Grams metrics (Yu et al., 2024). As our results highlight, these metrics provide interesting insight into model performance. Such insight was used to steer the development of the solution. However, the legal field and documents are known to be lengthy and complex (Beauchemin et al., 2020; Beauchemin and Khoury, 2023). Thus, we are skeptical that only relying on this type of metrics is sufficient to develop robust systems; these metrics display an incomplete illustration of the system's response quality and cannot properly capture the legal and misinformation risks they pose to the public. Indeed, ROUGE and BLEU have been criticized for lacking semantic capabilities or correlating weakly with human judgment (Reiter, 2018; Tay et al., 2019; Beauchemin et al., 2023). Moreover, more recent approaches that leverage Transformer-based architecture, such as BertScore, have yet to be shown to achieve a strong correlation with human judgment (Beauchemin et al., 2023). For this reason, many RAG applications now focus on human evaluation (Yu et al., 2024). However, such an evaluation procedure is labour-intensive and costly, especially in specialized fields such as the legal domain. Our primary results show that one can use automatic metrics during development to steer one project. However, human evaluation should evaluate the final system qualitatively to assess a system's performance and risk properly, particularly in sensitive fields such as the legal domain.

7 Conclusion and Future Works

In conclusion, this paper introduced two new corpora: a Quebec automobile insurance expertise reference corpus and a corpus of expert answers to laypeople automobile insurance questions. To generate answers to the questions in our second corpus, we leverage an RAG architecture that uses our reference corpus. We experimented with six approaches: a zero-shot that did not use the RAG architecture, an RAG architecture without references, and four models that incrementally use more of our reference corpus. Our results demonstrate that, on average, using our complete reference corpus generates better responses based on both automatic and manual evaluation metrics. Our results show that between 5% to 13% of generated answers include a false statement that could mislead a customer, indicating that LLM-based technical and sensitive QA is not yet robust enough for mass utilization by the public.

In our future works, we plan to extend the references corpus to include AMF proprietary documents, such as their insurance representative training manual, and increase the number of expert-answered questions. Moreover, we would also like to experiment with other LLMs, and to conduct a real-life evaluation using real insurance customers. Finally, we plan to improve performance with prompt engineering and LLM fine-tuning.

Limitations

First, despite our efforts to make our systems more factually grounded using Quebec insurance references, our proposed framework remains at risk of generating hallucinations in its answers, as shown in Table 3.

Second, since our reference documents are available online, it is possible that GPT-4o and other LLMs could have been trained with some or all of our reference documents. Thus, the results we obtained may include some overfitting, which could make it difficult to generalize to unseen data.

Third, our study is limited to monolingual French documents and QA, and to a single application domain. Though we expect our results to be consistent in other languages and domains, we did not study that question.

Fourth, we acknowledge that our prompt might be considered too simplistic; our focus was not to rabbit-hole ourselves with prompt engineering but instead study the quantitative and qualitative capabilities of out-of-the-box solutions and minimalist RAG to assess the limitations of such technology.

Finally, consistent with prior studies (Krishna et al., 2021; Xu et al., 2023; Louis et al., 2024), we observe that conventional automatic metrics may not accurately mirror answer quality, leading to potential misinterpretations.

Ethical considerations

As highlighted by Beauchemin et al. (2020), the premature deployment of legal NLP solutions, such as an insurance RAG system for the Quebec Insurance domain, poses a tangible risk to laypeople, who may uncritically rely on the answers it provides and thus inadvertently exacerbate their circumstances. Indeed, a layperson might use this kind of innovation as a viable source of information. Thus, the quality of the response needs to be as precise as possible. Furthermore, the use of AI in the legal field poses significant risks because of the presence of bias in corpora and the systems where many might be considered illegal (Bender et al., 2021; Beauchemin and Monty, 2022). We are committed to limiting the use of our dataset strictly to research purposes to ensure the responsible development of legal aid technologies and limit the risk of illegal, biased use.

Hardware & Librairies

Computations are performed on two 12 GO NVIDIA GTX 1080 TI and with proprietary OpenAI LLM and embeddings model using their API; one experimentation over the six approaches cost around 30 USD, the overall OpenAI budget was 1,050 USD.

Acknowledgements

This research was made possible thanks to the support of a Canadian insurance company, NSERC research grant RDCPJ 537198-18 and FRQNT doctoral research grant. We thank the reviewers for their comments regarding our work.

A Evaluation Annotation Interface

Figure 4 presents the evaluation interface used for our evaluation (in French). It is a custom adaptation of the Prodigy annotation tool (Montani and Honnibal, 2018).

B Ablation Study

Table 5 presents the ablation study based on the references used for the RAG, namely using only one source reference instead of the cumulative approach. Our results show that using the cumulative approach yields better results than using only one. We did not conduct the manual evaluation of our ablation study.

References

Ayyoub Ajmi. 2024. Revolutionizing Access to Justice: The Role of AI-Powered Chatbots and Retrieval-Augmented Generation in Legal Self-Help. In *The Brief*, volume 53-10.

Autorité des marchés financiers AMF. AMF approved forms. Accessed online (14-08-2024) `https://lautorite.qc.ca/en/professionals/insurers/automobile-insurance/amf-approved-forms`.

Autorité des marchés financiers AMF. 2018. *Mémoire présenté à la Commission des finances publiques sur le Projet de loi 141 : Loi visant principalement à améliorer l'encadrement du secteur financier, la protection des dépôts d'argent et le régime de fonctionnement des institutions financières.* Autorité des marchés financiers.

Autorité des marchés financiers AMF. 2019. *Québec Financial Education Strategy for 2019-2022 - Orientations and Action Plan.* Autorité des marchés financiers.

Figure 4: The Prodigy annotation interface (in French) used for evaluation.

	ROUGE			BERTScore	MeaningBERT	BLEU			METEOR
	1	2	L			Average	1	4	
All references	0.375±0.14	0.18±0.15	0.25±0.14	71.99±5.9	78.87±10.17	10.68±11.71	33.77±16.66	5.98±9.91	33.61±14.69
F.P.Q. 1	0.212±0.10	0.09±0.06	0.16±0.06	66.93±4.33	71.42±11.21	4.10±4.25	21.28±10.63	1.39±2.63	24.23±7.61
AMF	0.210±0.19	0.13±0.08	0.19±0.06	70.46±4.54	76.17±10.45	7.06±6.16	33.63±14.63	3.05±5.00	27.02±9.68
Educative Resources	0.240±0.08	0.13±0.07	0.19±0.09	71.26±4.34	77.55±10.22	7.36±5.16	33.17±12.62	3.44±5.01	27.38±9.68

Table 5: Automatic metrics average and one standard deviation over the five restarts on our questions-answering corpus of our ablation study.

Autorité des Marchés Financiers AMF. 2024a. Mission. Accessed online (14-08-2024) https://lautorite.qc.ca/en/general-public/about-the-amf/mission.

Autorité des Marchés Financiers AMF. 2024b. Practice Examination Questions. Accessed online (14-08-2024) https://lautorite.qc.ca/en/becoming-a-professional/damage-insurance/examinations/practice-examination-questions.

Satanjeev Banerjee and Alon Lavie. 2005. METEOR: An Automatic Metric for MT Evaluation With Improved Correlation With Human Judgments. In *Proceedings of the acl workshop on intrinsic and extrinsic evaluation measures for machine translation and/or summarization*, pages 65–72.

Jérôme Baray, Alain Decrop, and Gérard Cliquet. 2024. Modèle standardisé d'évaluation des ia génératives en soutien à la recherche marketing: Test de chatgpt. In *Colloque international de l'Association Tunisienne de Marketing*.

David Beauchemin, Nicolas Garneau, Eve Gaumond, Pierre-Luc Déziel, Richard Khoury, and Luc Lamontagne. 2020. Generating Intelligible Plumitifs Descriptions: Use Case Application with Ethical Considerations. In *Proceedings of the International Conference on Natural Language Generation*, pages 15–21.

David Beauchemin and Richard Khoury. 2023. RISC: Generating Realistic Synthetic Bilingual Insurance Contract. *Proceedings of the Canadian Conference on Artificial Intelligence*. Https://caiac.pubpub.org/pub/k18zu6c9.

David Beauchemin and Marie-Claire Monty. 2022. La discrimination en intelligence artificielle est-elle suffisamment encadrée ? Preprint.

David Beauchemin, Horacio Saggion, and Richard Khoury. 2023. MeaningBERT: Assessing Meaning Preservation Between Sentences. *Frontiers in Artificial Intelligence*, 6.

Belairdirect. 2024. FAQ. Accessed online (14-08-2024) https://www.belairdirect.com/en/faq.html.

Emily M Bender, Timnit Gebru, Angelina McMillan-Major, and Shmargaret Shmitchell. 2021. On the Dangers of Stochastic Parrots: Can Language Models Be Too Big? In *Proceedings of the ACM conference on fairness, accountability, and transparency*, pages 610–623.

Beneva. 2024. FAQ - Car Insurance. Accessed online (14-08-2024) https://www.beneva.ca/en/car-insurance/help.

Umar Butler. 2023. Open Australian Legal QA.

Chambre de l'Assurance de Dommages ChAD. 2024. About Us. Accessed online (14-08-2024) https://chad.ca/en/about-us/.

Mathieu Alexandre Chartier, Nabil Dakkoune, Guillaume Bourgeois, and Stéphane Jean. 2024. Évaluation des capacités de réponse de larges modèles de langage (llm) pour des questions d'historiens. In *24ème conférence francophone sur l'Extraction et la Gestion des Connaissances*, 40, pages 155–166.

Harrison Chase. 2022. LangChain.

Anthony Chen, Gabriel Stanovsky, Sameer Singh, and Matt Gardner. 2019. Evaluating Question Answering Evaluation. In *Proceedings of the workshop on machine reading for question answering*, pages 119–124.

Xin Cheng, Xun Wang, Xingxing Zhang, Tao Ge, Si-Qing Chen, Furu Wei, Huishuai Zhang, and Dongyan Zhao. 2024. xRAG: Extreme Context Compression for Retrieval-augmented Generation with One Token. *arXiv:2405.13792*.

Bourget Claire, Lacombe Marie-Eve, Godbout René, Lanctôt Sébastien, Rajaobelina Lova, Ducharme Guillaume, Lavoie Annie, and Maynard Marie-Guy. 2018. *Assurance de dommages à l'ère du numérique*. Centre facilitant la recherche et l'innovation dans les organisations.

Junyun Cui, Xiaoyu Shen, and Shaochun Wen. 2023. A Survey on Legal Judgment Prediction: Datasets, Metrics, Models and Challenges. *IEEE Access*.

Desjardins Assurances. 2024. Insurance FAQ. Accessed online (14-08-2024) `https://www.desjardins.com/qc/en/insurance/faq.html`.

Minwei Feng, Bing Xiang, Michael R Glass, Lidan Wang, and Bowen Zhou. 2015. Applying Deep Learning to Answer Selection: A Study and an Open Task. In *IEEE workshop on automatic speech recognition and understanding*, pages 813–820. IEEE.

Rudolf Flesch. 1948. A Readability Formula in Practice. *Elementary English*, 25(6).

Groupement des Assureurs Automobiles GAA. 2024. About Us. Accessed online (14-08-2024) `https://gaa.qc.ca/en/who-are-we/`.

Yunfan Gao, Yun Xiong, Xinyu Gao, Kangxiang Jia, Jinliu Pan, Yuxi Bi, Yi Dai, Jiawei Sun, and Haofen Wang. 2023. Retrieval-Augmented Generation for Large Language Models: A Survey. *arXiv:2312.10997*.

Ryan Greene, Arvind Neelakantan, Lilian Weng, and Ted Sanders. 2022. New and Improved Embedding Model.

Dan Hendrycks, Collin Burns, Anya Chen, and Spencer Ball. CUAD: An Expert-Annotated NLP Dataset for Legal Contract Review. In *Conference on Neural Information Processing Systems Datasets and Benchmarks Track*.

Matthew Honnibal, Ines Montani, Sofie Van Landeghem, and Adriane Boyd. 2020. SpaCy: Industrial-strength Natural Language Processing in Python.

Insurance Bureau of Canada IBC and Groupement des Assureurs Automobiles GAA. 2024. Infoassurance - About Us. Accessed online (14-08-2024) `https://infoassurance.ca/en/utility-menu/about-us/`.

Intact Insurance. 2024. FAQ. Accessed online (14-08-2024) `https://www.intact.ca/en/faq`.

Christopher Johnson. 2018. Projet de loi 141 et vente par internet: où en est le RCCAQ? `https://www.rccaq.com/cgi/page.cgi/_article_fr.html/Categories/Dans_la_mire/Projet_de_loi_141_et_vente_par_internet_o_en_est_le_RCCAQ_`.

Daniel Martin Katz, Dirk Hartung, Lauritz Gerlach, Abhik Jana, and Michael James Bommarito. 2023. Natural Language Processing in the Legal Domain. *Available at SSRN 4336224*.

Tannon Kew, Alison Chi, Laura Vásquez-Rodríguez, Sweta Agrawal, Dennis Aumiller, Fernando Alva-Manchego, and Matthew Shardlow. 2023. BLESS: Benchmarking Large Language Models on Sentence Simplification. *arXiv:2310.15773*.

Kalpesh Krishna, Aurko Roy, and Mohit Iyyer. 2021. Hurdles to Progress in Long-form Question Answering. In *Proceedings of the Conference of the North American Chapter of the Association for Computational Linguistics: Human Language Technologies*, pages 4940–4957. Association for Computational Linguistics.

Mosh Levy, Alon Jacoby, and Yoav Goldberg. 2024. Same Task, More Tokens: the Impact of Input Length on the Reasoning Performance of Large Language Models.

Chin-Yew Lin and FJ Och. 2004. Looking for a Few Good Metrics: ROUGE and Its Evaluation. In *Ntcir workshop*.

Nelson F Liu, Kevin Lin, John Hewitt, Ashwin Paranjape, Michele Bevilacqua, Fabio Petroni, and Percy Liang. 2024. Lost in the Middle: How Language Models Use Long Contexts. *Transactions of the Association for Computational Linguistics*, 12:157–173.

Antoine Louis, Gijs van Dijck, and Gerasimos Spanakis. 2024. Interpretable Long-Form Legal Question Answering With Retrieval-Augmented Large Language Models. In *Proceedings of the AAAI Conference on Artificial Intelligence*, volume 38, pages 22266–22275.

Jorge Martinez-Gil. 2023. A Survey on Legal Question–Answering Systems. *Computer Science Review*, 48:100552.

Monisha Mohanan. 2024. *Competitive Analysis of Embedding Models in Retrieval-Augmented Generation for Indian Motor Vehicle Law Chat Bots*. Ph.D. thesis, Dublin Business School.

Ines Montani and Matthew Honnibal. 2018. Prodigy: A Modern and Scriptable Annotation Tool for Creating Training Data for Machine Learning Models.

Seon-Ok Na, Young-Min Kim, and Seung-Hwan Cho. 2022. Insurance Question Answering via Single-turn Dialogue Modeling. In *Proceedings of the Second Workshop on When Creative AI Meets Conversational AI*, pages 35–41.

Mohammad Nuruzzaman and Omar Khadeer Hussain. 2020. IntelliBot: A Dialogue-Based Chatbot for the Insurance Industry. *Knowledge-Based Systems*, 196:105810.

Kishore Papineni, Salim Roukos, Todd Ward, and Wei-Jing Zhu. 2002. BLEU: A Method for Automatic Evaluation of Machine Translation. In *Proceedings of the annual meeting of the Association for Computational Linguistics*, pages 311–318.

Nicholas Pipitone and Ghita Houir Alami. 2024. LegalBench-RAG: A Benchmark for Retrieval-Augmented Generation in the Legal Domain.

Quebec. 2016. Code de la sécurité routière 2016.

Quebec. 2024. Loi sur l'assurance automobile 2024.

Ehud Reiter. 2018. A Structured Review of the Validity of BLEU. *Computational Linguistics*, 44(3):393–401.

Recueil des lois et des règlements du Québec RLRQ. 2004. Act Respecting the Regulation of the Financial Sector.

Société de l'Assurance Automobile du Québec SAAQ. 2024. Québec's Public Automobile Insurance Plan in Brief. Accessed online (14-08-2024) `https://saaq.gouv.qc.ca/en/traffic-accident/public-automobile-insurance-plan/in-brief`.

Abhay Shukla, Paheli Bhattacharya, Soham Poddar, Rajdeep Mukherjee, Kripabandhu Ghosh, Pawan Goyal, and Saptarshi Ghosh. 2022. Legal Case Document Summarization: Extractive and Abstractive Methods and their Evaluation. In *Proceedings of the Conference of the Asia-Pacific Chapter of the Association for Computational Linguistics and the International Joint Conference on Natural Language Processing*, pages 1048–1064. Association for Computational Linguistics.

Sonnet. 2024. Frequently Asked Questions. Accessed online (14-08-2024) `https://www.sonnet.ca/faqs`.

Wenyi Tay, Aditya Joshi, Xiuzhen Jenny Zhang, Sarvnaz Karimi, and Stephen Wan. 2019. Red-Faced ROUGE: Examining the Suitability of ROUGE for Opinion Summary Evaluation. In *Proceedings of the Annual Workshop of the Australasian Language Technology Association*, pages 52–60.

Xiaohua Wang, Zhenghua Wang, Xuan Gao, Feiran Zhang, Yixin Wu, Zhibo Xu, Tianyuan Shi, Zhengyuan Wang, Shizheng Li, Qi Qian, et al. 2024. Searching for Best Practices in Retrieval-Augmented Generation. *arXiv:2407.01219*.

Nirmalie Wiratunga, Ramitha Abeyratne, Lasal Jayawardena, Kyle Martin, Stewart Massie, Ikechukwu Nkisi-Orji, Ruvan Weerasinghe, Anne Liret, and Bruno Fleisch. 2024. CBR-RAG: Case-Based Reasoning for Retrieval Augmented Generation in LLMs for Legal Question Answering. In *International Conference on Case-Based Reasoning*, pages 445–460. Springer.

Nirmalie Wiratunga and Ashwin Ram. 2011. *Case-Based Reasoning Research and Development*. Springer.

Fangyuan Xu, Yixiao Song, Mohit Iyyer, and Eunsol Choi. 2023. A Critical Evaluation of Evaluations for Long-form Question Answering. In *Proceedings of the Annual Meeting of the Association for Computational Linguistics*, pages 3225–3245. Association for Computational Linguistics.

Antonio Jimeno Yepes, Yao You, Jan Milczek, Sebastian Laverde, and Leah Li. 2024. Financial Report Chunking for Effective Retrieval Augmented Generation. *arXiv:2402.05131*.

Hao Yu, Aoran Gan, Kai Zhang, Shiwei Tong, Qi Liu, and Zhaofeng Liu. 2024. Evaluation of Retrieval-Augmented Generation: A Survey. *arXiv:2405.07437*.

Tianyi Zhang, Varsha Kishore, Felix Wu, Kilian Q Weinberger, and Yoav Artzi. 2019. BERTScore: Evaluating Text Generation with BERT. In *International Conference on Learning Representations*.

Éducaloi. 2024. Governance. Accessed online (14-08-2024) `https://educaloi.qc.ca/en/governance/`.

Rethinking Legal Judgement Prediction in a Realistic Scenario in the Era of Large Language Models

Shubham Kumar Nigam[1] **Aniket Deroy**[2] **Subhankar Maity**[2] **Arnab Bhattacharya**[1]
[1]Indian Institute of Technology Kanpur (IIT-K)
[2]Indian Institute of Technology Kharagpur (IIT-Kgp)
{sknigam, arnabb}@cse.iitk.ac.in
{roydanik18, subhankar.ai}@kgpian.iitkgp.ac.in

Abstract

This study investigates judgment prediction in a realistic scenario within the context of Indian judgments, utilizing a range of transformer-based models, including InLegalBERT, BERT, and XLNet, alongside LLMs such as Llama-2 and GPT-3.5 Turbo. In this realistic scenario, we simulate how judgments are predicted at the point when a case is presented for a decision in court, using only the information available at that time, such as the facts of the case, statutes, precedents, and arguments. This approach mimics real-world conditions, where decisions must be made without the benefit of hindsight, unlike retrospective analyses often found in previous studies. For transformer models, we experiment with hierarchical transformers and the summarization of judgment facts to optimize input for these models. Our experiments with LLMs reveal that GPT-3.5 Turbo excels in realistic scenarios, demonstrating robust performance in judgment prediction. Furthermore, incorporating additional legal information, such as statutes and precedents, significantly improves the outcome of the prediction task. The LLMs also provide explanations for their predictions. To evaluate the quality of these predictions and explanations, we introduce two human evaluation metrics: *Clarity* and *Linking*. Our findings from both automatic and human evaluations indicate that, despite advancements in LLMs, they are yet to achieve expert-level performance in judgment prediction and explanation tasks.

1 Introduction

Predicting case outcomes based on judge-summarized narratives is an important task. Unlike previous studies (Malik et al., 2021; Nigam et al., 2024) and (Vats et al., 2023), we aim to simulate realistic scenarios where legal judgment prediction systems are used to predict and explain judgments as cases arrive on the bench for adjudication. Our approach focuses on the core factual components of the case—specifically, the events that led to the case being filed, which serve as the basis for judgment prediction. These facts are the foundation of legal arguments and provide the context needed for making judicial decisions. In contrast to previous works that have included the entire case text (including proceedings), our focus on facts mirrors real-world conditions, where judges rely primarily on the case facts when delivering judgments.

In addition to the facts of the case, we incorporate additional legal information such as statutes, precedents, and arguments. Statutes represent codified legal principles, while precedents provide case-specific rulings that help guide decision-making. Together, these legal frameworks offer a structured basis upon which judges rely when formulating their rulings. By extracting and integrating these elements into our models, we aim to enhance both the prediction and explanation tasks by grounding the analysis in actual legal texts and the governing principles that are applied in real cases.

We explore the efficacy of various transformer-based models investigate the impact of summarizing legal judgments (Deroy et al., 2021; Deroy and Maity, 2023; Nigam et al., 2023a; Deroy et al., 2024b) using techniques (Deroy et al., 2023, 2024c,a; Nigam and Deroy, 2023) such as BERT-Sum (Liu, 2019), CaseSummarizer (Polsley et al., 2016), LetSum (Farzindar, 2004), and SummaRuNNer (Nallapati et al., 2017). Our findings suggest that leveraging summarized information yields decent results in judgment prediction.

To further enhance the quality of prediction, we introduce hierarchical transformer models that utilize the entirety of judgment facts, demonstrating superior performance compared to traditional summarization methods. Additionally, our examination of LLMs, including Llama-2 (13b & 70b) (Touvron et al., 2023) and GPT-3.5 Turbo (Brown, 2020), highlights the exceptional performance of GPT-3.5 Turbo in the context of Indian legal judgment pre-

Proceedings of the Natural Legal Language Processing Workshop 2024, pages 61–80
November 16, 2024 ©2024 Association for Computational Linguistics

diction. We find that augmenting our models with additional legal information, such as statutes, precedents, and arguments, significantly improves the quality of both tasks.

In addition to focusing on the accuracy of legal judgment prediction, it is equally important to assess the quality of the explanations provided by the models. For this reason, we introduce two novel human evaluation metrics: *Clarity* and *Linking*. *Clarity* refers to how well the predictions and explanations are structured and whether they convey the reasoning in a clear and understandable manner. This is critical in the legal domain, where complex legal concepts must be communicated effectively. *Linking*, on the other hand, evaluates the logical consistency between the explanation and the final judgment. It assesses whether the explanation effectively ties back to the outcome and supports the predicted decision. These metrics are vital because, while models may produce accurate predictions, their explanations often lack coherence or fail to justify the decision meaningfully. By incorporating these metrics, we aim to ensure that models provide not only accurate outcomes but also transparent and interpretable explanations that can be trusted by legal professionals.

The key contributions of this study are:

1. We focus on evaluating the performance of several transformer-based models and hierarchical transformer models, specifically on factual data, to mirror real-world conditions in judgment prediction. This approach contrasts with previous works that utilized full case texts.
2. We utilize LLMs to assess their capabilities in legal judgment prediction and explanation tasks.
3. We define two human evaluation metrics, *Clarity* and *Linking*, to assess the quality of LLM-generated judgment predictions and explanations, providing a comprehensive assessment of the overall task performance.

To ensure reproducibility, both the code and dataset have been made publicly available via our repository[1]. Additionally, for convenience, we have uploaded the data[2] and models[3] to Huggingface.

[1]https://github.com/ShubhamKumarNigam/Realistic_LJP

[2]huggingface.co/collections/L-NLProc/Realistic_LJP-models

[3]huggingface.co/collections/L-NLProc/Realistic_LJP-datasets

2 Related Work

The field of Legal Judgment Prediction (LJP) has seen significant advancements, driven by the need to automate legal case outcome forecasting and alleviate the burden of overwhelming caseloads. Early works by (Aletras et al., 2016), (Chalkidis et al., 2019), and (Feng et al., 2021) laid the foundation for LJP, emphasizing the importance of explainability in AI predictions. Benchmark datasets such as CAIL2018 (Xiao et al., 2018), ECHR-CASES (Chalkidis et al., 2019), and others have spurred research in this area, inspiring models like TopJudge and MLCP-NLN. However, there remains a gap between machine and human performance.

In the Indian context, datasets like ILDC (Malik et al., 2021), PredEx (Nigam et al., 2024) and (Nigam et al., 2022; Malik et al., 2022; Nigam et al., 2023b) have highlighted the growing role of AI in legal judgments, with an emphasis on explainability. Research in LJP with LLMs, such as (Vats et al., 2023) and (Nigam et al., 2024), has experimented with models like GPT-3.5 Turbo and Llama-2 on Indian legal datasets. Other studies, such as (Masala et al., 2021) on Romanian legal texts and (Hwang et al., 2022) on Korean legal language, have demonstrated LJP's adaptability across legal systems.

Cross-jurisdictional work, including (Zhao et al., 2018), showcases LJP's applicability in different legal frameworks, with research expanding to multilingual considerations, as seen in (Niklaus et al., 2021) and (Kapoor et al., 2022) for Hindi legal documents. Recent innovations, such as event extraction and multi-stage learning (Feng et al., 2022), continue to push the boundaries of LJP research.

3 Task Definition

This study focuses on Supreme Court of India (SCI) judgments, and the Court Judgment Prediction with Explanation task consists of two subtasks:

Task A: Judgment Prediction: This subtask is framed as a binary classification problem specific to SCI cases. Given a segment of the legal judgment as input, the goal is to predict whether the decision favors or is against the appellant. The prediction is represented by binary labels: $\{1, 0\}$, where 1 indicates that the appeal is accepted (i.e., if any part of the appeal is accepted, the decision is considered in favor of the appellant). Although some cases might involve multiple heads of appeal, where an appellant might win on some grounds and lose on others, for the purposes of this task, the outcome is simplified to a binary decision. Cases with mixed outcomes are excluded or reduced to this binary format for prediction.

Task B: Rationale Explanation: This subtask involves generating a coherent explanation or rationale that justifies the predicted decision, based on the provided segment of the judgment. The explanation seeks to clarify the reasoning behind the predicted outcome.

The workflow of the system, as illustrated in Figure 1, captures the entire process—from extracting facts and additional legal information (such as statutes, precedents, and lower court rulings) to feeding this data into transformer models, hierarchical transformers, and LLMs. The diagram visually represents the pipeline of both tasks, highlighting how the prediction and explanation processes interact to form a comprehensive legal judgment prediction system.

4 Datasct

We utilize the ILDC-multi dataset, as described by (Malik et al., 2021), which comprises a total of 34,816 legal judgments from the Supreme Court of India, collected from 1947 to April 2020 via the Indian Kanoon website[4]. This dataset is divided into three subsets: training, validation, and test which contains 32,305, 994, and 1,517 judgments correspondingly. It is specifically designed to support the tasks of Court Judgment Prediction and Explanation (CJPE), with a portion of the legal judgment serving as input for both prediction and explanation processes. Additionally, a subset of this corpus is annotated with gold-standard explanations provided by legal experts, enhancing its utility for developing automated systems that predict and explain judicial outcomes.

5 Methodology

5.1 Extraction of Facts and Additional Information from Judgments

To extract relevant sentences from legal judgments, we employ a Hierarchical BiLSTM-CRF classifier, focusing on different rhetorical roles as identified by (Ghosh and Wyner, 2019). To create a realistic scenario for our model, we utilize the factual and additional contextual information such as statutes and precedents of the judgments as input for transformer models and LLMs.

[4]https://indiankanoon.org/

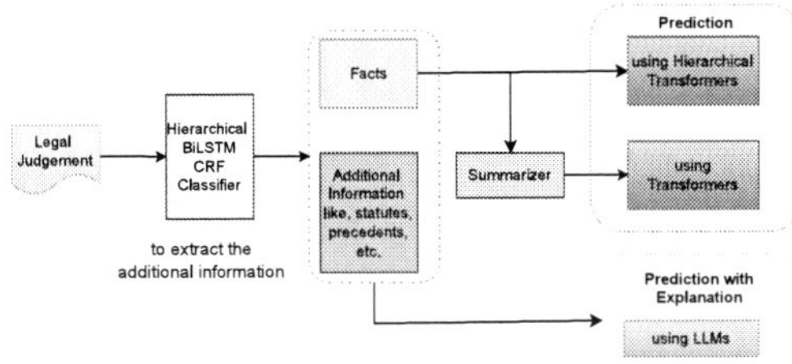

Figure 1: Workflow for Legal Judgment Prediction with explanation.

5.2 Transformer and Hierarchical Transformer Models

The extracted facts undergo summarization using various techniques, including CaseSummarizer (Polsley et al., 2016), BertSum (Liu, 2019), SummaRuNNer (Nallapati et al., 2017), and LetSum (Farzindar, 2004), to ensure they fit within the input constraints of transformer models. Given that models like XLNET-large (Yang et al., 2019), BERT (Devlin et al., 2018), and InLegalBERT (Paul et al., 2022) can process a maximum input length of 512 tokens, we summarize the facts accordingly. Additionally, we utilize hierarchical transformer models that allow us to input the entire set of facts without the need for summarization. This approach facilitates the handling of comprehensive legal information during the prediction task, which is a binary classification problem.

5.3 Prediction with Explanation using LLMs

For the explanation task, we leverage LLMs such as Llama-2 (70b & 13b) (Touvron et al., 2023) and GPT-3.5 Turbo (Brown, 2020), employing a prompting strategy. Given that the combined input and response length for these models is 4096 tokens, we segment the inputs into chunks of 2048 words. This segmentation allows us to generate judgment predictions, as one token corresponds to approximately three-quarters of a word, translating to about 750 words for 1000 tokens[5]. We then aggregate the outputs from multiple chunks using a majority voting mechanism to determine the final judgment; in the event of a tie, the judgment is considered in favor of the appellant. For inputs shorter than 2048 words, we directly input the entire text into the LLM without requiring majority voting. We explore two prompting techniques:

Normal Prompting: The prompt states, "You are asked to be a judge of a legal case and pro-

[5]what-are-tokens-and-how-to-count-them

vide a judgment of the following legal judgment: <Legal judgment>."

Chain-of-Thought Prompting (CoT): Following the chain-of-thought approach proposed by (Wei et al., 2022), the prompt is modified to include, "Think Step by Step."

We investigate six variations for each model input including sentences from:

V1: Only facts.

V2: V1 + statutes, and precedents.

V3: V2 + rulings by lower courts.

V4: V3 + arguments.

V1+CoT: Similar to V1, but incorporates the CoT prompt, "Think Step by Step."

V4+CoT: Similar to V4, but includes the CoT.

Variations V1 and V2 simulate realistic scenarios where only essential elements, such as facts, statutes, and precedents, are provided to the LLM. These components mirror how judges typically approach cases by relying on the factual context and legal frameworks. V3 accounts for cases where a lower court has previously ruled on the matter, adding another layer of realism by simulating situations where an appeal is being heard. V4 enhances the prediction process by including arguments from legal counsel, simulating the complexity of real courtroom proceedings.

Prompting strategies engage both Task A (prediction) and Task B (explanation), thereby facilitating a comprehensive approach to judgment prediction and rationale generation.

6 Evaluation of Model Performance

6.1 Automatic Evaluation

Table 1 summarizes the performance of judgment predictions made by different LLMs through prompting. The results demonstrate that relying solely on factual information leads to lower performance scores. However, incorporating additional legal case-specific information, such as statutes, precedents, rulings from lower courts, and arguments, significantly enhances the quality of predictions. Among the evaluated models, GPT-3.5 Turbo demonstrates the best overall performance.

Table 2 provides further insights into the performance of various hierarchical transformer models and other transformer architectures. The results show that hierarchical transformer models outperform traditional summarization methods. Notably, models specifically pre-trained on Indian legal data, such as InlegalBERT, exhibit superior performance compared to those trained on generic datasets like BERT. The results indicate that LLMs have yet to reach the performance level of legal experts, who demonstrate a 94% agreement rate, as noted by (Malik et al., 2021).

Metric	V1	V2	V3	V4	V1+CoT	V4+CoT
Llama-2-13b						
Precision	0.6443	0.6839	0.6941	0.6997	0.6821	**0.7221**
Recall	0.6292	0.6246	0.6228	0.6416	0.6319	**0.6824**
F1-score	0.6365	0.6528	0.6445	0.6693	0.6560	**0.7016**
Llama-2-70b						
Precision	0.7011	0.7344	0.7416	**0.7518**	0.7322	0.7416
Recall	0.6644	0.6851	0.7147	0.6952	0.6817	**0.7234**
F1-score	0.6822	0.7088	0.7278	0.7223	0.7059	**0.7323**
GPT-3.5 Turbo						
Precision	0.7016	0.7014	0.7411	0.7609	0.7261	**0.7687**
Recall	0.6894	0.6914	0.6949	**0.7155**	0.6847	0.7132
F1-score	0.6953	0.6962	0.7172	0.7374	0.7047	**0.7398**

Table 1: Performance Metrics for the Judgment Prediction Task on the ILDC-multi dataset using different LLMs across various input configurations (V1, V2, V3, V4, V1+CoT, V4+CoT), utilizing both normal prompting and CoT prompting. Bold values indicate the highest score for each metric and model.

6.2 Expert Evaluation

For the expert evaluation, we selected 25 explanations generated by the GPT-3.5 Turbo model, corresponding to different judgments, and enlisted three legal experts to assess these outputs. Each expert rated the explanations on a scale of 1 to 5 based on two criteria: (i) Clarity, the quality and coherence of the rationale behind the legal judgment, and (ii) Linking, the degree to which the explanation is logically connected to the final outcome of the judgment.

To ensure consistency and reliability in the evaluation, the experts were provided with clear guidelines. They were first instructed to familiarize themselves with both the legal judgments and the model-generated outputs to ensure informed assessments. For each explanation, they evaluated:

Clarity: This criterion focuses on how well the rationale is presented. A clear explanation should have a logical flow, use appropriate terminology, and be easily understood by both legal professionals and laypeople. The experts were asked to consider whether the explanation was coherent and if the reasoning behind the judgment was easy to follow.

Linking: This metric captures how well the explanation ties back to the final outcome. A strong

Metric	HT	CS	SR	BS	LS
			XLNET-large		
Precision	0.6424	0.6313	**0.6478**	0.6227	0.5778
Recall	**0.6036**	0.5713	0.5472	0.5683	0.5602
F1-score	**0.6223**	0.5998	0.5993	0.5942	0.5689
			InlegalBERT		
Precision	0.6534	0.6415	0.6338	**0.6604**	0.6010
Recall	**0.6202**	0.5673	0.5613	0.5885	0.5532
F1-score	**0.6363**	0.6022	0.5954	0.6223	0.5761
			BERT		
Precision	**0.6039**	0.5557	0.5589	0.5592	0.5475
Recall	**0.5838**	0.5540	0.5589	0.5589	0.5457
F1-score	**0.5936**	0.5548	0.5589	0.5590	0.5466

Table 2: Comparative Performance of Transformer Models on the Judgment Prediction Task on the ILDC-multi Dataset. These models are with fact summarization techniques such as CaseSummarizer (CS), SummaRuNNer (SR), BertSum (BS), and LetSum (LS), as well as Hierarchical Transformer (HT) models using the complete facts. Bold values indicate the highest score for each metric and model.

linking score indicates that the rationale clearly leads to the conclusion of the judgment, without any gaps or inconsistencies. The experts were tasked with identifying whether the explanation logically and explicitly supports the final decision. The evaluators used the following rating scales:

- **For Clarity:**
  [1]: Very Poor (Unclear rationale)
  [2]: Poor (Some clarity but weak rationale)
  [3]: Fair (Moderately clear rationale)
  [4]: Good (Clear rationale)
  [5]: Excellent (Very clear rationale)

- **For Linking:**
  [1]:Very Poor (Unclear and disconnected explanation)
  [2]:Poor (Weak linkage between explanation and judgment)
  [3]:Fair (Moderate linking, some gaps)
  [4]: Good (Clear linkage to the judgment)
  [5]:Excellent (Strong and coherent linking)

These ratings, calculated as the average scores for each criterion across the three experts, are presented in Table 3. To ensure objectivity and ethical standards, the experts were instructed to maintain impartiality and avoid conflicts of interest throughout the evaluation process.

The results indicate that Variation 4 with chain-of-thought prompting (V4+CoT) achieved the highest scores for both clarity and linking, demonstrating its effectiveness in producing coherent and well-connected explanations. The average Fleiss' Kappa scores for Clarity and Linking were 0.64 and 0.70, respectively, indicating substantial agreement among the evaluators.

Metric	V1	V2	V3	V4	V1+ CoT	V4+ CoT
Clarity	3.13	3.20	3.33	3.47	3.20	**3.73**
Linking	3.66	3.80	3.87	4.00	3.73	**4.27**

Table 3: Expert Evaluation Results for the Explanation Task Using GPT-3.5 Turbo. Bold values indicate the highest scores for each metric.

The combination of automatic and human evaluations offers a comprehensive assessment of the models' performance, revealing areas for improvement and confirming the efficacy of specific prompting techniques—such as chain-of-thought (CoT) in enhancing the quality of legal judgment prediction and explanation.

7 Conclusions

In this study, we explored the effectiveness of various LLMs and transformer architectures in the task of judgment prediction and explanation using the ILDC-multi dataset. Our results demonstrate that incorporating additional case-specific information significantly enhances the prediction accuracy compared to using only factual information. The results also highlight the superiority of hierarchical transformer models over traditional summarization techniques, suggesting that a comprehensive approach to input data yields better predictive outcomes. Despite the promising results, our evaluations reveal that automated metrics still fall short of matching the performance levels of human legal experts, who demonstrate a high degree of agreement in judgment assessments. This gap underscores the need for further refinement of LLMs and transformer models to improve their interpretability and reliability in legal contexts.

Limitations

This study is focused solely on Supreme Court of India (SCI) judgments, which may limit the generalizability of the models to other courts or jurisdictions. Legal systems in different countries, or even lower courts within the same system, may have distinct structures, procedures, and nuances that are not captured in this study.

Additionally, the judgment prediction task is simplified as a binary classification problem. In real-world cases, particularly in multi-issue appeals, an appellant may win on some points and lose on others. This complexity is not fully addressed here, as our model reduces the outcome to a binary decision, which may overlook the nuances of cases with multiple heads of appeal.

While we incorporate facts, statutes, precedents, and arguments to simulate a realistic scenario, this approach still does not capture the full range of judicial reasoning. Judges often rely on implicit legal reasoning, judicial discretion, and a wider array of contextual factors that may not be explicitly mentioned in legal documents, limiting the comprehensiveness of our model's predictions.

The large language models (LLMs) used in this study, such as GPT-3.5 Turbo and Llama-2, offer promising results, but their high computational requirements make them resource-intensive. This could restrict their practical application in many legal environments, especially in resource-constrained settings.

Furthermore, the human evaluation metrics—*Clarity* and *Linking*—are based on subjective assessments from legal experts. Although we provided detailed guidelines to standardize the evaluation process, differences in interpretation among experts can introduce variability into the results.

Future research will focus on addressing these limitations by exploring multi-label classification to account for more complex case outcomes, expanding the applicability of models to other legal domains and jurisdictions, and refining evaluation metrics to minimize subjectivity.

Ethical Considerations

In conducting this research, we adhered to ethical standards, particularly in the context of data usage and expert evaluation. The legal judgments used in our experiments were publicly available, and no private or sensitive data was accessed. For the human evaluation of judgment predictions and explanations, we engaged PhD scholars from the Rajiv Gandhi School of Intellectual Property Law as legal experts. Their participation was voluntary, and we provided monetary compensation for their time and expertise. This ensured that the evaluation process was both fair and conducted with proper acknowledgment of the experts' contributions.

References

Nikolaos Aletras, Dimitrios Tsarapatsanis, Daniel Preoţiuc-Pietro, and Vasileios Lampos. 2016. Predicting judicial decisions of the european court of human rights: A natural language processing perspective. *PeerJ computer science*, 2:e93.

Tom B Brown. 2020. Language models are few-shot learners. *arXiv preprint arXiv:2005.14165*.

Ilias Chalkidis, Ion Androutsopoulos, and Nikolaos Aletras. 2019. Neural legal judgment prediction in english. *Association for Computational Linguistics (ACL)*.

Aniket Deroy, Naksatra Kumar Bailung, Kripabandhu Ghosh, Saptarshi Ghosh, and Abhijnan Chakraborty. 2024a. Artificial intelligence (ai) in legal data mining. *arXiv preprint arXiv:2405.14707*.

Aniket Deroy, Paheli Bhattacharya, Kripabandhu Ghosh, and Saptarshi Ghosh. 2021. An analytical study of algorithmic and expert summaries of legal cases. In *Legal Knowledge and Information Systems*, pages 90–99. IOS Press.

Aniket Deroy, Kripabandhu Ghosh, and Saptarshi Ghosh. 2023. How ready are pre-trained abstractive models and llms for legal case judgement summarization? *arXiv preprint arXiv:2306.01248*.

Aniket Deroy, Kripabandhu Ghosh, and Saptarshi Ghosh. 2024b. Applicability of large language models and generative models for legal case judgement summarization. *Artificial Intelligence and Law*, pages 1–44.

Aniket Deroy, Kripabandhu Ghosh, and Saptarshi Ghosh. 2024c. Ensemble methods for improving extractive summarization of legal case judgements. *Artificial Intelligence and Law*, 32(1):231–289.

Aniket Deroy and Subhankar Maity. 2023. Questioning biases in case judgment summaries: Legal datasets or large language models? *arXiv preprint arXiv:2312.00554*.

Jacob Devlin, Ming-Wei Chang, Kenton Lee, and Kristina Toutanova. 2018. Bert: Pre-training of deep bidirectional transformers for language understanding. *arXiv preprint arXiv:1810.04805*.

Atefeh Farzindar. 2004. Atefeh farzindar and guy lapalme,'letsum, an automatic legal text summarizing system in t. gordon (ed.), legal knowledge and information systems. jurix 2004: The seventeenth annual conference. amsterdam: Ios press, 2004, pp. 11-18. In *Legal knowledge and information systems: JURIX 2004, the seventeenth annual conference*, volume 120, page 11. IOS Press.

Yi Feng, Chuanyi Li, Jidong Ge, Bin Luo, and Vincent Ng. 2021. Recommending statutes: A portable method based on neural networks. *ACM Transactions on Knowledge Discovery from Data (TKDD)*, 15(2):1–22.

Yi Feng, Chuanyi Li, and Vincent Ng. 2022. Legal judgment prediction via event extraction with constraints. In *Proceedings of the 60th Annual Meeting of the Association for Computational Linguistics (Volume 1: Long Papers)*, pages 648–664, Dublin, Ireland. Association for Computational Linguistics.

Saptarshi Ghosh and Adam Wyner. 2019. Identification of rhetorical roles of sentences in indian legal judgments. *Legal Knowledge and Information Systems: JURIX*, page 3.

Wonseok Hwang, Dongjun Lee, Kyoungyeon Cho, Hanuhl Lee, and Minjoon Seo. 2022. A multi-task benchmark for korean legal language understanding and judgement prediction. *Advances in Neural Information Processing Systems*, 35:32537–32551.

Arnav Kapoor, Mudit Dhawan, Anmol Goel, Arjun T H, Akshala Bhatnagar, Vibhu Agrawal, Amul Agrawal, Arnab Bhattacharya, Ponnurangam Kumaraguru, and Ashutosh Modi. 2022. HLDC: Hindi legal documents corpus. In *Findings of the Association for Computational Linguistics: ACL 2022*, pages 3521–3536, Dublin, Ireland. Association for Computational Linguistics.

Yang Liu. 2019. Fine-tune bert for extractive summarization. *arXiv preprint arXiv:1903.10318*.

Vijit Malik, Rishabh Sanjay, Shouvik Kumar Guha, Angshuman Hazarika, Shubham Kumar Nigam, Arnab Bhattacharya, and Ashutosh Modi. 2022. Semantic segmentation of legal documents via rhetorical roles. In *Proceedings of the Natural Legal Language Processing Workshop 2022*, pages 153–171, Abu Dhabi, United Arab Emirates (Hybrid). Association for Computational Linguistics.

Vijit Malik, Rishabh Sanjay, Shubham Kumar Nigam, Kripabandhu Ghosh, Shouvik Kumar Guha, Arnab Bhattacharya, and Ashutosh Modi. 2021. ILDC for CJPE: Indian legal documents corpus for court judgment prediction and explanation. In *Proceedings of the 59th Annual Meeting of the Association for Computational Linguistics and the 11th International Joint Conference on Natural Language Processing (Volume 1: Long Papers)*, pages 4046–4062, Online. Association for Computational Linguistics.

Mihai Masala, Radu Cristian Alexandru Iacob, Ana Sabina Uban, Marina Cidota, Horia Velicu, Traian Rebedea, and Marius Popescu. 2021. jurbert: A romanian bert model for legal judgement prediction. In *Proceedings of the Natural Legal Language Processing Workshop 2021*, pages 86–94.

Ramesh Nallapati, Feifei Zhai, and Bowen Zhou. 2017. Summarunner: A recurrent neural network based sequence model for extractive summarization of documents. In *Proceedings of the AAAI conference on artificial intelligence*, volume 31.

Shubham Nigam, Anurag Sharma, Danush Khanna, Noel Shallum, Kripabandhu Ghosh, and Arnab Bhattacharya. 2024. Legal judgment reimagined: PredEx and the rise of intelligent AI interpretation in Indian courts. In *Findings of the Association for Computational Linguistics ACL 2024*, pages 4296–4315, Bangkok, Thailand and virtual meeting. Association for Computational Linguistics.

Shubham Kumar Nigam and Aniket Deroy. 2023. Fact-based court judgment prediction. In *Proceedings of the 15th Annual Meeting of the Forum for Information Retrieval Evaluation*, pages 78–82.

Shubham Kumar Nigam, Aniket Deroy, Noel Shallum, Ayush Kumar Mishra, Anup Roy, Shubham Kumar Mishra, Arnab Bhattacharya, Saptarshi Ghosh, and Kripabandhu Ghosh. 2023a. Nonet at semeval-2023 task 6: Methodologies for legal evaluation. *arXiv preprint arXiv:2310.11049*.

Shubham Kumar Nigam, Navansh Goel, and Arnab Bhattacharya. 2022. nigam@ coliee-22: Legal case retrieval and entailment using cascading of lexical and semantic-based models. In *JSAI International Symposium on Artificial Intelligence*, pages 96–108. Springer.

Shubham Kumar Nigam, Shubham Kumar Mishra, Ayush Kumar Mishra, Noel Shallum, and Arnab Bhattacharya. 2023b. Legal question-answering in the indian context: Efficacy, challenges, and potential of modern ai models. *arXiv preprint arXiv:2309.14735*.

Joel Niklaus, Ilias Chalkidis, and Matthias Stürmer. 2021. Swiss-judgment-prediction: A multilingual legal judgment prediction benchmark. *arXiv preprint arXiv:2110.00806*.

Shounak Paul, Arpan Mandal, Pawan Goyal, and Saptarshi Ghosh. 2022. Pre-training transformers on indian legal text. *arXiv preprint arXiv:2209.06049*.

Seth Polsley, Pooja Jhunjhunwala, and Ruihong Huang. 2016. Casesummarizer: a system for automated summarization of legal texts. In *Proceedings of COLING 2016, the 26th international conference on Computational Linguistics: System Demonstrations*, pages 258–262.

Hugo Touvron, Louis Martin, Kevin Stone, Peter Albert, Amjad Almahairi, Yasmine Babaei, Nikolay Bashlykov, Soumya Batra, Prajjwal Bhargava, Shruti Bhosale, et al. 2023. Llama 2: Open foundation and fine-tuned chat models. *arXiv preprint arXiv:2307.09288*.

Shaurya Vats, Atharva Zope, Somsubhra De, Anurag Sharma, Upal Bhattacharya, Shubham Nigam, Shouvik Guha, Koustav Rudra, and Kripabandhu Ghosh. 2023. Llms–the good, the bad or the indispensable?: A use case on legal statute prediction and legal judgment prediction on indian court cases. In *Findings of the Association for Computational Linguistics: EMNLP 2023*, pages 12451–12474.

Jason Wei, Xuezhi Wang, Dale Schuurmans, Maarten Bosma, Fei Xia, Ed Chi, Quoc V Le, Denny Zhou, et al. 2022. Chain-of-thought prompting elicits reasoning in large language models. *Advances in Neural Information Processing Systems*, 35:24824–24837.

Chaojun Xiao, Haoxi Zhong, Zhipeng Guo, Cunchao Tu, Zhiyuan Liu, Maosong Sun, Yansong Feng, Xianpei Han, Zhen Hu, Heng Wang, et al. 2018. Cail2018: A large-scale legal dataset for judgment prediction. *arXiv preprint arXiv:1807.02478*.

Zhilin Yang, Zihang Dai, Yiming Yang, Jaime Carbonell, Russ R Salakhutdinov, and Quoc V Le. 2019. Xlnet: Generalized autoregressive pretraining for language understanding. *Advances in neural information processing systems*, 32.

Jieyu Zhao, Yichao Zhou, Zeyu Li, Wei Wang, and Kai-Wei Chang. 2018. Learning gender-neutral word embeddings. In *Proceedings of the 2018 Conference on Empirical Methods in Natural Language Processing*, pages 4847–4853, Brussels, Belgium. Association for Computational Linguistics.

A Expert Evaluation

Table 4 shows scores provided by three legal experts for V1. Table 5 shows scores provided by three legal experts for V2. Table 6 shows scores provided by three legal experts for V3. Table 7 shows scores provided by three legal experts for V4. Table 8 shows scores provided by three legal experts for V1+CoT. Table 9 shows scores provided by three legal experts for V4+CoT.

Table 10 shows scores provided by three legal experts for V1. Table 11 shows scores provided by three legal experts for V2. Table 12 shows scores provided by three legal experts for V3. Table 13 shows scores provided by three legal experts for V4. Table 14 shows scores provided by three legal experts for V1+CoT. Table 15 shows scores provided by three legal experts for V4+CoT.

Document	Legal Expert 1	Legal Expert 2	Legal Expert 3
Document 1	3	3	4
Document 2	3	4	3
Document 3	5	5	5
Document 4	4	4	4
Document 5	3	4	4
Document 6	4	4	4
Document 7	5	5	5
Document 8	2	2	4
Document 9	2	2	2
Document 10	1	2	2
Document 11	3	3	4
Document 12	3	3	4
Document 13	3	3	4
Document 14	3	3	4
Document 15	2	2	3
Document 16	5	5	5
Document 17	4	4	5
Document 18	2	2	2
Document 19	2	3	2
Document 20	2	2	2
Document 21	2	2	2
Document 22	2	2	2
Document 23	4	4	4
Document 24	1	2	1
Document 25	3	4	3

Table 4: Clarity ratings from three legal experts in V1

Document	Legal Expert 1	Legal Expert 2	Legal Expert 3
Document 1	4	4	4
Document 2	3	4	4
Document 3	3	4	3
Document 4	5	5	5
Document 5	2	2	2
Document 6	2	3	3
Document 7	4	4	4
Document 8	2	2	2
Document 9	3	3	3
Document 10	3	3	3
Document 11	5	5	5
Document 12	3	3	3
Document 13	2	2	2
Document 14	3	3	4
Document 15	4	4	4
Document 16	2	2	2
Document 17	2	2	3
Document 18	5	5	5
Document 19	3	3	4
Document 20	4	4	4
Document 21	1	2	2
Document 22	2	2	3
Document 23	3	3	4
Document 24	2	2	3
Document 25	5	5	5

Table 5: Clarity ratings from three legal experts in V2

Document	Legal Expert 1	Legal Expert 2	Legal Expert 3
Document 1	2	3	3
Document 2	5	5	5
Document 3	3	4	4
Document 4	2	2	2
Document 5	4	4	4
Document 6	3	3	3
Document 7	3	4	4
Document 8	2	2	3
Document 9	4	4	4
Document 10	5	5	5
Document 11	3	3	3
Document 12	1	2	3
Document 13	2	3	3
Document 14	5	5	5
Document 15	3	3	4
Document 16	2	3	4
Document 17	3	3	3
Document 18	4	5	5
Document 19	4	4	5
Document 20	2	3	3
Document 21	2	2	2
Document 22	3	3	3
Document 23	2	2	2
Document 24	4	4	4
Document 25	5	4	4

Table 6: Clarity ratings from three legal experts in V3

Document	Legal Expert 1	Legal Expert 2	Legal Expert 3
Document 1	5	5	5
Document 2	3	3	4
Document 3	3	3	4
Document 4	5	5	5
Document 5	2	2	3
Document 6	2	2	3
Document 7	5	5	5
Document 8	3	3	3
Document 9	3	3	3
Document 10	3	3	3
Document 11	2	3	3
Document 12	4	4	4
Document 13	3	4	3
Document 14	3	4	4
Document 15	5	5	5
Document 16	4	4	5
Document 17	2	3	3
Document 18	4	4	4
Document 19	3	3	3
Document 20	2	3	3
Document 21	2	2	3
Document 22	3	3	4
Document 23	4	4	4
Document 24	4	4	4
Document 25	2	2	2

Table 7: Clarity ratings from three legal experts in V4

Document	Legal Expert 1	Legal Expert 2	Legal Expert 3
Document 1	2	3	3
Document 2	4	4	4
Document 3	5	5	5
Document 4	3	3	4
Document 5	2	2	2
Document 6	3	3	4
Document 7	3	3	4
Document 8	1	1	2
Document 9	2	2	2
Document 10	5	5	5
Document 11	2	3	2
Document 12	3	3	3
Document 13	5	5	5
Document 14	4	4	4
Document 15	2	2	3
Document 16	3	3	4
Document 17	4	4	4
Document 18	3	3	4
Document 19	4	4	4
Document 20	3	3	4
Document 21	2	3	3
Document 22	2	3	2
Document 23	5	5	5
Document 24	3	3	3
Document 25	2	3	2

Table 8: Clarity ratings from three legal experts for V1+CoT

Document	Legal Expert 1	Legal Expert 2	Legal Expert 3
Document 1	5	5	5
Document 2	2	3	2
Document 3	4	4	5
Document 4	4	4	5
Document 5	3	4	3
Document 6	4	5	4
Document 7	4	4	4
Document 8	2	2	2
Document 9	3	4	3
Document 10	4	4	5
Document 11	5	5	5
Document 12	3	3	4
Document 13	4	4	5
Document 14	2	3	3
Document 15	4	4	4
Document 16	2	2	3
Document 17	4	4	4
Document 18	3	3	4
Document 19	5	5	5
Document 20	4	4	4
Document 21	2	2	3
Document 22	3	3	4
Document 23	5	5	5
Document 24	2	2	3
Document 25	4	4	4

Table 9: Clarity ratings from three legal experts for V4+CoT

Document	Legal Expert 1	Legal Expert 2	Legal Expert 3
Document 1	3	4	4
Document 2	3	4	3
Document 3	5	5	5
Document 4	3	4	3
Document 5	5	5	4
Document 6	3	4	3
Document 7	4	5	5
Document 8	3	4	4
Document 9	3	4	1
Document 10	3	3	2
Document 11	3	3	4
Document 12	3	3	4
Document 13	4	4	4
Document 14	5	5	4
Document 15	3	3	3
Document 16	4	5	4
Document 17	4	4	5
Document 18	5	5	2
Document 19	4	5	2
Document 20	3	3	2
Document 21	4	5	2
Document 22	4	5	1
Document 23	4	4	4
Document 24	4	4	1
Document 25	4	4	3

Table 10: Linking ratings from three legal experts for V1

Document	Legal Expert 1	Legal Expert 2	Legal Expert 3
Document 1	3	4	4
Document 2	3	4	4
Document 3	5	5	5
Document 4	3	4	4
Document 5	5	5	5
Document 6	3	4	4
Document 7	4	4	4
Document 8	3	4	3
Document 9	3	4	4
Document 10	3	4	4
Document 11	3	4	4
Document 12	3	3	3
Document 13	4	4	4
Document 14	5	5	5
Document 15	3	4	4
Document 16	4	4	3
Document 17	4	4	4
Document 18	5	5	5
Document 19	4	5	5
Document 20	3	3	3
Document 21	4	4	3
Document 22	4	4	3
Document 23	3	3	2
Document 24	3	3	2
Document 25	3	3	3

Table 11: Linking ratings from three legal experts for V2

Document	Legal Expert 1	Legal Expert 2	Legal Expert 3
Document 1	4	5	4
Document 2	4	4	3
Document 3	5	5	4
Document 4	4	4	4
Document 5	5	5	5
Document 6	4	4	4
Document 7	4	4	3
Document 8	4	4	4
Document 9	4	4	4
Document 10	4	4	3
Document 11	4	4	3
Document 12	3	3	3
Document 13	4	4	4
Document 14	5	5	5
Document 15	4	4	3
Document 16	4	4	4
Document 17	4	4	4
Document 18	5	5	3
Document 19	5	5	4
Document 20	3	3	3
Document 21	4	4	4
Document 22	4	2	3
Document 23	3	2	2
Document 24	3	2	2
Document 25	3	2	2

Table 12: Linking ratings from three legal experts for V3

Document	Legal Expert 1	Legal Expert 2	Legal Expert 3
Document 1	3	2	2
Document 2	3	2	3
Document 3	3	3	2
Document 4	4	4	3
Document 5	4	4	4
Document 6	4	4	4
Document 7	5	5	4
Document 8	4	4	3
Document 9	4	4	4
Document 10	4	4	3
Document 11	5	4	4
Document 12	5	5	5
Document 13	4	3	5
Document 14	4	4	3
Document 15	4	4	5
Document 16	5	5	4
Document 17	5	4	5
Document 18	5	5	5
Document 19	5	5	5
Document 20	5	5	5
Document 21	5	3	4
Document 22	5	4	5
Document 23	5	4	5
Document 24	5	5	5
Document 25	5	3	5

Table 13: Linking ratings from three legal experts for V4

Document	Legal Expert 1	Legal Expert 2	Legal Expert 3
Document 1	2	3	3
Document 2	4	4	4
Document 3	5	5	5
Document 4	3	3	4
Document 5	2	2	2
Document 6	3	3	4
Document 7	3	1	4
Document 8	1	1	2
Document 9	2	2	5
Document 10	5	5	2
Document 11	2	3	2
Document 12	3	3	3
Document 13	5	5	5
Document 14	4	4	4
Document 15	2	2	4
Document 16	3	3	5
Document 17	4	4	4
Document 18	3	3	4
Document 19	4	3	4
Document 20	3	3	4
Document 21	2	3	3
Document 22	2	3	2
Document 23	5	5	5
Document 24	3	3	2
Document 25	2	3	5

Table 14: Linking ratings from three legal experts for V1+CoT

Document	Legal Expert 1	Legal Expert 2	Legal Expert 3
Document 1	2	2	2
Document 2	4	4	4
Document 3	5	3	5
Document 4	4	4	4
Document 5	3	3	3
Document 6	4	4	3
Document 7	4	3	4
Document 8	2	2	2
Document 9	3	3	4
Document 10	5	5	4
Document 11	3	3	3
Document 12	4	5	3
Document 13	5	4	3
Document 14	4	3	3
Document 15	5	4	4
Document 16	4	4	3
Document 17	5	4	4
Document 18	4	4	4
Document 19	5	5	4
Document 20	3	3	3
Document 21	3	3	2
Document 22	5	5	2
Document 23	4	4	4
Document 24	3	2	2
Document 25	3	5	4

Table 15: Linking ratings from three legal experts for V4+CoT

The CLC-UKET Dataset: Benchmarking Case Outcome Prediction for the UK Employment Tribunal

Huiyuan Xie[1] **Felix Steffek**[2] **Joana Ribeiro de Faria**[2]
Christine Carter[2] **Jonathan Rutherford**[2]
[1]Department of Computer Science and Technology, University of Cambridge
[2]Faculty of Law, University of Cambridge

Abstract

This paper explores the intersection of technological innovation and access to justice by developing a benchmark for predicting case outcomes in the UK Employment Tribunal (UKET). To address the challenge of extensive manual annotation, the study employs a large language model (LLM) for automatic annotation, resulting in the creation of the CLC-UKET dataset. The dataset consists of approximately 19,000 UKET cases and their metadata. Comprehensive legal annotations cover facts, claims, precedent references, statutory references, case outcomes, reasons and jurisdiction codes. Facilitated by the CLC-UKET data, we examine a multi-class case outcome prediction task in the UKET. Human predictions are collected to establish a performance reference for model comparison. Empirical results from baseline models indicate that finetuned transformer models outperform zero-shot and few-shot LLMs on the UKET prediction task. The performance of zero-shot LLMs can be enhanced by integrating task-related information into few-shot examples. We hope that the CLC-UKET dataset, along with human annotations and empirical findings, can serve as a valuable benchmark for employment-related dispute resolution.

1 Introduction

In recent years, there has been great interest in adopting natural language processing techniques in the legal domain. One notable application is the prediction of outcomes for legal disputes in various jurisdictions (Xiao et al., 2018; Poudyal et al., 2020; Hwang et al., 2022; Henderson et al., 2022; Niklaus et al., 2023). However, the AI-based prediction of UK court decisions is still under-explored.

This paper investigates the prediction of dispute outcomes in the UK Employment Tribunal (UKET). The UKET serves a crucial function in the UK justice system, specifically dealing with employment-related disputes. Cases heard at the UKET cover a wide range of issues, such as unfair dismissal, discrimination and breach of contract. The possibility to apply to the UKET for a decision ensures that employment rights can be enforced. Knowing the likely outcome of a court procedure improves access to justice and facilitates amicable dispute resolution.

The contributions of this paper are as follows:

1. We constructed a large-scale CLC-UKET dataset based on the Cambridge Law Corpus (CLC) (Östling et al., 2023). CLC-UKET includes two components: CLC-UKET$_{anno}$ and CLC-UKET$_{pred}$. CLC-UKET$_{anno}$ consists of a selection of 19,090 UKET case judgments heard between 2011 and 2023 (inclusive). All cases come with metadata including a unique case identifier, the hearing date and jurisdiction codes. We further provided detailed legal annotations for all cases, including (a) facts, (b) claims, (c) references to legal statutes, acts, regulations, provisions and rules, (d) references to precedents and other court decisions, (e) general case outcome and (f) detailed order and remedies. We further curated CLC-UKET$_{pred}$, specifically designed to facilitate a multi-class case outcome prediction task. CLC-UKET$_{pred}$ consists of 14,582 cases, each supplemented with statements detailing the facts, claims and the general outcomes of the cases.

2. We assessed human performance on the UKET outcome prediction task on CLC-UKET$_{pred}$ with the aim of setting a human performance reference to calibrate prediction models.

3. We experimented with a range of baseline models to predict the general case outcomes based on information about facts and claims of UKET cases.

Proceedings of the Natural Legal Language Processing Workshop 2024, pages 81–96
November 16, 2024 ©2024 Association for Computational Linguistics

The CLC-UKET dataset and the empirical explorations aim to supplement the standard CLC dataset and facilitate future research on employment-related dispute resolution in the UK legal system. We will make the CLC-UKET dataset available via the official CLC website[1].

2 UK Legal System and UKET

The UK has a special category of judicial body, the employment tribunals, which deal exclusively with employment disputes. The UKET is one of the three largest tribunals in the greater tribunals system (Judicial Office, 2016). The UKET aims to provide a procedure which is easily accessible, informal, speedy and inexpensive (BEIS, 2020, p. 23). The form of employment tribunal proceedings is adversarial rather than investigatory, as each party has to present and prove its case (Deakin et al., 2021). Claimants must comply with procedural and substantive requirements to be successful. For instance, claimants must submit their claims on time, comply with the orders of the tribunal, present required evidence or information in a timely manner, and avoid scandalous, unreasonable or vexatious conduct (which would make a fair trial impossible). These are usually considered as *procedural* requirements. Claimants must also comply with the substantive requirements of the rules supporting the claims. For example, in order to be successful with a discrimination claim on grounds of disability, the claimant must prove their status as an employee, demonstrate their disability and show that they faced discrimination, which are considered as *substantive* requirements of the case. These procedural and substantive requirements are not necessarily determined at one final hearing or included in one final judgment. Instead, they may be iteratively decided at different stages, which can result in multiple decisions.

The employee (claimant) and the employer (respondent) submit their claims and responses, respectively, through a standardised form (Rules 8 and 16 of the Employment Tribunals Rules of Procedure 2013, hereinafter referred to as Rules). The tribunal considers these forms and may dismiss a claim for procedural or substantive reasons, *e.g.*, for lack of jurisdiction or for lack of any reasonable prospect of success (Rules, r. 27). At any stage of the proceedings, the tribunal can determine a preliminary issue, make a procedural order (*e.g.*, a deposit order or require the presentation of additional documents) or make a final decision (*e.g.*, strike out the claim, Rules, r. 37). There may be multiple final hearings for different issues, for example, one hearing to determine whether a party is liable, another hearing to determine the remedy and another to determine the costs (Rules, r. 57). Each of these hearings results in a separate judgment, written out in a separate document. Finally, a party may request a reconsideration of a previous judgment, which will lead to another judgment (Rules, r. 70). As a consequence, the resolution of a dispute may not be covered by one judgment only, but may be determined by iterative multiple decisions resulting in various case documents.

Each decision is linked to one or multiple jurisdiction codes. In the case of the UKET, there are 54 jurisdiction codes in total, which are used to identify the matter of disputes. By way of example, the jurisdiction code "unfair dismissal" is used when claimants argue that they have been unfairly dismissed. This jurisdiction code is often employed in addition to other jurisdiction codes, such as unlawful deduction from wages, redundancy, protective award, breach of contract and working time regulations.

In stark contrast with typical UK judgments, UKET decisions are relatively clearly structured, not only because there are no dissenting opinions, but also because there are specific rulings that set out which elements a judgment must contain (Rules, r. 62(5)). Nevertheless, UKET judgments are not always consistent since there are no formal rules on the style to be used in drafting a decision. Most English judgments summarise their decisions in a paragraph, although this summary does not need to respect any particular form (Conseil d'État, 2012, p. 136). In the case of the UKET, the summary is often found at the beginning of the judgment. However, judgments on multiple claims are sometimes divided into chapters, each analysing one claim containing the relevant decision. Also, whilst a judgment may contain an initial statement that the claimant is successful, it may not be clear which claim(s) this relates to in cases where there are multiple claims.

[1]The CLC website: https://www.cst.cam.ac.uk/research/srg/projects/law.

3 Related Work

3.1 Analysis of Employment Judgments

Quantitative methods for analysing legal judgments have long been explored. In relation to employment law, Grunbaum and Newhouse (1965) analysed 20 US Supreme Court judgments to identify the variables which impacted outcomes. Similarly, Field and Holley (1982) identified factors which influenced outcomes of performance appraisal judgments. Brudney et al. (1999) analysed the extent to which extradoctrinal factors such as political party, gender and professional experience influenced outcomes.

Moreover, several studies explored correlations between specific demographic groups and the ability to pursue their employment rights in tribunal. In the US, Schuster and Miller (1984) analysed 153 federal court cases, focusing on age discrimination, whilst Schultz and Petterson (1992) investigated race and sex discrimination. In the UK, Barnard and Ludlow (2016) investigated whether EU-8 migrant workers were able to enforce their rights by bringing claims before the UKET.

Many of these studies occurred before judgments were published online, and therefore not only entailed costly journeys to the registers, but also required manual extraction and tagging of specific elements of court decisions. More recently, Blackham (2021) conducted quantitative analyses of employment decisions, but despite having access to online judgments, some of their tasks still required manual labour.

3.2 Legal Judgment Prediction

The advance of deep learning models alongside the development of large-scale legal datasets has greatly advanced the research on legal judgment prediction (LJP) (Xiao et al., 2018; Chalkidis et al., 2019; O'Sullivan and Beel, 2019; Ma et al., 2021; Chalkidis et al., 2023; Colombo et al., 2024). A large number of datasets have been created for both civil law systems (Poudyal et al., 2020; Yamada et al., 2022) and common law systems (Caselaw Access Project, 2018; Henderson et al., 2022; Östling et al., 2023; Butler, 2024).

Facilitated by large-scale datasets, there has been a surge in the application of deep learning models to LJP in recent years. Zhong et al. (2018) introduced TopJudge to address LJP using multi-task learning that combines three aspects: law articles, charges and terms of penalty. Another notable contribution is the work of Ma et al. (2021) where an end-to-end framework was built to predict dispute outcomes using multi-task supervision and multi-stage representation learning. To the best of our knowledge, the only notable LJP paper on UK law is Strickson and De La Iglesia (2020), which dates before the emergence of LLMs and is limited to the binary task of UK Supreme Court judges allowing or dismissing an appeal.

4 The CLC-UKET Dataset

We curated a large-scale dataset focusing on UK employment-related dispute resolution. The resulting CLC-UKET dataset consists of two components: CLC-UKET$_{anno}$ consisting of 19,090 cases with detailed legal annotations and CLC-UKET$_{pred}$ with 14,582 cases curated for case outcome prediction for the UKET. The CLC-UKET dataset is constructed based on the UKET subset of the CLC (Östling et al., 2023) by adding annotations for selected UKET cases. A common practice for collecting legal annotations is to ask legal experts to manually annotate texts. However, this can be costly and time-consuming. To alleviate the burden of manual annotation, we explored utilising large language models (LLMs) for automatic annotation.

The dataset curation pipeline of CLC-UKET$_{anno}$ consists of two steps: a *case preparation* module and an *LLM-aided case annotation* module.

4.1 Case Preparation

The raw UKET subset of the CLC contains 52,339 cases in total, covering employment-related cases heard at the UKET from January 2011 to August 2023 (inclusive).[2] After analysing these cases, we noticed that many cases only consist of one page as regards the tribunal decision. Based on the observations from de Faria et al. (2024), many of these cases involve straightforward procedural decisions, for example when claimants withdraw their cases or respondents do not respond at all such that a default judgment is made. As such cases do not contain substantial information on facts and substantive reasons, we excluded them at the case preparation step.

After this filtering step, we obtained a collection of 19,090 cases containing more than one page in their court decision files. For each case, we collected a list of metadata, including a unique

[2]The hearing dates of the cases in the UKET subset of the CLC range from 2011 to 2023, although some cases were submitted before 2011.

case identifier used in the UKET records, date of filing, date of decision, place of hearing, judges, claimant(s), respondent(s) and appearances at the hearing. We also obtained jurisdiction codes for all cases from the UKET website.[3] In legal contexts, a *jurisdiction code* typically refers to a numerical or alphanumeric code assigned to a specific legal jurisdiction, a certain subject matter or a geographic area. Legal jurisdictions are defined areas with a distinct set of laws and regulations. In the case of the UKET, there are a total of 54 jurisdiction codes, which are used to identify the dispute matter. Each UKET case can be associated to multiple jurisdiction codes that indicate the categorical areas of the case. As an example, the code *unfair dismissal* is used when claimants argue that they have been unfairly dismissed and submit a claim for payment of a certain sum, *e.g.*, basic award, compensatory award (lack of notice pay and loss of earnings between a period) and injury to feelings award. A full list of jurisdiction codes in the UKET is presented in Appendix B.3.

4.2 LLM-aided Case Annotation

The CLC provides raw texts of the decisions of UKET cases. These documents usually contain entangled statements about facts provided by parties and their lawyers, reasoning towards a decision, legal statutes and precedents applied to justify the reasoning and final decisions regarding the case outcome. In this step, we followed similar lines to de Faria et al. (2024) and utilised the GPT-4-turbo model (Achiam et al., 2023) to automatically extract legal information from UKET decisions.

We applied an iterative development process to find the optimal prompt for the purpose of legal information extraction. The final prompt that we opted for yielded the best results in terms of the accuracy of information extracted, the adequacy of necessary information contained therein and the level of detail. The final prompt that we used for LLM-aided case annotation is presented in Appendix A.2. After automatic annotation, we obtained detailed annotations on important legal factors for 19,090 CLC-UKET cases, covering (1) facts, (2) claims, (3) references to legal statutes, (4) references to precedents, (5) general case outcomes, (6) general case outcomes labelled as "claimant wins", "claimant loses", "claimant partly wins" and "other", (7) detailed orders and remedies and (8) reasons.

[3]https://www.gov.uk/employment-tribunal-decisions.

5 Case Outcome Prediction

The annotated CLC-UKET data (*i.e.*, CLC-UKET$_{anno}$) provides a large collection of court decisions augmented with rich legal annotations, which can readily be used for downstream legal AI tasks. In this paper, we showcase a use case of the CLC-UKET data by investigating a classic task in legal AI, i.e., case outcome prediction.

5.1 Task Definition

Given a set of facts and claims of a UKET case, the task of case outcome prediction aims to automatically generate an outcome label falling into one of the following four categories: "claimant wins", "claimant loses", "claimant partly wins" and "other". The facts and the claims are the judges' summarisation of the statements provided by the claimant(s) and respondent(s) prior to or during a hearing.

More formally, given a set of facts $F = f_1, f_2, \cdots, f_m$ and a set of claims $C = c_1, c_2, \cdots, c_n$ for a UKET case, a prediction model $\texttt{CLS}$ outputs a label g for the general case outcome:

$$g = \texttt{CLS}(F, C)$$

where $g \in$ ["claimant wins", "claimant loses", "claimant partly wins" and "other"].

Note that there is a debate concerning the difference between the legal judgment prediction (LJP) task and the case outcome classification (COC) task (Medvedeva et al., 2021; Santosh et al., 2022; Medvedeva et al., 2023; Medvedeva and Mcbride, 2023). In this paper, we opted for the terminology "prediction" over "classification" as we deliberately excluded explicit information about case outcomes from the input of the prediction task, and only kept descriptions of facts and claims in the input. As such, this task focuses on predicting case outcomes based solely on information about facts and claims. Similarly, the legal experts predicting outcomes had only access to facts and claims.

5.2 Data Preparation for the Prediction Task

We tailored the CLC-UKET$_{anno}$ data to construct a case outcome prediction task for the UKET. Three types of legal factors are needed for the prediction task, namely *facts*, *claims* and *general case outcomes*. The input to the prediction models is a sequence of fact statements concatenated with claim

	train	val	test
#Cases	11,838	1,373	1,371
#AvgFactLen	79	85	88
#MaxFactLen	409	463	321
#AvgClaimLen	34	34	34
#MaxClaimLen	187	164	150

Table 1: Data statistics of the CLC-UKET$_{pred}$ dataset. #Cases denotes the number of cases. #AvgFactLen denotes the average number of words per fact statement. #MaxFactLen denotes the maximum length of fact statements. #AvgClaimLen denotes the average number of words per claim statement. #MaxClaimLen denotes the maximum length of claim statements.

statements, in the form of "$fact_1, fact_2, \cdots, fact_n$ [SEP] $claim_1$, $claim_2$, $\cdots$, $claim_m$". The target output of the prediction task is a general outcome label, which is a categorical variable labelling potential case outcomes as *claimant wins*, *claimant partly wins*, *claimant loses* and *other*.

5.3 Data Statistics

From the 19,090 cases in the CLC-UKET$_{anno}$ dataset, we filtered out cases where no substantial information about *facts* and *claims* was extracted by GPT-4 at the LLM-aided case annotation step. After the filtering, we obtained a set of 14,582 UKET cases, supplemented with fact and claim statements extracted by GPT-4. We denote this prediction dataset as CLC-UKET$_{pred}$. Following general practice in machine learning research, we divided the 14,582 CLC-UKET$_{pred}$ cases into three splits: *training*, *validation* and *testing*. The details on data statistics of the train/val/test sets for CLC-UKET$_{pred}$ are summarised in Table 1.

Note that for the *training* and *validation* sets, all three legal factors - facts, claims and outcomes - were sourced from information automatically extracted by GPT-4, as detailed in Section 4.2. For the *testing* set, facts and claims were automatically extracted by GPT-4, whilst the case outcome labels were manually annotated by a legal expert[4]. The expert annotator carefully analysed the full court judgments and summarised the judges' decisions into general case outcome labels. These manually annotated outcome labels for the test cases represent the actual judicial decisions, serving as gold-standard references for prediction evaluation.

[4]The legal annotator is a PhD Candidate in Law.

6 Experiments and Results

6.1 Baseline Models

We experimented with two classes of baseline models:

1. Transformer-based (Vaswani et al., 2017) models, including BERT (Devlin et al., 2019) and T5 (Raffel et al., 2020);
2. LLM-based models, including GPT-3.5 (OpenAI, 2022) and GPT-4 (Achiam et al., 2023).

The two Transformer-based models were fine-tuned on our CLC-UKET$_{pred}$ data, whilst GPT-3.5 and GPT-4 were tested using zero-shot and few-shot settings without dedicated fine-tuning. Implementation details of the baseline models are presented in Appendix A.1.

BERT. We fine-tuned BERT (Devlin et al., 2019) on the training set of CLC-UKET$_{pred}$ with the Adam optimiser (Kingma and Ba, 2014) with a learning rate of 1e-4 and a batch size of 32. The final checkpoint was obtained after training the model for 5 epochs.

T5. The T5 model (Raffel et al., 2020) is also fine-tuned on the training set of CLC-UKET$_{pred}$. The model is optimised with a learning rate of 1e-4 for 5 epochs.

GPT-3.5-turbo and **GPT-4-turbo**. We tested GPT-based models with diverse settings, including (1) zero-shot prediction, (2) few-shot prediction with randomly selected examples and (3) few-shot prediction with examples selected according to jurisdiction codes. The prompts that we used for LLM experiments are presented in Appendix A.2.

- *Zero-shot prediction.* In this setting, the GPT-based models are directly asked to predict an outcome based on information about facts and claims of a case. No examples are provided to the models in the prompts.
- *Few-shot prediction with randomly selected examples.* We randomly selected a few examples from the training set and included them in the prompt to GPT-based models. We also investigated the effects of the number of examples on prediction performance by experimenting with two numbers (*i.e.*, 2 and 5) for examples included in the prompts.
- *Few-shot prediction with examples selected using jurisdiction codes.* This setting differs

from the above few-shot setting in that we deliberately sampled case examples according to jurisdiction code similarity. In other words, given a target case for which a case outcome is to be predicted, we first identified the set of jurisdiction codes associated with it. Next, we gathered a collection of cases that share at least one jurisdiction code with the target case. From this collection, we sampled a specified number (similarly, 2 and 5) of example cases to include in the few-shot prompt.

6.2 Human Prediction

We further investigated how well legal experts can predict UKET case outcomes given facts and claims. This investigation is of paramount importance, as human performance can establish a reference to calibrate model performance.

Two legal experts conducted the human prediction exercise. They are PhD candidates in Law with a focus on UK employment law. They were supervised by a professor of law based in the UK. Each test case in CLC-UKET$_{pred}$ was separately annotated by the two legal experts. We asked annotators to indicate what they think is the most likely case outcome after reading facts and claims of a case. They were also asked to indicate whether a prediction is of low confidence. Cases labelled with low confidence are usually cases that are hard to predict due to insufficient information contained in the given facts or claims or due to the intrinsic complexity of a case (in particular the claims raised).

At the beginning of the annotation process, both annotators were provided with annotation guidelines (see Appendix D for details). The annotation guidelines are consistent with our overarching experimentation design for the prediction task. Annotators were asked to make their judgments separately, avoiding discussions amongst themselves. We emphasised that human predictions should be made based on the same facts and claims that prediction models were evaluated on. Annotators were required not to search for the cases they were annotating on the internet.[5] Whenever questions regarding the implementation of the annotation arose during the annotation process, the annotators were provided with clarification by the supervisor.

[5]However, annotators were free to research other information that might be helpful for the annotations, for example, information on the applicable law.

Baseline	Accuracy	Precision	Recall	F-score
Random	0.241	0.340	0.241	0.276
BERT	0.446	**0.623**	0.446	0.427
T5	**0.624**	0.602	**0.624**	**0.564**
GPT-3.5$_{zero}$	0.535	0.553	0.535	0.525
GPT-3.5$_{rand2}$	0.540	0.567	0.540	0.535
GPT-3.5$_{rand5}$	0.532	0.561	0.532	0.532
GPT-3.5$_{juris2}$	0.544	0.568	0.544	0.542
GPT-3.5$_{juris5}$	0.549	0.570	0.549	0.550
GPT-4$_{zero}$	0.545	**0.623**	0.545	0.549
GPT-4$_{rand2}$	0.518	0.612	0.518	0.530
GPT-4$_{rand5}$	0.539	0.614	0.539	0.547
GPT-4$_{juris2}$	0.540	0.619	0.540	0.551
GPT-4$_{juris5}$	0.536	0.617	0.536	0.546
Human	0.693	0.680	0.693	0.672

Table 2: Overall evaluation results for the multi-class CLC-UKET$_{pred}$ prediction task. *Precision*, *recall* and *F-score* report the weighted average of precision/recall/F-score obtained across labels, accounting for label imbalance. *Random* refers to *random guess*. *Human* refers to the averaged scores of the outcome labels predicted by two human experts. All predicted outcomes were evaluated against gold-standard case outcome labels directly extracted from court decisions.

After annotating, we obtained two independent sets of predicted case outcome labels for the 1,371 test cases. The Cohen's Kappa score for all annotations is 0.421[6].

6.3 Results

Overall results. Table 2 presents the overall evaluation results for the CLC-UKET$_{pred}$ prediction task. The experiment findings reveal several key insights regarding the performance of different models. All models tested significantly outperform the random guess baseline, indicating the models' efficacy on this task. Among the models, the fine-tuned T5 emerges as the best performer overall, achieving the highest F-score. There is a noticeable gap between machine and human performance, with human expert predictions obtaining a 19.1% higher F-score compared to the fine-tuned T5, highlighting the superiority of human judgment in this domain in a baseline setting.

In terms of the two GPT-based models, GPT-4 generally outperforms GPT-3.5, reinforcing the advancements made in this newer model version. However, the margin of GPT-4's outperformance is rather small. The inclusion of few-shot examples proves beneficial for improving GPT-3.5's predic-

[6]The Cohen's Kappa score between two specialised legal experts ranges from 0.41 to 0.60 indicating moderate agreement, highlighting the inherent complexity in the UKET prediction task.

Baseline	Label	Precision	Recall	F-score
BERT	wins	0.459	0.828	0.591
	loses	0.869	0.215	0.345
	partly	0.381	0.364	0.372
	other	0.036	0.455	0.067
T5	wins	0.595	0.716	0.650
	loses	0.647	0.846	0.734
	partly	0.541	0.066	0.117
	other	0	0	0
GPT-3.5$_{juris5}$	wins	0.515	0.700	0.594
	loses	0.720	0.565	0.633
	partly	0.362	0.305	0.331
	other	0.143	0.455	0.217
GPT-4$_{juris2}$	wins	0.588	0.700	0.639
	loses	0.778	0.430	0.554
	partly	0.359	0.541	0.431
	other	0.082	0.364	0.133
Human	wins	0.627	0.815	0.708
	loses	0.792	0.812	0.802
	partly	0.554	0.302	0.391
	other	0	0	0

Table 3: Evaluation scores obtained by baseline models and human predictions for the four label categories: *claimant wins, claimant loses, claimant partly wins* and *other*. The numbers of cases for the four labels are 437, 618, 305 and 11, respectively. For GPT-3.5 and GPT-4, the variants that achieved the highest F-sclores across relevant settings are presented.

Baseline	Accuracy	Precision	Recall	F-score
BERT	0.443	**0.619**	0.443	0.421
T5	**0.535**	0.552	**0.535**	**0.480**
GPT-3.5$_{juris5}$	0.455	0.488	0.455	0.451
GPT-4$_{juris2}$	0.465	0.527	0.465	0.448
Human	0.477	0.507	0.477	0.448

Table 4: Evaluation results obtained by baseline models and human predictions on test cases which are considered as hard to predict by human experts.

Baseline	Accuracy	Precision	Recall	F-score
BERT	0.589	0.728	0.589	0.554
T5	**0.718**	**0.735**	**0.718**	**0.713**
GPT-3.5$_{juris5}$	0.699	0.710	0.699	0.697
GPT-4$_{juris2}$	0.675	0.713	0.675	0.663
Human	0.812	0.807	0.812	0.810

Table 5: Evaluation results obtained by baseline models and human predictions when the labels "wins" and "partly wins" are aggregated. *Human* refers to the averaged scores of the outcome labels predicted by two human experts. For GPT-3.5 and GPT-4, the variants that achieved the highest F-scores across relevant settings are presented.

tion performance. Specifically, using examples that share similar jurisdiction codes with the target case enhances the F-score of GPT-3.5's predictions more effectively than randomly sampled examples, validating the positive impact of incorporating task-specific information on GPT-3.5's prediction performance. In addition, the marginal gains observed when varying the number of few-shot examples provided to GPT-based models suggest that simply increasing the number of examples is not sufficient to significantly boost performance. Moreover, GPT-4, in its zero-shot setting, already achieves the highest precision among all baseline models. Providing two similar cases in the *juris-2* few-shot setting improves GPT-4's F-score compared to the zero-shot setting.

Results for individual classes. In Table 3 we report the individual scores achieved by baseline models and human predictions across various label categories. Most baseline models demonstrate a high recall and a relatively low precision when predicting "claimant wins" and in contrast achieve a high precision and a relatively low recall when predicting the "claimant loses" label. These findings underscore the distinct trade-offs that prediction models make between precision and recall. Human predictions exhibit strong performance in the "claimant wins" and "claimant loses" categories, where the F-scores are consistently high. The labels "partly wins" and "other" consistently receive lower evaluation scores across all models and the human predictors, which may be attributed to the inherent difficulty of identifying cases within these two categories, compounded by the imbalanced distribution of cases across four categories.

Performance on *low confidence* cases. In the human prediction process described in Section 6.2, expert annotators were asked to explicitly indicate whether a case was difficult for them to predict based on the given facts and claims (*i.e.*, a "low confidence" prediction). Using these annotations, we further analysed different baselines for cases that were considered difficult by the human experts. Comparing Table 4 with Table 2, it can be observed that human performance on predicting for the *low confidence* cases is significantly worse than for all cases, suggesting that human assessments of the difficulty level of the prediction task align well with the empirical results. Furthermore, all baseline models exhibit relatively lower scores when evaluated on the *low confidence* cases. This pattern indicates that cases that are more challenging for human experts are also more difficult for the models.

Ablation study. This paper explores a fine-grained prediction setting that differentiates between cases where the claimant wins outright and those where the claimant partially wins. This distinction inherently creates a more challenging prediction task, as accurately predicting *partly wins* requires a nuanced assessment of the claimant's initial claims and the most likely outcomes for each individual claim. To understand the added difficulty of our setting, we aggregated the judgments with outcomes of "wins" and "partly wins" (*i.e.*, treating both labels as "wins") and evaluated performance under this simplified setting. The overall evaluation results are presented in Table 5.[7] A comparison of the results in Table 2 and Table 5 shows that all baseline models exhibit consistent improvements in prediction performance across all metrics in the simplified setting, with T5 achieving the best overall performance. Human predictions achieved a precision of 0.807 and a recall of 0.812, indicating that human annotators can effectively predict case outcomes when there is no requirement to further distinguish between the two winning-related categories.

7 Further Discussions

7.1 Relevance of Scores

We would like to emphasise that the evaluation scores reported for the CLC-UKET$_{pred}$ prediction task are baseline results. Both the transformer-based and the LLM-based models could be improved further for the task at hand. For example, the latter could be further enhanced by incorporating retrieval-augmented generation (Lewis et al., 2020; Gao et al., 2023) or chain-of-thought (Wei et al., 2022; Diao et al., 2023; Kim et al., 2023). Similarly, human experts might achieve better predictions by investing more time and conducting further research. Those interested in the legal domain are, therefore, encouraged to apply caution when drawing conclusions for legal practice.

The prediction task has been designed from the perspective of the claimant. This perspective informs the outcomes "claimant wins", "claimant loses", "claimant partly wins" and "other". This approach makes sense as it is first for the claimant to decide whether they apply for a decision of the Tribunal. Once the claimant has taken this first step, it is for the defendant to decide how they react to the claim. Whilst the outcome prediction for the claimant is also of relevance for the defendant, it should be noted that both models and human predictors achieve different scores depending on whether "wins" or "loses" is predicted.

Against this background, it is worth discussing a few patterns in the scores. First, both models and legal experts achieve higher recall than precision scores for "wins" and higher precision scores than recall scores for "loses". Precision is a useful measure when the costs of a wrongly predicted positive are high. In a litigation context, this is the case when the costs of initiating litigation (*e.g.*, fees for legal and other advisers, court fees, time and stress involved) are high. Likewise, recall is a useful measure if the costs of missing a true positive are high. In the context of court proceedings, this is the case when the opportunity cost of not initiating likely successful litigation is high, for example, if the expected remedy has a high monetary value or otherwise has a high relevance for the potential claimant (*e.g.*, for emotional reasons). Hence, it depends on the specific situation of a potential claimant whether precision or recall provides better guidance. Since the UKET currently does not charge fees and claimants can represent themselves (thereby saving costs), *recall* may be the preferable score if the claim matters to the potential claimant. Second, it is worth noting that the F-score of GPT-4_{juris2} for "partly wins" outperforms the human predictors. This may indicate the LLM's ability to navigate more complex litigation, which involves multiple claims or multiple parties on either side.

7.2 Possible Reasons for Errors

Models and annotators, based on the extracted facts and claims, cannot always determine whether a tribunal's decision will finally resolve the claim or only address a preliminary issue. For example, in a disability discrimination case, the tribunal might first issue a judgment confirming the claimant's disability (preliminary issue), followed by a second judgment addressing the actual discrimination claim. The first judgment (which the claimant may win) is a necessary step but does not resolve the final claim, whilst the second judgment might conclude that there was no discrimination (such that the claimant ultimately loses). Preliminary issues are often contested, and some applications may solely seek a tribunal declaration on such issues (*e.g.*, confirming the claimant is an employee or disabled). The possibility of such multi-step proceedings increases the complexity of predictions

[7] We also present results for individual categories (*i.e.*, "wins", "loses" and "other") in Appendix C.

and has likely had a negative effect on the scores of both the models and the human predictors.

Further difficulties arise in cases where the UKET renders a procedural decision instead of deciding on the substance of the claim. Such cases are classified as "other". However, both models and human annotators may predict a substantive instead of a procedural decision and, therefore, suggest "claimant wins" or "claimant loses". According to our annotation guidelines, this affects, in particular, the categories of "claimant partly wins" and "other". This complexity may have contributed to low evaluation scores for "claimant partly wins" and "other".

More generally, the extracted facts, which are the basis for both the models' and the humans' predictions, may not include all the elements needed to form a prediction. This may be the result of GPT-4 not including all details in the facts section when extracting the facts from the underlying UKET judgments. For example, when there is an application for costs, which is highly dependent on the parties' behaviour, the models and legal experts may be limited in their prediction due to factual details missing. Additionally, certain outcomes may hinge on factors like the respondent's failure to challenge the claim or produce evidence, which might not be reflected in the extracted facts, leading to incorrect predictions. Although extracted facts may include procedural aspects, they do not always capture procedural facts that determine the outcome, such as the timing of a claim that is dismissed due to late submissions.

8 Conclusion

This paper explores the prediction of dispute outcomes for the UK Employment Tribunal (UKET). It also illustrates the utility of LLMs for automatic annotation to reduce the burden of extensive manual annotation. With LLM-aided annotation, we curated the CLC-UKET dataset with comprehensive, high-quality legal annotations. We showcased how the CLC-UKET data can be used to construct a prediction task to categorise case outcomes based on sequences of facts and claims. We fine-tuned and evaluated two widely used Transformer-based models on this prediction task. We also evaluated LLMs on the prediction task with a range of settings, and reported human performance on the task to facilitate model calibration. These empirical efforts serve as a useful benchmark for the UKET prediction task. We will make the CLC-UKET dataset publicly available[8] to facilitate future research in this field.

Ethics Statement

The curated dataset is developed on the basis of the Cambridge Law Corpus (CLC), which aggregates publicly available UK legal judgments. Both the decisions in the CLC and the jurisdiction codes of UKET are licensed for use under the Open Government Licence. This licence grants a worldwide, royalty-free, perpetual and non-exclusive licence. Access to the CLC is restricted to researchers with confirmed ethical clearance and requires compliance with the DPA and UK GDPR. Whilst UK legal judgments are not anonymised, Rule 50 of the Employment Tribunal Rules ensures that sensitive personal information is anonymised when necessary. Additionally, Schedule 2, Part 5 of the DPA provides derogations for academic research, alleviating the burden of notifying all individuals involved in judgments.

Our dataset does not go beyond publicly available information and includes established procedures for data removal if requested. Like the original CLC, access to the dataset created for this paper is limited to qualified researchers who adhere to the relevant ethical and legal standards. Given the public availability of the data and our efforts to democratise access to legal information, we believe that we meet the ethical requirements for this research.

For more details on the legal and ethical considerations concerning the underlying CLC dataset, see Östling et al. (2023).

Limitations

Whilst our study provides valuable insights into the prediction of dispute outcomes for the UK Employment Tribunal, it is important to acknowledge certain limitations of our findings.

Access to the *actual* facts and claims of the cases. The facts and claims used in this paper were extracted from tribunal decisions. This was necessary given the impossibility of obtaining actual facts and claims in the number necessary for this paper. Consequently, we employed the extracted facts and claims from the court judgments as a practical substitute, providing a tangible foundation for

[8]The CLC website: https://www.cst.cam.ac.uk/research/srg/projects/law.

our judgment prediction models.

This approach could potentially introduce information biases at the input stage of the prediction task. The facts and claims that we used in the CLC-UKET dataset were derived from the judges' written decisions at the end of the proceedings. Since the judges know the result of the case at this stage of the process, the texts they write may inherently contain biased information (Sargeant and Magnusson, 2024). For example, sentiment words in the judges' statements might implicitly reveal their inclinations towards certain decisions. The models might incorporate such factors when making predictions related to case outcomes. Similarly, the legal experts may have picked up such sentiments.

In subsequent research, we will explore alternative methods of identifying facts and claims to better approximate the original submissions to the court, thus fostering a more realistic modelling of judgment prediction.

Automatic information extraction. Manual annotation of legal texts requires extensive expert knowledge and can be costly. To alleviate these challenges, this research utilised GPT-4 for automatic information extraction. Whilst the use of GPT-4 offers notable advantages in terms of time and cost efficiency, and the extraction results are generally satisfactory according to the quality check conducted by legal experts in a related study (de Faria et al., 2024), this annotation practice is not without flaws. The quality of legal annotations could be further improved in future explorations. There is also room to explore the effect of extracting and providing more detailed facts compared to the relatively concise fact statements present in the current CLC-UKET dataset.

Dataset and evolution of law over time. We do not know whether the datasets employed are representative or include all decisions by the UKET in the relevant period. The dataset providing the cases to be predicted by the models and human experts covers the years 2011 to 2023. During this time, both employment and procedural law has evolved. Predicting a case outcome without knowing the precise decision date may lead to mistakes. Models and human predictors did not have direct access to the date at which the underlying case was decided. However, they may have inferred the decision date from the case identifier, which contains the year of the decision.

Acknowledgements

This project received funding support from the Cambridge Centre for Data-Driven Discovery and Accelerate Programme for Scientific Discovery, made possible by a donation from Schmidt Futures. We are grateful for the helpful comments from Ludwig Bull, Mateja Jamnik, Leif Jonsson, Chikako Kanki, Måns Magnusson, Holli Sargeant, Takenobu Tokunaga, Arvid Wenestam and the participants of the "Artificial Intelligence and Law" workshop at Hitotsubashi University in December 2023.

References

Josh Achiam, Steven Adler, Sandhini Agarwal, Lama Ahmad, Ilge Akkaya, Florencia Leoni Aleman, Diogo Almeida, Janko Altenschmidt, Sam Altman, Shyamal Anadkat, et al. 2023. GPT-4 Technical Report. *arXiv preprint arXiv:2303.08774*.

Catherine Barnard and Amy Ludlow. 2016. Enforcement of Employment Rights by EU-8 Migrant Workers in Employment Tribunals. *Industrial Law Journal*.

BEIS. 2020. Findings from the Survey of Employment Tribunal Applications 2018 (2020/007). Technical report, Department for Business, Energy and Industrial Strategy, United Kingdom Government.

Alysia Blackham. 2021. Enforcing Rights in Employment Tribunals: Insights from Age Discrimination Claims in a New 'Dataset'. *Legal Studies*, 41(3):390–409.

James J. Brudney, Sara Schiavoni, and Deborah Jones Merritt. 1999. Judicial Hostility Toward Labor Unions? Applying the Social Background Model to a Celebrated Concern. *Ohio State Law Journal*, 60:1675–1771.

Umar Butler. 2024. Open Australian Legal Corpus.

Caselaw Access Project. 2018. Caselaw Access Project.

Ilias Chalkidis, Ion Androutsopoulos, and Nikolaos Aletras. 2019. Neural Legal Judgment Prediction in English. In *Proceedings of the 57th Annual Meeting of the Association for Computational Linguistics*, pages 4317–4323.

Ilias Chalkidis, Nicolas Garneau, Catalina Goanta, Daniel Martin Katz, and Anders Søgaard. 2023. LeXFiles and LegalLAMA: Facilitating English Multinational Legal Language Model Development. In *Proceedings of the 61st Annual Meeting of the Association for Computational Linguistics*, pages 15513–15535.

Pierre Colombo, Telmo Pessoa Pires, Malik Boudiaf, Dominic Culver, Rui Melo, Caio Corro, Andre Martins, Fabrizio Esposito, Vera Lúcia Raposo, Sofia Morgado, and Michael Desa. 2024. SaulLM-7B: a pioneering large language model for law. *arXiv:2403.03883*.

Conseil d'État. 2012. Groupe de Travail sur la Rédactions des Décisions de la Jurisdiction Administrative. Technical report, Conseil d'État (France).

Joana Ribeiro de Faria, Huiyuan Xie, and Felix Steffek. 2024. Automatic information extraction from employment tribunal judgements using large language models. *arXiv preprint arXiv:2403.12936*.

Simon Deakin, Zoe Adams, Catherine Barnard, and Sarah Butlin. 2021. *Deakin and Morris' Labour Law*. Hart Publishing.

Jacob Devlin, Ming Wei Chang, Kenton Lee, and Kristina Toutanova. 2019. BERT: Pre-training of Deep Bidirectional Transformers for Language Understanding. In *Proceedings of the 2019 Conference of the North American Chapter of the Association for Computational Linguistics*, pages 4171–4186.

Shizhe Diao, Pengcheng Wang, Yong Lin, and Tong Zhang. 2023. Active Prompting With Chain-of-Thought for Large Language Models. *arXiv preprint arXiv:2302.12246*.

Hubert Field and William Holley. 1982. The Relationship of Performance Appraisal System Characteristics to Verdicts in Selected Employment Discrimination Cases. *The Academy of Management Journal*, 25(2):392–406.

Yunfan Gao, Yun Xiong, Xinyu Gao, Kangxiang Jia, Jinliu Pan, Yuxi Bi, Yi Dai, Jiawei Sun, and Haofen Wang. 2023. Retrieval-Augmented Generation for Large Language Models: A Survey. *arXiv preprint arXiv:2312.10997*.

Werner F. Grunbaum and Albert Newhouse. 1965. Quantitative Analysis of Judicial Decisions: Some Problems in Prediction. *Houston Law Review*, 3:201–220.

Peter Henderson, Mark Krass, Lucia Zheng, Neel Guha, Christopher D Manning, Dan Jurafsky, and Daniel Ho. 2022. Pile of Law: Learning Responsible Data Filtering From the Law and a 256GB Open-source Legal Dataset. *Advances in Neural Information Processing Systems*, pages 32537–32551.

Wonseok Hwang, Dongjun Lee, Kyoungyeon Cho, Hanuhl Lee, and Minjoon Seo. 2022. A Multi-Task Benchmark for Korean Legal Language Understanding and Judgement Prediction. *Advances in Neural Information Processing Systems*, pages 29217–29234.

Judicial Office. 2016. The Judicial System of England and Wales: A Visitor's Guide. Technical report, UK Judicial Office.

Seungone Kim, Se June Joo, Doyoung Kim, Joel Jang, Seonghyeon Ye, Jamin Shin, and Minjoon Seo. 2023. The CoT Collection: Improving Zero-Shot and Few-Shot Learning of Language Models via Chain-of-Thought Fine-Tuning. *arXiv preprint arXiv:2305.14045*.

Diederik P Kingma and Jimmy Ba. 2014. Adam: A Method for Stochastic Optimization. *arXiv preprint arXiv:1412.6980*.

Patrick Lewis, Ethan Perez, Aleksandra Piktus, Fabio Petroni, Vladimir Karpukhin, Naman Goyal, Heinrich Küttler, Mike Lewis, Wen-tau Yih, Tim Rocktäschel, et al. 2020. Retrieval-Augmented Generation for Knowledge-Intensive NLP Tasks. *Advances in Neural Information Processing Systems*, 33:9459–9474.

Luyao Ma, Yating Zhang, Tianyi Wang, Xiaozhong Liu, Wei Ye, Changlong Sun, and Shikun Zhang. 2021. Legal Judgment Prediction with Multi-Stage Case Representation Learning in the Real Court Setting. In *Proceedings of the 44th International ACM SIGIR Conference on Research and Development in Information Retrieval*, pages 993–1002.

Masha Medvedeva and Pauline Mcbride. 2023. Legal Judgment Prediction: If You Are Going To Do It, Do It Right. In *Proceedings of the Natural Legal Language Processing Workshop 2023*, pages 73–84.

Masha Medvedeva, Ahmet Üstün, Xiao Xu, Michel Vols, and Martijn Wieling. 2021. Automatic Judgement Forecasting for Pending Applications of the European Court of Human Rights. In *Proceedings of the Fifth Workshop on Automatec Semantic Analysis of Information in Legal Text*, pages 12–23.

Masha Medvedeva, Martijn Wieling, and Michel Vols. 2023. Rethinking the Field of Automatic Prediction of Court Decisions. *Artificial Intelligence and Law*, 31(1):195–212.

Joel Niklaus, Veton Matoshi, Pooja Rani, Andrea Galassi, Matthias Stürmer, and Ilias Chalkidis. 2023. LEXTREME: A Multi-Lingual and Multi-Task Benchmark for the Legal Domain. *Findings of the Association for Computational Linguistics: EMNLP 2023*, pages 3016–3054.

OpenAI. 2022. Introducing ChatGPT.

Andreas Östling, Holli Sargeant, Huiyuan Xie, Ludwig Bull, Alexander Terenin, Leif Jonsson, Måns Magnusson, and Felix Steffek. 2023. The Cambridge Law Corpus: A Dataset for Legal AI Research. In *Advances in Neural Information Processing Systems*, volume 36, pages 41355–41385.

Conor O'Sullivan and Joeran Beel. 2019. Predicting the Outcome of Judicial Decisions Made by the European Court of Human Rights. In *Irish Conference on Artificial Intelligence and Cognitive Science*, pages 272–283.

Prakash Poudyal, Jaromir Savelka, Aagje Ieven, Marie Francine Moens, Teresa Goncalves, and Paulo Quaresma. 2020. ECHR: Legal Corpus for Argument Mining. In *Proceedings of the 7th Workshop on Argument Mining*, pages 67–75.

Colin Raffel, Noam Shazeer, Adam Roberts, Katherine Lee, Sharan Narang, Michael Matena, Yanqi Zhou, Wei Li, and Peter J Liu. 2020. Exploring the Limits of Transfer Learning with a Unified Text-to-Text Transformer. *The Journal of Machine Learning Research*, 21(1):5485–5551.

Rules. 2013. Employment Tribunals (Constitution and Rules of Procedure) Regulations 2013.

TYS Santosh, Shanshan Xu, Oana Ichim, and Matthias Grabmair. 2022. Deconfounding Legal Judgment Prediction for European Court of Human Rights Cases Towards Better Alignment With Experts. *Proceedings of the 2022 Conference on Empirical Methods in Natural Language Processing*, pages 1120–1138.

Holli Sargeant and Måns Magnusson. 2024. Bias in Legal Data for Generative AI. In *Generative AI and Law (GenLaw '24')*.

Vicki Schultz and Stephen Petterson. 1992. Race, Gender, Work, and Choice: An Empirical Study of the Lack of Interest Defense in Title VII Cases Challenging Job Segregation. *University of Chicago Law Review*.

Michael Schuster and Christopher Miller. 1984. An Empirical Assessment of the Age Discrimination in Employment Act. *ILR Review*.

Benjamin Strickson and Beatriz De La Iglesia. 2020. Legal Judgement Prediction for UK Courts. In *Proceedings of the 3rd International Conference on Information Science and Systems*, pages 204–209.

Ashish Vaswani, Noam Shazeer, Niki Parmar, Jakob Uszkoreit, Llion Jones, Aidan N. Gomez, Lukasz Kaiser, and Illia Polosukhin. 2017. Attention is All You Need. In *Advances in Neural Information Processing Systems*, pages 6000–6010.

Jason Wei, Xuezhi Wang, Dale Schuurmans, Maarten Bosma, Fei Xia, Ed Chi, Quoc V Le, Denny Zhou, et al. 2022. Chain-of-Thought Prompting Elicits Reasoning in Large Language Models. *Advances in Neural Information Processing Systems*, 35:24824–24837.

Thomas Wolf, Lysandre Debut, Victor Sanh, Julien Chaumond, Clement Delangue, Anthony Moi, Pierric Cistac, Tim Rault, Remi Louf, Morgan Funtowicz, Joe Davison, Sam Shleifer, Patrick von Platen, Clara Ma, Yacine Jernite, Julien Plu, Canwen Xu, Teven Le Scao, Sylvain Gugger, Mariama Drame, Quentin Lhoest, and Alexander Rush. 2020. Transformers: State-of-the-Art Natural Language Processing. In *Proceedings of the 2020 Conference on Empirical Methods in Natural Language Processing*, pages 38–45.

Chaojun Xiao, Haoxi Zhong, Zhipeng Guo, Cunchao Tu, Zhiyuan Liu, Maosong Sun, Yansong Feng, Xianpei Han, Zhen Hu, Heng Wang, and Jianfeng Xu. 2018. CAIL2018: A Large-scale Legal Dataset for Judgment Prediction. *arXiv Preprint 1807.02478v1*.

Hiroaki Yamada, Takenobu Tokunaga, Ryutaro Ohara, Keisuke Takeshita, and Mihoko Sumida. 2022. Annotation study of Japanese judgments on tort for legal judgment prediction with rationales. In *Proceedings of the Thirteenth Language Resources and Evaluation Conference*, pages 779–790, Marseille, France. European Language Resources Association.

Haoxi Zhong, Zhipeng Guo, Cunchao Tu, Chaojun Xiao, Zhiyuan Liu, and Maosong Sun. 2018. Legal judgment prediction via topological learning. In *Proceedings of the 2018 Conference on Empirical Methods in Natural Language Processing*, pages 3540–3549, Brussels, Belgium. Association for Computational Linguistics.

A Implementation Details

A.1 Experiment Settings for Transformer Models

The implementation of the two Transformer-based models is based on the HuggingFace transformer library (Wolf et al., 2020). We used the *base* versions for both models, initialised from their pre-trained weights. The BERT-base checkpoint has 110 million parameters. The T5-base checkpoint has 220 million parameters. The maximum input sequence length was set to 512 tokens[9]. We tried different settings for other hyperparameters such as *weight decay* and the number of *warm-up steps*, and found that the values of those hyperparameters have an impact on how fast the model is trained, especially at the beginning steps, but do not have a strong impact on the final learning performance. For this reason, we set both *weight decay* and *warm-up steps* to 0 for ease of model implementation and future replication. All training processes were performed on an Nvidia RTX 8000 GPU.

A.2 Final Prompts Used in the GPT-based Experiments

We experimented with a number of prompts whilst exploring automatic legal annotation using GPT-4 and the prediction of case outcomes with GPT-3.5 and GPT-4. The final prompts that we used were selected based on the quality of the responses from GPT models for the task at hand.

The **information extraction** prompt that we used to extract data from UKET court decisions reads:

> You are a legal assistant. Your task is to read through the court decisions that I will send you, and extract the following information for each input: 1. facts of the case; 2. claims made; 3. any references to legal statutes, acts, regulations, provisions and rules, including the specific number(s), section(s) and article(s) of each of them, and including procedural tribunal rules; 4. references to precedents and other court decisions; 5. general case outcome; 6. general case outcome summarised using one of the four labels - 'claimant wins', 'claimant loses', 'claimant partly wins' and 'other'; 7. detailed order and remedies; 8. essential reasons for the decision (procedural and substantive). If there are multiple claimants or respondents, extract the case outcome for each and all of the claimants or respondents separately. Please stick strictly to the text contents that I will send.

The **zero-shot** prompt that we used for the GPT-3.5 and GPT-4 prediction experiments is:

> You are a legal assistant. Your task is to predict the most likely outcome for a case based on the facts and claims that I will send you. Please summarise the case outcome using one of the four labels - 'claimant wins', 'claimant loses', 'claimant partly wins' and 'other'. Note that the label 'other' is to be reserved for cases for which the result cannot be predicted or where the outcome cannot be described in terms of winning or losing (*e.g.*, a merely procedural decision such as a stay or an evidence collection). The output should be one of the four labels.

The **few-shot** prompt that we used for GPT-3.5 and GPT-4 prediction experiments is:

> You are a legal assistant. Your task is to read through a few examples of legal case outcome prediction that I will send you and predict the most likely outcome for a case based on the facts and claims that I will send you. Please summarise the case outcome using one of the four labels - 'claimant wins', 'claimant loses', 'claimant partly wins' and 'other'. Note that the label 'other' is to be reserved for cases for which the result cannot be predicted or where the outcome cannot be described in terms of winning or losing (*e.g.*, a merely procedural decision such as a stay or an evidence collection). The output should be one of the four labels.
>
> To give you a few examples:
>
> Case example #1
>
> Facts: <FACTS>
>
> Claims: <CLAIMS>
>
> The case outcome label is: <OUTCOME LABEL>

[9]All input texts to BERT and T5 are under this token length limit.

<OTHER CASE EXAMPLES>

Case to be predicted:

Facts: <FACTS>

Claims: <CLAIMS>

What is the most likely case outcome?

B Further Analysis of the CLC-UKET Dataset

B.1 Examples From the CLC-UKET Dataset

Table 6 presents facts, claims and general case outcomes for two cases in the CLC-UKET$_{pred}$ dataset. Facts and claims are extracted annotations from GPT-4. Facts and claims are concatenated to form the input to the prediction task. Outcome labels are manually extracted by a legal expert from court judgments and are used as the target output of the prediction task.

B.2 Page Count Distribution

We calculated the page counts for the 52,339 court decisions in the original UKET subset in the CLC, which gives an essential idea of the length distribution of case decisions heard by the UKET.

From Table 7, it can be observed that the majority of cases (approximately 62.8%) have a decision document consisting of just one page. Of these, many only contain short decisions due to procedural aspects, such as claimants withdrawing their claims or respondents not responding at all. In such instances, the court judgments do not provide substantial information on the actual facts and substantive reasoning. Against this background, we excluded most of these very brief cases when constructing the CLC-UKET dataset.

B.3 Jurisdiction Codes

There are 54 jurisdiction codes linked to UKET cases[10]. A case can be associated with multiple codes if it involves multiple issues.

Here is a comprehensive list of jurisdiction codes in UKET: employment-agencies-act-1973, rights-on-insolvency, statutory-discipline-and-grievance-procedures, religion-or-belief-discrimination, interim-relief, race-discrimination, time-to-train, notice-appeal, fixed-term-regulations, trade-union-membership, agency-workers, national-minimum-wage, written-statements, flexible-working, parental-and-maternity-leave, redundancy, harassment, human-rights, reorganisation, health-safety, unfair-dismissal, protective-award, victimisation-discrimination, written-pay-statement, maternity-and-pregnancy-rights, unlawful-deduction-from-wages, contract-of-employment, part-time-workers, sex-discrimination, equal-pay-act, disability-discrimination, practice-and-procedure-issues, public-interest-disclosure, right-to-be-accompanied, blacklisting-regulations, tax, sexual-orientation-discrimination-transexualism, time-limits, breach-of-contract, trade-union-rights, age-discrimination, certification-officer, pension, jurisdictional-points, temporary-employment, transfer-of-undertakings, working-time-regulations, renumeration, improvement-notice, european-material, time-off, reserved-forces-act, central-arbitration-committee-cac, national-security.

[10]These codes are available at the UKET website at https://www.gov.uk/employment-tribunal-decisions.

C Aggregating "wins" and "partly wins"

In Table 8, we present evaluation results for individual categories (*i.e.*, "wins", "loses" and "other") in the ablation study where the "wins" and "partly wins" labels are aggregated. The results show that when we no longer differentiate between "wins" and "partly wins", both the baseline models and human predictions achieve higher scores for the "wins" category.

D Human Prediction for UKET Case Outcomes

D.1 Annotation guidelines

D.1.1 Introduction

This UKET prediction project explores the intersection of technological innovation and access to law by predicting dispute outcomes in the UK Employment Tribunal (UKET). We implement a range of deep learning models as baselines for this task. To calibrate model performance, we are interested in investigating how well legal experts in the relevant field can predict the most likely outcomes given facts and claims of UKET cases. This investigation is of paramount importance as the human annotations can be used as a performance "upper bound" to facilitate more informative model comparison.

D.1.2 Data annotation

Each row in the distributed data sheet corresponds to a UKET case. The information provided for the case includes the case identifier, facts of the case

Facts	The Claimant, Mr. B Shaw, was employed as a Business Adviser by the 2nd Respondent from 10 April 2007 until 30 April 2015. His employment then transferred under TUPE to the 3rd Respondent until he was made redundant on 30 June 2015. At the time of redundancy, the Claimant was 70 years old and had been continuously employed for 8 complete years. His rate of pay was £124 per day for a 4 day week, which is £496 per week. Both the 2nd and 3rd Respondents were insolvent. The Claimant was never employed by the 4th Respondent.
Claims	The Claimant presented a claim for a redundancy payment to the Employment Tribunal.
Outcome	Claimant wins

(a) Case 3346845/2016.

Facts	Facts: The claimant, Mr P Soennecken, was employed by the respondent, Otis Limited, as a Lift Engineer. On 17 November 2017, he was asked to attend the M&S store in Newbury because two passengers were trapped in a lift. He arrived at the store, parked outside and entered carrying his test tool but without his personal protective equipment (PPE) or other equipment provided by the respondent to ensure protection of health and safety when working on lifts. He proceeded to rescue the passengers from the lift by helping them to jump from the lift to the floor, which was just over 30cm from the floor level. He did not use a barrier to protect the gap between the lift and the floor. After he had completed the rescue of the passengers, the claimant returned to his van and collected his PPE and other equipment and proceeded to repair the broken lift. This resulted in the passengers complaining to M&S about the claimant, which in turn led to M&S complaining to the respondent. On receipt of the complaint, the respondent suspended the claimant pending an investigation carried out by Barry Sanderson. The allegations were breach of the cardinal rule by failing to use effective barriers, breaches of health and safety by failing to wear safety cap and gloves, not following correct procedures when releasing passengers from a lift car, a complaint in the manner the claimant spoke to the trapped passengers. Having reviewed the evidence and the representations made on behalf of the claimant, Mr Jenkinson concluded that Allegations 1, 2 and 3 were made out and he took the decision to dismiss the claimant summarily for gross misconduct. This was notified to him by letter dated 24 January 2018. He was given the right of appeal against the decision. He appealed by letter dated 25 January 2018 and the appeal meeting was held on 6 February conducted by Alex Lampe. Having reviewed the evidence and the representations made on behalf of the claimant, Mr Lampe upheld the decision to dismiss.
Claims	The claimant's complaints of unfair dismissal and wrongful dismissal.
Outcome	Claimant loses

(b) Case 2204650/2018.

Table 6: Examples from the CLC-UKET$_{pred}$ dataset.

Page count	#Cases	Page count	#Cases
1	32,853	6	523
2	8,604	7	415
3	1,722	8	461
4	1,137	9	379
5	722	≥ 10	5,523

Table 7: Page count distribution of the 52,339 UKET cases in the CLC.

and claims made by the applicant(s). Annotators are asked to predict the most likely case outcome based on the facts and claims.

We have 1,371 cases to be annotated in total. Case assignments:

- Annotator A: rows 2 to 1372 (1,371 cases)
- Annotator B: rows 2 to 1372 (1,371 cases)

D.1.3 Annotation instructions

Annotators' prediction for a case outcome should be one of the following four labels: "Claimant Wins", "Claimant Loses", "Claimant Partly Wins" and "Other". Please use the dropdown menu under the "Annotator's Prediction (dropdown)" column to select your predicted case outcome label.

Cases should be annotated from the perspective of the Claimant, identified as such in the Facts section. By way of example, if the claim is withdrawn, the Claimant loses because the claim is not successful. In cases where there is an Appellant and a Respondent, the Appellant is to be treated as Claimant.

The label "Other" is to be reserved for cases for which the result cannot be predicted (in the sense that the litigation is not about winning or losing; this does not cover uncertainty on the annotator's side) or where the outcome cannot be described in terms of winning or losing (*e.g.*, instead of the final decision applied for, the court makes merely procedural decision such as a stay or an evidence collection). To be precise: if the Claimant applies for a procedural decision and the court awards it (does not award it), then the correct label is "Claimant Wins" ("Claimant Loses"). If the Claimant applies for a substantive decision (*e.g.*, payment) and the court makes a procedural decision, which does not

Baseline	Label	Precision	Recall	F-score
BERT	wins	0.620	0.902	0.735
	loses	0.869	0.215	0.345
	other	0.036	0.455	0.067
T5	wins	0.819	0.621	0.707
	loses	0.647	0.846	0.734
	other	0	0	0
GPT-3.5$_{juris5}$	wins	0.710	0.814	0.758
	loses	0.720	0.565	0.633
	other	0.143	0.455	0.217
GPT-4$_{juris2}$	wins	0.668	0.883	0.761
	loses	0.778	0.430	0.554
	other	0.082	0.364	0.133
Human	wins	0.832	0.823	0.828
	loses	0.792	0.812	0.802
	other	0	0	0

Table 8: Evaluation scores obtained by baseline models and human predictions for the three label categories when "wins" and "partly wins" are combined into a single category "wins". As such, *wins* refers to the aggregated labels "claimant wins" and "claimant partly wins". *Loses* and *other* refer to the labels "claimant loses" and "other", respectively. For GPT-3.5 and GPT-4, the variants that achieved the highest F-scores across relevant settings are presented.

finally resolve the substantive application (*e.g.*, by striking out an application for lack of jurisdiction), then the correct label is "Other".

The label "Claimant Partly Wins" can be used when there is just one claim made or when multiple claims are made. If only one claim is made, the label "Claimant Partly Wins" applies if the Claimant will generally win, however, not be successful with the entirety of the claim. This is the case, where a Claimant applies for damages of £100 but will likely only be awarded £50. Additionally, you may infer a "Claimant Partly Wins" from other information in the Facts and Claims section than amounts. If multiple claims are made, the label applied if the Claimant will likely be successful with at least one claim in part but not with all claims in full. This is the case, where a Claimant applies for payment of wages of £100 and damages of £100 and will likely only be awarded £100 wages (but no damages). Again, a "Claimant Partly Wins" label may be inferred from other information than amounts. If there are multiple claims or decisions combining an outcome of "Claimant Wins", "Claimant Loses" or "Claimant Partly Wins" with an outcome of "Other" the latter shall be ignored and the case overall is to be annotated as "Claimant Wins", "Claimant Loses" or "Claimant Partly Wins".

Please make predictions ONLY based on the facts and the claims. Please do not search for the case on the internet. You may consult general legal information (textbooks, internet databases, etc.) that do not refer to the specific case at hand.

For cases where the annotators are not confident about a prediction (defined as a confidence level below 50%), please still make a prediction using one of the four labels AND tick "Yes" in the "Low Confidence" column. This may be the case, for example, where there are only few facts or facts presented as claims the Claimant raises. Please leave the "Low Confidence" cell blank for cases where annotators are relatively confident about the predictions (*i.e.*, with a confidence level greater or equal than 50%). Please note down questions and comments that you may have whilst annotating the cases in the "Notes (if any)" column, especially if a case is complicated and hard to predict an outcome for, or if a case is interesting from the legal perspective and would be a good example for later case study. For example, it might occur that the facts section is absolutely insufficient to predict the label, in which case you should write "insufficient facts" in the "Notes (if any)" column. If there are multiple claims, and you are not confident only with regard to one of the claims, please indicate that the insufficient facts or the particular issue relate to one (and please state which one) particular claim, in the "Notes (if any)" section.

Annotators should make their judgments separately (*i.e.*, without discussions amongst themselves). This is crucial to ensure the robustness of the annotation results.

Label	Kappa Score
claimant wins	0.322
claimant loses	0.191
claimant partly wins	0.284
other	0.470

Table 9: Annotators' agreement across four label categories, measured by Cohen's Kappa scores.

E Annotators' agreement across label categories

In Table 9 we report Cohen's Kappa scores for the predictions of two annotators under four label categories - *claimant wins, claimant loses, claimant partly wins* and *other*.

Information Extraction for Planning Court Cases

Drish Mali
The University of Edinburgh
D.Mali@sms.ed.ac.uk

Rubash Mali
Himalaya College of Engineering
rubash@hcoe.edu.np

Claire Barale
The University of Edinburgh
claire.barale@ed.ac.uk

Abstract

Legal documents are often long and unstructured, making them challenging and time-consuming to apprehend. An automatic system that can identify relevant entities and labels within legal documents, would significantly reduce the legal research time. We developed a system to streamline legal case analysis from planning courts by extracting key information from XML files using Named Entity Recognition (NER) and multi-label classification models to convert them into structured form. This research contributes three novel datasets for the Planning Court cases: a NER dataset, a multi-label dataset fully annotated by humans, and newly re-annotated multi-label datasets partially annotated using LLMs. We experimented with various general-purpose and legal domain-specific models with different maximum sequence lengths. It was noted that incorporating paragraph position information improved the performance of models for the multi-label classification task. Our research highlighted the importance of domain-specific models, with LegalRoBERTa and LexLM demonstrating the best performance.

1 Introduction

The use of Artificial Intelligence (AI) techniques within the legal domain has been rapidly growing, transforming the way legal professionals handle their complex tasks (Jacey and Yuniarti, 2023). The advancement in Natural Language Processing (NLP) in legal informatics (Krasadakis et al., 2024; Quevedo et al., 2023) has significantly enhanced tasks such as question-answering, judgment predictions, and information extraction from legal text (Zhong et al., 2020; Barale et al., 2023; Licari et al., 2023). For countries with common-law jurisdictions like the UK and the US, legal research needs to be consistent with referencing similar past cases (Shulayeva et al., 2017). However, legal research is extremely time-consuming due to the extensive length of legal texts (Vági, 2023) and the need for domain expertise to navigate the specialised vocabulary and legal jargon (Cemri et al., 2022). Additionally, the unstructured nature of legal documents, such as court hearings, adds to the complexity (Li and Li, 2021). To address these challenges, an NLP-based technique that can automatically extract relevant information from unstructured legal cases into a structured format would be highly beneficial. The primary task is twofold: (1) structuring the raw document formats (PDF and XML) of these Planning Court cases, and (2) curating a novel dataset to support future research efforts. To achieve this, we apply Named Entity Recognition (NER) and multi-label classification techniques, which are effective at organizing and categorizing legal information.

Large Language Models (LLMs) have demonstrated strong capabilities in the legal sector (Fei et al., 2023a), but they require large amounts of domain-specific, accurate data (Lai et al., 2023).We choose to use traditional extractive methods, such as named-entity recognition, which are well suited to the need for precision in the legal workflow and do not yield hallucinations. We opt to build upon those methods that are widely used by legal search softwares and propose to improve them using LLMs. This research focuses on cases from the Planning Court, part of the Administrative Court of England and Wales [1], provided by the Find Case Law service of The National Archives UK. It addresses two main issues: structuring the initial document format (PDF and XML) of Planning Court cases using LLMs, and curating a novel dataset for future research. We have employed NER and multilabel classification to bring structure to it. The project will benefit:

- **Legal Professionals:** For legal professionals

[1] https://www.judiciary.uk/courts-and-tribunals/high-court/administrative-court/planning-court

Proceedings of the Natural Legal Language Processing Workshop 2024, pages 97–114
November 16, 2024 ©2024 Association for Computational Linguistics

this system will make the searching of similar cases easier and streamline the legal research process as compared to the traditional manual searching approach (Vági, 2023). It would improve efficiency in legal research, enabling professionals to make more consistent decisions and prepare better for new cases (Barale et al., 2023).

- **Legal NLP Researchers:** The generated structured data will be a valuable asset for various research areas such as judgment prediction, summarisation, drafting, and content selection tasks. The availability of such data facilitates the exploration of new research questions, reducing the challenge of finding high-quality human-labeled legal domain-specific datasets (Song et al., 2022). This study also contributes to filling knowledge gaps in research on Planning Court cases.

The primary research questions guiding the project are as follows:

1. **RQ1:** Can language models accurately extract legal entities such as court name, location, citation, judges, and date from legal cases?

2. **RQ2:** Can language models comprehend legal text and classify it as introduction, factual text, citations to other cases, and judgment?

3. **RQ3:** Do transformer-based models pre-trained in the legal domain perform better than general-purpose models in legal entity extraction and multi-label classification?

To address these research questions, this study investigated the utility of language models in extracting information from legal documents specific to the Planning Court. Our contributions are as follows: (1) we create a novel dataset of Planning Court cases specifically curated for NER and multi-label classification, (2) we propose an end-to-end pipeline to extract and structure this data using NER and multi-label classification to analyse those cases automatically by extracting legally relevant entities and paragraphs, (3) lastly we create a structured database from our results, allowing for a quick and efficient search based on the extracted entities.

2 Background and Related Work

2.1 Legal Named Entity Recognition (NER)

NER is a foundational task of Natural Language Processing (NLP), where algorithms are trained to detect and classify entities like location, date or person in the given text (Yu et al., 2020). NER models perform token classification. Research on NER approaches has been ongoing for decades, utilizing methods like graph-based dependency parsing, LSTM, maximum entropy (Yu et al., 2020; Chieu and Ng, 2003; Chiu and Nichols, 2015). With the current advancements in transformer-based models, the performance of NER tasks has been improving significantly. Models like T5 and XLM-RoBERTa have achieved state-of-the-art results (Tavan and Najafi, 2022; Pu et al., 2022). However, the challenge with legal texts is their length and complexity (Mamakas et al., 2022a). They are often difficult to understand due to their complex language, ambiguities, cross-references, frequent amendments, and the specialized legal jargon involved, which requires domain-specific knowledge(Cemri et al., 2022; Ganguly et al.; Otto and Antón, 2009). Additionally, the domain-specific entities like courts, judges, statutes, and articles make the general NER models incompatible with legal documents (Zhao et al., 2023). Transformer-based models have shown promising results even for legal NER tasks (Kalamkar et al., 2022; Barale et al., 2023; Li et al., 2022; Bernsohn et al., 2024). These models perform well across various languages and legal systems (Kalamkar et al., 2022; Păis et al., 2023; Luz de Araujo et al., 2018; Smădu et al., 2022).

For evaluation of the Legal NER systems previous research has used a macro-average F1 score, as there can be an imbalance in the distribution of entities in legal texts (Barale et al., 2023; Keshavarz et al., 2022; Skylaki et al., 2020). Precision and recall are "also crucial for advancing future research and meeting the needs of potential legal end users" (Barale et al., 2023). High precision means the model identifies mostly correct entities, while high recall ensures it finds most of the relevant entities.

2.2 Multi-label classification in legal context

Multi-label classification is a supervised learning method where a single instance of input, such as text, image, or sound, can have multiple labels from a predefined set (Pant et al., 2018; de Leon Ferreira de Carvalho and Freitas, 2009). Compared

to simple multi-class classification problems, multi-label classification is more complex as labels are not mutually exclusive leading to challenges such as label space dimensionality, label drifting, data imbalance, and label dependency (Pant et al., 2018). Multi-label problems can be addressed using multi-class algorithms with a Binary Relevance transformation (Pereira et al., 2018). But it would be extremely slow as for N labels we would require N number of binary classification models (one model for each class) which would not be feasible. Another issue in multi-label classification is choosing evaluation metrics, which can be label-based or instance-based. Popular metrics for such tasks include hamming loss, exact match, AUC PR score, precision, recall, and F1 score (Pereira et al., 2018; Riyanto et al., 2023).
For legal text, the main problem with the dataset is the imbalance of labels, as some labels occur frequently while others are rare. To tackle this problem, F1 score and hamming loss are good candidate metrics (ster et al., 2024; Pereira et al., 2018). Hamming loss evaluates the fraction of incorrectly predicted labels relative to the total number of labels, and the F1 score considers both precision and recall, providing a balance between them. Domain-specific encoder-based models like LEGAL-BERT and LegalRoBERTa (ster et al., 2024; Geng et al., 2021) have shown impressive performance, but as noted, the length of legal texts is large. Therefore, larger models like Longformer and BIGBIRD, which support a larger maximum sequence length, may be needed (Mamakas et al., 2022b). Recent advancements in legal research have led to even larger domain-specific models like LexLM, which offer both larger max sequences and domain knowledge (Chalkidis* et al., 2023).

2.3 Prompting and Few-shot learning

Prompting is the task of providing input instructions to large language models (LLMs) such that these pre-trained models generate output through analogical learning (Bhandari, 2024; Chang et al., 2024). Advancements in LLMs have made prompting a standard approach for various NLP tasks (Chang et al., 2024). However, such models are extremely resource-intensive and require significant effort from the human side to design effective prompts as each model has their prompt format.

While paid services like ChatGPT offer powerful options, cost-effective alternatives like open-source models such as LLaMA (Touvron et al., 2023) also exist. To mitigate the computational demands of open-source models, techniques like Post-Training Quantization can be applied (Zhang et al., 2023) where the size of weights of a neural network are reduced without any retraining. This approach can reduce the computing resource requirements but may also diminish the model's capabilities, creating a performance versus resource trade-off. One solution to this challenge is to use 4-bit quantization (Jin et al., 2024) along with the NF4 Quantization scheme(Dettmers et al., 2023), and use bfloat16 format for performing computations, which aims to balance both the accuracy and efficiency of LLMs. Acquiring adequate amounts of labeled data is quite difficult (Bahrami et al., 2023) in today's day and age, especially with legal data being complex, unstructured, and rare to find. One of the boons of the emerging research in LLMs is their ability to learn patterns and perform specific tasks with few examples, a method called few-shot learning. Few-shot learning involves providing tasks based on a few particular examples in the prompt, allowing LLMs to understand the task, analyse the given examples, and infer accordingly (Brown et al., 2020). This technique has shown promising results in various NLP tasks, including text classification, and sentiment analysis (Min et al., 2021) with larger models like GPT4 and LLaMA performing well in the legal domain (Fei et al., 2023b). However, using few-shot examples alone is not always efficient, especially for complex domain-specific tasks (Naguib et al., 2024; Jayakumar et al., 2023), for such cases domain-specific models are required.

3 Data Collection and Exploratory Data Analysis (EDA)

3.1 Case data collection

We filtered data for Planning Court cases using the keyword search "planning court" on the Case Law service of The National Archives UK, yielding 845 cases. These documents were available in both PDF and XML formats, and we chose XML to avoid data inaccuracies associated with OCR processing of PDFs. These cases can be divided into two sections: the cover section (which contains the initial page of case with typical information as the neutral citation of the case, judges involved, date of the judgment.), the main section (includes the hearing cases from introduction to judgment). By analysing the XML document structure and using the National Archives of the LegalDocM-

L/Akoma Ntoso XML format (Palmirani and Vitali, 2011), it was identified that the cover section was located within the header tag and the main section within the <judgmentBody>tag. We extracted case-wise cover section data by retrieving text inside the <p>tags within the header tag, and the main section data by retrieving text inside the <p>tags within the <judgmentBody>tag. The cover text data was used to train the NER model, while the main section data was used to train the multi-label classification model as illustrated in Figure 1.

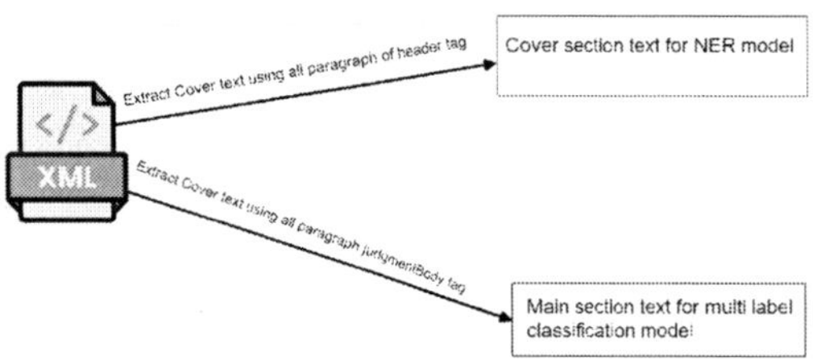

Figure 1: Overall workflow of the data extraction from XML file.

3.2 Cover Section Data Annotation and EDA

We obtained 845 cover sections and used the IOB (Inside, Outside, Beginning) format for annotating entities (Krishnan and Ganapathy, 2005). The entities we extracted using the NER model are 'Citation', 'Court', 'Judge', 'Location' and 'Date' (further descriptions and examples of these entities are listed in the appendix section). These categories were chosen for their crucial role in legal search workflows. 'Citation' aids in linking relevant cases, while 'Court' and 'Judge' allow filtering by jurisdiction or authority. 'Location' helps with regional relevance, and 'Date' enables chronological tracking of cases. For data labeling and creating the NER dataset, we utilised the UBIAI platform.

To understand the data better, we examined the word count of each cover section and the number of labeled entities present in this NER dataset. The descriptive statistics for the word count of all cases are detailed in Table 1. From observing the word counts, it became clear that models with at least a maximum token capacity of 2048 are required. Seventy-five percent of documents have cover sections with fewer words than 1339, about 1741 tokens (1 word is about 1.3 tokens [2]). Further analysis revealed that about 85% of cases have a cover section with fewer than 1500 words (about 2000 tokens), reinforcing the need for models with a 2048 maximum token capacity.

Table 1: Descriptive Statistics of Word Count for Cover Section Data

Statistic	Value
Average Word Count	1199.421
Minimum Word Count	94
Q1 (25%) of Word Count	960
Median (50%) of Word Count	1132
Q3 (75%) of Word Count	1339
Maximum Word Count	5877

The bar plot depicted in Figure 2 shows the counts of various entities within an NER dataset, highlighting the distribution of different entity types. The entity DATE has the highest frequency, appearing 1645 times, while CITATION is the least frequent with 971 occurrences. This visualisation underscores the prevalence of DATE entities in the dataset compared to others and indicates that the dataset is not balanced.

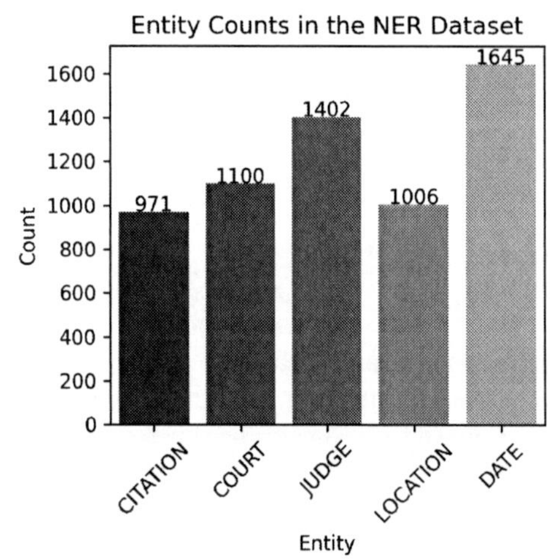

Figure 2: Distribution of Entities in NER Dataset

3.3 Main Section Data Annotation and EDA

We collected 140,377 paragraphs from 845 cases and decided to use four labels: introduction, fact, citation, and judgment for the multi-label classification task. These labels were chosen after discussions and suggestions from domain experts. The core motivation for selecting these four labels was to identify text segments that are important to legal professionals and to ensure that the annotation could be done without requiring specialised legal domain expertise. Due to time constraints and the

[2]https://platform.openai.com/tokenizer.

labor-intensive nature of manual annotation, we decided to annotate 400 out of 845 cases, resulting in 59,302 annotated paragraphs. Descriptive statistics for the word count of paragraphs in the main section are provided in Table 2, detailed descriptions with examples of each label are included in the Appendix. We initially grouped all the paragraphs

Table 2: Descriptive Statistics for Main Section Data

Statistic	Value
Total Number of paragraphs	140377
Average Word Count	359.85
Minimum Word Count	4
Q1 (25%) of Word Count	94
Median (50%) of Word Count	255
Q3 (75%) of Word Count	516
Maximum Word Count	4408

according to cases and manually labeled them. To visualise the data we plotted a bar chart showing the count of paragraphs and their respective labels, as illustrated in Figure 3. The distribution is imbalanced, with the 'fact' label having the highest count (15,511 paragraphs), while the 'introduction' and 'judgment' labels have the lowest counts (1,792 and 422 paragraphs, respectively). This imbalance is expected, as a case usually has a single paragraph for the conclusion, a few for the introduction, but many paragraphs presenting facts.

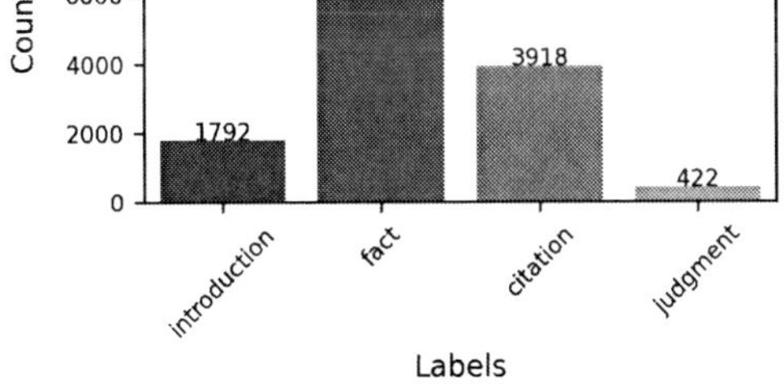

Figure 3: Distribution of label in multi-label Dataset

3.4 Main Section Data re-annotation and EDA

We re-annotated the data after identifying that separating paragraphs using tags disrupted the context needed for accurate labeling. An example of such a case is presented in Figure 4 where the context of the first paragraph is crucial to understanding the second paragraph. The first paragraph mentions the rule CPR, and the second paragraph elaborates on it. If examined individually, the first paragraph should have a fact label of 1 and the second paragraph a fact label of 0. However, as the second paragraph continues from the first, both should be labeled with a fact label of 1. To address this, we restructured and re-annotated the data.

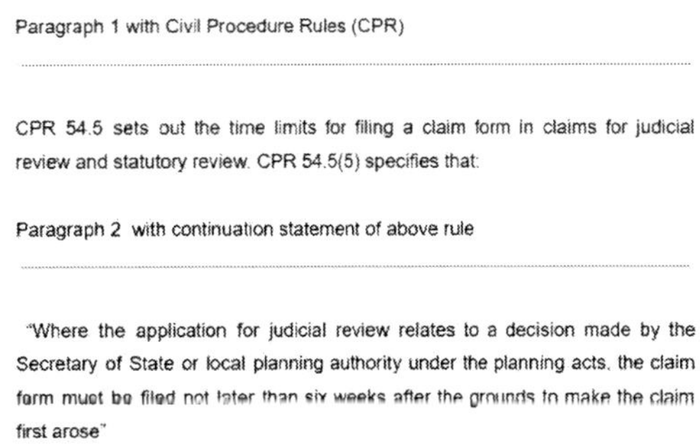

Figure 4: Example of paragraphs needing context from preceding paragraph

We improved paragraph extraction from the XML files by using the <num>tag with a style attribute, which allowed connected paragraphs to be treated as a single and made paragraphs longer. This approach resolved the previous issue as mentioned in Figure 4, enabling the extraction of 69,881 paragraphs from 845 cases. Similar to above approach, we looked into the descriptive statistics of the word count of paragraphs presented in Table 3 and 85% of the paragraphs contained fewer than 1,200 words, indicating that models with a maximum token size of around 1,536 tokens would be appropriate for this task.

Table 3: Descriptive Statistics for Re-annotation Data

Statistic	Value
Total Number of paragraphs	69,881
Average Word Count	766.75
Minimum Word Count	4
Q1 (25%) of Word Count	341
Median (50%) of Word Count	579
Q3 (75%)of Word Count	938
Maximum of Word Count	46,559

For the re-annotation process, we utilised both manual and automated methods. We manually labeled the 'introduction' and 'judgment' categories by reviewing the initial and final paragraphs of each case. For the 'fact' and 'citation' labels, we employed large language models (LLMs) due to the need for detailed paragraph analysis. We employed the LLaMA 3 70B model with 18 few-shot examples to predict whether paragraphs contained 'citation', achieving 86% accuracy (345 correct out of 400 randomly sampled paragraphs), the prompt for this task is presented in Figure 8. For the 'fact' label, LLaMA 3's performance was unsatisfactory, so we used ChatGPT 3.5, which accurately labeled 241 out of 300 randomly sampled paragraphs (about 80% accuracy) using five examples for a few-shot classification. We used a combination of 4-bit quantization along with double quantization, utilizing the NF4 quantization scheme, and performing computations in bfloat16 to achieve efficient and accurate LLaMA 3 model inference. As shown in Figure 5, the re-annotated data remains highly imbalanced, with the 'fact' label dominating at 45,774 paragraphs, while 'introduction' and 'judgment' labels have 3,429 and 948 paragraphs, respectively.

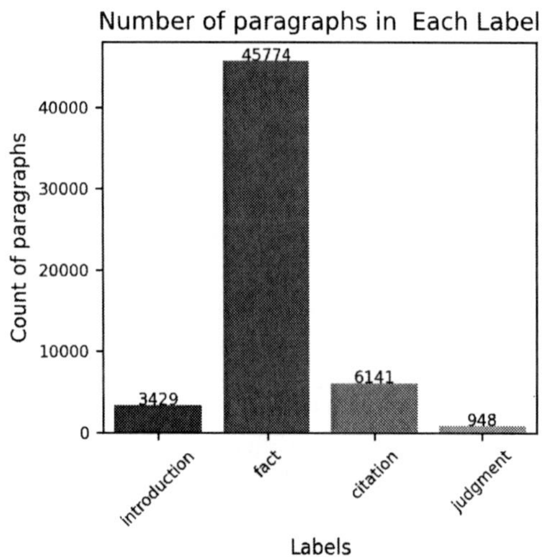

Figure 5: Distribution of label for re-annotated multi-label Dataset

4 Experimental Setup and Modeling

Experimental Setup for NER task: Literature suggests that models like LEGAL-BERT (Chalkidis et al., 2020) have been performing very well for NER tasks in the legal domain (Barale et al., 2023; Keshavarz et al., 2022; Kalamkar et al., 2022). However, the maximum sequence size of such BERT (Devlin et al., 2019) based models is just 512 tokens. Our EDA of NER data (Section 3.2) indicated that we would need models with larger maximum sequence lengths than 512 tokens, making it necessary to explore models with larger maximum sequence lengths. For legal text, such a smaller token size can be restrictive (Mamakas et al., 2022c). In our search for other legal domain-specific models, we identified two additional options: LegalRoBERTa (Geng et al., 2021) that still had 512 tokens as max sequence size limit, and LexLM supports 4096 tokens (Chalkidis et al., 2023). Further research led us to Google's BIGBIRD (Zaheer et al., 2021) model that also supports 4096 tokens. Given these findings, we decided to experiment with these four models which were available in the huggingface platform (Wolf et al., 2020). This selection allows us to evaluate both general-purpose and legal domain-specific models, and also compare the performance of models with smaller (512 tokens) and larger (4096 tokens) maximum sequence lengths. We had a total of 845 cases from which we got 845 cover sections, we split the data in a 70:15:15 ratio for train, test, and validation splits respectively. The models were trained on an NVIDIA A100 GPU with the following training configurations: Learning Rate: 1×10^{-5}, Number of Epochs: 200, Weight Decay: 0.01, Per Device Train Batch Size: 16, Per Device Eval Batch Size: 16, LR Scheduler Type: Cosine, Warmup Ratio: 0.1, Evaluation Strategy: Epoch, Save Strategy: Epoch, and Early Stopping Patience: 30.

As illustrated in Figure 2, the dataset is slightly imbalanced. To account for this, we report the Area Under the Precision-Recall Curve (AUC-PRC) score, which "measures the fraction of true positives among positive predictions" and varies with the ratio of positives to negatives (Saito and Rehmsmeier, 2015). Although the imbalance was not severe with the least frequent entity, 'citation,' still occurring 971 times, the variation in class frequencies was significant enough to warrant consideration. Therefore, we chose to report the F1 score, precision, and recall for each model.

Experimental Setup for multi-label classification: Multi-label classification in the legal domain is challenging due to severe label imbalance and complex label co-occurrence patterns (Forster et al., 2024). Models like LEGAL-BERT, DistilBERT (Sanh et al., 2020), LegalRoBERTa, and LexLM (Forster et al., 2024; Chalkidis et al., 2023; Wei et al., 2023; Geng et al., 2021) have shown impressive performance in legal multi-label text classification task. From our EDA in Section 3.3, it became clear that we would need models with sequence sizes of about 1,000 tokens. Similar to our NER experiment setup, we explored variations using legal domain-specific and general-purpose models with different maximum sequence sizes. To add another model with a larger maximum sequence size, we again selected the BIGBIRD model. Hence, we decided to use the five models mentioned above. The models were trained on three NVIDIA A100 Tensor Core GPUs using accelerate package [3]. Similar to the NER task, we had 845 cases with 59,302 paragraphs. We opted to split the data case-wise rather than label-wise to maintain the distribution of labels as they would appear in actual case documents. The data was divided into a 70:15:15 ratio for training, testing, and validation splits. The configuration for training is as follows: Per Device Train Batch Size: 16, Per Device Eval Batch Size: 16, Number of Epochs: 30, Evaluation Strategy: Epoch, Save Strategy: Epoch, Checkpoint Limit: 2, and Early Stopping Patience: 15.

Figure 3 highlighted the significant imbalance in the label distribution. To address this issue, we decided to report the F1 score as one of our primary evaluation metrics. The AUC-ROC score was selected because it balances precision and recall, while the Hamming loss was chosen for its sensitivity to class imbalance, capturing errors across all labels, including the rare ones. To check an individual model performance across each label, we assessed performance by reporting the F1 score, AUC-ROC score, recall, precision, and accuracy.

Experimental Setup for re-annotated multi-label classification: In evaluating the re-annotated multi-label data, we used the same four models: LEGAL-BERT, LegalRoBERTa, and LexLM, excluding DistilBERT due to its poor performance with the multi-label data. The evaluation metrics and train test evaluation splits ratio were consistent with those used for the original multi-label data. The only change in the training configuration was a reduction in batch size to 8, which was necessary to manage the increased memory requirements. This adjustment was made because the re-annotated data contained more words, as shown in Table 3, resulting in more tokens per paragraph.

[3]https://github.com/huggingface/accelerate.

5 Evaluation

5.1 Named Entity Recognition (NER) Evaluation

We evaluated these models using these metrics: average precision, recall, F1 score, and AUC-PR score. The results are presented in Table 4. The results clearly show that the LexLM model performed best in terms of precision, and AUC-PR. Meanwhile, LegalRoBERTa excelled in recall and F1 score. As anticipated, the general-purpose Google BIGBIRD model performed the worst among the models tested.

Table 4: Evaluation metrics for different legal models for the NER task

Model	Precision	Recall	F1	AUC PR
LexLM	**0.802**	0.795	0.798	**0.943**
Legal-BERT	0.799	0.804	**0.802**	**0.943**
Legal-RoBERTa	0.791	**0.813**	**0.802**	0.939
Google BigBird	0.731	0.724	0.727	0.926

5.2 Multi-label classification task Evaluation

During data annotation, we observed that "Introduction" typically appears in earlier paragraphs, while labels like "Judgment" appear towards the end. Based on this observation, we decided to test models with and without paragraph position information. The paragraph information was added to the text by explicitly mentioning the paragraph number before the paragraph content. Table 5 and Table 6 show the overall performance metrics for each model, including ROC AUC score, Hamming loss, and F1 score. Including paragraph position information in the models significantly improved their performance across all metrics. Without this information, LegalRoBERTa consistently outperformed other models in most metrics except recall, where it lagged slightly. With the inclusion of this information, the performance differences among models became more balanced. This suggested that models can better interpret and classify legal text with this additional contextual information. Additionally, the models exhibited varied strengths across different labels, indicating that no single model was universally superior. LegalRoBERTa and LexLM were particularly effective, demonstrating strong adaptability and consistent performance enhancements with the added paragraph position context.

Table 5: Evaluation metrics for different models for the multi-label dataset

Model	ROC AUC	Hamming Loss	F1 Score
DistilBERT	0.803	**0.048**	0.675
LexLM	0.800	0.053	0.643
LEGAL-BERT	0.820	**0.048**	0.669
LegalRoBERTa	**0.849**	**0.048**	**0.707**
Google BigBird	0.739	0.053	0.538

Table 6: Evaluation metrics for different models for the multi-label dataset with paragraph information

Model	ROC AUC	Hamming Loss	F1 Score
DistilBERT	0.825	0.046	0.721
LexLM	**0.847**	0.046	0.665
LEGAL-BERT	0.840	0.051	0.734
LegalRoBERTa	0.843	**0.042**	**0.745**
Google BigBird	0.812	0.049	0.654

5.3 Re-annotation Multi-label Task Evaluation

We experimented with three models: LegalRoBERTa, LexLM, and Google BIGBIRD for the re-annotated data. LEGAL-BERT was not used it was not performing best in evaluation criteria for multi-label classification task with paragraph information as illustrated in Table 6. We reported the average ROC AUC score, F1 score and Hamming loss as presented in Table 7. LexLM achieved the highest overall F1 score (0.851), indicating a strong balance between precision and recall, though it had the worst ROC AUC score, and tied for the lowest Hamming loss (0.063) with Google BIGBIRD. LegalRoBERTa demonstrated the highest ROC AUC score (0.877), highlighting its effectiveness in class separation. Its F1 score (0.850) was impressive, just slightly behind LexLM. Google BIGBIRD, while having the lowest F1 score (0.829), excelled in minimising Hamming loss (0.063).

Table 7: Evaluation metrics for different legal models for multi-label classification on re-annotated data

Method	ROC AUC	Hamming Loss	F1 Score
LegalRoBERTa	**0.877**	0.065	0.850
Google BigBird	0.866	**0.063**	0.829
LexLM	0.837	**0.063**	**0.851**

6 Discussion and Conclusion

Our study focused on planning court cases of the Administrative Court of England and Wales, where we designed and experimented with various models to extract important entities and label paragraphs. We added significant contributions to the legal research domain by creating a novel Named Entity Recognition (NER) dataset and a multi-label paragraph dataset which were both fully annotated by humans. Additionally, we developed another multi-label dataset with improved paragraph separation. We applied few-shot learning techniques using state-of-the-art models such as ChatGPT-3.5 and LLaMA 3 70B instruct model to generate two labels: 'fact' and 'citation' respectively.
For the NER task, it became clear that legal domain-specific models performed reasonably well even with smaller maximum sequence sizes. Notably, LegalRoBERTa achieved the highest recall of 0.813 and an F1 score of 0.802. This strong performance was likely because the entities often appeared early in the text, as we observed during the annotation process. LexLM model also excelled in various evaluation criteria and achieved the highest scores in precision (0.802), and AUC PR score (0.943). While Google BIGBIRD (a general-purpose model with a large maximum sequence length) performed the worst across all evaluation metrics. The success of LegalRoBERTa and LexLM highlights the importance of using specialised models for domain-specific applications. Conversely, the poor performance of the general-purpose Google BIGBIRD model reinforces the need for tailored approaches in legal text analysis and research.

In the multi-label task, incorporating paragraph position information had increased the model's performance. For the fully human-annotated dataset, LegalRoBERTa had the best performance. However, when paragraph information was added we found that there was no single superior model; both LegalRoBERTa and LexLM performed well in various metrics. As expected, Google BIGBIRD did not perform on par with the other models.

For re-annotated data, we tested only LegalRoBERTa, Google BIGBIRD, and LexLM. The LegalRoBERTa performed well in various metrics. However, the general-purpose model with a large max sequence like Google BIGBIRD, did not perform well further reinforcing the importance of domain-specific models. These findings from both the NER and multi-label classification tasks underscore the importance of using specialized models tailored to the legal domain to achieve superior performance, advancing legal research in this area.

7 Limitations and Future Work

One limitation of this research is that the re-extracted data was not fully annotated by humans. Due to time and cost constraints, we used LLMs to annotate the 'citation' and 'fact' labels. Future studies can leverage newer state-of-the-art models like LLaMA 3.1 and ChatGPT 4 for more accurate annotation or even fully human annotation can also be done. Another limitation is the dependency on powerful GPUs for fine-tuning and inferencing transformer-based models, which may not always be available in legal or academic settings. Additionally, the generalization performance of our methods has not been tested on other similar datasets.

For future work, we could explore more advanced models for annotation and extract paragraphs and cover section text from all cases within the Administrative Court to build a larger corpus. Additionally, testing our methods on other similar datasets and reporting their metrics would help assess the generalization of our approach.

8 Ethics Statement

The curated dataset contains sensitive information, including the names of claimants and appellants. Our research utilizes data that is already publicly available and not anonymous. We have obtained permission to use this data under the Open Justice Licence provided by the Find Case Law service, which allows us to copy, publish, distribute, and transmit the information. Our primary task is to transform this semi-structured data into a structured format. While we acknowledge the potential concerns regarding dual use, we focus on streamlining the analysis of legal cases, making the likelihood of such concerns minimal.

References

Morteza Bahrami, Muharram Mansoorizadeh, and Hassan Khotanlou. 2023. Few-shot learning with prompting methods. *2023 6th International Conference on Pattern Recognition and Image Analysis (IPRIA)*, pages 1–5.

Claire Barale, Michael Rovatsos, and Nehal Bhuta. 2023. Automated refugee case analysis: A NLP pipeline for supporting legal practitioners. In *Findings of the Association for Computational Linguistics: ACL 2023*, pages 2992–3005, Toronto, Canada. Association for Computational Linguistics.

Dor Bernsohn, Gil Semo, Yaron Vazana, Gila Hayat, Ben Hagag, Joel Niklaus, Rohit Saha, and Kyryl Truskovskyi. 2024. LegalLens: Leveraging LLMs for legal violation identification in unstructured text. In *Proceedings of the 18th Conference of the European Chapter of the Association for Computational Linguistics (Volume 1: Long Papers)*, pages 2129–2145, St. Julian's, Malta. Association for Computational Linguistics.

Prabin Bhandari. 2024. A survey on prompting techniques in llms. *arXiv.org*.

Tom B. Brown, Benjamin Mann, Nick Ryder, Melanie Subbiah, Jared Kaplan, Prafulla Dhariwal, Arvind Neelakantan, Pranav Shyam, Girish Sastry, Amanda Askell, Sandhini Agarwal, Ariel Herbert-Voss, Gretchen Krueger, Tom Henighan, Rewon Child, Aditya Ramesh, Daniel M. Ziegler, Jeffrey Wu, Clemens Winter, Christopher Hesse, Mark Chen, Eric Sigler, Mateusz Litwin, Scott Gray, Benjamin Chess, Jack Clark, Christopher Berner, Sam McCandlish, Alec Radford, Ilya Sutskever, and Dario Amodei. 2020. Language models are few-shot learners. *Preprint*, arXiv:2005.14165.

Mert Cemri, Tolga Çukur, and Aykut Koç. 2022. Unsupervised simplification of legal texts. *arXiv.org*.

Ilias Chalkidis, Manos Fergadiotis, Prodromos Malakasiotis, Nikolaos Aletras, and Ion Androutsopoulos. 2020. LEGAL-BERT: The muppets straight out of law school. In *Findings of the Association for Computational Linguistics: EMNLP 2020*, pages 2898–2904, Online. Association for Computational Linguistics.

Ilias Chalkidis*, Nicolas Garneau*, Catalina Goanta, Daniel Martin Katz, and Anders Søgaard. 2023. LeXFiles and LegalLAMA: Facilitating English Multinational Legal Language Model Development. In *Proceedings of the 61st Annual Meeting of the Association for Computational Linguistics*, Toronto, Canada. Association for Computational Linguistics.

Ilias Chalkidis, Nicolas Garneau, Catalina Goanta, Daniel Martin Katz, and Anders Søgaard. 2023. Lexfiles and legallama: Facilitating english multinational legal language model development. *Preprint*, arXiv:2305.07507.

Kaiyan Chang, Songcheng Xu, Chenglong Wang, Yingfeng Luo, Xiao Tong, and Jingbo Zhu. 2024. Efficient prompting methods for large language models: A survey. *arXiv.org*.

Hai Leong Chieu and Hwee Tou Ng. 2003. Named entity recognition with a maximum entropy approach. In *Conference on Computational Natural Language Learning*.

Jason P. C. Chiu and Eric Nichols. 2015. Named entity recognition with bidirectional lstm-cnns. *Transactions of the Association for Computational Linguistics*, 4:357–370.

André Carlos Ponce de Leon Ferreira de Carvalho and Alex Alves Freitas. 2009. A tutorial on multi-label classification techniques. In *IEEE Symposium on Foundations of Computational Intelligence*.

Tim Dettmers, Artidoro Pagnoni, Ari Holtzman, and Luke Zettlemoyer. 2023. Qlora: Efficient finetuning of quantized llms. *Preprint*, arXiv:2305.14314.

Jacob Devlin, Ming-Wei Chang, Kenton Lee, and Kristina Toutanova. 2019. Bert: Pre-training of deep bidirectional transformers for language understanding. *Preprint*, arXiv:1810.04805.

Zhiwei Fei, Xiaoyu Shen, Dawei Zhu, Fengzhe Zhou, Zhuo Han, Songyang Zhang, Kai Chen, Zongwen Shen, and Jidong Ge. 2023a. Lawbench: Benchmarking legal knowledge of large language models. *arXiv.org*.

Zhiwei Fei, Xiaoyu Shen, Dawei Zhu, Fengzhe Zhou, Zhuo Han, Songyang Zhang, Kai Chen, Zongwen Shen, and Jidong Ge. 2023b. Lawbench: Benchmarking legal knowledge of large language models. *Preprint*, arXiv:2309.16289.

Martina Forster, Claudia Schulz, Prudhvi Nokku, Melicaalsadat Mirsafian, Jaykumar Kasundra, and Stavroula Skylaki. 2024. The right model for the job: An evaluation of legal multi-label classification baselines. *Preprint*, arXiv:2401.11852.

Debasis Ganguly, Jack G. Conrad, Kripabandhu Ghosh, Saptarshi Ghosh, Pawan Goyal, Paheli Bhattacharya, Shubham Kumar Nigam, and Shounak Paul. Legal ir and nlp: The history, challenges, and state-of-the-art. In *Advances in Information Retrieval*, Lecture Notes in Computer Science, pages 331–340. Springer Nature Switzerland, Cham.

Saibo Geng, Rémi Lebret, and Karl Aberer. 2021. Legal transformer models may not always help. *arXiv.org*.

Precia Jacey and Siti Yuniarti. 2023. Artificial intelligence: Implementation in legal services (comparative study on china, united stated and indonesia). *Proceedings of the International Conference on Industrial Engineering and Operations Management*.

Thanmay Jayakumar, Fauzan Farooqui, and Luqman Farooqui. 2023. Large language models are legal but they are not: Making the case for a powerful legalllm. *ArXiv*, abs/2311.08890.

Renren Jin, Jiangcun Du, Wuwei Huang, Wei Liu, Jian Luan, Bin Wang, and Deyi Xiong. 2024. A comprehensive evaluation of quantization strategies for large language models. *Preprint*, arXiv:2402.16775.

Prathamesh Kalamkar, Astha Agarwal, Aman Tiwari, Smita Gupta, Saurabh Karn, and Vivek Raghavan. 2022. Named entity recognition in indian court judgments. *arXiv.org*.

Hossein Keshavarz, Zografoula Vagena, Pigi Kouki, Ilias Fountalis, Mehdi Mabrouki, Aziz Belaweid, and Nikolaos Vasiloglou. 2022. Named entity recognition in long documents: An end-to-end case study in the legal domain. In *2022 IEEE International Conference on Big Data (Big Data)*, pages 2024–2033.

Panteleimon Krasadakis, Evangelos Sakkopoulos, and Vassilios S. Verykios. 2024. A survey on challenges and advances in natural language processing with a focus on legal informatics and low-resource languages. *Electronics (Basel)*, 13(3):648–.

Vijay Krishnan and Vignesh Ganapathy. 2005. Named entity recognition. `https://cs229.stanford.edu/proj2005/KrishnanGanapathy-NamedEntityRecognition.pdf`. [Accessed 13-04-2024].

Jinqi Lai, Wensheng Gan, Jiayang Wu, Zhenlian Qi, and Philip S Yu. 2023. Large language models in law: A survey. *arXiv.org*.

Jing Li, Aixin Sun, Jianglei Han, and Chenliang Li. 2022. A survey on deep learning for named entity recognition. *IEEE transactions on knowledge and data engineering*, 34(1):50–70.

Xiao Li and Jing Li. 2021. Law - net: A new method for legal text mining.

Daniele Licari, Praveen Bushipaka, Gabriele Marino, Giovanni Comandé, and Tommaso Cucinotta. 2023. Legal holding extraction from italian case documents using italian-legal-bert text summarization. In *Proceedings of the Nineteenth International Conference on Artificial Intelligence and Law*, ICAIL '23, page 148–156, New York, NY, USA. Association for Computing Machinery.

Pedro Henrique Luz de Araujo, Teófilo E. de Campos, Renato R. R. de Oliveira, Matheus Stauffer, Samuel Couto, and Paulo Bermejo. 2018. Lener-br: A dataset for named entity recognition in brazilian legal text. In *Computational Processing of the Portuguese Language*, pages 313–323, Cham. Springer International Publishing.

Dimitris Mamakas, Petros Tsotsi, Ion Androutsopoulos, and Ilias Chalkidis. 2022a. Processing long legal documents with pre-trained transformers: Modding legalbert and longformer. *arXiv.org*.

Dimitris Mamakas, Petros Tsotsi, Ion Androutsopoulos, and Ilias Chalkidis. 2022b. Processing long legal documents with pre-trained transformers: Modding LegalBERT and longformer. In *Proceedings of the Natural Legal Language Processing Workshop 2022*, pages 130–142, Abu Dhabi, United Arab Emirates (Hybrid). Association for Computational Linguistics.

Dimitris Mamakas, Petros Tsotsi, Ion Androutsopoulos, and Ilias Chalkidis. 2022c. Processing long legal documents with pre-trained transformers: Modding legalbert and longformer. *Preprint*, arXiv:2211.00974.

Sewon Min, Michael Lewis, Hannaneh Hajishirzi, and Luke Zettlemoyer. 2021. Noisy channel language model prompting for few-shot text classification. *ArXiv*, abs/2108.04106.

Marco Naguib, Xavier Tannier, and Aur'elie N'ev'eol. 2024. Few shot clinical entity recognition in three languages: Masked language models outperform llm prompting. *ArXiv*, abs/2402.12801.

Paul N. Otto and Annie I. Antón. 2009. Managing legal texts in requirements engineering.

Monica Palmirani and Fabio Vitali. 2011. Akoma-ntoso for legal documents. In *Legislative XML for the Semantic Web*, Law, Governance and Technology Series, pages 75–100. Springer Netherlands, Dordrecht.

Pooja Pant, A. Sai Sabitha, Tanupriya Choudhury, and Prince Dhingra. 2018. Multi-label classification trending challenges and approaches. In *Emerging Trends in Expert Applications and Security*, volume 841 of *Advances in Intelligent Systems and Computing*, pages 433–444. Springer Singapore Pte. Limited, Singapore.

Rafael B. Pereira, Alexandre Plastino, Bianca Zadrozny, and Luiz H.C. Merschmann. 2018. Correlation analysis of performance measures for multi-label classification. *Information processing management*, 54(3):359–369.

Keyu Pu, Hongyi Liu, Yixiao Yang, Jiangzhou Ji, Wenyi Lv, and Yaohan He. 2022. Cmb ai lab at semeval-2022 task 11: A two-stage approach for complex named entity recognition via span boundary detection and span classification. In *International Workshop on Semantic Evaluation*.

Vasile Păis, Maria Mitrofan, Carol Luca Gasan, Alexandru Ianov, Corvin Ghit, ă, Vlad Silviu Coneschi, and Andrei Onut. 2023. Legalnero: A linked corpus for named entity recognition in the romanian legal domain. *Semantic Web*, pages 1–14.

Ernesto Quevedo, Tomas Cerny, Alejandro Rodriguez, Pablo Rivas, Jorge Yero, Korn Sooksatra, Alibek Zhakubayev, and Davide Taibi. 2023. Legal natural language processing from 2015-2022: A comprehensive systematic mapping study of advances and applications. *IEEE access*, pages 1–1.

Slamet Riyanto, Imas Sukaesih Sitanggang, Taufik Djatna, and Tika Dewi Atikah. 2023. Comparative analysis using various performance metrics in imbalanced data for multi-class text classification. *International Journal of Advanced Computer Science and Applications*.

Takaya Saito and Marc Rehmsmeier. 2015. The precision-recall plot is more informative than the roc plot when evaluating binary classifiers on imbalanced datasets. *PloS one*, 10(3):e0118432–e0118432.

Victor Sanh, Lysandre Debut, Julien Chaumond, and Thomas Wolf. 2020. Distilbert, a distilled version of bert: smaller, faster, cheaper and lighter. *Preprint*, arXiv:1910.01108.

Olga Shulayeva, Advaith Siddharthan, and Adam Wyner. 2017. Recognizing cited facts and principles in legal judgements. *Artificial intelligence and law*, 25(1):107–126.

Stavroula Skylaki, Ali Oskooei, Omar Bari, Nadja Herger, and Zac Kriegman. 2020. Named entity recognition in the legal domain using a pointer generator network. *Preprint*, arXiv:2012.09936.

Răzvan-Alexandru Smădu, Ion-Robert Dinică, Andrei-Marius Avram, Dumitru-Clementin Cercel, Florin Pop, and Mihaela-Claudia Cercel. 2022. Legal named entity recognition with multi-task domain adaptation. In *Proceedings of the Natural Legal Language Processing Workshop 2022*, pages 305–321, Abu Dhabi, United Arab Emirates (Hybrid). Association for Computational Linguistics.

Dezhao Song, Andrew Vold, Kanika Madan, and Frank Schilder. 2022. Multi-label legal document classification: A deep learning-based approach with label-attention and domain-specific pre-training. *Information systems (Oxford)*, 106:101718–.

Martina ster, Claudia Schulz, Prudhvi Nokku, Melicaalsadat Mirsafian, Jaykumar Kasundra, and Stavroula Skylaki. 2024. The right model for the job: An evaluation of legal multi-label classification baselines. *arXiv.org*.

Ehsan Tavan and Mary Najafi. 2022. Marsan at semeval-2022 task 11: Multilingual complex named entity recognition using t5 and transformer encoder. In *International Workshop on Semantic Evaluation*.

Hugo Touvron, Thibaut Lavril, Gautier Izacard, Xavier Martinet, Marie-Anne Lachaux, Timothée Lacroix, Baptiste Rozière, Naman Goyal, Eric Hambro, Faisal Azhar, Aurelien Rodriguez, Armand Joulin, Edouard Grave, and Guillaume Lample. 2023. Llama: Open and efficient foundation language models. *Preprint*, arXiv:2302.13971.

Renátó Vági. 2023. How could semantic processing and other nlp tools improve online legal databases? *TalTech Journal of European Studies*, 13(2):138–151.

Fusheng Wei, Robert Keeling, Nathaniel Huber-Fliflet, Jianping Zhang, Adam Dabrowski, Jingchao Yang, Qiang Mao, and Han Qin. 2023. Empirical study of llm fine-tuning for text classification in legal document review. *2023 IEEE International Conference on Big Data (BigData)*, pages 2786–2792.

Thomas Wolf, Lysandre Debut, Victor Sanh, Julien Chaumond, Clement Delangue, Anthony Moi, Pierric Cistac, Tim Rault, Rémi Louf, Morgan Funtowicz, Joe Davison, Sam Shleifer, Patrick von Platen, Clara Ma, Yacine Jernite, Julien Plu, Canwen Xu, Teven Le Scao, Sylvain Gugger, Mariama Drame, Quentin Lhoest, and Alexander M. Rush. 2020. Huggingface's transformers: State-of-the-art natural language processing. *Preprint*, arXiv:1910.03771.

Juntao Yu, Bernd Bohnet, and Massimo Poesio. 2020. Named entity recognition as dependency parsing. In *Proceedings of the 58th Annual Meeting of the Association for Computational Linguistics*, pages 6470–6476, Online. Association for Computational Linguistics.

Manzil Zaheer, Guru Guruganesh, Avinava Dubey, Joshua Ainslie, Chris Alberti, Santiago Ontanon, Philip Pham, Anirudh Ravula, Qifan Wang, Li Yang, and Amr Ahmed. 2021. Big bird: Transformers for longer sequences. *Preprint*, arXiv:2007.14062.

Jinjie Zhang, Yixuan Zhou, and Rayan Saab. 2023. Post-training quantization for neural networks with provable guarantees. *SIAM journal on mathematics of data science*, 5(2):373–399.

Junzhe Zhao, Yingxi Wang, Nicolay Rusnachenko, and Huizhi Liang. 2023. Legal_try at semeval-2023 task 6: Voting heterogeneous models for entities identification in legal documents. In *International Workshop on Semantic Evaluation*.

Haoxi Zhong, Chaojun Xiao, Cunchao Tu, Tianyang Zhang, Zhiyuan Liu, and Maosong Sun. 2020. How does nlp benefit legal system: A summary of legal artificial intelligence. *arXiv.org*.

A Appendix A: Document layout

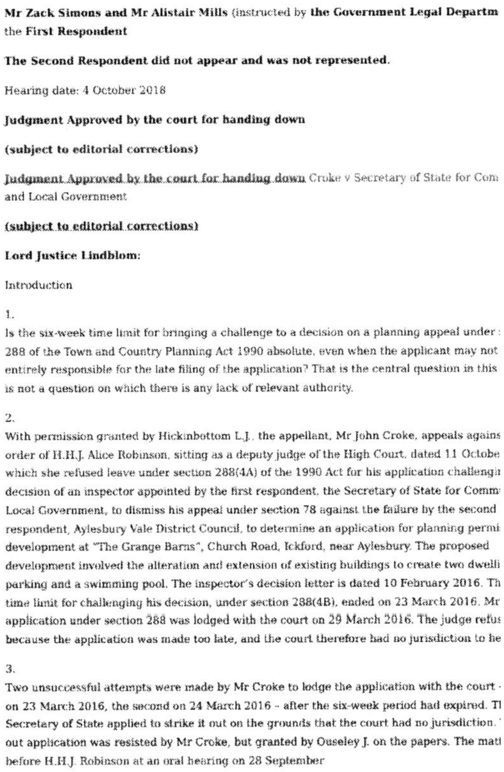

Mr Zack Simons and Mr Alistair Mills (instructed by **the Government Legal Departm** the **First Respondent**

The Second Respondent did not appear and was not represented.

Hearing date: 4 October 2018

Judgment Approved by the court for handing down

(subject to editorial corrections)

Judgment Approved by the court for handing down Croke v Secretary of State for Com and Local Government

(subject to editorial corrections)

Lord Justice Lindblom:

Introduction

1.
Is the six-week time limit for bringing a challenge to a decision on a planning appeal under : 288 of the Town and Country Planning Act 1990 absolute, even when the applicant may not entirely responsible for the late filing of the application? That is the central question in this is not a question on which there is any lack of relevant authority.

2.
With permission granted by Hickinbottom L.J., the appellant, Mr John Croke, appeals agains order of H.H.J. Alice Robinson, sitting as a deputy judge of the High Court, dated 11 Octobe which she refused leave under section 288(4A) of the 1990 Act for his application challengi decision of an inspector appointed by the first respondent, the Secretary of State for Comm Local Government, to dismiss his appeal under section 78 against the failure by the second respondent, Aylesbury Vale District Council, to determine an application for planning permi development at "The Grange Barns", Church Road, Ickford, near Aylesbury. The proposed development involved the alteration and extension of existing buildings to create two dwelli parking and a swimming pool. The inspector's decision letter is dated 10 February 2016. Th time limit for challenging his decision, under section 288(4B), ended on 23 March 2016. Mr application under section 288 was lodged with the court on 29 March 2016. The judge refu because the application was made too late, and the court therefore had no jurisdiction to he

3.
Two unsuccessful attempts were made by Mr Croke to lodge the application with the court on 23 March 2016, the second on 24 March 2016 – after the six-week period had expired. Tl Secretary of State applied to strike it out on the grounds that the court had no jurisdiction. out application was resisted by Mr Croke, but granted by Ouseley J. on the papers. The mat before H.H.J. Robinson at an oral hearing on 28 September

Figure 6: Snapshot of an example of main section

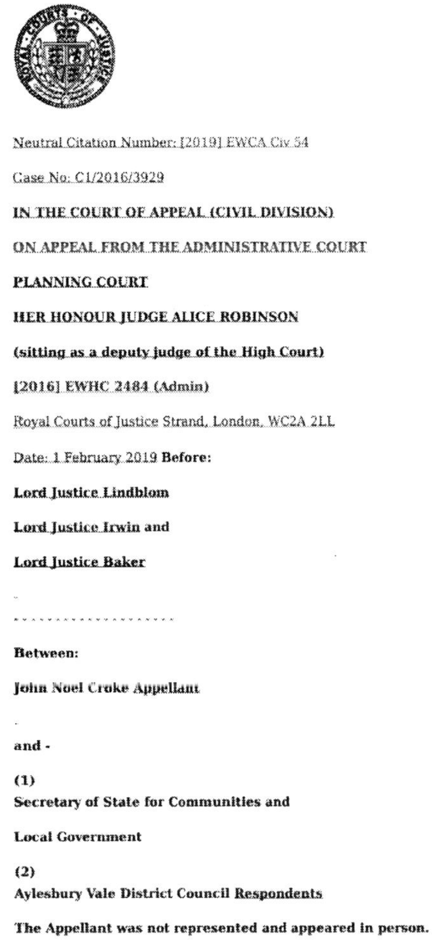

Neutral Citation Number: [2019] EWCA Civ 54

Case No: C1/2016/3929

IN THE COURT OF APPEAL (CIVIL DIVISION)

ON APPEAL FROM THE ADMINISTRATIVE COURT

PLANNING COURT

HER HONOUR JUDGE ALICE ROBINSON

(sitting as a deputy judge of the High Court)

[2016] EWHC 2484 (Admin)

Royal Courts of Justice Strand, London, WC2A 2LL

Date: 1 February 2019 **Before:**

Lord Justice Lindblom

Lord Justice Irwin and

Lord Justice Baker

Between:

John Noel Croke Appellant

and -

(1)
Secretary of State for Communities and

Local Government

(2)
Aylesbury Vale District Council Respondents

The Appellant was not represented and appeared in person.

Figure 7: Snapshot of an example of main section

B Appendix B: Links to Models and Platforms Used

- **LEGAL-BERT:** https://huggingface.co/nlpaueb/legal-bert-base-uncased
- **LegalRoBERTa:** https://huggingface.co/Saibo-creator/legal-roberta-base
- **LexLM:** https://huggingface.co/lexlms/legal-longformer-large
- **BIGBIRD:** https://huggingface.co/google/bigbird-roberta-base
- **DistilBERT:** https://huggingface.co/distilbert/distilbert-base-uncased
- **GitHub Repository:** https://tinyurl.com/d434zc34

C Appendix C: Individual metrics for classes for re-annotated data

Table 8: Evaluation metrics for different legal models across various labels for re-annotated data.

method	label	f1	roc auc	precision	recall	accuracy
google BIGBIRD	introduction	0.781	0.897	0.754	0.811	0.975
	fact	0.844	**0.731**	**0.783**	0.916	**0.783**
	citation	0.974	0.992	0.960	0.983	0.995
	judgment	0.719	0.845	0.747	0.694	0.992
LexLM	introduction	**0.799**	0.906	**0.775**	0.824	**0.977**
	fact	**0.846**	0.719	0.777	0.935	0.781
	citation	0.977	**0.993**	0.964	0.986	0.996
	judgment	0.785	**0.904**	0.759	**0.812**	**0.993**
LegalRoBERTa	introduction	0.788	**0.913**	0.740	**0.844**	0.975
	fact	0.840	0.705	0.761	**0.938**	0.771
	citation	**0.980**	**0.993**	**0.970**	**0.991**	**0.998**
	judgment	**0.793**	0.897	**0.787**	0.798	**0.993**

D Appendix D: Individual metrics for classes for multi-label classification

Table 9: Evaluation metrics for different models across various labels for multi-label dataset

method	label	f1 score	roc auc	precision	recall	accuracy
DistilBERT	introduction	0.388	0.657	**0.472**	.329	**0.960**
	fact	0.759	0.831	0.766	0.752	0.866
	citation	0.851	0.929	0.832	0.870	0.979
	judgment	0.704	0.797	**0.864**	0.594	**0.996**
LexLM	introduction	0.351	0.642	0.424	0.300	0.957
	fact	0.756	0.833	0.742	0.770	0.860
	citation	0.832	0.917	0.817	0.848	0.977
	judgment	0.635	0.811	0.645	0.625	0.995
LEGAL-BERT	introduction	0.357	0.656	0.385	0.332	0.954
	fact	0.757	0.829	**0.770**	0.745	0.866
	citation	0.856	0.931	**0.840**	0.874	**0.980**
	judgment	0.707	0.866	0.681	0.734	**0.996**
LegalRoBERTa	introduction	**0.425**	**0.687**	0.465	**0.392**	0.959
	fact	**0.788**	**0.865**	0.734	**0.850**	**0.871**
	citation	**0.862**	**0.950**	0.816	**0.914**	**0.980**
	judgment	**0.756**	**0.897**	0.718	**0.797**	**0.996**
google BIGBIRD	introduction	0.285	0.598	0.466	0.205	**0.960**
	fact	0.764	0.852	0.694	**0.850**	0.853
	citation	0.859	0.938	0.831	0.889	**0.980**
	judgment	0.247	0.570	**1.000**	0.141	0.994

Table 10: Evaluation metrics for different legal models across various labels for multi-label dataset with paragraph information.

method	label	f1	roc_auc	precision	recall	accuracy
DistilBERT	introduction	0.631	0.767	**0.762**	0.541	0.978
	fact	0.757	0.834	0.733	0.780	0.859
	citation	**0.868**	0.929	0.863	0.867	0.982
	judgment	0.631	0.772	0.745	0.594	0.993
LexLM	introduction	0.621	0.774	0.701	0.558	0.974
	fact	0.748	0.827	0.739	0.757	0.857
	citation	0.850	0.920	0.817	0.870	0.978
	judgment	0.444	**0.869**	0.316	0.251	**0.996**
LegalRoBERTa	introduction	**0.654**	0.787	0.749	0.518	**0.979**
	fact	0.804	0.833	0.767	0.804	0.858
	citation	0.867	**0.941**	**0.937**	**0.894**	**0.984**
	judgment	0.656	0.811	0.685	0.625	0.992
LEGAL-BERT	introduction	0.630	0.784	0.699	0.572	**0.979**
	fact	0.752	0.836	0.707	0.803	0.859
	citation	0.837	0.936	0.802	0.871	0.981
	judgment	**0.719**	0.820	0.790	**0.656**	0.995
google BIGBIRD	introduction	0.638	**0.798**	0.670	**0.603**	0.964
	fact	**0.866**	**0.940**	**0.842**	0.834	**0.980**
	citation	0.865	0.940	0.842	**0.834**	0.980
	judgment	0.247	0.570	**1.000**	0.140	0.993

F Appendix F: Individual metrics for classes for NER task

Table 11: Performance metrics for different legal models for each class of NER dataset.

	LexLM			LEGAL-BERT			LegalRoBERTa			google BIGBIRD		
class	precision	recall	f1-score	precision	recall	f1-score	precision	recall	f1-score	precision	recall	f1-score
O	0.97	**0.99**	**0.98**	**0.98**	0.98	**0.98**	**0.98**	0.98	**0.98**	**0.98**	0.97	**0.98**
B-CITATION	0.98	0.95	**0.96**	0.98	0.95	**0.96**	**1**	0.93	**0.96**	0.93	**0.97**	0.95
I-CITATION	0.99	0.98	**0.98**	0.99	**0.99**	**0.98**	**1**	0.96	**0.98**	0.98	**0.99**	**0.98**
B-DATE	**0.97**	0.96	0.96	0.96	0.96	0.96	**0.97**	**0.97**	**0.97**	**0.97**	0.95	0.96
I-DATE	0.93	0.98	**0.96**	**0.96**	0.91	0.93	0.92	**1**	0.95	0.95	0.94	**0.95**
B-JUDGE	0.68	0.77	0.72	**0.72**	0.71	0.71	0.69	**0.79**	**0.74**	0.68	0.61	0.65
I-JUDGE	0.90	0.87	0.89	0.89	0.86	0.86	**0.91**	**0.90**	**0.90**	0.90	0.81	0.84
B-LOCATION	0.72	0.61	0.66	0.66	0.64	0.74	0.68	**0.67**	**0.77**	**0.77**	**0.67**	0.62
I-LOCATION	**0.95**	0.82	0.88	0.88	**0.88**	**0.92**	0.90	0.84	0.88	0.89	0.62	0.86
B-COURT	**0.92**	0.73	**0.81**	0.81	**0.91**	0.75	0.82	0.65	0.74	0.74	0.62	0.75
I-COURT	**0.98**	0.82	**0.89**	0.89	**0.98**	0.86	0.92	0.82	**0.89**	0.89	0.80	0.87

F Appendix F: Description of Labels used in multi-label classification with examples

Table 12: Labels used in multi-label classification with description and examples.

Labels	Description with example
Introduction	Text containing the topic of discussion in court, usually preceding facts, history, and background. *Example:* What is the scope of the "presumption in favour of sustainable development" in the National Planning Policy Framework ("the NPPF")? That is the basic question in this appeal. Judges in the Planning Court have differed in their answers to it.
Fact	Text containing rules, facts, or references such as section 10, s.10, S 10, article 10, CPR (Civil Procedure Rule), regulations, etc. *Example:* Section 70(2) of the 1990 Act requires that, in dealing with an application for planning permission, a local planning authority must have regard to the provisions of the development plan, so far as is material to the application, and any "other material considerations".
Citation	Text containing references to cases, including neutral citations of different cases. *Example:* Time starts to run on the day after the date of the decision letter itself, not the day on which it is received by the applicant (see Griffiths v Secretary of State for the Environment [1983] 1 All E.R. 439).
Judgment	Text consisting of outcomes of cases and appeal (successful or dismissed). *Example:* For the reasons I have given, I would dismiss this appeal.

G Appendix G: Description of Entities used in NER with examples

Table 13: Entities used for NER model with description and examples.

Entities	Description with Examples
CITATION	A unique identifier for cases consisting of the year, jurisdiction, court, and case number. *Examples:* [2023] EWHC 2629 (KB), [2018] EWCA Civ 2532, [2011] UKSC 7
JUDGE	Name of the judges involved. *Examples:* Lord Justice Lindblom, MR JUSTICE JAY, MR JUSTICE HOLGATE
COURT	Name of the court where the case is heard. *Examples:* High Court (Administrative Court), Court of Appeal (Civil Division), High Court (Planning Court)
LOCATION	Location where the case was heard. *Examples:* Bristol Civil Justice Centre, Strand, London, WC2A 2LL, Manchester Civil Justice Centre
DATE	Date when the case was heard. *Examples:* 14 November 2018, 20/10/2023, 12/10/2015

H Appendix H: Few shot prompt example labeling the fact using ChatGPT

Here is the prompt used in the labeling the 'fact' using ChatGPT 3.5, the prompt is similar for LLaMA 3 70B which has 18 examples (used to label 'citation').

```
{
    "role": "system",
        "content": f"""**Task:** For the given text and determine whether it contains a fact content. Assign the label 1 only when you are extremely certain that the fact content is present (as mostly don't have fact content); otherwise, assign the label 0. You must generate an label for every given input and ouput the label only. The description of text with fact content is delimited by << >>.
    <<
        Fact content: Text containing rules, facts like section (like section 10, s 10 ,S10). Act, article, Amendment, rule, policy,local plan, paragrapgh from NPPF, CPR (civil preceding rule) etc.

    >>
      The few shot examples are delimited by ``` ```
    ```
        1) Input text : For all the above reasons, these second applications to reconsider must fail. They fail to meet any – let alone all – of the criteria set out in CPR 52.30. These are not exceptional cases. There has been no injustice to the applicant. There is no probability of a different result. There was never any tenable basis for an appeal, for the reasons given by both the judge and Lewison L.J.. We consider that neither application for reconsideration was justifiable. The applications before us are therefore dismissed.

      Output: 1

        2) Input text: In Lawal v Circle 33 Housing Trust [2014] EWCA Civ 1514, [2015] 1 P. & C.R. 12, Sir TerenceEtherton, then the Chancellor of the High Court, said at paragraph 65 that the paradigm case for reopening "is where the litigation process has been corrupted, such as by fraud or bias or where the judge read the wrong papers". He reiterated that the broad principle was that "for an appeal to be reopened, the injustice that would be perpetrated if the appeal is not reopened must be so grave as to overbear the pressing claim of finality in litigation". Finally, he said:
          "It also follows that the fact that a wrong result was reached earlier, or that there is fresh evidence, or that the amounts in issue are very large, or that the point in issue is very important to one or more of the parties or is of general importance is not of itself sufficient to displace the fundamental public importance of the need for finality."

      Output: 0

        3) Input text : These and other statements of principle were brought together in the judgment of this court inGoring-on-Thames Parish Council, to which we have already referred. Importantly, at paragraph 15,emphasis was placed on the requirement that "there must be a powerful probability that the decision in question would have been different if the integrity of the earlier proceedings had not been critically undermined". More recently, the scope of the jurisdiction was summarised byHickinbottom L.J.in Balwinder Singh v Secretary of State for the Home Department [2019] EWCA Civ 1504, paragraph 3, in terms with which we entirely agree:"This is an exceptional jurisdiction, to be exercised rarely: "the injustice that would be perpetrated if the appeal is not reopened must be so grave as to overbear the pressing claim of finality in litigation"(Lawal v Circle 33 Housing Trust [2014] EWCA Civ 1514; [2015] HLR 9 at [65] per Sir TerenceEtherton VC (as he then was)). The jurisdiction will therefore not be exercised simply because the determination was wrong, but only where it can be demonstrated that the integrity of the earlier proceedings has been "critically undermined" (R (Goring-on-Thames Parish Council) v SouthOxfordshire District Council [2018] EWCA Civ 860; [2018] 1 WLR 5161 at [10]-[11]."

      Output: 0

        4) Input : There were several delays prior to the Secretary of State's decision owing to additional consultations,which included a consultation on the Court of Appeal's decision in East Northamptonshire DistrictCouncil v Secretary of State for Communities and Local Government (the Barnwell Manor case)[2014] EWCA Civ 137. The Court of Appeal interpreted section 66(1) of the Planning (Listed Buildings And Conservation Areas) Act 1990 as requiring the decision-maker to give "the desirability of preserving the [relevant] building or its setting" not merely careful consideration but considerable importance and weight when balancing the advantages of the proposed development against the harmit might do.
      Output: 1

        5) Input: For these reasons, which are somewhat different from those of the judge, I would dismiss this appeal. I agree.
      Output: 0
    ```
    **Note the output should be 1 or 0. So return only 0 or 1 accordingly**

  The legal text is {paragraph}"""
      }
```

Figure 8: prompt for labeling fact

I Appendix I: Screen shot of the Data generated by the models

NEUTRAL CITATION	COURT	LOCATION	DATE	JUDGE	introduction	judgement	facts	citation
[2023] EWHC 171 (Admin)	THE HIGH COURT OF JUSTICE	2 Redcliff Street, Bristol BS	2023, 8 & 9 November 2022	MR JUSTICE LANE, MR JUSTICE LANE	['1. Climate change, with its consequences f...	['257. This judicial review is dismissed.']	['1. Climate change, with its consequences f...	['13. DL 78 to 82 are headed "Climate change...
[2022] EWHC 2406 (Admin)	THE HIGH COURT OF JUSTICE	Strand , London	2022, 7 July 2022	MR C M G OCKELTON , VICE PRESIDENT OF THE UPP...	['1. The Claimant is the registered propriet...	['31. I therefore hold that on its true cons...	['1. The Claimant is the registered propriet...	['5. The issue to be decided is therefore a ...
[2022] EWHC 2991 (Admin)	THE HIGH COURT OF JUSTICE	Strand , London	25 November 2022, 10 November 2022	JUDGE JARMAN KC	["1. The second interested party in these pr...	['38. In my judgment, each of the grounds of...	["1. The second interested party in these pr...	['27. He points out that the inspector did n...
[2022] EWHC 3317 (Admin)	THE HIGH COURT OF JUSTICE, COURT	Strand , London	2022, 8 December 2022	JUDGE JARMAN KC	['1. The claimant challenges a decision of a...	['37. I would therefore quash the decision a...	['1. The claimant challenges a decision of a...	['12. In contrast, the GPDO specifies those ...

Figure 9: Screenshot of data generated by the Named Entity Recognition (NER) and multi-label classification models. The NER model extracts key entities such as Neutral Citation, Court, Location, Date, and Judge. Meanwhile, the multi-label classification model generates relevant sections including Introduction, Judgment, Facts, and Citations.

Automated Anonymization of Parole Hearing Transcripts

Abed El Rahman Itani
University of Passau
itani01@ads.uni-passau.de

Wassiliki Siskou
University of Konstanz
University of Passau
wassiliki.siskou@uni-konstanz.de

Annette Hautli-Janisz
University of Passau
annette.hautli-janisz@uni-passau.de

Abstract

Responsible natural language processing is more and more concerned with preventing the violation of personal rights that language technology can entail (Weidinger et al., 2022). In this paper we illustrate the case of parole hearings in California, the verbatim transcripts of which are made available to the general public upon a request sent to the California Board of Parole Hearings. The parole hearing setting is highly sensitive: inmates face a board of legal representatives who discuss highly personal matters not only about the inmates themselves but also about victims and their relatives, such as spouses and children. Participants have no choice in contributing to the data collection process, since the disclosure of the transcripts is mandated by law. As researchers who are interested in understanding and modeling the communication in these hierarchy-driven settings, we face an ethical dilemma: publishing raw data as is for the community would compromise the privacy of all individuals affected, but manually cleaning the data requires a substantive effort. In this paper we present an automated anonymization process which reliably removes and pseudonymizes sensitive data in verbatim transcripts, while at the same time preserving the structure and content of the data. Our results show that the process exhibits little to no leakage of sensitive information when applied to more than 300 hearing transcripts.

1 Introduction

The growing need for anonymized datasets in computational social science such as NLP applications in law, criminology, sociology and political science is driven by the importance of ethical compliance, legal requirements, reduction of bias, and, ultimately, by the necessity for data sharing. In the context of spoken and transcribed dialogue data, anonymized datasets are particularly scarce. This holds especially for dialogues in legal settings, such as parole suitability hearings, where inmates who were originally sentenced to life-long imprisonment engage in discussions with a board of commissioners, requesting to be released from prison before the completion of their sentence. In California, the verbatim transcripts of these hearings can be requested at the California Board of Parole Hearings, but sharing them publicly raises ethical concerns: they include personally identifiable information (PII), such as names, inmate IDs, dates and other sensitive details about the people involved, and the participants do not have a choice as to whether they want to take part in the data collection process. Researchers who wish to make these transcripts available to ensure academic transparency face ethical dilemmas, as publishing the data would compromise the privacy of those affected. The contribution of our work is twofold: First, we introduce a robust automatic anonymization process for dialogue transcripts in criminal law, ensuring consistent entity replacement throughout each transcript. Second, we provide an evaluation of our process based on a subset of 100 manually anonymized parole hearing transcripts and show our system's minimal risk of data leakage demonstrated by the systems high precision.

2 Related Work

While anonymization has mainly been applied to data in the legal and clinical domain, researchers from other disciplines also feel the need to protect sensitive information in their datasets. In the specific case of Californian parole hearings, the dataset has not been made available to the public in its entirety (Hong et al., 2021b), with the available data only restricted to individual examples (Todd et al., 2020; Hong et al., 2021a). In a similar case for German, the entire dataset was manually redacted (Espinoza et al., 2024) and double-checked by a second person to ensure correctness.

Proceedings of the Natural Legal Language Processing Workshop 2024, pages 115–128

Regarding automatic anonymization, previous work mainly relies on written legal and clinical documents, applying methods such as masking, falsification or pseudonymization. ANOPPI uses a combination of automatic and semi-automatic processes, utilizing statistics and rule-based Named Entity Recognition (NER) methods to identify and remove personal information in Finnish court documents (Oksanen et al., 2019). It consistently replaces sensitive data with categorical labels, preserving both the semantic meaning and readability of the documents. PSILENCE uses a combination of NER tools and Coreference Resolution to ensure consistent labelling of entities in written legal documents (Cabrera-Diego and Gheewala, 2024). Schamberger (2021) proposes a customization solution to anonymize German legal court rulings using domain-specific NER in order to mask entities according to predefined rules. In the clinical domain, Ribeiro et al. (2023) proposes INCOGNITUS to automatically anonymize clinical notes by using a combination of NER tools like Conditional Random Field. For the anonymization of spoken language, Gardiner et al. (2024) use an Automatic Speech Recognition (ASR) system to generate transcripts from phone and video conversations and then enhance Google Data Loss Prevention service to improve PII detection.

The data underlying this paper falls between audio data (unpredictable and unstructured) and written legal documents (structured and manually curated): parole hearing transcripts exhibit some inherent structure with clearly identified speakers and roles, while dialogue is characterized by repair sentences, filled pauses, elliptical content as well as cut-off and spelled-out names with PII. While the aforementioned work on anonymization of written language does not directly translate to verbatim transcripts, the approach we take in the paper is similar in that we combine Named Entity Recognition and regular expressions with rule-based post-processing to identify sensitive information in the transcripts and replace it with categorical tags[1]. In this way we adjust the approach by INCOGNITUS (Oksanen et al., 2019) and apply it to dialogues from criminal law.

3 Data

The dataset comprises 334 parole suitability hearing transcripts in PDF format, which we officially requested from the California Department of Corrections and Rehabilitation (CDCR)[2]. All hearings took place between August and September 2021. The corpus consists of 21,874 pages and 5,013,156 words in total, with an average of 15,009 words and 65 pages per file. The transcripts share a standardized format, which we can exploit for anonymization: The first page of the PDF contains the names of the participants present in the hearing, the location such as the prison or facility of the inmate, as well as the date and time of the hearing. The second page contains the index, indicating the page number of each section (such as pre-commitment factors, post-commitment factors and decision) of the hearing. The subsequent pages comprise the main body of the transcript, containing the verbatim transcription of the dialogue, uniformly formatted with the speaker tag and the according text. The document also includes the closing statements of all participants and the final decision. The last pages of the document are reserved for a declaration of the transcriber as well as their signature. For anonymization, all transcripts are converted to text files. The index of each transcript is ignored during conversion as it does not contain PII. The final text file is formatted so that each utterance appears on a separate line to facilitate reading and processing.

4 Automatic Identification of Sensitive Information

4.1 Categories of Sensitive Information

Pre-defining categories of sensitive information is a key prerequisite for effective automatic data anonymization. The identification of privacy-relevant data categories involved an iterative approach to capture the full spectrum of sensitive information in parole hearing transcripts. This process entailed multiple rounds of manual review, with each iteration refining the list of categories to be anonymized.

Given the standardized format of the hearing

[1]We decided against masking as an anonymization technique, as the sensitive information would have only been redacted (e.g. "****") but not replaced with context-sensitive tags, thereby reducing the semantic and pragmatic expressiveness of the transcript. Additionally, we ruled out falsification, which replaces real data with generated false data, as it carries the risk of generating real names of individuals, potentially causing unintended consequences when publishing the falsified dataset.

[2]Parole hearing transcripts can be requested under the California Public Record Act. https://www.cdcr.ca.gov/bph/psh-transcript/

transcripts, most of the relevant data can be found in the front page of the documents. These include mainly the names of each person present in the hearing, the inmate's identification number (CDCR ID from now), the location, as well as time and date. Other forms of parole hearing specific sensitive data include spelled names, as well as fractions of spelled names (such as "V as in Victor"). We define those as *direct* identifiers and consider those to be the most important information to remove, as they significantly increase the risk of re-identification. Consequently, their removal is a priority.

The above mentioned comprehensive examination of the transcripts yields a list of *indirect* identifiers such as company names, organizations, age, height, nationality, religion, political group, phone numbers, URLs and email addresses that need to be redacted in order to ensure coverage of all privacy-relevant information of the individuals involved. Table 1 provides descriptions of all direct and indirect identifiers.

4.2 Automatic Entity Labeling

We employ a multi-tool approach for Named Entity Recognition to detect the different direct and indirect identifiers in the transcripts. We mainly use Presidio[3](Mendels and Balter, 2020), an open-source tool by Microsoft, to identify most PII in the text as it allows to manually add custom recognizers based on Regular Expressions. We developed a set of regular expressions tailored to detect entities unique to parole hearings, including SPELLED_NAME, SPELLED_OUT_ITEM and CDCR_ID. We additionally use spaCy[4] (Honnibal et al., 2020) and StanfordNER[5] (Finkel et al., 2005) to cover entities like PERSON, LOCATION, ORGANIZATION, as well as TIME and DATE. Although the latter two NERs already search for any occurrence of these entity types, we implemented custom recognizers in Presidio for these categories too, to complement the detection process, therefore reducing the risk of data leakage. Table 1 specifies which tool or combination of tools are used for each entity type.

By using multiple NER tools simultaneously on a single transcript, we leverage the strengths of each tool. While there is overlap in detecting common types such as PERSON and LOCATION, the tools complement each other by expanding coverage, thereby improving the overall accuracy of the anonymization process. In case one tool misses a piece of sensitive information, the likelihood of another tool detecting it gets increased, resulting in a more reliable entity identification process.

4.3 Automatic Filtering

A thorough manual iteration through the generated results shows some common errors in the labeling, e.g., context-specific non-sensitive terms of parole hearings that are needed in the transcript for information preservation such as "Board of Parole Hearings" is frequently misidentified as an ORGANIZATION entity. This process yields a whitelist of 290 named entities to prevent over-anonymization.

The main goal of our cleaning process however is the elimination of duplicate and overlapping labels generated by different NER tools. We define duplicates as those with identical start and end index positions. Formally, given two labeled entities $A_1(s_1, e_1)$ and $A_2(s_2, e_2)$, where s and e represent the start and end positions, we remove A_2 if:

$$s_1 = s_2 \text{ and } e_1 = e_2$$

For overlapping entities, we apply a series of rules for filtering. Labels that share the same start point but differ in end points, we keep the longer label. Formally, given $A_1(s_1, e_1)$ and $A_2(s_1, e_2)$, we keep A_1 if:

$$s_1 = s_2 \text{ and } e_1 > e_2$$

Similarly, for labels with the same endpoint but different start points, we preserve the longer annotation. Given $A_1(s_1, e_1)$ and $A_2(s_2, e_1)$, we keep A_1 if:

$$e_1 = e_2 \text{ and } s_1 < s_2$$

In cases where entities overlap, but do not share start and end index, we adjust their boundaries to create distinct, non-overlapping labels. For $A_1(s_1, e_1)$ and $A_2(s_2, e_2)$, where:

$$e_1 > s_2$$

we modify e_1 to ensure that it precedes s_2:

$$e_1 = s_2 - 1$$

[3]https://github.com/microsoft/presidio

[4]https://spacy.io/models

[5]https://nlp.stanford.edu/software/CRF-NER.html

Entity Type	Description	NER Source
PERSON	Names of individuals involved in the hearings are listed on the first page of the transcript. PERSON entities often include prefixes such as titles (e.g., Doctor, Miss, Commissioner). We remove these titles from the annotations to ensure that only the names themselves are removed in the final transcript.	Presidio, spaCy, StanfordNER
SPELLED_NAME	A custom label from a custom recognizer in Presidio is used to handle cases where names in parole hearings are spelled with letters separated by dashes (e.g., "J-O-H-N")..	Presidio
SPELLED_OUT_ITEM	A custom label from a custom recognizer in Presidio is used to handle cases where names are phonetically spelled out (e.g., "V as in Victor").	Presidio
CDCR_ID	A custom label added in Presidio to detect inmates CDCR ID, typically starting with a letter and followed by a series of numbers (e.g., "V12345").	Presidio
LOCATION	An umbrella term for locations, including states, countries, cities, etc.	Presidio, spaCy, StanfordNER
ORGANIZATION	Includes company names and organizations.	Presidio, StanfordNER
DATE	SpaCy's DATE entity detects dates, durations, ages, and time under a single category. To isolate actual dates, the duration, age, and time data are filtered out and reassigned to their specific entities. Additionally, a custom Presidio recognizer is employed to enhance the detection of typical date formats by assigning them to the DATE entity.	Presidio, spaCy
TIME	This combines a custom Presidio recognizer with spaCy's DATE entity to identify time patterns (such as XX:XX) and label them as TIME entities.	Presidio, spaCy
AGE	Identified using a combination of a custom Presidio recognizer as well as the age and duration data extracted from spaCy's DATE entity.	Presidio, spaCy
HEIGHT	Custom label detected by a custom Presidio recognizer. It detects numbers followed by height units (e.g., feet, inches).	Presidio
NRP	Presidio entity representing Nationality, Religion, or Political group.	Presidio
PHONE_NUMBER	Covers telephone numbers.	Presidio
EMAIL_ADDRESS	Covers email addresses.	Presidio
URL	Covers web addresses.	Presidio

Table 1: Entity types detected during the automatic annotation and anonymization process, alongside a small explanation of each type and the corresponding NER source.

This approach ensures that each word in the text is associated with at most one entity to prevent ambiguities in the anonymization process. A brief example of the filtering process is presented in Appendix A (step 1 to 3).

A total of 573,024 entities were labeled by the NER tools and regular expressions across the entire dataset. Table 2 displays the counts of labels that were filtered out. By applying the whitelist, handling duplicates, and resolving overlapping labels, 372,714 annotations were removed, with PERSON entities accounting for the highest number of removed annotations (306,567). As personal names are the most prevalent in parole hearing transcripts and all three NER tools are tasked with identifying them, this high degree of overlap is expected. Entities such as SPELLED_NAME and CDCR_ID are identified using regular expressions. Due to the transcription guidelines, the transcripts often include instances of stuttering (e.g., "I-I-I"), where repeated letters mimic the format of spelled names (e.g., "J-O-H-N"). This causes the regular expressions to incorrectly label stuttering as spelled names. To avoid incorrect labeling, we check if the repeated letters are identical, and if so, the label is getting removed. As a result, 418 SPELLED_NAMES labels were removed. The removal of certain CDCR_ID labels is due to overlaps where short IDs were detected as part of a larger CDCR_ID. In such cases, the filtering process merges the overlapping IDs into one and discards the redundant labels. Additionally, there are instances where commissioners begin spelling an ID but need to correct themselves partway through, leading to duplicate labels. As a result, 4 CDCR_ID labels needed to be removed.

The remaining 200,310 identified entities are clean, unique and usable annotations.

Annotation Type	Count
PERSON	306,567
LOCATION	14,787
ORGANIZATION	5,072
SPELLED_NAME	418
CDCR_ID	4
DATE	24,918
TIME	4,326
AGE	1,735
URL	4
NRP	360
Numerical values (non-sensitive)	14,523
Total annotations filtered-out	**372,714**
Final correct annotations	**200,310**

Table 2: Filtered annotation counts by entity and results of the automatic filtering process.

4.4 Results

We evaluate the performance of the automatic entity labelling based on a manually annotated subcorpus of 100 parole hearing transcripts. While the results presented in Table 3 primarily reflect the accuracy of the identification of sensitive entities, they directly impact the effectiveness of the anonymization process, as the replacements of each entity are based on these results. The table presents the precision, recall and F1-score for each entity type, based on a gold standard created by one of the authors. The results show a generally strong performance, with several entity types achieving high scores.

Entity Type	Precision	Recall	F1-score
PERSON	0.981	0.989	0.985
LOCATION	0.846	0.946	0.893
ORGANIZATION	0.768	0.739	0.754
SPELLED_NAME	1.000	0.995	0.997
CDCR_ID	0.933	0.996	0.964
DATE	0.883	0.968	0.923
TIME	0.977	0.943	0.960
AGE	0.903	0.926	0.914
HEIGHT	1.000	0.800	0.889
EMAIL_ADDRESS	1.000	0.750	0.857
URL	0.667	1.000	0.800
NRP	0.765	0.830	0.796
SPELLED_OUT_ITEM	1.000	1.000	1.000
PHONE_NUMBER	1.000	1.000	1.000
OVERALL	**0.955**	**0.972**	**0.963**

Table 3: Precision, Recall and F1-score of spaCy, Presidio and StanfordNER combined for different entity types across 100 hearing transcripts.

As stated in §4.1, we prioritize the detection of direct identifiers, which pose a higher risk of re-identification, such as PERSON, SPELLED_NAME, SPELLED_OUT_ITEM, CDCR_ID, LOCATION, TIME and DATE. For all of these entities our entity labeling approach achieves high or very high F1-scores. Notably, we observe an impressive F1-score of 0.985 for the PERSON entity type, showing the effectiveness of our multi-tool approach in accurately detecting individual names. Similarly, entities such as SPELLED_NAME, SPELLED_OUT_ITEM and PHONE_NUMBER achieve perfect or near-perfect scores (F1 $\geq$ 0.997). These high scores in performance can be attributed to the use of custom recognizers and regular expressions, which are particularly suited for the consistent structure and formatting of these entity types.

It is important to note that entities such as EMAIL_ADDRESS, URL and PHONE_NUMBER are quite rare, with HEIGHT and SPELLED_OUT_ITEMS, being the only ones occurring more than 20 times in the 100 transcripts analyzed. Additionally, the transcription conventions of parole hearings ensure a standardized format for these entities, which makes their detection through regular expressions straightforward. CDCR_ID and TIME entities both achieved F1-scores above 0.95. Among the direct identifiers entities related to LOCATION (F1 = 0.893) and DATE (F1 = 0.923) are the ones that show moderate performance but leave room for improvement.

The ORGANIZATION entity type posed significant challenges, resulting in the lowest F1-score of 0.754. We attribute this underperformance to the excessive use of abbreviations for programs, procedures and acts within the hearings, which are often misclassified by the NERs as organizations. For example, the abbreviation "CBA" for "Criminal Behavior Assessment" is incorrectly labelled as an organization, leading to confusing anonymization results in the end. The URL entity is amongst the rarest entities in the transcripts. It has a precision of 0.667 and an F1-score of 0.8 due to a single case of false positive, thus reaching to the conclusion that the automatic annotation process struggles with detecting URL entities.

Although some indirect identifiers exhibit lower F1-scores, this does not undermine the effectiveness of our approach. The high precision in recognizing direct identifiers significantly mitigates the risk of re-identification, ensuring the protection of privacy even if indirect identifiers are not perfectly detected.

Table 5 in Appendix B presents the performance of each NER tool when run individually on the subcorpus of 100 transcripts, with Presidio serving as baseline for comparison. Notably. Presidio achieves an F1-score of 0.989 for the PERSON entity, thus outperforming both StanfordNER and spaCy in this specific category. However, Presidio's performance falls short in other categories, with spaCy demonstrating better results for temporal data such as DATE, TIME and AGE. Presidio relies on regular expressions for such entities and therefore only serves to boost spaCy's results when used in combination. The F1-scores for entities such as LOCATION and ORGANIZATION are also lower when the tools are used by themselves. For instance, StanfordNER and Presidio show a low performance in the ORGANIZATION entity with F1-scores less than 0.600. In contrast, Table 3 demonstrates higher F1-scores when all tools are combined by improving the F1-score by 0.154 for the ORGANIZATION category.

This comparison underscores the complementary nature of the multi-tool approach, where the combination of tools compensates for weaknesses of the individual tools. Overall, an F1-score of 0.963 is achieved across all entities with the multi-tool approach. The values reported show a strong performance across most entity types, indicating that, once anonymized, the final transcripts will effectively protect individual's privacy and make re-identification difficult.

Our results are comparable to those reported in previous work by Schamberger (2021) and their domain-specific NER models achieving an F1-score between 0.802 and 0.811 for the identification of personal names. Our process achieves a higher F1-score for PERSON entities (0.985), indicating improved handling of names within legal settings, though it performs lower in detecting LOCATION and ORGANIZATION data, with F1-scores of 0.893 and 0.754, respectively. We attribute the higher performance for PERSON entities to the document format, where the names of participants are listed on the cover page of each transcript. In contrast, the lower scores for LOCATION and ORGANIZATION are likely due to domain-specific abbreviations, which lead to misclassifications (see also §5.1).

We conducted an ablation study, to evaluate the impact of the information given by the first page of the transcripts. We therefore executed the automatic annotation process without incorporating the names of the participants, the inmate's name, as well as the time and date of the hearing, typically found on the first page. Table 7 (Appendix D) shows the results of this experiment. A standard run (i.e. with first page information included) of the anonymization process yields a total of 573,024 unfiltered annotations, while running the code without the incorporation of the first page information only resulted in 447,216 unfiltered annotations. Integrating the names and organizations from the first page into Presidio improves it's accuracy of name detection, a step that particularly proves valuable in identifying names that were spelled or appear in incomplete form in the transcript.

The impact of incorporating the first page information into Presidio is evident in Table 8 in Appendix D. This table illustrates the differences in F1-scores for PERSON, LOCATION and ORGANIZATION entities. Without the first page information, these scores were 0.944, 0.713, and 0.630 respectively. These values are lower compared to the scores achieved when the anonymization process includes the first page data.

During a standard run, there is less confusion between the entities, resulting in more accurate annotations.

5 Pseudonymization

Pseudonymization involves assigning unique labels to each distinct entity within the dataset for the purpose of anonymization, meaning that reappearing entities are consistently replaced by the same tag. This is done through the use of a dictionary, which stores the original entity along with their pseudonymized category label. The primary function of this dictionary is to ensure the correct tag is consistently assigned throughout the transcript to the specific entities. In practice, entities are anonymized by combining the entity type with a sequential number. For example, names within the transcript are replaced by tags like [PERSON_1], [PERSON_2] and so forth. This approach is applied not only to names but to all recurring entities, ensuring consistent labeling across the dataset. Appendix A (step 4) showcases a practical illustration of how the anonymized final transcript appears after the replacement of PII by categorical tags.

For PERSON entities, all full names are extracted and each part of the full name is assigned a unique tag, which is then stored in a dictionary to ensure consistency across the transcript. We decided to use this approach, as commissioners often refer to the inmates by their last name alone. Each part of a PERSON entity is labeled with a sequential number, and the corresponding SPELLED_NAME is normalized and assigned the same sequential number as the matching PERSON entity. For CDCR ID entities, each unique value is assigned an individual tag. Example (1) demonstrates how these direct identifiers (in 1a) are anonymized within the transcripts (in 1b):

(1) a. **Original:**
We have a John Doe and the victim is Jane Smith. That's D-O-E. Case ID M23515.

b. **Anonymized:**
We have a [PERSON_1] [PERSON_2] and the victim is [PERSON_3] [PERSON_4]. That's [SPELLED_NAME_2]. Case ID [CDCR_ID_1].

Given that specific information such as the offender's name, hearing date and time are publicly available online on the CDCR's hearing calendar web page[6], we remove numerical values, such as date, time and age, by replacing the original data with fine-grained labels, using manually crafted rules consistently across all transcripts. The full date value is split into individual components and replaced by a type-specific label based on specific conditions. For instance, ordinal numbers ("1st", "2nd", ...) in the context of dates are replaced with the label [DAY]. Months and days of the week are detected using regular expressions and replaced with [MONTH] and [DAY_OF_WEEK] labels respectively. Four digit numbers under the DATE entity represent years and are replaced with [YEAR]. Decades ("20s", "30s", ...) are replaced with the label [DECADE]. Formatted dates that resemble patterns like "MM/DD/YYYY" are simply replaced by [DATE]. Any other numbers that do not satisfy the aforementioned conditions are replaced with [NUMBER]. Example (2) illustrates the handling of these specific entities.

(2) a. **Original:**
Today is 05/13/2012, 10:30, he was convicted back on Monday the 15th of June, 2011 at the age of 33 years old.

b. **Anonymized:**
Today is [DATE], [TIME], he was convicted back on [DAY_OF_WEEK] the [DAY] of [MONTH], [YEAR] at the age of [AGE] years old.

To generate more fine-grained and accurate pseudonymization labels for NRP, LOCATION and ORGANIZATION, we use BART, a zero shot classification model by Facebook (Facebook, 2024). BART is trained on the Multi-Genre Natural Language Inference (MultiNLI) dataset (Williams et al., 2018), which includes a diverse range of written and spoken data sources, including letters, Oxford University Press, press releases from government websites as well as transcriptions of face-to-face conversations and telephone calls.
The NRP entity, derived from Presidio, combines an individual's Nationality, Religion, and Political group affiliations – three distinct yet interrelated types of sensitive information. Similarly, LOCATION entities are complex, including diverse geographical information such as states, counties, cities, and countries.
BART's role is to distinguish and categorize the data within these multifaceted entities. By doing so, it enhances the contextual relevance and overall utility of the final dataset. This approach allows for more precise and meaningful pseudonymization while maintaining the analytical value of the data. Example (3) illustrates the conversion of each entity type into appropriate category labels, demonstrating the granularity and accuracy achieved through this method.

(3) a. **Original:**
He lived in Connecticut but then moved to California. He is a Canadian citizen from Canada and works with the California City Police Department.

b. **Anonymized:**
He lived in [STATE_1] but then moved to [STATE_2]. He is a [NATIONALITY_1] citizen from [COUNTRY_1] and works with the [POLICE_DEPARTMENT_1].

[6]https://www.cdcr.ca.gov/bph/2024/02/07/august-2024-hearing-calendar

For the remaining entities, each unique occurrence is replaced with the specific category label and their corresponding sequential number.

Appendix C shows that PERSON entities are the most frequent throughout parole hearing transcripts, accounting for 34.92% per 1000 tokens. This result is none of a surprise, as discussions typically revolve around the inmate, their victims, accomplices and family members. DATE, AGE and LOCATION entities, while important, appear at varying frequencies with only DATE occurring just over 3% per 1000 tokens. This reflects the importance of discussing the inmate's age at specific life events, such as the crime or key moments during incarceration, as well as references to locations related to their past or to future parole plans. Similarly, the frequent mention of DATE and LOCATION entities can be attributed to discussions about important milestones in the inmate's history or potential locations for future parole plans.

5.1 Challenges & Limitations

Despite the promising results we obtained from the detection of PII through NER tools and the pseudonymization technique, certain issues and constraints still need to be addressed. By law, all parole hearings transcripts are required to provide verbatim records of the dialogue. This standardized format presents both advantages and challenges to the anonymization process. We identified two primary categories of issues: (1) errors stemming from the NER tools that result in misclassified entities, and (2) entities that are completely missed by the NER tools, leading to unintended leakage of sensitive information.

Table 4 shows the number of misclassified entities we observed in the 100 manually analyzed transcripts. The most common misclassifications occur between LOCATION and PERSON. This is mainly caused by names that refer to both people and places (e.g. Georgia or Dallas) and are often incorrectly tagged as LOCATION by the NER tools.

Classification errors between ORGANIZATION and PERSON entities occurred 45 times, primarily because people's names appeared within official organization names. Misclassifications between CDCR ID and LOCATION entities are due to the regular expressions for CDCR ID entities matching zipcodes and post office box (PO Box) numbers. The least frequent mismatches, such as NRP | ORGANIZATION and EMAIL_ADDRESS | PERSON come from specific cases where an abbreviation was incorrectly misclassified by the NER tools as an NRP and a part of the email including a person's name is misclassified as a PERSON.

Mismatched entity pairs	Count
LOCATION | PERSON	127
ORGANIZATION | PERSON	45
LOCATION | ORGANIZATION	26
AGE | DATE	33
CDCR_ID | LOCATION	20
DATE | TIME	3
AGE | TIME	3
NRP | ORGANIZATION	1
EMAIL_ADDRESS | PERSON	1

Table 4: Counts of misclassified entity labels in 100 analyzed transcripts. In the format "LABEL A" | "LABEL B", the first label represents the incorrect classification by the NER, while the second label indicates the correct classification.

As already reported on in §4.4, the misclassification of non-sensitive entities that do not require anonymization, such as abbreviations of parole hearing-specific terms, frequently results in their attribution to the ORGANIZATION category, resulting in an over-anonymization of the data. Expanding the whitelist can help address this challenge.

Another issue was found in cases where the CDCR ID's first letter was spelled out phonetically by using a corresponding name. For example, "Victor 12345" was used to indicate that the CDCR ID begins with "V", resulting in the full CDCR ID "V12345". The NER tools misclassified "Victor" as a PERSON entity, leading to incorrect pseudonymization. Changing PERSON entities followed by CDCR IDs to just CDCR ID might seem like a straightforward solution, but is complicated by the fact that the inmates' names are often immediately followed by their CDCR ID, without any separating punctuation. We decided to accept these minor errors in the pseudomized text and will address the requirement of a more nuanced approach for phonetically spelled out names in the future.

The pseudonymization approach relies on a dictionary to assign distinct tags to each identified PERSON entity (e.g. PERSON_1, PERSON_2). This procedure ensures maintenance of privacy, while simultaneously allowing different individuals to remain distinguishable. However, this method faces challenges whenever a name that has already been assigned a label is later misspelled and therefore not found in the dictionary. As a result, a new and incorrect label is generated, leading to multiple labels for the same person, compromising the consistency and reliability of the redacted transcript. Example (4) showcases the erroneous anonymization of names due to typos. Even though the same person is referenced in both sentence fragments, two different tags are generated for the last name due to the misspelling. This issue might not leak PII, but compromises the data's integrity and underscores the dependence on error-free transcriptions for anonymization.

(4) a. **Original name:**
Mark | Stevenson | is present.
Mark | Stevenston | here is...
b. **Anonymized name:**
[Person_1] | [Person_2] | is present.
[Person_1] | [Person_3] | here is...

Due to the nature of spoken language, the transcripts include passages where multiple speakers talk simultaneously, leading to fragmented utterances appearing on separate lines. This can cause sensitive information to be split between lines and potentially remain undetected by the NERs.

While incorrect category labels reduce the utility of the anonymized transcripts and can lead to confusion, the consequences of missed entities are more severe, as they result in the direct leakage of PII.

Our approach to anonymization faces several challenges that highlight the inherent trade-offs between data privacy and and analytical utility. One notable decision we made was to not anonymize gender information, including gender specific pronouns in the text, given that the majority of inmates seeking parole in California are male.

Another significant limitation stems from the temporal context of the hearings. In the specific case of our dataset, many transcripts contain references to the COVID-19 pandemic, which inadvertently narrows the timeframe of the hearings to 2019 and 2021. This temporal information, while valuable for understanding the unique circumstances of conducting the hearings via video conferencing, also increases the potential for re-identification.

The same applies to high-profile cases that received significant media attention, such as parole hearings for individuals involved in the Manson murders. For these instances, achieving complete anonymization is especially difficult. The risk of re-identification cannot be entirely eliminated without significantly compromising the analytical utility of the transcripts.

While some of the identified limitations are inherent to the nature of the data and cannot be fully resolved, we hope to address the remaining in future work by enhancing the automatic detection of sensitive data. However, to ensure that no sensitive information has been overlooked, a final manual review before publication of the data is essential to prevent unintended data exposure and maintain ethical standards.

6 Conclusion

We introduced a novel approach for the anonymization of direct and indirect identifiers in parole hearing transcripts, offering a way to protect sensitive personal information while preserving the utility of the data for different kind of research purposes. Our methodology combines Named Entity Recognition tools with pseudonymization techniques and addresses the challenges posed by this specific type of legal dialogue. Despite the limitations of current NER tools, leading to misclassified entity types and errors arising from misspelled names, our approach successfully cleans the transcripts from sensitive data in the majority of cases. While our approach provides a strong methodology to reliably pseudonymize parole hearing transcripts, a thorough manual review of the transcripts before publication is still mandatory in order to avoid any unintended data leakage. Future research should focus on addressing the remaining limitations, with the ultimate goal of enhancing data privacy without sacrificing data utility.

Ethical considerations

While unanonymized parole hearing transcripts can be officially requested via email from the Board of Parole Hearings in California, our goal is to protect the privacy of the individuals involved. At the same time, we want to enable researchers to investigate linguistic strategies in parole hearings, which could lead to improved understanding of decision-making processes and potentially contribute to more equitable outcomes. However, we acknowledge that despite our best efforts at anonymization, a small risk of re-identification remains. This is especially true for high-profile cases. We would like to note that while we are using a technically publicly available dataset, we cannot guarantee that all participants, especially victims and their next of kin, are fully aware that these transcripts can be requested by anyone, regardless of scientific usage or other purposes. This underscores our commitment to robust anonymization and ethical handling of the data.

Despite the promising results of our anonymization process, we still wait for official confirmation that the anonymized dataset can be published online. We will also seek ethical clearance before releasing the anonymized dataset to confirm compliance with relevant regulations and standards. We have published the code for the anonymization process on GitHub[7].

Acknowledgements

We want to thank the California Department of Corrections and Rehabilitation (CDCR) for providing us with the parole hearing transcripts.
The work reported on in this paper was funded by the Deutsche Forschungsgemeinschaft (DFG – German Research Foundation) under Germany's Excellence Strategy – EXC-2035/1 – 390681379 as part of the project "Inequality in Street-level Bureaucracy: Linguistic Analysis of Public Service Encounters".

References

Luis Adrián Cabrera-Diego and Akshita Gheewala. 2024. PSILENCE: A Pseudonymization Tool for International Law. In *Proceedings of the Workshop on Computational Approaches to Language Data Pseudonymization (CALD-pseudo 2024)*, pages 25–36. Association for Computational Linguistics.

Ingrid Espinoza, Steffen Frenzel, Laurin Friedrich, Wassiliki Siskou, Steffen Eckhard, and Annette Hautli-Janisz. 2024. PSE v1.0: The First Open Access Corpus of Public Service Encounters. In *Proceedings of the 2024 Joint International Conference on Computational Linguistics, Language Resources and Evaluation (LREC-COLING 2024)*, pages 13315–13320, Torino, Italia. ELRA and ICCL.

Facebook. 2024. BART-Large-MNLI: A Zero-Shot Classification Model. https://huggingface.co/facebook/bart-large-mnli. Accessed: 2024-08-04.

[7]https://github.com/abedit/Automated-Anonymization-of-Parole-Hearing-Transcripts

Jenny Rose Finkel, Trond Grenager, and Christopher Manning. 2005. Incorporating Non-local Information into Information Extraction Systems by Gibbs Sampling. In *Proceedings of the 43rd Annual Meeting of the Association for Computational Linguistics (ACL 2005)*, pages 363–370. https://nlp.stanford.edu/software/CRF-NER.html.

Shayna Gardiner, Tania Habib, Kevin Humphreys, Masha Azizi, Frederic Mailhot, Anne Paling, Preston Thomas, and Nathan Zhang. 2024. Data Anonymization for Privacy-Preserving Large language Model Fine-Tuning on Call Transcripts. In *Proceedings of the Workshop on Computational Approaches to Language Data Pseudonymization (CALD-pseudo 2024)*, pages 64–75, St. Julian's, Malta. Association for Computational Linguistics.

Jenny Hong, Derek Chong, and Christopher Manning. 2021a. Learning from Limited Labels for Long Legal Dialogue. In *Proceedings of the Natural Legal Language Processing Workshop 2021*, pages 190–204, Punta Cana, Dominican Republic. Association for Computational Linguistics.

Jenny Hong, Catalin Voss, and Christopher Manning. 2021b. Challenges for Information Extraction from Dialogue in Criminal Law. In *Proceedings of the 1st Workshop on NLP for Positive Impact*, pages 71–81, Online. Association for Computational Linguistics.

Matthew Honnibal, Ines Montani, Sofie Van Landeghem, and Adriane Boyd. 2020. spaCy: Industrial-strength Natural Language Processing in Python.

Omri Mendels and Avishay Balter. 2020. Presidio: Context Aware, Pluggable and Customizable Data Protection and De-identification SDK for Text and Images. Microsoft.

Arttu Oksanen, Minna Tamper, Jouni Tuominen, Aki Hietanen, and Eero Hyvönen. 2019. ANOPPI: A Pseudonymization Service for Finnish Court Documents. In *Legal Knowledge and Information Systems*, pages 251–254. IOS Press.

Bruno Ribeiro, Vitor Rolla, and Ricardo Santos. 2023. INCOGNITUS: A Toolbox for Automated Clinical Notes Anonymization. In *Proceedings of the 17th Conference of the European Chapter of the Association for Computational Linguistics: System Demonstrations*, pages 187–194, Dubrovnik, Croatia. Association for Computational Linguistics.

Tom Schamberger. 2021. Customizable Anonymization of German Legal Court Rulings using Domain-specific Named Entity Recognition. Master's thesis, Department of Mathematics, Technical University Munich. Master's Thesis.

Graham Todd, Catalin Voss, and Jenny Hong. 2020. Unsupervised anomaly detection in parole hearings using language models. In *Proceedings of the Fourth Workshop on Natural Language Processing and Computational Social Science*, pages 66–71, Online. Association for Computational Linguistics.

Laura Weidinger, Jonathan Uesato, Maribeth Rauh, Conor Griffin, Po-Sen Huang, John Mellor, Amelia Glaese, Myra Cheng, Borja Balle, Atoosa Kasirzadeh, Courtney Biles, Sasha Brown, Zac Kenton, Will Hawkins, Tom Stepleton, Abeba Birhane, Lisa Anne Hendricks, Laura Rimell, William Isaac, Julia Haas, Sean Legassick, Geoffrey Irving, and Iason Gabriel. 2022. Taxonomy of risks posed by language models. In *Proceedings of the 2022 ACM Conference on Fairness, Accountability, and Transparency*, FAccT '22, page 214–229, New York, NY, USA. Association for Computing Machinery.

Adina Williams, Nikita Nangia, and Samuel Bowman. 2018. A Broad-Coverage Challenge Corpus for Sentence Understanding through Inference. In *Proceedings of the 2018 Conference of the North American Chapter of the Association for Computational Linguistics: Human Language Technologies, Volume 1 (Long Papers)*, pages 1112–1122, New Orleans, Louisiana. Association for Computational Linguistics.

A Automatic Annotation Example

The following is an extract from one of the hearing transcripts. To preserve the privacy of the people involved, the names and IDs have been altered. The labels are visually marked according to the tool that detected them: labels coming from spaCy are in blue, labels from Presidio are in green, and StanfordNER labels are in red.

1. PRESIDING COMMISSIONER JONES: All right. Good afternoon. Today's date, September 1st, 2021. Time is, uh, 1:30 PM. This is the initial parole suitability hearing for inmate- Correction. This is the first subsequent parole suitability hearing for inmate Kevin Richardson, R-I-C-H-A-R-D-S-O-N, CDCR number L90314. Inmate Richardson is not present at the hearing room at San Quentin State Prison. Uh, we were notified today that the inmate is currently out at the hospital and, uh, is currently unavailable for his hearing. Uh, so, uh, let's uh, take appearances. Uh, we are conducting this hearing by video conference. So, let's take appearances on who's here today. Uh, we'll have the Panel members go first. My name is Alyssa Jones J-O-N-E-S, Commissioner with the Board of Parole Hearings.

In this step, invalid labels are filtered out and the remaining labels are cleaned. The identification of "Board of Parole Hearing" as ORGANIZATION is dropped, as it is a non-sensitive term. The same applied to the DATE label of "Today's", since it does not contain a numerical component.

2. PRESIDING COMMISSIONER JONES: All right. Good afternoon. Today's date, September 1st, 2021. Time is, uh, 1:30 PM. This is the initial parole suitability hearing for inmate- Correction. This is the first subsequent parole suitability hearing for inmate Kevin Richardson, R-I-C-H-A-R-D-S-O-N, CDCR number L90314. Inmate Richardson is not present at the hearing room at San Quentin State Prison. Uh, we were notified today that the inmate is currently out at the hospital and, uh, is currently unavailable for his hearing. Uh, so, uh, let's uh, take appearances. Uh, we are conducting this hearing by video conference. So, let's take appearances on who's here today. Uh, we'll have the Panel members go first. My name is Alyssa Jones J-O-N-E-S, Commissioner with the Board of Parole Hearings.

Finally, any overlapping labels are separated.

3. PRESIDING COMMISSIONER JONES: All right. Good afternoon. Today's date, September 1st, 2021. Time is, uh, 1:30 PM. This is the initial parole suitability hearing for inmate- Correction. This is the first subsequent parole suitability hearing for inmate Kevin Richardson, R-I-C-H-A-R-D-S-O-N, CDCR number L90314. Inmate Richardson is not present at the hearing room at San Quentin State Prison. Uh, we were notified today that the inmate is currently out at the hospital and, uh, is currently unavailable for his hearing. Uh, so, uh, let's uh, take appearances. Uh, we are conducting this hearing by video conference. So, let's take appearances on who's here today. Uh, we'll have the Panel members go first. My name is Alyssa Jones J-O-N-E-S, Commissioner with the Board of Parole Hearings.

The pseudonymization method is applied. The changed entities are in bold.

4. PRESIDING COMMISSIONER **[PERSON_2]**: All right. Good afternoon. Today's date, **[MONTH] [DAY]**, **[YEAR]**. Time is, uh, **[TIME]** PM. This is the initial parole suitability hearing for inmate- Correction. This is the first subsequent parole suitability hearing for inmate **[PERSON_7] [PERSON_8]**, **[SPELLED_NAME_PERSON_8]**, CDCR number **[ID_1]**. Inmate **[PERSON_8]** is not present at the hearing room at **[PRISON_1]**. Uh, we were notified today that the inmate is currently out at the hospital and, uh, is currently unavailable for his hearing. Uh, so, uh, let's uh, take appearances. Uh, we are conducting this hearing by video conference. So, let's take appearances on who's here today. Uh, we'll have the Panel members go first. My name is **[PERSON_1] [PERSON_2]**, **[SPELLED_NAME_PERSON_2]**, Commissioner with the Board of Parole Hearings.

B Metrics of Presidio, spaCy and StanfordNER

Entity Type	Presidio			spaCy			StanfordNER		
	P	R	F1	P	R	F1	P	R	F1
PERSON	0.982	0.995	0.989	0.984	0.899	0.939	0.978	0.789	0.873
LOCATION	0.932	0.905	0.919	0.903	0.590	0.714	0.769	0.848	0.807
ORGANIZATION	0.976	0.341	0.505	—	—	—	0.688	0.487	0.571
SPELLED_NAME	1.000	0.995	0.997	—	—	—	—	—	—
CDCR_ID	0.933	0.996	0.964	—	—	—	—	—	—
DATE	0.647	0.611	0.628	0.921	0.780	0.845	—	—	—
TIME	0.880	0.621	0.728	0.973	0.796	0.875	—	—	—
AGE	0.931	0.126	0.222	0.903	0.921	0.912	—	—	—
HEIGHT	1.000	0.800	0.889	—	—	—	—	—	—
EMAIL_ADDRESS	1.000	0.750	0.857	—	—	—	—	—	—
URL	0.667	1.000	0.800	—	—	—	—	—	—
NRP	0.750	0.830	0.788	—	—	—	—	—	—
SPELLED_OUT_ITEM	1.000	1.000	1.000	—	—	—	—	—	—
PHONE_NUMBER	1.000	1.000	1.000	—	—	—	—	—	—
Overall	**0.953**	**0.885**	**0.918**	**0.971**	**0.801**	**0.878**	**0.951**	**0.629**	**0.757**

Table 5: Precision (P), Recall (R), and F1-score (F1) for the automatic labeling process run by each tool separately. Blank cells are due to spaCy and StanfordNER not covering certain entities, while Presidio covers every entity.

C Pseudonymization Statistics

Entity Type	Total	Average	Frequency
PERSON	153,495	459.57	34.9242%
LOCATION	8,410	25.18	1.9135%
ORGANIZATION	5,758	17.24	1.3101%
SPELLED_NAME	2,141	6.41	0.4871%
CDCR_ID	1,565	4.69	0.3561%
DATE	13,735	41.12	3.1251%
TIME	3,194	9.56	0.7267%
AGE	11,092	33.21	2.5237%
HEIGHT	103	0.31	0.0234%
EMAIL_ADDRESS	4	0.01	0.0009%
URL	17	0.05	0.0039%
NRP	735	2.20	0.1672%
SPELLED_OUT_ITEM	57	0.17	0.0130%
PHONE_NUMBER	4	0.01	0.0009%

Table 6: Number of entities pseudonymized, as well as the average of each entity per file and how frequently each entity is pseudonymized per 1000 tokens.

D Ablation Study

Entity Type	Standard process	Excluding 1st page
PERSON	460,062	333,223
LOCATION	23,197	25,245
ORGANIZATION	10,830	9,826
SPELLED_NAME	2,559	2,559
CDCR_ID	1,569	1,569
DATE	38,653	38,653
TIME	7,520	7,520
AGE	12,827	12,827
HEIGHT	103	103
EMAIL_ADDRESS	4	4
URL	21	21
NRP	1,095	1,082
SPELLED_OUT_ITEM	57	57
PHONE_NUMBER	4	4
Numerical values	14,523	14,523
Total	**573,024**	**447,216**

Table 7: Comparison of entity detection results: standard process vs. process excluding first page information.

Entity Type	Standard process			Excluding 1st page		
	P	R	F1	P	R	F1
PERSON	0.981	0.989	0.985	0.979	0.911	0.944
LOCATION	0.846	0.946	0.893	0.592	0.895	0.713
ORGANIZATION	0.768	0.739	0.754	0.721	0.560	0.630
SPELLED_NAME	1.000	0.995	0.997	1.000	0.995	0.997
CDCR_ID	0.933	0.996	0.964	0.933	0.996	0.964
DATE	0.883	0.968	0.923	0.883	0.968	0.923
TIME	0.977	0.943	0.960	0.977	0.943	0.960
AGE	0.903	0.926	0.914	0.903	0.926	0.914
HEIGHT	1.000	0.800	0.889	1.000	0.800	0.889
EMAIL_ADDRESS	1.000	0.750	0.857	1.000	0.750	0.857
URL	0.667	1.000	0.800	0.667	1.000	0.800
NRP	0.765	0.830	0.796	0.765	0.830	0.796
SPELLED_OUT_ITEM	1.000	1.000	1.000	1.000	1.000	1.000
PHONE_NUMBER	1.000	1.000	1.000	1.000	1.000	1.000
Overall	**0.955**	**0.972**	**0.963**	**0.930**	**0.907**	**0.918**

Table 8: Performance metrics comparison: standard process vs. process excluding first page information on a subcorpus of 100 transcripts.

Towards an Automated Pointwise Evaluation Metric for Generated Long-Form Legal Summaries

Shao Min Tan
Thomson Reuters Labs
Landis + Gyr-Strasse 3
6300 Zug, Switzerland
shaomin.tan@tr.com

Quentin Grail
Thomson Reuters Labs
Landis + Gyr-Strasse 3
6300 Zug, Switzerland
quentin.grail@tr.com

Lee Quartey
Thomson Reuters Labs
3 Times Square
New York, NY 10036, USA
lee.quartey@tr.com

Abstract

Long-form abstractive summarization is a task that has particular importance in the legal domain. Automated evaluation metrics are important for the development of text generation models, but existing research on the evaluation of generated summaries has focused mainly on short summaries. We introduce an automated evaluation methodology for generated long-form legal summaries, which involves breaking each summary into individual points, comparing the points in a human-written and machine-generated summary, and calculating a recall and precision score for the latter. The method is designed to be particularly suited for the complexities of legal text, and is also fully interpretable. We also create and release a small meta-dataset for the benchmarking of evaluation methods, focusing on long-form legal summarization. Our evaluation metric corresponds better with human evaluation compared to existing metrics which were not developed for legal data.

1 Introduction

Generative text models, including large language models (LLMs), have made huge strides in performance in the last few years, and are now increasingly deployed in many domains in business and science. However, research on effective automated evaluation metrics for generated text has yet to catch up, and basic methodologies such as ROUGE (Lin, 2004) and others (see Section 2) are still used to judge the performance of new models. In the sub-field of text summarization, existing research on and meta-datasets for the evaluation of generated text summaries have focused mainly on shorter summaries consisting of a few sentences, while very little work has been done on long-form summaries (see the survey Koh et al., 2022).

Long-form abstractive summarization is a task that has particular importance in the legal domain. Legal documents such as court judgments (which are documents written by judges, detailing the background of a court case and the reasons for a ruling) are often many tens of pages long, and summaries of these can be several pages long. The UK Supreme Court, for instance, releases press summaries of 2-3 pages for the cases it decides (The Supreme Court of the United Kingdom, 2024).

Modern LLMs, with their long context windows, are a natural tool for automatically generating such summaries from the original legal document. There is a pressing need, therefore, for effective automated evaluation metrics for the resulting long-form summaries.

In this paper, we propose an automated method for the evaluation of long-form generated legal summaries, which involves breaking each summary into individual points, comparing the points in a human-written reference and machine-generated candidate summary, and calculating a recall or precision score. We call our method the *pointwise evaluation methodology*.

The idea of splitting summaries into discrete units to obtain reliable manual evaluation scores is well-known (Nenkova and Passonneau, 2004), and automated methods based on this idea have been explored (Liu et al., 2023b). Our proposed method expands upon previous work by: 1) adapting the methodology to be usable for long-form summaries and 2) using more advanced models to deal with the greater nuance and complexity of legal text.

To evaluate this method against existing ones, we also create and release a small meta-dataset for benchmarking evaluation methodologies for long-form legal summarization. To our knowledge, this is the first such dataset to be made available.

Proceedings of the Natural Legal Language Processing Workshop 2024, pages 129–142
November 16, 2024 ©2024 Association for Computational Linguistics

2 Survey of Existing Approaches and Prior Work

2.1 Manual Evaluation Methodologies

Manual evaluation is considered to be the gold-standard for scoring the outputs of machine learning models. The following papers present systematic methods for collecting manual scores for generated text.

Pyramid (Nenkova and Passonneau, 2004) introduced a reliable method of obtaining human evaluations of generated summaries against a set of human-written reference summaries. The authors introduce the concept of Summarization Content Units (SCUs) — parts of a text that are no bigger than a single clause. The SCUs are manually extracted from each reference summary. If SCUs from multiple references have near-identical meanings, these are considered to be a single SCU, and this SCU is given a higher weight based on how many reference summaries it appears in.

The extracted SCUs are then used to objectively evaluate the candidate summaries. For each candidate summary, the human annotator determines which SCUs are contained within the candidate. The candidate is then assigned a score based on the weights of the SCUs it contains.

LitePyramid (Shapira et al., 2019) simplifies the Pyramid method by using statistical sampling rather than exhaustive SCU extraction and analysis, making the process less error-prone and more suited for crowdsourced workers. Instead of merging similar SCUs that appear in multiple documents, each SCU is considered individually during the annotation of candidate texts. A fact that is important will be repeated in different reference summaries and thus be "weighted" more strongly during the scoring process.

REALSumm (Bhandari et al., 2020) presents a meta-dataset for evaluation based on the CNN/Daily Mail dataset, produced by adapting the LitePyramid method to be used with only one human reference summary.

2.2 Automated Evaluation Metrics

Because human evaluation is time-consuming, automated evaluation metrics are often used to measure the quality of generated texts. While such automated methods are convenient, they may not correlate well with manual evaluation.

ROUGE-N (Lin, 2004) measures the overlap of n-grams between the reference and candidate texts.

ROUGE-L (Lin, 2004) measures the length of the longest common subsequence between the two texts, normalised by the length of one of the texts.

SEMScore (Aynetdinov and Akbik, 2024) measures the cosine similarity between the embeddings of the two texts.

BERTScore (Zhang et al., 2020) calculates the document similarity as a combination of the similarity between contextual BERT embeddings of individual tokens in the reference and candidate texts.

BARTScore (Yuan et al., 2021) is based on calculating the probability that the BART model would produce the candidate text given the reference text (or vice-versa).

FActScore (Min et al., 2023) calculates a factuality score for a generated text by breaking the generated text into atomic facts and calculating the percentage of facts supported by a reliable knowledge source. The authors focused on generated biographies.

AlignScore (Zha et al., 2023) measures the factual consistency between two texts using a general function of information alignment, developed using a variety of data sources from common NLP tasks.

A^{2}CU (Liu et al., 2023b) automates the LitePyramid method by 1) fine-tuning a T-Zero 3B model (Sanh et al., 2022) to extract content units from reference summaries, and 2) using a BERT-based (Devlin et al., 2019) Natural Language Inference (NLI) model to check whether each content unit is present in a generated candidate summary. The authors also developed a single-step metric (A^{3}CU). The authors trained and tested their models on short summaries (several sentences long) from the RoSE dataset (Liu et al., 2023a).

2.3 Meta-Datasets for Evaluation of Evaluation Metrics

TAC 2008 and TAC 2009 (Dang and Owczarzak, 2008): These datasets contain 100-word summaries of multiple documents, and include human evaluation of machine-generated summaries.

REALSumm CNNDM dataset (Bhandari et al., 2020): The authors created a meta-evaluation dataset based on the CNN/Daily Mail news summarization dataset. The gold summaries are an average of 3 - 4 sentences long.

RoSE dataset (Liu et al., 2023a): Meta-evaluation dataset of short-form summaries based on 3 datasets: CNN/Daily Mail, XSum (single-sentence summaries of news articles), and SAMSum (dialogue summaries).

2.4 Text Summarization in the Legal Domain

Hachey and Grover, 2006 developed an extractive summarization method for UK court judgments using the rhetorical status of sentences.

In Shukla et al., 2022, the authors explored and evaluated various extractive and abstractive methods of summarizing legal case documents. They also performed a meta-evaluation study, and found that the results of several automated evaluation metrics (ROUGE and BERTScore) correlate poorly with human ratings. The authors did not release their meta-evaluation dataset.

3 Pointwise Evaluation Method

3.1 Introduction

We expand upon previous work by developing an interpretable, two-step evaluation methodology suited for legal text. The steps consist of:

1. Breaking the reference and candidate texts into individual points;

2. Determining, for each point in the reference text, whether there is a point in the candidate text that is saying the same thing (though it may be phrased differently), and vice-versa.

These steps can either be done manually (see Section 4) or using automated methods (see Section 5). A recall and precision score can then be calculated.

3.2 Differences from Existing Approaches

Our method differs from existing approaches in the following ways.

Granularity of Semantic Units

Nenkova and Passonneau, 2004 and Liu et al., 2023b break the text to be evaluated down into basic units of a single clause, as shown in the example in Figure 1 (a1). Basic units of this size can work well with news article summaries, which tend to concentrate on facts.

Legal documents such as court judgments, however, are more complex and often involve logical reasoning. The example in Figure 1 (a2) shows a legal sentence and what it would look like if broken into single-clause units. These units, however, are not a good representation of the original sentence in the context of a legal case. The first point, that the Court of Appeals disagreed with the High Court, is true but not useful without the additional information about which point they disagreed on. The Court of Appeals may well have agreed with the High Court on another legal issue while disagreeing on this one. The second point, that "the listings were not targeted at UK consumers", is stated as a fact, when in the original sentence it was the High Court's opinion. It is important to distinguish who says something in a legal case, because the parties and courts involved often have differing opinions.

We therefore use longer points as our base unit of text.

Handling Long-Form Summaries

The entailment models used in Liu et al., 2023b have been trained on short summaries and perform less well on long-form summaries.

In addition, long documents sometimes require greater contextual understanding of the document in order to determine whether two sentences are making the same point. Consider the example in Figure 1 (b). These two sentences are making the same point in the context of the court's reasoning, but one needs to know the context of the factors mentioned in the second sentence in order to be sure of this.

Handling Greater Nuance and Complexity of Legal Text

Because legal texts involve complex reasoning, it is a more difficult task to determine whether two sentences are making the same point in the context of a legal case. For example, consider the two sentences in Figure 1 (c). The two sentences are not making the same point, nor does either entail the other. However, the logic involved in the sentences is somewhat convoluted.

We therefore make use of more advanced models, such as state-of-the-art LLMs, which are better able to handle such nuanced reasoning tasks, especially when given examples in the prompt.

4 Meta-Dataset for Evaluation of Long-Form Legal Summaries

We create a small meta-dataset for the evaluation of evaluation methods for long-form legal summarization, consisting of 7 cases from the UK Supreme Court (UKSC) [1]. For each decided case, the UKSC writes and releases a 2-3-page-long press summary.

[1]Contains public sector information licensed under the Open Government License v3.0.

(a) Granularity of semantic units

a1) News text:

Chelsea weren't awarded a penalty for David Ospina's 51st-minute clash with Oscar.

Single-clause semantic units:

- Chelsea weren't awarded a penalty.
- David Ospina clashed with Oscar.
- The clash occurred in the 51st minute.

a2) Legal text:

The Court of Appeals disagreed with the High Court's conclusion that the listings were not targeted at UK consumers.

Single-clause semantic units (do not capture full meaning):

- The Court of Appeals disagreed with the High Court's conclusion.
- The listings were not targeted at UK consumers.

(b) Contextual understanding required

1. Significant factors pointing in the direction of targeting include a message on the landing page and almost all subsequent pages offering to deliver to the UK.
2. The Supreme Court relies on various factors, including the "Deliver to United Kingdom" message displayed to UK consumers.

(c) Nuance and complexity of legal text

1. The company's targeting of consumers in the UK infringed the trademarks.
2. Even if the goods were not targeted at consumers in the UK, the company nonetheless infringed the trademarks.

Figure 1: Examples of the nuances involved in legal language and how it differs from other types of text such as news. The examples are explained in Section 3.2. Example (a1) is adapted from Liu et al., 2023b.

We use this press summary as the human-written reference summary of the case.

For each court decision, we generate 5 LLM-written summaries, using different models (Claude 3 Opus and Sonnet, GPT-4o, and Titan Text G1 Premier) and prompts. We then use a variation of the LitePyramid method to create the meta-dataset, following the two-step procedure described in Section 3.1.

Step 1: Point Extraction. We manually break each summary (human-written reference and LLM-generated candidates) down into discrete units, which we call *points*. As explained in Section 3.2, these points tend to be more complex than the units used in previous work using the Pyramid method.

Step 2: Point Matching. For a given candidate summary, we step through each point in the reference summary, and find the best-matching candidate point (if any).

Further details can be found in Appendices A.1 and A.2.

4.1 Recall Score

To calculate the overall recall score of the candidate summary, we consider the percentage of reference points which have a matching candidate point, with a weighting scheme applied. The weighting scheme is described in Appendix A.3.

The pointwise evaluation method can also be used to obtain precision scores. However, in accordance with the literature, we concentrate on recall-based scoring when creating the dataset.

4.2 Dataset Split

Some of the automated methods discussed in the next section require training examples. We use 3 of the UKSC cases (each with 1 human-written and 5 LLM-generated summaries) as the training and validation set, and the remaining 4 cases (each with 1 human-written and 5 LLM-generated summaries) as the test set for calculating the performance of the automated methods.

5 Automating the Pointwise Evaluation Method

Each step in the two-step approach described in Section 3.1 can be automated.

5.1 Step 1: Point Extraction

In Step 1, we break the text into individual points. We investigate the following automated methods.

5.1.1 Fine-tuned T5 Model

Chen et al., 2023 introduced a semantic unit which the authors call *atomic expressions of meaning* or *propositions*. The authors fine-tuned a Flan T5-large model (Chung et al., 2024) on the FACTOID-WIKI dataset to extract propositions from an input passage. We have found that their model splits the text into longer segments than the content units presented in Nenkova and Passonneau, 2004 and Liu et al., 2023b, making it more suitable for legal text. To further increase the suitability of the model, we fine-tune the model on our dataset.

5.1.2 LLM Prompted with Examples

We prompt an LLM (Claude 3.5 Sonnet, which in our experience is the best-performing Anthropic model for similar tasks) to split a paragraph into individual points, giving it similar instructions to those in Appendix A.1. We also provide it with about 25 examples from the training dataset.

For both of these methods, we pass each paragraph of the summary separately through the model.

5.2 Step 2: Point Matching

In Step 2, we compare the points in the reference and candidate texts, to determine whether the same points exist in both. In other words, for each point in the reference text, we need to evaluate whether there is a point in the candidate text that is stating the same idea. This boils down to determining whether two sentences are making the same point in the context of the legal case (though they may be phrased differently).

We investigate the following methods (ranging from simple to complex) to automate this step.

5.2.1 Cosine Similarity

We calculate the embeddings of the two points, using the Sentence Transformers (Reimers and Gurevych, 2019) *all-mpnet-base-v2* model (the current top-performing Sentence Transformers model (Sentence Transformers, 2024)). Cosine similarity is then computed between these embeddings. All pairs passing a threshold are considered a match. The threshold is selected to optimize one of the downstream metrics (*reference point based F1*, described in Section 6.2) on the training set.

5.2.2 NLI Model

We use the NLI model from Liu et al., 2023b to check whether each reference point is present in the candidate summary. Their NLI model is a DeBERTa model (He et al., 2021) that has been fine-tuned on the RoSE dataset. Having been trained on short summaries, the NLI model does not perform well when presented with more than a few sentences, even though the model can theoretically take in longer text.

To adapt the model for long-form summaries, we make use of the paragraph structure of these summaries. For each reference point, we ask the NLI model whether each paragraph in the candidate summary entails the reference point. If at least one candidate paragraph entails it, the reference point is considered present in the candidate summary.

Additionally, we fine-tune this NLI model on our legal dataset.

5.2.3 LLM with Contextual Prompt and Examples

As described in Section 3.2, legal text involves greater nuance than news text, and sometimes requires understanding of the context of the whole legal case. To best handle these complexities, we use a state-of-the-art LLM to determine whether two points are making the same point in the context of a legal case. We chose Claude 3.5 Sonnet as our LLM, since in our experience it is the best-performing Anthropic model for similar tasks.

The LLM is provided with the following information in the prompt:

- Examples from other court cases
- The full reference summary, which gives the LLM the context of the court case
- The context for each of the two points to be compared (the context consists of the point itself and the preceding and following point, in order of appearance)
- The two points to be compared
- An explanation of what "making the same point" means in the context of a court case (shown in Appendix A.4)
- An instruction to the LLM to give a one-sentence explanation, followed by a binary rating ("Yes" or "No")

We experimented with two regimes for providing examples in the prompt:

Few-Shot Regime: We provide around 10 examples which include edge cases that are particularly tricky to distinguish. For each example, an explanation is provided, followed by the correct answer.

Many-Shot Regime: We carried out many-shot prompting (a concept explored in Agarwal et al., 2024) by providing the LLM with several hundred examples. To create these examples, we used 2 UKSC cases from our training set. For each case, we collated the few-shot-prompted LLM responses for the reference-candidate point pairs from one of the generated summaries. We extracted all the point pairs for which the LLM gave a true positive, false positive, or false negative response. Because there were many more true negatives, we extracted only a subset of these point pairs; for each reference point, we chose the candidate point with the highest cosine similarity that was an LLM true negative. The incorrect LLM explanations (false positives or negatives) were then corrected by hand; in some cases the true positive explanations were also edited.

These examples were included in the many-shot prompt as follows: We first include the example court case summary, followed by a list of the example point pairs in that case. For each example point pair, we provided the hand-corrected explanation followed by the final "Yes" or "No" answer.

Pre-Selecting Candidates: To cut down on computation, we did not pass every reference-candidate point pair through the LLM. Rather, for each reference point, we pre-select the 5 candidate points that have the closest cosine similarity to the reference point.

5.2.4 Ensuring 1-1 Matching

For the Cosine Similarity and LLM automated methods, we carry out a further step. Sometimes a single candidate point may be matched to multiple reference points. We further disambiguate the situation by finding the best-matching reference point for each candidate point that has more than one reference match. To do so, we developed the assignment algorithm described in Appendix A.5.

5.3 Calculating the Candidate Summary Recall Score

The weighted percentage of reference points that have at least one match, according to the automated method, is the candidate summary recall score given by the method. The weighting of reference points is described in Appendix A.3.

6 Results

6.1 Step 1: Point Extraction

To evaluate the performance of automated models for point extraction, we employed the *easiness* scores introduced in Zhang and Bansal, 2021 and further extended by Nawrath et al., 2024. This score assesses the similarity between generated points and human-written ones, and is described in Appendix A.6.

We compare our approaches with the following baselines:

Sentence split: A baseline approach where the list of generated points is simply the list of sentences from the given text.

A^{2}CU-Generator (Liu et al., 2023b): See section 2.2.

	E_R	E_P
Sentence split	.70	.81
A^{2}CU-Generator	.80	.72
Dense X	.85	.85
Fine-tuned Dense X	.88	**.91**
LLM with multi-shot prompt	**.91**	.89

Table 1: *Easiness* scores (Zhang and Bansal, 2021; Nawrath et al., 2024) for point extraction. E_R and E_P represent the recall- and precision-oriented *easiness* scores respectively.

Dense X (Chen et al., 2023): See section 5.1.1.

Performance

Table 1 presents the results for the point extraction task. Dense X is a strong baseline. Our fine-tuned model and our LLM approach achieve an improvement of 3-6 percentage points over this baseline.

A qualitative analysis of the extracted points is also instructive. As seen in the examples in Figure 2, the A^{2}CU-Generator, which was trained on non-legal data, produces points that are too granular and that do not capture the complex meaning of the original text. Some of the points are not proper propositions (they do not make a declarative statement). The fine-tuned Dense X model output is better but still contains inaccuracies. In particular, the last point in the example in the Figure is incorrectly stated as if it were a fact. In contrast, the LLM produces points that are correct and properly capture the original meaning.

6.2 Step 2: Point Comparison

We first evaluate the performance of automated methods for Step 2 using gold Step 1 points extracted by human annotators. We calculate two sets of performance metrics as follows.

Pairwise Matching Scores: Using the automated method, we predict whether each reference-candidate pair is a match, and compare this to the gold annotation. We then calculate a precision and recall score for the Step 2 method. This indicates how closely the method's predictions align with human labels, for every reference-candidate point pair. We call these the *pairwise matching* scores, and they are an indication of how well the automated method can distinguish whether two sentences are making the same point in the context of a court case. This calculation is done before the assignment algorithm described in section 5.2.4.

Reference Point Based Scores: After performing the assignment algorithm (for the Cosine and

Original Text

Relevant to the question of whether an order should be made and, if so, what order, will be a number of factors such as the financial benefit which the applicant has already received, or whether the applicant has failed to take advantage of a right under the foreign law to claim financial relief.

Points created by A²CU-Generator

- Relevant to the question of whether an order should be made
- relevant to the question of what order should be made
- Relative to the question of whether an order should be made will be a number of factors
- Relative to the question of whether an order should be made and, if so, what order, will be a number of factors
- The financial benefit which the applicant has already received
- The financial benefit which the applicant has failed to take advantage of
- The financial benefit which the applicant has failed to take advantage of under the foreign law
- The applicant has failed to take advantage of a right
- The applicant has failed to take advantage of a right under the foreign law to claim financial relief

Points created by Fine-tuned Dense X

- Relevant to the question of whether an order should be made and, if so, what order, will be a number of factors.
- The financial benefit which the applicant has already received will be relevant factors.
- The applicant has failed to take advantage of a right under the foreign law to claim financial relief.

Points created by LLM

- A number of factors will be relevant to the question of whether an order should be made and, if so, what order.
- One relevant factor is the financial benefit which the applicant has already received.
- Another relevant factor is whether the applicant has failed to take advantage of a right under the foreign law to claim financial relief.

Figure 2: Examples of points produced by different automated Step 1 models. The A^{2}CU-Generator, which was trained on non-legal data, produces points that are too granular and that do not capture the complex meaning of the original text. Some of the points are not proper propositions (they do not make a declarative statement). The fine-tuned Dense X model output is better, but still not quite right – the last point, in particular, is incorrectly stated as if it were a fact. The LLM produces points that are correct and properly capture the original meaning.

LLM methods only), we then calculate another set of precision and recall scores for the method, from the frame of view of each reference point. Here, we are asking, for each reference point: if the automated method says there is a match, is there actually a match according to the gold annotation (and vice-versa)? This is regardless of which candidate point is matched. We call these scores the *reference point based* scores. These scores are an indication of how well the automated method can pick out which reference points are covered by the candidate summary. Since the summary recall score of the candidate summary is the percentage of reference points that are covered by the candidate summary, the *reference point based* scores also give an indication of how accurate the resulting summary recall score is likely to be.

Further details are given in Appendix A.7.

	Pairwise matching			Reference point based		
	P	R	F1	P	R	F1
Cosine similarity	.20	.67	.31	.62	.70	.66
A^{2}CU-NLI	n/a	n/a	n/a	.69	.49	.57
A^{2}CU-NLI$_{\text{fine-tuned}}$	n/a	n/a	n/a	.55	**.86**	.67
LLM, few-shot	.60	**.82**	**.70**	**.87**	.83	**.85**
LLM, many-shot	**.61**	.81	.69	**.87**	.84	**.85**

Table 2: Precision (P), recall (R) and F1-score of automated methods for Step 2. The *pairwise matching* scores are an indication of how well the method can distinguish whether two sentences are making the same point in a legal context. The *reference point based* scores indicate how well the method can pick out which reference points are covered by the candidate summary.

Performance

Table 2 shows the results of the automated methods for Step 2. Note that pairwise metrics were not calculated for the NLI-based method, because this method does not perform matching between two points, but rather asks if a candidate paragraph entails a reference point.

The F1 scores show that the LLM performs much better at this task than the other methods. This indicates that the LLM can better distinguish the nuances in complex legal statements than simpler models. The LLM many-shot and few-shot regimes perform similarly.

The absolute *pairwise matching* precision scores are not high. This indicates that, though it may seem a simple task to compare two sentences to see if they make the same point, this appears to be quite tricky for automated methods, even state-of-the-art LLMs that are given full context.

Because many of the false positives involve the same candidate point being matched to multiple reference points, the assignment algorithm in Section 5.2.4 mitigates the effect of these errors on the downstream summary recall score calculation, because each candidate point is only allowed to match to one reference point.

	Pearson Correlation			RMSE
	Summ.	Sys.	Pop.	
ROUGE-1	.350	.421	.523	.171
ROUGE-2	.651	.684	.595	.139
ROUGE-L	.656	.739	.676	.134
BERTScore	.596	.722	.589	.325
A^2CU	.830	.909	.638	.093
A^3CU	.477	.607	.048	.146
Pointwise $_{\text{DX-ft, NLI-ft}}$	.838	.883	.807	.236
Pointwise $_{\text{LLM, LLM-FS}}$	**.938**	**.987**	.940	.037
Pointwise $_{\text{LLM, LLM-MS}}$	.923	.975	**.950**	**.035**

Table 3: Pearson correlation (summary-, system- and population-level) of automated methods with human evaluation, as well as root mean squared error (RMSE) between automated metrics and human scores.

6.3 Comparison with Human Evaluation

We run Step 1 and Step 2 in a fully automated manner, obtaining recall scores for each candidate summary. We then calculate the correlation of these automatically-calculated recall scores with the recall scores obtained from human annotation (described in Section 4).

Due to computational resource limitations, we focused on only these combinations of Step 1 and Step 2 methods:

Pointwise $_{\text{DX-ft, NLI-ft}}$ is the non-LLM version, using the fine-tuned Dense X model for Step 1 and fine-tuned A^2CU-NLI model for Step 2.

Pointwise $_{\text{LLM, LLM-FS}}$ uses the LLM for Step 1 and few-shot-prompted LLM for Step 2.

Pointwise $_{\text{LLM, LLM-MS}}$ uses the LLM for Step 1 and many-shot-prompted LLM for Step 2.

We calculate three types of correlation scores. The summary-level score is the average (over all m cases) of the correlation across the n candidate summaries for each case. The system-level score first averages (over all m cases) the scores of the candidate summaries for each system (i.e. LLM and prompt that generated the summary), then calculates the correlations across the n systems using these average scores. In addition, we calculate a population-level correlation score, where the $m \times n$ candidate summaries are each considered as an individual datapoint in the correlation.

The correlation results are shown in Table 3. The LLM-based pointwise methods produce higher correlations (for all three correlation types) than the baselines. The non-LLM-based Pointwise $_{\text{DX-ft, NLI-ft}}$ performs better in some of the correlation categories than the baselines, but not as well as the LLM-based pointwise methods. This shows that the use of advanced LLM models yields a significant advantage in this task involving complex legal text.

We calculate the significance (p-value) of the improvement in correlation of our best-performing method over the best baseline, using the PERM-BOTH permutation algorithm described in Deutsch et al., 2021. Because the summary- and system-level correlations involve averaging over the cases, each correlation is calculated over only 5 systems, which is too small a number to achieve significance. For the population-level correlation, however, our method shows a strongly statistically significant improvement ($p < 0.001$) over the best baseline.

In addition, the root mean squared error between the LLM-based pointwise metric and the human metric is less than half that of the best baseline.

Figure 3 plots the summary recall scores obtained from several automated metrics against the human scores. We see that the pointwise metric corresponds much more closely with human evaluation than the baselines do. The pointwise metric has a narrower spread, and a best-fit line much closer to the ideal line, than the baselines.

7 Discussion and Conclusions

The improvement in correlation of our method over the baselines is particularly pronounced for the population-level correlation. This is an indication that our method produces consistent results across all the court cases in our dataset. In other words, it does not merely rank the candidate summaries for each case in the correct order from best to worst, but also gives a recall score that is well-correlated with the human score on an individual candidate summary level.

In addition, the root mean squared error between the LLM-based pointwise metric and the human metric is much smaller than that of the baselines. This indicates that our method produces absolute recall scores that are close to the human scores, thus giving an accurate idea of the absolute quality of a single LLM summary (and not just the comparatative quality of multiple LLM summaries).

The plots in Figure 3 illustrate these points further.

Apart from performance, one of the advantages of the pointwise evaluation method over existing ones its its interpretability and explainability. The method allows us to see exactly which reference points are included or missing in the candidate summary. This allows us to improve the candidate

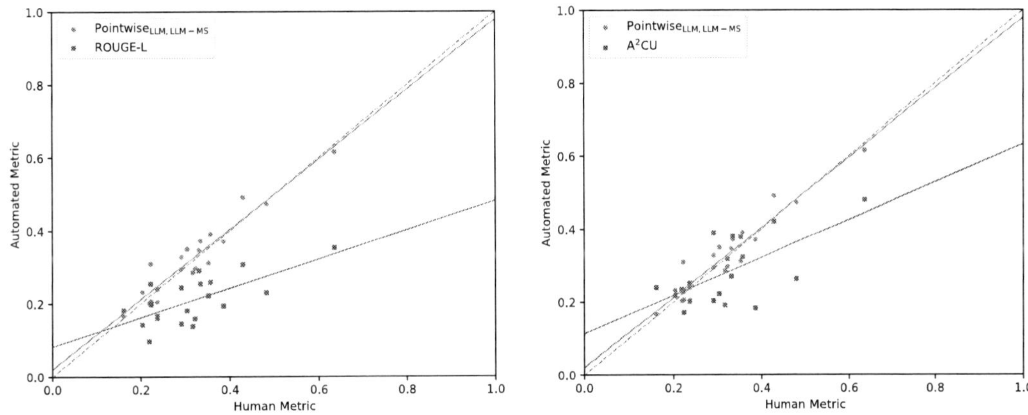

Figure 3: Correspondence of automated metrics with human evaluation. These plots show one of the LLM-based pointwise metrics (red circles), as well as the two best baselines, A^{2}CU and ROUGE-L (blue squares). Each individual point in the scatterplot represents one generated candidate summary. The best-fit lines are also shown. The gray dashed line represents a perfect match. The pointwise metric has a narrower spread, and a best-fit line much closer to the ideal gray dashed line, than the baselines.

summaries in a targeted manner, for example by editing the prompts to tell the summarizing LLM to focus more on the type of information that the current summaries do not include. We can also see which points in each candidate summary were not included in the reference (and thus are probably irrelevant), and can thus also improve the LLM prompts to avoid these.

8 Limitations and Further Work

The pointwise evaluation methodology focuses on the content of a summary, and does not account for (more subjective) aspects of a text, such as writing style and flow. These aspects are nevertheless an important part of a well-written legal summary.

Creating a meta-evaluation dataset for long-form legal summaries is very resource-intensive, and we were thus only able to create a small dataset. Future work to extend the dataset to more cases and across more jurisdictions would allow for more representative and statistically significant tests.

The pointwise method currently compares candidate summaries to a single human-written summary. Using multiple human-written references, as done in the original Pyramid (Nenkova and Passonneau, 2004) and LitePyramid methods (Shapira et al., 2019), could improve the robustness of the method.

It would also be instructive to explore the use of other LLMs (other than Claude 3.5 Sonnet) for the Step 2 task of determining whether two points are saying the same thing in a legal context.

The greedy assignment method described in section 5.2.4 may not always assign a candidate point to the correct reference point. A more complex, non-greedy algorithm may improve the matching and be closer to how a human would pick the best pairwise matches between two sets of points.

Because of the complexities involved in legal reasoning, perfect one-to-one matches between points may not always be possible; this could be an interesting direction for future work.

The pointwise method is more computationally-intensive than baselines such as ROUGE, but the computations can be parallelised for greater efficiency.

We developed the pointwise evaluation methodology for the specific task of evaluating legal summaries. It is appropriate for use cases where there is an objective standard for the content that should or should not be included in a text. It would be less appropriate for use cases where there are many possible interpretations of a topic, such as arguing for or against a particular issue.

9 Ethics

The impacts – and potential harms – of artificial intelligence are ever-increasing, and sensitive domains like legal technology can often experience outsized effects from misuse. Over the course of the research performed, we sought to ensure that any data and results – generated or derived – were free of such harms. Our work was built upon court opinions and judgments that reference real parties, locations, and accusations, though we took care to ensure this information remained neutral and without commentary during the model development processes. Further, we took steps to ensure that no individual, entity, or party was unfairly targeted or identified, opting to leverage very high visibility cases drawn from the UK Supreme Court.

Despite managing all items under the scope of our control in the manner described above, the work and experimentation performed under this research effort does leverage pretrained large language models for tasks such as data augmentation, passage extraction, and pointwise comparison (among others). Such models are generally built and hosted by third parties, and may hold inherent biases, shortcomings, or factual inconsistencies based on the processes and data with which they were trained. These potential limitations were not *exhaustively* studied under the work contained in this paper, though we reviewed the results to the best of our determinative ability to ensure they met these ethical standards.

Nonetheless, we implore researchers who wish to leverage this work to likewise verify that potential hallucinations are limited, biases are minimized, and model-based decision making is fair and explainable. We discourage leveraging this work for critical decision making in any legal, personal, or high-risk domain without thorough review of results by a trained subject-matter expert (e.g., a licensed attorney specializing in the area of interest). Further, we invite future researchers to ensure that similarly appropriate disclosures are made to any end users consuming data or insights drawn from this work.

References

Rishabh Agarwal, Avi Singh, Lei M. Zhang, Bernd Bohnet, Luis Rosias, Stephanie Chan, Biao Zhang, Ankesh Anand, Zaheer Abbas, Azade Nova, John D. Co-Reyes, Eric Chu, Feryal Behbahani, Aleksandra Faust, and Hugo Larochelle. 2024. Many-shot in-context learning. *Preprint*, arXiv:2404.11018.

Ansar Aynetdinov and Alan Akbik. 2024. Semscore: Automated evaluation of instruction-tuned llms based on semantic textual similarity. *Preprint*, arXiv:2401.17072.

Manik Bhandari, Pranav Narayan Gour, Atabak Ashfaq, Pengfei Liu, and Graham Neubig. 2020. Re-evaluating evaluation in text summarization. In *Proceedings of the 2020 Conference on Empirical Methods in Natural Language Processing (EMNLP)*, pages 9347–9359, Online. Association for Computational Linguistics.

Tong Chen, Hongwei Wang, Wenhao Yu, Kaixin Ma, Xinran Zhao, Hongming Zhang, and Dong Yu. 2023. Dense x retrieval: What retrieval granularity should we use? *Preprint*, arXiv:2312.06648.

Hyung Won Chung, Le Hou, Shayne Longpre, Barret Zoph, Yi Tay, William Fedus, Yunxuan Li, Xuezhi Wang, Mostafa Dehghani, Siddhartha Brahma, Albert Webson, Shixiang Shane Gu, Zhuyun Dai, Mirac Suzgun, Xinyun Chen, Aakanksha Chowdhery, Alex Castro-Ros, Marie Pellat, Kevin Robinson, Dasha Valter, Sharan Narang, Gaurav Mishra, Adams Yu, Vincent Zhao, Yanping Huang, Andrew Dai, Hongkun Yu, Slav Petrov, Ed H. Chi, Jeff Dean, Jacob Devlin, Adam Roberts, Denny Zhou, Quoc V. Le, and Jason Wei. 2024. Scaling instruction-finetuned language models. *Journal of Machine Learning Research*, 25(70):1–53.

Hoa Trang Dang and Karolina Owczarzak. 2008. Overview of the TAC 2008 update summarization task. In *Proceedings of the First Text Analysis Conference, TAC 2008, Gaithersburg, Maryland, USA, November 17-19, 2008*. NIST.

Daniel Deutsch, Rotem Dror, and Dan Roth. 2021. A statistical analysis of summarization evaluation metrics using resampling methods. *Transactions of the Association for Computational Linguistics*, 9:1132–1146.

Jacob Devlin, Ming-Wei Chang, Kenton Lee, and Kristina Toutanova. 2019. BERT: Pre-training of deep bidirectional transformers for language understanding. In *Proceedings of the 2019 Conference of the North American Chapter of the Association for Computational Linguistics: Human Language Technologies, Volume 1 (Long and Short Papers)*, pages 4171–4186, Minneapolis, Minnesota. Association for Computational Linguistics.

Ben Hachey and Claire Grover. 2006. Extractive summarisation of legal texts. *Artificial Intelligence and Law*, 14(4):305–345.

Pengcheng He, Xiaodong Liu, Jianfeng Gao, and Weizhu Chen. 2021. Deberta: decoding-enhanced bert with disentangled attention. In *9th International Conference on Learning Representations, ICLR 2021, Virtual Event, Austria, May 3-7, 2021*. OpenReview.net.

Huan Yee Koh, Jiaxin Ju, Ming Liu, and Shirui Pan. 2022. An empirical survey on long document summarization: Datasets, models, and metrics. *ACM Comput. Surv.*, 55(8).

Chin-Yew Lin. 2004. ROUGE: A package for automatic evaluation of summaries. In *Text Summarization Branches Out*, pages 74–81, Barcelona, Spain. Association for Computational Linguistics.

Yixin Liu, Alex Fabbri, Pengfei Liu, Yilun Zhao, Linyong Nan, Ruilin Han, Simeng Han, Shafiq Joty, Chien-Sheng Wu, Caiming Xiong, and Dragomir Radev. 2023a. Revisiting the gold standard: Grounding summarization evaluation with robust human evaluation. In *Proceedings of the 61st Annual Meeting of the Association for Computational Linguistics (Volume 1: Long Papers)*, pages 4140–4170, Toronto, Canada. Association for Computational Linguistics.

Yixin Liu, Alexander Fabbri, Yilun Zhao, Pengfei Liu, Shafiq Joty, Chien-Sheng Wu, Caiming Xiong, and Dragomir Radev. 2023b. Towards interpretable and efficient automatic reference-based summarization evaluation. In *Proceedings of the 2023 Conference on Empirical Methods in Natural Language Processing*, pages 16360–16368, Singapore. Association for Computational Linguistics.

Sewon Min, Kalpesh Krishna, Xinxi Lyu, Mike Lewis, Wen-tau Yih, Pang Koh, Mohit Iyyer, Luke Zettlemoyer, and Hannaneh Hajishirzi. 2023. FActScore: Fine-grained atomic evaluation of factual precision in long form text generation. In *Proceedings of the 2023 Conference on Empirical Methods in Natural Language Processing*, pages 12076–12100, Singapore. Association for Computational Linguistics.

Marcel Nawrath, Agnieszka Nowak, Tristan Ratz, Danilo Walenta, Juri Opitz, Leonardo Ribeiro, João Sedoc, Daniel Deutsch, Simon Mille, Yixin Liu, Sebastian Gehrmann, Lining Zhang, Saad Mahamood, Miruna Clinciu, Khyathi Chandu, and Yufang Hou. 2024. On the role of summary content units in text summarization evaluation. In *Proceedings of the 2024 Conference of the North American Chapter of the Association for Computational Linguistics: Human Language Technologies (Volume 2: Short Papers)*, pages 272–281, Mexico City, Mexico. Association for Computational Linguistics.

Ani Nenkova and Rebecca Passonneau. 2004. Evaluating content selection in summarization: The pyramid method. In *Proceedings of the Human Language Technology Conference of the North American Chapter of the Association for Computational Linguistics: HLT-NAACL 2004*, pages 145–152, Boston, Massachusetts, USA. Association for Computational Linguistics.

Nils Reimers and Iryna Gurevych. 2019. Sentence-bert: Sentence embeddings using siamese bert-networks. In *Proceedings of the 2019 Conference on Empirical Methods in Natural Language Processing*. Association for Computational Linguistics.

Victor Sanh, Albert Webson, Colin Raffel, Stephen H. Bach, Lintang Sutawika, Zaid Alyafeai, Antoine Chaffin, Arnaud Stiegler, Arun Raja, Manan Dey, M Saiful Bari, Canwen Xu, Urmish Thakker, Shanya Sharma Sharma, Eliza Szczechla, Taewoon Kim, Gunjan Chhablani, Nihal V. Nayak, Debajyoti Datta, Jonathan Chang, Mike Tian-Jian Jiang, Han Wang, Matteo Manica, Sheng Shen, Zheng Xin Yong, Harshit Pandey, Rachel Bawden, Thomas Wang, Trishala Neeraj, Jos Rozen, Abheesht Sharma, Andrea Santilli, Thibault Févry, Jason Alan Fries, Ryan Teehan, Teven Le Scao, Stella Biderman, Leo Gao, Thomas Wolf, and Alexander M. Rush. 2022. Multitask prompted training enables zero-shot task generalization. In *The Tenth International Conference on Learning Representations, ICLR 2022, Virtual Event, April 25-29, 2022*. OpenReview.net.

Sentence Transformers. 2024. Pretrained models. `https://sbert.net/docs/sentence_transformer/pretrained_models.html`.

Ori Shapira, David Gabay, Yang Gao, Hadar Ronen, Ramakanth Pasunuru, Mohit Bansal, Yael Amsterdamer, and Ido Dagan. 2019. Crowdsourcing lightweight pyramids for manual summary evaluation. In *Proceedings of the 2019 Conference of the North American Chapter of the Association for Computational Linguistics: Human Language Technologies, Volume 1 (Long and Short Papers)*, pages 682–687, Minneapolis, Minnesota. Association for Computational Linguistics.

Abhay Shukla, Paheli Bhattacharya, Soham Poddar, Rajdeep Mukherjee, Kripabandhu Ghosh, Pawan Goyal, and Saptarshi Ghosh. 2022. Legal case document summarization: Extractive and abstractive methods and their evaluation. In *Proceedings of the 2nd Conference of the Asia-Pacific Chapter of the Association for Computational Linguistics and the 12th International Joint Conference on Natural Language Processing (Volume 1: Long Papers)*, pages 1048–1064, Online only. Association for Computational Linguistics.

The Supreme Court of the United Kingdom. 2024. Decided cases. `https://www.supremecourt.uk/decided-cases/index.html`.

Weizhe Yuan, Graham Neubig, and Pengfei Liu. 2021. Bartscore: Evaluating generated text as text generation. In *Advances in Neural Information Processing Systems*, volume 34, pages 27263–27277. Curran Associates, Inc.

Yuheng Zha, Yichi Yang, Ruichen Li, and Zhiting Hu. 2023. AlignScore: Evaluating factual consistency with a unified alignment function. In *Proceedings of the 61st Annual Meeting of the Association for Computational Linguistics (Volume 1: Long Papers)*, pages 11328–11348, Toronto, Canada. Association for Computational Linguistics.

Shiyue Zhang and Mohit Bansal. 2021. Finding a balanced degree of automation for summary evaluation. In *Proceedings of the 2021 Conference on Empirical Methods in Natural Language Processing*, pages 6617–6632, Online and Punta Cana, Dominican Republic. Association for Computational Linguistics.

Tianyi Zhang, Varsha Kishore, Felix Wu, Kilian Q. Weinberger, and Yoav Artzi. 2020. Bertscore: Evaluating text generation with BERT. In *8th International*

Conference on Learning Representations, ICLR 2020, Addis Ababa, Ethiopia, April 26-30, 2020. OpenReview.net.

A Appendix

A.1 Step 1: Point Extraction

In breaking down the summary into discrete points, we use the following heuristics based on the nature of legal text.

- If a sentence specifies who said something (or which law specifies something), this is included in the resulting point(s).
- If there is a list of multiple factors that are considered, each factor is split into a separate point.
- A sentence that follows a *because-therefore* structure can be split into separate points.
- A sentence that has a conditional structure and cannot be split without changing the meaning of the sentence should be left as a single point, even if the resulting point is quite long.

Examples are shown in Figure 4.

A.2 Step 2: Point Matching

For each reference point, we find the best-matching point in the candidate summary (if any).

A one-to-one match is done where possible – i.e. each reference point should be matched to at most one candidate point, and vice-versa. If one or more candidate points each only cover part of the reference point's content, we mark these as "partial matches".

Sometimes multiple candidate points are sufficiently similar to the reference point to be considered a match. In such cases the best match is annotated as a full match, and the rest are noted as "other relevant matches". Sometimes there may be multiple reference points talking about the same thing – such as where the court, in its reasoning, repeated a point already stated in the case background for emphasis. If these multiple similar reference points may match to a single candidate point, the reference point with the most similar context to the candidate point is marked as the "full match", and the remaining reference points get the candidate point as an "other relevant match".

A.3 Weighting Scheme for Recall Score

A single sentence in the original summary may be broken down into multiple reference points, with many shared words between the points. This is particularly the case when there are multiple factors mentioned in the original sentence (see the first example in Figure 4). In such cases, the resulting points would have an oversized effect on the final recall score of the document.

To mitigate this problem, we apply the following weighting scheme to the reference points, where the weight W_p of each reference point p (containing lemmas each denoted with l) is:

$$W_p = \frac{\sum\limits_{l \subset p} W_l}{\sum\limits_{p}\sum\limits_{l \subset p} W_l},$$

where

$$W_l = \begin{cases} \min(\frac{N_{l,\text{ para}}}{N_{l,\text{ points}}}, 1) & \text{if lemma in paragraph} \\ 0 & \text{otherwise.} \end{cases}$$

Here, $N_{l,\text{ para}}$ is the number of times the lemma appears in the original paragraph, and $N_{l,\text{ points}}$ is the total number of times the lemma appears in all the points extracted from that paragraph. This weighting scheme down-weights points which "share" many lemmas with other points, where these lemmas did not appear as often in the original paragraph.

In addition, we also consider the type of match (full or partial): a reference point with a full-matching candidate point will count fully towards the recall score. A reference point that has no full match but one or more partial matches has its contribution reduced by a factor of 0.5.

A.4 Explanation Provided to Step 2 LLM

The following text is included in the prompt for the LLM for Step 2 (point matching), to specify what "making the same point" means in the context of a legal summary:

```
Two sentences make the same point if they
explain the same legal reasoning step,
describe the same part of a legal test or
rule, describe the same conclusion by the
same court, or give the same background
information about the facts and events
about a case.
Note in particular the following
situations when two sentences do NOT make
the same point:
If the sentences seem to be making the
same argument, but the argument is being
```

Original Text	Points
The court agreed that the scale of the publications, the plaintiff's situation, and the gravity of the statements themselves supported the finding of serious harm.	• The court agreed that the scale of the publications supported the finding of serious harm. • The court agreed that the plaintiff's situation supported the finding of serious harm. • The court agreed that the gravity of the statements themselves supported the finding of serious harm.

Original Text	Points
There were uncertainties surrounding the underlying facts of the case, making it difficult to ascertain the precise scope of the doctrine.	• There were uncertainties surrounding the underlying facts of the case. • These uncertainties made it difficult to ascertain the precise scope of the doctrine.

Original Text	Points
Section 103A provides that a dismissal is unfair if the reason for the dismissal is that the employee made a protected disclosure.	• Section 103A provides that a dismissal is unfair if the reason for the dismissal is that the employee made a protected disclosure.

Figure 4: Examples of how complex legal texts are split into points.

```
made by different parties (e.g. the court
and the plaintiff), the sentences are not
considered to be making the same point.
If the sentences seem to be making the
same argument, but the argument is being
made by different courts (e.g. the Supreme
Court and the Court of Appeal), the
sentences are not considered to be making
the same point.
If the sentences are describing two
different parts of the same legal test
or rule, they are not making the same
point.
If one sentence talks about a conclusion
and one sentence focuses on the reasoning
behind the conclusion, they are not making
the same point.
```

A.5 Assignment Algorithm to Ensure 1-1 Matching

To find the best-matching reference point for each candidate point that has more than one reference match, we developed the following greedy algorithm (combined with a further prompt to an LLM in the LLM case).

Let the set of candidate points that have at least one reference match be C. The set of reference points that the candidate points in C match to is R. For each candidate point c_m in C, if c_m has only one reference match r_i, this reference is assigned to c_m. r_i and c_m are then removed from the pools R and C. This algorithm is run recursively until there are no more candidate points in C that have only one reference match.

We then sort the remaining candidate points in C in increasing order of the number of reference points they each match to. We then find the best match for each candidate point c_n in C thus:

- For the cosine case, we assign to c_n the reference point with the smallest cosine distance from c_n. We then run the algorithm described in the previous paragraph again.
- For the LLM method, we use a further prompt to an LLM. We run the candidate point c_n through an LLM prompt, together with all the reference points it matches to, and ask the LLM which of the reference points is the closest match. The LLM is prompted with instructions for what is and is not considered a similar point in the context of a legal case. The LLM's answer r_j is assigned to c_n, and r_j and c_n are removed from the pools R and C. After each LLM call (which makes one assignment of an r to a c), we then run the previously-described algorithm again.

We proceed in this way until all candidate points which had multiple reference matches have been assigned a single reference point.

A.6 Easiness Score Calculation for Point Extraction

The *easiness* score (Zhang and Bansal, 2021; Nawrath et al., 2024) is composed of a recall-based and a precision-based metric computed between human-labeled points (P^H) and generated points (P^G). The recall-oriented metric (E_R) measures whether for each human-written point, there is a closely matching generated point. The precision-oriented score (E_P) measures whether for each generated point, there is a closely matching human-written counterpart.

For a given passage with M human-written points and N generated points, these scores are defined as follows:

$$E_P = \frac{\sum Acc_j}{N},$$

where

$$Acc_j = \max_m Rougel_{F1}(P_j^G, P_m^H).$$

The recall-based score is then computed in the reverse direction:

$$E_R = \frac{\sum Acc_j}{M},$$

where

$$Acc_j = \max_n Rougel_{F1}(P_j^H, P_n^G).$$

The ROUGE score is used here (rather than, for example, embedding similarity) because we expect point extraction (which more closely resembles a chunking process than a paraphrasing one) to preserve the original lemmas for the most part.

A.7 Step 2 Performance Metrics

For each reference point, we pre-select the 5 candidate points that have the closest cosine similarity to the reference point. This forms the pre-filtered set of reference-candidate pairs for which we will calculate a precision and recall score for the method. For the purposes of calculating pure Step 2 performance of the LLM method, if there are gold matches that do not make it into the top 5 candidate points, we include these pairs as well. This allows us to calculate the real performance of the LLM method even if the cosine method produces a false negative.

We compare the automated method predictions to the gold labels as follows to calculate the pairwise matching score. Where the gold annotation indicates a "full match" or "other relevant match" and the automated method indicates a match, count this as a True Positive. Where the gold annotation indicates a "partial match" and the automated method indicates a match, count this as half a True Positive. Where the human annotation indicates no match at all, and the method indicates a match, count this as a False Positive. Where the human annotation indicates a "full match" or "other relevant match", and the automated method does not indicate a match, this is a False Negative. Where the gold annotation indicates a "partial match" and the automated method does not indicate a match, this is half a False Negative. All other cases are True Negatives.

A.8 LLM Prompts

The LLM prompts for proposition extraction, proposition comparison, and the assignment algorithm are available upon request.

Enhancing Contract Negotiations with LLM-Based Legal Document Comparison

Savinay Narendra, Kaushal Shetty, Adwait Ratnaparkhi
Machine Learning Center of Excellence, JPMorgan Chase & Co.
{savinay.narendra, kaushal.shetty, adwait.ratnaparkhi}@jpmchase.com

Abstract

We present a large language model (LLM) based approach for comparing legal contracts with their corresponding template documents. Legal professionals use commonly observed deviations between templates and contracts to help with contract negotiations, and also to refine the template documents. Our comparison approach, based on the well-studied natural language inference (NLI) task, first splits a template into key concepts and then uses LLMs to decide if the concepts are entailed by the contract document. We also repeat this procedure in the opposite direction — contract clauses are tested for entailment against the template clause to see if they contain additional information. The non-entailed concepts are labelled, organized and filtered by frequency, and placed into a *clause library*, which is used to suggest changes to the template documents. We first show that our LLM-based approach outperforms all previous work on a publicly available dataset designed for NLI in the legal domain. We then apply it to a private real-world legal dataset, achieve an accuracy of 96.46%. Our approach is the first in the literature to produce a natural language comparison between legal contracts and their template documents.

1 Introduction

In the dynamic landscape of contract management, the ability to efficiently negotiate, draft, and manage contracts is paramount for organizations seeking to mitigate risks and streamline operations. This paper explores a comprehensive approach to enhancing contract management processes through the implementation of systematic clause variation analysis, which can be further used to create pre-negotiated Master Service Agreements (MSAs), advanced contract classification and summarization techniques. By leveraging historical contract data and automating key aspects of contract management, organizations can significantly reduce negotiation time frames and improve the consistency and quality of their contractual agreements.

Our work includes several key components aimed at improving contract management through the use of advanced language models:

Demonstrating the Performance of Large Language Models for Natural Language Inference Tasks: We investigate the efficacy of large language models (LLMs) such as Mixtral and GPT-4 in performing Natural Language Inference (NLI) tasks on the contractNLI dataset (Koreeda and Manning, 2021a). This involves not only assessing the models' ability to understand and infer contractual language but also identifying evidence for each NLI task. By demonstrating the superior performance of these models when compared to (Koreeda and Manning, 2021b), we aim to highlight their potential in automating complex contract analysis tasks, thereby enhancing the efficiency and accuracy of contract management processes. The ability of these models to accurately perform NLI tasks is crucial for understanding the nuances and implications of various contract clauses, which in turn supports more informed decision-making during contract negotiations.

Discover Clause Variations: We present the first approach using LLMs to develop clause comparison of contracts agreements with respect to the template agreement as an NLI task. This can be further used to create a comprehensive catalog of approved contract terms based on historical contracts. We explore the application of LLMs in contract management, particularly in reviewing contracts against a template to compare clause variations. To facilitate this, we developed a Retrieval Augmented Generation (RAG) pipeline, which enhances the ability to retrieve relevant clauses and generate appropriate variations. This enables organizations to maintain a high level of consistency and compliance in their contractual agreements, while also speeding up the negotiation process.

Proceedings of the Natural Legal Language Processing Workshop 2024, pages 143–153
November 16, 2024 ©2024 Association for Computational Linguistics

We also show how to use LLMs to modify master contracts by incorporating amendments. This involves leveraging the capabilities of advanced language models to automatically generate and integrate amendments into existing contracts. Through these initiatives, our research aims to provide a robust framework for leveraging advanced language models and historical contract data to enhance the efficiency, consistency, and quality of contract management processes. By automating key aspects of contract analysis and negotiation, organizations can achieve significant improvements in operational efficiency and risk mitigation. This paper demonstrates how the integration of LLMs into contract management can transform traditional practices, leading to more streamlined and effective contract lifecycle management.

2 Related Work

Legal contracts are characterized by their intricate logical structures, specialized vocabulary, and the necessity for precise interpretation. The ability to perform document-level Natural Language Inference (NLI) in this context is crucial for various applications, including contract review, compliance checking, and automated legal reasoning. However, existing NLI datasets and models are not well-suited for these tasks, as they are primarily designed for sentence-level inference and lack the context and complexity of full documents.

Reviewing a contract is a time-consuming and complex process that incurs large expenses for companies. To address this gap, (Koreeda and Manning, 2021b)) introduced ContractNLI: A Dataset for Document-level Natural Language Inference for Contracts. This is further discussed in Section 3.1. The task involves using a Span NLI BERT model to classify whether each hypothesis (a sentence) is entailed by, contradicts, or is not mentioned by (neutral to) the contract, and to identify evidence for the decision as spans in the contract. The Span NLI BERT performed significantly better than existing Transformer-based models in terms of NLI. Our task closely parallels their problem statement, as we aim to determine whether each clause in the template agreement is covered (entails or contradicts) or not covered (neutral) in the contract agreement.

The application of large language models (LLMs) in the context of legal contracts has been extensively explored by (Roegiest et al., 2023). Their problem setup involves legal questions with several answer options, focusing on structured answers rather than generating free text. They employ an embedding-based approach to predict the answer option with the highest similarity to the question text and develop question-specific prompts, eventually landing on a smaller set of reusable prompt templates.

(Lam et al., 2023) present a multi-step method for drafting contract clauses, which includes comparing an input clause to clauses in a trusted repository to yield a set of similar clauses, extracting keyphrase vectors, and clustering these vectors to provide suggestions for modifying the input clause. This method uses the LEDGAR dataset of SEC filings as the trusted repository, offering a robust framework for clause comparison and modification. LegalBench, introduced by (Guha et al., 2024), is a benchmark constructed through a collaborative effort involving legal experts, NLP researchers, and practitioners. LegalBench includes a diverse set of tasks covering various aspects of legal reasoning, from understanding and interpreting legal texts to applying legal principles in specific contexts. This benchmark represents a significant advancement in the intersection of NLP and legal technology, enabling systematic evaluation and comparison of LLMs on legal reasoning tasks and facilitating the development of more sophisticated models tailored to the needs of the legal profession.

Our work differs from the aforementioned studies in several key aspects. While previous research has focused on sentence-level NLI, structured question answering, clause drafting, and benchmarking legal reasoning tasks, our approach is the first to leverage LLMs for the direct comparison of legal contracts with their corresponding template documents. By splitting both templates and contracts into sub-clauses and using LLMs to determine entailment in both directions, we create a comprehensive clause library that aids in refining template documents and assisting in contract negotiations. Our method not only outperforms existing models on a publicly available NLI dataset in the legal domain but also demonstrates high accuracy on a private real-world legal dataset, showcasing its practical applicability and effectiveness.

3 Datasets

3.1 ContractNLI

Before applying large language models (LLMs) to our internal dataset, we wanted to experiment with an external dataset to evaluate their effectiveness and potential. Hence, we utilized the ContractNLI dataset, designed for document-level natural language inference (NLI) specifically tailored to contracts, aiming to automate and support the labor-intensive process of contract review. It is the first dataset to apply NLI to contracts and is the largest annotated corpus of its kind as of September 2021. The dataset includes 607 non-disclosure agreements (NDAs), each annotated with 17 fixed hypotheses, resulting in a substantial corpus for training and evaluating NLI models. The primary tasks involve classifying each hypothesis as Entailment, Contradiction, or NotMentioned, and identifying evidence spans for Entailment and Contradiction labels. For evidence extraction, we need to identify a list of exact spans from the dataset that either contradict or entail the hypothesis, based on the label. This is applicable only when the NLI label is Entailment or Contradiction. The ContractNLI dataset includes evidence as a list of span indices. Each index in the array corresponds to a span where the hypothesis either entails or contradicts the span in the contract.

3.2 Internal Dataset

The internal dataset consists of 25 master contracts, which serve as the primary documents for our analysis. Out of these 25 master contracts, 5 include associated amendments. These amendments reflect changes or additions to the original contract terms, offering a richer context for understanding the evolution of contractual agreements over time. The contracts in the dataset span a significant temporal range, with effective dates ranging from June 2007 to August 2023. This extensive timeframe allows for the examination of contractual language and practices over a period of more than 15 years, providing insights into how contract terms and structures have evolved.

The dataset includes a diverse array of contract types, reflecting the various agreements between JP Morgan and its suppliers. These contract types are:

1. Software and Maintenance Agreement
2. Professional Services Agreement
3. Software License Agreement
4. Application Service Provider Agreement
5. Hardware Agreement

We systematically segmented each clause from the template into distinct key concepts. Subsequently, we employed these segmented concepts within a natural language inference (NLI) framework. In this framework, each key concept from the template was treated as a hypothesis, while the entire contract document was considered the premise. The objective was to predict whether the contract document either contradicts, entails or remains neutral towards the given concept/hypothesis. Additionally, we performed a reverse analysis in which each key concept from the contract clauses were compared against the template document, to identify concepts in the contract that were not covered in the template.

4 Motivation

Contract review is a very labor-intensive process and there is a growing need to streamline and automate the process of contract review, which is critical in legal and business environments. Traditional methods of contract analysis are time-consuming, prone to human error, and often require significant expertise. Contract review involves meticulously reading through lengthy and complex documents to identify key clauses, obligations, exceptions, and potential risks. This process demands a deep understanding of legal language and the ability to interpret nuanced terms and conditions, which can vary significantly between contracts. Additionally, the need to cross-reference multiple documents and ensure compliance with relevant laws and regulations further complicates the task. By leveraging advanced natural language processing (NLP) techniques, specifically large language models (LLMs), we aim to enhance the efficiency and accuracy of contract review. Our initial experiments with the ContractNLI dataset provide a valuable opportunity to assess the capabilities of LLMs in handling complex legal language and inference tasks. This research not only contributes to the field of NLP by addressing the unique challenges posed by legal documents but also has practical implications for improving contract management processes in various industries.

5 Experiments on ContractNLI Dataset

In our experiments, we explored the application of large language models to the ContractNLI dataset, focusing on two primary tasks: (1) classifying the relationship between a given contract and a set of hypotheses, and (2) identifying evidence within the contract that supports the classification decision. To guide the models' responses, we employed specific prompts tailored to each task. We tested the performance of both commercial and open-source models, including the GPT-4 model, which is accessed via a commercial API. GPT-4 (OpenAI et al., 2024) is a large-scale, multimodal model that exhibits human-level performance on various professional and academic benchmarks.

Additionally, we fine-tuned the Mixtral 8x7B (Jiang et al., 2024), a Sparse Mixture of Experts (SMoE) language model, which combines multiple expert networks to improve performance while maintaining efficiency. We chose this Mixtral model as it was one of the open-source models available at that time with demonstrated superior performance and reduced inference costs.

To fine-tune the Mixtral model, we employed Low-Rank Adaptation (LoRA) (Hu et al., 2021), which freezes the pre-trained model weights and injects trainable rank decomposition matrices into each layer of the Transformer architecture, greatly reducing the number of trainable parameters for downstream tasks.

We maintained consistent training parameters for both tasks. Specifically, we used the following settings that included a per-device training batch size to 1 and used gradient accumulation to effectively manage memory usage, with accumulation steps also set to 1. Gradient check-pointing was enabled to further conserve memory during training. The total number of training steps was capped at 4000. A small learning rate of 2.5e-5 was selected to ensure stable and gradual fine-tuning of the model. Training was conducted using bf16 precision to optimize computational resources.

Here are the explanations for the two tasks within the ContractNLI dataset.

Natural Language Inference The first task involves classifying the relationship between a contract and a set of hypotheses. Each hypothesis is a single sentence, and the goal is to determine whether the hypothesis is entailed by, contradicts, or is neutral with respect to the contract.

Evidence Extraction The second task focuses on identifying evidence within the contract that supports the classification decision made in the first task.

5.1 Prompts

Here are the prompts that we used for the two tasks described above respectively. We used the same prompts between the two large language models to ensure consistency in inference over the test set. Prompt 1 is used for NLI and prompt 2 is used for evidence identification.

1. Given a document and a hypothesis, determine whether the document entails or contradicts the hypothesis. Answer strictly as "Entailment" or "Contradiction"

2. Given a document and a hypothesis, if the label is 'Entailment' extract evidence verbatim from the document that support the hypothesis. If the label is 'Contradiction', extract evidence verbatim from the document that contradicts the hypothesis \n Evidence:

In the ContractNLI dataset, we did not evaluate whether the hypothesis and the contract are neutral to each other, as our focus was on evidence extraction based on NLI results, applicable only when the NLI label is Entailment or Contradiction.

5.2 Results

	F1(C)	F1(E)	Acc.
GPT-4	0.70	0.91	
	-	-	0.87
Mixtral	0.74	0.93	
	-	-	0.90
Span NLI BERT	0.389	0.839	
	-	-	0.87

Table 1: Comparison of GPT-4(OpenAI et al., 2024), Mixtral 8x7B(Jiang et al., 2024) and Span NLI Bert(Koreeda and Manning, 2021b) on NLI task for ContractNLI test dataset.

In the table above, C refers to Contradiction label while E refers to Entailment Label. The dataset contains a significantly smaller number of instances labeled as Contradiction. We We observe that GPT-4 and Mixtral model achieves a significantly higher F1 score on the Contradiction label compared to the Span NLI BERT model (Koreeda and Manning, 2021b). Additionally, both the LLMs demonstrates superior performance in calculating the F1 score for the Entailment label. In the ContractNLI dataset, we conducted NLI in just one direction, assessing whether the hypothesis contradicts or entails a given contract, as we aimed to compare how LLMs would outperform the results of (Koreeda and Manning, 2021b)

Model	Mean Average Precision
GPT 4	92.68%
Mixtral	79.8%
Span NLI Bert	92.2%

Table 2: Comparison of performance of GPT-4, Mixtral and Span NLI BERT on evidence identification for ContractNLI test dataset

We observe that GPT-4 model also achieve superior performance on Evidence Identification as compared to the fine-tuned Span NLI Bert model. The mean average precision for Evidence Identification is calculated by averaging the precision across each evidence predicted by the model with respect to the true evidence for that instance at each recall level where a relevant token is retrieved.

6 Proposed solution for Internal Dataset

In our internal problem setting, we are tasked with comparing a negotiated contract against a pre-established template for the contract. These contracts frequently undergo several amendments that add, delete, or modify the original clauses. This scenario closely resembles a Natural Language Inference (NLI) task, wherein we seek to determine whether each concept (hypothesis) in the template clauses is either covered (contradicted or entailed) or not covered (neutral) in relation to the contract agreement. Additionally, since the documents are often available as scanned PDFs, we must explore OCR solutions to accurately convert them into text for further analysis.

One of the main challenges we faced was that many of the documents were images embedded in PDF files, making it difficult to extract and segment the text based on sections. Our initial experiments using Tesseract-OCR were unsuccessful due to errors introduced during OCR and the difficulty of segmenting free-flowing text without clear delimiters. To address this, we used a document image transformer model capable of identifying sections using boundaries and then performing OCR on the bounded boxes. Once the text from each section was extracted, we used GPT-4 model using tailored prompts to extract the correct clauses and compare them with template clauses. This approach allowed us to effectively process and analyze the complex legal language and structure of the contracts, demonstrating the potential of LLMs in automating and enhancing the contract review process.

6.1 PDF Extraction using OCR

The input documents for our tool were PDF documents, and we begin with extracting text from these PDFs. Traditional PDF extraction tools proved inadequate because the PDFs contained text embedded as images. Consequently, we could not rely on regular extraction methods. To address this challenge, we explored two distinct approaches. The first approach involved using Tesseract OCR, while the second approach utilized a Document Image Transformer (DiT) model combined with EasyOCR.

6.1.1 Tesseract OCR

Traditional OCR tools like Tesseract (Smith, 2007) have been widely used for text extraction from various document formats. However, when dealing with PDFs where text is embedded as images, several limitations become apparent including high character error rate, lack of document segmentation and scalability issues.

6.1.2 Document Image Transformer

To address the limitations of traditional OCR tools, we explored the use of a Document Image Transformer (DiT) model(Li et al., 2022). This model serves as the backbone network for a variety of vision-based Document AI tasks, including document image classification, layout analysis, table detection, and text detection for OCR.

Bounding Box Identification: The first step in our approach involved using the DiT model to identify bounding boxes for each section of the document. This segmentation process is crucial for accurately isolating different parts of the document, accommodating the diverse styles and layouts found in image-embedded PDFs. The DiT model's self-supervised pre-training enables it to achieve high accuracy in this task, setting the stage for effective text extraction.

Text Extraction with EasyOCR: Once the sections were identified, we utilized EasyOCR (Baek et al., 2019; Shi et al., 2015), an open-source OCR engine, to extract text from each bounding box. EasyOCR's robust text recognition capabilities complement the DiT model's segmentation, resulting in a more reliable extraction process. By focusing on smaller, well-defined sections, EasyOCR can achieve higher accuracy compared to processing entire pages at once.

6.2 Large Language Models

Clause Variability Analysis One of the primary tasks in our experiments was to identify the variabilities of specific clauses in the master contract agreements compared to the template master agreements. The clauses analyzed include Limitations of Liability, Insurance, Indemnity, Representations and Warranties, Red Flags, System Modifications, Assignment, Source Code Escrow and Audits.

By comparing these clauses between the master agreements and the template agreements, we aimed to understand the common deviations and variations that occur during contract negotiations and amendments.

6.2.1 Handling Amendments with GPT-4

For contracts that include amendments, we created modified contracts by incorporating all the amendments into the original master agreements. One key observation was that GPT-4 requires very specific context to accurately amend the original master contract agreement. To address this, we employed intelligent chunking of the document using a fine-tuned Document Information Transformer (DiT) model, which helped in breaking down the document into various subsections. The process involved the following steps:

Summarizing Amendments: First, a summary of the amendment document was created to capture all the sections and subsections that needed modification using prompt 1 in Appendix. The amendment was essential to isolate and focus solely on the modified sections of the document. This approach aims to eliminate extraneous information, thereby reducing the potential for errors within the model.

Extracting Key Data: Upon extracting the relevant sections and associated text from the amendments in JSON format, the modified master contract, incorporating these amendments, was generated using prompts 2 and 3 in Appendix.

Concept Extraction from Template Clauses: To further analyze the clauses, we divided the template master agreements into multiple concepts or hypotheses using the prompt 4 in Appendix. This step allowed us to break down each template clause into its fundamental concepts, making it easier to compare and analyze against the master agreements.

The term "concept" refers to a specific segment of the original clause, maintaining the integrity and context of the clause. Each clause is divided into multiple concepts. A sample concept/sub-clause generated from the template agreement for the "Red Flags" clause using GPT-4 is shown in table 3.

6.2.2 Retrieval Augmented Generation (RAG) Pipeline

Once the concepts were extracted from each template clause, we implemented a Retrieval Augmented Generation (RAG) pipeline in figure 1 to ask question to the document for each concept in template clause using prompt 5.

For each chunk retrieved in response to the above question, cross-references to other sections were appended to the chunk. This approach ensured that we could accurately determine whether each concept was present in the contract document, providing a comprehensive analysis of clause coverage and variability.

We also did a reverse comparison in which we asked the following question as specified in prompt 6 to find out if there are any additional concepts mentioned in the contract clause not included in the template contract.

These experiments with large language models, particularly GPT-4, demonstrated the importance of providing specific context and intelligent document chunking to accurately amend and analyze contracts. By leveraging advanced NLP techniques and fine-tuned models, we were able to systematically identify clause variabilities, handle amendments, and extract key concepts, thereby enhancing our understanding and management of contractual agreements.

6.3 Prompts

All the prompts used in our work can be found at Appendix A. One of the most challenging aspects of contract review was the incorporation of multiple amendments into the master contract. To address this challenge, we utilized the GPT-4 model to summarize each amendment. The model was prompted to generate output in JSON format, specifying the parent section, the child section, and

"Red Flags" Clause	Sub-Clauses/Concepts
Whenever the Deliverables set forth in ... Supplier having unencrypted ... that contains consumer information, Supplier will have policies and procedures in order to detect ... , practices, or other specific activity that indicates the possible existence of identity theft ("Red Flags") and will either report the Red Flags to ... prevent or mitigate identity theft.	• Deliverables may include Supplier having unencrypted ... containing consumer information. • Supplier must have policies and procedures to detect, ... identity theft indicators ("Red Flags"). • Supplier is responsible ... to prevent or mitigate identity theft.

Table 3: Red Flags Clause Concept Extraction

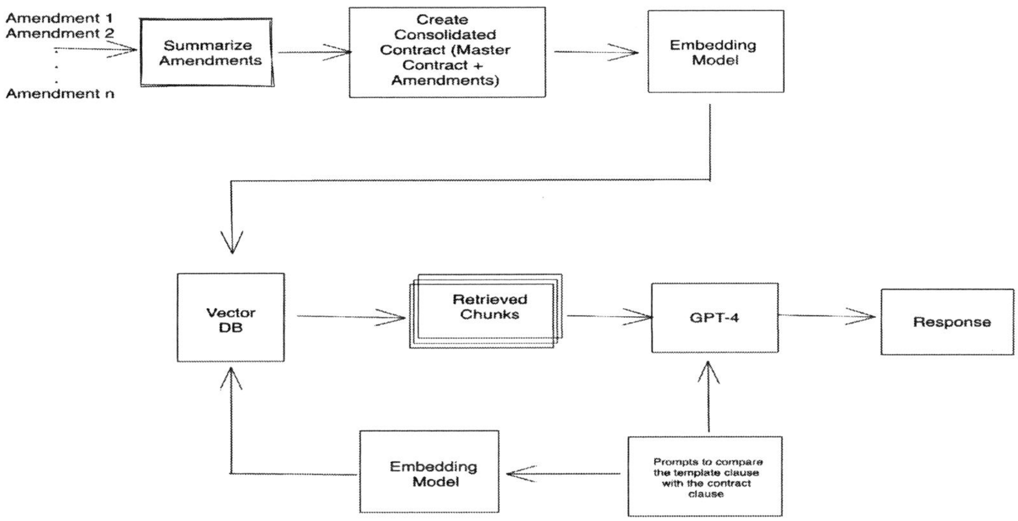

Figure 1: Pipeline to find deviations between Template Clause and Contract Clause

the verbatim text to be added or deleted from the master contract.

7 Results

The clause variations generated by the GPT-4 model using the pipeline in Figure 1 on the internal dataset were annotated by the annotation team at JP Morgan. The annotators are experienced with handling legal documentation, but may not be able to judge the output at the level of a trained lawyer. The quality of the annotations is deemed sufficient for practical applications. On our internal dataset, the model achieved an accuracy of 96.46%. The accuracy is determined by dividing the total number of correctly identified concepts within each clause by the model, based on their classification as entailed, contradicted, or neutral with respect to the contract document. Refer to Figure 2 for performace of the model on each clause across the dataset.

7.1 Sample Outputs

7.1.1 Comparing Concept in Template Clause with Contract Clause

Here, we show a sample clause variation to determine whether the concept in the template clause "Representations and Warranties" is entailed, contradicted, or neutral with respect to the corresponding clause in the contract. The output from the model offers a natural language explanation of the similarities(entailment) and differences(contradiction) between the template agreement and contract agreement. Please refer to table 4.

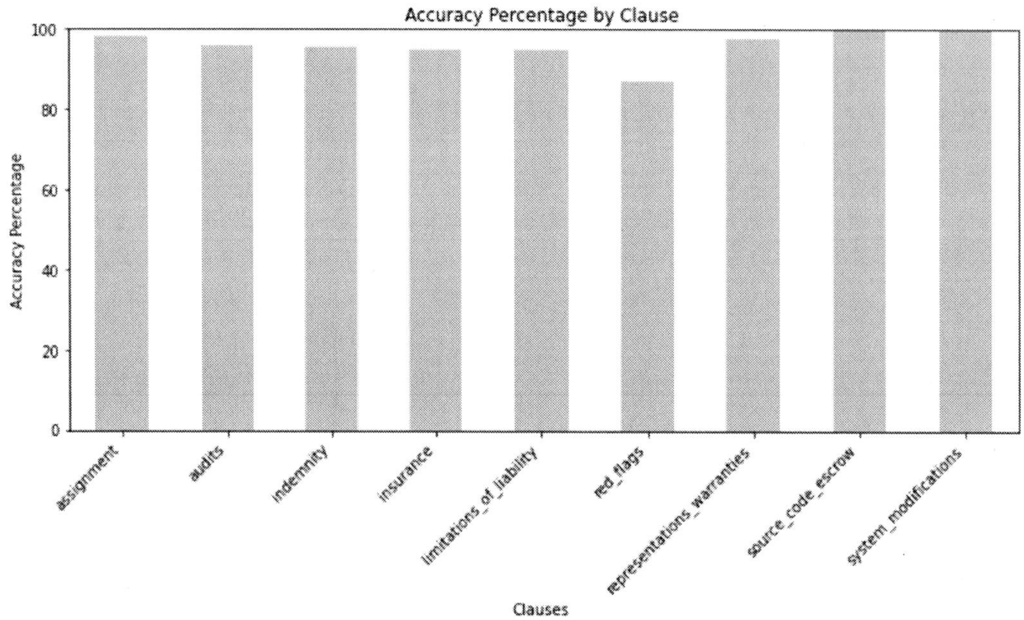

Figure 2: Accuracy Percentage by Clause using GPT-4

The model also generates output that assists a lawyer in identifying any additional sub-clauses present in the contract but absent from the template.

8 Discussion

Our experiments and results on the ContractNLI dataset reveal that both the GPT-4 and Mixtral models outperform the SpanNLI BERT model introduced by Koreeda and Manning (2021) on Natural Language Inference (NLI) tasks. For NLI, GPT-4 achieved an F1 score of 0.91 on the Entailment label, compared to 0.834 by the SpanNLI BERT model. Additionally, GPT-4 attained an F1 score of 0.70 on the Contradiction label, significantly higher than the 0.357 achieved by the SpanNLI BERT model. For evidence identification, GPT-4 achieved slightly superior performance than the Span NLI Bert model and demonstrated a mean average precision of 92.68%. These results demonstrate the potential of leveraging state-of-the-art language models for enhancing the accuracy and reliability of NLI tasks and evidence identification in legal contexts.

The results on the internal dataset demonstrate the efficacy of Large Language Models (GPT-4) in generating outputs that are highly accurate when applied to our internal dataset. The model achieved an impressive accuracy of 96.46%, indicating a high level of precision in its outputs and can be used as a very effective tool by legal professionals in comparing contracts and simplifying the contract negotiation process. The insights provided by the model can help in informed decision-making, further improving the quality of contract review. Additionally, the analysis of clause variations enabled the creation of a clause library, focusing on the most frequent additions and deletions of sub-clauses/concepts. Due to the highly confidential nature of the data, we are unable to disclose the specific modified clauses.

The integration of the GPT-4 model into the contract negotiation process has the potential to significantly improve outcomes and streamline operations for legal professionals. However, one potential risk in our study is that, although the annotators are experienced in handling legal documentation, their evaluations may lack the nuanced judgment and expertise of a trained lawyer. This could potentially impact the accuracy and reliability of the annotations, particularly in complex legal scenarios.

9 Conclusion

In this study, we explore the efficacy of our novel approach on the Contract-NLI dataset, a publicly available dataset designed for natural language inference and evidence identification within legal

Concept from template	The deliverables will not contain any malware, .. malicious programs and will not store any data on computers, systems, or network.
GPT-4 output from comparing template concept to contract	"The document does not explicitly state that the deliverables will not contain any malware, .. will not store any data on computers, systems, or network. However, it does mention that the supplier will comply with certain security and risk management policies, and that the supplier is responsible for assessing and remediating security vulnerabilities."
Sources from the Contract	• "5.10 Application Security." • "5.5 Critical Vulnerabilities."

Table 4: Sample Clause Variation Comparing a Concept in the Template Clause "Representations and Warranties" with the Contract

contracts. Our methodology demonstrates superior performance compared to all previously established techniques for NLI task and Evidence Identification on the Contract-NLI dataset.

We introduce the first approach that leverages large language models (LLMs) to generate natural language comparisons between legal contracts and their corresponding templates, conceptualized similarly to a natural language inference (NLI) problem on the internal dataset, where we have achieved high accuracy. Additionally, we illustrate the capability of LLMs to perform comparative analysis against both the source text and the text of citations cross-referenced elsewhere in the document.

Our approach involves framing the comparisons as an NLI problem, thereby enabling a more structured and interpretable analysis. The results indicate that our approach not only outperforms existing methods on the Contract-NLI dataset but also provides a robust framework for the natural language comparison of legal documents. The implications of these findings suggest significant advancements in the automation of legal document analysis and the potential for broader applications in the legal domain.

References

Youngmin Baek, Bado Lee, Dongyoon Han, Sangdoo Yun, and Hwalsuk Lee. 2019. Character region awareness for text detection.

Neel Guha, Julian Nyarko, Daniel Ho, Christopher Ré, Adam Chilton, Alex Chohlas-Wood, Austin Peters, Brandon Waldon, Daniel Rockmore, Diego Zambrano, et al. 2024. Legalbench: A collaboratively built benchmark for measuring legal reasoning in large language models. *Advances in Neural Information Processing Systems*, 36.

Edward J. Hu, Yelong Shen, Phillip Wallis, Zeyuan Allen-Zhu, Yuanzhi Li, Shean Wang, Lu Wang, and Weizhu Chen. 2021. Lora: Low-rank adaptation of large language models.

Albert Q. Jiang, Alexandre Sablayrolles, Antoine Roux, Arthur Mensch, Blanche Savary, Chris Bamford, Devendra Singh Chaplot, Diego de las Casas, Emma Bou Hanna, Florian Bressand, Gianna Lengyel, Guillaume Bour, Guillaume Lample, Lélio Renard Lavaud, Lucile Saulnier, Marie-Anne Lachaux, Pierre Stock, Sandeep Subramanian, Sophia Yang, Szymon Antoniak, Teven Le Scao, Théophile Gervet, Thibaut Lavril, Thomas Wang, Timothée Lacroix, and William El Sayed. 2024. Mixtral of experts.

Yuta Koreeda and Christopher Manning. 2021a. ContractNLI: A dataset for document-level natural language inference for contracts. In *Findings of the Association for Computational Linguistics: EMNLP 2021*, pages 1907–1919, Punta Cana, Dominican Republic. Association for Computational Linguistics.

Yuta Koreeda and Christopher D Manning. 2021b. Contractnli: A dataset for document-level natural language inference for contracts. In *Findings of the Association for Computational Linguistics: EMNLP 2021*, pages 1907–1919.

Kwok-Yan Lam, Victor CW Cheng, and Zee Kin Yeong. 2023. Applying large language models for enhancing contract drafting. In *Proceedings of the Third International Workshop on Artificial Intelligence and Intelligent Assistance for Legal Professionals in the Digital Workspace (LegalAIIA 2023)*.

Junlong Li, Yiheng Xu, Tengchao Lv, Lei Cui, Cha Zhang, and Furu Wei. 2022. Dit: Self-supervised pre-training for document image transformer.

OpenAI, Josh Achiam, Steven Adler, Sandhini Agarwal, Lama Ahmad, Ilge Akkaya, Florencia Leoni Aleman, Diogo Almeida, Janko Altenschmidt, Sam Altman, Shyamal Anadkat, Red Avila, Igor Babuschkin, Suchir Balaji, Valerie Balcom, Paul Baltescu, Haiming Bao, Mohammad Bavarian, Jeff Belgum, Irwan Bello ..., and Barret Zoph. 2024. Gpt-4 technical report.

Adam Roegiest, Radha Chitta, Jonathan Donnelly, Maya Lash, Alexandra Vtyurina, and Francois Longtin. 2023. Questions about contracts: Prompt templates for structured answer generation. In *Proceedings of the Natural Legal Language Processing Workshop 2023*, pages 62–72.

Baoguang Shi, Xiang Bai, and Cong Yao. 2015. An end-to-end trainable neural network for image-based sequence recognition and its application to scene text recognition.

R. Smith. 2007. An overview of the tesseract ocr engine. In *Ninth International Conference on Document Analysis and Recognition (ICDAR 2007)*, volume 2, pages 629–633.

A Appendix A: Prompts

1. You are a US attorney that reviews the amendments made to a master agreement and modifies the master agreement based on that.

   MASTER AGREEMENT:

   {master_agreement}

   Edit the master agreement with the changes in the following amendment compared to master agreement. Only edit the master agreement. Follow the instructions in the amendment below to modify the master agreement. Add the amendments text to the relevant sections verbatim. If the amendment instructs to add the text, add it to the relevant section in the master agreement at the appropriate position. Figure out where the amendment should be made and then add it at the relevant position.

   AMENDMENT:

   {amendment}

   OUTPUT:

   {{amended_master_agreement}}

   Strictly follow the instructions below to produce the output:

   If the amendment is not at all related to the text in the master agreement, only output the master agreement as it is.

   (a) Only output the modified master agreement.
   (b) Do not make up facts.
   (c) Do not add the prompt text to the final output.
   (d) Do not add reason to the final output on how the output was generated.

2. You are a US attorney that works on extracting the amendments from the document below that need to be amended in the master agreement.

   Extract the exact section number where the modification has to take place in the original document, the text that needs to be replaced and the modified text verbatim in a RFC8259 compliant JSON format. Sections are identified with numbers. Include the section header in `parent_section_no` and `child_section_no`. Do not include any explanation or comment.

   AMENDMENT DOCUMENT:

   `{amendment}`

   The output should be strictly in the format as below without any comments. The output is RFC8259 compliant JSON. Follow the below format strictly. Do not add any comment to the answer. Only return the JSON.

   `[[parent_section_no: , parent_title: , child_section_no:, child_title:, amendment_text: , parent_section_no: , parent_title: ,child_section_no:, child_title:, amendment_text: ]]`

   The `parent_section_no` is the parent section number that needs to be modified in the master agreement. The `parent_title` is the title of the parent section number that needs to be modified in the master agreement. The `child_section_no` is the child section number that needs to be modified in the master agreement. The `child_title` is the title of the child section number that needs to be modified in the master agreement.

   HERE IS AN EXAMPLE OF HOW THE FINAL JSON OUTPUT SHOULD LOOK LIKE:

   AMENDMENT DOCUMENT:

   Section 2, Indemnity is hereby amended as follows:

   The first paragraph of Section 2.2, Indirect Damages, is hereby deleted and replaced with the following: «amendment_text»

OUTPUT:

parent_section_no: «2», parent_title: «Indemnity» , child_section_no: «.2», child_title: «Indirect Damages» , amendment_text: «amendment_text»" parent_section_no: «3» parent_title:«Communications» , child_section_no: «(g)», child_title:«Publicity» , amendment_text: «amendment_text»" parent_section_no: «», parent_title: «Pricing Schedule Exhibit» , child_section_no: «», child_title: «» , amendment_text: «amendment_text»"

INSTRUCTIONS WHILE CREATING THE OUTPUT:

- In cases, when there are section numbers specified, extract the section header and add it to parent_section_no.
- Do not add the list item numbers in the document as parent_section_no.
- Create a RFC8259 compliant JSON.
- Check for double quotes (") in amendment_text key and replace them with single quotes.

3. Given the document below, the section number and the title, determine whether this is the right section where the chunk should be added. Return True if this is the document where the chunk should be added, else return False.

   Information:

   Parent Section Number: {parent_section_number}
   Child Section Number: {child_section_number}
   Parent title: {parent_title}
   Child title: {child_title}
   Document Chunk: {chunk}

4. You are a US attorney that helps your clients extract key and broad concepts from the clauses.

   Only extract key and broad points from the template clause below each separated by a new line. Each bulleted point mentioned is a single concept. Include all key points within each bulleted point.

   Template Clause: {template_clause}

5. Is the following concept covered within the document? ALWAYS return a "SOURCES" part in your answer. Don't try to make up an answer.

   CONCEPT: {question} {section_text} ——————— FINAL ANSWER:
   SOURCES:

6. Based on the following key points below from the template, answer the following question. ALWAYS return a "SOURCES" part in your answer.

   If the answer is "Yes" and there is additional information in the contract document not included in the template, include the "SUB CLAUSE" from the contract which is included else include "NA" in "SUB CLAUSE".
   QUESTION: What additional information is in the contract clause {key} that is not included in the template concepts below?
   ALL CONCEPTS: {all_template_concepts}
   ———————

   FINAL ANSWER:
   SOURCES:
   SUB CLAUSE:

Attributed Question Answering for Preconditions in the Dutch Law

Felicia Redelaar[1,2], Romy van Drie[2], Suzan Verberne[1], Maaike de Boer[2]

[1]Leiden Institute of Advanced Computer Science, Einsteinweg 55, Leiden, The Netherlands
[2]Dep. Data Science, TNO, Anna van Buerenplein 1, The Hague, The Netherlands
Correspondence: s.verberne@liacs.leidenuniv.nl, maaike.deboer@tno.nl

Abstract

In this paper, we address the problem of answering questions about preconditions in the law, e.g. "When can the court terminate the guardianship of a natural person?". When answering legal questions, it is important to attribute the relevant part of the law; we therefore not only generate answers but also references to law articles. We implement a retrieval augmented generation (RAG) pipeline for long-form answers based on the Dutch law, using several state-of-the-art retrievers and generators. For evaluating our pipeline, we create a dataset containing 102 legal QA pairs with attributions. Our experiments show promising results on our extended version for the automatic evaluation metrics from the Automatic LLMs' Citation Evaluation (ALCE) Framework and the G-EVAL Framework. Our findings indicate that RAG has significant potential in complex, citation-heavy domains like law, as it helps laymen understand legal preconditions and rights by generating high-quality answers with accurate attributions.

1 Introduction

Many people encounter civil justice problems at some point in their lives, whether they are disagreements with landlords or issues at work. However, not everyone knows their rights or how to resolve these problems, leaving them unsure of what to do next (Balmer et al., 2010). Studies have shown that the main obstacles to getting justice are the costs involved and a lack of awareness about legal rights and available options (Hoekstra and Teeuwen, 2023). This issue is not just local – it is a global problem. Over 1.4 billion people around the world have unresolved civil justice needs (Ponce et al., 2019), and in a global survey, 43% of respondents said that legal issues had negatively affected their personal lives (Ponce et al., 2019).

Automated legal Question Answering (QA) could provide affordable assistance to a wide audience. One concern is that many countries still lack a digital legal aid system, as each country operates under its own legal framework (Wiggers, 2023) and in their local language. This requires language-specific QA solutions, such as those explored by Louis et al. (2023), which focuses on developing a system capable of answering legal questions in French for Belgian law. Prior initiatives have been undertaken to assist individuals by creating legal chatbots for various languages, including French, Thai, and Indonesian (Queudot et al., 2020; Socatiyanurak et al., 2021; Firdaus et al., 2020).

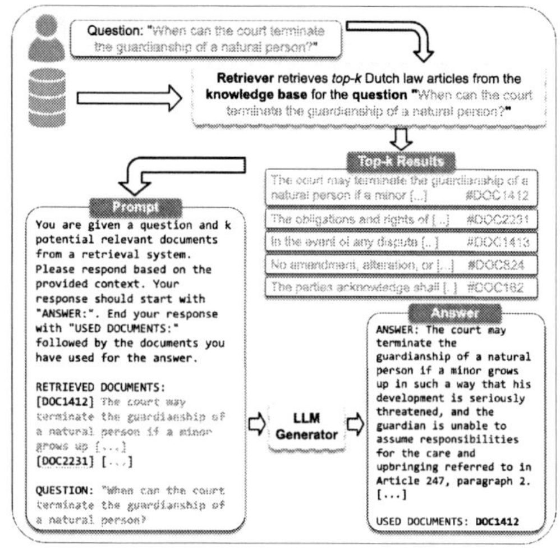

Figure 1: Our RAG framework for legal attributed QA with an example

An important requirement of legal QA systems is that they should provide verifiable sources in their responses, so-called **attributions**, in order to increase the verifiability of the responses. Additionally, the answers generated by these systems should be tailored to an individual's specific legal situation and provide detailed information about their legal options. Furthermore, the responses should not be too brief, such as simple "yes" or "no" answers (Do

Proceedings of the Natural Legal Language Processing Workshop 2024, pages 154–165
November 16, 2024 ©2024 Association for Computational Linguistics

et al., 2017), which fail to capture the complexity of legal issues.

In this paper we focus on **precondition**-related questions. We define a precondition to refer to the specific requirements, criteria, or circumstances that must be fulfilled before a specific action, event, decision, or outcome can legally occur or be finalized. Some examples of precondition-related questions are: "When is a student eligible for student financing?" and "What are the requirements for entering into a marriage?". The answer to the first question contains preconditions such as having a Dutch nationality. The latter question can be answered with the precondition of being at least 18 years old.

We address **Attributed QA (AQA) for the Dutch law**. Our aim is to answer legal questions with a tailored answer, including attributions to the relevant law article. Attributions have the form of references to specific documents, in our case articles of the Dutch law.

To this end, we create and publish a Dutch legal QA dataset, consisting of 102 question-answer pairs with attributions to Dutch law articles. We implement and evaluate a Retrieval Augmented Generation (RAG) pipeline that generates informative long-form answers to Dutch law questions, where each generated answer contains a list of attributions (references) to sources. Our approach is illustrated in Figure 1. Our contributions are as follows:

- We implement a RAG solution for attributed QA for the Dutch law.
- We have created and released an annotated dataset for (attributed) QA for the Dutch law that can be used in legal QA tasks. The dataset consists of 102 question-and-answer pairs that have an attribution to the used law articles. The answers have been verified by a legal expert on legal correctness.
- We extend an existing method for the automatic evaluation of attributed QA tasks. Our extended evaluation method is especially suitable when the answers in the dataset contain ground-truth attributions.

We publicly release our code and dataset at `https://gitlab.com/normativesystems/flintfillers/aqa_preconditions`.

2 Related work

2.1 Legal Question Answering

Legal questions can expect binary, multiple-choice, multi-span, or long-form answers (Martinez-Gil, 2023). QA systems are commonly implemented as two-stage pipelines, consisting of a retrieval step followed by an extraction or generation step (Martinez-Gil, 2023). Traditionally, the first stage of legal QA relied on sparse (keyword-based) retrieval techniques. With the rise of transformers, several works have incorporated dense retrievers to improve the first stage in their legal QA system (Hoppe et al., 2021; Khazaeli et al., 2021; Karpukhin et al., 2020). Dense retrievers embed both the query and the document as a vector in a continuous vector space, which allows to find relevant documents that have semantic similarity to the query but no or very little word overlap.

The most recent advancements in the field are in the second stage of the legal QA pipeline, using LLMs to generate fluent answers (Louis et al., 2023). This work employs the conventional two-stage method to answer long-form legal question, using an LLM to generate answers. Finally, their methodology involves generating rationale for answers that include a pointer towards a knowledge base.

Datasets for legal QA have been released in prior work: Zhong et al. (2020) released JEC-QA, a Chinese dataset for multiple-choice questions, sourced from legal exams. For long-form questions, Mansouri and Campos (2023); Chen et al. (2023) released English and Chinese datasets sourced from online forums, and Louis et al. (2023) released a French dataset sourced from lawyers. We are the first initiative creating, curating, and releasing a dataset for Dutch legal QA.

2.2 Attributed QA

In Attributed Question Answering (AQA), the input is a question, and the output is a tuple of an answer string and its attributions (Bohnet et al., 2022). The attributions are references to a knowledge corpus C. An example for the AQA task is the input question "Which movies have Cate Blanchet as a member of their cast?", which should produce an output answer string: "Carol, The Lord of the Rings, Tár, and Don't Look Up", with attribution references e.g. in the form [DOC1][DOC2]. These references are pointers to text segments in a knowledge corpus that support the given answer string.

AQA is commonly solved with RAG (Li et al., 2024; Muller et al., 2023; Stolfo, 2024; Hu et al., 2024; Menick et al., 2022). While most of these works achieve attributions through prompting, Ye et al. (2024) propose an approach in which they fine-tune an LLM to generate references. In the context of cross-lingual QA, Muller et al. (2023) improve attribution quality using Natural Language Inference.

2.3 Evaluation of AQA

Multiple studies have suggested methods for evaluating the answers and attributions generated by an LLM. Some studies involve manual human evaluation assessing whether the answer is supported by the given attributions and whether the answer itself is plausible (Menick et al., 2022). Kamalloo et al. (2023) introduced HAGRID, which measures whether the explanation directly answers the question and whether the explanation is attributable to the attributions. For automatic evaluation, several studies have proposed prompting LLMs to generate evaluations. In a study by Yue et al. (2023), the ATTRSCORE was proposed, which evaluates three binary metrics. These are whether the answer is attributable, extrapolatory, and contradictory. Additionally, Li et al. (2023) proposed KALMA, an automatic evaluation framework that assesses the generated text and its citations. The generated text is evaluated using G-EVAL (Liu et al., 2023), an evaluation suite that uses LLMs with chain-of-thoughts to measure coherence, consistency, fluency, and relevance. In KALMA, the citations are automatically evaluated using precision and recall.

Based on the work of Bohnet et al. (2022), Gao et al. (2023) introduced Automatic LLMs' Citation Evaluation (ALCE), which is the first benchmark for AQA. The benchmark contains three datasets: ASQA (Stelmakh et al., 2022), QAMPARI (Amouyal et al., 2022), and ELI5 (Fan et al., 2019). Our work will not use these benchmark datasets because they do not contain ground truth attributions to a knowledge corpus. ALCE serves as a framework for automatically evaluating answer strings and their corresponding cited attributions generated by LLMs. The authors of ALCE developed automatic metrics along three dimensions and demonstrated their strong correlation with human judgments. In our evaluation, we extend ALCE for the evaluation of AQA with ground truth references.

2.4 Retrieval Augmented Generation

RAG, introduced in the work by Lewis et al. (2020), is a technique that augments the prompt to an LLM with external knowledge. RAG is particularly relevant for attributed QA as it allows external knowledge to be used to answer questions, while the attributions can be generated by the LLM. The main components of RAG are the retriever and the generator. The retriever aims to find the most relevant documents in a large knowledge corpus for a specific query or question. An LLM is then used to generate an answer. The main motivation of RAG is two-fold. Firstly, to use custom data, since LLMs have been trained on a huge amount of data that might not be aligned for a specific task. On top of that, the data the LLM has been pre-trained with could be outdated or contain inaccuracies. Secondly, to give the user access to the sources of the generated information, allowing them to verify its correctness and ensure the information is accurate and reliable.

Substantial research has been dedicated to optimizing retrievers for QA tasks (Chen et al., 2017). Karpukhin et al. (2020) propose Dense Passage Retrieval and showed that a dense retriever can outperform sparse vector space models such as BM25 when adding enough data. SPLADE (Formal et al., 2021) is a retriever that combines dense and sparse retrieval and has been successfully used in RAG contexts. Lin et al. (2023) introduced DRAGON, which is a generalized dense retriever trained through progressive data augmentation. Ram et al. (2023) proposed RALM to optimize the retriever for in-context retrieval-augmented LLMs. In this paper, we follow this line of work and evaluate state-of-the-art retrieval models, both dense and sparse, in the context of RAG for attributed legal QA.

3 Dataset

3.1 Creating question-answer pairs

Our work aims to help users better understand when they are legally permitted to take certain actions, which is why we focus exclusively on precondition-related questions.

To select sources for our questions, we carefully review Dutch law texts via the official government website[1] and reading these on the **article** level. We filter out all technical or administrative legislation.

[1]https://wetten.overheid.nl/

These are laws that are intended to adjust, implement, or execute existing legislation without making policy changes.[2] From the remaining laws, we sample 25 laws at random for question formulation. These 25 laws comprise a total of 4441 articles.

We formulate the questions by looking for subordinating conjunctions such as "only if" or "on condition (that)". Whenever we find such conjunctions followed by actionable measures in a law text, we formulate a legal question. We formulate a ground truth answer to the question by referencing the relevant law texts, aiming to maintain the original meaning as closely as possible, considering the complexity and potential ambiguities in legal texts. In other words, we first look for the answers by finding pre-conditions in law texts, and then formulate legal questions around these pre-conditions. We formulated questions to 17 of the 25 laws and created 110 questions–answer pairs based on these laws.

Next, a legal expert is consulted for quality assurance, checking the legal correctness of all the questions and answers. The legal expert assessed whether the answer to the question was an accurate representation of the source document. We implement the expert's feedback regarding question and answer pairs, and discard questions that are too vague or contained answers that are too complex to verify for legal correctness according to the expert. Finally, the legal expert is consulted again to make sure the dataset quality is up to par in terms of legal correctness and completeness of the questions and answers. This yields a final number of 102 question-answer pairs, each with legal attribution references.

3.2 Knowledge corpus

We use the Dutch law as the knowledge corpus to provide references that a system can use when generating an answer.

The laws are publicly available and downloadable in XML format from the official government website.[1] With a parsing script we convert the laws from XML into a CSV file in which each row contains the text of a law article. Articles longer than 150 words are split into new rows to make the references in the answer easier to verify since some articles are over 1000 words in length. We use a hard cut-off after 150 words. This results in some law articles having multiple chunks in our knowledge corpus, each following the other on a word basis. A downside of the cut-off is some loss in the meaning of the split chunks which might affect retrieval and generation performance. Finally, for each created chunk, we assign a unique document ID to facilitate straightforward referencing by the system.

The resulting number of articles is 22,462 and the number of chunks is 30,803. Most articles (16,665) contain one chunk since their text consists of 150 words or less. The remaining articles are comprised of 2 to 20 chunks. By design, 100% of our curated QA pairs contain article-level references through chunks in the knowledge corpus. This approach ensures that each answer can be traced back to a specific legal article, enhancing the reliability and traceability of the dataset. By design, 100% of our questions–answer pairs contain article-level references. This approach ensures that each answer can be traced back to a specific legal article.

4 Methods: RAG system

4.1 Retrievers

We experiment with three types of retrievers: 1) sparse retrievers; 2) dense retrievers; 3) hybrid retrievers. Sparse retrievers focus on the lexical overlap of terms between the query and the documents, relying on traditional information retrieval methods such as term frequency-inverse document frequency (TF-IDF) (Sparck Jones, 1972). Our work uses the BM25 ranking model (Robertson et al., 1995) as a baseline retriever, which relies on TF-IDF.

While sparse retrievers are computationally efficient and interpretable, they are limited to word overlap between the query and the relevant documents. This means that sparse retrievers potentially miss relevant documents that do not share exact terms with the query. Dense retrievers do incorporate richer semantic information in the form of embeddings. In our work, we compare the following embedding models that we use as our dense retrievers:

- ALLNLI-GRONLP-BERT-BASE-DUTCH-

[2]These laws have the following words in their title: aanpassingswet (adjustment act), aanwijzingswet (designation act), verzamelwet (collection act), implementatiewet (implementation act), belastingplan (tax plan), intrekkingswet (withdrawal act), invoeringswet (introduction act), overige fiscale maatregelen (other fiscal measures), tijdelijke wet (temporary act), uitvoeringswet (execution act), wet aanpassing (law adjustment), wet aanvullende (supplementary law), and wijzigingswet (amendment act).

CASED: a sentence-BERT model (Reimers and Gurevych, 2019) trained on Dutch text;

- PARAPHRASE-MULTILINGUAL-MINILM-L12-V2: a multilingual sentence BERT model;
- MULTILINGUAL-E5, an open source text embedding model (Wang et al., 2024), the small, base and large version;
- DRAGON (Lin et al., 2023), trained using progressive data augmentation, but not multilingual (trained on English).

Note that several legal BERT models exist, but none of these was pre-trained for retrieval (in a bi-encoder or cross-encoder setting). Hybrid retrievers combine the strengths of sparse and dense retrievers to enhance the performance and accuracy of information retrieval systems by integrating precise keyword matching of sparse retrievers with the semantic understanding of dense retrievers. In this work, we use Sparse Lexical and Dense Embeddings (SPLADE) (Formal et al., 2021) as hybrid retriever. SPLADE has been trained on English datasets and is not a multilingual model.

4.2 Generators

After retrieving the most relevant documents, our generator is instructed through a prompt to generate a long-form answer using the potentially relevant retrieved documents and the corresponding question. We use one-shot in-context learning, and provide the prompt in the language (Dutch or English) in which the LLM has been mostly pre-trained on. Our prompt is shown in Table 4 in Appendix A.

We experiment with four commercial GPT models by OpenAI.[3] We choose the models GPT-3.5-TURBO and GPT-4O. The first model is a fast, inexpensive model used for simple tasks and the latter model is currently the fastest and most affordable flagship model by OpenAI.

Furthermore, we experiment with three open-source models. These are GEITJE-7B-ULTRA[4], LLAMA-3-8B-DUTCH[5], and FIETJE-2-INSTRUCT.[6] We select GEITJE-7B-ULTRA since it currrently is the largest open-source Dutch language model. The model is based on MISTRAL-7B, which reports to outperform LLAMA 2 on all benchmarks.[7] We select the LLAMA-3-8B-DUTCH model, since it has been trained on the same Dutch texts that GEITJE-7B-ULTRA has been trained on, but is based on Llama 3. Lastly, we experiment with FIETJE-2-INSTRUCT since we want to see the potential results of a substantially smaller model. Fietje is based on Microsoft's phi-2, further trained for Dutch. It has only 2.7 billion parameters. The instruct version of the model was created by finetuning the base model on Dutch-language chat datasets.

5 Experiments

We first conduct experiments to select the best retriever component for our RAG pipeline. Once the best-performing retriever for each scenario is identified, we proceed to conduct experiments on the entire RAG pipeline using the best-performing retriever based on its recall@k score.

5.1 Setup

Regarding the parameters used for the retrievers, we have generated the embeddings of all SBERT and MULTILINGUAL-E5 models using batches of $batchsize = 32$. Regarding the parameters used for the generators, all GPT models generated text using $temperature = 0.0$ and $max\_tokens = 1000$. The open source LLMs generated text using a $temperature = 0.2$ and with $max\_tokens = 5000$. The temperature parameters were selected to be as low as possible since we have a dataset on legal work, and we want to minimize chances for rewording or creative output. For the GPT models, we use a temperature of 0.0 since we want less "creative" results, and still see variations in the output of the OpenAI models. With a temperature of 0.0, the GPT models' output still is non-deterministic. For the open source models, we use a temperature of 0.2 to create deviation in the responses. Furthermore, the max_token differs between the GPT models and open-source models is due to the open-source LLMs often requiring more tokens since they first describe that analyzed all given documents to formulate their answer, before actually providing their answer.

We generate answers with the OpenAI models ten times for robust results. For the open-source models, we generate answers five timesfor computational cost reasons. Their output, however, often deviated from the instructed format. For example, the models frequently ignore the required structure

[3] https://platform.openai.com/docs/models

[4] https://huggingface.co/BramVanroy/GEITje-7B-ultra

[5] https://huggingface.co/ReBatch/Llama-3-8B-dutch

[6] https://huggingface.co/BramVanroy/fietje-2-instruct

[7] https://mistral.ai/news/announcing-mistral-7b/

and begin their responses with a detailed analysis for each document. This means that their answers needs to be extracted manually before automatic evaluation is possible. We use top-K sampling with $K = 50$. We instruct all models to respond starting with "ANSWER:" before giving their answer to the question and "DOC IDs:" before citing the used documents. We automatically process the model's answers using a regular expression. We select the answers using the following rules whenever the models do not respond in this format. Firstly, if a variation of "ANSWER:" is present, we select all text that comes afterward as their response til the term "DOC IDs" appears. We disregard all texts after "DOC IDs" that are not DOC IDs. If no variation of "ANSWER:" exists in their response, we select the entire response as the output.

To run the experiments, we either used a laptop with an *Intel i7-1225U* processor, *Intel Iris Xe graphics* with 8GB, 16GB of RAM, or to accelerate the process, a part of the clusters containing dual *AMD EPYC 9354* CPUs (2x 32-core), 1TB of RAM, 8TB of SSD storage, and 4x *Nvidia L40S* GPUs. As for software, we used Huggingface for the transformer models, Pyserini[8] for BM25 and TREC Eval[9] to calculate the $recall@k$ score.

5.2 Evaluation

We base our automatic evaluation framework on the Automatic LLMs' Citation Evaluation (ALCE) (Gao et al., 2023). This framework developed automatic metrics among three dimensions – fluency, correctness, and citation quality. We argue that this framework could be more suitable for the AQA task by implementing small adjustments and we present these in our work. In our method, we still use the three dimensions but introduce different automatic evaluation methods for each dimension. We will discuss these in more detail in the following sections. Table 1 provides an overview of our and ALCE's evaluation's dimensions, definitions, and metrics.

5.2.1 Fluency

The ALCE framework uses MAUVE (Pillutla et al., 2021) to evaluate the fluency of the output as a sanity check, as most LLMs are capable of generating fluent text. However, the authors discovered that MAUVE is sensitive to the length of the output and found that its results become unstable for responses longer than 100 words. We therefore believe that MAUVE should not be used because of its instability. We instead use G-EVAL (Liu et al., 2023) to evaluate the output's fluency. Using G-EVAL with GPT-3.5-turbo, we prompt a detailed instruction to evaluate the fluency and coherence of an answer. The fluency metric measures the quality of the language model's answer in terms of grammar, spelling, punctuation, word choice, and sentence structure. The answer should be easy to read and follow. Coherence measures the quality of all sentences collectively, as whether they fit together and sound naturally. This metric considers the quality of the answer as a whole and takes in the account whether the answer is well-structured.

5.2.2 Correctness

The ALCE framework uses three different datasets and a different method for each to calculate the model response's correctness: exact match recall, recall@5, and a Natural Language Inference (NLI) model that is fine-tuned to check whether the model output entails sub claims created by another model based of the original model's response. In our work, we propose to use four metrics for the correctness score. Firstly, we decide to use the common metrics ROUGE (Lin, 2004) and METEOR (Banerjee and Lavie, 2005). We are able to use ROUGE and METEOR since the dataset in our work contains ground truth answers. These metrics calculate the overlap between the ground truth and model's answer. Secondly, we add G-EVAL to calculate the consistency and relevance scores. The consistency measures the factual alignment between the human answer and the language model answer. A factually consistent answer contains only statements that are entailed by the source document. Answers are penalized when there are hallucinated facts. The relevance metric measures whether the answer merely contains important and relevant information to the question. Answers are penalized when containing redundancies and excess information.

5.2.3 Citation quality

The ALCE framework computes the citation quality using a Natural Language Inference (NLI) model. Specifically, the recall and precision of the entailment of each statement with its attribution (0 or 1) is averaged over all statements in the model response. The recall of a statement in the model's generated answer is 1 if the concatenation of all cited passages fully support the statement.

[8]https://github.com/castorini/pyserini

[9]https://github.com/cvangysel/pytrec_eval

Evaluation dimension	Definition	ALCE's Metrics	Our Metrics
1) Fluency	Whether the model's generated text is fluent and coherent	• MAUVE	• Fluency • Coherence
2) Correctness	Whether the answer is accurate and covers all aspects of interest	• Exact match recall • Recall@5, • Claim recall	• ROUGE-L • METEOR • Consistency • Relevance
3) Citation Quality	Whether the answer is well supported by the cited passages and no irrelevant passages are cited	• Citation recall • Citation precision	• Citation recall • Citation precision • HitRate@k

Table 1: Evaluation dimensions and associated metrics of ALCE and our work.

The NLI model is used to determine "full support". The precision in ALCE detects irrelevant citations. A cited passage is seen as irrelevant if the citation alone does not support a claim, and if removing it does not affect other citations combined to support the claim.

We use a more precise method for citation quality, which is possible since our dataset QA-pairs contain attribution ground truths. We simply use regular recall and precision for the citation quality.

6 Results

6.1 Retrieval

Table 2 shows the results on the retrieval part of the RAG. We compare the baseline model BM25 to dense and hybrid retrievers. We can see that the E5-MULTILINGUAL$_{\text{LARGE}}$ model provides the highest performance on all metrics.

6.2 Generation

Table 3 shows the results for our RAG pipeline using our QA dataset with the knowledge corpus. In this setup, *k=3*, and the MULTILINGUAL-E5-BASE model was used for the retrieval of the documents. Regarding the correctness of the answers and the citation metrics, the GPT models perform substantially better than the open-source LLMs. Specifically, GPT-4O showed the best performance across most metrics, while the GPT-3.5-TURBO model had the highest precision score. An example of the output of the generation per model is shown in Appendix B.

7 Discussion

The results show that our RAG system can generate fluent and correct answers with an 83.0% hit-rate. The answers are often highly coherent with the ground truth, and the models are capable of citing their sources accurately.

Looking at the retrievers, there are substantial differences. DRAGON consistently underperformed our baseline model, BM25. We hypothesize that this might be because DRAGON is a dense retriever trained solely in the English language, lacking multilingual capabilities. The E5 models, which were the best retriever models in our RAG system, were also trained using contrastive learning. Following E5, the hybrid model SPLADE, and the Dutch-trained SBERT performed best. This is an interesting finding, especially considering that SPLADE was trained only for the English language, leading us to hypothesize that its performance could be attributed to its partly sparse characteristics, enabling lexical overlap. While the models (4, 5, and 6 in Table 2) performed similarly in retrieval, using the best model improves the likelihood of correct attributions in the generated answers.

The results on the generation show that the proprietary models scored higher on all evaluation metrics than the open-source models. There are several explanations for the substantial difference, but the main one probably lies in the parameter sizes between the models. Although the number of parameters for the proprietary models used in our work remains undisclosed, it is reasonable to assume that they are significantly larger than the open-source models that we have used for our work which are relatively small models ranging between

	Model	#Param	R@3	R@5	R@10	Hit@3	Hit@5	Hit@10
Sparse								
1	BM25	-	0.586	0.672	0.739	0.696	0.775	0.873
Dense								
2	$\text{SBERT}_{\text{MULTILINGUAL}}$	117.7M	0.404	0.426	0.500	0.510	0.529	0.627
3	$\text{SBERT}_{\text{DUTCH}}$	109.1M	0.516	0.583	0.616	0.618	0.696	0.745
4	$\text{E5-multilingual}_{\text{SMALL}}$	117.7M	0.674	0.732	0.803	0.794	0.853	0.912
5	$\text{E5-multilingual}_{\text{BASE}}$	278.0M	0.696	0.755	0.816	0.843	0.892	0.941
6	$\text{E5-multilingual}_{\text{LARGE}}$	559.9M	**0.729**	**0.780**	**0.845**	**0.873**	**0.922**	**0.961**
7	DRAGON	109.5M	0.251	0.300	0.366	0.314	0.382	0.461
Hybrid								
8	SPLADE	109.5M	0.508	0.589	0.678	0.627	0.735	0.843

Table 2: Retrieval scores of sparse, dense, and hybrid retrievers using only the text from the article of each document in the knowledge corpus consisting of 273 laws.

		Fluency		Correctness				Citation quality		
		COH	FLU	ROU	MET	CON	REL	R	P	Hit
GPT										
1	GPT-3.5-turbo-0125	0.807 ±0.8	0.974 ±0.1	0.561 ±0.7	0.732 ±0.3	0.943 ±0.4	0.964 ±0.2	0.510 ±0.0	0.615 ±1.1	0.784 ±0.0
2	GPT-4o	0.847 ±0.7	0.970 ±0.2	0.629 ±0.4	0.754 ±0.4	0.934 ±0.3	0.961 ±0.1	0.539 ±0.3	0.692 ±0.5	0.830 ±0.5
Open source LLMs										
3	GEITje-7B-ultra	0.794 ±2.8	0.952 ±1.3	0.382 ±1.8	0.369 ±1.7	0.822 ±2.3	0.856 ±1.7	0.146 ±2.3	0.189 ±1.4	0.225 ±3.6
4	Llama-3-8B-dutch	0.744 ±3.1	0.957 ±1.1	0.341 ±2.0	0.427 ±1.9	0.632 ±3.4	0.728 ±3.4	0.237 ±2.5	0.274 ±1.7	0.365 ±3.9

Table 3: Performances of the LLMs on our dataset with the knowledge corpus using the best performing retriever, $mE5_{large}$, with $k = 3$. We show the mean and standard deviation scaled by a factor of 100. The performances are evaluated on Fluency, Correctness and Citation through nine evaluation metrics: *G-EVAL Coherence* (COH), *G-EVAL Fluency* (FLU), *ROUGE-L* (ROU), *METEOR* (MET), *G-EVAL Consistency* (CON), *G-EVAL Relevance* (REL), *Precision* (P), *Recall* (R), and *Hitrate@5* (Hit)

2 and 7 billion parameters. It is well established that larger model sizes often result in better performance due to a better natural language understanding and ability to handle larger context windows. Additionally, we noted that GEITJE produced the most fluent responses, while LLAMA generated the most correct answers and maintained the highest citation quality across all settings. We hypothesize that GEITJE is more proficient in Dutch, while LLAMA is better in understanding instructions.

8 Conclusion

In this paper, we create and evaluate a retrieval augmented generation (RAG) pipeline for attributed Question Answering for the Dutch law, generating long-form answers to precondition questions. We experiment with several state-of-the-art retrievers and generators. For evaluating our pipeline, we create and release a dataset containing 102 legal QA pairs with attributions, as well as an automated evaluation framework suited to this task. The results show that our RAG system can generate fluent and largely correct answers with an 83.0% hit-rate.

Future work includes an extension of the dataset with other document types such as jurisdictions, include more retrievers such as a multilingual hybrid retriever and compare the results from the evaluation framework with human judgements.

Limitations

One of the limitations of this work is that, although we validated the answers with a domain expert, it is not validated whether the answers are indeed understandable to laypeople, or whether multiple experts agree with each other. Another limitation is that the legislative provisions selected often include conditional phrases. This raises the question of whether the retrieval approach may have been inadvertently biased towards these specific linguistic patterns.

References

Samuel Joseph Amouyal, Ohad Rubin, Ori Yoran, Tomer Wolfson, Jonathan Herzig, and Jonathan Berant. 2022. Qampari: An open-domain question answering benchmark for questions with many answers from multiple paragraphs. *ArXiv, abs/2205.12665.*

Nigel J Balmer, Alexy Buck, Ash Patel, Catrina Denvir, and Pascoe Pleasence. 2010. Knowledge, capability and the experience of rights problems. *London: PLEnet.*

Satanjeev Banerjee and Alon Lavie. 2005. Meteor: An automatic metric for mt evaluation with improved correlation with human judgments. In *Proceedings of the acl workshop on intrinsic and extrinsic evaluation measures for machine translation and/or summarization*, pages 65–72.

Bernd Bohnet, Vinh Q Tran, Pat Verga, Roee Aharoni, Daniel Andor, Livio Baldini Soares, Massimiliano Ciaramita, Jacob Eisenstein, Kuzman Ganchev, Jonathan Herzig, et al. 2022. Attributed question answering: Evaluation and modeling for attributed large language models. *arXiv preprint arXiv:2212.08037.*

Andong Chen, Feng Yao, Xinyan Zhao, Yating Zhang, Changlong Sun, Yun Liu, and Weixing Shen. 2023. Equals: A real-world dataset for legal question answering via reading chinese laws. In *Proceedings of the Nineteenth International Conference on Artificial Intelligence and Law*, pages 71–80.

Danqi Chen, Adam Fisch, Jason Weston, and Antoine Bordes. 2017. Reading wikipedia to answer open-domain questions. *arXiv preprint arXiv:1704.00051.*

Phong-Khac Do, Huy-Tien Nguyen, Chien-Xuan Tran, Minh-Tien Nguyen, and Minh-Le Nguyen. 2017. Legal question answering using ranking svm and deep convolutional neural network. *arXiv preprint arXiv:1703.05320.*

Angela Fan, Yacine Jernite, Ethan Perez, David Grangier, Jason Weston, and Michael Auli. 2019. Eli5: Long form question answering. *arXiv preprint arXiv:1907.09190.*

VAH Firdaus, PY Saputra, and D Suprianto. 2020. Intelligence chatbot for indonesian law on electronic information and transaction. In *IOP Conference Series: Materials Science and Engineering*, volume 830, page 022089. IOP Publishing.

Thibault Formal, Benjamin Piwowarski, and Stéphane Clinchant. 2021. Splade: Sparse lexical and expansion model for first stage ranking. In *Proceedings of the 44th International ACM SIGIR Conference on Research and Development in Information Retrieval*, pages 2288–2292.

Tianyu Gao, Howard Yen, Jiatong Yu, and Danqi Chen. 2023. Enabling large language models to generate text with citations. *arXiv preprint arXiv:2305.14627.*

MS Hoekstra and G Teeuwen. 2023. Drempels in de toegang tot het recht.

Christoph Hoppe, David Pelkmann, Nico Migenda, Daniel Hötte, and Wolfram Schenck. 2021. Towards intelligent legal advisors for document retrieval and question-answering in german legal documents. In *2021 IEEE Fourth International Conference on Artificial Intelligence and Knowledge Engineering (AIKE)*, pages 29–32. IEEE.

Nan Hu, Jiaoyan Chen, Yike Wu, Guilin Qi, Sheng Bi, Tongtong Wu, and Jeff Z. Pan. 2024. Benchmarking large language models in complex question answering attribution using knowledge graphs. *arXiv preprint arXiv:2401.14640.*

Ehsan Kamalloo, Aref Jafari, Xinyu Zhang, Nandan Thakur, and Jimmy Lin. 2023. Hagrid: A human-llm collaborative dataset for generative information-seeking with attribution. *arXiv preprint arXiv:2307.16883.*

Vladimir Karpukhin, Barlas Oğuz, Sewon Min, Patrick Lewis, Ledell Wu, Sergey Edunov, Danqi Chen, and Wen-tau Yih. 2020. Dense passage retrieval for open-domain question answering. *arXiv preprint arXiv:2004.04906.*

Soha Khazaeli, Janardhana Punuru, Chad Morris, Sanjay Sharma, Bert Staub, Michael Cole, Sunny Chiu-Webster, and Dhruv Sakalley. 2021. A free format legal question answering system. In *Proceedings of the Natural Legal Language Processing Workshop 2021*, pages 107–113.

Patrick Lewis, Ethan Perez, Aleksandra Piktus, Fabio Petroni, Vladimir Karpukhin, Naman Goyal, Heinrich Küttler, Mike Lewis, Wen-tau Yih, Tim Rocktäschel, et al. 2020. Retrieval-augmented generation for knowledge-intensive nlp tasks. *Advances in Neural Information Processing Systems*, 33:9459–9474.

Xinze Li, Yixin Cao, Liangming Pan, Yubo Ma, and Aixin Sun. 2023. Towards verifiable generation: A benchmark for knowledge-aware language model attribution. *arXiv preprint arXiv:2310.05634.*

Xinze Li, Yixin Cao, Liangming Pan, Yubo Ma, and Aixin Sun. 2024. Towards verifiable generation: A benchmark for knowledge-aware language model attribution. In *Findings of the Association for Computational Linguistics ACL 2024*, pages 493–516, Bangkok, Thailand and virtual meeting. Association for Computational Linguistics.

Chin-Yew Lin. 2004. Rouge: A package for automatic evaluation of summaries. In *Text summarization branches out*, pages 74–81.

Sheng-Chieh Lin, Akari Asai, Minghan Li, Barlas Oguz, Jimmy Lin, Yashar Mehdad, Wen-tau Yih, and Xilun Chen. 2023. How to train your dragon: Diverse augmentation towards generalizable dense retrieval. *arXiv preprint arXiv:2302.07452.*

Yang Liu, Dan Iter, Yichong Xu, Shuohang Wang, Ruochen Xu, and Chenguang Zhu. 2023. Gpteval: Nlg evaluation using gpt-4 with better human alignment. *arXiv preprint arXiv:2303.16634*.

Antoine Louis, Gijs van Dijck, and Gerasimos Spanakis. 2023. Interpretable long-form legal question answering with retrieval-augmented large language models. *arXiv preprint arXiv:2309.17050*.

Behrooz Mansouri and Ricardo Campos. 2023. Falqu: Finding answers to legal questions. *arXiv preprint arXiv:2304.05611*.

Jorge Martinez-Gil. 2023. A survey on legal question–answering systems. *Computer Science Review*, 48:100552.

Jacob Menick, Maja Trebacz, Vladimir Mikulik, John Aslanides, Francis Song, Martin Chadwick, Mia Glaese, Susannah Young, Lucy Campbell-Gillingham, Geoffrey Irving, et al. 2022. Teaching language models to support answers with verified quotes. *arXiv preprint arXiv:2203.11147*.

Benjamin Muller, John Wieting, Jonathan H Clark, Tom Kwiatkowski, Sebastian Ruder, Livio Soares, Roee Aharoni, Jonathan Herzig, and Xinyi Wang. 2023. Evaluating and modeling attribution for cross-lingual question answering. In *Proceedings of the 2023 Conference on Empirical Methods in Natural Language Processing*, pages 144–157.

Krishna Pillutla, Swabha Swayamdipta, Rowan Zellers, John Thickstun, Sean Welleck, Yejin Choi, and Zaid Harchaoui. 2021. Mauve: Measuring the gap between neural text and human text using divergence frontiers. *Advances in Neural Information Processing Systems*, 34:4816–4828.

Alejandro Ponce, Sarah Chamness Long, Elizabeth Andersen, Camilo Gutierrez Patino, Matthew Harman, Jorge A Morales, Ted Piccone, Natalia Rodriguez Cajamarca, Adriana Stephan, Kirssy Gonzalez, Jennifer VanRiper, Alicia Evangelides, Rachel Martin, Priya Khosla, Lindsey Bock, Erin Campbell, Emily Gray, Amy Gryskiewicz, Ayyub Ibrahim, Leslie Solis, Gabriel Hearn-Desautels, and Francesca Tinucci. 2019. *Global Insights on Access to Justice 2019: Findings from the World Justice Project General Population Poll in 101 Countries*. World Justice Project.

Marc Queudot, Éric Charton, and Marie-Jean Meurs. 2020. Improving access to justice with legal chatbots. *Stats*, 3(3):356–375.

Ori Ram, Yoav Levine, Itay Dalmedigos, Dor Muhlgay, Amnon Shashua, Kevin Leyton-Brown, and Yoav Shoham. 2023. In-context retrieval-augmented language models. *Transactions of the Association for Computational Linguistics*, 11:1316–1331.

Nils Reimers and Iryna Gurevych. 2019. Sentence-BERT: Sentence embeddings using Siamese BERT-networks. In *Proceedings of the 2019 Conference on Empirical Methods in Natural Language Processing and the 9th International Joint Conference on Natural Language Processing (EMNLP-IJCNLP)*, pages 3982–3992, Hong Kong, China. Association for Computational Linguistics.

Stephen E Robertson, Steve Walker, Susan Jones, Micheline M Hancock-Beaulieu, Mike Gatford, et al. 1995. Okapi at trec-3. *Nist Special Publication Sp*, 109:109.

Vorada Socatiyanurak, Nittayapa Klangpornkun, Adirek Munthuli, Phongphan Phienphanich, Lalin Kovudhikulrungsri, Nantawat Saksakulkunakorn, Phonkanok Chairaungsri, and Charturong Tantibundhit. 2021. Law-u: Legal guidance through artificial intelligence chatbot for sexual violence victims and survivors. *IEEE Access*, 9:131440–131461.

Karen Sparck Jones. 1972. A statistical interpretation of term specificity and its application in retrieval. *Journal of documentation*, 28(1):11–21.

Ivan Stelmakh, Yi Luan, Bhuwan Dhingra, and Ming-Wei Chang. 2022. Asqa: Factoid questions meet long-form answers. *arXiv preprint arXiv:2204.06092*.

Alessandro Stolfo. 2024. Groundedness in retrieval-augmented long-form generation: An empirical study. In *Findings of the Association for Computational Linguistics: NAACL 2024*, pages 1537–1552.

Liang Wang, Nan Yang, Xiaolong Huang, Linjun Yang, Rangan Majumder, and Furu Wei. 2024. Multilingual e5 text embeddings: A technical report. *arXiv preprint arXiv:2402.05672*.

G Wiggers. 2023. *The relevance of impact: bibliometric-enhanced legal information retrieval*. Ph.D. thesis, Leiden University.

Xi Ye, Ruoxi Sun, Sercan Arik, and Tomas Pfister. 2024. Effective large language model adaptation for improved grounding and citation generation. In *Proceedings of the 2024 Conference of the North American Chapter of the Association for Computational Linguistics: Human Language Technologies (Volume 1: Long Papers)*, pages 6237–6251.

Xiang Yue, Boshi Wang, Ziru Chen, Kai Zhang, Yu Su, and Huan Sun. 2023. Automatic evaluation of attribution by large language models. In *Findings of the Association for Computational Linguistics: EMNLP 2023*, pages 4615–4635, Singapore. Association for Computational Linguistics.

Haoxi Zhong, Chaojun Xiao, Cunchao Tu, Tianyang Zhang, Zhiyuan Liu, and Maosong Sun. 2020. Jec-qa: a legal-domain question answering dataset. In *Proceedings of the AAAI Conference on Artificial Intelligence*, volume 34, pages 9701–9708.

A Example prompt

You will be given a question and a list of 5 documents that are retrieved by BM25. The retrieved documents contain content that are the most relevant to the question from a large corpus.
Your task is to generate 2 things as an output. 1: An answer to the question based on the set of documents provided, and 2: A list of attributions to the documents you have used to generate your answer. Note that not all of these 5 documents are relevant to the answer. BM25 simply returned the documents most likely to be relevant to the question.

Please make sure you read and understand these instructions carefully. Please keep this document open while reviewing, and refer to it as needed.

Steps:
1. Read the question carefully and identify the main topic and key points.
2. Read the documents provided by BM25 and check if they contain information that are directly relevant for the answer to the question.
3. Generate the answer string that answers the question based on the documents provided. Starting your answer with "ANSWER:".
4. Create a list of the document IDs that you have used for your answer, so the user can cross-check. Do only use the IDs of documents you have actually used to generate your answer. Start your answer with "DOC IDS:".

Example 1:
Question (EXAMPLE OF THE INPUT YOU WILL RECEIVE):
Question: Wanneer wordt een ongewenstheid verklaring opgeheven?

Documents (EXAMPLE OF THE INPUT YOU WILL RECEIVE):
Potential relevant documents: $\{document1\}, \{document2\}, \{...\}, \{documentk\}$

(EXAMPLE OF YOUR OUTPUT - ALWAYS DO IT IN THIS FORMAT, CAPITALIZING THE "ANSWER:"):
ANSWER: De ongewenstheid verklaring wordt opgeheven bij de volgende condities: Indien de vreemdeling tien jaar onafgebroken buiten Nederland verblijf heeft gehad en de vreemdeling niet ongewenst is verklaard.

(EXAMPLE OF YOUR OUTPUT - ALWAYS DO IT IN THIS FORMAT, CAPITALIZING "DOC IDS:", THERE CAN BE ONE OR MORE.):
DOC IDS: DOC0226

REMEMBER, YOUR TASK IS TO GENERATE AN ANSWER STRING AND A LIST FOR THE DOCUMENT IDs USED IN YOUR ANSWER. ALWAYS START THE ANSWER WITH: "ANSWER:", AND THE ATTRIBUTION WITH "DOC IDS:". ALWAYS USE CAPITALIZATION FOR ANSWER AND DOC IDS IN YOUR OUTPUT! DO NOT HAVE ANY OTHER OUTPUT.

Here comes your task:

Question: $\{question\}$
Potential relevant documents: $\{document1\}, \{document2\}, \{...\}, \{documentk\}$

Table 4: Prompt template to generate long-form answers. Blue text is the input data that is different for each question.

B Comparison of Generation outputs

Question: When can the court terminate a parent's custody?
Human answer: The court can terminate a parent's custody if: a. a minor is growing up in such a way that their development is seriously threatened, and the parent is not capable of taking responsibility for the care and upbringing, as referred to in Article 247, second paragraph, within a time frame that can be deemed acceptable for the person and development of the minor, or b. the parent abuses their custody.
GPT-4o: The court can terminate a parent's custody if a minor is growing up in such a way that their development is seriously threatened and the parent is not capable of taking responsibility for the care and upbringing within an acceptable time frame, or if the parent abuses their custody. Custody can also be terminated if it has been suspended, provided that the mentioned conditions are met.
GPT-3.5: The court can terminate a parent's custody if a minor is growing up in such a way that their development is seriously threatened, and the parent is not able to take responsibility for the care and upbringing within a time frame that can be deemed acceptable for the person and development of the minor, or if the parent abuses their custody.
GEITje-7B-ultra: The court can terminate a parent's custody if: a. a minor is growing up in such a way that their development is seriously threatened, and the parent is not capable of taking responsibility for the care and upbringing, as referred to in Article 247, second paragraph, within a time frame that can be deemed acceptable for the person and development of the minor, or if the parent abuses their custody. The custody of the parent can also be terminated if the custody has been suspended, provided that the conditions of the first paragraph are met. b. If both parents jointly exercise custody, after the termination of one parent's custody, the other parent will henceforth exercise custody alone. In the case of the termination of custody of a parent who exercises custody alone, the other parent can at any time request the court to be granted custody. This request will be granted if the court deems it necessary in the interest of the minor. The court that has rejected the request referred to in the previous paragraph can always change this decision. However, it will only do so at the request of the parent involved, and only based on circumstances that the court could not have taken into account when making the decision. c. The parent whose custody has been terminated can, at their request, be reinstated in custody if: the reinstatement of custody is in the best interest of the minor, and the parent is capable of permanently taking responsibility for the care and upbringing of the minor, as referred to in Article 247, second paragraph. If, at the time of termination of custody, custody has been assigned to the other parent, the court will not assign custody to the parent whose custody was terminated, and who makes the request referred to in the first paragraph, unless circumstances have changed after the decision assigning custody to the other parent, or the decision was based on incorrect or incomplete information. Article 253e applies correspondingly.
Llama-3-8B-dutch: The court can terminate a parent's custody when a minor is growing up in such a way that their development is seriously threatened and the parent is not capable of taking responsibility for the care and upbringing within a time frame that can be deemed acceptable for the person and development of the minor, or if the parent abuses their custody
Fietje-2B: Royal authority can be terminated if the king has not reached the age of eighteen.

Table 5: Translated examples of long-form answers from various generators for the same setup, receiving the same input chunks from the E5 retriever.

Algorithm for Automatic Legislative Text Consolidation

Matias Etcheverry
Doctrine
Ecole Nationale Supérieure Paris-Saclay
matias.etcheverry@doctrine.fr

Thibaud Real
Doctrine
thibaud.real-del-sarte@doctrine.fr

Pauline Chavallard
Doctrine
pauline@doctrine.fr

Abstract

This study introduces a method for automating the consolidation process in a legal context, a time-consuming task traditionally performed by legal professionals. We present a generative approach that processes legislative texts to automatically apply amendments. Our method employs light quantized generative model, fine-tuned with LoRA, to generate accurate and reliable amended texts. To the authors knowledge, this is the first time generative models are used on legislative text consolidation. Our dataset is publicly available on HuggingFace[1]. Experimental results demonstrate a significant improvement in efficiency, offering faster updates to legal documents. A full automated pipeline of legislative text consolidation can be done in a few hours, with a success rate of more than 63% on a difficult bill.

1 Introduction

Every year in France, the *Projet de Loi Finance*[2] (PLF), annually introduces numerous modifications to the General Tax Code (484 in 2024). The objective of this study is to automate the process of legislative text consolidation, which is the act of combining modifications from a `modification section`, contained inside the PLF, to an `existing article` to generate a `modified article`. Example 1 illustrates a dummy consolidation, where the original text of a law is updated by incorporating amendments directly into it, resulting in a revised, coherent version.

Legislative text consolidation is a critical yet time-consuming task, traditionally performed manually by legal professionals. A sample of the PLF is presented in Example[3] 2. It modifies `article 1586 ter` and `article 1586 quater` of the General Tax Code.

Example 1: Illustration of legislative consolidation

```
Existing article: Paris is the
capital of France.
Modification section:
I.- Replace the word « is »
with « has been ».
II.- Add « since the late 10th
century » at the end of the
sentence.
Modified article: Paris has
been the capital of France
since the late 10th century.
```

The conventions represented on Figure 1 are adhered to:

- A legislative bill is composed of multiple articles[4].
- An article comprises several sections. A section is defined as a collection of paragraphs that enact modifications to a single article.
- A section may effectuate either a singular modification or multiple modifications. For instance, section `A.-` implements a single modification, whereas section `B.-` introduces four modifications.

Three primary modification categories are identified: a deletion, involving the removal of a word, sentence, or paragraph; an addition, encompassing the insertion of a word, sentence, or paragraph and a substitution, where a word, sentence, or paragraph is exchanged for another. Example 2 demonstrates one instance of addition and four instances of substitutions.

The automation of legislative text consolidation has the potential to significantly expedite

[1]Link to dataset

[2]Link to *Projet de Loi Finance* for 2024

[3]All examples are translated from French to English.

[4]An article would be the equivalent of a section in a bill in common-law countries.

Proceedings of the Natural Legal Language Processing Workshop 2024, pages 166–175
November 16, 2024

Example 2: Extract of article 79 of the PLF 2024

Modification sections:

I.-The General Tax Code is amended as follows:
A.-The following words are added to the first sentence of the second paragraph of 1 of II of Article 1586 ter: « , as it stood prior to Finance Act 2023-1322 of 29 December 2023 for 2024 »;
B.-Article 1586 quater is amended as follows:
1° I is amended as follows
a) The second paragraph of b and c is amended as follows:
-at the beginning, the rate: « 0.125% » is replaced by the rate: « 0.094% »;
-at the beginning, the rate: « 0.094% » is replaced by the rate: « 0.063% »;
b) The second paragraph of c is amended as follows:
-the rate: « 0.225% » is replaced by the rate: « 0.169% »;
-the rate: « 0.113% » is replaced by the rate: « 0.056% »;

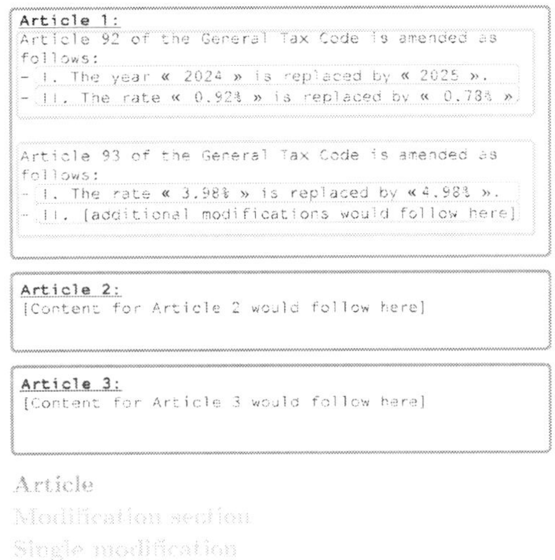

Figure 1: General structure of the PLF

this process, offering a rapid update of legal documents post-enactment and potentially pre-enactment, thereby enhancing the accessibility and reliability of legal information.

2 Related works

2.1 Information extraction approaches

Modification sections typically follow a consistent lexical structure. Arnold-Moore (1995, 1997) and Mazzei et al. (2009) exploit this formal consistency to extract amendments and construct a structured tree representation, applying information extraction techniques.

Subsequently, a clear trend is drawn in information extraction between tagging-based methods and generative methods. Tagging-based methods are designed to classify individual tokens (token-based methods) or clusters of tokens (span-based methods). In contrast, generative methods are oriented towards producing textual content that is inherently construed as a relationship triplet. Hence, Shi and Lin (2019) undertake a notably question answering adaptation of the BERT model to facilitate generation across a diverse corpus, achieving a remarkably good baseline. In more recent times, generative models appear to exhibit superior performance. Josifoski et al. (2022) introduce the GenIE model, which succeeds in generating generation triplets through its utilization of the BART architecture.

In recent developments, models dedicated to text editing have garnered interest for their utility in tasks that necessitate the rearrangement of words and text spans, such as summarization. Malmi et al. (2019) introduced `LaserTagger`, an approach that assigns one of several tags to tokens, including `KEEP`, `DELETE`, `SWAP`, or `PRONOMINALIZE`, to facilitate text editing. Concurrently, Mallinson et al. (2020) developed a two-stage algorithm wherein the first model tags tokens, and the subsequent model is responsible for the rearrangement of these tagged tokens.

2.2 Generative approaches

Generative approaches rapidly took the lead to reinterpret any task of extraction, classification, or edition as generative problems under certain frameworks (Raffel et al., 2019). Building upon this foundational work, Chung et al. (2022) expanded the utility of these models through the fine-tuning process to accommodate a broad spectrum of human instructions, thereby enhancing their applicability. This advancement has catalyzed subsequent research endeavors, focusing extensively on the exploration of instruction-based fine-tuning within the realm of generative models.

Instruction tuning It is crucial to recognize that fine-tuning the model for a specific task is pivotal (Brown et al., 2020; Wei et al., 2022). In specific-use Pretrained Large Language Models (PLLMs), such as for legislative text consolidation, we may use instruction tuning to ensure that our model consolidates the provided legal text in all cases.

Finetuning Existing parameter-efficient tuning methods still lag behind full fine-tuning on higher-resource and challenging tasks, but often succeed when dealing simple tasks, as consolidation would be (He et al., 2022). These approaches enable instruction tuning to be performed on cost-effective GPUs.

On one hand, prompt tuning methods involve concatenating the embeddings of input tokens with a trainable tensor. This tensor can be optimized through backpropagation to enhance the modeling performance for a specific task. Remarkably, prompt tuning achieves modeling performance comparable to fine-tuning all layers, yet only necessitates training 0.1% of the parameters (Li and Liang, 2021; Liu et al., 2021). On the other hand, adaptation methods involve the insertion of fully connected layers into the transformer blocks (Houlsby et al., 2019). These techniques achieve equivalent performance to prompt tuning, albeit slightly more parameter-intensive. He et al. (2022) finds an equivalence between prompt tuning and adapter methods: adapter tuning is prompt tuning in series.

Ultimately, the LoRA method has garnered significant popularity (Hu et al., 2021). This technique involves adding a low-rank matrix to certain matrices within the PLLM. The underlying notion is that low-rank matrices encapsulate all the required information for precise task fine-tuning, while PLLM matrices encompass the full spectrum of information from pretraining. Notably, this method is not restricted solely to instruction embedding; it is applicable to a broad array of fine-tuning tasks. Furthermore, when utilized in conjunction with model quantization methods, LoRA extends the capability of fine-tuning numerous PLLMs (Dettmers et al., 2023).

3 Dataset

Our first objective is to construct a dataset for automatic consolidation. Each sample in this dataset is a triplet of texts `(existing article, modification section, modified article)` in which the `modification section` specifies the changes to be made to the `existing article` to obtain the `modified article`. Our research shall primarily concentrate on the national consolidation. On a national scope, laws, decrees, and regulations revise existing legal regulations.

The publication of legal texts has seen significant growth over the past 20 years. Figure 2 shows the evolution of the number of modifying articles recorded in France. In 2022, 17487 texts were published from 2512 laws providing modifications on existing laws. We create a dataset of 5000 triplets `(existing article, modification section, modified article)`. We only keep `existing articles` that are modified only once. This condition helps avoid `existing articles` modified by two `modification sections` simultaneously.

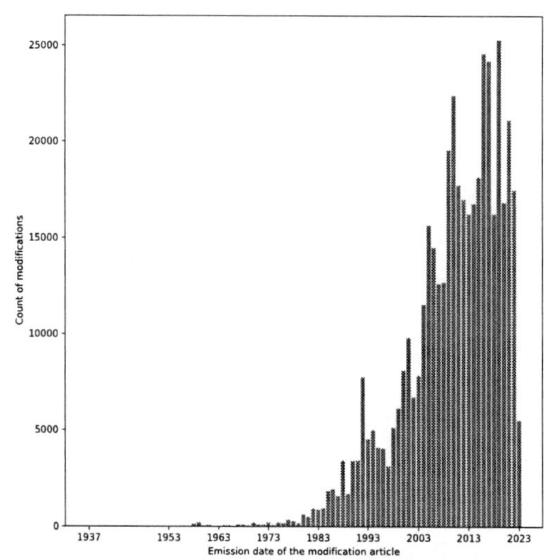

Figure 2: Number of modification sections published per year in France

The links between `(existing article, modification section, modified article)` are publicly available through the Légifrance platform. In the end, we accumulated a dataset comprising 3124 triplets. Example 3 shows a complete sample of the dataset, publicly available on HuggingFace[5].

Example 3: Sample of the dataset
Existing article: *Article 10:*
`Appointments are made each year in the last week of August. The general meeting of the order meets at the courthouse.`
Modification section: *Article 5:*
`Article 10 is amended as follows:`
`1° The words « in the last week of August » are replaced by the words « during the month of December »;`
`2° The second sentence is deleted.`
Modified article: *Article 10:*
`Appointments are made each year during the month of December.`

4 Approaches & developped methods

The objective is to modify an existing article by incorporating alterations delineated within a modification document. Initially, a foundational baseline employing a span extraction methodology was developed. Subsequently, this baseline is evaluated against our advanced methodology, which encompasses the fine-tuning of a pre-trained language model.

4.1 Baseline: span extraction through question answering

We aim to establish the baseline outlined in Section 2.1, which involves adapting a BERT model for the question answering task (Shi and Lin, 2019). Two distinct models are employed for this purpose. The first model is designed to extract spans that need to be added within the modification section, while the second model identifies spans for deletion within the existing article. Consequently, the span of words identified by the second model can be overwritten by the span generated by the first model. Both approaches utilize the same architecture, employing a CamemBERT Model with a span classification head [6]. This head consists of a linear layer on top of the hidden-state outputs to compute span start logits and span end logits. This model comprises 110M parameters. The batch size is 16 and the learning rate for the Adam optimizer is 2×10^{-5}. We train for 15 epochs.

Labeling and input format Example 4 illustrates the labeling for a sample of the dataset, where spans highlighted in red are predicted by an initial model and subsequently overwritten by spans highlighted in green, as predicted by a second model. This labeling schema facilitates the modeling of three modification types: additions are seamlessly integrated into existing text by substituting blank spaces. Moreover, we introduced the token `[NL]` (New Line) prior to the commencement of each paragraph and at the conclusion of each text, as it is denoted that the consolidation process often refers to paragraph. The models acquisition of this token contribute to improved performance in instances exhibiting such patterns.

Example 4: Labels in the span extraction dataset for a substitution
Existing article: `[NL] the duties corresponding to the post of Chief State Public Works Engineer in the second group referred to in Article 8 of this Decree are, for the post reporting to the Minister for Foreign Affairs: [NL] Charged with the duties of Deputy Director of Real Estate Operations in the Real Estate Affairs Department within the General Administration Department. [NL]`

Modification section: `[NL] The second paragraph of Article 1 of the above-mentioned Order of 4 May 2007 is replaced by the following provisions: [NL] « Assistant to the Deputy Director of Real Estate Operations. » [NL]`

Legend: Span to be predicted by the first model. Span to be predicted by the second model to be overwritten by the first span.

When inputting data into the model, the existing article and the modification section are concate-

[5]Link to dataset
[6]Camembert for question answering

nated with a [SEP] token in between. The modification section serves as the "Question" while the existing article acts as the "Paragraph"

Test set and metrics To assess the model's performance, we test the model on a dataset comprising 302 triplets. Once the spans are predicted, the consolidated text can be reconstructed accordingly. Therefore, it becomes pertinent to utilize a end-to-end oriented metric: word error. Commonly applied in speech-to-text algorithms, the word error measures the number of errors in the transcription of a speech. In our context, this metric assesses the error count within the predicted consolidated text relative to the expected version.

4.2 Text generation

Our aim is to leverage generative models to directly predict consolidated texts. Whereas the span extraction method can lead to linguistically nonsensical outcomes in case of prediction errors, generative models ensure the grammatical correctness of generated texts.

4.2.1 Fune-tuning & Instruction tuning

We opt to fine-tune a generative model using the LoRA approach (Dettmers et al., 2023). Given that we are solely focusing on a single task for fine-tuning, it did not seem particularly advantageous to employ a prompt tuning method, which is particularly suited for datasets containing diverse types of instructions. The LoRA technique was applied to the projection layers of the query, key and value components of the pretrained language model, targeting approximately 3% of the parameters from the original model.

The prompt format is straightforward and adheres to the conventions commonly employed in instruction tuning. Example 5 illustrates the input format during training. The `Instruction` corresponds to the modification to be performed, i.e., the modification section. The `Input` corresponds to the existing article on which the modification is to be applied. Lastly, the expected `Response` pertains to the modified article. During inference, the `Response` field is left empty, and the model is tasked with predicting it.

We are employing open-source models that are open for commercial use. Our baseline model is OpenLLama, which is a replication of LLaMa with less intrusive licenses. This model has undergone the same pretraining process as LLaMa and is available in various sizes, ranging from 3 to 13 billion parameters. For training these models, we will utilize Nvidia T4 GPUs with 16GB of memory or Nvidia A10G GPUs with 24GB of memory, depending on the model size.

Example 5: Example of prompt

```
### Instruction:
Article 10 is amended as
follows:
1° The words « in the last week
of August » are replaced by
the words « during the month of
December »;
2° The second sentence is
deleted.
### Input:
Appointments are made each year
in the last week of August.
The general meeting of the
order meets at the courthouse.
### Response:
Appointments are made each year
during the month of December.
```

Consistently across the conducted experiments, certain hyperparameters were kept uniform: the learning rate was set at 3×10^{-4}, and the LoRA dropout rate was sustained at 5%. A 4-bit quantization is employed. Only prompts containing fewer than 1024 tokens were selected for use. The micro batch size was determined to be 4, with gradient checkpointing applied after processing every 128 samples. The training duration was limited to 2 epochs.

4.2.2 Training on the modified article only

The first experiment involved comparing two models trained with the same prompt, which includes the `Instruction`, `Input`, and `Response` fields. However, the tasks differ: one model is trained to predict the entire prompt (i.e., all three fields: `Instruction`, `Input`, and `Response`), while the other model is trained solely to predict the `Response` field. In both cases, the full prompt is provided as input during training. Two opposing intuitions were considered. On one hand, training the model to predict the complete prompt could enhance its comprehension of legislative semantics. On the other hand, training the model to predict solely `Response` field removes certain constraints. For this experiment, we selected two Open-LLaMa models with

3 billion parameters each. The Table 1 below summarizes the results. Notably, training a model exclusively on the `Response` field yields superior performance, of +9.4%.

Model trained on	Average Word Error	Median Word Error
Whole prompt	18.6	10.5
Modified article	17.0	7.0

Table 1: Training on the whole prompt vs. training on the modified article only

4.2.3 Influence of cleaning the dataset

We also aimed to examine the influence of dataset quality on consolidation performance. To this end, we selected two OpenLLaMa models with 3 billion and trained them using two distinct consolidation datasets. The second dataset was a cleaned version of the open-sourced dataset, where all consolidation cases that did not involve any modification or involved tables were removed, comprising 1784 triplets.

The results of this comparison highlight the impact of dataset quality on consolidation performance, as shown in Table 2. By using a cleaner dataset that focuses exclusively on meaningful consolidation examples, the model tends to achieve better outcomes, even when compared to a larger dataset that includes less relevant instances. This underscores the significance of dataset quality in influencing model performance for the consolidation task.

Dataset	Average Word Error	Median Word Error
Full dataset	17.0	7.0
Curated dataset	12.0	4.0

Table 2: Influence of the quality of the training dataset

4.2.4 Influence of the size of the low rank matrix

The LoRA finetuning method encompasses two hyperparameters: the rank r of the added matrices and the multiplier α. The multiplier α operates as a learning rate for the added matrices and exhibits relatively modest effects once it reaches a sufficiently high value. It was set as twice the value of r. The matrix rank r significantly impacts the model's performance. A smaller r suggests limited fine-tuning, where the model requires minimal adaptation to accomplish the intended task. In contrast, a larger r implies extensive retraining, almost akin to starting from scratch. Table 3 showcases the performance of two models, each utilizing different r values. Notably, the model with the higher r value attains slightly better consolidation capabilities. It can be observed that the model with a higher rank value r trains faster but eventually converges to a similar value as the other model.

Rank r	Average Word Error	Median Word Error
16	12.0	4.0
64	11.7	4.0

Table 3: Influence of the rank of the added matrices

4.2.5 Influence of the size of the PLLM

We also examined the impact of the PLLM size on consolidation performance. To do so, we compared three OpenLLaMa models with 3 billion, 7 billion, and 13 billion parameters, respectively trained on a curated dataset with a large low-rank r. Despite being more challenging to fine-tune, larger models generally exhibit better performance due to their increased information retention capacity. We further compared these models with a 13-billion-parameter OpenLLaMa model that had already undergone an initial round of fine-tuning on an instruction dataset.

Table 4 outlines the results. It's observed that, on average, the number of errors is lower for the 3-billion-parameter model compared to the 7-billion-parameter model. However, the number of errors is higher in terms of median values. The 7-billion-parameter model generally predicts better modified articles, but in some cases, the modified article is significantly worse from the expected text. This can be attributed to the fact that the 7-billion-parameter model possesses a larger generative capacity. As a result, in complex consolidation examples, the 7-billion-parameter model might "hallucinate" and generate interpretations of the texts, whereas the 3-billion-parameter model tends to generate the unconsolidated existing article. This effect disappear in the 13-billion-parameter model which showcases a considerable performance gap. The 13-billion-parameter model, which was pre-fine-tuned on an instruction dataset, further enhances consolidation performance.

Model size	Average Word Error	Median Word Error
3b	10.0	2.0
7b	13.5	0.5
13b	6.07	0
13b pre-finetuned	5.09	0

Table 4: Influence of the size of the PLLM

4.3 Comparing all methods

We now proceed to compare the different approaches employed: span extraction and the generative method, on a more challenging dataset. While it would have been ideal to maintain the same test set as used in previous sections, it became evident that the models were insufficiently distinguishable based on that test set alone. Therefore, we opted to construct a second, more complex test set, utilizing the legal provisions from the previous year's PLF. Additionally, we compare our results with OpenAI's GPT-3.5 and GPT-4 models to further contextualize model performance.

Approach	Prompt size	Average Word Error (95% CI)
Span Extraction	512	36.2*(31.4)
Generative models		
Open-LLaMA 3b	1024	65.5 (29.2)
Open-LLaMA 13b	1024	**20.7** (7.79)
GPT3.5-turbo-0613	4k	44.8 (27.5)
GPT4-0613	8k	**9.41** (3.58)

* Computed only on single modifications

Table 5: Comparison of the proposed approach with the baseline

The results are denoted in Table 5. We first observe that the generative models yield the best performances. While these models generally produce highly accurate consolidations, in certain cases, the consolidation can result in aberrations, leading to hallucinations and the generation of lengthy texts, resulting in substantial consolidation errors. The distributions of word errors for each model and error type (addition, deletion, substitution) are depicted in Figure 3. Additionally, it is notable that GPT4 demonstrates superior performance, while our best model (Open-LLaMa 13b) falls between GPT3.5 and GPT4.

5 Application on a bill

Encouraged by our model's promising performance, we embarked on live automatic consolidation of the *Projet de Loi de Finance 2024* from September 2023 to December 2023. This bill was proposed on 26th of September, 2023 and contained 60 articles. After multiples debates at the parliements, the bill was promulgated on 29th of December, 2023 with 264 articles. This is a highly complex bill.

5.1 Pipeline

Our consolidation pipeline is depicted in Figure 4. This pipeline was up during the four months of life of the bill. The pre-processing consists of three primary steps.

5.1.1 Section splitter

A bill is structured into articles, each specifying modifications to current laws on particular topics. Consequently, a bill's article might introduce several changes to numerous laws. A section division using regular expressions is therefore created to break down the bill's article into these distinct sections. This splitter leverages the hierarchical structure of the bill's article to efficiently segment it into components.

5.1.2 Entity recognition

We employ an already fine-tuned entity recognition model system to identify the specific law articles targeted by each section. Upon identifying these articles, we retrieve their contents for further processing.

5.1.3 Our consolidation algorithm

We use our best model to generate the consolidated text.

5.2 Results

In this section, we delineate the consolidation process undertaken as of 16th of December, 2023. At this juncture, the legislative bill comprised 271 articles. Upon division, this legislative text was found to encompass 1399 simple modifications applicable to 606 articles of law.

Our pipeline incorporates two instances of human intervention, symbolized by hand icons, primarily focused on verification rather than labeling. The law article detection phase, leveraging an existing entity recognition component, achieved an 82.0% success rate. To quantify the success rate

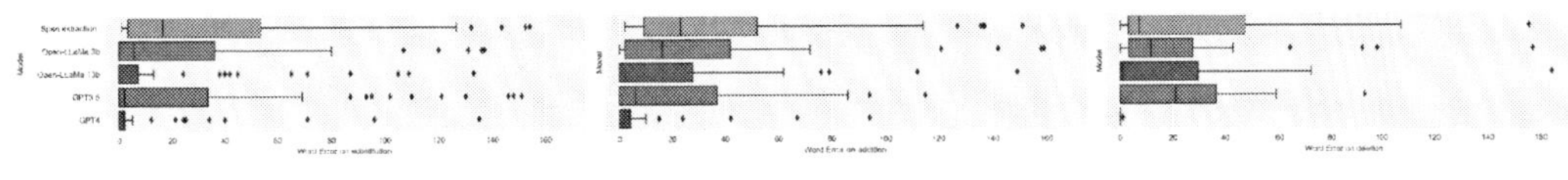

Figure 3: Word error distributions per model per modification type

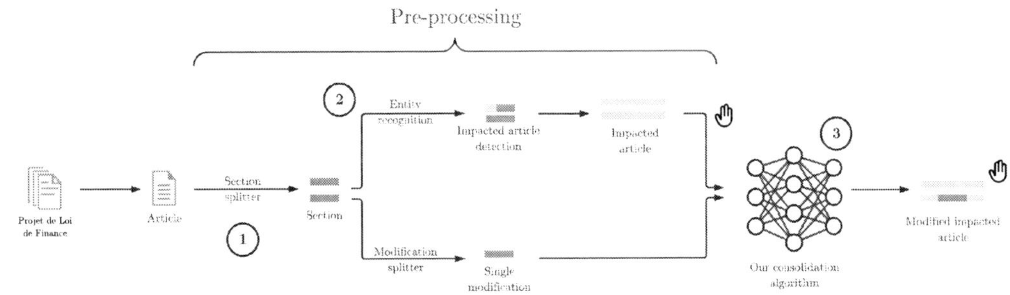

Figure 4: Full consolidation pipeline

of our algorithm, we executed the consolidation process on the legislative bill using both GPT-4 and our best model, OpenLLaMa-13, generating two sets of predictions. Subsequently, we scrutinized and amended the predictions made by GPT-4 to produce a third set, representing human annotations. For a prediction and an annotation, we removed special characters from each string, such as accents, commas, and line breaks, to facilitate the comparison of the raw texts. However, it exists two cases where the consolidation process can't be done: the presence of tables and lengthy prompts. Table 6 presents the rate of possible consolidations along the rate of correct consolidation for both algorithms.

Model	Rate of possible consolidations	Correctness rate among possible consolidations
Our model	49.8%	63.2%
GPT4-0613	91.3%	61.4%

Table 6: Correct consolidation rate

Our Open-LLaMa-13b model faces challenges due to its limited context size, allowing application in only 49.8% of consolidation cases. Conversely, GPT4-0613 encounters difficulties in consolidating only 8.7% of cases, all related to the inclusion of tables. In terms of correctness rates, both models achieve 63.2% and 61.4% respectively, considering their respective possible consolidations. While our algorithm appears to achieve a higher correctness rate, it's crucial to note that it consolidates far fewer samples with much smaller prompt sizes compared to GPT4, which consolidates most of them.

In Figure 5, we depict the correctness rate against the full prompt length, including the generated `Response`, for both models in cases possible for our Open-LLaMa-13b. Here, GPT4-0613 achieves a 73.6% correctness rate. Notably, the full prompt length for the GPT-4 model slightly differs due to the inclusion of few-shot examples. Both models exhibit differing behaviors in correctness rates against full prompt length. Open-LLaMa-13b peaks for full prompt lengths below 1000 tokens, with performance gradually decreasing for larger prompts, highlighting attention mechanism limitations. Conversely, GPT4-0613 demonstrates consistent performance across varying prompt lengths, showing no impact from larger prompts.

6 Conclusion

This research implements a generative method to automate legislative text consolidation, demonstrating a significant capability to process and automatically apply changes to legislative texts. We determined that the quality of the dataset and the size of the pre-trained model were two parameters that most significantly influenced consolidation performance. Despite exceptional performances of GPT4, in the end, we ideally prefer to use an open-source model for handling legal data due to its sensitivity. The consolidation, led on a real-time legislative bill, proved to be highly effective, although occasional issues in the generation process could result

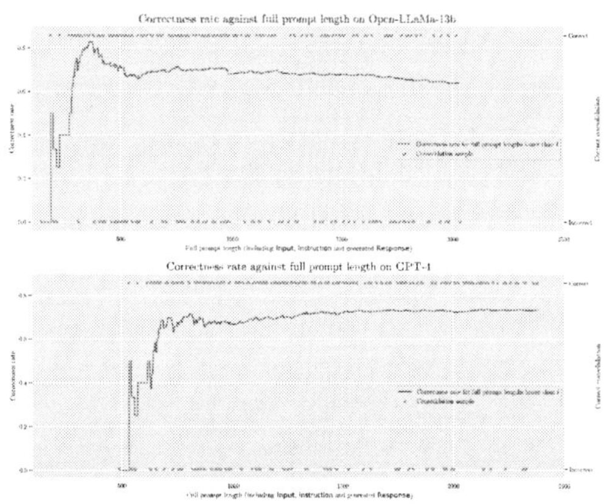

Figure 5: The correctness rates against prompt length are plotted for Open-LLaMa-13b and GPT-4 on the same consolidation samples (49.8% of the PLF). Each dot represents a sample of the PLF consolidation, indicating whether it is correct or not. The curve at prompt length i illustrates the rate of correct consolidation among samples with a prompt length less than i.

in nonsensical consolidations.

Moving forward, our objective is to delve into advanced fine-tuning strategies and broaden our methodology to encompass additional models. On one side, there exists a variety of models equipped with commercial licenses, such as LLaMA 3.1, that offer new possibilities for exploration. These models often feature larger context windows, enabling the consolidation of more samples. On the other side, innovative fine-tuning techniques are being developed, such as the Mixture of LoRA Experts approach. This technique is designed to fine-tune each expert within a Mixture of Experts.

This research opens promising avenues for integrating generative methods into legal processes, with the hope of radically transforming legal practice.

References

Timothy Arnold-Moore. 1995. Automatically processing amendments to legislation. In *Proceedings of the 5th International Conference on Artificial Intelligence and Law*, ICAIL '95, page 297–306, New York, NY, USA. Association for Computing Machinery.

Timothy Arnold-Moore. 1997. Automatic generation of amendment legislation.

Tom B. Brown, Benjamin Mann, Nick Ryder, Melanie Subbiah, Jared Kaplan, Prafulla Dhariwal, Arvind Neelakantan, Pranav Shyam, Girish Sastry, Amanda Askell, Sandhini Agarwal, Ariel Herbert-Voss, Gretchen Krueger, Tom Henighan, Rewon Child, Aditya Ramesh, Daniel M. Ziegler, Jeffrey Wu, Clemens Winter, Christopher Hesse, Mark Chen, Eric Sigler, Mateusz Litwin, Scott Gray, Benjamin Chess, Jack Clark, Christopher Berner, Sam McCandlish, Alec Radford, Ilya Sutskever, and Dario Amodei. 2020. Language models are few-shot learners. *Preprint*, arXiv:2005.14165.

Hyung Won Chung, Le Hou, Shayne Longpre, Barret Zoph, Yi Tay, William Fedus, Yunxuan Li, Xuezhi Wang, Mostafa Dehghani, Siddhartha Brahma, Albert Webson, Shixiang Shane Gu, Zhuyun Dai, Mirac Suzgun, Xinyun Chen, Aakanksha Chowdhery, Alex Castro-Ros, Marie Pellat, Kevin Robinson, Dasha Valter, Sharan Narang, Gaurav Mishra, Adams Yu, Vincent Zhao, Yanping Huang, Andrew Dai, Hongkun Yu, Slav Petrov, Ed H. Chi, Jeff Dean, Jacob Devlin, Adam Roberts, Denny Zhou, Quoc V. Le, and Jason Wei. 2022. Scaling instruction-finetuned language models. *Preprint*, arXiv:2210.11416.

Tim Dettmers, Artidoro Pagnoni, Ari Holtzman, and Luke Zettlemoyer. 2023. Qlora: Efficient finetuning of quantized llms. *Preprint*, arXiv:2305.14314.

Junxian He, Chunting Zhou, Xuezhe Ma, Taylor Berg-Kirkpatrick, and Graham Neubig. 2022. Towards a unified view of parameter-efficient transfer learning. *Preprint*, arXiv:2110.04366.

Neil Houlsby, Andrei Giurgiu, Stanislaw Jastrzebski, Bruna Morrone, Quentin de Laroussilhe, Andrea Gesmundo, Mona Attariyan, and Sylvain Gelly. 2019. Parameter-efficient transfer learning for nlp. *Preprint*, arXiv:1902.00751.

Edward J. Hu, Yelong Shen, Phillip Wallis, Zeyuan Allen-Zhu, Yuanzhi Li, Shean Wang, Lu Wang, and Weizhu Chen. 2021. Lora: Low-rank adaptation of large language models. *Preprint*, arXiv:2106.09685.

Martin Josifoski, Nicola De Cao, Maxime Peyrard, Fabio Petroni, and Robert West. 2022. Genie: Generative information extraction. *Preprint*, arXiv:2112.08340.

Xiang Lisa Li and Percy Liang. 2021. Prefix-tuning: Optimizing continuous prompts for generation. *Preprint*, arXiv:2101.00190.

Xiao Liu, Yanan Zheng, Zhengxiao Du, Ming Ding, Yujie Qian, Zhilin Yang, and Jie Tang. 2021. Gpt understands, too. *Preprint*, arXiv:2103.10385.

Jonathan Mallinson, Aliaksei Severyn, Eric Malmi, and Guillermo Garrido. 2020. Felix: Flexible text editing through tagging and insertion. *Preprint*, arXiv:2003.10687.

Eric Malmi, Sebastian Krause, Sascha Rothe, Daniil Mirylenka, and Aliaksei Severyn. 2019. Encode, tag, realize: High-precision text editing. *Preprint*, arXiv:1909.01187.

Alessandro Mazzei, Daniele P. Radicioni, and Raffaella Brighi. 2009. Nlp-based extraction of modificatory provisions semantics.

Colin Raffel, Noam Shazeer, Adam Roberts, Katherine Lee, Sharan Narang, Michael Matena, Yanqi Zhou, Wei Li, and Peter J. Liu. 2019. Exploring the limits of transfer learning with a unified text-to-text transformer. *Preprint*, arXiv:1910.10683.

Peng Shi and Jimmy Lin. 2019. Simple bert models for relation extraction and semantic role labeling. *Preprint*, arXiv:1904.05255.

Jason Wei, Maarten Bosma, Vincent Y. Zhao, Kelvin Guu, Adams Wei Yu, Brian Lester, Nan Du, Andrew M. Dai, and Quoc V. Le. 2022. Finetuned language models are zero-shot learners. *Preprint*, arXiv:2109.01652.

Measuring the Groundedness of Legal Question-Answering Systems

Dietrich Trautmann, Natalia Ostapuk, Quentin Grail, Adrian Alan Pol, Guglielmo Bonifazi, Shang Gao and **Martin Gajek**
Thomson Reuters Labs, Zug, Switzerland
{first.last}@tr.com

Abstract

In high-stakes domains like legal question-answering, the accuracy and trustworthiness of generative AI systems are of paramount importance. This work presents a comprehensive benchmark of various methods to assess the groundedness of AI-generated responses, aiming to significantly enhance their reliability. Our experiments include similarity-based metrics and natural language inference models to evaluate whether responses are well-founded in the given contexts. We also explore different prompting strategies for large language models to improve the detection of ungrounded responses. We validated the effectiveness of these methods using a newly created grounding classification corpus, designed specifically for legal queries and corresponding responses from retrieval-augmented prompting, focusing on their alignment with source material. Our results indicate potential in groundedness classification of generated responses, with the best method achieving a macro-F1 score of 0.8. Additionally, we evaluated the methods in terms of their latency to determine their suitability for real-world applications, as this step typically follows the generation process. This capability is essential for processes that may trigger additional manual verification or automated response regeneration. In summary, this study demonstrates the potential of various detection methods to improve the trustworthiness of generative AI in legal settings.

Query

When does the duty to preserve documents end? Focus on SDNY case law.

Response A

The duty to preserve evidence arises when a party reasonably anticipates litigation. This duty generally requires the party to suspend its routine document retention/destruction policy and put in place a 'litigation hold' to ensure the preservation of relevant documents. The duty to preserve evidence ends when the litigation is resolved or when the party no longer reasonably anticipates litigation.

Response B

The duty to preserve evidence arises when a party reasonably anticipates litigation. This duty generally requires the party to suspend its routine document retention/destruction policy and put in place a 'litigation hold' to ensure the preservation of relevant documents. The duty to preserve evidence ends when the litigation is resolved or when the party files a motion to dismiss.

Figure 1: Example query and corresponding LLM responses with **grounded** and erroneous spans (Procedural Errors). The retrieved context used for grounding the responses was omitted due to its length. The remaining sentences in both responses are identical and grounded, but not highlighted to emphasize the differences.

1 Introduction

Generative AI systems are increasingly employed in high-stakes domains such as legal question-answering, where accuracy and trust are paramount (Monroy et al., 2009; Vold and Conrad, 2021; Khazaeli et al., 2021; Martinez-Gil, 2023). A significant challenge in these applications is the detection of outputs that are not grounded in the input data (context), which can compromise user trust and diminish the application's value (Maynez et al., 2020; Rawte et al., 2023). This work addresses this challenge by conducting a comprehensive benchmarking to assess the groundedness of AI-generated legal responses, thereby enhancing their reliability.

Our methodology investigates diverse approaches to classify responses based on their foundation in the provided source material (cf. Fig. 1). We utilize:

1. *Similarity-based techniques*, employing various text similarity metrics to quantify the alignment between the generated text and the input data at the sentence-level.

2. *Natural language inference* models to determine if the generated response sentences are entailed by or contradict the sentences in the source material.

3. Diverse *prompting strategies* for large language models (LLMs) to detect ungrounded responses. (Bubeck et al., 2023).

Proceedings of the Natural Legal Language Processing Workshop 2024, pages 176–186
November 16, 2024 ©2024 Association for Computational Linguistics

We evaluate these approaches on a new corpus of legal queries and responses, annotated for their degree of groundedness.

Experimental results demonstrate the effectiveness of many methods in the detection of potentially ungrounded answers. We also discuss the trade-offs between task performance and computational efficiency, highlighting the capabilities of particular approaches to operate with minimal added latency in real-world applications.

Furthermore, we investigated the types of errors present in the responses, categorizing them into six distinct classes: *Factual Inaccuracies*, *Contextual Misinterpretations*, *Procedural Errors*, *Reasoning Errors*, *Misattributions*, and *Terminological Errors*. Our analysis reveals that factual inaccuracies are the most prevalent type of errors. Importantly, we found that the misclassification rates in the overall groundedness assessment task are not uniform across these error categories, providing valuable insights for targeted improvements in AI-generated legal responses.

Our findings underscore the potential of automated groundedness assessment tools to improve the reliability and utility of generative AI in legal settings, ensuring that the generated responses are consistently accurate and trustworthy. The error analysis further contributes to a nuanced understanding of the challenges in this domain, paving the way for more refined and effective AI systems in legal applications.

2 Related Work

2.1 Grounding of Generated Responses

Grounding and factual consistency in language model outputs, especially for summarization and question-answering tasks, have been a focal point of recent research. Kryściński et al. (2020) introduced a weakly-supervised, model-based approach to verify factual consistency between source documents and generated summaries. This method uniquely combines consistency checks with the extraction of supporting and contradictory spans.

Building on this, Maynez et al. (2020) performed an extensive human evaluation of neural abstractive summarization systems. Their results showed a significant amount of ungrounded content in model-generated summaries and found that textual entailment measures correlate more strongly with faithfulness than standard metrics. This finding closely relates to our interest in assessing the groundedness of AI-generated legal responses.

The Chain-of-Knowledge (CoK) framework (Li et al., 2023) marks a major advance in reducing hallucinations. By dynamically incorporating grounding information from various sources, CoK enhances factual accuracy in knowledge-intensive tasks.

In essence, grounding of LLM-generated responses aims to ensure that outputs are factually consistent with input data, thereby enhancing reliability and reducing ungrounded LLM-generated content.

2.2 Hallucination Detection

Advancements in hallucination detection have been pivotal in developing more reliable and grounded LLMs, particularly for question-answering (QA) systems.

The *HaluEval-Wild* benchmark (Zhu et al., 2024) offers a novel approach to evaluating LLM hallucinations in real-world settings. By categorizing challenging user queries into five distinct types, this tool provides essential insights for enhancing LLM reliability in scenarios that mirror real-world interactions, which is crucial for QA systems.

Wang et al. (2024) contribute with *MIGRES*, a method that uses LLMs' ability to identify missing information for targeted knowledge retrieval and extraction. This approach promises to improve the groundedness of responses by ensuring comprehensive information gathering.

In long-form question answering, Rosenthal et al. (2024) introduced *ClapNQ*, a benchmark designed for retrieval-augmented generation (RAG) systems. Its emphasis on concise, cohesive answers grounded in source passages makes it particularly relevant for evaluating QA systems that require detailed, well-supported responses.

An empirical evaluation of AI-driven legal research tools (Magesh et al., 2024) challenges claims of "hallucination-free" systems, underscoring the necessity for rigorous evaluation in assessing the groundedness of legal QA systems.

Additionally, Hong et al. (2024) have launched the *Hallucinations Leaderboard*, an open initiative for measuring and comparing hallucinations across various LLMs and tasks. This resource offers a valuable opportunity for benchmarking the groundedness of QA systems against a diverse range of models and applications.

3 Grounding Definition

Grounding in legal question-answering systems refers to the extent to which an AI-generated response is firmly rooted in, supported by, and directly attributable to the provided legal source material. It ensures the model's output aligns with and accurately represents the information in the input data, avoiding fabrication, extraneous details, or misleading content. A well-grounded response should adhere closely to the facts, legal principles, and reasoning presented in the source material, without introducing unsupported claims or misrepresenting the legal context (Chandu et al., 2021).

Several key aspects ensure the reliability of AI-generated legal responses. Factual alignment and relevance are crucial, ensuring the content reflects the source documents and addresses the legal query accurately. Source attribution allows tracing information back to specific input texts, while legal interpretation fidelity ensures conclusions are substantiated by the provided materials. This involves not only accurately conveying factual information but also maintaining the integrity of legal procedures, correctly interpreting the context, and using appropriate legal terminology. The generated responses must adhere to the given context, avoiding unsupported claims or extrapolations, and preserving the nuances and complexities of legal language and concepts (Magesh et al., 2024).

The assessment of grounding in legal AI responses involves a comprehensive evaluation of how faithfully the generated content aligns with the retrieved legal context. This evaluation considers various aspects of the response, including its factual accuracy, the appropriateness of legal interpretations, the coherence of legal reasoning, and the proper use of legal terminology. Grounding is vital in legal applications to maintain the integrity of legal advice, ensure compliance with laws and precedents, and prevent misinformation. By ensuring strong grounding, legal question-answering systems can provide more reliable, trustworthy, and legally sound responses, which is crucial in the high-stakes environment of legal practice and decision-making.

4 Dataset Creation

In this section, we will describe and list all the steps involved in creating the *Groundedness Classification* dataset used in our benchmarking.

4.1 Data Source

The dataset originates from proprietary data in the *Casetext* Legal Research Skill[1]. We limited the data selection to the internal users only, primarily consisting of diverse sales demonstrations as well as domain experts and engineering-related testing sessions. All queries, however, are realistic representations of everyday research in the legal domain. Additionally, we performed a deduplication process on the input queries.

The dataset comprises input queries (e.g., questions about particular legal use cases) accompanied by LLM-generated responses and retrieved context data. During development, legal professionals verified these responses to ensure they were grounded in the context provided to the LLM (as part of the prompt). The context data is derived from a retrieval system with access to the *Casetext* database for legal research, which includes case law, statutes, regulations, and legal texts authored by internal legal experts and lawyers.

The ground truth responses (LLM-based answers) were generated using custom instructions in a prompt to *GPT-4* in the current production environment. At this stage of the dataset creation process, we had compiled a selection of legal user queries, gold responses, and their corresponding contexts.

4.2 Synthetic Adaptation

The next step in our dataset creation process involved generating evoked ungrounded responses to evaluate both grounded and ungrounded outputs. We instructed *GPT-4o* to make subtle and unintrusive variations to the original grounded responses, preserving most of the meaning while introducing minor deviations from the provided context. In the prompt, we included the original query and context alongside the gold response and these instructions.

These adapted responses, which we consider partially ungrounded[2], complement our final dataset. The inclusion of both grounded and ungrounded responses allows for a more comprehensive evaluation of response quality and adherence to provided context. An example of this subtle deviation from the source material in the generated response was depicted in the leading example in Fig. 1.

[1] https://casetext.com/cocounsel/

[2] Only some sentences ended up with slight modifications, while most were kept as the original sentences.

Split	#Queries	#Responses	#Response Sentences
Training	400	1080	5671
Development	58	162	797
Testing	115	316	1516
Total	573	1558	7984

Table 1: Data Set Statistics

4.3 Data Splits

We divided the dataset into training, development, and test sets using a ratio of 70 : 10 : 20, respectively. This split ensures a representative distribution across all subsets while maintaining a sufficiently large test set for robust evaluation.

The resulting counts for each split are presented in Table 1. It is noteworthy that the number of responses is not exactly twice the number of queries. This discrepancy arises from our dataset creation process, where we retained multiple significant variations of generated responses for certain queries to enhance the diversity and coverage of our dataset.

To maintain the integrity of our evaluation, we ensured that all responses corresponding to a particular query were assigned to the same split. This approach prevents potential leakage between the training and evaluation sets, thereby providing a more accurate assessment of model performance on unseen data.

5 Benchmarking Methodologies

This section overviews the diverse methodologies employed in our benchmark study for quantifying response grounding, systematically evaluating approaches that assess adherence of generated responses to provided context.

5.1 Similarity-based Approaches

Similarity-based approaches compare each response sentence against all context sentences, allowing for detailed grounding assessment. We aggregate these sentence-level estimations for the final response-level prediction.

Semantic Similarity We embedded sentences using the *nlpaueb/legal-bert-base-uncased* model with the Sentence-Transformers library. Matching pairs were identified using cosine similarity, with an optimized threshold determined on the development set for final grounding prediction.

Quoted Information Precision Adapting the *QuIP-score* (Weller et al., 2024), we examined character n-gram overlap between LLM responses and context sentences. We optimized both the n-gram size (21 in our setup) and similarity threshold on the development set for grounding determination in the final evaluation.

5.2 Natural Language Inference

FactKB Evaluating factual consistency in natural language generation is crucial, especially for complex domains. We employed FactKB[3], an approach leveraging pre-training with facts from external knowledge bases, to address challenges in entity and relation errors (Feng et al., 2023).

FactKB has shown state-of-the-art performance in factual consistency evaluation across various domains. We used it to compute factuality scores of generated response sentences against source context sentences.

Our grounding determination process involved identifying the highest-scoring source sentence for each target sentence based on *FactKB* scores, then applying an optimized threshold to classify grounding sufficiency. This threshold, determined using our development set, balanced precision and recall in grounding classification, adapting *FactKB* to our specific task of response grounding quantification.

Hallucination Evaluation Models The Hallucination Evaluation Model (HEM), developed by Vectara (Hughes et al., 2023), is designed to detect hallucinations in LLM-generated responses. HEM is available in two versions: *V1*, a fine-tuned model based on *cross-encoder/nli-deberta-v3-base*, and *V2*, an improved version using *flan-t5-base*.

Built on research in factual consistency for summarization, HEM classifies whether a summary is factually consistent with its source. The model was fine-tuned on diverse documents to ensure robustness across content types and is publicly available on Hugging Face under the Apache 2 license.

[3]https://hf.co/bunsenfeng/FactKB

HEM evaluates LLM responses by comparing them to source documents, classifying summaries as consistent or inconsistent. For our study, we implemented a fine-grained approach, scoring individual sentences against corresponding contexts. This granular analysis provides a nuanced assessment of hallucinations at the sentence level, offering deeper insights into model performance.

5.3 Prompting Approaches

Direct Prompting One straight-forward approach for groundedness classification via prompting is asking either the same or another LLM whether a particular response for a query is grounded in a context or not (Trautmann et al., 2022). Therefore, we utilized several LLMs with a custom prompt and collected the binary classification as the prompt-based baselines. We used the specialized open access model *Lynx-v1.1* (Ravi et al., 2024) and the general purpose public LLMs *GPT-4o* and *Claude Sonnet 3.5*. All three LLMs were evaluated with the same prompt from Ravi et al. (2024).

In principle, this approach has similarities with *Reflexion* by Shinn et al. (2024), where a *Self-Reflection* LLM should reflect on a previous answer and if necessary to update its prediction. The authors showed that this was helpful, especially for more complex tasks.

Amazon RefChecker RefChecker (Hu et al., 2024) introduces a framework for hallucination detection using knowledge triplets to capture fine-grained assertions. The process involves three steps: claim extraction, hallucination checking, and aggregation. This decoupled process is also known as prompt chaining (Trautmann, 2023).

An LLM identifies knowledge triplets from the response to the original query. Zero-shot checkers then predict hallucination labels for each triplet (entailment, contradiction, or neutral). Finally, these labels are integrated to compute an overall hallucination score for the response.

RefChecker's computational demands are notable: for n triplets extracted, the LLM is prompted with the entire original context n times, significantly impacting processing time and resource consumption. This approach balances granular analysis with computational intensity, offering a detailed but resource-intensive method for hallucination detection.

SelfCheckGPT We adapt the approach of Manakul et al. (2023), which assesses hallucination likelihood in LLM-generated sentences by evaluating their consistency with multiple answers from the same query. SelfCheckGPT assumes that grounded sentences should be consistent with other sampled answers.

The method generates new responses using the initial prompt with increased temperature. It then calculates a hallucination score for each sentence as the average of contradiction probabilities with these new samples. The response-level score is the maximum of sentence-level scores, with the threshold optimized on the training set.

We enhance this approach with a novel context-based evaluation (*ContextNLI*) using the *potsawee/deberta-v3-large-mnli* model. This compares each answer sentence against context sentences, identifying the minimum contradiction score as the hallucination probability. The maximum score across all sentences represents the answer's overall hallucination likelihood.

We implement two variants of this approach: *Multi-Gen*, which follows the original consistency checks, and our novel *ContextNLI*, which incorporates the context-based evaluation, thus providing complementary methods for assessing the groundedness of LLM-generated content.

DeepEval: Claims Extraction and Verification We adapt the *Faithfulness* metrics from Ip (2023) to detect contradictions between source documents and generated answers. This approach divides the task into two subtasks: claims extraction and claim verification (prompt chains, Trautmann (2023)).

First, we use an LLM to extract claims independently from both source documents and generated answers using a custom prompt. Then, a second LLM call with another custom prompt identifies claims from the generated answer not factually supported by the source document claims. If any generated claim contradicts a source claim, we consider the answer inaccurate.

This method requires three LLM calls in total: two for claims extraction and one for comparison. We utilize *Claude Sonnet 3.5* for all these calls, balancing task complexity reduction with comprehensive analysis.

5.4 Fine-Tuning

In addition to our primary methods, we fine-tuned a Cross-Encoder classifier (*DeBERTa v3* as the base model) specifically tailored to our dataset. To ensure the integrity of our evaluation, we meticulously prepared a specialized training and evaluation corpus based on the initial data splits, thereby avoiding any potential contamination between sets.

Our fine-tuning approach focused on the nuanced differences between grounded and ungrounded responses. For each pair of such responses, we isolated the sentences that differed between them. This selective process allowed us to concentrate on the most informative elements for distinguishing between grounded and ungrounded content.

To establish ground truth for the grounded responses, we employed a semantic similarity measure (as described in Section 5.1). For each sentence in the grounded response, we identified the most semantically similar sentence from the context and assigned it the corresponding cosine similarity score. These scores typically ranged from 0.8 to 0.99, indicating high levels of semantic alignment.

Conversely, for the ungrounded responses, we paired each sentence with the same context sentence used for its grounded counterpart. However, we assigned these pairs a score of 1 minus the cosine similarity, effectively inverting the grounding measure. This approach provided a balanced representation of both grounded and ungrounded examples in our training data.

Through this methodology, we compiled a balanced dataset comprising 558 samples for training and 75 for development. This carefully curated dataset served as the foundation for our fine-tuning process, enabling the Cross-Encoder to learn the subtle distinctions between grounded and ungrounded content within our specific corpus.

The outcomes of our fine-tuning efforts (after hyper-parameter optimization), are comprehensively presented (macro averaged) in Tab. 2.

Model Name	M-Prec	M-Rec	M-F1	Acc
deberta-v3-base	0.459	0.466	0.450	0.493
deberta-v3-large	0.736	0.739	0.733	0.733

Table 2: DEV set metrics for DeBERTa models

Following the fine-tuning stage, we integrated this grounding classification (GC) model into our benchmark, employing a methodology analogous to that used for the NLI approaches described in Section 5.2.

6 Experimental Set-Up

Our benchmarking study aimed to evaluate various methods for classifying LLM responses as grounded or ungrounded relative to a given context and query.

Methodology Despite the varied granularity of approaches (response-level vs. sentence-level), we standardized outputs to binary classifications for consistent comparison. We developed each method on the training set, optimized parameters on the development set, and conducted final evaluations on the test set.

Performance Metrics We assessed classification accuracy (including macro-averaged f1, precision, and recall) and computational efficiency through latency measurements. Latency was computed as the average processing time across all samples in the development set. These metrics provide insights into each approach's practical applicability.

Computational Resources Local approaches utilized Amazon EC2 G5 Instances (8xlarge)[4]. Prompting-based methods were executed via Azure OpenAI Services[5], AWS Bedrock (Anthropic's Claude)[6], and Anthropic's API directly, ensuring diverse and robust evaluation environments.

7 Groundedness Classification Results

Our benchmark evaluation of groundedness classification approaches revealed insightful performance trade-offs, as shown in Tab. 3. The metrics include classification precision, recall, F1-score, and accuracy, providing a comprehensive view of each method's applicability.

The multi-stage prompt chaining approach, *DeepEval Claims Verify*, achieved top classification metrics, but with high latency (26.1 seconds per request). In contrast, *direct prompting* with *GPT-4o* achieved the second-highest scores with significantly lower latency (2.2 seconds), as illustrated in Fig. 2.

A clear speed-performance trade-off emerged across methods. Similarity-based approaches (*COS_SIM* and *QUIP*) were fastest but struggled with ungrounded response identification. NLI methods showed improved performance at the cost

[4]https://aws.amazon.com/ec2/instance-types/g5/

[5]https://azure.microsoft.com/en-us/products/ai-services/openai-service

[6]https://aws.amazon.com/bedrock/claude/

#	Model Name	Development Set				Test Set			
		Precision	Recall	Macro-F1	Accuracy	Precision	Recall	Macro-F1	Accuracy
1	COS_SIM	0.525	0.520	0.494	0.520	0.497	0.497	0.493	0.497
2	QUIP	0.648	0.533	0.421	0.533	0.560	0.509	0.379	0.509
3	HEM V1	0.640	0.640	0.640	0.640	0.598	0.595	0.592	0.595
4	HEM V2	0.580	0.580	0.580	0.580	0.564	0.563	0.562	0.563
5	FACT_KB	0.527	0.527	0.526	0.527	0.510	0.510	0.508	0.510
6	GC-large	0.694	0.667	0.655	0.667	0.628	0.620	0.615	0.620
7	LYNX v1.1	0.764	0.460	0.571	0.460	0.792	0.503	0.597	0.503
8	Sonnet 3.5	0.728	0.727	0.726	0.727	0.724	0.715	0.712	0.715
9	GPT-4o	0.783	0.773	0.771	0.773	**0.802**	0.763	0.755	0.763
10	RefChecker (Haiku)	0.511	0.506	0.450	0.506	0.514	0.507	0.435	0.508
11	RefChecker (Sonnet 3)	0.500	0.500	0.366	0.500	0.500	0.500	0.386	0.500
12	DeepEval Claims Verify	**0.801**	**0.800**	**0.800**	**0.800**	0.779	**0.774**	**0.774**	**0.775**
13	SCGPT (Multi-Gen)	0.627	0.627	0.627	0.627	0.679	0.667	0.661	0.667
14	SCGPT (ContextNLI)	0.620	0.620	0.620	0.620	0.610	0.604	0.600	0.604

Table 3: Performance comparison of different models on Development and Test sets

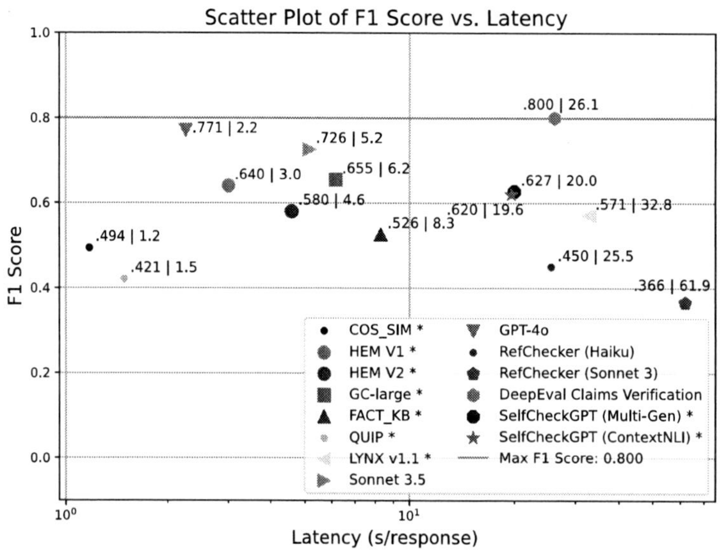

Figure 2: Development set results for our benchmark. We report the F1-scores (y-axis) for each method and the corresponding latency (x-axis) in seconds per response. Approach names denoted with * were run on an AWS *ml.8xlarge* instance.

of increased latency. Within NLI, *HEM V1* outperformed *HEM V2*, and fine-tuning on our corpus further improving results.

Unexpectedly, complex prompt chaining approaches like *RefChecker* and *SelfCheckGPT* underperformed, highlighting challenges in developing universally effective methods across diverse contexts.

These findings emphasize the importance of balancing task performance and computational efficiency when selecting a groundedness classification approach, with optimal choices depending on specific application requirements and resource constraints.

8 Error Analysis

We conducted a detailed investigation into the types of response errors present in our benchmark dataset to gain deeper insights into ungrounded content.

Through examination of error spans in the training set, we identified six distinct error types. The models were instructed to select from our predefined error types (Tab. 5, App. A.2).

Focusing on the development set, our analysis revealed interesting patterns. The LLMs achieved exact agreement on the hallucination type in 29% of cases, with at least one overlapping error type for each response. *GPT-4o* typically predicted a

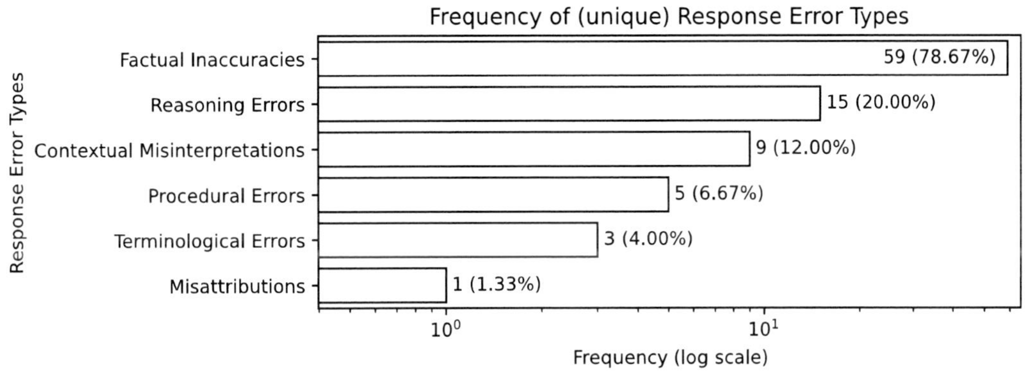

Figure 3: Counts of unique error types in the development set. Some responses contained up to three different error types. The frequency axis is in log-scale.

Error Type	Misclassified	Total	Percentage
Terminological Errors	2	3	66.7%
Factual Inaccuracies	12	59	20.3%
Procedural Errors	1	5	20.0%
Reasoning Errors	2	15	13.3%
Contextual Misinterpretations	1	9	11.1%
Misattributions	0	1	0.0%

Table 4: Development set misclassification of the best performing model by error types.

single error type, while *Claude-3.5-Sonnet* often suggested multiple types per response.

We aggregated predictions where both LLMs agreed. The distribution of unique error types is visualized in Fig. 3, with per-response occurrences in Fig. 4 (App. A.1). *Factual Inaccuracies* were most common, followed by *Reasoning Errors*. All initially defined error types were represented, validating our classification scheme.

This analysis provides valuable insights into response error types and ungrounded content in language model outputs, crucial for developing targeted strategies to improve response generation.

Misclassification Analysis We conducted a misclassification analysis on our best-performing model, *DeepEval Claims Verify*, to gain deeper insights into its performance across different error types. As summarized in Tab. 4, *Terminological Errors* showed the highest misclassification rate (67%), despite their low frequency, followed by *Factual Inaccuracies* (20%) and *Procedural Errors* (20%). These findings reveal the varying challenges posed by different error categories and highlight areas for potential improvement in groundedness classification models, particularly in handling less common but difficult-to-classify error types.

9 Conclusion

Our comprehensive benchmark study on groundedness classification of legal question-answering systems has revealed significant insights into performance and efficiency trade-offs. The multi-stage prompt chaining approach, *DeepEval Claims Verify*, emerged as the top performer with an F1 score of 0.80, closely followed by direct prompting using *GPT-4o* at 0.77, which demonstrated lower latency. These results highlight the potential of advanced prompting techniques in achieving high accuracy.

Similarity-based and natural language inference methods, while less accurate, offered fast processing times. Our response error type classification identified *Factual Inaccuracies* and *Reasoning Errors* as the most prevalent types of ungrounded content, providing direction for future improvements.

The study underscores the critical balance between task performance, computational efficiency, and ease of implementation when selecting groundedness classification methods. With top-performing methods achieving F1 scores of 0.80, this benchmark represents a significant advancement in the reliable assessment of AI-generated content across diverse applications.

Limitations

While our study offers valuable insights into the performance of various groundedness classification approaches, it is essential to acknowledge several limitations inherent in our experimental setup and the methods we evaluated.

Firstly, our dataset, though carefully curated, is limited in size and domain scope. The responses were generated using specific language models and may not fully represent the diverse range of hallucinations or ungrounded content that could occur across different models or domains. This limitation potentially affects the generalizability of our findings to broader contexts or more specialized applications.

Secondly, the binary classification of responses as either grounded or ungrounded may oversimplify the nuanced nature of language model outputs. In reality, responses often contain a mix of grounded and ungrounded elements, and a more granular assessment might provide deeper insights into model behavior.

Our evaluation metrics, while standard in the field, may not capture all aspects of response quality or usefulness. For instance, a response that is technically grounded but irrelevant or poorly structured might still receive a high rating within our current framework.

The computational resources required for some of the more complex approaches, particularly those involving multiple API calls or large language models, pose scalability challenges. This limitation may restrict the practical applicability of these methods in real-time or resource-constrained environments.

Additionally, our error type classification, while informative, relies on the agreement between two specific language models. This approach may introduce biases or limitations based on the particular characteristics of these models.

Lastly, the rapid pace of development in language model technology means that our findings may quickly become outdated as new models and techniques emerge. The performance gaps we observed between different approaches may shift with the introduction of more advanced models or refined methodologies.

Future work should address these limitations by expanding the dataset to include a broader range of domains and increasing its size. Developing more nuanced classification frameworks that can capture the complexity of language model outputs would also be beneficial. Furthermore, exploring scalable methods that can be applied in real-time or resource-constrained environments, as well as continuously updating the evaluation framework to reflect the latest advancements in language model technology, will be crucial for the ongoing relevance of this research.

Ethics Statement

This study on groundedness classification methods aims to improve the reliability and trustworthiness of AI-generated content, which has significant ethical implications. By developing more accurate methods to detect ungrounded or hallucinated information, we contribute to the broader goal of mitigating the spread of misinformation and enhancing the integrity of AI-assisted communication. Our work aligns with the principles of beneficence and non-maleficence, as it seeks to maximize the benefits of language models while minimizing potential harms associated with inaccurate or misleading information.

We acknowledge that the development and deployment of these classification methods may have broader societal impacts. We emphasize the importance of transparent and responsible use of these methods, respecting principles of fairness and privacy. Furthermore, we encourage ongoing dialogue and collaboration within the NLP community to address the ethical challenges associated with AI-generated content and its evaluation.

References

Sébastien Bubeck, Varun Chandrasekaran, Ronen Eldan, Johannes Gehrke, Eric Horvitz, Ece Kamar, Peter Lee, Yin Tat Lee, Yuanzhi Li, Scott Lundberg, et al. 2023. Sparks of artificial general intelligence: Early experiments with gpt-4. arxiv. *arXiv preprint arXiv:2303.12712*.

Khyathi Raghavi Chandu, Yonatan Bisk, and Alan W Black. 2021. Grounding 'grounding' in NLP. In *Findings of the Association for Computational Linguistics: ACL-IJCNLP 2021*, pages 4283–4305, Online. Association for Computational Linguistics.

Shangbin Feng, Vidhisha Balachandran, Yuyang Bai, and Yulia Tsvetkov. 2023. Factkb: Generalizable factuality evaluation using language models enhanced with factual knowledge. In *Proceedings of the 2023 Conference on Empirical Methods in Natural Language Processing*, pages 933–952.

Giwon Hong, Aryo Pradipta Gema, Rohit Saxena, Xiaotang Du, Ping Nie, Yu Zhao, Laura Perez-

Beltrachini, Max Ryabinin, Xuanli He, and Pasquale Minervini. 2024. The hallucinations leaderboard–an open effort to measure hallucinations in large language models. *arXiv preprint arXiv:2404.05904*.

Xiangkun Hu, Dongyu Ru, Lin Qiu, Qipeng Guo, Tianhang Zhang, Yang Xu, Yun Luo, Pengfei Liu, Yue Zhang, and Zheng Zhang. 2024. Refchecker: Reference-based fine-grained hallucination checker and benchmark for large language models. *arXiv preprint arXiv:2405.14486*.

Simon Hughes, Minseok Bae, and Miaoran Li. 2023. Vectara Hallucination Leaderboard.

Jeffrey Ip. 2023. Deepeval: A tool for deep learning model evaluation. GitHub repository.

Soha Khazaeli, Janardhana Punuru, Chad Morris, Sanjay Sharma, Bert Staub, Michael Cole, Sunny Chiu-Webster, and Dhruv Sakalley. 2021. A free format legal question answering system. In *Proceedings of the Natural Legal Language Processing Workshop 2021*, pages 107–113.

Wojciech Kryściński, Bryan McCann, Caiming Xiong, and Richard Socher. 2020. Evaluating the factual consistency of abstractive text summarization. In *Proceedings of the 2020 Conference on Empirical Methods in Natural Language Processing (EMNLP)*, pages 9332–9346.

Xingxuan Li, Ruochen Zhao, Yew Ken Chia, Bosheng Ding, Shafiq Joty, Soujanya Poria, and Lidong Bing. 2023. Chain-of-knowledge: Grounding large language models via dynamic knowledge adapting over heterogeneous sources. In *The Twelfth International Conference on Learning Representations*.

Varun Magesh, Faiz Surani, Matthew Dahl, Mirac Suzgun, Christopher D Manning, and Daniel E Ho. 2024. Hallucination-free? assessing the reliability of leading ai legal research tools. *arXiv preprint arXiv:2405.20362*.

Potsawee Manakul, Adian Liusie, and Mark Gales. 2023. Selfcheckgpt: Zero-resource black-box hallucination detection for generative large language models. In *Proceedings of the 2023 Conference on Empirical Methods in Natural Language Processing*, pages 9004–9017.

Jorge Martinez-Gil. 2023. A survey on legal question–answering systems. *Computer Science Review*, 48:100552.

Joshua Maynez, Shashi Narayan, Bernd Bohnet, and Ryan McDonald. 2020. On faithfulness and factuality in abstractive summarization. In *Proceedings of the 58th Annual Meeting of the Association for Computational Linguistics*, pages 1906–1919, Online. Association for Computational Linguistics.

Alfredo Monroy, Hiram Calvo, and Alexander Gelbukh. 2009. Nlp for shallow question answering of legal documents using graphs. In *International Conference on Intelligent Text Processing and Computational Linguistics*, pages 498–508. Springer.

Selvan Sunitha Ravi, Bartosz Mielczarek, Anand Kannappan, Douwe Kiela, and Rebecca Qian. 2024. Lynx: An open source hallucination evaluation model. *arXiv preprint arXiv:2407.08488*.

Vipula Rawte, Amit Sheth, and Amitava Das. 2023. A survey of hallucination in large foundation models. *arXiv preprint arXiv:2309.05922*.

Sara Rosenthal, Avirup Sil, Radu Florian, and Salim Roukos. 2024. Clapnq: Cohesive long-form answers from passages in natural questions for rag systems. *arXiv preprint arXiv:2404.02103*.

Noah Shinn, Federico Cassano, Ashwin Gopinath, Karthik Narasimhan, and Shunyu Yao. 2024. Reflexion: Language agents with verbal reinforcement learning. *Advances in Neural Information Processing Systems*, 36.

Dietrich Trautmann. 2023. Large language model prompt chaining for long legal document classification. *arXiv preprint arXiv:2308.04138*.

Dietrich Trautmann, Alina Petrova, and Frank Schilder. 2022. Legal prompt engineering for multilingual legal judgement prediction. *arXiv preprint arXiv:2212.02199*.

Andrew Vold and Jack G Conrad. 2021. Using transformers to improve answer retrieval for legal questions. In *Proceedings of the Eighteenth International Conference on Artificial Intelligence and Law*, pages 245–249.

Keheng Wang, Feiyu Duan, Peiguang Li, Sirui Wang, and Xunliang Cai. 2024. Llms know what they need: Leveraging a missing information guided framework to empower retrieval-augmented generation. *arXiv preprint arXiv:2404.14043*.

Orion Weller, Marc Marone, Nathaniel Weir, Dawn Lawrie, Daniel Khashabi, and Benjamin Van Durme. 2024. "according to . . . ": Prompting language models improves quoting from pre-training data. In *Proceedings of the 18th Conference of the European Chapter of the Association for Computational Linguistics (Volume 1: Long Papers)*, pages 2288–2301, St. Julian's, Malta. Association for Computational Linguistics.

Zhiying Zhu, Zhiqing Sun, and Yiming Yang. 2024. Halueval-wild: Evaluating hallucinations of language models in the wild. *arXiv preprint arXiv:2403.04307*.

A Response Error Types

A.1 Dev Set Error Types

A.2 Description and Examples

See the table 5 for our six response error types with their descriptions and examples.

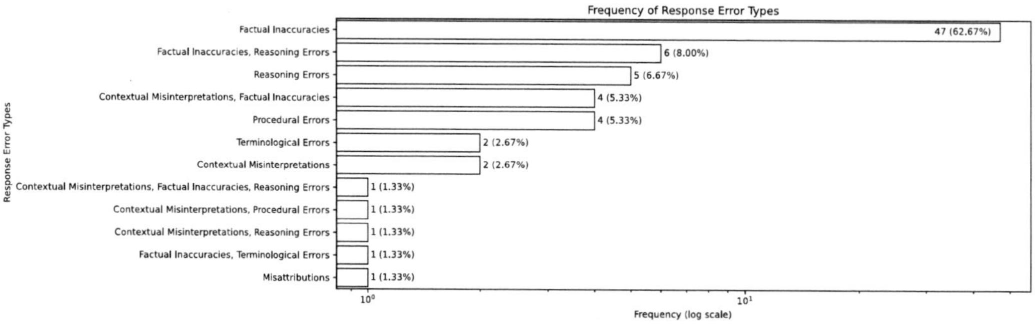

Figure 4: Counts of response error types in the development set. The frequency axis is in log-scale.

Error Type	**Short Description**	**Examples**
Factual Inaccuracies	Misrepresentation of established facts, dates, or details	1. Brown v. Board of Education was decided in 1964. 2. The First Amendment protects only written speech.
Contextual Misinterpretations	Misapplication of legal principles or inappropriate analogies	1. Applying Miranda rights to a civil tax dispute. 2. Using Roe v. Wade precedent in a Second Amendment case.
Procedural Errors	Mistakes in describing legal procedures or processes	1. A case goes directly from district court to the Supreme Court, skipping the appellate court. 2. Claiming that jury selection occurs after opening statements in a trial.
Reasoning Errors	Flawed arguments or unsupported legal conclusions	1. Since the Fourth Amendment protects against unreasonable searches, all warrantless searches are unconstitutional. 2. Because the Supreme Court ruled on abortion in Roe v. Wade, states cannot pass any abortion laws.
Misattributions	Incorrect assignment of opinions, quotes, or actions	1. Justice Scalia wrote the majority opinion in Obergefell v. Hodges. 2. The phrase "separate but equal" originated from Brown v. Board of Education.
Terminological Errors	Misuse or misinterpretation of legal terms or concepts	1. "Habeas corpus" refers to the right to a speedy trial. 2. "Strict scrutiny" means that a law is automatically unconstitutional.

Table 5: Response error types with a description and examples

Transductive Legal Judgment Prediction Combining BERT Embeddings with Delaunay-Based GNNs

Hugo Attali and **Nadi Tomeh**
LIPN, CNRS UMR 7030, Université Paris Sorbonne Nord, France

Abstract

This paper presents a novel approach to legal judgment prediction by combining BERT embeddings with a Delaunay-based Graph Neural Network (GNN). Unlike inductive methods that classify legal documents independently, our transductive approach models the entire document set as a graph, capturing both contextual and relational information. This method significantly improves classification accuracy by enabling effective label propagation across connected documents. Evaluated on the Swiss-Judgment-Prediction (SJP) dataset, our model outperforms established baselines, including larger models with cross-lingual training and data augmentation techniques, while maintaining efficiency with minimal computational overhead.

1 Introduction

Modeling legal texts have attracted lots of interest recently in two directions (Cui et al., 2023). The first is to gather large collections of legal text such as the MultiLegalPile corpus (Niklaus et al., 2024) and train legal large language models (LLMs) such as (Colombo et al., 2024). The second focuses on smaller, manually annotated and specialized datasets and benchmarks such as the Swiss Judgment Prediction[1] (SJP) dataset (Niklaus et al., 2021), LexGLUE (Chalkidis et al., 2022) and LEXTREME (Niklaus et al., 2023), and train smaller supervised models, mainly by finetuning BERT-like models, sometimes applying cross-lingual transfer and data augmentation (Niklaus et al., 2022).

General-purpose LLMs like ChatGPT often perform poorly on legal tasks in zero and few-shot settings (Chalkidis, 2023; Niklaus et al., 2023), though they can be useful as components in larger frameworks (Wu et al., 2023). Specialized models, fine-tuned with supervised learning (Niklaus et al., 2021, 2022, 2023), require significant resources to improve performance, such as applying cross-lingual transfer, adapter-based fine-tuning, or tripling the dataset size with machine-translated documents (Niklaus et al., 2022). The suboptimal performance is likely due to the complexity of legal texts, which are long, dense, and filled with specialized terminology that generic pre-trained models struggle to understand. Additionally, these models lack sufficient exposure to the contextual and nuanced nature of legal reasoning, requiring more domain-specific data to adapt effectively.

In this paper, we hypothesize that transductive learning techniques (Gammerman et al., 1998; Joachims, 1999) are well adapted to Legal Judgment Prediction (LJP) as it has been shown to work well in few-shot scenarios (Liu et al., 2019; Colombo et al., 2023) and on small training datasets (Li et al., 2021; Lin et al., 2021). Along these lines, we construct a single graph with all training (labeled) and test (unlabeled) documents as nodes, allowing a Graph Neural Network (GNN) to learn from the entire dataset simultaneously. This approach leverages the relationships between documents for effective label propagation and context-aware classification, improving generalization by using both labeled and unlabeled data. It also captures domain-specific knowledge through connections like citations and shared terminology, adapts dynamically to the test set, and reduces overfitting by integrating test data into the learning process.

Our model (§3) is a simple and efficient graph-based approach that achieves state-of-the-art results on the Swiss Judgment Prediction (SJP) task (Niklaus et al., 2021) without additional resources. It is also simpler than existing transductive graph-based models for document classificaiton (Lin et al., 2021). Experiments (§4) show it outperforms strong baselines from the literature and a new zero-shot SaulLM-7B baseline (Colombo et al., 2024).

[1] We use the term prediction in the machine learning sense and not in the juridical sense (Medvedeva and Mcbride, 2023).

Proceedings of the Natural Legal Language Processing Workshop 2024, pages 187–193
November 16, 2024 ©2024 Association for Computational Linguistics

2 Related Work

Transductive GNNs for Text Classification GNNs (Goller and Kuchler, 1996) have demonstrated effectiveness across various domains (Wu et al., 2020; Nathani et al., 2019; Schlichtkrull et al., 2018; Vashishth et al., 2020), and have been applied to various text processing tasks (Nikolentzos et al., 2020; Wang et al., 2024). Most similar to our work is their use in transducive models. For instance, BertGCN (Lin et al., 2021) which builds a heterogeneous graph over a dataset, representing documents as nodes using BERT embeddings and modeling semantic relationships between them, allowing both labeled and unlabeled data to contribute to learning. Our model differs by using Delaunay triangulation for simpler graph construction, avoiding joint BERT and GCN training to reduce memory usage, and not requiring interpolation with a separate BERT-based classifier, resulting in more efficient graph construction and faster training. KnnGCN (Benamira et al., 2019) constructs corpus-level graphs using a KNN approach, which is less suited to GNNs than our Delaunay-based method. In contrast, TextGTL (Li et al., 2021) builds three non-heterogeneous graphs (Semantic, Syntax, and Context Text Graphs) using complex techniques like canonical correlation analysis and dependency parsing, whereas our model employs simpler graph construction techniques. Furthermore, none of the previous models have been specifically applied to LJP.

Graph-Based Methods in Legal Text Graph-based models have been explored for legal judgment prediction, similar to our approach. Zhao et al. (2022) use a graph network with heterogeneous text graphs and a GCN to predict outcomes, while LADAN (Xu et al., 2020) employs a graph neural network and attention mechanism to distinguish between confusing law articles. However, neither constructs a comprehensive graph for all documents, as we do. Other methods focus on different tasks, such as LegalGNN (Yang et al., 2021) for legal recommendations, using a heterogeneous graph with user queries, and CaseGNN (Tang et al., 2024) for legal case retrieval by modeling document-level relationships.

3 Method

In this section we describe our architecture, also depicted in Figure 1.

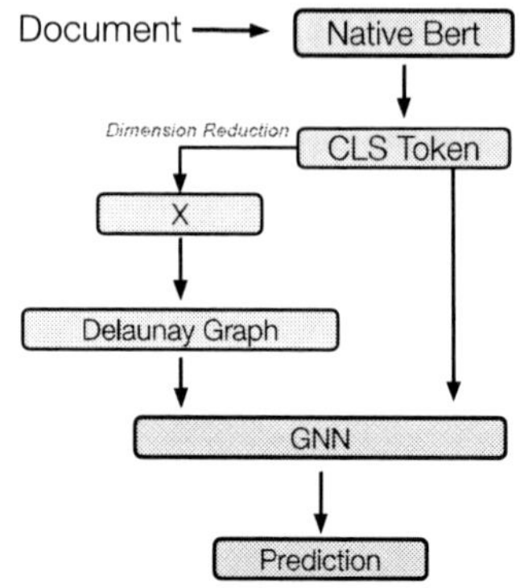

Figure 1: Our model architecture. A document is processed through a BERT model to obtain CLS tokens, which are then used alongside the Delaunay graph of documents for classification using a GNN.

Document Encoder We begin by modeling documents as a graph, using the `[CLS]` tokens extracted from a standard BERT model (Devlin, 2018) (up to 512 tokens) to represent each document. While this approach leverages BERT's document representation, our method is flexible and can easily incorporate other encoders that provide document representations. Documents that are longer than BERT context capacity are cut off. In contrast to our simple approach, some of the baselines we present in §4.2 handle long documents hierarchically or using larger models.

Delaunay Graph To effectively model documents as a graph, we propose using a a Delaunay graph (Attali et al., 2024). This kind of graph is particularly advantageous for information propagation by a GNN. It helps mitigating common challenges such as oversquashing (Alon and Yahav, 2021) – information loss due to bottleneck structures in the graph, and oversmoothing (Oono and Suzuki, 2020; Cai and Wang, 2020) – information mixing which can blur distinctions between nodes. In fact, Delaunay graphs do not have tight bottlenecks and large cliques (Nguyen et al., 2023). Additionally, Delaunay triangulation correlates with improved *homophily* of the graph, meaning it better captures the similarity between connected nodes.

In our approach, each document to be classified is represented as a node within this graph. To construct the graph, we employ a strategy similar to that used in Attali et al. (2024). First, we perform a Delaunay triangulation in a 2-dimensional feature space, where each `[CLS]` token represents the document's embedding. Since the `[CLS]` token is typically high-dimensional, we reduce its dimensionality using UMAP (McInnes et al., 2018) that preserves the local structure of data. Delaunay graphs basically establish relationships between documents based on their distances in feature space. This operation is computationally efficient and scalable as we show in our experiments §4.

GNN-Based Classification Finally, for classification, we use a simple GCN (Kipf and Welling, 2017). Our GCN takes as input the [CLS] output from BERT, which represents the document (node) embeddings, and the adjacency matrix of the Delaunay graph. We construct a single graph for training, validation and test sets.

Training To maintain simplicity and modularity, we adopt a two-stage training approach. In the first stage, we add a binary classification MLP on top of BERT's [CLS] token and train both BERT and the MLP to minimize the binary cross-entropy loss using the true labels from the training set. The MLP is used only during this training phase. In the second stage, we train the GNN on the Delaunay graph constructed from all document embeddings, using the same binary classification loss on the training set labels.

4 Experiments

4.1 Dataset

To assess the effectiveness of our method, we utilize the task of Legal Judgment Prediction, aiming to forecast the verdict of a case based on the provided facts (Aletras et al., 2016; Zhong et al., 2018; Chalkidis et al., 2019a; Niklaus et al., 2021; Cui et al., 2023). For this evaluation, we use the Swiss-Judgment-Prediction dataset (Niklaus et al., 2021), a comprehensive multilingual resource comprising 85,000 cases from the Swiss Federal Supreme Court (FSCS). Each case in this dataset is annotated with a binarized judgment outcome, indicating either approval or dismissal. See Table 1 for dataset statistics.

Dataset	#Train	#Val	#Test	#Time
Italian	3,072	408	812	$\approx 11s$
German	35,452	4,705	9,725	$\approx 50s$
French	21,179	3,095	6,820	$\approx 30s$

Table 1: Dataset statistics. Time indicates the total time required to construct the graph, including the time spent on dimensionality reduction.

4.2 Baselines

Finetuned LMs We compare our architecture with three types of **monolingual** baselines as presented by Niklaus et al. (2021). The simplest ones use standard BERT (Devlin, 2018) for German (Branden Chan and Yeung, 2019), French (Martin et al., 2019), and Italian (Parisi et al., 2020), handling up to 512 tokens. Long BERT is an extended version of Standard BERT that includes additional positional encodings, allowing it to process longer texts of up to 2048 tokens. Hierarchical BERT, on the other hand, first processes text segments of up to 512 tokens each with a standard BERT, and then combines these segment encodings using a BiLSTM (Chalkidis et al., 2019b). We also compare to **multilingual** baselines that use pre-trained XLM-R (Conneau, 2019) along with **data augmentation** techniques based on machine translation and cross-lingual transfer as presented by Niklaus et al. (2022).

Zero-shot LLM (SaulLM-7B) In this baseline, we use a role-based prompt instructing the model to evaluate legal cases as a Swiss judge, analyzing the facts step-by-step and determining whether to dismiss or approve the request in a chain-of-thought style (Wei et al., 2024). SaulLM-7B (Colombo et al., 2024) is employed through a text generation pipeline, generating responses with a limit of 600 tokens. The outputs are parsed using regular expressions and conflict resolution rules to identify patterns indicating each class.

4.3 Experimental Setup

For the experiments, we follow the same training procedure as described in (Niklaus et al., 2021). For our method, we use the standard BERT [CLS] token embedding (up to 512 tokens). For the final classification we use a GCN (Kipf and Welling, 2017). We fix the number of layers to 2 and the dropout rate to 0.5, in line with (Pei et al., 2020; Attali et al., 2024). We fine-tune the learning rate, testing values of {0.005, 0.0005, 0.0001}, and the weight decay among {5e-05, 5e-6, 5e-07} on the validation set. The main results are presented in Table 2, where we report the average macro-averages F1-score for each method across 5 runs. We use the macro-averaged F1-score instead of the micro-average to give equal weight to all classes, ensuring that the performance on less frequent classes is fairly represented.

Model	De	Fr	It
Majority	44.5	44.9	44.8
Stratified	50.0	50.0	48.8
Linear (BoW)	52.6	56.6	53.9
BERT	63.7	58.6	55.2
Long BERT	67.9	68.0	59.8
Hierarchical BERT	68.5	70.2	57.1
Hierarchical BERT+MT	70.0	71.0	71.9
XLM-R+Adapters+CL	69.9	71.8	70.7
XLM-R+Adapt.+CL+MT	70.3	72.1	72.3
SaulLM-7B	51.0	52.0	52.0
BERT+Delaunay+GCN	**79.2**	**77.5**	**74.4**

Table 2: Main results. The baselines including BERT and XLM-R are taken from (Niklaus et al., 2021, 2022). Best scores are in bold. Our method achieves standard deviations ranging between 0.5 and 0.7 across different languages, making it the most stable method compared to the baselines.

4.4 Results

Main Findings Our model achieves the highest scores across all languages as presented in Table 2. This demonstrates that our approach, which builds on top of a fine-tuned BERT outperforms the BERT baseline with *negligible computational overhead* and without retraining BERT. Despite being a smaller model, BERT+Delaunay+GCN outperforms Hierarchical BERT and Long BERT, and XLM-R models with cross-lingual training and data augmentation techniques like machine translation. Additionally, our transductive approach seems to mitigate the lack of resources, as seen in the results for the Italian dataset. While the Italian scores are generally lower than those for German and French, mainly due to the smaller dataset size. This underscores our model's robustness, particularly for lower-resource languages. Finally, our model outperforms the specialized legal LLM (SaulLM-7B), confirming findings from the literature that generic, powerful language models like ChatGPT underperform on this task (Niklaus et al., 2023; Chalkidis, 2023).

Running Time The Delaunay graph can be constructed efficiently including dimensionality reduction as presented in Table 1. Adding a GCN-based classification layer is highly scalable and computationally efficient. On average, a single run of classification takes 91 seconds on the German dataset, 42 seconds on the French dataset, and 5 seconds on the Italian dataset when using a T4 GPU.

	De	Fr	It
SBERT + Delaunay+GCN	44.8	47.6	51.9
BERT + KMeans	52.0	74.2	66.4
BERT + Delaunay+GCN	**79.2**	**77.5**	**74.4**

Table 3: Results of our ablation study.

Ablations To demonstrate the necessity of both (a) fine-tuning document representations for the task at hand and (b) enriching them through GNNs, we conducted a series of comparisons. First, we replaced the Delaunay+GCN part of the architecture with KMeans unsupervised clustering on `[CLS]` tokens which does not need any training. In a second experiments, we replaced the finetuned BERT with pre-trained SBERT (Reimers, 2019) without any further finetuning on the task to generate document embeddings. The results are shown in Table 3.

The results show that our method consistently outperforms both KMeans clustering and SBERT-based encoding, emphasizing the importance of first fine-tuning document representations for task-specific alignment and then further refining them with graph-based methods like Delaunay GNN. This approach effectively captures structural relationships, enhancing representation quality and leading to more accurate classification.

5 Conclusions

This paper demonstrates that a transductive legal judgment prediction method, combining BERT embeddings with Delaunay-based GNNs, significantly outperforms traditional inductive classification methods by effectively utilizing contextual and relational information between legal documents for more accurate label propagation and classification. In future work, we will study the necessity of retraining the model whenever a new batch of documents are to be classified. We will also explore semi-supervised training approaches to study the dependency of the performance on annotated data.

6 Limitations

Our study is limited by its exclusive focus on the SJP dataset, which may affect its generalizability to other legal systems. The model may also inherit biases from the training data, and we have not performed a bias analysis. While our approach improves performance, it may not fully capture all the complex factors influencing judicial decisions and may face scalability challenges with larger datasets.

7 Ethics Statement

Our work uses machine learning techniques for legal judgment prediction based on SJP dataset. We acknowledge that models trained on historical data may inherit biases, such as disparities in legal decisions or underrepresentation of certain groups. Since our model is based on cases from the Swiss Federal Supreme Court, it may not generalize to other jurisdictions or legal systems with different laws or cultural contexts. We have not tested its applicability outside the Swiss judicial system, and extending it to other settings would require careful adaptation and validation.

Our method is not intended to replace human judgment but to provide supplementary insights to legal professionals. Its outputs should be viewed as probabilistic suggestions, not definitive conclusions, and should always be used alongside human oversight to consider the broader context and ethical implications not captured in the training data.

To mitigate risks of bias and unjust outcomes, we recommend integrating our model in a way that enhances, rather than replaces, human decision-making. Any deployment should include mechanisms for regular monitoring and auditing to detect and address potential biases promptly, ensuring its alignment with fair legal practices.

References

Nikolaos Aletras, Dimitrios Tsarapatsanis, Daniel Preotiuc-Pietro, and Vasileios Lampos. 2016. Predicting judicial decisions of the european court of human rights: a natural language processing perspective. *PeerJ Comput. Sci.*, 2:e93.

Uri Alon and Eran Yahav. 2021. On the bottleneck of graph neural networks and its practical implications. In *International Conference on Learning Representations*.

Hugo Attali, Davide Buscaldi, and Nathalie Pernelle. 2024. Delaunay graph: Addressing over-squashing and over-smoothing using delaunay triangulation. In *Forty-first International Conference on Machine Learning*.

Adrien Benamira, Benjamin Devillers, Etienne Lesot, Ayush K. Ray, Manal Saadi, and Fragkiskos Malliaros. 2019. Semi-Supervised Learning and Graph Neural Networks for Fake News Detection. In *ASONAM 2019 - IEEE/ACM International Conference on Advances in Social Networks Analysis and Mining*, Vancouver, Canada.

Malte Pietsch Tanay Soni Branden Chan, Timo Möller and Chin Man Yeung. 2019. German bert. https://deepset.ai/german-bert.

Chen Cai and Yusu Wang. 2020. A note on over-smoothing for graph neural networks. *Graph Representation Learning*.

Ilias Chalkidis. 2023. Chatgpt may pass the bar exam soon, but has a long way to go for the lexglue benchmark. *Preprint*, arXiv:2304.12202.

Ilias Chalkidis, Ion Androutsopoulos, and Nikolaos Aletras. 2019a. Neural legal judgment prediction in English. In *Proceedings of the 57th Annual Meeting of the Association for Computational Linguistics*, pages 4317–4323, Florence, Italy. Association for Computational Linguistics.

Ilias Chalkidis, Ion Androutsopoulos, and Nikolaos Aletras. 2019b. Neural legal judgment prediction in english. *arXiv preprint arXiv:1906.02059*.

Ilias Chalkidis, Abhik Jana, Dirk Hartung, Michael Bommarito, Ion Androutsopoulos, Daniel Katz, and Nikolaos Aletras. 2022. LexGLUE: A benchmark dataset for legal language understanding in English. In *Proceedings of the 60th Annual Meeting of the Association for Computational Linguistics (Volume 1: Long Papers)*, pages 4310–4330, Dublin, Ireland. Association for Computational Linguistics.

Pierre Colombo, Michael Desa, Telmo Pires, Malik Boudiaf, Dominic Culver, Rui Melo, Caio Corro, André Martins, Fabrizio Esposito, Vera Raposo, and Sofia Morgado. 2024. SaulLM-7B: A pioneering Large Language Model for Law. Working paper or preprint.

Pierre Colombo, Victor Pellegrain, Malik Boudiaf, Myriam Tami, Victor Storchan, Ismail Ayed, and Pablo Piantanida. 2023. Transductive learning for textual few-shot classification in API-based embedding models. In *Proceedings of the 2023 Conference on Empirical Methods in Natural Language Processing*, pages 4214–4231, Singapore. Association for Computational Linguistics.

A Conneau. 2019. Unsupervised cross-lingual representation learning at scale. *arXiv preprint arXiv:1911.02116*.

Junyun Cui, Xiaoyu Shen, and Shaochun Wen. 2023. A survey on legal judgment prediction: Datasets, metrics, models and challenges. *IEEE Access*, 11:102050–102071.

Jacob Devlin. 2018. Bert: Pre-training of deep bidirectional transformers for language understanding. *arXiv preprint arXiv:1810.04805*.

Alexander Gammerman, Volodya Vovk, and Vladimir Vapnik. 1998. Learning by transduction. In *UAI '98: Proceedings of the Fourteenth Conference on Uncertainty in Artificial Intelligence, University of Wisconsin Business School, Madison, Wisconsin, USA, July 24-26, 1998*, pages 148–155. Morgan Kaufmann.

Christoph Goller and Andreas Kuchler. 1996. Learning task-dependent distributed representations by backpropagation through structure. In *Proceedings of International Conference on Neural Networks (ICNN'96)*, volume 1, pages 347–352. IEEE.

Thorsten Joachims. 1999. Transductive inference for text classification using support vector machines. In *Proceedings of the Sixteenth International Conference on Machine Learning*, ICML '99, page 200–209, San Francisco, CA, USA. Morgan Kaufmann Publishers Inc.

Thomas N. Kipf and Max Welling. 2017. Semi-Supervised Classification with Graph Convolutional Networks. In *Proceedings of the International Conference on Learning Representations*, ICLR.

Chen Li, Xutan Peng, Hao Peng, Jianxin Li, and Lihong Wang. 2021. Textgtl: Graph-based transductive learning for semi-supervised text classification via structure-sensitive interpolation. In *Proceedings of the Thirtieth International Joint Conference on Artificial Intelligence, IJCAI-21*, pages 2680–2686. International Joint Conferences on Artificial Intelligence Organization. Main Track.

Yuxiao Lin, Yuxian Meng, Xiaofei Sun, Qinghong Han, Kun Kuang, Jiwei Li, and Fei Wu. 2021. BertGCN: Transductive text classification by combining GNN and BERT. In *Findings of the Association for Computational Linguistics: ACL-IJCNLP 2021*, pages 1456–1462, Online. Association for Computational Linguistics.

Yanbin Liu, Juho Lee, Minseop Park, Saehoon Kim, Eunho Yang, Sung Ju Hwang, and Yi Yang. 2019. Learning to propagate labels: Transductive propagation network for few-shot learning. In *7th International Conference on Learning Representations, ICLR 2019, New Orleans, LA, USA, May 6-9, 2019*. OpenReview.net.

Louis Martin, Benjamin Muller, Pedro Javier Ortiz Suárez, Yoann Dupont, Laurent Romary, Éric Villemonte de La Clergerie, Djamé Seddah, and Benoît Sagot. 2019. Camembert: a tasty french language model. *arXiv preprint arXiv:1911.03894*.

Leland McInnes, John Healy, and James Melville. 2018. Umap: Uniform manifold approximation and projection for dimension reduction. *arXiv preprint arXiv:1802.03426*.

Masha Medvedeva and Pauline Mcbride. 2023. Legal judgment prediction: If you are going to do it, do it right. In *Proceedings of the Natural Legal Language Processing Workshop 2023*, pages 73–84, Singapore. Association for Computational Linguistics.

Deepak Nathani, Jatin Chauhan, Charu Sharma, and Manohar Kaul. 2019. Learning attention-based embeddings for relation prediction in knowledge graphs. *arXiv preprint arXiv:1906.01195*.

Khang Nguyen, Nong Minh Hieu, Vinh Duc Nguyen, Nhat Ho, Stanley Osher, and Tan Minh Nguyen. 2023. Revisiting over-smoothing and over-squashing using ollivier-ricci curvature. In *International Conference on Machine Learning*, pages 25956–25979. PMLR.

Joel Niklaus, Ilias Chalkidis, and Matthias Stürmer. 2021. Swiss-judgment-prediction: A multilingual legal judgment prediction benchmark. In *Proceedings of the Natural Legal Language Processing Workshop 2021*, pages 19–35, Punta Cana, Dominican Republic. Association for Computational Linguistics.

Joel Niklaus, Veton Matoshi, Pooja Rani, Andrea Galassi, Matthias Stürmer, and Ilias Chalkidis. 2023. LEXTREME: A multi-lingual and multi-task benchmark for the legal domain. In *Findings of the Association for Computational Linguistics: EMNLP 2023*, pages 3016–3054, Singapore. Association for Computational Linguistics.

Joel Niklaus, Veton Matoshi, Matthias Stürmer, Ilias Chalkidis, and Daniel Ho. 2024. MultiLegalPile: A 689GB multilingual legal corpus. In *Proceedings of the 62nd Annual Meeting of the Association for Computational Linguistics (Volume 1: Long Papers)*, pages 15077–15094, Bangkok, Thailand. Association for Computational Linguistics.

Joel Niklaus, Matthias Stürmer, and Ilias Chalkidis. 2022. An empirical study on cross-X transfer for legal judgment prediction. In *Proceedings of the 2nd Conference of the Asia-Pacific Chapter of the Association for Computational Linguistics and the 12th International Joint Conference on Natural Language Processing (Volume 1: Long Papers)*, pages 32–46, Online only. Association for Computational Linguistics.

Giannis Nikolentzos, Antoine Tixier, and Michalis Vazirgiannis. 2020. Message passing attention networks for document understanding. In *Proceedings of the AAAI Conference on Artificial Intelligence*, AAAI, pages 8544–8551.

Kenta Oono and Taiji Suzuki. 2020. Graph neural networks exponentially lose expressive power for node classification. *Proceedings of the International Conference on Learning Representations*.

Loreto Parisi, Simone Francia, and Paolo Magnani. 2020. Umberto: an italian language model trained with whole word masking. *Original-date*, 55:31Z.

Hongbin Pei, Bingzhe Wei, Kevin Chen-Chuan Chang, Yu Lei, and Bo Yang. 2020. Geom-gcn: Geometric graph convolutional networks. *arXiv preprint arXiv:2002.05287*.

N Reimers. 2019. Sentence-bert: Sentence embeddings using siamese bert-networks. *arXiv preprint arXiv:1908.10084*.

Michael Schlichtkrull, Thomas N Kipf, Peter Bloem, Rianne Van Den Berg, Ivan Titov, and Max Welling.

2018. Modeling relational data with graph convolutional networks. In *The Semantic Web: 15th International Conference, ESWC 2018, Heraklion, Crete, Greece, June 3–7, 2018, Proceedings 15*, pages 593–607. Springer.

Yanran Tang, Ruihong Qiu, Yilun Liu, Xue Li, and Zi Huang. 2024. Casegnn: Graph neural networks fornbsp;legal case retrieval withnbsp;text-attributed graphs. In *Advances in Information Retrieval: 46th European Conference on Information Retrieval, ECIR 2024, Glasgow, UK, March 24–28, 2024, Proceedings, Part II*, page 80–95, Berlin, Heidelberg. Springer-Verlag.

Shikhar Vashishth, Soumya Sanyal, Vikram Nitin, and Partha Talukdar. 2020. Composition-based multi-relational graph convolutional networks. ICLR.

Kunze Wang, Yihao Ding, and Soyeon Caren Han. 2024. Graph neural networks for text classification: a survey. *Artificial Intelligence Review*, 57(8).

Jason Wei, Xuezhi Wang, Dale Schuurmans, Maarten Bosma, Brian Ichter, Fei Xia, Ed H. Chi, Quoc V. Le, and Denny Zhou. 2024. Chain-of-thought prompting elicits reasoning in large language models. In *Proceedings of the 36th International Conference on Neural Information Processing Systems*, NIPS '22, Red Hook, NY, USA. Curran Associates Inc.

Yiquan Wu, Siying Zhou, Yifei Liu, Weiming Lu, Xiaozhong Liu, Yating Zhang, Changlong Sun, Fei Wu, and Kun Kuang. 2023. Precedent-enhanced legal judgment prediction with LLM and domain-model collaboration. In *Proceedings of the 2023 Conference on Empirical Methods in Natural Language Processing*, pages 12060–12075, Singapore. Association for Computational Linguistics.

Zonghan Wu, Shirui Pan, Fengwen Chen, Guodong Long, Chengqi Zhang, and S Yu Philip. 2020. A comprehensive survey on graph neural networks. In *IEEE transactions on neural networks and learning systems*, volume 32, pages 4–24. IEEE.

Nuo Xu, Pinghui Wang, Long Chen, Li Pan, Xiaoyan Wang, and Junzhou Zhao. 2020. Distinguish confusing law articles for legal judgment prediction. In *Proceedings of the 58th Annual Meeting of the Association for Computational Linguistics*, pages 3086–3095, Online. Association for Computational Linguistics.

Jun Yang, Weizhi Ma, Min Zhang, Xin Zhou, Yiqun Liu, and Shaoping Ma. 2021. Legalgnn: Legal information enhanced graph neural network for recommendation. *ACM Trans. Inf. Syst.*, 40(2).

Qihui Zhao, Tianhan Gao, Song Zhou, Dapeng Li, and Yingyou Wen. 2022. Legal judgment prediction via heterogeneous graphs and knowledge of law articles. *Applied Sciences*, 12(5).

Haoxi Zhong, Zhipeng Guo, Cunchao Tu, Chaojun Xiao, Zhiyuan Liu, and Maosong Sun. 2018. Legal judgment prediction via topological learning. In *Proceedings of the 2018 Conference on Empirical Methods in Natural Language Processing*, pages 3540–3549, Brussels, Belgium. Association for Computational Linguistics.

Cross Examine: An Ensemble-based approach to leverage Large Language Models for Legal Text Analytics

Saurav Chowdhury[1], Suyog Joshi[2], Lipika Dey[2]
[1]Indian Institute of Technology, Jodhpur, India, [2]Ashoka University, India,
Email: chowdhury.4@iitj.ac.in, suyog.joshi_asp25@ashoka.edu.in, lipika.dey@ashoka.edu.in

Abstract

Legal documents are complex in nature, describing a course of argumentative reasoning that is followed to settle a case. Churning through large volumes of legal documents is a daily requirement for a large number of professionals who need access to the information embedded in them. Natural Language Processing(NLP) methods that help in document summarization with key information components, insight extraction and question answering play a crucial role in legal text processing. Most of the existing document analysis systems use supervised machine learning, which require large volumes of annotated training data for every different application and are expensive to build. In this paper we propose a legal text analytics pipeline using Large Language Models (LLMs), which can work with little or no training data. For document summarization, we propose an iterative pipeline using retrieval augmented generation to ensure that the generated text remains contextually relevant. For question answering, we propose a novel ontology-driven ensemble approach similar to cross-examination that exploits questioning and verification principles. A knowledge graph, created with the extracted information, stores the key entities and relationships reflecting the repository content structure. A new dataset is created with Indian court documents related to bail applications for cases filed under POCSO [1] Act. Analysis of insights extracted from the answers reveal patterns of crime and social conditions leading to those crimes, which are important inputs for social scientists as well as legal system.

1 Introduction

Legal language is inherently complex (Marmor, 2014), characterized by formality, precision, and complexity along with use of specialized vocabulary. Legal documents are often lengthy, with intricate reasoning about laws, acts, clauses, and provisions, with redundancy and repetition, as is necessary in the legal domain. Legal professionals, who have to wade through large volumes of legal text daily, therefore look for text processing tools that can help them in searching through the documents, and retrieve relevant information efficiently. Insights extracted from large collections of legal documents benefit different stakeholders like legal practitioners, clients, social scientists as well as law makers. Consequently legal document summarization, sentence / paragraph labeling using classification models and question answering from legal documents have been popular applications of Natural Language Processing(NLP) (Deroy et al., 2021), (Bhattacharya et al., 2021).

Advances in the area of Natural Language Processing(NLP) have inspired a large volume of work in the area of legal analytics across the world. Legal document summarization, both extractive and abstractive, in different languages have been reported all over the world. Legal data analytics is a relatively new area, but gaining rapid popularity. It may be noted that most of the earlier systems were developed using supervised machine learning methods, where the models were trained with large volumes of carefully annotated data, obtaining which is prohibitively expensive. Besides, each system catered to a specific use case, for which it was trained, therefore requiring substantial rework for extension to other legal domains or jurisdictions. With the evolution of Large Language Models (LLMs)(Topsakal and Akinci, 2023), trained on massive volumes of heterogeneous data from a wide variety of sources, the domain of text processing is seeing a paradigm shift. Applying them for legal text analytics is also being explored. However, one of the key challenges of working with these models is the restricted context length on which

[1]Protection of Children from Sexual Offences Act (POCSO), 2012 : Indian law to protect children from sexual offences

Proceedings of the Natural Legal Language Processing Workshop 2024, pages 194–204
November 16, 2024 ©2024 Association for Computational Linguistics

they can work, which is far less than a standard legal document. Another challenge stems from the fact that LLMs are known to hallucinate, or generate text that may not be contextually relevant or correct, which is also not quite acceptable for legal text processing tasks. The current work was motivated by these challenges and sought to explore whether these challenges can be overcome or bypassed, thereby easing the tasks of legal document summarization and question answering for analytical insight generation.

This paper proposes an LLM-driven legal text processing pipeline that first generates contextually relevant summaries from long court proceedings, and subsequently uses the summaries to extract legal information to build a knowledge graph from a legal text repository. The knowledge graph is designed following a legal ontology design that stores the core legal concepts and relationships among them. The summarization process uses a "summary of summaries" approach along with Retrieval-Augmented Generation (RAG) (Lewis et al., 2020) and LLMs (Topsakal and Akinci, 2023). Legal information extraction from the summaries is realized using an ontology-driven LLM-powered question-answering system that employs a novel ensemble-based approach. The ensemble approach was motivated by the method of "cross examination" that is used during legal trials to challenge the credibility and reliability of a witness's testimony, uncover inconsistencies, and present an alternative interpretation of the facts. This process is crucial in legal systems to ensure a thorough and fair examination of the evidence. In the current context, the term "cross-examination" is used metaphorically and the key idea is to follow a multi-pronged information retrieval over two phases. In the first phase, for a given type of information to be extracted from a legal document, a set of paraphrased questions are formulated using ontology definitions of concepts and relations. In the second phase, a set of verification questions are formulated with the retrieved answers. The above design of the ensemble of questions is aimed at establishing the validity of LLM-generated answers by analyzing them from multiple perspectives. Answer to a single question can be compared with its counterparts generated by the paraphrases, and also verified against the original document before it is accepted. Our experiments also show that the quality of answers obtained from the summaries are often better than those obtained from the original document. Based on the fact that LLMs work better on shorter contexts than longer ones, this result is as expected.

Besides the presentation of a novel workflow, contribution of this work also lies in creating a new dataset consisting of Indian court proceedings related to Protection of Children from Sexual Offences (POCSO) Act, 2012. The POCSO Act, 2012 is a gender-neutral law that was passed to protect children from offences including Sexual Assault, harassment, threatening and child pornography. Analyzing cases under the purview of POCSO Act can unravel insights about the nature of the crimes, social and economic circumstances related to the event of crime, existence of bias, if any, in the judicial system, and also uncover the dynamics of how such cases proceed (Damodharan et al., 2021). The knowledge graph contains all details extracted from the court proceedings related to bail applications from the accused. Experiments and evaluations on this collection show promising and interesting results, thereby establishing the feasibility of the proposed methods in setting up a legal text analytics pipeline in a completely unsupervised way. The repository is publicly available.

The rest of the paper is organized as follows. Section 2 presents a review of earlier work in the area of legal text analytics. Section 3 presents the details of the proposed pipeline for summary generation and question answering from the summaries. Section 4 presents details of dataset creation, experimentation and results obtained. Section 5 discusses the experiments and the results. Section 6 concludes with a discussion of some limitations, which are addressed in Section 7, followed by the dataset link in Section 8.

2 Legal Text Analytics - review of earlier work

Automated summarization of legal documents has been an active area of research for quite some time. Two types of summaries are prevalent—extractive and abstractive. Extractive summaries contain a subset of sentences identified as important from the original document. Abstractive summaries may contain new words and sentences, which are strewn together to convey the original content with a reduced size but without losing the original meaning. In Bhattacharya et al. (2021), authors have emphasized the use of extractive summaries for legal documents to ensure that the characteristic of legal language is retained in the summary.

Abstractive summarization stores the essence of a document, but does not preserve exact sentential structures. Masked language models like T5, BART, etc., were found to work well for summarization. In Zmiycharov et al. (2021), a T5-based abstractive summary generation model was proposed for EU legal documents. In Elaraby and Litman (2022), a BART-based model, that could capture the argumentative structure of legal documents by integrating argument role labeling into the summarization process, was proposed. In Feijo and Moreira (2023) proposed an abstractive text summarization approach using an encoder-decoder architecture. Most of the above approaches required a large training corpus to train the models. The models were not transferable and hence not usable in a context other than for which they were designed. To overcome the challenges of high-quality training data, a transfer learning based approach that exploits extractive and abstractive techniques simultaneously, was proposed in Moro et al. (2023). Though Large Language Models (LLMs) can summarize content pretty well and are known to work with little or no supervision, legal document summarizing still pose a challenge since these are very large and often do not fit into acceptable context lengths.

Legal question answering and text analytics beyond summarization is emerging as an important area. Martinez-Gil (2023) presents results of a quantitative and qualitative survey carried out to document the existing challenges in the area, the primary one being the fact that the task is time-consuming and error-prone. Guha et al. (2024) reports a study on the adoption of Large Language Models(LLMs) by the legal community. They present a collaboratively constructed legal reasoning benchmark consisting of 162 tasks covering six different types of legal reasoning called Legal Bench.

Summarizing documents from Indian court proceedings using NLP techniques is a relatively less explored area. Recently, platforms like SCC Online (SCC Online, 2024), Manupatra (Manupatra, 2024), and Indian Kanoon (Kanoon, 2024) have started hosting vast repositories of digitized court proceedings with advanced search capabilities. Bhattacharya et al. (2023) presents transformer-based models for rhetorical role labeling to assign labels such as Fact, Argument, Final Judgement, etc., to sentences of a court case document. Quevedo et al. (2023) presents a detailed study on the readiness of general-purpose LLMs for abstractive summarization of legal documents. They propose a human-in-the-loop approach for obtaining functional summaries with LLMs.

3 Ontology-driven framework for Legal Document Summarization and Analytics using Large Language Models

Though Large Language Models (LLMs), trained over very large repositories are known to be good for general - purpose language generation tasks like summarization or question answering, performance of similar tasks over specialized domains can greatly benefit from the use of ontologies or knowledge graphs (Agrawal et al., 2024). This is true for all specialized domains like health, climate or legal repositories. A legal ontology is well structured framework that defines the relationships between various legal concepts, entities, principles and processes enabling a systematic understanding of law and legal domain. Legal documents are an important part of the ontology (Van Engers et al., 2008). While some legal documents store information about the legal processes, statutes etc. and are more permanent in nature, legal documents arising out of legal proceedings contain details about a specific case, referring to other legal concepts. Each legal proceeding usually gives rise to a number of legal documents of different types. Figure 1 presents a portion of the legal ontology used for our work. This ontology is created from concepts and relations presented in Leone et al. (2020).

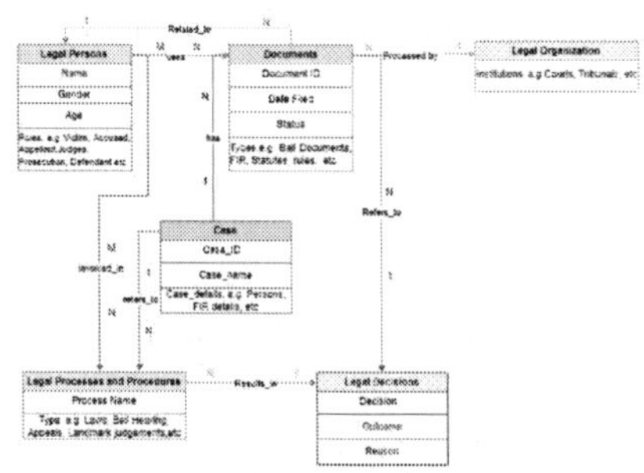

Figure 1: Legal Ontology Diagram

The ontology depicts the interplay between legal professionals, persons, documents, organisations, principles and process. For instance, it shows that accused, victim, lawyer, judge all are "Legal Persons", with various properties like gender, age etc. Legal documents encompass a large category of documents like case files, bail applications, court proceedings, judgements, contracts etc. Each has its own characteristic (not shown in the figure). The ontology plays a key role in information extraction from document summaries, explained in section 3.2. But before that, in the next subsection we present the mechanism for creating document summaries from legal documents using LLMs. Though the ontology is not used for the task of summarization, it plays a key role in its evaluation, wherein it provides the list of key concepts and relations that should be present in the summary.

3.1 Legal Document Summarization using summary of summaries

Legal document summarization aims to generate shorter versions of long documents retaining crucial legal information components like the judgements, citations, bills under process, acts and laws etc. Long documents are broken into fixed size chunks, say, D1, D2, ..., Dn. Vector embeddings of each chunk are created and passed on to the LLM for generating summaries using the following prompt - "*summarize the provided text. This is just part of a larger document, so do not add any extra information and narration. Provide details about the victim and accused, including gender, age, legal status (minor or adult), relationship between appellant and accused, familiarity between victim and accused, specific charges, repeat offenses, bail approval, final judicial decision, rationale provided by the judge, and relevant legal principles or precedents referenced, do not write anything extra, just reduce the words: {text}.*" The chunk summaries are concatenated to create an intermediate document, which is passed on as context to the LLM for a second time with the same prompt to generate the final summary. Figure 2 for an architectural diagram of the approach.

This approach has multiple advantages. In the first pass, it allows the query to focus on each part of the document and include the contextually relevant parts in its summary. In the second pass, it eliminates redundancies. The two passes ensure that if a piece of relevant information is present in multiple chunks but in different contexts representing different perspectives of its use, these are retained in each chunk-summary and also in the final. This holds for citations which are references to past cases, and are often found in both the arguments and judgment sections, but may or may not be used from the same perspective. On the contrary, a piece of information like ones that describe the accused or circumstances of crime, are repeated in different chunks to emphasize on the same truth. These may be retained in the individual chunk summaries in the first pass, but multiple occurrences are eliminated from the final summary.

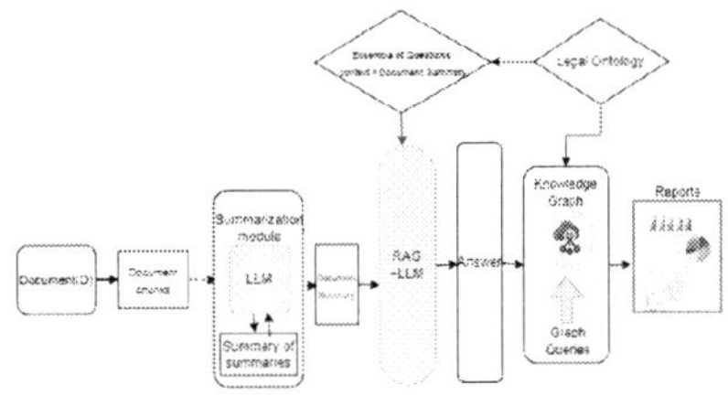

Figure 2: Architecture

3.2 Ontology-driven Information Extraction from Legal documents - an Ensemble-based approach

Retrieval-Augmented Generation (RAG) is a mechanism to improve the performance of LLMs over longer contexts (Fan et al., 2024), by combining the powers of information retrieval and generative models. In this framework, long documents are partitioned into smaller units like sentences or paragraphs, which are converted into text vectors using an embedding language model. The vectors are stored in a knowledge library, from which components relevant to a given query are retrieved and passed on to the generative models for answer generation. RAG based frameworks are gaining popularity as they help generate more accurate, informed and contextually relevant outputs from local repositories.

We now present how the RAG framework is used along with the "cross-examination" motivated ensemble approach to generate answers from legal documents using LLMs. For question answering with LLMs, a key problem that needs to be addressed is to obtain some assurance about the quality of answers, especially since these models are known to generate out-of-context answers, which are sometimes outright wrong. To address this issue we propose the idea of creating an ensemble of legal questions in a controlled manner, using the legal ontology. Lawyers often examine witnesses by paraphrasing an earlier question. Rephrasing a questions helps test the consistency of a witness's testimony. Lawyers also pose clarification questions, wherein questions are formulated with the answers, and the witness has to verify its truth. This is used as a tool to reconfirm or disprove answers given by the witness. The proposed ensemble design is motivated by this idea of cross-examination.

It is assumed that the information components to be extracted from the legal documents are part of the legal ontology presented earlier. Thus each component not only has a definition, but is known to be constrained by its relationships with other concepts. For a given entity e, a set of questions $Q_p(e)$, which are paraphrases of each other, are generated using its definition from the ontology and an LLM prompt. The questions can also be generated using a mixture of human-paraphrasing and LLM-paraphrasing. Each question in $Q_p(e)$ is passed on to the LLM again for generating answers, this time with a specific legal document summary as the context. Further to paraphrasing, an added layer of confidence in the answers is derived through verification. This is done by creating a second set of questions, denoted by $Q_v(e)$, whose purpose is to verify the answers generated for questions in $Q_p(e)$. Let a_i denote the answer to a question $q_i \in Q_p(e)$. A verification question q_i^v is created for q_i to verify whether the answer a_i is supported by the document. Verification questions are designed as a prompt that will generate either "Yes" or "No" as answer, when the question is passed on to the LLM along with the document as context. A verification question typically looks like *Given the following context, is a_i true?* or *"Given the following context, does a_i follow q_i?"*. For a single question q, thus a multitude of answers is generated with multiple accesses to the LLM.

The above steps are followed for each information component to generate an ensemble of questions for each one of them. The legal document summaries generated in the earlier step, are now passed as context one at a time, along with the questions. Since the questions in $Q_p(q)$ ask the same thing in different ways, it is expected that if all the answers are similar, and each are verified to be correct by the second set of questions, then the answer is right. However, this does not provide an absolute guarantee. Answers to legal questions can be either objective or subjective. Asking about the appellant's name or gender, the police station under which a crime event was registered etc. are examples of objective answers. Subjective answers do not call for a fixed word composition, but need to convey the right sense. The measures defined below are used to determine similarity of two answers:

- ROUGE-L score: This is used to compute the similarity of two texts based on the Longest Common Subsequence (LCS) shared between them. LCS is the longest sequence of words that appear in both the candidate and reference summaries, while keeping the order of the words intact.
- METEOR (Metric for Evaluation of Translation with Explicit ORdering) Score: This metric is used for evaluating text generation. It considers synonyms, stemming (matching word roots) and paraphrases while computing similarity. This score reflects semantic similarities that are not captured by ROUGE-L. It calculates precision and recall, giving more weight to recall.
- BERT Cosine-similarity: This measures the cosine similarity of two texts based on their BERT embeddings, capturing the semantic similarity between the two texts.

Based on the definitions, it can be seen that ROUGE-L and METEOR help in verifying whether the expected key concepts are present in a machine-generated summary, while BERT cosine similarity measure captures the semantic similarity of two texts. While question answering is expected to work similarly whether it is done for full documents or document summaries, experiments show that the performance of the process is better for summaries. This could be due to the fact that summaries have almost no repetitions and hence provide easy context to the LLMs. Table 1 shows examples of paraphrased questions and sample answers along with verification questions and answers. The verification questions are automatically picked up from a set of templates curated for the purpose along with the corresponding text from answers returned by the LLM. It can be seen that, while the first and third answers overlap, the second one is not useful. The verification question also proves this.

3.3 Knowledge Graph generation and graph analytics

The extracted information from answers obtained from the questions discussed in Section 3.2 are used to populate a knowledge graph, that follows the legal ontology design presented earlier. The nodes in the knowledge graph represent different kinds of legal entities like case documents as well

Table 1: QA - Sample question and answers with Primary, Paraphrased and Verification questions

Primary Question	Answer	Verification Question	Ans.
Which legal principle, landmark judgment, or precedent was adhered to in the decision?	The Special Court designated under the Protection of Children from Sexual Offences (POCSO) Act has the exclusive power to deal with applications under Section 438 of the Code of Criminal Procedure (Cr.P.C.) related to offenses under the POCSO Act, even before registering an FIR.	Is *answer to question* correct from given context?	Yes
What guiding legal principle, significant case law, or past judicial precedent influenced the document?	Not available	Is it true that the legal principle, significant case law, or past judicial precedent influenced the ruling are *answer to question*?	No
Which principles, landmark judgments, or legal precedents are mentioned as reference points in the document?	Section 438 of Cr.P.C.	Is *answer to question* mentioned as legal principle, significant case law, or past judicial precedent which served as a reference point?	Yes

as laws and sections cited, names of defendants and accused entities along with their properties like age and gender, if retrieved. A set of people-people relations that are not a part of the ontology design and added to the knowledge graph based on the knowledge graph answers. Since LLM generated answers are rather verbose, and not fixed in nature, a named entity extractor is first applied to extract the legal entities from the answers. The extracted entities are then resolved document-wise, using the methods presented in (Kalamkar et al., 2022). For example, a particular statute may be referred to in a legal document multiple times, sometimes with its full name like *Indian Penal Code* and sometimes as *IPC*. A second level of resolution is needed to resolve the entity mentions across the documents, since only one instance of a named entity should be ideally retained in the knowledge graph. For inter-document entity resolutions, we apply a clustering algorithm that uses locality sensitive hashing (LSH) to group similar strings together. Querying a knowledge graph thereafter yields interesting insights about how cases, people or organizations, statutes etc. may be linked to each other.

4 Dataset Creation

We now present the details of the dataset that has been created for this work. This dataset was created keeping in mind an important application of legal text mining, namely analysis of crimes against children. According to National Crime Records Bureau (NCRB), India, 43.44% of POCSO cases end in no convictions due to lack of evidence (Nigudkar et al., 2023). It was also mentioned that only in about 6% of the cases involved an unfamiliar accused and victim pair. In almost 23% of cases, the victim and accused are known to each other, which includes an approximate estimate of 4% of cases where the accused is a family member. According to the NCRB report of 2022, out of 38,444 cases analyzed, 414 or 1% of the cases involved male victims, while the rest involved female victims. The results stated above were manually curated, and have not been updated for last three years. We belive that with proposed mechanisms, one can do these kind of analysis regularly in an automated way. To check the applicability and validity of the proposed framework for insight generation, a repository of 50 POCSO bail applications filed after 2020 has been created. These were collected from two sites eCourts India (2024) and Kanoon (2024). The second site also contains human-generated summaries for these applications, along with human annotations for various sections of the documents, which have been used for evaluation purposes. The questions were designed to extract insights like those mentioned by NCRB. The full list of questions is presented in Appendix 1 (10.1).

5 Experiments and Results

All experiments were done using the Langchain (Tian et al., 2023), (Muludi et al., 2024) platform which facilitates Retrieval-Augmented Generation. Results are provided for LLAMA 2 (Touvron, 2023) and GPT-3.5-Turbo (OpenAI, 2023). The details of evaluation and results obtained are presented in the following subsections. All experiments were run thrice and average results are presented.

5.1 Evaluation of LLM-generated summaries

For evaluating the summaries generated, two experiments were conducted. In the first experiment, GPT-3.5 and LLama 2 were deployed to generate summaries from the whole document. Though GPT 3.5 could generate the summaries, Llama

2 failed to generate summaries from the whole document. In the second experiment, the summaries were obtained using the proposed summary of summaries approach, using document chunks. The summaries were compared with original summaries and notes available in Kanoon (2024) using ROUGE-L, METEOR and BERT similarity scores. Table 2 shows the results obtained for both the experiments. Clearly summaries generated using the proposed summary of summaries approach fared better, when compared to human summaries. We conclude that the restricted context of a chunk helps it to pick up more relevant material for the final summary, than when it works on the entire document at one go. While the higher ROUGE-L scores indicate higher presence of actual legal terms in the second set, the higher BERT similarity scores indicate higher semantic similarity and the METEOR scores indicate lexical matching, semantic meaning, and content coverage. It is also observed that the free Llama2 model performs slightly better than the subscription based model GTP-3.5 Turbo. Compression ratio for a summary is obtained as

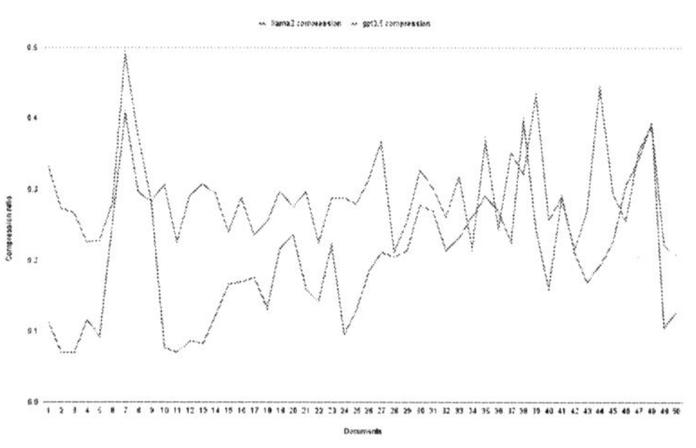

Figure 3: Compression Ratio: Number of tokens in Summary vs Original Document

the ratio of number of tokens in summary against the original document. GPT 3.5 Turbo consistently generates briefer summaries than LLAMA2. Figure 3 presents the compression ratio for the entire set for both the LLMs. The correlation between the results is 0.48, which is quite high.

Manual Assessment of Quality of Summaries: One of the key concerns expressed by legal professionals about automatically generated legal document summaries is the loss of rigour that is a characteristic of legal language. Since the rigor actually stems from the redundancy and repetition, which are dispensed off in a machine-generated, the summaries cannot be used as legal documents themselves, but can help in quick assimilation of content

Table 2: Average Scores for Generated Summaries from 50 Bail Documents for POCSO cases

Context	LLM	Rouge-L	BERT	METEOR
Full Document	GPT-3.5 turbo	0.17	0.80	0.24
Full Document	Llama2	-	-	-
Summary of Summaries	GPT-3.5 turbo	0.21	0.83	0.26
Summary of Summaries	LLAMA2	0.26	0.84	0.36

and answer legal questions posed by lawyers while doing their background research. For that purpose the summaries need to be factually correct in terms of all entities and their roles, cite the correct laws and statutes, be causally correct while reasoning about facts and arguments, and also be readable. Since this is an expert-intensive task, we could obtain expert evaluation for 25 summaries. The ones generated by Llama2 were selected for evaluation. The experts were requested to assign scores between 1 to 5, 1 being the lowest and 5 the highest on the following parameters (i). Correctness of facts (ii). Laws and Statutes (iii). Legal Language (iv). Reasoning correctness. Table 3 shows the average scores obtained.

Table 3: Evaluation Parameters and Averages

Parameters	LLAMA 2	GPT-3.5 turbo
Correctness of facts	3.66	3.2
Laws and Statutes	3.66	3.3
Legal Language	2.67	2.9
Reasoning correctness	3.33	3.25

5.2 Evaluation of Question Answering based Information Extraction

We now present evaluation scores for answers to the cross-examination comprising a set of 15 questions, along with their paraphrases and verification questions. For each question a gold-standard human answer was obtained from experts or from Kanoon (2024). The machine-generated answers of the paraphrased questions were compared with the human answers using ROUGE-L, BERT similarity and METEOR (Metric for Evaluation of Translation with Explicit ORdering) scores. Each of these scores were then multiplied by a factor of 1 or 0, depending on whether the corresponding verification answer was true / false. A weighted average was thereafter computed for each question, for each measure for each document. Figure 4 presents the ROUGE-L, BERT cosine similarity and METEOR scores for this set, averaged for all document summaries. It can be seen that the ROUGE-L scores are fairly consistent across all questions and both the LLMs, and much lower than the corresponding BERT scores. This is expected. However METEOR scores are almost similar in case of answers generated by LLAMA2 but are higher in case of answers generated by GPT 3.5. Figure 4 shows that GPT 3.5 generated answers in general score better than LLAMA2 for most questions, and particularly for those that need inferring, like questions 7 (about relationship between victim and accused), and 9 (whether accused is repeat offender). This also holds for questions 1 to 4, which though appear to be simple, need inferences to be drawn, as these may not be explicitly mentioned in the documents. LLAMA2 does a better job of identifying citations and section numbers etc. It may be surmised that since LLAMA 2 summaries were longer than GPT 3.5 Turbo summaries, they preserved information components better than the later.

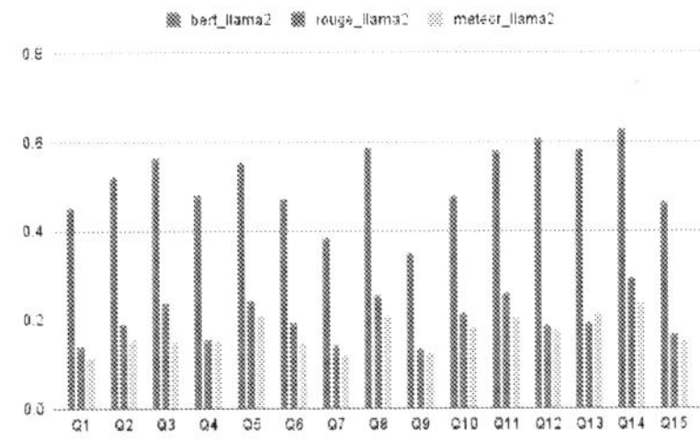

A. Scoring LLAMA2-generated answers against human answers

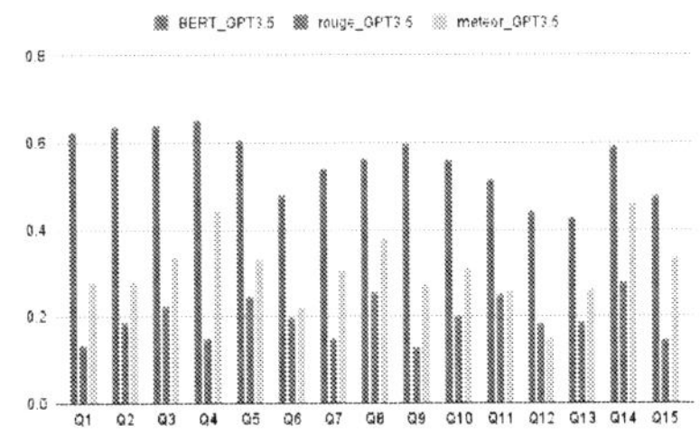

B. Scoring GPT-3.5 Turbo answers against human answers

Figure 4: Comparing LLM-generated Answers with human answers using BERT Similarity, METEOR, and ROUGE-L scores

5.3 Knowledge Graph from Legal Repository: Obtaining Insights from the graph

We have used the Neo4j (Neo4j, Inc., 2023) platform to store and query the knowledge graph generated from the current repository. Figure 5 shows a portion of the knowledge graph with case documents and their references to statutes and laws. For insight generation and analytics we query the graph database using graph query language CYPHER. Besides obtaining the most referred to laws and sections, the most important application of the knowledge graph is to find similar cases, where similar cases are those that might be discussing about similar crimes and hence referring to same or overlapping set of laws. Neo4J identifies similar nodes using a graph based similarity computation, which takes into account structural similarity. Figure 6 shows two such case documents which were inferred as similar. It was found that both these documents refer to similar sets of sections awarded for *gang rape*.

Among other insights found from the answers, we report that 5 out of the 50 cases, i.e. 10% of the cases involved male victims, which is higher than the figures reported earlier, and can be investigated further. Only 24% of the cases led to acquittal of the accused. A clique of 10 cases citing *Scheduled Castes and Scheduled Tribes Act*, suggest subjugation of marginalised section. In more than 50% of the cases, reference to Section 29, indicates that unlike other court proceedings which hinge on the accused's innocence till proved guilty, for POCSO cases, it is presumed that the accused has committed the offence, until contrary is proved. Degree analysis reveals that, most of the cases involved heinous crimes falling under Sections 3 and 5 of POCSO which deals with penetrative assault. Around 10 % cases involved handling of child pornography.

6 Conclusion

In this paper, we have explored how LLMs can be leveraged to perform legal text analytics. We have proposed an efficient mechanism to generate summaries for legal documents using LLMs, with no further training. We have also proposed a mechanism to generate a knowledge graph from a repository of case documents, using across-examination

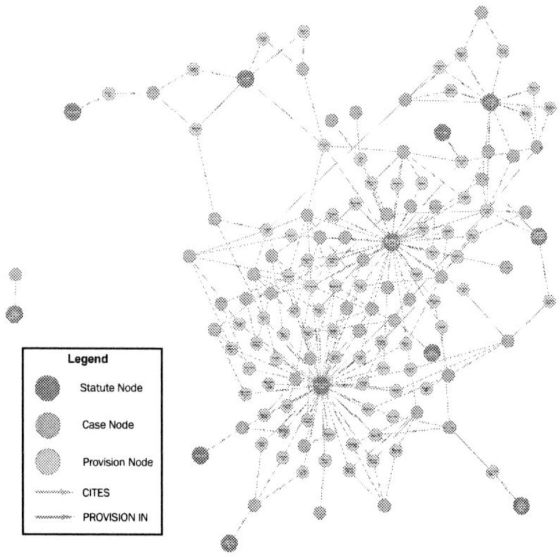

Figure 5: POCSO:citation Knowledge Graph

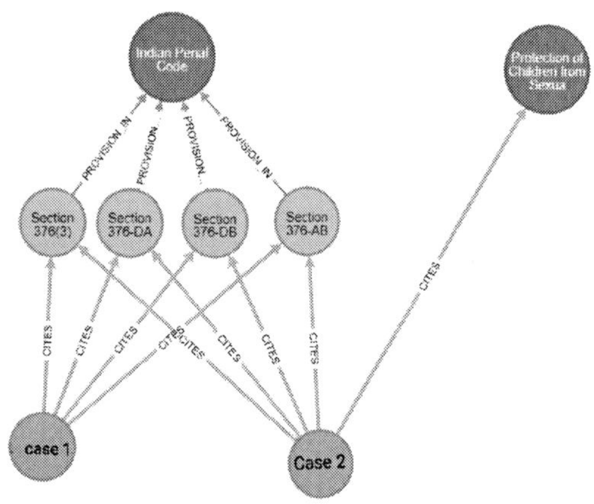

Figure 6: POCSO:citation Knowledge Graph

like technique of posing a set of questions and cross-verifying the answers. Going ahead, we intend to build a completely automated pipeline for legal document analytics and summarization. The dataset has been shared in Section 8. Along with building a large knowledge base, one aspect of research will be focused on automated evaluation of LLM-generated content. Validating the answers through external causal frameworks is also being explored.

7 Limitations

The novel approaches have been tested on a small dataset, so this needs to be thoroughly evaluated on a larger dataset.Going forward we plan to expand the dataset. Further, we plan to implement the pipeline on Large Language Models (LLMs) with larger context window size. Better evaluation scores and methods need to be evolved for legal text analytics.

8 Dataset- Link

The dataset can be found at this GitHub link.

9 Ethics Statement

Our research adheres to the ethical standards, ensuring data privacy by anonymizing all collected data and conducting a thorough bias analysis to mitigate potential harms. All data and dataset used and created are adopted from publicly available resources and adhering to the usage policy. All research paper, journals, websites used in the paper have been duly cited.

References

Garima Agrawal, Tharindu Kumarage, Zeyad Alghamdi, and Huan Liu. 2024. Can knowledge graphs reduce hallucinations in LLMs? : A survey. In *Proceedings of the 2024 Conference of the North American Chapter of the Association for Computational Linguistics: Human Language Technologies (Volume 1: Long Papers)*, pages 3947–3960, Mexico City, Mexico. Association for Computational Linguistics.

Paheli Bhattacharya, Shounak Paul, Kripabandhu Ghosh, Saptarshi Ghosh, and Adam Wyner. 2023. Deeprhole: deep learning for rhetorical role labeling of sentences in legal case documents. *Artificial Intelligence and Law*, pages 1–38.

Paheli Bhattacharya, Soham Poddar, Koustav Rudra, Kripabandhu Ghosh, and Saptarshi Ghosh. 2021. Incorporating domain knowledge for extractive summarization of legal case documents. pages 22–31.

Dinakaran Damodharan, Lakshmi Sravanti, R KiragasuruMadegowda, and John Vijay Sagar. 2021. The protection of children from sexual offences (pocso) act, 2012. *Forensic Psychiatry In India*, 66.

Aniket Deroy, Paheli Bhattacharya, Kripabandhu Ghosh, and Saptarshi Ghosh. 2021. *An Analytical Study of Algorithmic and Expert Summaries of Legal Cases.*

eCourts India. 2024. ecourts - services for indian judiciary. Accessed: October 10, 2024.

Mohamed Elaraby and Diane Litman. 2022. Arglegalsumm: Improving abstractive summarization of legal documents with argument mining. *arXiv preprint arXiv:2209.01650.*

Wenqi Fan, Yujuan Ding, Liangbo Ning, Shijie Wang, Hengyun Li, Dawei Yin, Tat-Seng Chua, and Qing Li. 2024. A survey on rag meeting llms: Towards retrieval-augmented large language models. In *Proceedings of the 30th ACM SIGKDD Conference on Knowledge Discovery and Data Mining*, pages 6491–6501.

Diego de Vargas Feijo and Viviane P Moreira. 2023. Improving abstractive summarization of legal rulings through textual entailment. *Artificial intelligence and law*, 31(1):91–113.

Neel Guha, Julian Nyarko, Daniel Ho, Christopher Ré, Adam Chilton, Alex Chohlas-Wood, Austin Peters, Brandon Waldon, Daniel Rockmore, and Diego Zambrano. 2024. Legalbench: A collaboratively built benchmark for measuring legal reasoning in large language models. *Advances in Neural Information Processing Systems*, 36.

Prathamesh Kalamkar, Astha Agarwal, Aman Tiwari, Smita Gupta, Saurabh Karn, and Vivek Raghavan. 2022. Named entity recognition in indian court judgments. *arXiv preprint arXiv:2211.03442*.

Indian Kanoon. 2024. Indian kanoon - search engine for indian law. Accessed: October 10, 2024.

Valentina Leone, Luigi Di Caro, and Serena Villata. 2020. Taking stock of legal ontologies: a feature based comparative analysis. *Artificial Intelligence and Law*, 28(2):207–235.

Patrick Lewis, Ethan Perez, Aleksandra Piktus, Fabio Petroni, Vladimir Karpukhin, Naman Goyal, Heinrich Küttler, Mike Lewis, Wen-tau Yih, Tim Rocktäschel, et al. 2020. Retrieval-augmented generation for knowledge-intensive nlp tasks. *Advances in Neural Information Processing Systems*, 33:9459–9474.

Manupatra. 2024. Manupatra - legal search engine. Accessed: 2024-05-31.

Andrei Marmor. 2014. *The language of law*. OUP Oxford.

Jorge Martinez-Gil. 2023. A survey on legal question–answering systems. *Computer Science Review*, 48:100552.

Gianluca Moro, Nicola Piscaglia, Luca Ragazzi, and Paolo Italiani. 2023. Multi-language transfer learning for low-resource legal case summarization. *Artificial Intelligence and Law*, pages 1–29.

Kurnia Muludi, Kaira Milani Fitria, and Joko Triloka. 2024. Retrieval-augmented generation approach: Document question answering using large language model. *International Journal of Advanced Computer Science & Applications*, 15(3).

Neo4j, Inc. 2023. Neo4j. Accessed: 2024-10-14.

Dr. Mohua Nigudkar, Dr. Upneet Lalli, and Soledad Herrero. 2023. Svp national police academy journal june, 2023 vol. lxxii, no. 1. *SVP National Police Academy Journal June, 2023 Vol. LXXII, No. 1*, page 246.

OpenAI. 2023. Gpt-3.5 turbo. https://openai.com/. Accessed: 2023-06-16.

Ernesto Quevedo, Tomas Cerny, Alejandro Rodriguez, Pablo Rivas, Jorge Yero, Korn Sooksatra, Alibek Zhakubayev, and Davide Taibi. 2023. Legal natural language processing from 2015-2022: A comprehensive systematic mapping study of advances and applications. *IEEE Access*.

SCC Online. 2024. Scc online - comprehensive legal research. Accessed: 2024-05-31.

Ying Tian, Tianyu Shi, Jerry Gao, and Luheng He. 2023. Langchain: A universal api for integrating language models. Accessed: 2024-06-16.

Oguzhan Topsakal and Tahir Cetin Akinci. 2023. Creating large language model applications utilizing langchain: A primer on developing llm apps fast. In *International Conference on Applied Engineering and Natural Sciences*, volume 1, pages 1050–1056.

Hugo Touvron. 2023. Llama 2: Open foundation and fine-tuned chat models. *Preprint*, arXiv:2307.09288.

Tom Van Engers, Alexander Boer, Joost Breuker, André Valente, and Radboud Winkels. 2008. Ontologies in the legal domain. *Digital Government: E-Government Research, Case Studies, and Implementation*, pages 233–261.

Valentin Zmiycharov, Milen Chechev, Gergana Lazarova, Todor Tsonkov, and Ivan Koychev. 2021. A comparative study on abstractive and extractive approaches in summarization of european legislation documents. In *Proceedings of the International Conference on Recent Advances in Natural Language Processing (RANLP 2021)*, pages 1645–1651.

10 Appendix

10.1 Appendix 1: Primary Questions along with two paraphrases of each.

Q1.1 What is the gender of the victim?

Q1.2 Please find the gender of the victim.

Q1.3 What gender does the victim identify as?

Q2.1 Is the victim a minor or not minor?

Q2.2 Please mention if the victim is legally considered a minor or not minor under the age of majority.

Q2.3 Does the victim's age classify them as being under the legal age of adulthood or not adult?

Q3.1 What is the gender of the accused?

Q3.2 Please find the gender of the accused.

Q3.3 What gender does the accused identify as?

Q4.1 Is the accused a minor or not minor?

Q4.2 Please mention if the accused is legally considered a minor or not minor under the age of majority.

Q4.3 Does the accused's age classify them as being under the legal age of adulthood?

Q5.1 Who filed the bail application?

Q5.2 Regarding the bail application, can you mention the name appellant?

Q5.3 Please mention the name who initiated the process of filing the bail application?

Q6.1 How is the appellant related to the accused?

Q6.2 Please mention the nature of the relationship between the appellant and the accused?

Q6.3 Please provide details on the connection between the appellant and the accused?

Q7.1 Was the accused known to the victim?

Q7.2 Did the victim have any prior acquaintance with the accused?

Q7.3 Was there any pre-existing familiarity between the victim and the accused?

Q8.1 Under which sections have the accused been booked?

Q8.2 Under what legal provisions was the accused charged?

Q8.3 What are the specific sections of the law under which the accused was implicated?

Q9.1 Has the accused committed repeat offense?

Q9.2 Has the accused engaged in a repeated offense?

Q9.3 Did the accused commit the same offense again?

Q10.1 Was bail granted to the accused?

Q10.2 Did the accused receive bail approval?

Q10.3 Was bail approval given to the accused?

Q11.1 What was the final decision of the judge for this application?

Q11.2 What was the final verdict of the judge for the case?

Q11.3 Did the judge finally grant bail to the accused for the case?

Q12.1 What were the judge's reasons for the decision?

Q12.2 What rationale did the judge provide for the verdict?

Q12.3 What were the judge's justifications for the ruling?

Q13.1 Which legal principle, landmark judgment, or precedent was adhered to in the decision?

Q13.2 What guiding legal principle, significant case law, or past judicial precedent influenced the document?

Q13.3 Which principles, landmark judgments, or legal precedents are mentioned as reference points in the document?

Q14.1 What jurisdiction does the case fall under?

Q14.2 In which jurisdiction does the case fall?

Q14.3 Under which jurisdiction does the case lie?

Q15.1 In which police station was the case reported?

Q15.2 At which police station was the case reported?

Q15.3 Where was the case reported to the police?

LLMs to the Rescue: Explaining DSA Statements of Reason with Platform's Terms of Services

Marco Aspromonte[1]
marco.aspromonte2@unibo.it

Andrea Filippo Ferraris[1]
andrea.ferraris3@unibo.it

Federico Galli[1,2]
federico.galli7@unibo.it

Giuseppe Contissa[1,2]
giuseppe.contissa@unibo.it

[1] **Alma AI, Alma Mater Studiorum, University of Bologna**
[2] Department of Legal Studies, Alma Mater Studiorum, University of Bologna

Abstract

The Digital Services Act (DSA) requires online platforms in the EU to provide "statements of reason" (SoRs) when restricting user content, but their effectiveness in ensuring transparency is still debated due to vague and complex terms of service (ToS). This paper explores the use of NLP techniques, specifically multi-agent systems based on large language models (LLMs), to clarify SoRs by linking them to relevant ToS sections. Analysing SoRs from platforms like Booking.com, Reddit, and LinkedIn, our findings show that LLMs can enhance the interpretability of content moderation decisions, improving user understanding and engagement with DSA requirements.

1 Introduction

The Digital Services Act (DSA), adopted by the European Union on November 1, 2022, represents a significant milestone in the EU regulation of online platforms, as it establishes a global standard for transparency and accountability in content moderation.

A key innovation of the DSA is the requirement for intermediary hosting services to provide "statements of reason" (SoRs) when restricting user-generated content (Article 17). The SoR must specify the action taken, the factual circumstances, any use of automated systems in the moderation process, and the legal or contractual grounds for deeming the content illegal or incompatible with the platform's terms of service (ToS), along with an explanation and other metadata. It should also inform users of available redress options, ensuring clarity and precision to allow users to contest the decision.

Article 24(5) further requires online platforms to submit SoRs, as outlined in Article 17, to the European Commission for inclusion in a publicly accessible, machine-readable database. In response to this mandate, the European Commission launched the DSA Transparency Database (TD) in September 2023.

The scheme of the TD roughly reflects the content of the SoR pursuant to Article 17.[1] Each SoR instance is composed of several mandatory attributes, such as the content type (e.g. text, image, etc.) and language, the type and period of restriction, the ground for the decision, the category of restricted content, the fact relied upon on the decision, etc. Attribute values are to be selected by the provider from a list of options or can be typed into as free text (generally with character limitations). Other attributes are only optional. As for the ground for the provider's decision (field "decision_ground"), the TD presents only two possible options: `"ILLEGAL_CONTENT"` and `"INCOMPATIBLE_CONTENT"`. Moreover, the TD typifies 14 distinct "categories" of statements as potential grounds for restriction (see Table 1).

The TD is intended as a critical tool for scrutinizing content moderation practices, revealing how well platforms comply with the requirements set by the DSA. However, the effectiveness of the TD in fulfilling its promises of transparency and accountability remains a subject of ongoing debate (Trujillo et al., 2024; Kaushal et al., 2024). In particular, there are doubts about whether the SoR provides sufficient information to allow users to understand the reasons for content restriction and to contest its lawfulness. This is especially true when it comes to the asserted incompatibility with ToS. These are often lengthy and complex documents

[1] Available at: transparency.dsa.ec.

Proceedings of the Natural Legal Language Processing Workshop 2024, pages 205–215
November 16, 2024

(Melinat et al., 2014) drafted in legal jargon (Butt, 2001), and the complexity and lack of understanding and awareness of legal texts of this kind is an old and well-known issue (Masson and Waldron, 1994).

Given this background, the present paper explores the potential of NLP techniques, particularly multi-agent systems based on large language models (LLMs), to enhance the transparency and user-friendliness of SoRs submitted to the TD. We propose and evaluate a method that uses LLMs to contextualise explanations in SoRs related to ToS incompatibility within the platform's content policy guidelines. Our focus on ToS incompatibility stems from its frequency as the main reason for content removal and its suitability for uniform LLM-based analysis, unlike removals based on national laws, which vary across the EU and add complexity. ToS, being unique to each platform, offer a more consistent and manageable basis for explanation.

2 Background

Our work builds on and merges three emerging research strands: 1) existing works applying computational techniques to analyse the DSA Transparency Report; 2) the application of NLP techniques to enhance accessibility and legibility of transparency legal requirements; 3) the use of LLMs in the legal field.

2.1 Computational Analysis of DSA Transparency Database

Since the launch of the DSA Transparency Database, several studies have used computational methods to analyze and extract aggregated insights from its data. The database contains vast amounts of raw data on content moderation practices by online platforms, making automated tools essential for understanding its contents effectively.

For instance, Drolsbach et al. (Drolsbach and Pröllochs, 2024) examined 156 million SoRs over two months, highlighting content restrictions categorized under "Scope of Platform Service" (49.06%), reflecting ambiguities in this classification. Similarly, another work (Trujillo et al., 2024) analysed 195 million SoRs, incorporating cross-references with Article 15 Transparency Reports[2]. They found inconsistencies across platforms like TikTok, YouTube, and Snapchat.

[2] Article 15 of the DSA mandates annual transparency reports from platforms on content moderation actions and their justifications.

A key related study (Kaushal et al., 2024) to our paper analysed a representative sample of the Transparency Database (131m SoRs) submitted in November 2023 to evaluate platform content moderation practices. They provided several findings, such as the prevalence of SoR reported as ToS violations (99.8%) compared to illegal content (0.2%). They show that all (99.9%) of ToS violations do not report the URL to the relevant platforms' ToS. With regard to ToS, they also point to a critical lack of precision in stating the "fact underlying the decision", namely the motivation of the decision taken. This does not generally allow users to identify what elements of their content are violating norms, leading to restriction.

Overall, current research indicates that online platforms heavily rely on their ToS as the basis for content restriction decisions, which is, per se, compliant with the DSA. However, when content is deemed incompatible with the ToS, the communication often lacks specificity, providing only a generic statement without a clear reference to the exact grounds for removal. In our study, we investigate whether NLP techniques can be employed to link ToS to the relevant sections of online platforms' ToS or content guidelines, thereby giving users more detailed information about the reasons for content restrictions.

2.2 NLP for Legal Transparency Enhancement

NLP offers significant potential for enhancing transparency and regulatory compliance in the legal domain (Thimm, 2023; Cejas et al., 2023). By automating the analysis and generation of complex legal texts, NLP can improve business compliance, reduce human errors and improve the clarity of legal communications (Katz et al., 2023). This capability is particularly valuable in contexts where legal requirements are intricate and frequently updated - such as the digital environment - ensuring that organisations can maintain compliance consistently and transparently (Zhou et al., 2022).

For example, NLP can be employed to automatically extract relevant clauses from regulatory documents and cross-reference them with a company's internal policies to ensure alignment with legal standards (Bizzaro et al., 2024; Hendrycks et al., 2021). In another scenario, NLP tools can analyse public statements or contractual terms to identify potential legal risks and unfair clauses and enable proactive compliance management (Lippi et al., 2019).

Furthermore, NLP can play a crucial role by making complex legal language more accessible to users (Garimella et al., 2022). Automated systems can translate intricate legal jargon into plain language, helping users understand the rationale behind moderation decisions and, if necessary, challenge those decisions effectively. This not only enhances user engagement but also builds trust in platform governance by providing transparency into the legal reasoning that underpins content moderation.

2.3 LLMs for Legal Applications

LLMs are rapidly transforming legal practice by automating complex tasks such as interpreting legal texts, generating documents, and providing preliminary legal advice (Qin and Sun, 2024; Yang et al., 2024; Martin et al., 2024). These models are particularly valuable in domains that involve the processing of large volumes of intricate and nuanced language, offering the potential to significantly enhance both transparency and understandability, and efficiency in various legal processes.

The application of LLMs is notably expanding across various legal domains. They are increasingly employed to draft legal documents that comply with specific regulatory requirements (Lin and Cheng, 2024), automate the extraction of relevant clauses from extensive legal texts (Bizzaro et al., 2024), and even predict the outcomes of legal disputes based on historical data (de Menezes-Neto and Clementino, 2022). This growing interest highlights the transformative role LLMs can play in streamlining legal processes, which are traditionally reliant on significant human expertise and time.

In the context of content moderation, LLMs show considerable promise as tools both for supporting platforms in their content moderation activity (Kumar et al., 2024; Kolla et al., 2024) as well as for helping users understand and, if necessary, challenge platform decisions (Guan et al., 2023). By analysing Statements of Reason provided when content is removed or restricted, LLMs can leverage their advanced NLP capabilities to interpret SoRs and assess whether moderation actions comply with the DSA and platform-specific ToS (Atreja et al., 2023).

3 Data

For this study, we compiled a custom dataset using resources from the DSA Transparency Database.

We focused on Statements of Reasons (SoRs) specifically related to content removal due to violations of terms of services (ToS) from three major online platform providers: Booking.com, Reddit, and LinkedIn. This selection was made to capture a diverse range of online environments. Booking.com, as a leading e-commerce platform in the travel industry, provides insights into ToS enforcement concerning commercial content; Reddit, a large social media forum, illustrates content moderation challenges in a user-generated, community-driven space; and LinkedIn, a professional networking platform, reflects ToS enforcement in a setting focused on professional conduct and business communication. This approach enables a comprehensive examination of SoRs across platforms with varying purposes, user bases, and content policies.

To ensure a representative sample, we selected SoRs from a specific time frame, spanning from March 2024 to August 2024.

The content of each SoR consists of four key attributes included in the TD, which are intended to provide context for explaining the decision that affects users' content. The attributes are the UUID, the ground for incompatible content (`"incompatible_content_ground"`), the explanation for incompatible content (`"incompatible_content_explanation"`) and the facts relevant for the decision (`"decision_facts"`).

We did not rely on the current versions of the ToS available on the platforms' websites, as they may overlook regulatory changes or evolving industry standards that could impact the interpretation of the SoRs. Using the historical ToS in force at the time the SoRs were issued was crucial, as relying on updated versions could render certain SoRs outdated or irrelevant.

The selected dataset consists of 7000 SoRs, among which 3000 were issued by Booking.com, 2000 by LinkedIn and 2000 by Reddit.

Figure 1 shows the distribution of the selected SoRs across the three online platforms and the 14 typified restrictions, while Table 1 represents the pairs between each category and its acronym. LinkedIn and Booking.com have high scores in the "Scope of Platform Service" (SOPS) category, reflecting their specific and well-defined content purposes. Booking.com also shows a high number of SoRs for "Data Protection and Privacy Violations" (DPAPV) due to its frequent handling of sensitive user data.

Reddit scores highest in "Non-Consensual Be-

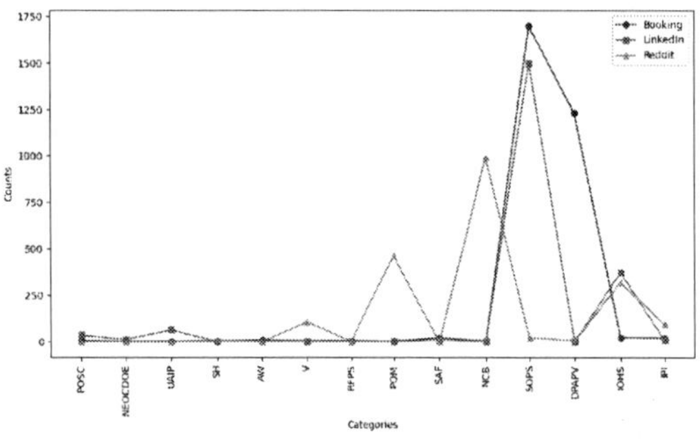

Figure 1: Distribution of categories in linear scale

Category	Acronym
PORNOGRAPHY_OR_SEXUALIZED_CONTENT	POSC
NEGATIVE_EFFECTS_ON_CIVIC_DISCOURSE_OR_ELECTIONS	NEOCDOE
UNSAFE_AND_ILLEGAL_PRODUCTS	UAIP
SELF_HARM	SH
ANIMAL_WELFARE	AW
VIOLENCE	V
RISK_FOR_PUBLIC_SECURITY	RFPS
PROTECTION_OF_MINORS	POM
SCAMS_AND_FRAUD	SAF
NON_CONSENSUAL_BEHAVIOUR	NCB
SCOPE_OF_PLATFORM_SERVICE	SOPS
DATA_PROTECTION_AND_PRIVACY_VIOLATIONS	DPAPV
ILLEGAL_OR_HARMFUL_SPEECH	IOHS
INTELLECTUAL_PROPERTY_INFRINGEMENTS	IPI

Table 1: Categories and Their Acronyms

havior" (NCB), likely due to its large, diverse user base and the anonymity it offers, which can lead to issues like doxxing, harassment, and the unauthorised sharing of personal information. On the contrary, categories such as Animal Welfare (AW), Self-Harm (SH), and Risk for Public Security (RFPS) have relatively low SoR frequencies across all platforms, as these are less common restrictions in the contexts analysed. Overall, Reddit addresses the most diverse harmful content, while LinkedIn and Booking.com focus on specific issues related to their platform's nature.

In addition to the Statements of Reasons (SoRs), we collected the relevant Terms of Service (ToS) in effect when the selected SoRs were issued to understand the basis for content removals. We relied on both the ToS, as the binding contract, and the community guidelines, which provide additional context for applying the ToS. Though not part of the formal contract, community guidelines are valuable as they offer practical interpretations of the ToS. Integrating both allowed us to better align the explanations of content removals with their intended meaning and scope, providing context that might be missing from the ToS alone.

Both the ToS and community guidelines were pre-processed to extract relevant content moderation clauses, enabling the LLM to match them with the SoRs for more accurate and contextually relevant explanations of the moderation decisions.

4 Architecture and Methods

The proposed architecture is based on a multi LLM-based-agent system (Guo et al., 2024) and a Retrieval-Augmented Generation (RAG) process (Gao et al., 2024). It employs two autonomous LLM-based agents, each assigned specific roles: the "Refiner Agent" and the "Explainer Agent". These agents operate independently, coordinating their actions to process and interpret platform documents (ToS and SoRs), enhancing both the accuracy and contextual relevance of the system's output. Through this division of tasks and inter-agent interaction, our approach aligns with the principles of multi-agent systems by enabling collaborative decision-making and specialised behaviour.

We tested the agent-based architecture with two pre-trained LLMs: `"Mistral-7b-instruct-v0.3"` (Jiang et al., 2023), and `"Gpt4o-mini"` [3]. During each test run, only one of these models is used, enabling a direct comparison of their outputs. Each model is independently evaluated for its ability to interpret retrieved documents, refine them, and generate expert-like explanations.

The Mistral-7b model was used in an optimised version with 4-bit quantisation, which allows it to handle complex prompts efficiently while minimising memory usage. This makes it suitable for resource-constrained environments (Pan et al., 2023). On the other hand, the GPT4o-mini model has a unique architecture that adds additional depth and nuance to the evaluation process.

These models were integrated into the architecture using the Hugging Face Transformers library [4] for the Mistral model and the OpenAI API for the GPT4o-mini model. This integration enables comprehensive performance assessments across different computational scenarios. By combining the transparency and replicability of open-source models with the enhanced performance of proprietary models, this dual approach facilitates a thorough comparison of the models' effectiveness in interpreting and evaluating content moderation actions.

The architecture is hosted on a public GitHub

[3]See: Gpt-4o-mini-OpenAI
[4]See: huggingface.co

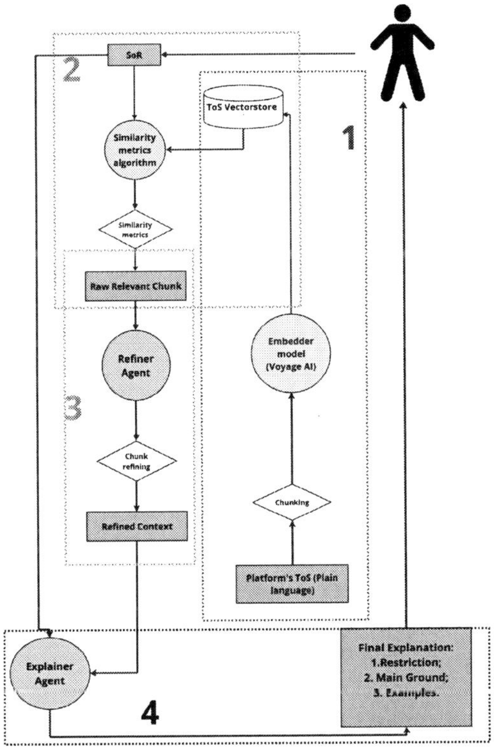

Figure 2: Visual representation of the pipeline

repository [5] and is presented in Figure 2, and it is divided into 4 modules, each marked with a coloured box and pairing number.

- Module 1 (blue): Vector Store Creation;
- Module 2 (red): Retriever and similarity;
- Module 3 (green): Agentic refinement;
- Module 4 (black): Agentic explanation.

We analyse each module in the following subsections.

4.1 Vector Store Creation

The first module, computed once for each online platform provider, is designed to create a chunked version of the relevant ToS. We achieved this by dividing the ToS into chunks, ensuring each chunk corresponds to a complete paragraph or section, thereby preserving the text's original structure and semantic meaning.

We then initialised an embedding model using `VoyageAIEmbeddings`[6], which converts the text into high-dimensional vectors within a dense vector space to effectively capture its semantic meaning. Specifically, we utilised the `Voyage-2-Law` large pre-trained embedding model,[7] which is tailored for legal texts. We opted for Voyage-2-Law over general-purpose models because it is specifically trained on legal documents, enabling it to capture the nuances and context of legal language more accurately.

The generated embeddings were stored in the open-source vector database, Chroma DB (Chroma).[8] These chunked ToS serve as a knowledge base, facilitating the retrieval of relevant sections of the ToS in relation to a given SoR.

4.2 Retriever and Similarity

The primary goal of this module is to extract from the database all ToS chunks that are relevant to the given SoR. It begins by analysing the SoR and focuses on retrieving the most semantically relevant chunks from the vector store. To achieve this, we adopted a hybrid approach[9], combining Cosine Similarity metrics (a semantic-based method) (Lahitani et al., 2016) with the Probabilistic Relevance framework (specifically, BM25) (Robertson and Zaragoza, 2009).

We selected the top two results from each method and merged them into a single file consisting of a list of chunks (referred to as "Raw Relevant Chunks" in 2). To avoid redundancy, we opted to filter out the identical chunks from the file "Raw Relevant Chunks" in case the chunks retrieved using Cosine Similarity overlap with those obtained via BM25. This process results in a list that may contain only two chunks. The file is then passed to the next module, the Agentic Refiner, for further processing.

4.3 Agentic Refinement

The third module focuses on refining the chunks extracted by the second module to streamline and optimise the information that will be provided to the agent responsible for generating the user explanation. Following a novel approach explored by Xu et al. (2024), we employ the first LLM-based agent to refine the chunks obtained from the previous module.

[5]See: framework's GitHub repository
[6]See: `https://www.voyageai.com/`
[7]See: Voyage-2-Law overview
[8]See: `https://github.com/chroma-core/chroma`
[9]See: Hybrid Search: Combining BM25 and Semantic Search

In this module, the agent is provided with the target SoR and the "Raw relevant chunks". Using techniques of prompt engineering (Sahoo et al., 2024), the agent is instructed to extract only the information from the raw chunks that directly relates to the target SoR, removing any irrelevant content and eliminating noise that may be present in the raw data.[10]

4.4 Agentic Explanation

The fourth and final module, the Agentic Explanation module, is responsible for explaining the SoR in relation to the platform's ToS. Drawing on the work of Feng et al. (2023), which highlights the effectiveness of large language models (LLMs) in rephrasing and simplifying complex legal texts, this module utilizes the SoR and the refined sections of the ToS to link the moderation action to the platform's contractual justifications.

The output provides a structured explanation to enhance users' understanding of the legal grounds for content moderation. The agent situates the SoR within the platform's policy framework by identifying the ground or rule that the content violated (rule-based explanation) and offering examples to demonstrate how the ground applies to different forms of content (explanation by example) (van der Waa et al., 2021).

It is important to note that this kind of explanation does not extend to the platform's internal decision-making process or the criteria used to assess a particular content for restriction. This limitation is due to the fact that the TD does not provide data on the actual moderated content. As a result, the agent cannot explain why a particular piece of content was deemed problematic under the platform's rules or account for any contextual factors influencing the moderation decision. Nonetheless, the output can still help users who are already familiar with the content in question to better understand the reasons behind the restriction.

5 Validation

The validation process focuses on evaluating the performance of two LLM-based agents: the "Refiner", which extracts relevant sections from the ToS, and the "Explainer", which aims to clarify the content of a SoR in light of the relevant platform's ToS.

A human evaluation approach was chosen to assess the quality of the outputs generated by both agents. Human evaluation was selected due to its capacity to provide a nuanced and contextual assessment that goes beyond what current automated metrics can offer (Chang et al., 2024). It allows for more accurate and comprehensive feedback on semantic and qualitative aspects of the generated responses, which is particularly important with legal content.

The evaluation process was designed to achieve statistical significance, ensuring that the results are robust and credible. In particular, we observed that, within each provider, the SoRs pertaining to the same category are remarkably similar in their formulation. Given this high degree of standardisation or consistency per category, we selected one representative sample from each category per online platform.

The criteria for validating the outputs of the two agents were based on four key metrics, each rated on a 1-to-5 scale:

1. **Relevance**: Assesses whether the output is appropriate and significant with regard to the Statement of Reasons (SoR) and the refined ToS. High scores indicate that the refined content is directly relevant to the SoR/refined ToS, while lower scores suggest a lack of alignment or relevance.

2. **Accuracy**: Evaluates whether all relevant arguments and information from the original ToS (for the "Refiner") and the refined ToS (for the "Explainer") are retained. A high score reflects comprehensive retention, whereas a low score indicates omissions.

3. **Coherence**: Measures the consistency of the output with the original ToS intent. Under this metric, the "Refiner" is evaluated in terms of linguistic coherence, namely its capacity to faithfully represent original text. The "Explainer" is assessed in terms of its capacity not to hallucinate and introduce meanings and examples which are not directly taken by the refined ToS. Higher scores signify that the output faithfully reflects the original content without modification/hallucination.

4. **Readability** (specific to the "explainer"

[10]The prompt includes specific instructions to the model, detailing the background and context for evaluation. It ensures that the model considers the statement of reason provided by the platform, the relevant sections of the ToS, and the legal framework context outlined in Article 17.

agent): Assesses the clarity and ease of understanding of the generated explanations. Higher scores suggest that the output is easy to read, with a smooth flow and consistent tone and style.

The evaluation was conducted by a panel of three independent human evaluators, each with specialised expertise in content moderation practices and regulatory compliance under the DSA[11].

6 Experimental Results

This section presents the experimental results obtained from evaluating the two LLM-based agents, the "Refiner Agent" and the "Explainer Agent", using the selected pre-trained models: "Mistral-7b-instruct-v0.3" and "GPT4o-mini".

Table 2 summarises the performance metrics for the Refiner Agent across the different criteria and analysed platforms.

The Explainer Agent was evaluated separately to measure its effectiveness in providing user-friendly explanations that contextualise the legal reasons behind content moderation decisions. Table 3 shows the performance metrics for the Explainer Agent.

The scores (1-5) were averaged for both agents, outlining a global statistical significance and providing a clear comparison of the models' outputs.

Platform	Model	Relevance	Accuracy	Coherence
Booking.com	GPT4o-mini	**4.69**	3.84	4.38
Booking.com	Mistral-7b	4.07	**4.28**	4.5
Reddit	GPT4o-mini	4.45	3.80	4.60
Reddit	Mistral-7b	4.0	4.05	4.5
LinkedIn	GPT4o-mini	4.56	4.0	**4.68**
LinkedIn	Mistral-7b	3.81	3.75	4.37

Table 2: Results for Refiner Agent across platforms

Platform	Model	Relevance	Accuracy	Coherence	Readability
Booking.com	GPT4o-mini	**4.85**	4.57	**4.85**	4.71
Booking.com	Mistral-7b	4.71	**4.73**	4.14	4.9
Reddit	GPT4o-mini	4.71	4.12	4.62	**5.0**
Reddit	Mistral-7b	4.7	3.8	4.2	4.73
LinkedIn	GPT4o-mini	4.0	4.4	4.7	4.8
LinkedIn	Mistral-7b	4.75	4.0	4.12	4.62

Table 3: Results for Explainer Agent across Platforms

We used standard deviation to quantify the variability in the scores provided by different evaluators across the relevant metrics. To facilitate comparison across different metrics and model/platforms, we also normalised the standard deviation values to a range a range [0, 1].

[11]The dataset and the evaluation results can be found at the following GitHub repository: `https://github.com/sustaz/DAFNE_4_NLLP`

Table 4 and Table 5 present the standard deviation values across the different criteria per model-platform, respectively for the Refiner and the Explainer Agent. The lower variability scores show the higher inter-annotator agreement.

Platform	Model	Relevance	Accuracy	Coherence
Booking	gpt4mini	**0.29**	0.43	0.30
Booking	mistral-7b	0.58	**0.41**	0.46
Reddit	gpt4mini	0.31	0.49	**0.23**
Reddit	mistral-7b	0.43	0.47	0.25
LinkedIn	gpt4mini	0.39	0.47	0.34
LinkedIn	mistral-7b	0.46	0.47	0.43

Table 4: Standard Deviation for Refiner Agent

Platform	Model	Relevance	Accuracy	Coherence	Readability
Booking	gpt4mini	0.30	0.38	0.41	0.30
Booking	mistral-7b	0.30	0.44	0.44	0.51
Reddit	gpt4mini	**0.00**	0.36	**0.22**	**0.27**
Reddit	mistral-7b	0.25	0.40	0.20	0.39
LinkedIn	gpt4mini	0.40	**0.28**	0.23	**0.27**
LinkedIn	mistral-7b	0.43	0.49	0.42	0.47

Table 5: Standard Deviation for Explainer Agent

7 Discussion

We detail the discussion in the subsections below, separately for the two agents and then comparatively on the performance of the two models.

7.1 Refiner Agent Results

The Refiner Agent was evaluated on relevance, accuracy, and coherence. The results across platforms show notable differences between the two LLM models used — `GPT4o-mini` and `Mistral-7b`.

For relevance, `GPT4o-mini` generally outperformed Mistral-7b across all platforms, achieving the highest scores on Booking.com (4.69) and LinkedIn (4.56), with strong evaluator agreement indicated by low standard deviations (0.29 on Booking.com and 0.23 on Reddit). This indicates gpt4o-mini's ability to retrieve the most relevant sections of the ToS for the given Statement of Reasons (SoR). Mistral-7b, though slightly lower in relevance scores, still performed consistently, particularly on Booking.com (4.07) and Reddit (4.0).

Accuracy scores demonstrate that Mistral-7b surpassed GPT4o-mini in most cases, particularly on Booking.com (4.28) and Reddit (4.05). This suggests that Mistral-7b performed better at retaining and faithfully representing the necessary arguments from the original ToS. However, the higher standard deviations for Mistral-7b in coherence (0.46 on Booking.com and 0.43 on LinkedIn) suggest more inconsistent outputs in terms of logical structure and clarity. Also, on LinkedIn, GPT4o-mini performed better (4.0), possibly due to the platform's more structured and formal ToS, which may have aligned better with its training data.

In terms of coherence, GPT4o-mini again showed stronger results, particularly on LinkedIn (4.68) and Reddit (4.6), suggesting its capacity to maintain a logical flow in refining the ToS. Mistral-7b was slightly lower but still consistent, scoring 4.5 on both Booking.com and Reddit.

7.2 Explainer Agent Results

The Explainer Agent was evaluated on four metrics: relevance, accuracy, coherence, and readability. Similar trends emerged across the platforms, with GPT4o-mini showing the strongest performance in most categories, particularly in readability.

For relevance, GPT4o-mini achieved the highest scores, especially on Booking.com (4.85) and Reddit (4.71), with perfect evaluator agreement on Reddit (0.00). Mistral-7b performed comparably well on Booking.com (4.71) and Reddit (4.7) and even surpassed GPT4o-mini on LinkedIn (4.75), but with the highest variability in terms of inter-annotator agreement.

Accuracy scores followed a similar trend, with Mistral-7b outperforming GPT4o-mini on Booking.com (4.73), but showing greater variability in readability with higher standard deviations on LinkedIn (0.47) and Booking.com (0.51). However, GPT4o-mini performed better on Reddit (4.12) and LinkedIn (4.4), with the lowest deviations between annotators (0.27), again suggesting its effectiveness in explaining less complex ToS.

All in all, the Explainer Agent, both with GPT4o-mini and Mistral-7b, scores higher in accuracy than the Refiner Agent. This suggests that, although it is useful for reducing context to explain the SoR with ToS, the refinement exercise may lead to the loss of information needed to provide a faithful explanation.

Coherence, i.e. whether the explanation logically connects the SoR to the ToS, showed GPT4o-mini excelling, particularly on Booking.com (4.85) and Reddit (4.62). This indicates the model's capability to provide clear, structured reasoning without introducing extraneous information.

In terms of readability, GPT4o-mini scored particularly high, achieving a perfect score on Reddit (5.0) and 4.71 on Booking.com. This suggests that GPT4o-mini generates explanations that are easier to read and understand, which is crucial for users engaging with the platform. Mistral-7b also performed well in readability, particularly on Booking.com (4.9), but showed a drop on Reddit (4.73), indicating slightly less user-friendly outputs.

The Box 7.2 portrays an example of an explanation of a Reddit's SoR produced with Mistral-7B.

Explanation Example

RESTRICTION: Your content was restricted because it violated Rule 3 of the platform's Terms and Conditions.
MAIN GROUND: The main ground for the restriction is the sharing of intimate or sexually-explicit media of someone without their consent.
EXAMPLE: Examples of content that the Platform may remove under this ground include:
- Images or videos of intimate parts of a person's body, even if the person is clothed or in public, if contextualized in a salacious manner (such as "creepshots" or "upskirt" imagery).
- Fake or "lookalike" depictions of intimate media.
- Leaked, stolen, or privately-shared content of someone who does not consent to sharing it on Reddit.
- Images or video of another person posted for the specific purpose of faking explicit content or soliciting "lookalike" pornography (e.g. "deepfakes" or "bubble porn").

7.3 Models Comparative Evaluation

Across the two agentic tasks, gpt4o-mini generally outperforms Mistral-7b across most metrics, particularly in relevance, coherence, and readability. This performance is further supported by lower standard deviations in these metrics, indicating greater consistency in GPT4o-mini's outputs. This can likely be attributed to gpt4o-mini's advanced architecture, which better handles the structured legal language in the ToS, making it well-suited for user-facing applications where clarity and accessibility are essential.

Mistral-7b, on the other hand, excels in accuracy, faithfully retaining details from the original ToS. This makes Mistral-7b a promising tool for tasks like legal document processing or back-end content moderation, where accuracy is key. However, Mistral-7b showed higher standard deviations in readability (e.g., 0.51 on Booking.com and 0.47 on LinkedIn), suggesting more variability in its user-friendliness.

Platform-specific variations further underscore

the importance of ToS. For example, gpt4o-mini performed better on LinkedIn due to the structured nature of its ToS, while Mistral-7b excelled on Booking.com, where detailed ToS favoured accuracy.

Overall, both models produced useful outputs. Gpt4o-mini delivered more coherent and user-friendly explanations, which is ideal for front-end roles, while Mistral-7b prioritised accuracy, making it reliable for back-end tasks.

8 Limitations

We acknowledge a few limitations in our study, many of which stem from the inherent limitations of the DSA Transparency Database.

One major constraint is the absence of direct links or detailed descriptions of the moderated content. This limitation affects our system's ability to provide fact-specific explanations for content removal decisions. Instead, the model is forced to generate more generic, rule-based, or example-based explanations, which, despite their usefulness, can limit users' ability to fully understand how their content violated the platform's TOS.

Another limitation is the lack of multilingual testing. The models have only been tested on English-language data, as the database contains no non-English SoRs. Multilingual support is essential for broader applicability, especially across the EU.

Lastly, the system has not been evaluated on other platforms, which may provide different contexts for content restrictions and reasons for ToS violations. Such differences may impact the models' performance, and future work should address this by testing on more varied scenarios.

9 Conclusion and Future Work

This study demonstrated the potential of large language models, like GPT4o-mini and Mistral-7b, in enhancing transparency and user comprehension in content moderation decisions under the DSA.

However, challenges remain, particularly in handling the complexity of legal texts. LLMs struggle with nuanced, context-specific legal language (Homoki and Ződi, 2024), as the one used in ToS, as well as accuracy issues regarding reliance on static datasets, which may become outdated (Jayakumar et al., 2023).

Moreover, the "black box" nature of LLMs, where the decision-making process is opaque, poses a significant challenge in legal contexts (Lin et al., 2024). In legal applications, where the rationale behind decisions must be clear and defensible (Rotolo and Sartor, 2023), the inability to trace or explain the reasoning of LLMs undermines their reliability.

A valuable direction for future work is conducting an ablation study to better understand the contributions of various components in our system, particularly the role of the Refiner Agent. Preliminary results indicate that the Refiner Agent performs with slightly lower accuracy than the final model, prompting a closer examination of its role.

From a legal point of view, we intend to expand our work by linking the agentic explanations to more refined legal grounds for content removal contained in the ToS, possibly attaching them to relevant regulatory frameworks. The potential is not merely to provide an explanation of content restriction but also the legal justification to challenge the platform's decision.

10 Ethical Statement

There are several ethical strengths to our work. Data contained in the TD are anonymised. So, no personal data processing is involved in the study. The focus on explainability and transparency aims to empower platforms' users to better understand content moderation decisions in the context of ToS, possibly supporting their right to challenge the decision, contest the legality of ToS and seek redress.

Ethical concerns are related to the system's accuracy. Limited detail in platform reports can result in vague explanations. In some cases, the AI may "hallucinate" by generating incorrect or invented information which does not reflect the ToS content. These issues could mislead users and negatively impact their ability to effectively appeal decisions, potentially undermining their right to remedy.

Acknowledgement

This research was supported by the PRIN 2022 PNRR Project DAFNE (Democratic governance of Automated systems for Fake NEws, GA. P2022R7RS9) under the MUR National Recovery and Resilience Plan funded by the European Union – Next Generation EU.

References

Shubham Atreja, Jane Im, Paul Resnick, and Libby Hemphill. 2023. Appealmod: Shifting effort from moderators to users making appeals. *arXiv preprint arXiv:2301.07163*.

Pietro Giovanni Bizzaro, Elena Della Valentina, Maurizio Napolitano, Nadia Mana, and Massimo Zancanaro. 2024. Annotation and classification of relevant clauses in terms-and-conditions contracts. *Preprint*, arXiv:2402.14457.

Peter Butt. 2001. Legalese versus plain language. *Amicus Curiae*, 35:28.

Orlando Amaral Cejas, Muhammad Ilyas Azeem, Sallam Abualhaija, and Lionel C Briand. 2023. NLP-based Automated Compliance Checking of Data Processing Agreements against GDPR. *arXiv preprint arXiv:2209.09722v2*. Submitted to IEEE for possible publication.

Yupeng Chang, Xu Wang, Jindong Wang, Yuan Wu, Linyi Yang, Kaijie Zhu, Hao Chen, Xiaoyuan Yi, Cunxiang Wang, Yidong Wang, et al. 2024. A survey on evaluation of large language models. *ACM Transactions on Intelligent Systems and Technology*, 15(3):1–45.

Jacob de Menezes-Neto and M. B. M. Clementino. 2022. Using deep learning to predict outcomes of legal appeals better than human experts: A study with data from Brazilian federal courts. *PloS one*, 17(7):e0272287.

Chiara Patricia Drolsbach and Nicolas Pröllochs. 2024. Content Moderation on Social Media in the EU: Insights From the DSA Transparency Database. In *Companion Proceedings of the ACM on Web Conference 2024*, pages 939–942.

Yutao Feng, Jipeng Qiang, Yun Li, Yunhao Yuan, and Yi Zhu. 2023. Sentence simplification via large language models. *Preprint*, arXiv:2302.11957.

Yunfan Gao, Yun Xiong, Xinyu Gao, Kangxiang Jia, Jinliu Pan, Yuxi Bi, Yi Dai, Jiawei Sun, Meng Wang, and Haofen Wang. 2024. Retrieval-augmented generation for large language models: A survey. *Preprint*, arXiv:2312.10997.

Aparna Garimella, Abhilasha Sancheti, Vinay Aggarwal, Ananya Ganesh, Niyati Chhaya, and Nanda Kambhatla. 2022. Text simplification for legal domain: Insights and challenges. In *Proceedings of the 1st Workshop on Natural Language Legal Processing (NLLP)*, pages 224–234.

Yanchu Guan, Dong Wang, Zhixuan Chu, Shiyu Wang, Feiyue Ni, Ruihua Song, Longfei Li, Jinjie Gu, and Chenyi Zhuang. 2023. Intelligent Virtual Assistants with LLM-based Process Automation. *Preprint*, arXiv:2312.06677.

Taicheng Guo, Xiuying Chen, Yaqi Wang, Ruidi Chang, Shichao Pei, Nitesh V. Chawla, Olaf Wiest, and Xiangliang Zhang. 2024. Large language model based multi-agents: A survey of progress and challenges. *Preprint*, arXiv:2402.01680.

Dan Hendrycks, Collin Burns, Anya Chen, and Spencer Ball. 2021. Cuad: An expert-annotated nlp dataset for legal contract review. *Preprint*, arXiv:2103.06268.

Péter Homoki and Zsolt Ződi. 2024. Large language models and their possible uses in law. *Research Article*, pages 435–455. Online Publication Date: 15 Apr 2024.

Thanmay Jayakumar, Fauzan Farooqui, and Luqman Farooqui. 2023. Large Language Models are Legal but they are not: Making the Case for a Powerful LegalLLM. In *Proceedings of the Natural Legal Language Processing Workshop 2023*, pages 223–229, December 7, 2023. Association for Computational Linguistics.

Albert Q. Jiang, Alexandre Sablayrolles, Arthur Mensch, Chris Bamford, Devendra Singh Chaplot, Diego de las Casas, Florian Bressand, Gianna Lengyel, Guillaume Lample, Lucile Saulnier, Lélio Renard Lavaud, Marie-Anne Lachaux, Pierre Stock, Teven Le Scao, Thibaut Lavril, Thomas Wang, Timothée Lacroix, and William El Sayed. 2023. Mistral 7b. *Preprint*, arXiv:2310.06825.

Daniel Martin Katz, Dirk Hartung, Lauritz Gerlach, Abhik Jana, and Michael J. Bommarito II au2. 2023. Natural language processing in the legal domain. *Preprint*, arXiv:2302.12039.

Rishabh Kaushal, Jacob van de Kerkhof, Catalina Goanta, Gerasimos Spanakis, and Adriana Iamnitchi. 2024. Automated Transparency: A Legal and Empirical Analysis of the Digital Services Act Transparency Database. In *Proceedings of the ACM Conference on Fairness, Accountability, and Transparency (ACM FAccT '24)*, page 19 pages, Rio de Janeiro, Brazil. ACM.

Mahi Kolla, Siddharth Salunkhe, Eshwar Chandrasekharan, and Koustuv Saha. 2024. LLM-Mod: Can Large Language Models Assist Content Moderation? In *Extended Abstracts of the 2024 CHI Conference on Human Factors in Computing Systems*, CHI EA '24, New York, NY, USA. Association for Computing Machinery.

Deepak Kumar, Yousef AbuHashem, and Zakir Durumeric. 2024. Watch your language: Investigating content moderation with large language models. *arXiv preprint arXiv:2309.14517v2*.

Alfirna Rizqi Lahitani, Adhistya Erna Permanasari, and Noor Akhmad Setiawan. 2016. Cosine similarity to determine similarity measure: Study case in online essay assessment. In *2016 4th International Conference on Cyber and IT Service Management*, pages 1–6.

Chun-Hsien Lin and Pu-Jen Cheng. 2024. Legal documents drafting with fine-tuned pre-trained large language model. *Preprint*, arXiv:2406.04202.

Zhen Lin, Shubhendu Trivedi, and Jimeng Sun. 2024. Generating with confidence: Uncertainty quantification for black-box large language models. *Transactions on Machine Learning Research*.

Marco Lippi, Przemysław Pałka, Giuseppe Contissa, Francesca Lagioia, Hans-Wolfgang Micklitz, Giovanni Sartor, and Paolo Torroni. 2019. Claudette: an automated detector of potentially unfair clauses in online terms of service. *Artificial Intelligence and Law*, 27(2):117–139.

Lauren Martin, Nick Whitehouse, Stephanie Yiu, Lizzie Catterson, and Rivindu Perera. 2024. Better Call GPT, Comparing Large Language Models Against Lawyers. *Preprint*, arXiv:2401.16212.

M. E. J. Masson and M. A. Waldron. 1994. Comprehension of legal contracts by non-experts: Effectiveness of plain language redrafting. *Applied Cognitive Psychology*, 8:67–85. P. 16.

Peter Melinat, Tolja Kreuzkam, and Dirk Stamer. 2014. Information overload: A systematic literature review. https://doi.org/10.13140/2.1.4293.7606.

Jiayi Pan, Chengcan Wang, Kaifu Zheng, Yangguang Li, Zhenyu Wang, and Bin Feng. 2023. Smoothquant+: Accurate and efficient 4-bit post-training weightquantization for llm. *Preprint*, arXiv:2312.03788.

Weicong Qin and Zhongxiang Sun. 2024. Exploring the nexus of large language models and legal systems: A short survey. *Preprint*, arXiv:2404.00990.

Stephen Robertson and Hugo Zaragoza. 2009. The Probabilistic Relevance Framework: BM25 and Beyond. *Found. Trends Inf. Retr.*, 3(4):333–389.

Antonino Rotolo and Giovanni Sartor. 2023. Argumentation and explanation in the law. *Frontiers in Artificial Intelligence*, 6.

Pranab Sahoo, Ayush Kumar Singh, Sriparna Saha, Vinija Jain, Samrat Mondal, and Aman Chadha. 2024. A systematic survey of prompt engineering in large language models: Techniques and applications. *Preprint*, arXiv:2402.07927.

Heiko Thimm. 2023. Data modeling and NLP-based scoring method to assess the relevance of environmental regulatory announcements. *Environmental Systems and Decisions*, 43:416–432.

Amaury Trujillo, Tiziano Fagni, and Stefano Cresci. 2024. The DSA Transparency Database: Auditing self-reported moderation actions by social media. *arXiv preprint arXiv:2312.10269*.

Jasper van der Waa, Elisabeth Nieuwburg, Anita Cremers, and Mark Neerincx. 2021. Evaluating xai: A comparison of rule-based and example-based explanations. *Artificial intelligence*, 291:103404.

Shicheng Xu, Liang Pang, Mo Yu, Fandong Meng, Huawei Shen, Xueqi Cheng, and Jie Zhou. 2024. Unsupervised information refinement training of large language models for retrieval-augmented generation. *Preprint*, arXiv:2402.18150.

Xiaoxian Yang, Zhifeng Wang, Qi Wang, Ke Wei, Kaiqi Zhang, and Jiangang Shi. 2024. Large language models for automated Q&A involving legal documents: a survey on algorithms, frameworks and applications. *International Journal of Web Information Systems*, 20(4):413–435.

Yu-Cheng Zhou, Zhe Zheng, Jia-Rui Lin, and Xin-Zheng Lu. 2022. Integrating NLP and context-free grammar for complex rule interpretation towards automated compliance checking. *Computers in Industry*, 142:103746.

BLT: Can Large Language Models Handle Basic Legal Text?

Andrew Blair-Stanek[1,2] **Nils Holzenberger**[3] **Benjamin Van Durme**[1]
[1] Johns Hopkins University, [2] University of Maryland School of Law,
[3] Télécom Paris - Institut Polytechnique de Paris

Abstract

We find that the best publicly available LLMs like GPT-4 and Claude currently perform poorly on basic legal text handling. This motivates the creation of a benchmark consisting of examples that lawyers and paralegals would expect LLMs to handle zero-shot, such as looking up the text at a line of a witness deposition or at a subsection of a contract. LLMs' poor performance on this benchmark casts into doubt their reliability as-is for legal practice. However, fine-tuning on our training set brings even a small model to near-perfect performance. This benchmark will be useful for fine-tuning LLMs for downstream legal tasks, as well as for tracking LLMs' reliability as-is for basic legal tasks.

1 Introduction

There has been much excitement about the potential of large language models (LLMs) to handle complex reasoning tasks. In the legal domain, recent work has focused on LLMs' ability to perform high-level tasks such as passing the bar exam, identifying hearsay evidence, or navigating the tax code. These results have led to predictions that LLMs will imminently revolutionize law practice.

However, no prior work has investigated LLMs' ability to handle the most very basic text tasks done in daily legal practice. In this paper, we introduce a benchmark for **B**asic **L**egal **T**ext (BLT) handling. BLT mimics simple tasks done by lawyers and paralegals, including looking up citations to the record, finding statutory citations containing particular text or definitions, or finding the text in a contract that another lawyer has explicitly cited.

BLT is designed so that a paralegal, new lawyer, or even non-subject matter expert could perform zero-shot at or near 100%. But we find that leading publicly available LLMs perform poorly out-of-the-box. An example of this poor performance is in Figure 1, where GPT-4o fails to retrieve the text on the specified line of a deposition transcript excerpt that is a mere 15 lines long.

1: MR. MACEJKA: Object to form.
2: A. The medical invoice from the MAO would be
3: the medical claims data. So we're already in
4: receipt of that.
5: BY MR. PENNEKAMP:
6: Q. That's what you referred to a medical
7: invoice, is the claims data?
8: MR. MACEJKA: Object to form.
9: A. That essentially is what the medical
10: claims data is.
11: BY MR. PENNEKAMP:
12: Q. Do you ask the providers for their
13: invoices for the medical services?
14: MR. MACEJKA: Object to form.
15: A. We will request for EOBs or billing

What is the exact text of just line 7 above?

The exact text of line 7 is: "Q. That's what you referred to a medical"

Figure 1: GPT-4o incorrectly answering a simple question about a page from a line-numbered witness deposition transcript. Line numbers, exactly as shown above, are passed to GPT-4o, which incorrectly answers 13% of such one-page, 15-line deposition retrieval prompts.

Yet we find that fine-tuning a less-advanced model, GPT-3.5-turbo, on BLT's training set leads to near-human (i.e., 100%) performance. We also find that this fine-tuned model also performs better on a more complex legal task, demonstrating BLT's value for fine-tuning LLMs for legal applications.

The BLT dataset has additional strengths. Our code[1] can generate unlimited new examples never before seen in corpora. Moreover, BLT is scalable to different window sizes and is one of the few datasets taking full advantage of LLMs with window sizes of 64k or 128k tokens.

[1] `https://github.com/blairstanek/blt`.

Proceedings of the Natural Legal Language Processing Workshop 2024, pages 216–232
November 16, 2024 ©2024 Association for Computational Linguistics

2 Background

Law is a largely text-based profession and thus is often used to demonstrate LLMs' capabilities. OpenAI's GPT-4 technical report (OpenAI, 2023b) mentioned only a single benchmark in the abstract itself: GPT-4 had passed the bar exam, with the score in the 90th percentile.

OpenAI's developer livestream by co-founder Greg Brockman introducing GPT-4 (OpenAI, 2023a) used four examples to show GPT-4's capabilities. One involved U.S. tax law, where Brockman prompted GPT-4 with several tax-code sections and had it calculate the taxes of hypothetical taxpayers Alice and Bob. Brockman proclaimed that GPT-4 can "do taxes."

2.1 Legal Use of LLMs

Legal NLP is concerned with a diverse range of tasks, reflecting the diversity of tasks lawyers perform. Examples include legal judgment prediction (Medvedeva and McBride, 2023; Chalkidis et al., 2019; Xiao et al., 2018), contract review (Hendrycks et al., 2021), document review (Lewis et al., 2023), and retrieving relevant case law (Kim et al., 2022). There has been extensive discussion of how NLP can benefit the legal system (Zhong et al., 2020; Aidid and Alarie, 2023). LLMs have been deployed for a wide range of legal tasks, including case analysis (Savelka et al., 2023), discovery (Pai et al., 2023), and analyzing contracts (Roegiest et al., 2023).

Several LLMs have been fine-tuned on legal materials (Colombo et al., 2024) and for legal tasks. Dominguez-Olmedo et al. (2024) discovered that for some legal tasks, a 8-billion parameter LLM that has been lightly pretrained on legal tasks substantially outperforms GPT-4, which has several orders of magnitude more parameters.

Many legal benchmarks for LLMs have been created (Chalkidis et al., 2022; Fei et al., 2023), with many incorporated into the broad LegalBench project (Guha et al., 2022). These are all much higher-level tasks than BLT, including identifying testimony to which the hearsay doctrine applies or whether contractual terms impose particular restrictions (Hendrycks et al., 2021).

The SARA (StAtutory Reasoning Assessment) dataset (Holzenberger et al., 2020) is one of the higher-level tasks in LegalBench. It consists of nine tax-related sections of the U.S. Code, plus 376 hand-crafted "cases" consisting of facts and a question that can be unambiguously answered applying the nine sections to the facts. Because SARA is a higher-level task clearly predicated on lower-level text handling (specifically, finding text at a citation), we use it to measure the effectiveness of fine-tuning with BLT, discussed in Section 5.

The ability of GPT-3 to handle SARA was evaluated in Blair-Stanek et al. (2023), with lackluster performance found. Qualitatively, GPT-3 often retrieved text from the wrong part of the given statute. For example, GPT-3 was prompted with the text of the U.S. tax code's section 152, some facts about Alice and Bob, and the question of whether Alice's relationship to Bob fell under section 152(d)(2)(C). GPT-3's response analyzed the question using the text of section 152(d)(2)(**D**), with the result that GPT-3 answered the question about Alice and Bob incorrectly. This inability to retrieve clearly specified text – resulting in incorrect answers to legal questions – was a motivation behind the BLT dataset and this paper.

LLMs have seen much of the internet during their training. To evaluate LLMs' ability to handle novel legal questions, Nay et al. (2023) generate synthetic multiple-choice legal questions. Similarly, to test whether LLMs can handle truly novel legal texts, Blair-Stanek et al. (2023) generate synthetic sections constructed with nonces (phonetically plausible nonsense words) and probe GPT-3's ability to reason over these synthetic sections. BLT incorporates such synthetic sections, albeit for simpler tasks than statutory reasoning.

2.2 Related LLM Evaluations

Numerous evaluation metrics have been developed for LLMs (Shahriar et al., 2024; Chang et al., 2023). For example, BIG-Bench (Srivastava et al., 2023) includes basic word handling tasks like word sorting and text editing. Parsing software logs is evaluated by (Le and Zhang, 2023). Simplifying complex sentences is evaluated in (Wu and Arase, 2024). LLMs can solve quite complicated tasks by being prompted to provide a chain of thought (Kojima et al., 2022), including in the legal domain (Yu et al., 2022). More generally, choosing the appropriate way to prompt LLMs, called prompt engineering, often has a substantial impact on LLM performance (White et al., 2023; Liu et al., 2023b). A complementary approach has been to decompose the task at hand into tasks the LLM can handle (Dua et al., 2022; Khot et al., 2023). LLMs have been evaluated in various professional domains, including medicine (Beaulieu-Jones et al., 2024) and accounting (Zhao and Wang, 2024).

LLMs have been trained or otherwise induced to use "Tools" (Schick et al., 2023; Paranjape et al., 2023). For example, an LLM might detect that it needs to call a calculator tool to handle a math problem posed to it in text form. In theory, tools could be written to handle the BLT tasks and then be integrated into LLMs. But the BLT prompts are oversimplified versions of tasks lawyers need LLMs to do seamlessly. A lawyer will not ask an LLM for the citation to the record where the plaintiff says "I have therapy tomorrow." But a lawyer might expect an LLM to insert a citation to the record that proves a plaintiff receives psychological care, and a basic text-matching tool would not handle that.

Some of BLT's prompts are quite long, which is realistic because lawyers regularly handle long texts. Liu et al. (2023a) investigated how LLMs handle retrieval from long prompts. They found that LLMs' accuracy followed a U-curve with respect to the information's position, with information in the middle of the prompt used much less than if it were at the start or end. They connected this to the "serial-position" effect exhibited by humans, who best remember material presented near the beginning or end.

3 The BLT Benchmark

The BLT benchmark involves three different types of legal text, each of which has between two and five different tasks run on it.

3.1 Deposition Transcripts

In litigation in the U.S., depositions of witnesses under oath are a key factfinding tool. The depositions typically occur in lawyers' offices and allow lawyers to ask witnesses questions on virtually any topic. Professional court reporters transcribe the depositions into transcripts, typically with 25 numbered lines per page, often running over 100 pages for a single witness deposition. Attorneys must cite relevant portions of the resulting transcripts in subsequent motions, such as those asking the court to grant their side summary judgment. Portions of transcripts are cited by page and line number.

One basic legal text-handling task a lawyer must do is finding the page and line of a transcript where particular text appears. This motivates the **text→cite** task, where the prompt consists of one or more pages of actual deposition transcript followed by the question, "What are the page number and line number of the line above with the text "__"?" (after single pages, the prompt does not ask for the page number). To ensure there is only one clearly correct answer, prompts are not constructed asking about lines with less than four words, that are subsets of another line, or that are too similar to other lines (defined as Levenshtein distance under four (Levenshtein et al., 1966)).

The converse is another basic text-handling task: given a citation to a transcript, find the text at the cited location. Lawyers must do this basic task in order to evaluate the opposing side's motions. Paralegals do it on their side's own motions before submitting them (ProParalegal, 2017). This motivates the **cite→text** task, where the prompt consists of one or more pages of a deposition transcript followed by the question "What is the exact text of just line __ of page __ above?" (after single pages, the prompt omits the page number). An example of GPT-4o failing this task appears in Figure 1.

BLT's deposition transcript tests are built from a novel corpus we constructed of 33,176 lines of actual deposition transcripts filed with federal district courts and downloaded via Bloomberg Law from the Public Access to Court Electronic Records (PACER) system. They are from a variety of cases; our main criterion was that the transcripts be cleanly OCR'ed and could be fully cleaned with regular expressions. This corpus can be extended *ad infinitum* by downloading further transcripts and cleaning them, as deposition transcripts are not copyrightable.[2] The existing page and line numbers are stripped out, and random spans of appropriate length are selected, with new page numbers and line numbers, in case the LLM saw the original numbering during training.

The size of the prompt is scalable, which was a key goal of BLT. For BLT-4k (the version fitting within a 4,000 token window), we use a mix of 1 and 2 page subsets of depositions. Larger versions have larger subsets. For BLT-128k (fitting inside a 128,000 token window), we use a mix of 120 and 140-page subsets of depositions. Appendix B details the sizes used.

[2]Lipman v. Massachusetts, 311 F. Supp. 593 (D. Mass. 1970); 1 Nimmer on Copyright §5.12[C]. Even in the unlikely event transcripts are copyrightable, this use of them is likely fair use. 17 U.S.C. §107.

Section 5217. Definition of cleight.
(a) General rule. The term "cleight" means any baitisolist or any roussiont.
(b) The term "baitisolist" means any ballinated or any caset.
(c) The term "roussiont" means any dicemercu or any accodpoileare.

What is the exact citation above where the term "roussiont" is defined? (Use standard legal formatting like section 1001(b)(2)).

Section 5217(b)

Figure 2: Example of GPT-4 incorrectly answering **defined→cite** question with a 2-deep, 2-wide synthetic section. The correct answer is "section 5217(c)".

3.2 Synthetic Sections

Lawyers regularly work with hierarchical text, including statutes, contracts, regulations, treaties, court rules, and corporate charters. Hierarchical text is often organized into sections, subsections, paragraphs, subparagraphs, etc. Being able to navigate such hierarchical text is a basic legal text-handling task required of all lawyers, whether they are litigators arguing that a statute applies to their case or are transactional lawyers negotiating contract terms.

We generate synthetic hierarchical sections, following the approach of Blair-Stanek et al. (2023). They use repeated application of the logical form $A \Rightarrow B$, with two parameters: depth, the maximum number of times it is applied; and width, the number of times it is applied to each B. The terms defined are nonces that are not real words but are pronounceable. These synthetic sections can be arbitrarily large, by adjusting the width and depth, thus making tasks based on them scalable to different-sized token windows. For example, BLT-4k has synthetic sections ranging from 2-wide, 2-deep, as in Figure 2, which are very short, up to 3-wide, 4-deep, which takes up much of the 4k token window. At the highest end, BLT-128k has a variety ranging from 60-wide, 2-deep to 5-wide, 5-deep, which (because size is exponential with respect to depth) takes up much of the 128,000-token window. For the full list of sizes in each BLT-*, see Appendix A. Being synthetic ensures they are novel and not seen by LLMs during training. This simulates the challenges faced by lawyers in handling newly drafted contracts, legislation, or other hierarchical text. Nearly unlimited quantities of synthetic sections of any sizes can be generated by permuting the nonces.

A basic legal text-processing skill is finding the citation, in a hierarchical text, of the text to which you are pointing a court or another lawyer. This motivates applying the **text→cite** task on synthetic sections, where the prompt consists of one synthetic section followed by the question "What is the exact citation above of the text "__"? (Use standard legal formatting like section 1001(b)(2))." The code we use to generate synthetic sections guarantees there is only a single correct answer.

The converse legal skill is, given a hierarchical citation, finding the text at it. Hence we apply the **cite→text** task to synthetic sections, with the prompt consisting of one synthetic section followed by the question "What is the exact text of just section __ above?"

We ask this question only of "leaves" in the statute, meaning they have no subsections underneath them. This ensures there is only a single correct answer. For example, suppose that section 573(a) was not a leaf, perhaps with paragraphs 573(a)(1) and 573(a)(2) underneath it. If you asked for the text of section 573(a), it is ambiguous whether you should also return the text of 573(a)(1) and 573(a)(2). Such ambiguity is avoided by considering only leaves.

We also include two other basic legal text-handling tasks on the synthetic sections. Terms are defined in hierarchical texts and often referenced elsewhere in the same hierarchical text. Lawyers must be able to cite a term's precise definition. With **defined→cite**, the prompt is one synthetic section followed by the question "What is the exact citation above where the term "__" is defined? (Use standard legal formatting like section 1001(b)(2))." Conversely, when given such a citation by another lawyer, a lawyer must be able to find the term, which motivates **cite→define**. There, the prompt is one synthetic section followed by the question "What is the term defined at section __?" An example of GPT-4 incorrectly answering a defined→cite problem appears in Figure 2.

3.3 U.S. Code

The U.S. Code is the official compilation of general and permanent U.S. federal statutes. The U.S. Code is a large corpus of hierarchical text. We apply to the U.S. Code all four tasks that we applied to synthetic sections: **text→cite**, **cite→text**,

defined→cite, and **cite→defined**. For these four tasks on the U.S. Code, the prompt is the same as for synthetic sections.

During training, LLMs have doubtless seen all of the U.S. Code, which is not copyrighted and is publicly available on multiple websites. To test whether LLMs' familiarity with U.S. Code sections causes errors, we add a fifth test for U.S. Code sections: **cite→amended**. In all but one respect, this test is identical to cite→text, in that it has the text of one or more sections and asks "What is the exact text of just section __ above?" about a leaf.

The sole difference is that we make a small but semantically-important change to the text in that leaf to see if the LLM returns the original text or the changed text (which is the correct answer). This tests a basic legal skill: applying a given newly-amended statute, rather than its old version. If the leaf contains any numbers, we add or subtract one from the last appearing number (although we never move from 1 to 2 or from 2 to 1 since that would also require changing singular nouns to plural or vice versa). Otherwise, we tweak the last appearing citation from, say, "(D)" to "(A)". Otherwise, we toggle the last "and" to "or" or vice versa. Otherwise, we toggle the last "shall" to "may" or vice versa. If none of these changes are available, we insert "unless otherwise provided by section 101," at the start of the leaf.

For all tasks on the U.S. Code, we do not use sections containing tables, which are not purely text. Examples include the income tax tables at 26 U.S.C. §1, and 5,946 sections are excluded for this reason. We do not use sections, like 5 U.S.C. §9507 and 25 U.S.C. §5329, with quoted hierarchical text such as model contracts, which are hard for even a human lawyer to read. We never use any of the cites that Congress has sloppily added twice, such as the two subsection (e)'s in 42 U.S.C. §1397hh.

For text→cite, we do the same test as with transcripts, not using lines that are under four words long, are subsets of any line appearing elsewhere in the prompt, or that have a Levenshtein distance under four from another line in the prompt. For defined→cite, we do not use terms defined in more than one place in the prompt.

Unlike synthetic sections, which can be generated in unlimited quantities in arbitrarily large sizes, there are a limited number of U.S. Code sections. But it is a huge corpus, with 43,916 sections that meet the criteria discussed above, 447,037 leaves, and 23,562 unique definitions. Although 94% of sections are under 2,000 GPT-4 tokens, that still leaves 2,602 sections over 2,000 tokens, including 813 sections over 4,000 tokens and 196 sections over 8,000 tokens. When there are insufficient numbers of large enough sections, we can generate prompts of any desired size *ad infinitum* by adding randomly selected other sections of approximately the same size. We randomly shuffle the order of the sections in the prompt so that the target section's position is not a cue to the model.

Having multiple sections in a prompt resembles how OpenAI's Greg Brockman pasted nine tax-related sections into GPT-4 during the livestream introducing GPT-4. This is realistic: lawyers handling real-world issues often must apply several statutes in conjunction, not just one.

3.4 General Considerations

For each of the 11 tests, and for each possible size (ranging from BLT-4k to BLT-128k), we generate a training/test split of 1000/100 prompts.[3] Why only 100 test prompts for each test split? Three reasons. First, there are 11 tests, thus 1,100 test prompts for each size of BLT-*. Second, the monetary cost of calling many LLMs with just 1,100 BLT-8k prompts with around 5,000 tokens per prompt is already nontrivial. Third, any LLM deployed for real-world legal practice should be at or near 100%, and as accuracy approaches 100% the t-statistic goes to zero.

Prompt engineering is not our focus, because the BLT tasks are expressly designed to be subsidiary tasks: legal users would not ask LLMs to solve the BLT tasks themselves. Rather, LLMs being able to handle the BLT tasks will generally be a prerequisite to accomplishing higher-level tasks, like drafting court documents citing statutes and deposition transcripts. Moreover, lawyers are unlikely to engage in more than rudimentary prompt engineering. We do try different prompts, as discussed in section 4.1 and appendices E and F.

4 Results and Discussion

We tested four models from OpenAI: GPT-3.5-turbo, GPT-4, and GPT-4-turbo, and GPT-4o. From Google, we tested the chat-bison-32k variant of

[3]All BLT data can be downloaded from:
`http://nlp.jhu.edu/law/blt/BLT-4k.zip`
`http://nlp.jhu.edu/law/blt/BLT-8k.zip`
`http://nlp.jhu.edu/law/blt/BLT-16k.zip`
`http://nlp.jhu.edu/law/blt/BLT-32k.zip`
`http://nlp.jhu.edu/law/blt/BLT-64k.zip`
`http://nlp.jhu.edu/law/blt/BLT-128k.zip`.

	model	transc.		synthetic section				U.S. Code					mean
		text→cite	cite→text	text→cite	cite→text	defined→cite	cite→defined	text→cite	cite→text	cite→amended	defined→cite	cite→defined	
BLT-4k	GPT-3.5-turbo	53	32	72	38	83	79	89	52	56 (0)	77	98	66.3
	GPT-4	82	78	88	97	90	100	98	93	93 (0)	98	100	92.5
	GPT-4-turbo	87	88	85	63	76	95	98	84	77 (7)	96	99	86.2
	chat-bison-32k	84	29	7	77	37	92	83	90	89 (1)	81	97	69.6
	Claude-2.1	54	38	74	71	78	85	97	87	87 (1)	96	95	78.4
	GPT-4o	88	84	99	90	98	98	99	91	94 (0)	97	100	94.4
	Claude-3.5	96	80	100	99	100	100	100	97	97 (0)	98	100	97.0
BLT-8k	GPT-4	44	26	64	49	82	83	94	74	76 (0)	88	97	70.6
	GPT-4-turbo	57	53	66	45	75	74	94	80	71 (3)	98	99	73.8
	chat-bison-32k	59	6	9	29	48	59	70	83	86 (1)	80	89	56.2
	Claude-2.1	35	11	58	51	70	54	91	81	79 (4)	94	92	65.1
	GPT-4o	79	37	86	73	88	87	97	85	86 (3)	99	96	83.0
	Claude-3.5	75	66	94	72	99	99	100	100	94 (1)	100	99	90.1
BLT-16k	GPT-4-turbo	30	20	78	36	83	83	90	64	58 (5)	93	95	66.4
	chat-bison-32k	42	6	36	30	69	57	25	54	52 (2)	43	58	42.9
	Claude-2.1	21	5	64	48	76	61	82	66	65 (4)	85	85	59.8
	GPT-4o	59	17	93	86	98	96	96	65	63 (2)	93	96	78.4
	Claude-3.5	69	36	94	68	97	96	99	72	73 (2)	94	95	78.4
BLT-32k	GPT-4-turbo	23	11	42	7	64	63	77	38	36 (1)	82	85	48.0
	chat-bison-32k	13	0	8	10	39	32	12	32	36 (0)	30	36	22.5
	Claude-2.1	20	3	45	24	54	38	76	45	43 (3)	71	70	44.5
	GPT-4o	50	17	82	64	83	76	96	48	44 (6)	95	95	68.2
	Claude-3.5	72	35	62	33	82	72	90	57	56 (6)	91	88	67.1
BLT-64k	GPT-4-turbo	17	4	27	10	60	54	51	19	16 (4)	55	66	34.5
	Claude-2.1	5	1	52	26	56	35	58	31	29 (4)	55	66	37.6
	GPT-4o	65	16	87	61	92	88	95	53	53 (1)	91	93	72.2
BLT-128k	GPT-4-turbo	9	3	3	0	20	17	34	12	12 (0)	51	56	19.7
	Claude-2.1	10	0	11	3	16	21	47	21	18 (1)	45	60	22.9
	GPT-4o	53	10	36	18	72	49	79	30	28 (1)	88	88	50.1

Table 1: Accuracy in percent of several models against all the different sizes of BLT. GPT-4o and Claude-3.5 are broken out separately since their training cutoff was several months after the BLT dataset was made public online, so they may have seen the BLT test data during training. Under cite→amended, the number in parentheses is how often the model erred by returning the unamended U.S. Code text rather than the amended text provided to the model in the prompt, results discussed in Subsection 4.4.

PaLM 2. From Anthropic, we tested Claude-2.1 and Claude-3.5 Sonnet. (Due to token limits, we were not able to test Claude-3.5 on our two largest test sets, BLT-64k and -128k.)

Crucially, GPT-4o and Claude-3.5's training cutoffs were several months after we released the BLT test and training data sets on the internet in November 2023. They may have seen the BLT test sets during training, artificially boosting their performance. Accordingly, they are broken out separately in Table 1.

Table 1 contains our results. All tests were by API call, with temperature set to 0.0 to maximize reproducibility and minimize hallucination. Each number in Table 1 (other than the means and the numbers in parentheses) corresponds to 100 calls to the relevant LLM's API – one call each for each of the 100 prompts in each test set. For example, there are 100 prompts in test for text→cite for synthetic sections in BLT-4k. Our code measures accuracy with forgiving rules, ignoring case and whitespace. Our code uses handwritten rules to classify errors, a feature we draw on in the discussion below.

We note that accuracy monotonically decreases as prompt size increases, with each model achieving higher accuracy on BLT-4k than BLT-8k, higher accuracy on BLT-8k than BLT-16k, and so on.

4.1 GPT-4 on transcript text→cite

All GPT-4 models (GPT-4, GPT-4-turbo, and GPT-4o) performed under 90 percent on transcript text→cite for BLT-4k. To further investigate this poor performance, we generate 1,000 new prompts in the same format (25-lines per page, with half being one-page and half being two-page) and pass them to GPT-4. GPT-4 achieves 87.5% on these 1,000. Qualitatively, most errors are either identifying the line after the correct one or before the correct one. The full error breakdowns are in Appendix D.

The biggest determinant of performance is whether the transcript was a single page or two pages. GPT-4 correctly answered 91% of single-page transcript prompts, but just 84% of 2-page transcript prompts. This makes sense, since 2-page transcripts have 50 lines of text, whereas 1-page transcripts have just 25 lines of text. (An example of GPT-4 getting a wrong answer on a 2-page transcript appears in Appendix C.)

To see whether the problem is the greater number of lines or having the text split into two pages, we generate 500 new prompts with single pages but with 50 lines per page. (In other words, the transcript quotation is all one page, but with line numbers starting at "1:" and ending at "50:", followed by the question). We find GPT-4 achieves 84.8% accuracy, nearly identical to the two-page transcripts, indicating the problem is length, not being split into two pages.

To investigate how the location, within the transcripts, of the text impacts accuracy, we generate 5,000 new two-page prompts, and run against GPT-4. The results are the red dashed line in Figure 3. We see a generally downwards trend. We do not see the distinct U-pattern observed by Liu et al. (2023a) in accuracy versus position of requested information within a long prompt.

We also perform a sensitivity analysis, trying four question formats other than "What are the page number and line number of the line above

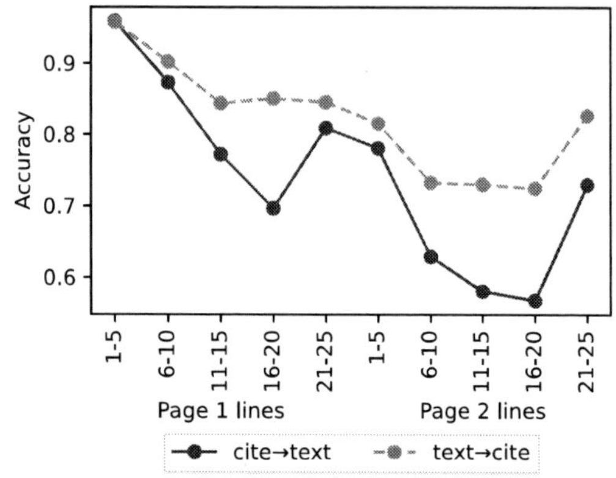

Figure 3: Graph of location of relevant line versus accuracy on both transcript **cite→text** and **text→cite** on 5,000 prompts to GPT-4.

with the text "__"?" appearing after the quotations. (Details in Appendix E.) We find the biggest improvement simply by swapping the question from the end to the beginning and changing "above" to "below". We tried the same switch – moving the question from the bottom to the top – for all of BLT-4k and re-ran against GPT-4. The results are in Appendix F. It turns out that moving the question from the end to the start actually hurt performance in 7 of 11 tasks, indicating no general trend.

4.2 GPT-4 on transcript cite→text

All models performed poorly on transcript cite→text for BLT-4k. For example, Claude-3.5 got 80%, GPT-4 got 78%, and GPT-4o got 84%. To further investigate, we generated 1,000 new prompts in the same format and passed them to GPT-4, which got got 75.7% accuracy on these 1,000. We found little difference between one-page and two-page transcripts, on which GPT-4 got 76.6% and 74.8% respectively.

To investigate how accuracy varies with the location of the requested cite, within the transcripts, we generate 5,000 new two-page prompts, and pass them to GPT-4. The results are the solid blue line in Figure 3. We see a trend towards lower accuracy further into the transcript, with higher accuracy near the beginning and end of each page.

4.3 Poor Performance on synthetic cite→text

Several models have their worst performance, among synthetic section tasks, on cite→text. Each BLT-* has a variety of different size sections, shown in Appendix A. Some of the worst BLT-4k performance is on 3-wide, 4-deep synthetic sec-

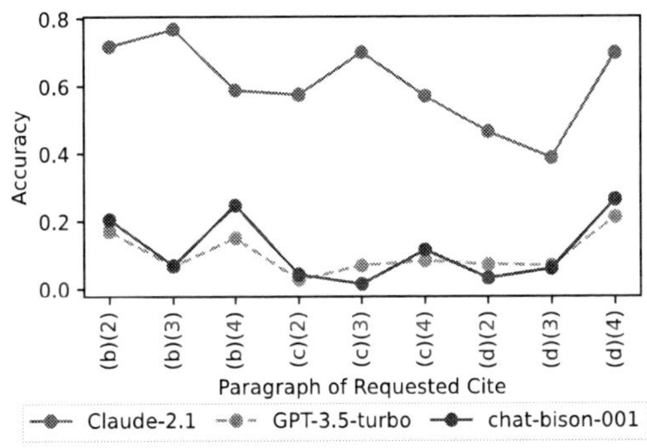

Figure 4: Graph of location of requested cite versus accuracy for 5,000 synthetic **cite→text** prompts, all using 3-wide, 4-deep synthetic sections, which are 127 lines long. Note that each first subdivision (e.g., (a), (1)) is used for a "General Rule" that has few lines, so such subdivisions are not included in this graph.

text and task	not tuned	fine-tuned
transcript text→cite	53	100
transcript cite→text	32	99
synthetic text→cite	72	98
synthetic cite→text	38	100
synthetic defined→cite	83	100
synthetic cite→defined	79	100
uscode text→cite	89	100
uscode cite→text	52	100
uscode cite→amendedtext	56	100
uscode defined→cite	77	100
uscode cite→defined	98	100

Table 2: Results of fine-tuning GPT-3.5-turbo on 9,900 training samples from BLT-4k. Both numerical columns contain percent accuracy on BLT-4k's test prompts. Fine-tuning GPT-3.5-turbo improves it to near perfect.

tions. To see if location within the section plays a role in accuracy, we generated 5,000 prompts using 3-wide, 4-deep synthetic sections, and we ran all against three models with poor performance on synthetic cite→text. The results are in Figure 4. Once again, in contrast to Liu et al. (2023a), there is no U-pattern. We found the same lack of discernible pattern in accuracy versus location with all models and all tasks involving either synthetic sections or the U.S. Code.

4.4 Problem Revealed by cite→amended

Recall that for cite→amended we make a minimal, but semantically-important, change to the subsection of the U.S. Code section being requested. The correct answer is returning the subsection's text with this amendment. Many of the errors involve returning the text of the wrong subsection. But one type of error is particularly concerning: an LLM returning the subsection *without* the amendment, presumably relying on the original U.S. Code text seen during training.

In practice, this error means that, even if a lawyer or paralegal pastes in the new version of legislation, the LLM ignores it. The LLM will act as if the legislation had never been amended.

The occurrence of this error is in parentheses under the cite→amended column in Table 1, showing that several LLMs make this error a nontrivial number of times. To investigate further, we generated 1,000 new BLT-4k style cite→amended prompts. On these, Claude-2.1 incorrectly returned the original text 17 times (1.7%), chat-bison-32k did so 4 times (0.4%), GPT-4o did so 10 times (1%), and GPT-4-turbo did so fully 44 times (4.4%).

5 Fine-Tuning

We fine-tune the 4,000-token version of GPT-3.5-turbo with BLT-4k's training set. For each of the 11 task types, BLT-4k has a training set with 1,000 prompts and answers, for a total of 11,000 prompts and answers. Recall that the training set and test set are generated in the same way, with the same code. Of the 11,000 prompts and answers in the training set, we use 90% for training, leaving 10% as a possible evaluation set for future work. We train for two epochs with all hyperparameters, like learning rate, set to the defaults. The results of the fine-tuning are in Table 2. We find that fine-tuning brings GPT-3.5-turbo, which is far from OpenAI's most advanced model, to near the 100% performance expected of lawyers and paralegals.

We tested how this fine-tuned GPT-3.5-turbo performs on the SARA dataset (Holzenberger et al., 2020), using the 276 cases where the answer is entail/contradict. Each prompt consists of each U.S. Code section(s) mentioned in the case, plus the facts (i.e., the premise) and the hypothesis (i.e., the question). Without fine-tuning, GPT-3.5-turbo's accuracy was 54.3% (150 / 276), but with our fine-tuning it rises to 60.9% (168 / 276). Qualitatively, the fine-tuned model's answers focus on applying only the relevant statutory provisions. (An example is in Appendix H.)

This result shows the utility of fine-tuning LLMs

on BLT's training data to improve performance on higher-level legal tasks. Also, this result is in line with the findings of Dominguez-Olmedo et al. (2024) that small LLMs that have been lightly fine-tuned on legal tasks often substantially outperform larger LLMs on legal tasks.

6 LLMs Trained After BLT Release

We generally see the best performance from Claude-3.5 and GPT-4o, the two most recently released LLMs that we test. There are three possible, non-exclusive explanations. First, these models may be more advanced and thus better at most tasks. Second, we released the BLT test sets on the internet in November 2023, several months before these models' training cutoff dates, so there may have been test-set leakage, with the models already having seen the answers during training. Third, the BLT training sets (which are ten times larger than the test sets) were also released in November 2023, before these models' training cutoffs. As the fine-tuning experiments in Section 5 demonstrate, training on the BLT training data can substantially improve performance. Seeing the BLT training data may have improved these models' basic legal text handling.

7 Conclusion

The chief innovation officer at a large international law firm observed to the *New York Times* of LLMs, "At its best, the technology seems like a very smart paralegal." (Lohr, 2023). We find LLMs are more like sloppy paralegals.

Currently available LLMs perform poorly out-of-the-box on basic legal text handling. The BLT tasks are designed to be truly basic, with humans able to perform them at or near 100%. The GPT-4 family, PaLM 2, and Claude-2.1 all fall far short. Only one model, Claude-3.5, comes close, with 97.0% aggregate performance, and then only on our smallest test set, BLT-4k. Yet even Claude-3.5 achieves only 80% on retrieving the text on a line of one or two pages of deposition transcript.

We find that fine-tuning on our training set brings performance up to near 100%. We expect BLT to be a useful resource for those fine-tuning LLMs for much more complicated legal tasks, as well as a benchmark for LLMs' ability to do basic legal text handling without fine-tuning.

Ethics Statement

LLMs can be misused by legal professionals and laypersons alike to address legal problems properly requiring the full attention of a legal professional. One of our goals is to alert potential users of the failings of existing LLMs at basic legal tasks. Users may misconstrue our findings on the value of fine-tuning to assume incorrectly that an LLM with such fine-tuning can handle legal matters. Even if an LLM gets 100% on BLT, that does not mean the LLM can handle legal matters.

Acknowledgments

This work has been supported by the U.S. National Science Foundation under grant 2204926. Any opinions, findings, and conclusions or recommendations expressed in this article are those of the authors and do not necessarily reflect the views of the National Science Foundation. We would like to thank Susan McCarty and Orion Weller for valuable assistance.

References

Abdi Aidid and Benjamin Alarie. 2023. *The Legal Singularity: How Artificial Intelligence Can Make Law Radically Better*. University of Toronto Press.

Brendin R Beaulieu-Jones, Margaret T Berrigan, Sahaj Shah, Jayson S Marwaha, Shuo-Lun Lai, and Gabriel A Brat. 2024. Evaluating capabilities of large language models: Performance of gpt-4 on surgical knowledge assessments. *Surgery*.

Steven Bird, Ewan Klein, and Edward Loper. 2009. *Natural language processing with Python: analyzing text with the natural language toolkit*. " O'Reilly Media, Inc.".

Andrew Blair-Stanek, Nils Holzenberger, and Benjamin Van Durme. 2023. Can GPT-3 Perform Statutory Reasoning? In *Proceedings of the Nineteenth International Conference on Artificial Intelligence and Law*, ICAIL '23, page 22–31.

Ilias Chalkidis, Ion Androutsopoulos, and Nikolaos Aletras. 2019. Neural legal judgment prediction in English. In *Proceedings of the 57th Annual Meeting of the Association for Computational Linguistics*, pages 4317–4323, Florence, Italy. Association for Computational Linguistics.

Ilias Chalkidis, Abhik Jana, Dirk Hartung, Michael Bommarito, Ion Androutsopoulos, Daniel Katz, and Nikolaos Aletras. 2022. LexGLUE: A benchmark dataset for legal language understanding in English. In *Proceedings of the 60th Annual Meeting of the Association for Computational Linguistics (Volume*

1: Long Papers), pages 4310–4330, Dublin, Ireland. Association for Computational Linguistics.

Yupeng Chang, Xu Wang, Jindong Wang, Yuan Wu, Linyi Yang, Kaijie Zhu, Hao Chen, Xiaoyuan Yi, Cunxiang Wang, Yidong Wang, et al. 2023. A survey on evaluation of large language models. *ACM Transactions on Intelligent Systems and Technology.*

Pierre Colombo, Telmo Pessoa Pires, Malik Boudiaf, Dominic Culver, Rui Melo, Caio Corro, Andre F. T. Martins, Fabrizio Esposito, Vera Lúcia Raposo, Sofia Morgado, and Michael Desa. 2024. Saullm-7b: A pioneering large language model for law. *arXiv.*

Ricardo Dominguez-Olmedo, Vedant Nanda, Rediet Abebe, Stefan Bechtold, Christoph Engel, Jens Frankenreiter, Krishna Gummadi, Moritz Hardt, and Michael Livermore. 2024. Lawma: The power of specialization for legal tasks. *arXiv.*

Dheeru Dua, Shivanshu Gupta, Sameer Singh, and Matt Gardner. 2022. Successive prompting for decomposing complex questions. In *Proceedings of the 2022 Conference on Empirical Methods in Natural Language Processing*, pages 1251–1265, Abu Dhabi, United Arab Emirates. Association for Computational Linguistics.

Zhiwei Fei, Xiaoyu Shen, Dawei Zhu, Fengzhe Zhou, Zhuo Han, Songyang Zhang, Kai Chen, Zongwen Shen, and Jidong Ge. 2023. Lawbench: Benchmarking legal knowledge of large language models. *Preprint*, arXiv:2309.16289.

Neel Guha, Daniel E. Ho, and Julian Nyarko et al. 2022. Legalbench: Prototyping a collaborative benchmark for legal reasoning. *Preprint*, arXiv:2209.06120.

Dan Hendrycks, Collin Burns, Anya Chen, and Spencer Ball. 2021. Cuad: An expert-annotated NLP dataset for legal contract review. *Advances in Neural Information Processing Systems.*

Nils Holzenberger, Andrew Blair-Stanek, and Benjamin Van Durme. 2020. A dataset for statutory reasoning in tax law entailment and question answering. In *Proceedings of the Natural Legal Language Processing Workshop 2020 co-located with the 26th ACM SIGKDD International Conference on Knowledge Discovery & Data Mining (KDD 2020), Virtual Workshop, August 24, 2020*, volume 2645 of *CEUR Workshop Proceedings*, pages 31–38. CEUR-WS.org.

Tushar Khot, Harsh Trivedi, Matthew Finlayson, Yao Fu, Kyle Richardson, Peter Clark, and Ashish Sabharwal. 2023. Decomposed prompting: A modular approach for solving complex tasks. In *The Eleventh International Conference on Learning Representations, ICLR 2023, Kigali, Rwanda, May 1-5, 2023.* OpenReview.net.

Mi-Young Kim, Juliano Rabelo, Randy Goebel, Masaharu Yoshioka, Yoshinobu Kano, and Ken Satoh. 2022. COLIEE 2022 summary: Methods for legal document retrieval and entailment. In *New Frontiers in Artificial Intelligence - JSAI-isAI 2022 Workshop, JURISIN 2022, and JSAI 2022 International Session, Kyoto, Japan, June 12-17, 2022, Revised Selected Papers*, volume 13859 of *Lecture Notes in Computer Science*, pages 51–67. Springer.

Takeshi Kojima, Shixiang Shane Gu, Machel Reid, Yutaka Matsuo, and Yusuke Iwasawa. 2022. Large language models are zero-shot reasoners. *Advances in neural information processing systems*, 35:22199–22213.

Van-Hoang Le and Hongyu Zhang. 2023. An evaluation of log parsing with chatgpt. *arXiv preprint arXiv:2306.01590.*

Vladimir I Levenshtein et al. 1966. Binary codes capable of correcting deletions, insertions, and reversals. In *Soviet physics doklady*, volume 10, pages 707–710. Soviet Union.

David D. Lewis, Lenora Gray, and Mark Noel. 2023. Confidence sequences for evaluating one-phase technology-assisted review. In *Proceedings of the Nineteenth International Conference on Artificial Intelligence and Law*, ICAIL '23, page 131–140.

Nelson F. Liu, Kevin Lin, John Hewitt, Ashwin Paranjape, Michele Bevilacqua, Fabio Petroni, and Percy Liang. 2023a. Lost in the middle: How language models use long contexts. *Preprint*, arXiv:2307.03172.

Pengfei Liu, Weizhe Yuan, Jinlan Fu, Zhengbao Jiang, Hiroaki Hayashi, and Graham Neubig. 2023b. Pretrain, prompt, and predict: A systematic survey of prompting methods in natural language processing. *ACM Comput. Surv.*, 55(9).

Steve Lohr. 2023. A.I. threatens lawyers? We've heard this before. *New York Times*, page B1.

Masha Medvedeva and Pauline McBride. 2023. Legal judgment prediction: If you are going to do it, do it right. In *Proceedings of the Natural Legal Language Processing Workshop 2023*, pages 73–84, Singapore. Association for Computational Linguistics.

John J. Nay, David Karamardian, Sarah B. Lawsky, Wenting Tao, Meghana Bhat, Raghav Jain, Aaron Travis Lee, Jonathan H. Choi, and Jungo Kasai. 2023. Large language models as tax attorneys: A case study in legal capabilities emergence. *Preprint*, arXiv:2306.07075.

OpenAI. 2023a. Gpt-4 developer livestream.

OpenAI. 2023b. Gpt-4 technical report. *Preprint*, arXiv:2303.08774.

Sumit Pai, Sounak Lahiri, Ujjwal Kumar, Krishanu Baksi, Elijah Soba, Michael Suesserman, Nirmala Pudota, Jon Foster, Edward Bowen, and Sanmitra Bhattacharya. 2023. Exploration of open large language models for eDiscovery. In *Proceedings of the Natural Legal Language Processing Workshop 2023,* pages 166–177, Singapore. Association for Computational Linguistics.

Bhargavi Paranjape, Scott Lundberg, Sameer Singh, Hannaneh Hajishirzi, Luke Zettlemoyer, and Marco Tulio Ribeiro. 2023. Art: Automatic multi-step reasoning and tool-use for large language models. *arXiv preprint arXiv:2303.09014*.

Drescher ProParalegal. 2017. Practice tip sheet.

Adam Roegiest, Radha Chitta, Jonathan Donnelly, Maya Lash, Alexandra Vtyurina, and Francois Longtin. 2023. Questions about contracts: Prompt templates for structured answer generation. In *Proceedings of the Natural Legal Language Processing Workshop 2023*, pages 62–72, Singapore. Association for Computational Linguistics.

Jaromír Savelka, Kevin D. Ashley, Morgan A. Gray, Hannes Westermann, and Huihui Xu. 2023. Can GPT-4 support analysis of textual data in tasks requiring highly specialized domain expertise? In *Proceedings of the 6th Workshop on Automated Semantic Analysis of Information in Legal Text co-located with the 19th International Conference on Artificial Intelligence and Law (ICAIL 2023), Braga, Portugal, 23rd September, 2023*, volume 3441 of *CEUR Workshop Proceedings*, pages 1–12. CEUR-WS.org.

Timo Schick, Jane Dwivedi-Yu, Roberto Dessì, Roberta Raileanu, Maria Lomeli, Luke Zettlemoyer, Nicola Cancedda, and Thomas Scialom. 2023. Toolformer: Language models can teach themselves to use tools. *arXiv preprint arXiv:2302.04761*.

Sakib Shahriar, Brady D. Lund, Nishith Reddy Mannuru, Muhammad Arbab Arshad, Kadhim Hayawi, Ravi Varma Kumar Bevara, Aashrith Mannuru, and Laiba Batool. 2024. Putting gpt-4o to the sword: A comprehensive evaluation of language, vision, speech, and multimodal proficiency. *Applied Sciences*, 14(17):7782.

Aarohi Srivastava, Abhinav Rastogi, Abhishek Rao, Abu Awal Md Shoeb, Abubakar Abid, and Adam Fisch et al. 2023. Beyond the imitation game: Quantifying and extrapolating the capabilities of language models. *Preprint*, arXiv:2206.04615.

Kristina Toutanova, Dan Klein, Christopher D. Manning, and Yoram Singer. 2003. Feature-rich part-of-speech tagging with a cyclic dependency network. In *Human Language Technology Conference of the North American Chapter of the Association for Computational Linguistics, HLT-NAACL 2003, Edmonton, Canada, May 27 - June 1, 2003*. The Association for Computational Linguistics.

Jules White, Quchen Fu, Sam Hays, Michael Sandborn, Carlos Olea, Henry Gilbert, Ashraf Elnashar, Jesse Spencer-Smith, and Douglas C. Schmidt. 2023. A prompt pattern catalog to enhance prompt engineering with chatgpt. *Preprint*, arXiv:2302.11382.

Xuanxin Wu and Yuki Arase. 2024. An in-depth evaluation of gpt-4 in sentence simplification with error-based human assessment. *Preprint*, arXiv:2403.04963.

Chaojun Xiao, Haoxi Zhong, Zhipeng Guo, Cunchao Tu, Zhiyuan Liu, Maosong Sun, Yansong Feng, Xianpei Han, Zhen Hu, Heng Wang, and Jianfeng Xu. 2018. CAIL2018: A large-scale legal dataset for judgment prediction. *CoRR*, abs/1807.02478.

Fangyi Yu, Lee Quartey, and Frank Schilder. 2022. Legal prompting: Teaching a language model to think like a lawyer. *CoRR*, abs/2212.01326.

Joanna Zhao and Xinruo Wang. 2024. Unleashing efficiency and insights: Exploring the potential applications and challenges of chatgpt in accounting. *Journal of Corporate Accounting & Finance*, 35(1):269–276.

Haoxi Zhong, Chaojun Xiao, Cunchao Tu, Tianyang Zhang, Zhiyuan Liu, and Maosong Sun. 2020. How does nlp benefit legal system: A summary of legal artificial intelligence. In *Proceedings of the 58th Annual Meeting of the Association for Computational Linguistics*, pages 5218–5230.

A Synthetic Section Sizes

Larger versions of BLT have longer and more complicated prompts. Below are the size of synthetic sections in each size of BLT. The generated prompts are distributed uniformly among these section sizes. For example, one-quarter of BLT-16k's synthetic statutes are 5-wide, 4-deep; one-quarter are 8-wide, 3-deep; and so on.

Version	Sizes
BLT-4k	2 wide, 2 deep
	2 wide, 3 deep
	2 wide, 4 deep
	2 wide, 5 deep
	3 wide, 2 deep
	3 wide, 3 deep
	3 wide, 4 deep
	4 wide, 2 deep
	4 wide, 3 deep
BLT-8k	2 wide, 6 deep
	3 wide, 5 deep
	4 wide, 4 deep
	7 wide, 3 deep
	20 wide, 2 deep
BLT-16k	5 wide, 4 deep
	8 wide, 3 deep
	9 wide, 3 deep
	30 wide, 2 deep
BLT-32k	3 wide, 6 deep
	4 wide, 5 deep
	6 wide, 4 deep
	12 wide, 3 deep
	11 wide, 3 deep
	44 wide, 2 deep
	40 wide, 2 deep
BLT-64k	7 wide, 4 deep
	16 wide, 3 deep
	15 wide, 3 deep
	14 wide, 3 deep
	13 wide, 3 deep
	60 wide, 2 deep
	65 wide, 2 deep
BLT-128k	4 wide, 6 deep
	5 wide, 5 deep
	8 wide, 4 deep
	9 wide, 4 deep
	20 wide, 3 deep
	80 wide, 2 deep

B Transcript Quotation Sizes

Larger versions of BLT have longer prompts. Below are the number of pages of deposition transcript quotation used in each size BLT model.

Version	Transcript Pages
BLT-4k	1, 2
BLT-8k	5, 10, 15
BLT-16k	25, 40
BLT-32k	30, 60, 80
BLT-64k	100, 130
BLT-128k	120, 140

The generated prompts are distributed uniformly among these page sizes. For example, half of BLT-4k's prompts have one-page deposition quotations and the other half have two-page deposition quotations.

C Example GPT-4 failing on a 2-page transcript text→cite Prompt

Page 68:
1: after the accident?
2: A. He called me – that same day,
3: he called me at nighttime and asked me how
4: I was.
5: Q. He called you and asked you how
6: you were?
7: A. Yes.
8: Q. What did you tell him?
9: A. I just told him that I wasn't
10: feeling good, that I was just laying in
11: bed.
12: Q. And what did he say?
13: A. He said take the pills I gave
14: you, you'll be ready and better by next
15: week. He was just giving me something like
16: a fast way for me to feel up, to cheer up.
17: It wasn't helping.
18: Q. Going back to your primary care
19: physician. You said she wanted to send you
20: to a specialist?
21: A. Yes.
22: Q. But then you called workers'
23: comp?
24: A. Yeah, that's when the issue
25: happened and I called workers' comp.

Page 69:
1: Q. Then who did you treat with
2: next?

3: A. I treated with CityMD.
4: Q. You said CityMD?
5: A. Yes.
6: Q. Was the place that you went to
7: the first time the same place that you went
8: like after you went to your primary care
9: physician?
10: A. Excuse me again?
11: MR. GROSSMAN: You said you
12: went to CityMD. She thinks you went
13: twice, did you go twice?
14: THE WITNESS: No.
15: MR. GROSSMAN: Then you're not
16: listening to the question. You went
17: to CityMD first, then you went to
18: your primary physician. Now, she
19: wants to know where you went next.
20: THE WITNESS: No, first I went
21: to the primary.
22: MR. GROSSMAN: First primary,
23: and then CityMD and then where did
24: you go?
25: THE WITNESS: I was in CityMD

What are the page number and line number of the line above with the text "your primary physician. Now, she"?

The page number is 69 and the line number is 19.

Note that GPT-4's answer above is wrong, since the requested text is on line 18, not 19.

D GPT-4 Errors on Transcripts

GPT-4 performs surprisingly poorly on transcripts, even the 1- and 2-page transcripts in BLT-4k. Below are GPT-4's errors on the large runs used to investigate the problem. Our API-calling code automatically categorizes the errors.

D.1 GPT-4's errors on transcript text→cite from BLT-4k

Recall that we generated 1,000 new BLT-4k style transcripts with text→cite prompts to investigate GPT-4's poor performance. Below is a tabulation of the lines returned by GPT-4 relative to the correct ones. We see that the overwhelming majority of errors are returning the line before or line after the correct one.

#	**Relative Error**
3	prior page
1	19 before
1	3 before
1	2 before
12	1 before (i.e. prior line)
76	1 after (i.e. next line)
1	2 after
1	3 after
1	next page

D.2 GPT-4's errors on transcript cite→text from BLT-4k

Recall that we generated 1,000 new BLT-4k style transcripts with cite→text prompts to investigate GPT-4's poor performance on that task. Below is a tabulation of the errors.

#	**Type of Error**
166	wrong line
48	superset
10	not found
9	subset wrong line
7	multiple wrong lines
3	subset

There was a difference in the type of errors on one-page versus two-page. Almost all (84%) the errors on two-page transcripts was returning the text from the wrong line (almost always the line before or after the correct one). But one-page transcripts were only 51% wrong-line errors, with 35% being superset errors, where GPT-4 returned not only the text of the requested line, but also part of adjacent lines. Here is an example of a superset error that occurred on this dataset:

...
22: MS. WOLVERTON: Objection. Vague. Whose
23: e-mail records?
24: Q Ms. Abedin's e-mail records located. I
25: apologize.

What is the exact text of just line 25 above?

GPT-4 returned "Q Ms. Abedin's e-mail records located. I apologize." which is actually lines 24 and 25, whereas the prompt asks for "the exact text of **just** line 25 above". These superset errors are much more understandable from a human perspective than an entirely wrong line, but they still fail according to the clear instructions in the prompt, with the word 'just'.

Of the 1,000 prompts, 166 were "wrong line" errors. Below shows the position, relative to the correct one, from which the text was incorrectly drawn:

#	Relative Error
2	prior page
4	same page, >3 lines before
1	3 lines before
6	2 lines before
81	prior line
39	next line
10	2 lines after
7	3 lines after
6	4 lines after
15	same page, >4 lines after
3	next page

As with text→cite, here we see the overwhelming majority of wrong line errors are returning either the prior line or next line.

E Sensitivity analysis on GPT-4's transcript text→cite errors

Recall that GPT-4 performs poorly on text→cite, so we attempted a sensitivity analysis, seeing how performance on the 100 test prompts for the task in BLT-4k changed with changes in the phrasing within the prompt. The results are below.

BLT-4k default **What are the page number and line number of the line above with the text "__"?**	82/100
Move question from end to beginning, so question is **What are the page number and line number of the line below with the text "__"?**	99/100
Keep question at end, adding "exact" so question is **What are the exact page number and the exact line number of the line above with the text "__"?**	84/100
Keep question at end, adding "precise" so question is **What are the precise page number and the precise line number of the line above with the text "__"?**	84/100
Keep default question at end, but add the following introduction at the start: **Below is a portion of a transcript, with each line starting with a number that is important for referring to that line.**	93/100

The improvement from moving the question to the start motivated further experimentation, below.

F Question at Start versus End

Because transcript text→cite on GPT-4 saw large improvements from moving the question from the bottom (which is the standard for all of BLT-* for all tasks) to the top, we attempted the same change for all BLT-4k, running against GPT-4:

text and task	question at...	
	end	start
transcript text→cite	82	99
transcript cite→text	78	85
synthetic text→cite	88	91
synthetic cite→text	97	82
synthetic defined→cite	90	82
synthetic cite→defined	100	98
uscode text→cite	98	96
uscode cite→text	93	82
uscode cite→amendedtext	93	82
uscode defined→cite	98	71
uscode cite→defined	100	100

We see that GPT-4 is quite sensitive to whether the question is at the top or bottom. But moving the question to the start actually produced worse results for 7 of the 11 tasks. This indicates that the improvement in transcript text→cite by moving the question to the top was an outlier.

G Sensitivity analysis on GPT-4's transcript cite→text errors

Recall that GPT-4 did poorly on transcript text→cite and that we performed a sensitivity analysis, discussed in Appendix E. Since GPT-4 also did pooorly on cite→text, we also do a sensitivity analysis on that.

BLT-4k default **What is the exact text of just line _ of page _ above?**	78/100
Move question from end to beginning, so question is **What is the exact text of just line _ of page _ below?**	85/100
Rephase as **Return the exact text of just line 4 of page 59 above?**	74/100
Change "exact" to "precise", so question is **What is the precise text of just line _ of page _ above?**	79/100
Add clarification, so question is **What is the exact text of just line _ of page _ above? Return just the text on that line and return none of the text on the line before or after, even if necessary for a full sentence.**	62/100
Keep default question at end, but add the following introduction at the start: **Below is a portion of a transcript, with each line starting with a number that is important for referring to that line.**	90/100

H Example of fine-tuned GPT-3.5-turbo performing better

Recall that fine-tuning GPT-3.5-turbo on part of BLT-4k's training set improved its performance on the SARA dataset (Holzenberger et al., 2020). Below we have an example SARA prompt used, plus both non-tuned GPT-3.5-turbo's answer and the fine-tuned version's answer. We see the fine-tuned version sticks much more closely to the relevant statutory text and thus comes to the correct answer.

The prompt (edited with ellipses for brevity):

We are going to be doing Entailment/Contradiction reasoning applying the statute(s) below:
§2. Definitions and special rules
(a) Definition of surviving spouse
(1) In general
For purposes of section 1, the term "surviving spouse" means a taxpayer-
(A) whose spouse died during either of the two years immediately preceding the taxable year, and
(B) who maintains as his home a household which constitutes for the taxable year the principal place of abode (as a member of such household) of a dependent (i) who (within the meaning of section 152) is a son, stepson, daughter, or stepdaughter of the taxpayer, and (ii) with respect to whom the taxpayer is entitled to a deduction for the taxable year under section 151.
***
(b) Definition of head of household
(1) In general ***
(2) Determination of status
Notwithstanding paragraph (1),
(A) an individual who is legally separated from his spouse under a decree of divorce or of separate maintenance shall not be considered as married;
(B) a taxpayer shall be considered as not married at the close of his taxable year if at any time during the taxable year his spouse is a nonresident alien; and
(C) a taxpayer shall be considered as married at the close of his taxable year if his spouse (other than a spouse described in subparagraph (B)) died during the taxable year.
***
Premise: Alice and Bob got married on Feb 3rd, 1992. Alice died on July 9th, 2014.
Hypothesis: Section 2(b)(2)(C) applies to Bob in 2014.
Answer:

Non-tuned GPT-3.5-turbo's incorrect answer:

To determine whether Section 2(b)(2)(C) applies to Bob in 2014, we need to analyze the relevant provisions of the tax code.

Section 2(b)(2)(C) states that a taxpayer shall be considered as married at the close of his taxable year if his spouse (other than a spouse described in subparagraph (B)) died during the taxable year.

In this case, Alice, Bob's spouse, died on July 9th, 2014. To determine if Section 2(b)(2)(C) applies to Bob in 2014, we need to consider whether Alice's death during the taxable year qualifies Bob as a surviving spouse.

According to Section 2(a)(1)(A), a surviving spouse is defined as a taxpayer whose spouse died during either of the two years immediately preceding the taxable year. In this case, Alice died in 2014, which is within the two years immediately preceding the taxable year.

Next, we need to consider Section 2(a)(1)(B), which states that a surviving spouse must maintain as his home a household that constitutes the principal place of abode of a dependent. The dependent must be a son, stepson, daughter, or stepdaughter of the taxpayer, and the taxpayer must be entitled to a deduction for the taxable year under Section 151.

In this case, we don't have information about whether Bob has a dependent who meets the criteria mentioned above. Therefore, we cannot determine if Bob meets the requirements of a surviving spouse under Section 2(a)(1)(B).

Since we cannot determine if Bob meets the requirements of a surviving spouse, we cannot conclude whether Section 2(b)(2)(C) applies to Bob in 2014.

Fine-tuned GPT-3.5-turbo's correct answer:

To determine if Section 2(b)(2)(C) applies to Bob in 2014, we need to consider the marital status of Bob and whether his spouse died during the taxable year.

According to the premise, Alice died on July 9th, 2014, and she was married to Bob. Therefore, we need to determine Bob's marital status at the close of the taxable year 2014.

Since Bob and Alice got married on Feb 3rd, 1992, and Alice died in 2014, Bob was married to Alice at the close of 2014.

Therefore, Section 2(b)(2)(C) applies to Bob in 2014 because his spouse (Alice) died during the taxable year.

I Dataset Statistics

We computed statistics on the BLT dataset using NLTK's tokenizers and Stanford's tagger (Bird

	transc.		synthetic section				U.S. Code				
	text→cite	cite→text	text→cite	cite→text	defined→cite	cite→defined	text→cite	cite→text	cite→amended	defined→cite	cite→defined
mean	11.3	11.3	51.3	51.5	30.5	30.6	48.7	48.6	48.6	48.6	48.5
stddev	11.4	11.4	58.5	58.6	29.3	29.3	93.9	95.0	95.0	93.4	93.8
median	7	7	37	37	22	22	29	29	29	29	29
min	1	1	3	3	3	3	2	1	1	1	1
max	286	286	490	490	250	250	6383	6383	6383	6383	6383

Table 3: Number of words per sentence in the training set. Statistics computed across all sizes of the BLT dataset. Sentence and word boundaries were determined using NLTK's standard tokenizer (Bird et al., 2009).

Adjective	3	3	1	1	2	2	7	7	7	7	7
Adverb	4	4	0	0	1	1	1	1	2	1	2
Conjunction	11	11	2	2	3	4	19	19	19	19	19
Determiner	7	8	15	15	25	23	11	11	11	11	11
Noun	19	21	28	29	29	29	29	29	29	29	30
Number	11	11	3	2	0	0	3	3	3	2	3
Pronoun	8	6	0	0	0	0	0	0	0	0	0
Punctuation	24	23	51	50	36	37	19	19	19	19	19
Verb	13	13	0	0	3	4	10	10	10	10	10

Table 4: Part-of-speech tags in % of occurrence, rounded to the closest percentage point. Statistics computed across all sizes of the BLT dataset, on a 1% subset drawn at random from the training set for each task. Sentence and word boundaries were determined using NLTK's standard tokenizer (Bird et al., 2009). Part-of-speech tags were inferred using Stanford's POS tagger (Toutanova et al., 2003).

et al., 2009; Toutanova et al., 2003). Number of sentences per document (Table 5) and number of words per sentence (Table 3) were computed on the entire training set. The distribution of part-of-speech tags (Table 4) was computed using 1% of the training set, chosen at random. Given that these automatic tools were trained on standard written English, they may give somewhat inaccurate results on legal English.

BLT		transc.		synthetic section				U.S. Code				
		text→cite	cite→text	text→cite	cite→text	defined→cite	cite→defined	text→cite	cite→text	cite→amended	defined→cite	cite→defined
4k	mean	34.5	33.7	25.0	24.0	25.0	24.0	58.9	58.7	58.7	63.8	63.1
	stddev	15.3	15.1	16.9	16.9	16.9	16.9	19.4	20.6	20.6	20.9	21.3
	median	32	31	21	20	21	20	58	58	58	63	62
	min	8	8	8	7	8	7	5	4	4	9	8
	max	81	79	57	56	57	56	119	219	219	133	132
8k	mean	215.4	214.6	93.6	92.6	93.6	92.6	121.4	119.7	119.7	127.1	127.4
	stddev	105.9	105.8	46.0	46.0	46.0	46.0	34.9	32.9	32.9	36.6	35.8
	median	205.5	205	98	97	98	97	124	122	122	127	129
	min	58	57	26	25	26	25	34	29	29	23	32
	max	472	471	165	164	165	164	213	210	210	240	238
16k	mean	722.4	721.6	104.5	103.5	104.5	103.5	231.7	231.7	231.7	233.5	231.5
	stddev	262.7	262.5	56.0	56.0	56.0	56.0	62.3	62.0	62.0	65.0	65.0
	median	644.5	643	95.5	94.5	95.5	94.5	231	231	231	240.5	235
	min	315	315	36	35	36	35	68	61	61	90	89
	max	1187	1186	191	190	191	190	435	401	401	389	390
32k	mean	1263	1263	234.7	233.7	234.7	233.7	461.8	460.4	460.4	462.6	458.0
	stddev	566.3	566.2	164.2	164.2	164.2	164.2	104.8	102.8	102.8	104.9	107.5
	median	1183	1181	174	173	174	173	469	473	473	478	470
	min	391	390	46	45	46	45	173	183	183	171	185
	max	2307	2305	489	488	489	488	768	767	767	740	752
64k	mean	2531	2530	226.2	225.2	226.2	225.2	873.1	874.4	874.4	884.9	884.1
	stddev	799.3	799.0	126.2	126.2	126.2	126.2	199.4	199.2	199.2	177.3	176.2
	median	2721	2720	230	229	230	229	875	874	874	883	882
	min	1365	1365	66	65	66	65	425	402	402	425	424
	max	3648	3646	461	460	461	460	1377	1375	1375	1318	1378
128k	mean	2874	2873	793.3	792.3	793.3	792.3	1817	1820	1820	1805	1818
	stddev	872.6	872.4	503.2	503.2	503.2	503.2	320.7	304.3	304.3	301.3	307.2
	median	3306	3305	788.5	787.5	788.5	787.5	1804	1825	1825	1794	1816
	min	1671	1671	86	85	86	85	904	903	903	983	923
	max	3929	3926	1710	1709	1710	1709	2752	2657	2657	2776	2751

Table 5: Number of sentences per document in the training set. At most 4 significant digits were kept. Sentence boundaries were determined using NLTK's standard tokenizer (Bird et al., 2009).

Multi-Property Multi-Label Documents Metadata Recommendation based on Encoder Embeddings

Nasredine Cheniki
Publications Office
of the European Union
nasredine.cheniki@ext.ec.europa.eu

Vidas Daudaravicius
European Commission
Joint Research Centre
vidas.daudaravicius@ec.europa.eu

Abdelfettah Feliachi
Publications Office
of the European Union
abdelfettah.feliachi
@ext.publications.europa.eu

Didier Hardy
Publications Office
of the European Union
didier.hardy@publications.europa.eu

Marc Wilhelm Küster
Publications Office
of the European Union
marc.kuster@publications.europa.eu

Abstract

The task of document classification, particularly multi-label classification, presents a significant challenge due to the complexity of assigning multiple relevant labels to each document. This complexity is further amplified in multi-property multi-label classification tasks, where documents must be categorized across various sets of labels. In this research, we introduce an innovative encoder embedding-driven approach to multi-property multi-label document classification that leverages semantic-text similarity and the reuse of pre-existing annotated data to enhance the efficiency and accuracy of the document annotation process. Our method requires only a single model for text similarity, eliminating the need for multiple property-specific classifiers and thereby reducing computational demands and simplifying deployment. We evaluate our approach through a prototype deployed at the European Commission for daily operations, which demonstrates superior performance over existing classification systems. Our contributions include improved accuracy without additional training, increased efficiency, and demonstrated effectiveness in practical applications. The results of our study indicate the potential of our approach to be applied across various domains requiring multi-property multi-label document classification, offering a scalable and adaptable solution for metadata annotation tasks.

1 Introduction

Metadata facilitates navigation through extensive document collections, offering insights into data usage, retrieval, traceability, and reusability. It also refines search processes within large datasets. Document classification, also known as document annotation, is crucial for information retrieval applications and involves tagging documents with various metadata. This task is laborious, especially when multiple labels per document are required. The complexity increases with multi-property multi-label classification tasks, where each property may contain multiple labels.

Recent advances in document classification (Song et al., 2022; Chalkidis et al., 2019) using natural language processing have significantly improved efficiency, accuracy, and completeness of metadata. However, these methods typically necessitate the development and training of separate models for each classification property, which is resource-intensive and time-consuming. Furthermore, the need for continuous retraining to update these models with new properties and labels presents challenges in scalability and adaptability.

In this paper, we introduce an innovative approach for multi-property, multi-label document classification that is driven by encoder embeddings. Our method capitalizes on semantic-text similarity,

Proceedings of the Natural Legal Language Processing Workshop 2024, pages 233–242
November 16, 2024 ©2024 Association for Computational Linguistics

using pre-annotated datasets to streamline the annotation process. It stands out by eliminating the need for additional model training or fine-tuning, which greatly reduces computational requirements and eases deployment. Our proposed approach is highly applicable in use-cases where multi-label annotated data already exists which is often a use case in various enterprises.

We leverage pre-trained models like BERT(Devlin et al., 2018) to avoid fine-tuning, making our solution more scalable and flexible. Our prototype, tested at the European Commission for daily operations, has outperformed existing systems, enhancing efficiency and accuracy in document annotation. The success of our approach suggests its applicability in various settings that require sophisticated document classification.

The key contributions of our study are as follows:

- Improved Accuracy Without Additional Training: We leverage pre-trained embeddings to enhance the accuracy of document classification without the need for further training. This approach not only speeds up the process but also yields better accuracy in annotating documents with various properties and labels.
- Enhanced Efficiency: Our technique utilizes a single text similarity model instead of multiple classifiers tailored to specific properties. This greatly simplifies deployment in practical settings where there are often limitations on computational resources and time.
- Proven Practical Effectiveness: Our method's integration into the daily operations of the European Commission. Empirical results shows that our approach outperforms existing systems in document classification tasks.

2 Related Work

Classifying large collections of documents is time intensive and consuming task. However, recent breakthroughs in NLP and the development of large language models (LLMs) have greatly improved the efficiency of this process. Avram et al. (2021) proposed a framework for classifying documents according to the EuroVoc framework in 22 different languages[1] by fine-tuning advanced Transformer-based pretrained language models. This method has shown significant improvements in classification accuracy. Nonetheless, it requires individual training for each language, leading to high computational demands and difficulties in scaling, particularly when new descriptors or languages need to be added.

Suominen (2019) introduced Annif, a tool that automates the labor-intensive process of subject indexing for librarians. It uses a combination of existing tools and various NLP algorithms to boost accuracy and versatility for different types of documents. However, its effectiveness might be limited in environments with constantly changing content.

Chalkidis et al. (2019) developed a technique for classifying legal documents using a dataset annotated with EuroVoc labels, comprising 57,000 texts. They found that self-attention mechanisms and domain-specific embeddings notably improve classification performance. However, this method is computationally expensive, particularly for long documents, due to the inclusion of GRU units.

Chang et al. (2020) created the X-Transformer model to address issues in extreme multi-label text classification, which involves dealing with vast output spaces and tackling the problem of label sparsity. Their model surpasses traditional models in various benchmarks and achieves top-tier results. However, this model requires considerable GPU resources and has scalability issues when faced with large sets of labels due to memory limitations.

Wan et al. (2019) tackled the challenge of classifying long legal documents by breaking them down into smaller sections. They found that this segmentation, along with the use of BiLSTM networks and simpler architectures, made it easier to process lengthy texts. The effectiveness of this approach depends heavily on the quality of the initial segmentation, as poor segmentation can lead to complications in the model's implementation and fine-tuning, especially if it doesn't correctly reflect the thematic or semantic divisions within the documents.

3 Background and Definitions

In this section, we provide detailed definitions of the terms and key concepts used in this paper, including Document, Context, Metadata , semantic text similarity, k-nearest neighbors.

3.1 Document and dataset

A document in the context of this study consists of two main components: text and metadata. Let d_i

[1] In 2024, the number of supported languages in EuroVoc is 27.

denote a document that belongs to a dateset DT, which can be formally described as:

$$d_i = (T_i, M_i) \in DT$$

where T represents the text component of the document and M represents the metadata associated with the document.

3.1.1 Text

A text is a primary component of a document that refers to the plain, natural language content that conveys information. This includes sentences, paragraphs, titles, abstracts, and other narrative elements. The text can be further decomposed into specific contexts $C_1, C_2, \ldots, C_n$, where each C_i denotes a specific part of the text relevant to the analysis.

$$T = \{C_1, C_2, \ldots, C_n\}$$

3.1.2 Metadata

Metadata is structured information which provides additional context and attributes that help to categorize and identify the document.

The metadata M consists of various properties $P_1, P_2, \ldots, P_m$ and their corresponding sets of values, where each property P_i is an attribute of the document, and $\{V_{i1}, V_{i2}, \ldots, V_{in_i}\}$ are the values assigned to that attribute. A property can have multiple values.

$$M = \{(P_i, \{V_{i,j}\})\}$$

3.1.2.1 Classification Properties

Classes are predefined categories or labels that are assigned to documents based on their content. Within this study, each class is denoted by V_{ij}, where i represents the property index, and j denotes the specific class within that property. A document d_i can belong to one or more of these classes based on the corresponding property.

Let V_{ij} represent a specific class for property p_i. The membership of a document d in multiple classes is represented as follows:

$$d \in \bigcup_{i,j} V_{ij}$$

Here, the notation $\bigcup_{i,j} V_{ij}$ indicates the union of classes to which the document d may belong, emphasizing that a document can be associated with multiple classes across different properties.

3.2 Embedding

Embedding is a technique used to convert the context of a document into a vector in a continuous vector space. This vector representation captures the semantics of the context, allowing for various computational operations such as similarity measurements and clustering. Let E_m denote an embedding function based on model m that maps the context of a document C to a vector $\mathbf{v}$ in an n-dimensional continuous vector space. Formally, the embedding function E_m can be described as:

$$E_m : C_i \to \mathbb{R}^n$$

where:

- C_i is the context of the document, which can be a sentence, paragraph, or any specific part of the text.
- $\mathbb{R}^n$ is the n-dimensional continuous vector space.
- $\mathbf{v_i} = E_m(C_i)$ is the resulting n-dimensional vector that represents the semantics of the context C_i.

Embeddings are typically obtained using neural network models trained on large text corpora, such as DistilBERT (Sanh et al., 2019), RoBERTa (Liu et al., 2020) or BERT (Reimers and Gurevych, 2019). The length of a context is delimited by the input size of such transformer language model.

3.3 K-Nearest Neighbors (K-NN)

K-Nearest Neighbors (K-NN) is a machine learning algorithm used to identify the most similar documents to a new document based on their embeddings.

For a given document d_x and its vector representation $\mathbf{v_x}$, K-NN aims to find the subset $S \subseteq D$ of k documents that are highly similar to d_x as measured by a specific distance metric μ (e.g., Euclidean distance).

$$S_{d_x} = \text{kNN}(\mathbf{v}_x, \mathbf{v}_i, \mu, k)$$

where:

- d_x: The new document for which we are finding the nearest neighbors.
- v_x: The vector embedding of the new document.
- $\mathbf{v}_i$: The vector embeddings of all documents in the dataset D.
- μ: The metric used for measuring distances (Euclidean or Manhattan).
- k: The number of nearest neighbors to retrieve.

The function maximizes the similarity between $\mathbf{v}_x$ and $\mathbf{v}_i$ to identify the nearest neighbors.

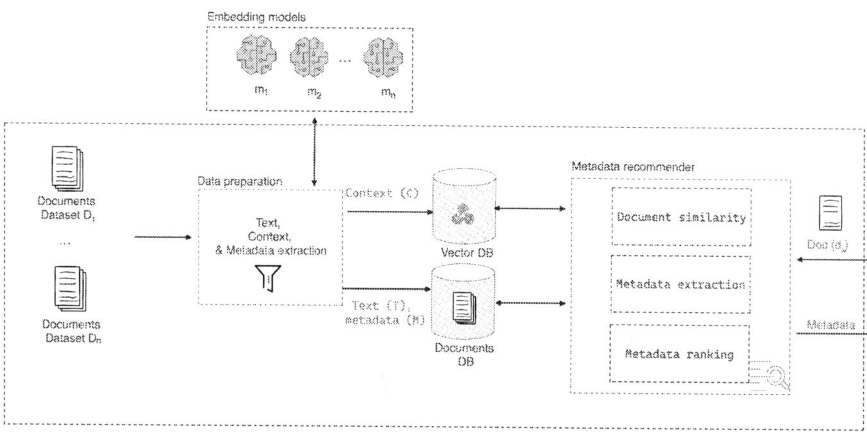

Figure 1: k–NN-based metadata replication framework

4 Multi-property Multi-label Documents Classification

In this section, we present our method for Multi-property Multi-label document classification. Figure 1 illustrates the key components of our approach, from document datasets to metadata recommendation.

4.1 Data Preparation

Initially, datasets retrieved from various sources undergo data cleaning and preparation. This step ensures that the data is consistent, accurate, and ready for processing. This preparation is crucial for effective feature extraction in later stages.

4.2 Context and Vector Embeddings

The number of contexts per document is not balanced among documents, sometimes can reach over 2000 contexts in a document, and it may lead a long document to be overvalued. Therefore, in this stage, only the first context C_1 is extracted from each document which is a title and a summary often. Context may include all textual content or parts of the document. Subsequently, this context is used in the embedding process, where an embedding model m converts the context into vector embeddings $\mathbf{v}_i$. These embeddings capture the semantics of the text and are stored in a vector database (Vector DB).

$$\mathbf{v} = E_m(C_1)$$

4.3 Metadata and Text Database

Parallel to embedding, metadata M_i and a first context C_1 from each document are extracted and stored in a vector database (vector DB). This database supports facilitates access to both the raw text and its associated metadata, ensuring that these elements are readily available for retrieval and analysis.

4.4 Metadata recommendation

This phase is central to our approach and involves several sub-processes designed to leverage the prepared data and embeddings for effective metadata recommendation.

4.4.1 Document Similarity

When a new document d_x is introduced, the system applies K-NN algorithm to find the n most similar documents from the Vector DB based on their vector embeddings $\mathbf{v}_i$. This process identifies k documents with the highest semantic similarity to d_x, suggesting a high potential relevance of their metadata for d_x.

$$\text{kNN}(\mathbf{v}_x, \mathbf{v}_i, \mu, k) \rightarrow \{d_1, d_2, \ldots, d_k\}$$

where: μ is the Euclidean distance metric used to measure the similarity between two vector embeddings. It is defined as:

$$\mu(\mathbf{v}_x, \mathbf{v}_i) = \sqrt{\sum_{j=1}^{n}(v_{xj} - v_{ij})^2}$$

4.4.2 Metadata Extraction

The metadata identified for document d_x in the previous stage is extracted and collected for further processing, where:

$$\text{Metadata}(d_1, \ldots, d_k; P) \rightarrow \{V_{P,1}^{(f_1)}, \ldots, V_{P,n}^{(f_m)}\}$$

where each $V_{P,i}$ is the values of a specific metadata property P and f_i is the frequency of occurrence of $V_{P,i}$ in the similar documents $d_1, d_2, \ldots, d_k$.

4.4.3 Metadata Ranking

Using a defined scoring function, such as frequency, the list of metadata associated with the retrieved top documents is then ranked. The scoring function can be formalized as follows:

$$\text{Scoring}(d_x, P) \rightarrow \left[\text{V}_{P,1}^{(s_1)}, \text{V}_{P,2}^{(s_2)}, \ldots, \text{V}_{P,m}^{(s_m)}\right]$$

where $\text{V}_{P,i}^{(s_i)}$ denotes the metadata value V_i of a property P, with a score s_i assigned based on the frequency of its occurrence in documents similar to d_x. The list is sorted in descending order of s_i, indicating that values with higher scores are deemed more relevant to d_x.

The ranked metadata from this comprehensive process is then used to classify the new document d_x.

5 Implementation

5.1 Overview

We conducted two evaluation experiments. The first experiment aimed to validate the hypothesis that 'similar documents should have similar metadata.' In this experiment, a random set of documents was selected and subjected to the metadata recommendation process. The metadata recommended by the process was then compared with the metadata previously attributed to these documents.

The second experiment involved deploying our prototype in a real-world scenario to collect user feedback for benchmark comparisons. This allowed us to directly compare the performance and effectiveness of our approach with existing annotation systems.

5.2 Documents dataset

In this experiment, we utilize CELLAR as the document dataset. CELLAR[2] is the semantic repository of the European Union (EU) official publications, managed by the EU Publications Office(Francesconi et al., 2015). Documents in CELLAR are manually annotated by human agents. There are many metadata attributes assigned to documents, including publication date, document type, EuroVoc thesaurus concepts, and more. In this study, we focus on recommending properties that provide classifications, such as EuroVoc concepts.

Accordingly, we define our document dataset as:

$$DT = \{\text{CELLAR}\}$$

All documents, along with their embedding vectors, are stored in an Elasticsearch database. Metadata is retrieved directly from CELLAR as needed using its SPARQL endpoint.[3]

5.3 Metadata

Various controlled vocabularies are used to label documents in CELLAR (see example in Table 1). The Common Data Model (CDM)[4] provides a variety of properties (predicates) for describing bibliographic resources (documents, agents, events, etc.). In our study we focus on the properties of CDM that are more likely to be related to the topic or the theme of documents. For this purpose, we identified a set of properties that fulfil our objectives. We selected the following metadata properties:

- *EuroVoc concepts*: EuroVoc[5], a multilingual interdisciplinary thesaurus, that allows assigning specific topics to the description of resources. With more than 8000 terms in EuroVoc thesaurus, selecting the correct values to annotate documents with an acceptable accuracy is a time consuming task, even for experts with knowledge about the content of EuroVoc and the documents to annotate.
- *rdf type*: generic document type. There are 505 document types to describe any document in Cellar. For instance, thematic domain, EuroVoc concept, etc.
- *Theme*: the subject of the publication
- *Resource type*: the resource type of a work.
- *Subject matter*: a legal document is about a concept expressed as a subject matter. Very often this property is similar to EuroVoc concepts but is used for different purposes.

Therefore, our classification properties are defined as follows:

$$P = \{\text{EuroVoc, RDF-Type, Theme, Subject, Resource-Type}\}$$

The example of various document properties can be found in Table 1.

[2] https://op.europa.eu/en/web/eu-vocabularies/news/-/blogs/new-brochure-about-cellar

[3] https://publications.europa.eu/webapi/rdf/sparql

[4] https://op.europa.eu/it/web/eu-vocabularies/cdm

[5] https://op.europa.eu/en/web/eu-vocabularies/dataset/-/resource?uri=http://publications.europa.eu/resource/dataset/eurovoc

Actual labels	Proposed labels	Frequency
	EuroVoc descriptors	
EU financial instrument, investment, structural policy, transmission network, transport network, EU programme, sustainable development, project of common interest, energy grid, trans-European network	**investment, project of common interest, energy grid, trans-European network**	3
	reduction of gas emissions, renewable energy, **EU financial instrument, structural policy, transmission network, transport network, EU programme, sustainable development**	2
	energy cooperation, consumer information, financial occupation, insurance, investment company, disclosure of information, financial legislation, financial services, risk management, financial risk, energy policy, investment promotion, emission trading, climate change, greenhouse gas, transition economy, climate change policy, EU energy policy, security of supply, electricity supply, gas supply, electrical energy	1
	Subject matter descriptors	
Trans-European network	**Trans-European network**, Energy	2
	Investments, Free movement of capital, Environment, Economic policy, Trans-European networks	1
	rdf type descriptors	
Work, Legal resource	**Work**	10
	Legal resource	4
	Secondary legislation, Consolidated act	2
	Other act of the Council	1
	Resource type descriptors	
Regulation	Proposal for a regulation, Consolidated text	2
	Regulation, Communication, Legislative resolution, Roadmap, Proposal for an act, Note[a]	1

[a]Some proposed concepts might be irrelevant to a document because the search space of similar documents is not adjusted for a specific document but all available documents are reused.

Table 1: Labels of various properties of CELEX:32021R1153 document

5.4 Embedding model and metadata properties

To compute the embedding for a CELLAR Document, we use the *all-distilroberta-v1* model. This model, a Sentence Transformer model, maps sentences and paragraphs to a 768-dimensional dense vector space. It is effectively utilized for tasks such as clustering or semantic search.

To establish the context, we utilized the first 5,000 characters from the beginning of each document.

$$C(d) = \text{first}(5000, d)$$

Therefore, our embedding space is defined as follows:

$$E_{all-distilroberta-v1} : C \to \mathbb{R}^{768}$$

5.5 Metadata inference from similar documents

To validate our hypothesis, we conducted a series of experiments based on English documents from CELLAR. We utilized a snapshot of documents up to the year 2019, which includes more than 500,000 documents along with their associated metadata.

In our initial hypothesis validation experiment, we aim to evaluate recall only which is more important than precision in cases such as automated annotation process. A more detailed results using F1-score is presented in Section 5.6.4.

- We randomly selected a set of 1,000 documents from the CELLAR repository, all of which already have their associated metadata.
- For each document, we identified the first 10 most similar documents (for K-NN, $k = 10$), the 10 least similar documents (ranked 91-100) returned by the metadata recommender, and 10 randomly chosen documents for comparison.
- We then verified the presence of any metadata in the selected documents. To ensure accuracy, the original document was always excluded from the list of similar documents and never appeared in the selection of 10 similar documents. We introduced a hyper-parameter, L, as an experimental parameter to filter metadata values based on the frequency of their occurrence in similar documents. For instance, if $L = 1$, the metadata value must appear at least once among the metadata of similar documents; if $L = 10$, the metadata value must appear in all 10 similar documents.

This experiment was iterated three times, with results averaged to assess the overall efficacy of the the metadata recommendation process.

The results of the experiments show (see Figure 2) that we were able to retrieve significant amount of related metadata for various metadata properties such as *EuroVoc* (Fig. 2a) with 60%, *Theme* (Fig. 2b) with 70%, and *Subject-matter* (Fig. 2c) with 25% recall. However, for *rdf:type* (Fig. 2d) and *resource-type* (Fig. 2e) results are similar in all selected subsets (most/less/random). This is due to the fact that the distribution of these property values are not even. The L parameter determines how many concepts are selected. The lower is L value the more concepts are selected. It results in higher recall which is important in use cases of automated annotation when human annotators are selecting from the narrow list of candidates instead of using full list of concepts. Nevertheless, the human annotator can adjust L value at any time which brings high flexibility for annotators.

5.6 Use-Case: Document Annotation

After validating the hypothesis that metadata could be inferred from similar documents, we conducted a second experiment.

5.6.1 Deployed prototype and collected feedback

We deployed a prototype that implements our approach in a real-world annotation system scenario. Cataloguers have access to a prototype application where they can upload documents and receive metadata recommendations. We have collected usage feedback to establish a benchmark for comparison. This has enabled us to directly compare the performance and effectiveness of our approach with existing annotation systems. Figure 3 displays the user interface of our annotation application following the submission of a document. Annotation candidates are displayed in a table, allowing users to filter the results and select the most relevant ones. Users can also provide feedback to assess the quality of the returned results, which is subsequently used for comparative analysis.

In total, 967 documents were submitted for annotation and feedback was collected.

5.6.2 Evaluation Metrics

Our evaluation framework employed several metrics to measure the performance of our document annotator in comparison to the aforementioned tools. Here is a summary of the metrics:

- **Precision (Average):** Measures the accuracy of the selected annotations, indicating how many are relevant.
- **Recall (Average):** Assesses the tool's ability to identify all relevant annotations within the documents.
- **F1 Score (Average):** Provides a balance between precision and recall, offering a single score that measures overall accuracy.
- **Micro F1 Score:** Aggregates the contributions of all classes to compute the average F1 score, reflecting overall classification performance.
- **NDCG Score (Average):** Evaluates the ranking quality of the annotations by measuring the grading consistency of recommended tags. The value of NDCG is determined by comparing the relevance of the items returned by the search engine to the relevance of the item that a hypothetical "ideal" search engine would return(Järvelin and Kekäläinen, 2002).

5.6.3 Other annotation tools

This evaluation focuses on comparing our document annotator with two other tools.

- **Annif** (Suominen, 2019): Annif is an open-source toolkit designed for automated subject indexing using a variety of machine learning and AI-based algorithms for efficient text classification. Our approach is compared to an existing deployment of Annif, available at the Open Data Portal of the Publications Office of the European Commission[6].
- Eurovoc classifier based on EUBERT[7]: EUBERT is a pretrained BERT model that utilizes the vast corpus of documents from the European Publications Office. It is specifically tailored for tasks like text classification, question answering, and language understanding. The classification model is built on top of EUBERT with 7331 Eurovoc labels.

Since the compared tools recommend only Eurovoc metadata, we limit evaluated properties to only Eurovoc thesaurus.

5.6.4 Comparison and discussion

The feedback and quantitative metrics indicate that our prototype (CELLAR Annotator) surpasses both Annif and the Eurovoc classifier in terms of the F1 score across various top k values. The selection of top k values for the CELLAR annotator is based on concept score evaluation described in Section 4.4.3 and using value L=1.

[6] https://data.europa.eu/annif
[7] github.com/racai-ai/pyeurovoc

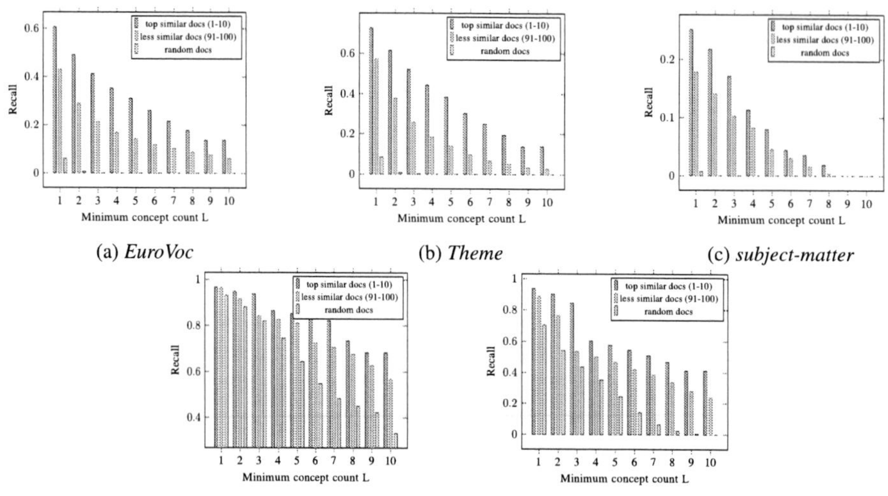

(a) *EuroVoc* (b) *Theme* (c) *subject-matter*

(d) *rdf:type* (e) *resource-type*

Figure 2: Metadata annotation results. X-axis is minimum concept frequency, y-axis is recall

As shown in Figure 4 (top left), the precision of Cellar Annotator consistently outperformed both Annif and EUBERT across all values of k. This indicates that Cellar Annotator has a higher accuracy in predicting relevant annotations, ensuring that the annotations provided are relevant and accurate. Specifically, the precision for Cellar Annotator remained above 0.9 for all values of $k <= 7$, highlighting its reliability in maintaining high precision even as the number of considered annotations increased.

In terms of recall (Figure 4, top right), Cellar Annotator significantly surpassed both Annif and EUBERT. This suggests that Cellar Annotator is more effective in retrieving all relevant annotations, thereby reducing the number of missed annotations. The recall values for Cellar Annotator consistently stayed above 0.55, while the other methods showed more variability and generally lower recall rates. This demonstrates the robust capability of Cellar Annotator to identify and recall relevant annotations comprehensively.

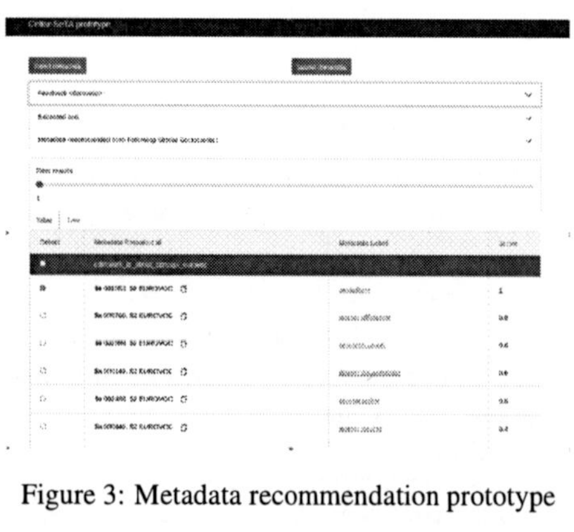

Figure 3: Metadata recommendation prototype

The micro F1 score, which balances precision and recall, further confirmed the superiority of Cellar Annotator (Figure 5, bottom left). The scores for Cellar Annotator were consistently higher, indicating a balanced performance in terms of both precision and recall. The micro F1 scores remained around 0.7 for Cellar Annotator, whereas Annif and EUBERT showed lower and more fluctuating scores. This balanced performance is crucial for applications where both high precision and recall are essential.

Finally, the NDCG scores (Figure 5, bottom right) demonstrated that Cellar Annotator also excels in ranking the most relevant annotations higher. With NDCG scores consistently around 0.75, Cellar Annotator ensures that the most pertinent annotations are prioritized, enhancing the overall utility and effectiveness of the annotation system. This metric is particularly important for user-facing applications where the relevance of top-ranked annotations significantly impacts user experience and satisfaction.

6 Conclusion and perspectives

In this paper, we present a novel method for multi-property multi-label document classification that leverages an encoder embedding-driven approach. Our technique aims to streamline the document an-

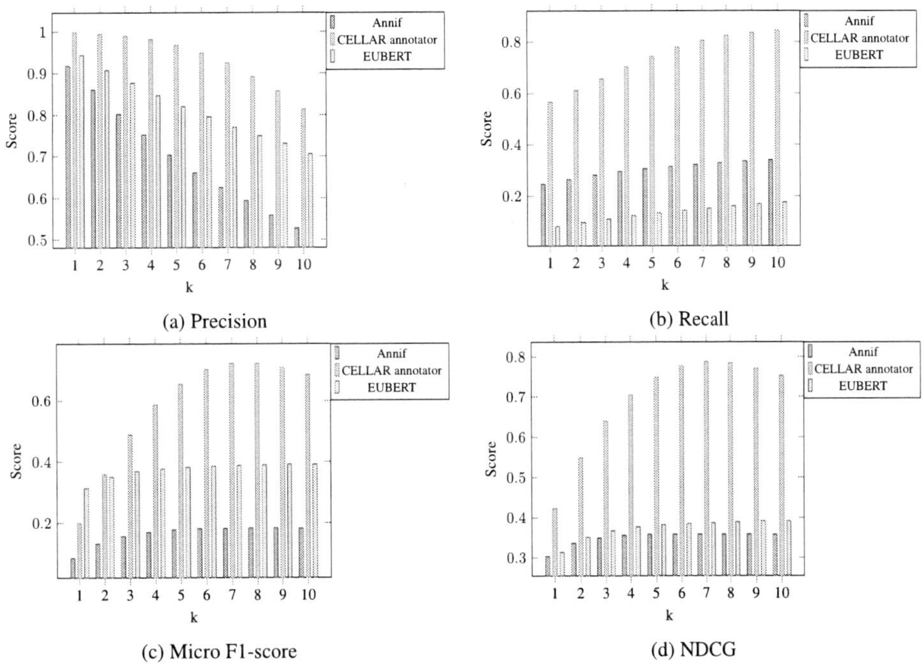

Figure 4: Precision, Recall, micro F1-score and NDCG results

notation process by utilizing semantic text similarity and the reuse of annotated data. This approach reduces the complexity associated with deploying multiple models, as it relies on a single model to assess text similarity, which results in enhanced efficiency compared to traditional classification methods.

The practical implementation of our prototype within the European Commission has yielded promising results. Empirical results show that our method surpasses the performance of existing systems, delivering superior accuracy and operational efficiency in practical settings.

For future work, we aim to assess additional state-of-the-art embedding models to further refine our approach. We also plan to expand our methodology by incorporating graph-based semantic similarity measures.

Limitations

One main limitation of the metadata replication approach is the sole focus on the reuse of the metadata data that has been used in the past. This may magnify labels related to the past manual captured metadata. All the possible values from the vocabularies are not necessarily present in the metadata regardless of their usefulness. This also sheds the light on an other limitation regarding the already used metadata: the distribution of the reuse of the values. The human bias induced in the manual metadata annotation could have an impact on the quality of the recommendations and should be further investigated and kept in mind for the industrialisation of this approach.

To address these limitations, we plan to introduce an option for exact matching of classes. This will facilitate the identification of new classes that have not been previously used for annotations, thereby expanding the scope and effectiveness of our metadata recommendations.

One significant constraint of metadata replication lies in its exclusive reliance on previously utilized metadata, potentially perpetuating biases linked to past manual annotations. Such an approach does not guarantee the inclusion of all valuable terms from controlled vocabularies, as not all possible values may be represented within the existing metadata. This limitation underscores another issue concerning the frequency of value reuse in metadata: the influence of human bias during manual annotation could affect the quality of generated recommendations, which merits closer examination and consideration during the process of operationalizing this methodology.

To mitigate these issues, we are proposing the integration of an exact matching feature for class identification. This enhancement aims to uncover novel classes that have not been employed in prior annotations, thus broadening the reach and improving the efficacy of our metadata recommendation system.

References

Andrei-Marius Avram, Vasile Pais, and Dan Ioan Tufis. 2021. PyEuroVoc: A tool for multilingual legal document classification with EuroVoc descriptors. In *Proceedings of the International Conference on Recent Advances in Natural Language Processing (RANLP 2021)*, pages 92–101, Held Online. INCOMA Ltd.

Ilias Chalkidis, Emmanouil Fergadiotis, Prodromos Malakasiotis, and Ion Androutsopoulos. 2019. Large-scale multi-label text classification on EU legislation. In *Proceedings of the 57th Annual Meeting of the Association for Computational Linguistics*, pages 6314–6322, Florence, Italy. Association for Computational Linguistics.

Wei-Cheng Chang, Hsiang-Fu Yu, Kai Zhong, Yiming Yang, and Inderjit S. Dhillon. 2020. Taming pre-trained transformers for extreme multi-label text classification. In *Proceedings of the 26th ACM SIGKDD International Conference on Knowledge Discovery & Data Mining*, KDD '20, page 3163–3171, New York, NY, USA. Association for Computing Machinery.

Jacob Devlin, Ming-Wei Chang, Kenton Lee, and Kristina Toutanova. 2018. BERT: pre-training of deep bidirectional transformers for language understanding. *CoRR*, abs/1810.04805.

Enrico Francesconi, Marc W. Küster, Patrick Gratz, and Sebastian Thelen. 2015. The ontology-based approach of the publications office of the eu for document accessibility and open data services. In *Electronic Government and the Information Systems Perspective*, pages 29–39, Cham. Springer International Publishing.

Kalervo Järvelin and Jaana Kekäläinen. 2002. Cumulated gain-based evaluation of ir techniques. *ACM Trans. Inf. Syst.*, 20:422–446.

Yinhan Liu, Myle Ott, Naman Goyal, Jingfei Du, Mandar Joshi, Danqi Chen, Omer Levy, Mike Lewis, Luke Zettlemoyer, and Veselin Stoyanov. 2020. Ro{bert}a: A robustly optimized {bert} pretraining approach.

Nils Reimers and Iryna Gurevych. 2019. Sentence-BERT: Sentence embeddings using Siamese BERT-networks. In *Proceedings of the 2019 Conference on Empirical Methods in Natural Language Processing and the 9th International Joint Conference on Natural Language Processing (EMNLP-IJCNLP)*, pages 3982–3992, Hong Kong, China. Association for Computational Linguistics.

Victor Sanh, Lysandre Debut, Julien Chaumond, and Thomas Wolf. 2019. Distilbert, a distilled version of bert: smaller, faster, cheaper and lighter. *ArXiv*, abs/1910.01108.

Dezhao Song, Andrew Vold, Kanika Madan, and Frank Schilder. 2022. Multi-label legal document classification: A deep learning-based approach with label-attention and domain-specific pre-training. *Information Systems*, 106:101718.

Osma Suominen. 2019. Annif: Diy automated subject indexing using multiple algorithms. *LIBER Quarterly: The Journal of the Association of European Research Libraries*, 29(1):1–25.

Lulu Wan, George Papageorgiou, Michael Seddon, and Mirko Bernardoni. 2019. Long-length legal document classification. *CoRR*, abs/1912.06905.

Comparative Study of Explainability Methods for Legal Outcome Prediction

Ieva Raminta Staliūnaitė
University of Cambridge
irs38@cam.ac.uk

Josef Valvoda
University of Copenhagen
jval@di.ku.dk

Ken Satoh
National Institute of Informatics
ksatoh@nii.ac.jp

Abstract

This paper investigates explainability in Natural Legal Language Processing (NLLP). We study the task of legal outcome prediction of the European Court of Human Rights cases in a ternary classification setup, where a language model is fine-tuned to predict whether an article has been claimed and violated (positive outcome), claimed but not violated (negative outcome) or not claimed at all (null outcome). Specifically, we experiment with three popular NLP explainability methods. Correlating the attribution scores of input-level methods (Integrated Gradients and Contrastive Explanations) with rationales from court rulings, we show that the correlations are very weak, with absolute values of Spearman and Kendall correlation coefficients ranging between 0.003 and 0.094. Furthermore, we use a concept-level interpretability method (Concept Erasure) with human expert annotations of legal reasoning, to show that obscuring legal concepts from the model representation has an insignificant effect on model performance (at most a decline of 0.26 F1). Therefore, our results indicate that automated legal outcome prediction models are not reliably grounded in legal reasoning.[1]

1 Introduction

Interpretability is at the core of legal practice. Lawyers and judges pour over legal text to interpret it in light of current affairs, the case at hand and the general zeitgeist (Valvoda et al., 2024). In the context of natural legal language processing, interpretability is no less important. Primarily, this is because the use of Machine Learning (ML) in law can have profound effects on human life (Hacker et al., 2020). This risk is widely acknowledged, as reflected in the EU's General Data Protection Regulation (GDPR), which mandates that legal decisions must be explainable (Hamon et al., 2020; Selbst and Powles, 2017).[2] As such, we advocate for interpretability to be a central focus of NLLP research.

Despite early contributions to the field, which include symbolic methods (Ashley, 1991; Collenette et al., 2020) as well as attention-based interpretability (Branting et al., 2021), and the emergence of recent domain-specific methods (Valvoda and Cotterell, 2024), there remains a lack of a comprehensive overview of the popular NLP interpretability tools that can be applied to legal contexts.

In this work, we offer such a comparative study. We focus on explainability of neural models in the context of the legal outcome prediction task - a popular NLLP task (Brüninghaus and Ashley, 2006; Zhong et al., 2018; Chalkidis et al., 2019; Long et al., 2019; Dong and Niu, 2021; Ma et al., 2021). In particular, we work on the recent reformulation of this task as a three-way classification (Valvoda et al., 2023) and compare three influential interpretability methods from general NLP on legal outcome prediction - Integrated Gradients (Sundararajan et al., 2017), Contrastive Explanations (Jacovi et al., 2021) and Concept Errasure (Ravfogel et al., 2022).

We first hypothesize that while different explainability methods might provide varying results in terms of what legal outcome prediction models use in their decision-making process, the models are likely to be using features which differ from those that a human would deem important. We put this hypothesis to the test by correlating the attributions from the methods of Integrated Gradients (Sundararajan et al., 2017) and Contrastive Explanations (Jacovi et al., 2021) with ground truth data from court rulings. Confirming our hypothesis, we measure a very weak correlation between the predicted importance scores and the ground truth labels, with the absolute values of the correla-

[1] Our code: https://github.com/ieva-raminta/XNLLP

[2] Specifically, Article 22 and provisions of Articles 13-15 of GDPR ask for a *'meaningful information about the logic involved'*.

Proceedings of the Natural Legal Language Processing Workshop 2024, pages 243–258
November 16, 2024

tion coefficients of Spearman (1904) and Kendall (1938) ranging between 0.003 and 0.094.

We further hypothesise that the outcome prediction models are not likely to perform complex legal reasoning, such as those captured in annotated datasets of legal arguments (Habernal et al., 2023) and concepts (Mumford et al., 2023). We test this by using the Concept Erasure method (Ravfogel et al., 2022). Indeed, we find that the outcome prediction models perform on par or at times even better when legal concepts are obscured from their representations, with F1 on the outcome prediction task decreasing by at most 0.26 - a statistically insignificant change.

We conclude that the subpar performance of neural models on negative outcome prediction task is symptomatic of a larger issue - the models do not reason like a human legal professional would.

2 Related Work

Over the years, different approaches have been proposed to address the question of how an ML model *reasons* (Ribeiro et al., 2016; Lundberg and Lee, 2017). Researchers have compared the faithfulness and cost of various interpretability methods (Lipton, 2018; Wiegreffe and Pinter, 2019; Jain and Wallace, 2019; Wang et al., 2020). The majority of these explainability methods link surface features in the model input to model predictions. Some research has emphasized that there is likely no single feature-based explanation for a given model prediction (Camburu, 2020). Thus, the development of alternative, concept-based methods has complemented their feature-based counterparts (Yeh et al., 2020). Furthermore, humans find the explanations of deceptive machine learning systems equally convincing as those of truthful models (Pataranutaporn et al., 2021), which stresses the importance of explanations being faithful as opposed to simply convincing (Alhindi et al., 2018; Piratla et al., 2023; Atanasova et al., 2023).

The earliest work in explainability in NLLP are the legal reasoning systems of HYPO (Ashley, 1991) and CATO (Aleven, 1997). These symbolic systems involve a manual extraction of factors that do not deterministically influence the case outcome, but rather weigh the decision positively or negatively with varying strength, depending on the context. Since then researchers have developed hybrid systems, using stochastic methods to extract the features that are then fed into a rule-based system. Falakmasir and Ashley (2017) have used tf-idf and Latent Dirichlet Allocation (LDA), while Mumford et al. (2023) employed transformer models (Vaswani et al., 2017), to extract factors to be used in rule-based systems.

Researchers have also studied explainability in fully probabilistic methods. Branting et al. (2019) and Branting et al. (2021) use attention as explanation. Yamada et al. (2024) solve the outcome prediction and rationale extraction tasks via a multitask approach. Norkute et al. (2021) evaluate the usefulness of attention scores as well as scores from a source attribution method based on word overlap, by measuring the increase in the speed of humans reviewing legal summaries. Strickson and De La Iglesia (2020) and Soh Tsin Howe (2024) use topic models along with other feature-extraction methods. Gray et al. (2023), Gray et al. (2024) and Drápal et al. (2023) use LLMs to extract factors in legal cases. Valvoda and Cotterell (2024) explore a novel interpretability method in NLLP, namely influence functions (Koh and Liang, 2017), in order to determine which cases in the training data influence the outcome predictions.

Some researchers have also addressed the problem that interpretability methods are difficult to evaluate, given that even humans disagree on what a correct explanation is. Malik et al. (2021) compare the results of an outcome prediction model with some parts of the input masked and without, which highlight the difference between the importance attributed by experts and the occlusion method. Salaün et al. (2022) have shown low agreement between integrated gradients scores of models and expert annotations. Feng et al. (2022) link the errors of outcome prediction models to their failure to detect the parts of the input that determine the judgment. Santosh et al. (2022) use deconfounding to align model predictions with expert reasoning. Xu et al. (2023) study human label variation with regard to the rationales explaining legal outcomes, and show low agreement not only between experts and models, but also among experts, which highlights the difficulty of the task. By and large, the models described in this subsection do not compare multiple interpretability methods.

Legal outcome prediction is the task of predicting the outcome of a case, i.e. whether a law has been violated, given the case facts, which describe the circumstances of the parties involved.[3] Over

[3]See appendix A for a condensed example of a case.

the years, predicting the outcome of a court case has been approached by many researchers in a number of jurisdictions (Virtucio et al., 2018; Chalkidis et al., 2019; Mumcuoğlu et al., 2021; Jacob de Menezes-Neto and Clementino, 2022; Cui et al., 2023). Perhaps due to its conceptual simplicity, the task is one of the cornerstones of NLLP research and is usually defined as a binary classification task (Feng et al., 2022; Cui et al., 2023). Different approaches to legal outcome prediction use the case facts (Shaikh et al., 2020), the complaints (Chalkidis et al., 2019; Semo et al., 2022), the contents of the laws (Zhong et al., 2018), and/or the facts of precedent cases (Cao et al., 2024).

Recent work has re-framed outcome prediction to reflect the reality of a court setting better (Valvoda et al., 2023). Instead of predicting if an article is violated or not, the task is to predict whether the article is claimed to be violated (simulating the role of a lawyer), and then whether it is actually found to be violated or not (simulating the role of a judge). This can be simplified as a three-way classification objective. In practice, a model is trained to predict **positive outcomes**, i.e. when a law has been claimed as violated and found as violated, **negative outcomes**, i.e. when a law has been claimed as violated but the judge found it was not violated, **null outcomes**, i.e. when a law has not even been claimed as violated and is irrelevant to the case.

3 Explainability for Models of Legal Outcome

In our explainability experiments, we focus on the re-framing of the legal outcome prediction task following Valvoda et al. (2023). We do this for three reasons. (1) The new formulation better reflects the actual legal process and outperforms prior work in the domain of the European Convention of Human Rights (ECHR). (2) legal outcome prediction models turn out to perform particularly poorly when having to predict negative outcomes. This is diametrically opposite to their excellence at predicting positive outcomes. Thus, at the core of our paper lies a natural question arising from this asymmetry. Why do the models struggle with negative outcome prediction? (3) Having three target classes instead of two, opens up new possibilities in terms of the explainability methods we can study.

We begin our work with the standard Explainable Artificial Intelligence (XAI) method - namely integrated gradients (Sundararajan et al., 2017). This method highlights the input tokens (in our setting facts) the model finds important for a given case. Then, we move to a contrastive explanation method (Jacovi et al., 2021). Since we work with a three-way classification problem we can employ contrastive explanations to infer which facts are particularly important to the model for distinguishing each target class from every other class. Our main interest here is to understand why the models struggle with negative outcomes.

Finally, we use the Concept Erasure method (Ravfogel et al., 2022) to perform a deeper analysis of whether any legal concepts are used by the model. Unlike the prior two methods where we study the effect of input tokens, here we study the effect of legal concepts encoded in the latent representations learned by the model. We describe each of the above approaches in more detail in section 5.

Given the ground-truth data of human annotated token sequences and legal concepts (Chalkidis et al., 2021; Habernal et al., 2023; Mumford et al., 2023), we can begin to study how well a model aligns with human judgement when it comes to legal reasoning. Furthermore, the chosen set of XAI approaches allows us to study the difference between superficial textual explanations versus explanations through concepts in the legal AI domain.

4 Parametrizing Legal Outcome Prediction Models

We finetune a sequence classification model on the ECtHR dataset to jointly predict the positive, negative and null outcomes, following the architecture of the ternary prediction setup from Valvoda et al. (2023). One modification made to the model architecture is replacing the multi-layer perceptron (MLP) with a simple linear classification layer. This change ensures that the setup is compatible with the interpretability methods discussed in Section 5, where linear classifiers are used.

We choose the LEGAL-BERT model (Chalkidis et al., 2020) due to its domain-specific training set and the fact that it yields the best performance for the ternary setup we are using for our experiments.[4] The model is trained on a single NVIDIA TU102 GPU with batch size 16, for a maximum of 10

[4]We replicate the experiments with other models too in order to ensure that the model results are not idiosyncratic to our chosen setup. Please see appendix C.

epochs, using early stopping by monitoring the loss.

The model performs the best on the null class, and yields particularly poor results on the negative cases, as shown in Table 1. The most common mistakes of the model are assigning the null label to the items from the positive and negative classes, as shown in Table 2.

Metric	null	positive	negative
precision	93.55	78.80	48.07
recall	98.68	77.93	10.33
F1	96.04	78.36	17.01

Table 1: Results of the three way outcome prediction LEGAL-BERT model on the ECtHR test set.

True \ Pred.	null	positive	negative
= null	12117	109	53
positive	258	1056	41
negative	580	175	87

Table 2: Confusion matrix of the three way outcome prediction LEGAL-BERT model on the ECtHR test set.

5 Interpretability Methods

This section describes the interpretability methods used in this study, along with their implementation.

5.1 Integrated Gradients

The Integrated Gradients method, or Axiomatic Attribution for Deep Networks (Sundararajan et al., 2017) is a gradient-based attribution method, which does not require any instrumentation of the network that it is being applied to. The model uses a baseline input as a counterfactual to each feature being tested for attribution. In the context of language, a sequence of the <PAD> tokens can be used for this purpose. Integrated gradients are obtained by accumulating the gradients collected along a path from the baseline to the input. In this work we use the implementation of Layer Integrated Gradients from the Captum package (Kokhlikyan et al., 2020), where we compute the attributions with regard to the BertEmbedding layer. This approach is chosen as a reliable yet simple interpretability method.

5.2 Contrastive Explanations

Jacovi et al. (2021) propose a Contrastive Explanations method for model interpretability that is inspired by cognitive science research. Since humans generate explanations contrastively, namely explaining why a certain occurrence happened instead of some alternative, they argue that XAI methods should mimic this type of reasoning. Hence, instead of comparing the input to a neutral input such as the baseline in the Integrated Gradients method, Jacovi et al. (2021) project the input representation onto a space which minimally separates two class labels as predicted by the model. The predicted label is called 'fact', and the alternative label 'foil'. The contrastive explanation can then be generated by computing the difference between the original representation and the contrastive projection. The method is also applicable to any neural classifier. The application of the contrastive approach is particularly interesting with the negative cases, given that they meaningfully contrast to the positive cases by virtue of not violating a given article, while contrasting to the null cases by allegedly violating the article.

5.3 Concept Erasure

A deeper interpretability method that we employ in this study, is at the level of concepts instead of surface level input features. Inspired by the idea of Jacovi et al. (2021) to use concept attribution for explainability, we apply Linear Adversarial Concept Erasure, presented by Ravfogel et al. (2022), to our task. That is, the method obscures concepts which may or may not influence the model predictions for the main task by projecting them to a space where a linear classifier can no longer recover the signal to determine the presence of the concept in the input. An adversarial model is trained with a constrained, linear minimax game to erase the concept while maintaining the performance on the main task. We interpret the outputs of this method to show the importance of a given concept to a trained model through the difference in model performance when the concept is erased from the input representation. The purpose of using this explainability method for the legal outcome prediction task is to investigate the use of actual legal concepts rather than relying on superficial input features.

In this study we adapt the Concept Erasure model to our multi-output concept prediction task, where for each concept the model solves a binary classification problem of predicting the presence of the given concept in the input document. We train a Logistic Regression model on the subset of the ECtHR training set which contains items annotated for the presence of legal concepts. We use a maximum of 4000 iterations, l2 penalty, saga solver and warm start. The input to the classifier is the encoded representation from the last hidden state of the trained LEGAL-BERT model described in Section 4.

6 Datasets

We use the European Court of Human Rights (ECtHR) dataset (Chalkidis et al., 2021)[5] and its extensions for the experiments in this study (see Table 3 for data statistics). We are using the version of the dataset presented by Valvoda et al. (2023), as it is more complete. Valvoda et al. (2023) also extend the task of outcome prediction to include prediction of negative outcomes. The *Allegedly Violated Articles* and *Violated Articles* together comprise information about *Positive* cases and *Negative* cases. Namely, if an article is both *Allegedly Violated* and *Violated*, the case is positive, whereas if an article is only *Allegedly Violated* but not *Violated*, then the case is negative. The Silver Allegation Rationales indicate the parts of the case facts which are referenced in the decision of the judge. These rationales are available for all the cases where a regular expression match is found between the judgment and the case facts. Similarly, Gold Allegation Rationales have been annotated by a legal expert as the important facts for the allegations. Only 50 cases have been annotated with gold rationales. The silver rationales are more abundant, but less reliable than the gold ones. In this study we are only using the Silver Rationales, due to the size of the annotated data.

In addition, we are also using annotations of legal concepts in ECtHR. Firstly, Habernal et al. (2023) annotate a corpus of 373 court decisions covering Articles 3, 7, and 8, with legal arguments being made in each case. The purpose of the dataset is to aid Legal NLP models in coming closer to legal reasoning in modeling outcomes. Secondly, Mumford et al. (2023) annotate 735 cases pertaining to Article 6, with legal concepts that correspond to factors in a rule-based legal reasoning system. The concepts used in this study are listed in appendix B.

[5]https://huggingface.co/datasets/AUEB-NLP/ecthr_cases

6.1 Dataset Preprocessing

Integrated Gradients and Contrastive Explanations. We use Silver Rationales annotations as the target labels for evaluating the interpretability methods. We adjust the level of granularity of the outputs from the Integrated Gradients and Contrastive Explanation methods in order to make them comparable. The token-wise attributions from the Integrated Gradient method are accumulated per paragraph in order to match the paragraph-wise ground truth in Silver Rationales. Similarly, due to the cost of masking every token in very lengthy case fact documents, when applying the Contrastive Explanations method to the ECtHR data, we modify the masking method to cover entire paragraphs rather than single tokens. When a paragraph is being masked, it is replaced by a sequence of <MASK> tokens of a length equal to the number of tokens in that paragraph.

Concept Erasure. The Legal Argument (Habernal et al., 2023) and Legal Reasoning (Mumford et al., 2023) labels are transformed to binary targets. That is, we convert the token-wise sequence tags indicating the presence of legal arguments from the Legal Argument dataset to a binary document-wise label, indicating whether the concept is present in the case. From the available annotations in Habernal et al. (2023) we use the Argument Type data as the legal concepts. Similarly, the mean annotator scores for the presence of concepts in the Legal Reasoning dataset are converted to a binary label using the ARGMAX of [positive ascription annotations, negative ascription annotations, no ascription annotations] scores, and interpreting both positive ascription and negative ascription to indicate a presence of that concept. For both datasets, we only use a concept if it appears in at least one but not all of the cases in the training set, so that it could theoretically be used as a factor for outcome prediction.

7 Evaluation Metrics

Spearman and Kendal Correlation Coefficients. In order to compare the importance scores attributed to the inputs and concepts by the different interpretability methods, we run each interpretability method on the inputs and evaluate the predictions with respect to the Silver Rationales annotations. We run a correlation study using Spearman (1904) and Kendall (1938) rank correlation coefficients and calculate statistical significance using a T-test. The differences assigned by the Contrastive

Annotation	Description	# of Cases Containing Annotation
Facts	A description of the case	11 000
Allegedly Violated Articles	A binary label indicating whether the lawyer claimed the article to be violated	11 000
Violated Articles	A binary label indicating whether the judge deemed the article violated	11 000
Positive/Negative/Null Cases	A three way label indicating whether the case was claimed and violated, not claimed, or claimed but not violated, respectively	11 000
Silver Allegation Rationales	Sentences from Facts referred to by the judge in the ruling	2 770
Gold Allegation Rationales	Sentences from Facts annotated by an expert as important	50
Legal Arguments	The presence of an argument	373
Legal Reasoning Concepts	The presence of a legal reasoning concept	735

Table 3: Data Statistics

Explanations method and the attributions of Integrated Gradients are treated as ranks.

Change in Accuracy and F1 scores. The method for evaluating the importance of legal concepts to the outcome prediction model is comparing the outcome prediction performance with and without the erasure of a given concept. We compare both accuracy and F1 scores of the predictions pre- and post-projection. In addition, we run a T-test to determine whether the predictions made pre- and post-projection are statistically significant.

8 Results

This section presents the quantitative and qualitative results of the interpretability methods. In order to ensure that the results cannot be accounted for by the short input sequence length of the LEGAL-BERT model (Chalkidis et al., 2020) or the ternary setup of the task (Valvoda et al., 2023), we replicate the results with the Longformer model (Beltagy et al., 2020) as well as the binary setup. The results of these experiments are presented in appendix C.

8.1 Integrated Gradients vs. Contrastive Explanations for Model Interpretability

A correlation method is applied to the results of the Integrated Gradients and Contrastive Explanations methods. In order to control for random effects, we compare to a random baseline, wherein the importance scores are assigned randomly to the inputs, within the same range as the scores of the interpretability methods.

The input paragraphs selected by both interpretability methods do not correlate with the Silver Rationales when looking at all the classes of the main task together, nor broken down by class. The effect size is very small, indicating that the models might not be relying on the information contained in the rationales for their predictions.

The breakdown between different facts and foils in Table 5 shows negligible correlations in all combinations of fact and foil.

Class	Method	Spearman		Kendall	
		coeff.	p-value	coeff.	p-value
null	IG	-0.036	**0.000**	-0.034	**0.000**
	CE	0.041	0.363	0.035	0.363
	random	0.011	0.490	0.009	0.491
pos	IG	-0.003	0.758	-0.003	0.758
	CE	0.088	**0.000**	0.070	**0.000**
	random	-0.016	0.362	-0.013	0.362
neg	IG	0.018	**0.000**	0.017	**0.000**
	CE	0.094	0.233	0.051	0.466
	random	0.045	0.511	0.042	0.511

Table 4: Results of the correlation study between the importance scores from Integrated Gradients (IG), Contrastive Explanations (CE) and random baseline on the one hand, and the Silver Rationales annotations on the other hand. The class refers to the ground truth. Statistically significant (p-value < 0.05) correlations are in bold.

To illustrate the types of paragraphs selected by the models as important, we look at one case in detail. Namely, in a case concerning the custody of a child, the lawyer has claimed that Articles 6 (Right to a fair trial) and 8 (Right to respect for private and family life) have been breached. However, the judge ruled that only Article 8 was violated, but not Article 6, meaning that the applicant is considered to have had a fair trial. Hence, this item has a negative label for Article 6, a positive label for Article 8, and null labels for all other articles. The model correctly predicts the negative label for Article 6.

The Contrastive Explanations method, using the positive label as a foil, lists the following sequence as the most important for this prediction: '*On 17 May 2005 the court dismissed the request for new access arrangements as the first applicant had failed to submit the required documents. It seems, however, that this decision did not become final as on 25 May 2005 the first applicant successfully requested that the proceedings be joined to pro-*

Fact	Foil	Method	Spearman coeff.	Spearman p-value	Kendall coeff.	Kendall p-value
null	pos	CE	0.020	**0.014**	0.017	**0.014**
		random	0.001	0.864	0.001	0.864
null	neg	CE	-0.017	**0.04**	-0.014	**0.04**
		random	0.005	0.570	0.004	0.570
pos	null	CE	-0.047	**0.000**	-0.039	**0.000**
		random	0.001	0.912	0.001	0.912
pos	neg	CE	-0.065	**0.000**	-0.053	**0.000**
		random	-0.007	0.428	-0.006	0.428
neg	null	CE	0.013	0.424	0.010	0.424
		random	-0.009	0.580	-0.007	0.580
neg	pos	CE	-0.062	**0.000**	-0.051	**0.000**
		random	-0.004	0.802	-0.003	0.802

Table 5: Results of the correlation study between the importance scores from Contrastive Explanations (CE) and the Silver Rationales annotations, compared to a random baseline, and broken down by fact and foil. Statistically significant (p-value < 0.05) correlations are in bold.

ceedings P 667/2003 (see paragraph 30 above)'.[6] This paragraph is also highlighted in the Silver Rationales data as one of the important factors for the case. This paragraph highlights that the applicant had failed to follow the required procedures for the trial, which is an argument as to why the court dismissing the request for new access arrangements is not deemed unlawful. This contrastive explanation indeed focuses on the reason why the claim was dismissed, rather than the reason why the claim was made in the first place. However, the paragraph selected as the second most important by the contrastive method is '*According to letters addressed to the court by the Šentjur Centre on 8 September 2003 and 3 May 2004, in the context of proceedings no. P 667/2003, the Šentjur Centre and the Unit attempted to organise supervised meetings between the applicants, but M.E. refused to cooperate.*'. As opposed to the first paragraph, these facts portray the reasons for accepting the claim, highlighting the refusal to cooperate of the second applicant, which could be interpreted as a breach of the right to a fair trial. These importance scores are contradictory to each other, both supporting and undermining the outcome.

Similarly, the Integrated Gradients method assigns the highest importance score to the following paragraph: '*On 1 August 2001 the Šentjur Centre issued an order granting the first applicant four hours a week with the second applicant, taking into account the expert committee's opinion and the fact that, at the supervised meeting between the applicants, the second applicant had not appeared to be afraid of the first applicant but, on the contrary, pleased to see him. The Šentjur Centre did not follow the first applicant's proposal that he should be allowed to pick the second applicant up at her nursery; instead it ordered M.E. to bring the second applicant to a meeting point at a local train station.*' This part of the input emphasizes the reasons for accepting the claim and assigning it a positive outcome, since the second applicant appears to be pleased to see the first applicant (the claimant). This could be interpreted as reasons to deem the trial unfair, as the text points to the circumstances in favour of the first applicant.

All in all, we observe through the qualitative analysis that the paragraphs selected by the interpretability methods appear to be relevant facts for the case, however not necessarily contributing to the predicted label. This suggests that they might not be particularly useful to an end user, given that they provide arguments for different outcomes to the predicted one.

8.2 Concept Erasure

The results of the Concept Erasure method on both the Legal Argument Mining (Habernal et al., 2023) and the Legal Reasoning Factors (Mumford et al., 2023) datasets are presented in Table 6. We confirm that the concepts are erased from the representation by observing that the Concept Prediction model performs at chance level, matching the majority accuracy, after the concept erasure. The F1 scores of the Concept Prediction task are often low even before the projection, however this matches the reportedly low legal concept prediction scores of Mumford et al. (2023) and Habernal et al. (2023). In order to ensure that concept erasure is happening, we perform the T-test on the predictions of the concept classification model before and after the projection. We find that in about half of the cases, the projection makes a significant difference to the predictions ($p<0.05$).

Overall, the results indicate that legal concepts are not absolutely necessary for the Outcome Prediction model, as the model performance is not significantly affected by the erasure of any of the legal concepts from both datasets. That is, the model with erased legal concepts is able to perform the task on par, or in some cases even better, than prior to the erasure.

[6]A larger subset of the facts from the case are presented in appendix A.

Erased Concept	Concept Task					Outcome Task			Concept Task					Outcome Task		
	Acc			F1		F1			Acc			F1		F1		
	maj	pre	post	pre	post	null	pos	neg	maj	pre	post	pre	post	null	pos	neg
None	–	–	–	–	–	.91	.55	.13	–	–	–	–	–	.93	.35	.39
	Legal Argument Mining (Habernal et al., 2023)															
	Development Set								**Test Set**							
1	.79	.79	.79	.25	.00	.93	.58	.40	.91	.86	.91	.40	.00	.92	.29	.13
2	.89	.86	.89	.33	.00	.93	.58	.50	.91	**.91**	**.91**	**.67**	**.00**	.92	.29	.19
3	.51	**.55**	**.48**	**.55**	**.29**	.93	.61	.46	.50	**.60**	**.50**	**.61**	**.15**	.92	.29	.13
4	.97	.97	.97	.00	.00	.93	.56	.50	.91	.91	.91	.00	.00	.92	.29	.13
5	.72	.79	.62	.84	.74	.93	.56	.47	.73	.63	.63	.73	.75	.92	.29	.13
6	.59	.52	.55	.50	.31	.93	.58	.50	.59	.59	.59	.53	.40	.92	.29	.13
7	.52	**.62**	**.41**	**.67**	**.56**	.93	.56	.46	.59	**.50**	**.36**	**.52**	**.53**	.92	.30	.20
	Legal Reasoning Factors (Mumford et al., 2023)															
	Development Set								**Test Set**							
1	.52	**.45**	**.51**	**.27**	**.00**	.91	.55	.13	.75	**.72**	**.75**	**.47**	**.00**	.92	.33	.39
2	.86	.83	.86	.00	.00	.91	.55	.12	.91	.91	.91	.00	.00	.93	.42	.40
3	.62	**.67**	**.62**	**.53**	**.00**	.92	.57	.13	.97	1.00	.97	1.00	.00	.92	.35	.38
4	.90	**.67**	**.90**	**.00**	**.00**	.92	.55	.06	.84	**.84**	**.84**	**.55**	**.00**	.93	.19	.39
5	.83	.83	.83	.00	.00	.91	.52	.06	.88	.84	.88	.00	.00	.93	.27	.38
6	.97	.97	.97	.00	.00	.92	.55	.12	.97	.97	.97	.00	.00	.93	.35	.39
7	.79	**.62**	**.79**	**.00**	**.00**	.92	.55	.13	.75	**.75**	**.75**	**.33**	**.00**	.93	.35	39
8	.83	**.79**	**.83**	**.88**	**.91**	.91	.48	.19	.75	**.81**	**.75**	**.88**	**.86**	.92	.36	.41
9	.62	**.83**	**.62**	**.78**	**.00**	.92	.55	.07	.75	**.72**	**.75**	**.40**	**.00**	.92	.29	.43
10	.83	**.86**	**.83**	**.60**	**.00**	.92	.48	.13	.78	.78	.78	.36	.00	.93	.27	.38
11	.93	.93	.93	.00	.00	.92	.55	.13	.94	.94	.94	.00	.00	.93	.35	.43
12	.76	**.86**	**.76**	**.67**	**.00**	.92	.55	.13	.88	**.72**	**.88**	**.00**	**.00**	.93	.35	.39
13	.90	**.76**	**.90**	**.00**	**.00**	.92	.55	.13	.84	**.66**	**.84**	**.00**	**.00**	.93	.38	.42
14	.90	.90	.86	.00	.00	.91	.55	.13	.88	.84	.88	.00	.00	.93	.35	.39
15	.90	.90	.90	.00	.00	.92	.55	.13	.97	.94	.97	.00	.00	.93	.36	.39
16	.93	**.86**	**.93**	**.33**	**.00**	.92	.52	.13	.75	**.72**	**.75**	**.30**	**.00**	.93	.34	.39
17	.97	.93	.97	.00	.00	.92	.55	.13	.94	.91	.94	.00	.00	.93	.35	.39
18	.76	.72	.76	.00	.00	.91	.55	.13	.84	.81	.84	.00	.00	.93	.35	.39
19	.97	.97	.97	.00	.00	.91	.55	.13	.97	.97	.97	.00	.00	.93	.35	.39
20	.79	**.69**	**.79**	**.31**	**.00**	.92	.52	.13	.66	**.75**	**.66**	**.63**	**.00**	.92	.36	.37

Table 6: Results of the Concept Erasure method: accuracy and F1 scores of the outcome prediction model as well as concept prediction model pre- and post-projection, including a majority class baseline for concept prediction. Statistically significant differences between pre- and post-projection predictions are marked in bold. The concepts are listed in appendix B.

9 Conclusion

We have studied three interpretability methods in the domain of legal outcome prediction. Our experimental results show a small variance in the correlation between the importance scores assigned by different interpretability methods and the ground truth. Worryingly, even removing the information a lawyer would consider essential for reasoning over the data has an insiginificant effect on the model performance. We interpret this result as a call for caution in using automated legal outcome prediction models as they do not appear to be grounded in legal reasoning to the extent that would be necessary for ensuring reliability.

Future work in NLLP should continue searching for ways to make legal outcome prediction models more transparent by investigating their legal expertise. Studying why predicting negative outcome prediction remains a difficult task is only one direction of such research. New directions could involve the study of biases that may be affecting the decision making of the models.

Limitations

This study is limited to only English language data. In future work, it should be extended to other languages as well as other jurisdictions. As far as the results of the study are concerned, the outputs of the explainability method depend on the performance of the outcome prediction model, which could itself be improved, especially on the negative case in the ternary setup. While we acknowledge that the explainability suffers from model errors, this is in line with the argument that improvements to the model should incorporate interpretable legal reasoning.

Ethics Statement

Our research indicates it is not safe to deploy outcome prediction models to the real world, as the predictions of the model do not have a strong basis in legal reasoning and therefore may be biased through dependence on spurious correlations.

Acknowledgments

Ieva Raminta Staliūnaitė is supported by Huawei. Josef Valvoda is funded by the Nordic Programme for Interdisciplinary Research Grant 105178 and the Danish National Research Foundation Grant no. DNRF169.

References

Vincent AWMM Aleven. 1997. *Teaching case-based argumentation through a model and examples*. Ph.D. Dissertation, University of Pittsburgh.

Tariq Alhindi, Savvas Petridis, and Smaranda Muresan. 2018. Where is your evidence: Improving fact-checking by justification modeling. In *Proceedings of the First Workshop on Fact Extraction and VERification (FEVER)*, pages 85–90, Brussels, Belgium. Association for Computational Linguistics.

Kevin D Ashley. 1991. Reasoning with cases and hypotheticals in hypo. *International journal of man-machine studies*, 34(6):753–796.

Pepa Atanasova, Oana-Maria Camburu, Christina Lioma, Thomas Lukasiewicz, Jakob Grue Simonsen, and Isabelle Augenstein. 2023. Faithfulness tests for natural language explanations. In *Proceedings of the 61st Annual Meeting of the Association for Computational Linguistics (Volume 2: Short Papers)*, pages 283–294, Toronto, Canada. Association for Computational Linguistics.

Iz Beltagy, Matthew E Peters, and Arman Cohan. 2020. Longformer: The long-document transformer. *arXiv e-prints*, pages arXiv–2004.

Karl Branting, Craig Pfeifer, Bradford Brown, Lisa Ferro, John Aberdeen, Brandy Weiss, Mark Pfaff, and Bill Liao. 2021. Scalable and explainable legal prediction. *Artificial Intelligence and Law*, 29:213–238.

Karl Branting, Brandy Weiss, Bradford Brown, Craig Pfeifer, A Chakraborty, Lisa Ferro, Mark Pfaff, and Alex Yeh. 2019. Semi-supervised methods for explainable legal prediction. In *Proceedings of the seventeenth international conference on artificial intelligence and law*, pages 22–31.

Stefanie Brüninghaus and Kevin D Ashley. 2006. Progress in textual case-based reasoning: predicting the outcome of legal cases from text. In *AAAI*, pages 1577–1580.

Oana-Maria Camburu. 2020. *Explaining Deep Neural Networks*. Ph.D. thesis, University of Oxford.

Lang Cao, Zifeng Wang, Cao Xiao, and Jimeng Sun. 2024. Pilot: Legal case outcome prediction with case law. In *Proceedings of the 2024 Conference of the North American Chapter of the Association for Computational Linguistics: Human Language Technologies (Volume 1: Long Papers)*, pages 609–621.

Ilias Chalkidis, Ion Androutsopoulos, and Nikolaos Aletras. 2019. Neural legal judgment prediction in english. In *Proceedings of the 57th Annual Meeting of the Association for Computational Linguistics*, pages 4317–4323.

Ilias Chalkidis, Manos Fergadiotis, Prodromos Malakasiotis, Nikolaos Aletras, and Ion Androutsopoulos. 2020. Legal-bert: The muppets straight out of law school. In *Findings of the Association for Computational Linguistics: EMNLP 2020*, pages 2898–2904.

Ilias Chalkidis, Manos Fergadiotis, Dimitrios Tsarapatsanis, Nikolaos Aletras, Ion Androutsopoulos, and Prodromos Malakasiotis. 2021. Paragraph-level rationale extraction through regularization: A case study on european court of human rights cases. In *Proceedings of the Annual Conference of the North American Chapter of the Association for Computational Linguistics*, Mexico City, Mexico. Association for Computational Linguistics.

Joe Collenette, Katie Atkinson, and Trevor Bench-Capon. 2020. An explainable approach to deducing outcomes in european court of human rights cases using adfs. In *Computational Models of Argument*, pages 21–32. IOS Press.

Junyun Cui, Xiaoyu Shen, and Shaochun Wen. 2023. A survey on legal judgment prediction: Datasets, metrics, models and challenges. *IEEE Access*.

Qian Dong and Shuzi Niu. 2021. Legal judgment prediction via relational learning. In *Proceedings of the 44th International ACM SIGIR Conference on Research and Development in Information Retrieval*, pages 983–992.

Jakub Drápal, H Westermann, J Savelka, et al. 2023. Using large language models to support thematic analysis in empirical legal studies. *Legal Knowledge and Information Systems*, pages 197–206.

Mohammad H Falakmasir and Kevin D Ashley. 2017. Utilizing vector space models for identifying legal factors from text. In *Legal Knowledge and Information Systems*, pages 183–192. IOS Press.

Yi Feng, Chuanyi Li, and Vincent Ng. 2022. Legal judgment prediction via event extraction with constraints. In *Proceedings of the 60th Annual Meeting of the Association for Computational Linguistics (Volume 1: Long Papers)*, pages 648–664.

Morgan Gray, Jaromir Savelka, Wesley Oliver, and Kevin Ashley. 2023. Automatic identification and empirical analysis of legally relevant factors. In *Proceedings of the Nineteenth International Conference on Artificial Intelligence and Law*, pages 101–110.

Morgan A Gray, Jaromir Savelka, Wesley M Oliver, and Kevin D Ashley. 2024. Empirical legal analysis simplified: reducing complexity through automatic identification and evaluation of legally relevant factors. *Philosophical Transactions of the Royal Society A*, 382(2270):20230155.

Ivan Habernal, Daniel Faber, Nicola Recchia, Sebastian Bretthauer, Iryna Gurevych, Indra Spiecker genannt Döhmann, and Christoph Burchard. 2023. Mining legal arguments in court decisions. *Artificial Intelligence and Law*, pages 1–38.

Philipp Hacker, Ralf Krestel, Stefan Grundmann, and Felix Naumann. 2020. Explainable ai under contract and tort law: legal incentives and technical challenges. *Artificial Intelligence and Law*, 28:415–439.

Ronan Hamon, Henrik Junklewitz, Ignacio Sanchez, et al. 2020. Robustness and explainability of artificial intelligence. *Publications Office of the European Union*, 207:2020.

Elias Jacob de Menezes-Neto and Marco Bruno Miranda Clementino. 2022. Using deep learning to predict outcomes of legal appeals better than human experts: A study with data from brazilian federal courts. *PloS one*, 17(7):e0272287.

Alon Jacovi, Swabha Swayamdipta, Shauli Ravfogel, Yanai Elazar, Yejin Choi, and Yoav Goldberg. 2021. Contrastive explanations for model interpretability. In *Proceedings of the 2021 Conference on Empirical Methods in Natural Language Processing*, pages 1597–1611.

Sarthak Jain and Byron C Wallace. 2019. Attention is not explanation. In *Proceedings of NAACL-HLT*, pages 3543–3556.

Maurice G Kendall. 1938. A new measure of rank correlation. *Biometrika*, 30(1-2):81–93.

Pang Wei Koh and Percy Liang. 2017. Understanding black-box predictions via influence functions. In *International conference on machine learning*, pages 1885–1894. PMLR.

Narine Kokhlikyan, Vivek Miglani, Miguel Martin, Edward Wang, Bilal Alsallakh, Jonathan Reynolds, Alexander Melnikov, Natalia Kliushkina, Carlos Araya, Siqi Yan, and Orion Reblitz-Richardson. 2020. Captum: A unified and generic model interpretability library for pytorch. *Preprint*, arXiv:2009.07896.

Zachary C. Lipton. 2018. The mythos of model interpretability: In machine learning, the concept of interpretability is both important and slippery. *Queue*, 16(3):31–57.

Shangbang Long, Cunchao Tu, Zhiyuan Liu, and Maosong Sun. 2019. Automatic judgment prediction via legal reading comprehension. In *Chinese Computational Linguistics: 18th China National Conference, CCL 2019, Kunming, China, October 18–20, 2019, Proceedings 18*, pages 558–572. Springer.

Scott M Lundberg and Su-In Lee. 2017. A unified approach to interpreting model predictions. *Advances in neural information processing systems*, 30.

Luyao Ma, Yating Zhang, Tianyi Wang, Xiaozhong Liu, Wei Ye, Changlong Sun, and Shikun Zhang. 2021. Legal judgment prediction with multi-stage case representation learning in the real court setting. In *Proceedings of the 44th International ACM SIGIR Conference on Research and Development in Information Retrieval*, pages 993–1002.

Vijit Malik, Rishabh Sanjay, Shubham Kumar Nigam, Kripabandhu Ghosh, Shouvik Kumar Guha, Arnab Bhattacharya, and Ashutosh Modi. 2021. Ildc for cjpe: Indian legal documents corpus for court judgment prediction and explanation. In *Proceedings of the 59th Annual Meeting of the Association for Computational Linguistics and the 11th International Joint Conference on Natural Language Processing (Volume 1: Long Papers)*, pages 4046–4062.

Emre Mumcuoğlu, Ceyhun E Öztürk, Haldun M Ozaktas, and Aykut Koç. 2021. Natural language processing in law: Prediction of outcomes in the higher courts of turkey. *Information Processing & Management*, 58(5):102684.

Jack Mumford, Katie Atkinson, and Trevor Bench-Capon. 2023. Combining a legal knowledge model with machine learning for reasoning with legal cases. In *Proceedings of the Nineteenth International Conference on Artificial Intelligence and Law*, pages 167–176.

Milda Norkute, Nadja Herger, Leszek Michalak, Andrew Mulder, and Sally Gao. 2021. Towards explainable ai: Assessing the usefulness and impact of added explainability features in legal document summarization. In *Extended Abstracts of the 2021 CHI Conference on Human Factors in Computing Systems*, CHI EA '21, New York, NY, USA. Association for Computing Machinery.

Pat Pataranutaporn, Valdemar Danry, Joanne Leong, Parinya Punpongsanon, Dan Novy, Pattie Maes, and Misha Sra. 2021. Ai-generated characters for supporting personalized learning and well-being. *Nature Machine Intelligence*, 3(12):1013–1022.

Vihari Piratla, Juyeon Heo, Sukriti Singh, and Adrian Weller. 2023. Estimation of concept explanations should be uncertainty aware. *arXiv preprint arXiv:2312.08063*.

Shauli Ravfogel, Michael Twiton, Yoav Goldberg, and Ryan D Cotterell. 2022. Linear adversarial concept erasure. In *International Conference on Machine Learning*, pages 18400–18421. PMLR.

Marco Tulio Ribeiro, Sameer Singh, and Carlos Guestrin. 2016. " why should i trust you?" explaining the predictions of any classifier. In *Proceedings of the 22nd ACM SIGKDD international conference on knowledge discovery and data mining*, pages 1135–1144.

Olivier Salaün, Fabrizio Gotti, Philippe Langlais, and Karim Benyekhlef. 2022. Why do tenants sue their landlords? answers from a topic model. In *Legal Knowledge and Information Systems*, pages 113–122. IOS Press.

Tyss Santosh, Shanshan Xu, Oana Ichim, and Matthias Grabmair. 2022. Deconfounding legal judgment prediction for european court of human rights cases towards better alignment with experts. In *Proceedings of the 2022 Conference on Empirical Methods in Natural Language Processing*, pages 1120–1138.

Andrew D Selbst and Julia Powles. 2017. Meaningful information and the right to explanation. *International Data Privacy Law*, 7(4):233–242.

Gil Semo, DorBernsohn BenHagag GilaHayat, and Joel Niklaus. 2022. Classactionprediction: A challenging benchmark for legal judgment prediction of class action cases in the us. *NLLP 2022*, 2022:31–46.

Rafe Athar Shaikh, Tirath Prasad Sahu, and Veena Anand. 2020. Predicting outcomes of legal cases based on legal factors using classifiers. *Procedia Computer Science*, 167:2393–2402.

Jerrold Soh Tsin Howe. 2024. Discovering significant topics from legal decisions with selective inference. *Philosophical Transactions of the Royal Society A*, 382(2270):20230147.

C Spearman. 1904. The proof and measurement of association between two things. *The American Journal of Psychology*, 15(1):72–101.

Benjamin Strickson and Beatriz De La Iglesia. 2020. Legal judgement prediction for uk courts. In *Proceedings of the 3rd International Conference on Information Science and Systems*, pages 204–209.

Mukund Sundararajan, Ankur Taly, and Qiqi Yan. 2017. Axiomatic attribution for deep networks. In *International conference on machine learning*, pages 3319–3328. PMLR.

Josef Valvoda and Ryan Cotterell. 2024. Towards explainability in legal outcome prediction models. In *Proceedings of the 2024 Conference of the North American Chapter of the Association for Computational Linguistics: Human Language Technologies (Volume 1: Long Papers)*, pages 7262–7282.

Josef Valvoda, Ryan Cotterell, and Simone Teufel. 2023. On the Role of Negative Precedent in Legal Outcome Prediction. *Transactions of the Association for Computational Linguistics*, 11:34–48.

Josef Valvoda, Alec Thompson, Ryan Cotterell, and Simone Teufel. 2024. The ethics of automating legal actors. *Transactions of the Association for Computational Linguistics*, 12:700–720.

Ashish Vaswani, Noam Shazeer, Niki Parmar, Jakob Uszkoreit, Llion Jones, Aidan N Gomez, Ł ukasz Kaiser, and Illia Polosukhin. 2017. Attention is all you need. In *Advances in Neural Information Processing Systems*, volume 30. Curran Associates, Inc.

Michael Benedict L Virtucio, Jeffrey A Aborot, John Kevin C Abonita, Roxanne S Avinante, Rother Jay B Copino, Michelle P Neverida, Vanesa O Osiana, Elmer C Peramo, Joanna G Syjuco, and Glenn Brian A Tan. 2018. Predicting decisions of the philippine supreme court using natural language processing and machine learning. In *2018 IEEE 42nd annual computer software and applications conference (COMPSAC)*, volume 2, pages 130–135. IEEE.

Junlin Wang, Jens Tuyls, Eric Wallace, and Sameer Singh. 2020. Gradient-based analysis of nlp models is manipulable. In *Findings of the Association for Computational Linguistics: EMNLP 2020*, pages 247–258.

Sarah Wiegreffe and Yuval Pinter. 2019. Attention is not not explanation. In *Proceedings of the 2019 Conference on Empirical Methods in Natural Language Processing and the 9th International Joint Conference on Natural Language Processing (EMNLP-IJCNLP)*. Association for Computational Linguistics.

Shanshan Xu, Santosh T.y.s.s, Oana Ichim, Isabella Risini, Barbara Plank, and Matthias Grabmair. 2023. From dissonance to insights: Dissecting disagreements in rationale construction for case outcome classification. In *Proceedings of the 2023 Conference on Empirical Methods in Natural Language Processing*, pages 9558–9576, Singapore. Association for Computational Linguistics.

Hiroaki Yamada, Takenobu Tokunaga, Ryutaro Ohara, Akira Tokutsu, Keisuke Takeshita, and Mihoko Sumida. 2024. Japanese tort-case dataset for rationale-supported legal judgment prediction. *Artificial Intelligence and Law*, pages 1–25.

Chih-Kuan Yeh, Been Kim, Sercan Arik, Chun-Liang Li, Tomas Pfister, and Pradeep Ravikumar. 2020. On completeness-aware concept-based explanations in deep neural networks. *Advances in neural information processing systems*, 33:20554–20565.

Haoxi Zhong, Zhipeng Guo, Cunchao Tu, Chaojun Xiao, Zhiyuan Liu, and Maosong Sun. 2018. Legal judgment prediction via topological learning. In *Proceedings of the 2018 conference on empirical methods in natural language processing*, pages 3540–3549.

A The Facts of Case 001-118248

'4. The first applicant, Mr Eberhard, was born in 1968 and lives in Ponikva. The second applicant, M., is his daughter.', '5. On 8 April 2001 the first applicant's wife, M.E., together with the second applicant, then aged four, moved out of the flat in which they had been living with the first applicant. M.E. subsequently filed a petition for divorce.', '6. On 4 May 2001 the first applicant and his wife, with whom the second applicant was living, signed an agreement on access arrangements.', '7. On 12 June 2001 the first applicant filed a request with the Šentjur Social Welfare Centre ("the Šentjur Centre") seeking formal determination of the access arrangements, claiming that since 12 May 2001 M.E. had denied him access to the second applicant.', '8. During the following month M.E. gave a number of statements at the Šentjur Centre, opposing contact between the applicants, stating that the first applicant represented a danger to her and the second applicant. She also lodged a criminal complaint against the first applicant for endangering their safety.', [...] '11. On 1 August 2001 the Šentjur Centre issued an order granting the first applicant four hours a week with the second applicant, taking into account the expert committee's opinion and the fact that, at the supervised meeting between the applicants, the second applicant had not appeared to be afraid of the first applicant but, on the contrary, pleased to see him. The Šentjur Centre did not follow the first applicant's proposal that he should be allowed to pick the second applicant up at her nursery; instead it ordered M.E. to bring the second applicant to a meeting point at a local train station.', [...] '19. On 15 June 2004 the Ministry quashed the impugned enforcement orders, finding that M.E. had not been informed of the first applicant's notices concerning non-compliance and had had no opportunity of participating in the proceedings and presenting arguments in her favour. [...] '24. On 6 June 2003 the first applicant lodged an application for custody of the second applicant, relying on the fact that M.E. was denying them contact. He also requested an interim order under which the second applicant would be placed in his custody pending the outcome of the proceedings, and the appointment of a curator ad litem to represent the second applicant's interests in the proceedings. [...] '29. However, as M.E. continued to refuse any contact between the applicants, on 16 August 2004 the first applicant requested that the proceedings be resumed and a hearing was scheduled for 7 October 2004. It was adjourned as the court decided, further to the first applicant's request, to appoint an expert psychologist. On 19 October 2004 the court appointed expert D.T. to produce an opinion in the case.', [...] In addition, the first applicant alerted the court to the fact that he had had no access to the second applicant in the past four and a half years, except on one occasion at her school.', '32. In the meantime, the appointed expert informed the court on 22 September 2005 that he was unable to prepare the opinion as M.E. had refused to cooperate. [...] Subsequently, on 26 May 2006, the court issued a decision rejecting the first applicant's application for provisional custody and upholding his alternative request for an interim access order. [...] '45. On 2 March 2007 the first applicant lodged a supervisory appeal, relying on section 6 of the Act on Protection of the Right to a Hearing without Undue Delay ("the 2006 Act").', [...] '62. On 17 May 2005 the court dismissed the request for new access arrangements as the first applicant had failed to submit the required documents. It seems, however, that this decision did not become final as on 25 May 2005 the first applicant successfully requested that the proceedings be joined to proceedings P 667/2003 (see paragraph 30 above).'

B Legal Concepts Used in this Study

The concepts from the Mumford et al. (2023) dataset:

1. Access to Court
2. Allowed Time and Facilities for Defence
3. Allowed to Defend in Person or Through Legal Assistance
4. Allowed to Fairly Examine Witnesses
5. Balance of Complexity and Circumstance
6. Conducted Publicly Where Appropriate
7. Equality of Arms and Adversarial Hearing
8. Fair
9. Had the Minimum Rights
10. Independent and Impartial
11. Informed Promptly
12. Integrity of Evidence
13. Legal Certainty is Upheld
14. No Adverse Effect from Alternative Proceedings
15. No adverse Prejudicial Statements
16. No Unreasonable Delays
17. Option of Free Access to Interpreter
18. Presumption of Innocence
19. Public Hearing
20. Reasonable Time

The concepts from the Habernal et al. (2023) dataset:

1. Distinguishing
2. Scope of Assessment
3. Consensus of the Procedural Parties
4. Meaning & Purpose Interpretation
5. Proportionality Test - Appropriateness
6. Proportionality Test - Legitimate Purpose
7. Proportionality Test - Legal Basis

C Longformer and Binary Setup Results

C.1 Longformer Three Way Classification Model

Tables 7 and 8 present the results of the Contrastive Explanation, Integrated Gradients and Concept Erasure on the Longformer three way outcome prediction model. The results corroborate the results seen in Section 8, namely low correlation scores between contrastive explanation and integrated gradients importance scores against silver rationales, and unchanged outcome prediction scores after concept erasure. Given the lack of difference between the results with the Longformer model and the LEGAL-BERT model, we conclude that the effect observed in this study is not due to some idiosyncratic behavior of LEGAL-BERT.

Class	Method	Spearman coeff.	Spearman p-value	Kendall coeff.	Kendall p-value
null	IG	-0.028	**0.000**	-0.026	**0.000**
	CE	0.011	0.180	0.009	0.180
	random	0.003	0.733	0.002	0.733
pos	IG	0.010	0.303	0.009	0.303
	CE	-0.060	**0.000**	-0.049	**0.000**
	random	-0.009	0.322	-0.007	0.322
neg	IG	-0.019	0.205	-0.018	0.205
	CE	-0.039	**0.013**	-0.032	**0.013**
	random	0.001	0.926	0.001	0.926

Table 7: Results of the correlation study between the importance scores from Integrated Gradients (IG), Contrastive Explanations (CE) and random baseline on the one hand, and the Silver Rationales annotations on the other hand. The class refers to the ground truth. Statistically significant (p-value < 0.05) correlations are in bold.

C.2 LEGAL-BERT Binary Classification Model

Tables 9 and 10 present the results of the Contrastive Explanation, Integrated Gradients and Concept Erasure on the LEGAL-BERT binary outcome prediction model. The results corroborate the results seen in Section 8, namely low correlation

Erased Concept	Concept Task					Outcome Task			Concept Task					Outcome Task		
	Acc			F1		F1			Acc			F1		F1		
	maj	pre	post	pre	post	null	pos	neg	maj	pre	post	pre	post	null	pos	neg
None	–	–	–	–	–	.93	.57	.36	–	–	–	–	–	.93	.38	.15
	Legal Argument Mining (Habernal et al., 2023)															
	Development Set								**Test Set**							
1	.79	.86	.76	.60	.22	.93	.57	.36	.91	.68	.86	.00	.40	.94	.38	.15
2	.90	.86	.90	.33	.00	.93	.57	.39	.91	**.82**	**.91**	**.33**	**.00**	.94	.38	.16
3	.52	**.48**	**.52**	**.35**	**.00**	.93	.57	.36	.50	**.50**	**.50**	**.42**	**.00**	.94	.38	.21
4	..97	.97	.97	.00	.00	.93	.57	.39	.91	.91	.91	.00	.00	.95	.38	.17
5	.72	**.72**	**.72**	**.79**	**.84**	.94	.57	.41	.73	**.68**	**.73**	**.76**	**.84**	.94	.38	.21
6	.59	**.59**	**.59**	**.46**	**.00**	.93	.55	.37	.59	**.64**	**.59**	**.43**	**.00**	.94	.38	.22
7	.52	.66	.59	.67	.63	.94	.57	.41	.59	.41	.27	.48	.43	.94	.38	.16
	Legal Reasoning Factors (Mumford et al., 2023)															
	Development Set								**Test Set**							
1	.52	**.52**	**.52**	**.30**	**.00**	.93	.45	.27	.75	**.66**	**.75**	**.15**	**.00**	.94	.29	.50
2	.86	.86	.83	.33	.00	.93	.48	.26	.91	.88	.91	.00	.00	.94	.27	.46
3	.62	**.69**	**.62**	**.47**	**.00**	.93	.48	.26	.97	.94	.97	.00	.00	.94	.29	.50
4	.90	**.79**	**.90**	**.40**	**.00**	.92	.48	.25	.84	**.78**	**.84**	**.22**	**.00**	.94	.32	.50
5	.83	**.76**	**.83**	**.22**	**.00**	.93	.50	.25	.88	**.78**	**.88**	**.36**	**.00**	.94	.29	.50
6	.97	.93	.97	.50	.00	.93	.48	.26	.97	.88	.94	.00	.00	.94	.30	.50
7	.79	**.66**	**.79**	**.17**	**.00**	.92	.50	.24	.75	**.56**	**.75**	**.13**	**.00**	.94	.32	.54
8	.83	**.66**	**.83**	**.78**	**.91**	.93	.48	.26	.75	**.59**	**.75**	**.70**	**.86**	.94	.29	.50
9	.62	.76	.79	.67	.75	.93	.48	.26	.75	.75	.75	.33	.56	.93	.32	.51
10	.83	**.66**	**.79**	**.17**	**.00**	.93	.50	.25	.78	.69	.78	.17	.22	.94	.32	.45
11	.93	.97	.93	.67	.00	.93	.48	.26	.94	.88	.94	.00	.00	.94	.29	.42
12	.76	**.90**	**.76**	**.80**	**.00**	.92	.48	.25	.88	**.81**	**.88**	**.25**	**.00**	.94	.33	.50
13	.90	**.79**	**.90**	**.00**	**.00**	.93	.50	.26	.84	**.75**	**.84**	**.20**	**.00**	.93	.32	.46
14	.90	.90	.90	.40	.00	.92	.48	.25	.88	**.72**	**.88**	**.00**	**.00**	.94	.30	.46
15	.90	.93	.90	.50	.00	.92	.48	.25	.97	1.00	.97	.67	.00	.94	.32	.45
16	.93	**.66**	**.93**	**.17**	**.00**	.92	.50	.24	.75	**.66**	**.75**	**.35**	**.00**	.94	.29	.47
17	.97	.97	.97	.67	.00	.93	.48	.26	.94	.94	.94	.00	.00	.94	.30	.46
18	.76	**.79**	**.76**	**.50**	**.00**	.93	.48	.26	..84	.84	.84	.29	.00	.94	.30	.42
19	.97	.90	.97	.40	.00	.93	.48	.26	.97	.94	.97	.50	.00	.94	.29	.46
20	.79	.69	.79	.47	.57	.93	.48	.26	.66	.72	.50	.61	.33	.94	.32	.54

Table 8: Results of the Concept Erasure method with the Longformer three way outcome prediction model: accuracy and F1 scores of the outcome prediction model as well as concept prediction model pre- and post-projection, including a majority class baseline for concept prediction. Statistically significant differences between pre- and post-projection predictions are marked in bold. The concepts are listed in appendix B.

between the importance scores assigned by contrastive explanation and integrated gradients methods against silver rationales, as well as no change in outcome prediction performance after concept erasure. Based on the lack of difference between the results observed with the ternary and binary setups, we conclude that the results cannot be accounted for by the more difficult three way classification task.

Class	Method	Spearman coeff.	Spearman p-value	Kendall coeff.	Kendall p-value
neg	IG	0.041	**0.000**	0.038	**0.000**
	CE	0.011	0.483	0.083	0.483
	random	0.010	0.371	0.008	0.371
pos	IG	0.015	0.388	0.014	0.388
	CE	0.026	0.367	0.021	0.367
	random	0.028	0.411	0.073	0.411

Table 9: Results of the correlation study between the importance scores from Integrated Gradients (IG), Contrastive Explanations (CE) and random baseline on the one hand, and the Silver Rationales annotations on the other hand. The class refers to the ground truth. Statistically significant (p-value < 0.05) correlations are in bold.

Erased Concept	Concept Task					Outcome Task	Concept Task					Outcome Task
	Acc			F1		F1	Acc			F1		F1
	maj	pre	post	pre	post		maj	pre	post	pre	post	
None	–	–	–	–	–	.76	–	–	–	–	–	.76
	Legal Argument Mining (Habernal et al., 2023)											
	Development Set						**Test Set**					
1	.79	.79	.79	.25	.00	.76	.93	.86	.91	.40	.00	.75
2	.90	.86	.90	.33	.00	.76	.93	**.91**	**.91**	**.00**	**.00**	.75
3	.52	**.55**	**.48**	**.55**	**.29**	.78	.50	**.59**	**.50**	**.61**	**.15**	.75
4	.97	.97	.97	.00	.00	.78	.91	.91	.91	.00	.00	.75
5	.72	.79	.62	.84	.74	.78	.73	.64	.64	.73	.75	.75
6	.59	.52	.55	.50	.38	.78	.59	.59	.59	.53	.40	.75
7	.52	**.62**	**.41**	**.67**	**.56**	.78	.59	**.50**	**.36**	**.52**	**.53**	.75
	Legal Reasoning Factors (Mumford et al., 2023)											
	Development Set						**Test Set**					
1	.52	**.45**	**.52**	**.27**	**.00**	.76	.75	**.72**	**.75**	**.47**	**.00**	.75
2	.86	.83	.86	.00	.00	.76	.91	.91	.91	.00	.00	.76
3	.62	.69	.62	.53	.00	.76	.97	**1.00**	**.97**	**1.00**	**.00**	.76
4	.90	**.69**	**.90**	**.00**	**.00**	.77	.84	**.84**	**.84**	**.55**	**.00**	.76
5	.83	.83	.83	.00	.00	.76	.88	.84	.88	.00	.00	.76
6	.97	.97	.97	.00	.00	.77	.97	.97	.97	.00	.00	.76
7	.79	**.62**	**.79**	**.00**	**.00**	.77	.75	**.75**	**.75**	**.33**	**.00**	.76
8	.83	**.79**	**.83**	**.88**	**.91**	.76	.75	**.81**	**.75**	**.88**	**.86**	.75
9	.62	**.83**	**.62**	**.78**	**.00**	.77	.75	**.72**	**.75**	**.40**	**.00**	.75
10	.83	**.86**	**.83**	**.60**	**.00**	.77	.78	**.78**	**.78**	**.36**	**.00**	.76
11	.93	.93	.93	.00	.00	.77	.94	.93	.93	.00	.00	.76
12	.76	**.86**	**.76**	**.67**	**.00**	.77	.88	**.72**	**.88**	**.00**	**.00**	.76
13	.90	**.76**	**.90**	**.00**	**.00**	.77	.84	**.66**	**.84**	**.00**	**.00**	.76
14	.90	.90	.86	.00	.00	.76	.88	.84	.88	.00	.00	.76
15	.90	.90	.90	.00	.00	.77	.97	.94	.97	.00	.00	.76
16	.93	**.86**	**.93**	**.33**	**.00**	.77	.75	**.72**	**.75**	**.31**	**.00**	.76
17	.97	.93	.97	.00	.00	.77	.94	.91	.94	.00	.00	.76
18	.76	.72	.76	.00	.00	.76	.84	.81	.84	.00	.00	.76
19	.97	.97	.97	.00	.00	.76	.97	.97	.97	.00	.00	.75
20	.79	**.69**	**.79**	**.31**	**.00**	.77	.66	**.75**	**.66**	**.63**	**.00**	.75

Table 10: Results of the Concept Erasure method with the LEGAL-BERT binary outcome prediction model: accuracy and F1 scores of the outcome prediction model as well as concept prediction model pre- and post-projection, including a majority class baseline for concept prediction. Statistically significant differences between pre- and post-projection predictions are marked in bold. The concepts are listed in appendix B.

Bonafide at LegalLens 2024 Shared Task: Using Lightweight DeBERTa Based Encoder For Legal Violation Detection and Resolution

Shikha Bordia
bordiashikha06@gmail.com

Abstract

In this work, we present two systems—Named Entity Resolution (NER) and Natural Language Inference (NLI)—for detecting legal violations within unstructured textual data and for associating these violations with potentially affected individuals, respectively. Both these systems are lightweight DeBERTa based encoders that outperform the LLM baselines. The proposed NER system achieved an F1 score of 60.01% on Subtask A of the LegalLens challenge, which focuses on identifying violations. The proposed NLI system achieved an F1 score of 84.73% on Subtask B of the LegalLens challenge, which focuses on resolving these violations by matching them with pre-existing legal complaints of class action cases. Our NER system ranked sixth and NLI system ranked fifth on the LegalLens leaderboard. We release the trained models and inference scripts[1].

1 Introduction

Social networks and other online platforms are increasingly becoming effective tools to address consumer complaints; however, the vast amount of unstructured textual data makes it challenging to identify valid complaints and if they are associated with any legal violations. There is a pressing need to develop sophisticated methods to identify these hidden breaches, as they have significant implications for individual rights and legal obligations, if any.

In this regard, Bernsohn et al. (2024) propose two subtasks —Subtask A, Legallens NER (Named Entity Recognition), to detect legal violations mentioned in the text and Subtask B, Legallens NLI (Natural Language Inference), to match the detected violations with resolved class action cases. To address these subtasks in this paper, we propose NER and NLI models based on training DeBERTaV3 encoders. We finetune task-specific encoders on our synthetically augmented dataset. In summary, we list our findings here:

1. Continuing to pretrain an already powerful general domain task-specific model on our subtask can boost the performance of our system.

2. While synthetic data can significantly boost the capabilities of models, it's crucial to recognize that surpassing specific thresholds of training data volumes may not necessarily result in proportional enhancements in performance.

3. Scaling laws suggest that Large Language Models (LLMs) show predictable performance improvements. However, smaller models can either match or perform better using appropriate training objectives and data, specifically for classification tasks.

In Section 2, we examine the related works on NER and NLI tasks. Section 3 provides an overview of the methodologies employed for the tasks. In Section 4, we describe the experimental setup. Section 5 discusses the results and findings; Section 6 discusses the conclusions.

2 Related Works

NER Research in NER has evolved from statistical models such as Maximum Entropy (Borthwick et al., 1998), Hidden Markov Models (Bikel et al., 1999), and Conditional Random Fields (CRF)(McCallum and Li, 2003), using bidirectional RNNs, often combined with CRF layers (Huang et al., 2015; Ma and Hovy, 2016; Lample et al., 2016) to using transformer-based models (Vaswani et al., 2017). This transition has enabled

[1] https://github.com/BordiaS/LegalLens_inference

Proceedings of the Natural Legal Language Processing Workshop 2024, pages 259–266
November 16, 2024 ©2024 Association for Computational Linguistics

Table 1: The distribution of number of words by entity type in the LegalLens NER training dataset

LAW	VIOLATED BY	VIOLATED ON	VIOLATION
4.14	2.19	3.24	12.39

accurate and robust entity recognition across various domains and languages. In legal domain, variations of BERT-based transformers (Devlin, 2018) like RoBERTa (Liu, 2019), DeBERTaV3 (He et al., 2021a), LegalBERT (Chalkidis et al., 2020), with BiLSTM and CRF layers on the top (Huo et al., 2023; Ningthoujam et al., 2023) have given state-of-the-art performance on legal NER tasks (Kalamkar et al., 2022; Modi et al., 2023). Legallens NER task has four sets of entity types that have not been previously explored in legal NER research. In this work, we use the recently proposed DeBERTaV3 based GLiNER (Zaratiana et al., 2023) architecture that outperforms both ChatGPT (Brown et al., 2020) and fine-tuned LLMs in zero-shot evaluations on various NER benchmarks.

NLI NLI classifies the logical relationship between a premise (a given statement) and a hypothesis (a proposed conclusion) as entailed, contradictory, or neutral. Early work on NLI focused on rule-based systems and logical inference (Giampiccolo et al., 2007). The advent of large-scale datasets, such as the SNLI (Bowman et al., 2015), MultiNLI corpus (Williams et al., 2017), XNLI (Conneau et al., 2018) enabled the development of sophisticated models. Transformer-based models such as RoBERTa (Liu, 2019) and XLNet(Yang, 2019) have pushed the limits of NLI performance by giving human-like scores.

NLI is a critical task in NLP that serves as a benchmark for natural language understanding. Although significant progress has been made, challenges remain in developing systems that can perform robust and generalizable inference across diverse domains and languages. In this work, we use Tasksource's NLI model and finetune it on the LegalLens NLI dataset. Tasksource is a framework that harmonizes data sets for multitask learning and evaluation in NLP by providing a collection of pre-processing methods (Sileo, 2024).

Data Augmentation The advent of LLMs has introduced a novel approach to data augmentation in machine learning tasks (He et al., 2021b; Gan and Ng, 2019; Hosseini et al., 2024). Leveraging the capabilities of these models, we employ two distinct strategies to enhance our datasets. For the NER task, we utilize few-shot learning techniques to expand the existing dataset. This method allows us to generate additional, contextually relevant examples based on a small number of initial samples. Concurrently, for the NLI dataset, we implement a paraphrasing approach. This technique involves reformulating the sentences—premise and hypothesis—while preserving their semantic content, thereby increasing the diversity and robustness of our training data. This approach also preserves the original label distribution. We use Mixtral 8x7B model (Jiang et al., 2024), a state-of-the-art LLM, to augment both the datasets. The specific prompts used for these augmentation tasks are detailed in the Appendix A for both the subtasks, ensuring transparency and reproducibility of our methods.

3 Methodology

In this section, we introduce our approach for each of the subtasks.

3.1 Subtask A: LegalLens NER

Problem Statement The NER task aims to detect legal violations in social media posts and online reviews. The training and development datasets consist of 710 and 617 data points. We specifically identify the following entities: `LAW` (law or regulation breached), `VIOLATION` (content describing the violation), `VIOLATED BY`(entity committing the violation) and `VIOLATED ON` (victim or affected party).The average number of words range between 2.19 and 4.14 for `LAW`, `VIOLATED BY` and `VIOLATED ON` while the average number of words for `VIOLATION` is 12.39 as shown in Table 1.

Contribution Our main contributions are as follows:

- We finetune a lightweight bidirectional transformer encoder GLiNER proposed by Zaratiana et al. (2023), that uses DeBERTaV3 (He et al., 2021a) as backbone. It is trained on Pile-NER dataset (Zhou et al., 2023).
- We experiment with the architectures—single, bi-encoder and polyencoder—proposed by Zaratiana et al. (2023)

All the pre-trained checkpoints of these models are taken from the Hugging Face hub repository.

Model	Precision	Recall	F1
gliner_small-v2.1	70.26	45.83	55.47
gliner_base	71.30	47.02	56.67
gliner_small	72.32	45.71	56.02
gliner-bi-base-v1.0	**83.30**	46.31	**59.53**
gliner-bi-small-v1.0	74.00	48.39	58.52
gliner-poly-small-v1.0	71.04	**49.64**	58.44

Table 2: Comparison of different GLiNER architectures on LegalLens NER development dataset. The table showcases the models and their respective performance

3.2 Subtask B: LegalLens NLI

Problem Statement The NLI task aims to link resolved class action cases with violations detected by the NER model. The premise comprises summaries of legal news articles, while the hypothesis consists of synthetically generated social media posts that mimic potential legal violations. The dataset includes 312 data points across four legal domains: Consumer Protection, Privacy, TCPA, and Wage.

Contribution

- We finetune a multitask DeBERTaV3 based encoder, Tasksource (Sileo, 2024), that casts all the classification tasks as natural language inference and trains the model on 600+ English tasks simultaneously to achieve state-of-the-art performance at its size.
- We propose synthetic data generation to enhance the performance of the model. We employ Mixtral 8x7B by Jiang et al. (2024) to generate paraphrases for each premise-hypothesis pair. The class labels (Entailed, Contradict, and Neutral) remain unchanged. This approach doubles the size of the training data while preserving the original class distribution.
- Augmenting the NLI dataset boosted the final F1 score metric by a significant margin of 7.65%.

4 Experimental Settings

NER We finetune the GLiNER models on the LegalLens NER dataset using a dropout rate of 0.5 and a batch size of 8. We employ AdamW optimizer with a base learning rate of 1e-5 for pre-trained layers (the transformer backbone, DeBERTaV3) and 5e-5 for non-pre-trained layers (FFN layers, span representation). The model is trained to a maximum of 10 epochs, starting with a 10% warm-up phase, followed by a decay phase using a linear scheduler. We save the best checkpoint and, subsequently, reduce the learning rate to 5e-6, and train this checkpoint until convergence. To address class imbalance, we use focal loss, instead of cross-entropy loss, with alpha 0.75 and gamma 2.

Entity Type	Precision	Recall	F1
LAW	73.40	92.00	81.66
VIOLATED BY	88.16	89.33	88.74
VIOLATED ON	71.43	73.33	72.37
VIOLATION	68.17	39.29	49.85
micro avg	71.93	51.49	**60.01**

Table 3: Entity level metrics of the best performing model **gliner-bi-base-v1.0** integrated with predefined rules

We experiment with three different architectures proposed by Zaratiana et al. (2023) and Knowledgator Engineering[2]—original GLiNER, the bi-encoder and the poly-encoder as shown in Table 2. During inference, we utilize a model threshold of 0.8 to compute performance metrics. Additionally, we implement a rule to eliminate false positive entities. In the event that multiple entities of the same type are extracted, we discard the entity with the lowest confidence score and retain the one with the highest score. This approach resulted in an improvement in the F1 score by 0.5%, reaching 60.01%.

NLI We train four models and test them on each legal domain. Each of these four models is trained on three domains at once and tested on the fourth to prevent data leakage as described by Bernsohn et al. (2024). For each domain, we finetune Tasksource's NLI model using a learning rate of 2e-5, a sequence length of 256, and a batch size of 8 for a maximum of 7 epochs using a cosine scheduler. We

[2]Knowledgator Blog link

Model	Consumer Protection	Privacy	TCPA	Wage	Macro F1
`tasksource` (orignal)	85.48	76.07	62.16	81.56	76.31
`tasksource` (augmented)	**88.71**	**85.88**	**79.72**	**84.61**	**84.73**

Table 4: Comparison of Tasksource's model performance on LegalLens NLI's dev dataset. The second row shows the improved performance using the augmented dataset over the original dataset as the training data by 7.65%

save the best checkpoint and reduce the learning rate to 2e-6, and further train it until convergence. As shown in Table 4, the synthetically augmented dataset boosted the performance of the models on the development dataset by 7.65%.

5 Results and Discussions

NER The original GLiNER architecture employs bi-directional encoder. The entity labels, separated by [SEP] token, and the input sequence are concatenated and then passed through the encoder model. The bi-encoder architecture decouples the entity labels and input sequence. The poly-encoder uses fuses the entity label and input sequence encoder representations together to capture the interactions between them. The bi-encoder model, `gliner-bi-base-v1.0`, has best performance with an F1 score of 59.53% and the highest precision of 83.30%. The polyencoder model, `gliner-poly-small-v1.0`, gave the highest recall of 49.64% as shown in Table 2.

Our experiments reveal that shuffling entity order and randomly dropping entities did not affect the metrics. After identifying the best model, we trained it on a synthetic dataset generated using few-shot learning. However, this approach did not yield any improvement in results. We then applied rule-based entity filtering, which improved the development dataset results by 0.5%, increasing the final F1 score from 59.53% to 60.01%. The system ranked sixth on the leaderboad with an F1 score of 33.00% on the test dataset (Hagag et al., 2024).

Table 1 illustrates the distribution of word count by entity type. The `VIOLATION` entity type averages 12.39 words, compared to a maximum of 4.14 for the other three types, increasing the complexity of the task. The model performs better on shorter entities, as shown in Table 3. Previous research has shown that NER models struggle with complex entities and tagging long sequences (Dai, 2018).

Although our model results did not surpass the baselines (Bernsohn et al., 2024), further exploration of medium and large variants of GLiNER could be beneficial. Due to limited computational resources, we were unable to include them in our experiments.

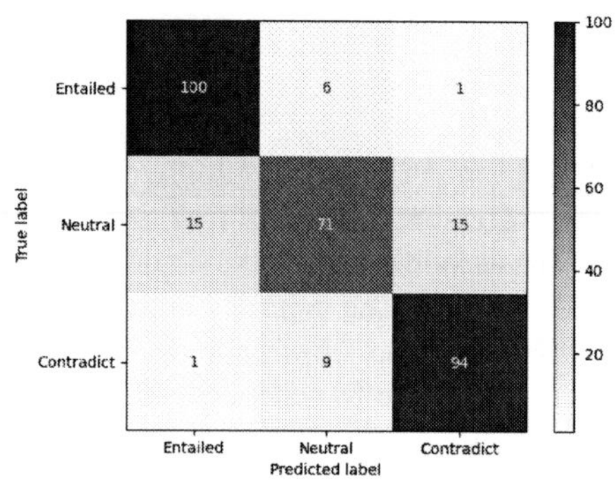

Figure 1: Final Confusion Matrix on the LegalLens NLI the dev dataset

NLI For each legal type category, we employ four distinct models. During the evaluation process on the unlabeled test set, we consider the collective assessment of all four models. The final label for a premise-hypothesis pair is determined by the model exhibiting the highest confidence score among the four. Our findings indicate that data augmentation proved beneficial, albeit to a certain extent. When we expanded the dataset to triple its original size by incorporating an additional set of paraphrases, we observed that the corresponding increase in F1 scores was not proportional to the increase in data volume. This suggests that there may be diminishing returns in terms of performance improvement beyond a certain threshold of data augmentation.

We compare our results with the baseline proposed by Bernsohn et al. (2024). They finetune Falcon 7B (Almazrouei et al., 2023) and report an F1 score of 81.02% compared to 84.73% for our model. The system ranked fifth on the leaderboad with an F1 score of 65.30% on the test dataset (Hagag et al., 2024).

In the error analysis of the final model, we see that both the models are capable of handling first class errors—confusions between `Contradict` and `Entailed`. However, our model does better with handling second-class errors—misclassification of `Contradict` or `Entailed` as `Neutral`; and Falcon 7B model does better with handling another class of errors—misclassification of `Neutral` as `Contradict` or `Entailed`. The confusion matrix for our model is shown in Figure 1.

It is interesting to note that a multitask DeBERTa based encoder surpassed the performance of a 7B parameter by 3.17%. Our model is capable of resolving the ambiguities and complexities related to wage norms. Finally, it can be stated that paraphrasing can serve as a data augmentation technique to enhance the natural language understanding capabilities of smaller models.

6 Conclusion

In conclusion, we present two systems developed for the LegalLens 2024 shared task, comprising a zero-shot bidirectional DeBERTa encoder with domain-adaptive pretraining for the NER subtask and a multitask DeBERTa encoder enhanced by data augmentation techniques for the NLI subtask. The experiments demonstrate that synthetic data generation can enrich datasets and improve the performance of encoder-based models. However, it is evident that more data does not necessarily translate to better performance. By optimizing on smaller but richer datasets and employing suitable training objectives, smaller models can outperform larger language models.

Further exploration of different augmentation strategies, with a particular focus on generating more contextually diverse synthetic data, employing adversarial data, or leveraging domain-specific paraphrasing techniques, may yield performance improvements for NER tasks. While rule-based filtering improved the F1 score by 0.5%, the adoption of more sophisticated post-processing strategies, such as probabilistic methods or ensemble techniques, holds the potential to further enhance the results.

Finally, the proposed systems secured the sixth and fifth ranks in the LegalLens NER and LegalLens NLI tasks, respectively, demonstrating their competitiveness in the shared task.

7 Acknowledgement

All experiments were carried out using Kaggle notebooks, which were equipped with a single NVIDIA P100 GPU. We extend our gratitude to Kaggle for their support in providing this computational resource.

References

Ebtesam Almazrouei, Hamza Alobeidli, Abdulaziz Alshamsi, Alessandro Cappelli, Ruxandra Cojocaru, Merouane Debbah, Etienne Goffinet, Daniel Heslow, Julien Launay, Quentin Malartic, et al. 2023. Falcon-40b: an open large language model with state-of-the-art performance.

Dor Bernsohn, Gil Semo, Yaron Vazana, Gila Hayat, Ben Hagag, Joel Niklaus, Rohit Saha, and Kyryl Truskovskyi. 2024. Legallens: Leveraging llms for legal violation identification in unstructured text. *arXiv preprint arXiv:2402.04335*.

Daniel M Bikel, Richard Schwartz, and Ralph M Weischedel. 1999. An algorithm that learns what's in a name. *Machine learning*, 34:211–231.

Andrew Borthwick, John Sterling, Eugene Agichtein, and Ralph Grishman. 1998. Nyu: Description of the mene named entity system as used in muc-7. In *Seventh Message Understanding Conference (MUC-7): Proceedings of a Conference Held in Fairfax, Virginia, April 29-May 1, 1998*.

Samuel R Bowman, Gabor Angeli, Christopher Potts, and Christopher D Manning. 2015. A large annotated corpus for learning natural language inference. *arXiv preprint arXiv:1508.05326*.

Tom Brown, Benjamin Mann, Nick Ryder, Melanie Subbiah, Jared D Kaplan, Prafulla Dhariwal, Arvind Neelakantan, Pranav Shyam, Girish Sastry, Amanda Askell, Sandhini Agarwal, Ariel Herbert-Voss, Gretchen Krueger, Tom Henighan, Rewon Child, Aditya Ramesh, Daniel Ziegler, Jeffrey Wu, Clemens Winter, Chris Hesse, Mark Chen, Eric Sigler, Mateusz Litwin, Scott Gray, Benjamin Chess, Jack Clark, Christopher Berner, Sam McCandlish, Alec Radford, Ilya Sutskever, and Dario Amodei. 2020. Language models are few-shot learners. In *Advances in Neural Information Processing Systems*, volume 33, pages 1877–1901. Curran Associates, Inc.

Ilias Chalkidis, Manos Fergadiotis, Prodromos Malakasiotis, Nikolaos Aletras, and Ion Androutsopoulos. 2020. Legal-bert: The muppets straight out of law school. *arXiv preprint arXiv:2010.02559*.

Alexis Conneau, Guillaume Lample, Ruty Rinott, Adina Williams, Samuel R Bowman, Holger Schwenk, and Veselin Stoyanov. 2018. Xnli: Evaluating cross-lingual sentence representations. *arXiv preprint arXiv:1809.05053*.

Xiang Dai. 2018. Recognizing complex entity mentions: A review and future directions. In *Proceedings of ACL 2018, Student Research Workshop*, pages 37–44.

Jacob Devlin. 2018. Bert: Pre-training of deep bidirectional transformers for language understanding. *arXiv preprint arXiv:1810.04805*.

Wee Chung Gan and Hwee Tou Ng. 2019. Improving the robustness of question answering systems to question paraphrasing. In *Proceedings of the 57th annual meeting of the association for computational linguistics*, pages 6065–6075.

Danilo Giampiccolo, Bernardo Magnini, Ido Dagan, and William B Dolan. 2007. The third pascal recognizing textual entailment challenge. In *Proceedings of the ACL-PASCAL workshop on textual entailment and paraphrasing*, pages 1–9.

Ben Hagag, Liav Harpaz, Gil Semo, Dor Bernsohn, Rohit Saha, Pashootan Vaezipoor, Kyryl Truskovskyi, and Gerasimos Spanakis. 2024. Legallens shared task 2024: Legal violation identification in unstructured text. *Preprint*, arXiv:2410.12064.

Pengcheng He, Jianfeng Gao, and Weizhu Chen. 2021a. Debertav3: Improving deberta using electra-style pretraining with gradient-disentangled embedding sharing. *Preprint*, arXiv:2111.09543.

Xuanli He, Islam Nassar, Jamie Kiros, Gholamreza Haffari, and Mohammad Norouzi. 2021b. Generate, annotate, and learn: Generative models advance self-training and knowledge distillation. *arXiv:2106.06168*.

Mohammad Javad Hosseini, Andrey Petrov, Alex Fabrikant, and Annie Louis. 2024. A synthetic data approach for domain generalization of nli models. *arXiv preprint arXiv:2402.12368*.

Zhiheng Huang, Wei Xu, and Kai Yu. 2015. Bidirectional lstm-crf models for sequence tagging. *arXiv preprint arXiv:1508.01991*.

Jingjing Huo, Kezun Zhang, Zhengyong Liu, Xuan Lin, Wenqiang Xu, Maozong Zheng, Zhaoguo Wang, and Song Li. 2023. AntContentTech at SemEval-2023 task 6: Domain-adaptive pretraining and auxiliary-task learning for understanding Indian legal texts. In *Proceedings of the 17th International Workshop on Semantic Evaluation (SemEval-2023)*, pages 402–408, Toronto, Canada. Association for Computational Linguistics.

Albert Q Jiang, Alexandre Sablayrolles, Antoine Roux, Arthur Mensch, Blanche Savary, Chris Bamford, Devendra Singh Chaplot, Diego de las Casas, Emma Bou Hanna, Florian Bressand, et al. 2024. Mixtral of experts. *arXiv preprint arXiv:2401.04088*.

Prathamesh Kalamkar, Astha Agarwal, Aman Tiwari, Smita Gupta, Saurabh Karn, and Vivek Raghavan. 2022. Named entity recognition in indian court judgments. *arXiv preprint arXiv:2211.03442*.

Guillaume Lample, Miguel Ballesteros, Sandeep Subramanian, Kazuya Kawakami, and Chris Dyer. 2016. Neural architectures for named entity recognition. In *Proceedings of the 2016 Conference of the North American Chapter of the Association for Computational Linguistics: Human Language Technologies*, pages 260–270, San Diego, California. Association for Computational Linguistics.

Yinhan Liu. 2019. Roberta: A robustly optimized bert pretraining approach. *arXiv preprint arXiv:1907.11692*.

Xuezhe Ma and Eduard Hovy. 2016. End-to-end sequence labeling via bi-directional LSTM-CNNs-CRF. In *Proceedings of the 54th Annual Meeting of the Association for Computational Linguistics (Volume 1: Long Papers)*, pages 1064–1074, Berlin, Germany. Association for Computational Linguistics.

Andrew McCallum and Wei Li. 2003. Early results for named entity recognition with conditional random fields, feature induction and web-enhanced lexicons. In *Proceedings of the Seventh Conference on Natural Language Learning at HLT-NAACL 2003*, pages 188–191.

Ashutosh Modi, Prathamesh Kalamkar, Saurabh Karn, Aman Tiwari, Abhinav Joshi, Sai Kiran Tanikella, Shouvik Kumar Guha, Sachin Malhan, and Vivek Raghavan. 2023. Semeval 2023 task 6: Legaleval-understanding legal texts. *arXiv preprint arXiv:2304.09548*.

Dhanachandra Ningthoujam, Pinal Patel, Rajkamal Kareddula, and Ramanand Vangipuram. 2023. Researchteam_hcn at semeval-2023 task 6: A knowledge enhanced transformers based legal nlp system. In *Proceedings of the 17th International Workshop on Semantic Evaluation (SemEval-2023)*, pages 1245–1253.

Damien Sileo. 2024. tasksource: A large collection of NLP tasks with a structured dataset preprocessing framework. In *Proceedings of the 2024 Joint International Conference on Computational Linguistics, Language Resources and Evaluation (LREC-COLING 2024)*, pages 15655–15684, Torino, Italia. ELRA and ICCL.

Ashish Vaswani, Noam Shazeer, Niki Parmar, Jakob Uszkoreit, Llion Jones, Aidan N Gomez, Lukasz Kaiser, and Illia Polosukhin. 2017. Attention is all you need.(nips), 2017. *Advances in Neural Information Processing Systems*, 10:S0140525X16001837.

Adina Williams, Nikita Nangia, and Samuel R Bowman. 2017. A broad-coverage challenge corpus for sentence understanding through inference. *arXiv preprint arXiv:1704.05426*.

Zhilin Yang. 2019. Xlnet: Generalized autoregressive pretraining for language understanding. *arXiv preprint arXiv:1906.08237*.

Urchade Zaratiana, Nadi Tomeh, Pierre Holat, and Thierry Charnois. 2023. Gliner: Generalist model for named entity recognition using bidirectional transformer. *Preprint*, arXiv:2311.08526.

Wenxuan Zhou, Sheng Zhang, Yu Gu, Muhao Chen, and Hoifung Poon. 2023. Universalner: Targeted distillation from large language models for open named entity recognition.

A Example Appendix

Prompts Figure 2 showcases few-shot learning approach to generate NER data points using three randomly selected examples from the training dataset.

Figure 3 and 4 showcase prompts to generate praphrases of premise and hypothesis of the NLI training dataset.

```
<s>[INST]**Objective:**
Produce a realistic social media post about legal violations that include
clearly identified named entities. Each entity should be meticulously labeled
according to its type for straightforward extraction.

**Format Requirements:**
- The output should be formatted in JSON, containing the text and the
corresponding entities list.
- Each entity in the text should be accurately marked and annotated in the
'entities' list.
- Meticulously follow all the listed attributes.

**Entity Annotation Details:**
- All entity types must be in uppercase. For example, use "TYPE" not "type".
- Entity types must be one of the four types:
1. LAW: law or regulation breached
2. VIOLATION: content describing the violation
3. VIOLATED BY: entity committing the violation)
4. VIOLATED ON: victim or affected party

- There should not be multiple entities of each type. If there are multiple
entities of VIOLATION, it should be mentioned as one single span

**Output Schema: **

<start>
{
  "text": "{text content}",
  "entities": [
    {"entity": "entity name", "types": ["type"]},
    ...
  ]
}
<end>

**Here are some real-world examples**:

{examples}


[\INST]
```

Figure 2: Prompt design for NER dataset with task description and few-shot examples

```
Produce a realistic paraphrasing of the given court settlement. It should
retain all the details.  The output should strictly consist of the rephrasing
and nothing else.

**Here's the text**

{text}
```

Figure 3: Prompt design to paraphrase the premise of the NLI training dataset.

```
Produce a realistic paraphrasing of the given social media post. It should
retain all the details. The output should strictly consist of the rephrasing
and nothing else.

**Here's the text**

{text}
```

Figure 4: Prompt design to paraphrase the hypothesis of the NLI training dataset.

LAR-ECHR: A New Legal Argument Reasoning Task and Dataset for Cases of the European Court of Human Rights

Odysseas S. Chlapanis[1,3], **Dimitrios Galanis**[2,3] and **Ion Androutsopoulos**[1,3]
[1]Department of Informatics, Athens University of Economics and Business, Greece
[2]Institute for Language and Speech Processing, Athena Research Center, Greece
[3]Archimedes Unit, Athena Research Center, Greece
odyhlapanis@aueb.gr, galanisd@athenarc.gr, ion@aueb.gr

Abstract

We present Legal Argument Reasoning (LAR), a novel task designed to evaluate the legal reasoning capabilities of Large Language Models (LLMs). The task requires selecting the correct next statement (from multiple choice options) in a chain of legal arguments from court proceedings, given the facts of the case. We constructed a dataset (LAR-ECHR) for this task using cases from the European Court of Human Rights (ECHR). We evaluated seven general-purpose LLMs on LAR-ECHR and found that (a) the ranking of the models is aligned with that of LegalBench, an established US-based legal reasoning benchmark, even though LAR-ECHR is based on EU law, (b) LAR-ECHR distinguishes top models more clearly, compared to LegalBench, (c) even the best model (GPT-4o) obtains 75.8% accuracy on LAR-ECHR, indicating significant potential for further model improvement. The process followed to construct LAR-ECHR can be replicated with cases from other legal systems.

Facts:	
Applicant married B, had daughter C.	
B abused applicant due to psychiatric disorders.	
B arrested, released; applicant moved to shelter.	
Marriage dissolved; B continued harassment.	
Preceding arguments:	
Government claimed it has established legal protections for domestic violence victims. The court noted B's repeated violence. All incidents concerned the same perpetrator and occurred in a continual manner, so the Court will examine them as a continuous situation.	
Continuation Options:	
(A) Psychiatric reports indicating mental disorders, tendency towards violence ...	✔
(B) Applicant's confinement in mental hospital ...	✘
(C) Police collected information about applicant ...	✘
(D) Complaint about psychiatric examination, ...	✘

Table 1: A cropped instance from LAR-ECHR.

1 Introduction

The rise of Large Language Models (LLMs) has impacted several sectors, including the legal one. In the United States, LLMs are being integrated into legal research and writing tools designed for both professionals and laypeople.[1] These advances are largely due to the effort of legal experts who contributed significantly in dataset development and manual evaluation (Guha et al., 2023; Magesh et al., 2024). Their involvement, however, is extremely costly, hence methods to construct and evaluate legal benchmarks semi-automatically are required.

LegalBench (Guha et al., 2023) is an example of a widely used legal reasoning benchmark. It consists of data for 162 tasks, hand-crafted by legal experts, that evaluate six types of legal reasoning of the US legal system, making it the most reliable dataset of this kind. MMLU-Law, a subset of MMLU (Hendrycks et al., 2021) that contains three US legal tasks only, is also commonly used. Similarly, LawBench (Fei et al., 2023) and IL-TUR (Joshi et al., 2024) were created for the Chinese and Indian regions; they comprise 20 and 8 tasks, respectively. For other legal systems, at least two other large multi-task legal benchmarks have been made available (Chalkidis et al., 2022; Niklaus et al., 2023). However, they include mostly text classification tasks that do not require understanding or generating chains of legal arguments (e.g., court arguments explaining the decisions of judges) and can be solved reasonably well using smaller BERT-based models (Chalkidis et al., 2020) or even linear classifiers (Aletras et al., 2016). Hence, it is questionable if they test legal reasoning abilities.

Motivated by the observations above, we introduce a novel task (§2), Legal Argument Reasoning (LAR), designed to evaluate the legal reasoning skills of LLMs. The task requires selecting the cor-

[1] https://www.americanbar.org/groups/law_practice/resources/tech-report/2023/2023-artificial-intelligence-ai-techreport/

Proceedings of the Natural Legal Language Processing Workshop 2024, pages 267–279
November 16, 2024 ©2024 Association for Computational Linguistics

rect next statement (from multiple choice options) in a chain of legal arguments from court proceedings, given the facts of the case. We have prepared a LAR dataset for EU law, LAR-ECHR (§3), using court arguments from the European Court of Human Rights (ECHR). It contains 403 instances; Table 1 shows a cropped example. Notably, the same process could be applied to construct LAR datasets for other legal systems as well.

We evaluate two closed-weight and 5 open-weight LLMs on LAR-ECHR (§4), comparing their performance and rankings against two legal benchmarks: LegalBench and MMLU-Law. For completeness, we also report scores on two general reasoning benchmarks: the entire MMLU (MMLU-Full) and HellaSwag (Zellers et al., 2019). We find that: (a) the ranking of the models on LAR-ECHR is aligned with that of LegalBench, even though the two benchmarks are from different legal systems (US, EU); (b) LAR-ECHR provides clearer distinctions among top models, compared to LegalBench; (c) even the best model (`GPT-4o`) obtains only 75.8% accuracy on LAR-ECHR, similar to the top accuracy on LegalBench (73.3%), indicating significant potential for further model improvement.

Our contributions are three-fold: (i) we introduce a novel task, Legal Argument Reasoning (LAR), to evaluate the legal reasoning abilities of state-of-the-art LLMs; (ii) we create and publicly release LAR-ECHR, a challenging EU-specific LAR dataset; (iii) we present a method to create LAR datasets for any other legal system using court proceedings with annotated arguments.

2 The LAR task

We introduce Legal Argument Reasoning (LAR), a novel task to evaluate the legal reasoning abilities of LLMs. The LLM is fed with the *facts* of the case (a list of sentences summarizing the events considered, see Table 1), a sequence of *preceding arguments* (statements) from the court proceedings, and *continuation options* (the correct next statement and distractors). The LLM has to select the correct next statement. (In court proceedings, 'arguments' are numbered statements documenting the legal reasoning of the court.)

LAR requires various types of legal and commonsense reasoning that extend beyond simple pattern recognition or memorization. As demonstrated by HellaSwag (Zellers et al., 2019), even predicting the next sentence in a generic corpus can be challenging and requires reasoning skills. In the legal domain, the complex terminology and inferences make the task of predicting a legal professional's next argument significantly harder (§4). The arguments embody the court's legal reasoning for its decisions. As Medvedeva and Mcbride (2023) state: "[J]udges usually offer explanations which serve to justify their decisions with reference to the facts found to be established and the relevant law. [These explanations] involve the exercise of legal reasoning". Merely understanding the legal terminology is insufficient, as the the facts and the relevant law must also be considered.

3 The LAR-ECHR dataset

The LAR-ECHR dataset contains arguments from the proceedings of the European Court of Human Rights (ECHR). An ECHR court decision typically begins with the facts of the case, followed by the 'Law' section, where the arguments of the parties and the court are presented, followed by the court's conclusion (e.g., verdict, fines). To create the dataset, we used statements from 'Law'.

To ensure that LAR-ECHR is challenging and effectively evaluates legal reasoning, we select appropriate arguments based on criteria derived from the annotations of the Legal Argument Mining ECHR (LAM:ECHR) dataset (Habernal et al., 2024) (§3.1). The criteria we use are described in §3.2 below. Instead of generating the distractors using a language model, as in HellaSwag (Zellers et al., 2019) and LegalLens (Bernsohn et al., 2024), we draw them from similar ECHR cases using an algorithm we developed (§3.3), to avoid introducing language model biases and hallucinations.

LAR-ECHR is based on 191 ECHR court cases. From the 191 cases, we derive 403 samples (like the example of Table 1), which we split randomly into three sets: 5 samples for few-shot prompts, 98 samples for development, 300 samples for testing. In our experiments, we use only the test set, but we release the full dataset for future research.[2] Below we describe in detail how the dataset was created.

3.1 The previous LAM:ECHR dataset

In the aforementioned LAM:ECHR dataset, the arguments of 373 ECHR court decisions were annotated for legal argument mining purposes. The

[2] `https://huggingface.co/datasets/AUEB-NLP/lar-echr`

cases pertain to alleged violations of Article 8 ('Respect for private and family life') and, to a lesser extent, Article 7 ('No punishment without law') of the European Convention on Human Rights. The arguments were annotated for the actors stating them ('ECHR', 'Applicant', 'State', 'Third Parties', 'Commission/Chamber') and the type of argument (16 types). The argument types are: 'Procedural', 'Interpretation' (five variations), 'Principle of proportionality' (four variations), 'Institutional' (three variations), 'Precedents', 'Decision', 'Application to the concrete case'. The latter type is the most common (57%), and we use only arguments of this type in the new LAR-ECHR dataset (§3.2).

There are 9,950 arguments (65%) labeled with the 'ECHR' actor in LAM:ECHR, 2,471 (16%) arguments labeled with 'Applicant', 2,399 (16%) labeled with 'State'. Only the remaining 385 (3%) arguments are associated with the last two actors; for simplicity, we discard these 385 statements.

The facts of each case are not included in LAM:ECHR, but they are included in the ECtHR B dataset (Chalkidis et al., 2021), which does not provide arguments. We unified the two datasets using regular expressions. A further complication is that LAM:ECHR was published after ECtHR B. The 373 cases of LAM:ECHR include 94 cases that are not covered by ECtHR B. Consequently, we used only the 279 cases covered by both datasets. Recently, a new dataset, ECtHR-PCR (T.y.s.s. et al., 2024), which contains both facts and arguments of ECHR cases (even the most recent ones), was released. Using this dataset, the missing cases will be included in an update of LAR-ECHR in the future.

From the remaining 279 cases, we selected the most appropriate *target arguments* (correct next statements) according to criteria described in §3.2 below. Some cases included multiple arguments that satisfied the criteria, while others none (88 cases). Consequently, we selected target arguments from the remaining 191 cases. The distractor arguments (incorrect next statements) were also selected from the 191 cases (§3.3). This process led to 403 instances, like the one of Table 1.

3.2 Selection of target arguments

Here we describe the process used to select the target arguments (correct next statements) of the new dataset from the 191 cases of §3.1.

As already noted, the 'Law' section of each case contains the arguments of the parties and the court. Actually, a case usually examines multiple *issues* and the 'Law' section contains the arguments of the parties, followed by the arguments of the court, separately per issue. For each issue, the arguments of the parties (in the court proceedings) are actually also written by the judges, in a way that supports the reasoning of the judges. Therefore, for each issue, the arguments (statements) of both the parties and the court actually form a reasoning chain. From that chain, we wish to focus on the arguments of the judges, especially those annotated as 'Application to the concrete case' in LAM:ECHR, which are the most demanding in terms of reasoning, as they consider and combine the arguments of the parties, the law, and the facts of the particular case. Those arguments are "concerned with determining the relation between the concrete case and the abstract legal norm by the subsumption of the facts of a case under a legal norm" (Habernal et al., 2024). In other words, they are parts of the reasoning that the judges follow to connect the law to the facts by 'subsumption', i.e., checking if the facts meet the conditions specified by the law.

Furthermore, in our experience, among the arguments of the judges, the first one (per issue) is the most difficult to predict; we leave an experimental validation of this claim for future work (§7). Therefore, we select as target arguments those that satisfy the following criteria: (i) the argument must be annotated as 'ECHR' (argument of the judges), (ii) the argument must be annotated as 'Application to the concrete case', and (iii) it must be the first one (per issue) after the arguments of the parties.

Due to the limited context length of LLMs, in LAR-ECHR the facts of each case are summarized (using `GPT-4o`) and only the last three of the arguments preceding the target one are retained.

3.3 Selection of distractors

Distractors are incorrect next statements, as opposed to the target argument, which is the correct one. Some studies use synthetic distractors generated by LLMs, e.g., HellaSwag (Zellers et al., 2019) and Legalens (Bernsohn et al., 2024). We opt to use arguments from the same dataset as distractors, following the approach in EntailmentBank (Dalvi et al., 2021). This approach avoids the introduction of biases and hallucinations of LLM generators, as reported in the work of HellaSwag.

The most suitable distractors are algorithmically selected. The algorithm adheres to the following desiderata. (a) The distractors must be *similar* to the target argument, i.e., they must have roughly

Text	Score
Target argument	
The Court notes that this complaint is not manifestly ill-founded within the meaning of Article 35 §3 ...	1.00
Candidate distractors	
The Court notes that *the application* is not manifestly ill-founded within the meaning of Article 35 §3 ...	0.95
The Court, having examined those complaints under Articles 5 §1 and 6 §1 of the Convention ...	0.85
The Court considers that this part of the application raises questions of law which are important ...	**0.79**
The Court notes that the Government put forward reasons for this complaint to be declared inadmissible ...	0.73

Table 2: Exploring the effect of the cosine similarity threshold τ on the candidate distractors.

the same style, length, and vocabulary. As seen in the example in Table 1, the target (correct) argument refers to an event about 'psychiatric reports', 'mental disorder', and 'tendency towards violence'; each one of the distractors mentions relevant terms ('mental hospital', 'police', 'psychiatric examination'). However, (b) the distractors should not be near-duplicates or paraphrases of the target argument or another distractor. With these desiderata, we developed the following algorithm.

Distractor selection algorithm: For each target argument, the candidate distractors are the target arguments of the other cases (of all the issues of the other 190 cases, §3.1). For each candidate distractor, its embedding is computed using an LLM.[3] The candidate distractors are then ranked based on their cosine similarity to the embedding of the target argument (desideratum (a)), from highest to lowest. While the top-3 ranked candidates could present the greatest challenge, they may also be paraphrases of the target argument or another distractor (desideratum (b)). Hence, before selecting the top-3 ranked candidate distractors, we discard candidate distractors whose similarity to the target argument or a more highly ranked candidate distractor exceeds a threshold τ.

Cosine similarity threshold: To select the τ threshold, we conducted the following experiment: for each one of a few target arguments of the development subset (§4.1), we ranked the candidate distractors as above, and manually inspected the texts of the target and the distractors and their similarity scores (see Table 2 for an example). We observed that for similarity scores above 0.9, the two texts were almost identical. For scores between 0.9 and 0.85, they shared several words. For lower similarity scores, no such issues were visible, so we set $\tau = 0.8$.

4 Experiments

4.1 Experimental setup

We evaluate the reasoning skills of seven general-purpose LLMs using the respective web APIs and three random seeds. We employed closed-weight OpenAI models (GPT family), namely `gpt-4o` (L), `gpt-4o-mini` (S) (OpenAI et al., 2024)[4]; open-weight models by Mistral (Mistral family), namely `open-mixtral-8x22b` (L), `open-mixtral-8x7b` (M), `open-mistral-7b` (S) (Jiang et al., 2024)[5]; and open-weight models by Meta (Llama family), namely `llama-3.1-70b` (L), `llama-3.1-8b` (S) (Dubey et al., 2024)[6] .

We report the average classification accuracy (over the three random seeds) and the standard deviation for each LLM on the test subset of LAR-ECHR. We also show results on two previous legal benchmarks (LegalBench, MMLU-Law) and two general benchmarks (MMLU-full, HellaSwag), as previously reported (Liang et al., 2023).

MMLU (Hendrycks et al., 2021) is the most widely used benchmark for evaluating the knowledge and reasoning abilities of instruction following LLMs (Liang et al., 2023). MMLU-Law is a subset of MMLU that contains three legal tasks ('International Law', 'Jurisprudence', 'Professional Law'). LegalBench is the largest (in terms of tasks) benchmark for the evaluation of legal reasoning (Magesh et al., 2024). It includes 162 tasks that assess 6 different reasoning types. HellaSwag (Zellers et al., 2019) is a dataset created automatically that only contains the next statement prediction task, similar to LAR-ECHR. However, in HellaSwag the texts are collected from online articles and not chains of legal arguments, as in LAR-ECHR. In the three previous benchmarks that have multiple tasks (MMLU, MMLU-Law, LegalBench), we report macro-average over their tasks.

[3]We use `openai-embed-small` (`https://openai.com/index/introducing-text-and-code-embeddings/`) (Neelakantan et al., 2022).

[4]`https://openai.com/index/hello-gpt-4o/`

[5]`https://mistral.ai/news/mixtral-8x22b/`

[6]`https://ai.meta.com/blog/meta-llama-3-1/`

Models	LAR-ECHR (Ours)	Legal Bench*	MMLU Law*	MMLU Full*	Hella Swag
GPT-4o (L)	**75.8** ± 1.8 **[1]**	**73.3 [1]**	**85.2 [1]**	**74.8 [1]**	**89.1 [1]**
GPT-4o-mini (S)	61.6 ± 2.2 [4]	65.3 [4]	79.6 [2]	66.8 [4]	83.4 [3]
Mistral-8x22B (L)	69.8 ± 1.3 [2]	70.8 [2]	79.1 [3]	70.1 [3]	79.6 [4]
Mistral-8x7B (M)	57.2 ± 1.6 [5]	63.0 [5]	74.3 [4]	64.9 [5]	70.5 [5]
Mistral-7B (S)	49.6 ± 1.9 [7]	33.1 [7]	63.2 [6]	58.4 [6]	60.7 [7]
Llama-3.1-70B (L)	67.2 ± 2.6 [3]	68.7 [3]	67.4 [5]	70.9 [2]	86.2 [2]
Llama-3.1-8B (S)	54.1 ± 1.6 [6]	34.2 [6]	57.3 [7]	50.0 [7]	68.0 [6]

Table 3: Comparison of LLMs from three families on LAR-ECHR, LegalBench, MMLU-Law, MMLU-Full. L, M, S denote the largest, medium, smallest models per family, respectively. Accuracy in %. Rankings in square brackets. LAR-ECHR results averaged over three random seeds. HellaSwag results on a subset of 1000 samples and one random seed. *Results from Liang et al. (2023).

4.2 Zero-shot prompting

All experiments are performed in a zero-shot setting with a Chain-of-Thought (CoT) prompt (Wei et al., 2023) we designed for LAR-ECHR (Table 4). The prompt explains the provided input (facts, preceding arguments, continuation options) and the task, asking the LLM to generate an output in three steps. In the first step ('Analysis'), the LLM reflects on the plausibility of each option (candidate next argument). In the second step ('Explanation'), the LLM explains its choice. In the last step ('Answer'), the LLM outputs only the letter (A, B, C, D) of its choice (to facilitate answer collection).

4.3 Experimental results

Table 3 presents the accuracy of the models on the five datasets (LAR-ECHR, LegalBench, MMLU-Law, MMLU-Full, HellaSwag). The large version of `GPT-4o` (L) achieves the best performance on all datasets, with accuracy 75.8% on LAR-ECHR, showing that there is room for model improvement on our dataset. The rankings (in square brackets) of all models on LAR-ECHR are identical to those of LegalBench, even though the two datasets are based on different legal systems (US, EU). Within each family of models, the largest model is the best on all datasets, as expected.

`Mistral` (L) is the second best model on LAR-ECHR and LegalBench, with a larger performance gap from the best model (6 pp), compared to the corresponding gap on LegalBench (2.5 pp), showing that LAR-ECHR distinguishes better than LegalBench the legal reasoning abilities of the top two models. When comparing models of the same family, LAR-ECHR also distinguishes better between `GPT-4o` (L) and `GPT-4o` (S), as shown in Fig. 1, and the same applies between `Mistral` (L) and `Mistral` (M). By contrast, LegalBench distinguishes substantially better between `Mistral` (L) and `Mistral` (S) (Fig. 1), as well as between `Llama`

Prompt:
You will be provided with the introductory Facts in a European Court of Human Rights (ECHR) case, an excerpt of arguments from that case and several possible continuations of these arguments. Your task is to determine which continuation accurately extends the original argument.
Output format:
- Analysis: Provide an in-depth evaluation of how each option relates to the initial argument.
- Explanation: Articulate why your chosen option is the correct continuation.
- Answer: State the letter of your selected answer.
Facts: ...
Preceding arguments: ...
Continuation options: ...
LLM response:
```
Analysis:
(A): Reinforces B's mental health issues and need for treatment.
(B): Discusses mental hospital confinement, unrelated to specific case facts.
(C): Introduces irrelevant information about police actions and examinations.
(D): Diverges to complaints about forced evaluations, not B's violence.
Explanation:
Option (A) criticizes Croatian authorities for not acting on B's known psychiatric issues and violent tendencies, aligning with the Court's view of ongoing abuse.
Answer: (A)
```

Table 4: Our CoT prompt for LAR-ECHR, a sample input (facts, preceding arguments, continuation options), and the response (analysis, explanation, answer) from `GPT-4o`. The '...' are as in Table 1. The full version of this table can be found in Appendix A.

(L) and Llama (S); this is due to the much lower scores the smaller Mistral (S) and Llama (S) obtain on LegalBench compared to LAR-ECHR.

Table 5 presents the performance of GPT and Llama models on LAR-ECHR when provided with the original, complete facts of the proceedings, for models with large enough context length. As expected, all models exhibit greater performance when using the complete facts. Notably, Llama models benefit more than GPT models. Differences between models within the same family are relatively small. These findings suggest that while summaries offer an effective workaround for models with limited context lengths, they can introduce bias, potentially favoring certain models.

5 Related work

The LAR task was inspired by the continuation task introduced by SWAG (Zellers et al., 2018) and later improved by HellaSwag (Zellers et al., 2019). It is a multiple-choice task where the model has to select the most likely continuation of an event description, such as "A woman sits at a piano" is followed by "She sets her fingers on the keys". The corpus is collected from various online sources such as wikiHow[7]. Similarly to LAR, HellaSwag is constructed automatically, via a technique called Adversarial Filtering (AF) which selects the most persuasive LLM-generated continuations as incorrect options. It is shown empirically that accurately predicting the correct continuation of an event in HellaSwag requires skills that are closely related to commonsense reasoning. The primary differences with our work, aside from our focus on the legal domain, are: (a) we employ official content from court proceedings instead of events from online articles of varying credibility, (b) we use (based on the respective annotations) the most appropriate chain of arguments, and (c) we utilize human-generated challenging distractors.

Our dataset builds on top of two previous works: LAM:ECHR (Habernal et al., 2024) and ECtHR B (Chalkidis et al., 2021). LAM:ECHR annotated, with the help of legal experts, the arguments of 373 ECHR decisions with *actor* and *argument type* labels, and trained and evaluated their RoBERTa-based models on both tasks. In ECtHR B the goal is to predict the articles of ECHR that were allegedly violated, given the facts of the case. To create LAR-ECHR we aligned the common instances of these datasets to combine the annotated arguments of LAM:ECHR with the facts of the cases from ECtHR B.

[7] https://www.wikihow.com/

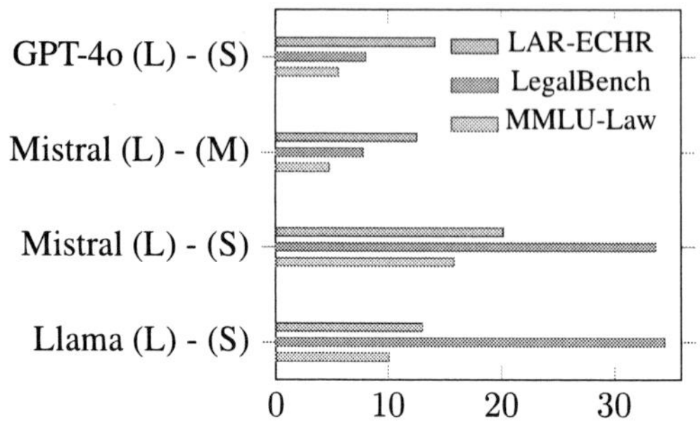

Figure 1: Performance gap within the same LLM family.

Models	LAR-ECHR (complete facts)
GPT-4o	**77.9** (+2.1)
GPT-4o-mini	64.3 (+2.7)
Llama-70B	73.3 (+6.1)
Llama-8B	58.0 (+3.9)

Table 5: Results on LAR-ECHR with complete facts. The difference in performance from the summarized version is shown in parentheses.

One of the most widely known benchmarks in legal NLP is LexGLUE (Chalkidis et al., 2022). It was one of the first large-scale collection of datasets dedicated to the legal domain. Its creation was inspired by the success of GLUE, a multi-task benchmark dataset (Wang et al., 2018), and the subsequent and more challening SuperGLUE (Wang et al., 2019). LexGLUE includes a variety of (English-only) classification tasks from both US and EU legal systems, however it does not contain any reasoning-specific tasks. LEXTREME (Niklaus et al., 2023) followed with a collection of 11 datasets, featuring tasks similar to those in LexGLUE, to establish a multilingual legal NLP benchmark. LegalLens (Bernsohn et al., 2024) introduced two classification tasks: detecting legal violations and identifying potentially affected individuals. The tasks were created using LLMs and then validated by human experts. The aforementioned benchmarks focus on specific classification tasks. They do not directly measure in-context learning capabilities or the understanding of legal reasoning explanations.

In the broader NLP landscape, several datasets have recently emerged for evaluating the few-shot learning capabilities and advanced reasoning skills of LLMs, replacing GLUE and SuperGLUE as the most widely used benchmarks. These new benchmarks are more aligned with the skills required by chatbot assistants designed to solve a wide range of tasks by following instructions, primarily through generating text rather than predefined labels. The most prominent of these is the Massive Multitask Language Understanding (MMLU) benchmark (Hendrycks et al., 2021), which is preferred for evaluating the knowledge and general capabilities of LLMs (Liang et al., 2023). It is a multiple-choice dataset that covers 57 tasks across diverse academic subjects, three of them being law-specific. ARC (Clark et al., 2018) is another multiple-choice question-answering dataset that includes science questions requiring various types of reasoning. Big Bench (Srivastava et al., 2023) is a challenging dataset of 204 tasks that focuses on various topics among them arithmetic, logical, common-sense and algorithmic reasoning as well as language understanding and world knowledge.

Inspired by the success of these benchmarks, several benchmarks for the legal domain, with the same orientation, were also made available. For example, the largest legal reasoning benchmark (in terms of number of tasks) is LegalBench (Guha et al., 2023), comprising 162 tasks that cover six different types of legal reasoning and focus on the US legal system. Bongard et al. (2022) created a challenging legal reasoning dataset by adapting questions from a textbook on US civil procedure which however is cast as a binary classification task and does not focus on continuations such as LAR-ECHR. A few datasets that are focused on other legal systems than the US were also made available. For example, LawBench (Fei et al., 2023) consists of 20 tasks on Chinese law that evaluate legal knowledge understanding of LLMs. IL-TUR (Joshi et al., 2024) covers a wide range of multilingual legal text understanding and reasoning tasks for English and 9 Indian languages. Our dataset, LAR-ECHR, differs from the datasets in these benchmarks in that (a) it uses the legal reasoning chain of the arguments of the judges, (b) it refers to EU law and (c) instances are collected semi-automatically from court proceedings using annotations, not handcrafted by legal experts.

6 Conclusion

In this study, we introduced LAR, a legal reasoning NLP task that requires selecting the correct next argument made by judges in a case. We constructed a dataset for this task, called LAR-ECHR, using cases from ECHR. We evaluated seven general-purpose LLMs from three families on this dataset. The best model obtained 75.8% accuracy, indicating significant potential for further model improvement. Model rankings were identical with those of LegalBench, even though the datasets are based on different legal systems. Despite that weak models obtained a substantially lower score in LegalBench, LAR-ECHR distinguished the top models more clearly. The process followed to construct LAR-ECHR can be replicated with cases from any court proceedings, even from different legal systems.

7 Future work

The semi-automatic creation of a LAR dataset requires a few design decisions, two of which we believe are most worth investigating further: (a) the impact of not selecting only the first arguments of the judges (per issue) as target arguments (which in our experience are the most difficult to predict) and (b) the impact of the similarity threshold τ in selecting candidate distractors.

Additionally, we plan to extend the dataset in various directions: (a) collect and align the missing ECHR cases that are annotated from LAM:ECHR, but they do not exist in ECtHR B, (b) include the rest of the articles of ECHR, apart from articles 7 and 8, to cover other domains of legal expertise, (c) annotate more cases to increase the dataset size. These extensions could lead to the inclusion of a training set for fine-tuning LLMs. These LLMs would be either open-source LLMs or smaller BERT-based models that have shown promise in legal reasoning tasks, such as (Chalkidis et al., 2020). Even though these legal-specific models do not exhibit few-shot learning capabilities, they would be ideal baseline models.

Independently of this extension, we plan to evaluate more general-purpose, but also legal-specific LLMs, and update the leaderboard of the dataset. It would be insightful to measure the impact of pretraining on the same or other legal systems. To our knowledge, there is currently only one publicly released family of legal LLMs that can follow instructions, `Saul-7B` (Colombo et al., 2024b), `Saul-54B` and `Saul-141B` (Colombo et al., 2024a).

Finally, the process followed to construct LAR-ECHR could be replicated with cases from other court proceedings to create new LAR datasets that are focused on other legal systems and/or languages.

Limitations

One limitation of our work has to do with the process followed to create the dataset. While the data were originally created by humans, the next statement prediction task is artificial. We employed semi-automatic techniques, based on legal expert annotations and embedding similarity of the arguments, to compile a challenging dataset. We also summarized the facts to fit in the context length of all the models. This process might have introduced biases and/or mistakes, as we have already discussed for the summaries of the facts (§ 4.3). The impact of these biases could only be measured by careful examination from legal experts and extensive comparisons with different variations (e.g. summaries from other models).

Furthermore, it should be noted that, as in many other legal NLP datasets, we are using the 'facts' of ECHR court decisions as if they are the factual information available prior to the final decision. However, due to the details of the legal process and the way that court proceedings are written, this is unrealistic (Medvedeva and Mcbride, 2023). The judges actually publish only the information that is supporting their final decision as the 'facts' of the case; not the original record that they had to consider in that process. To make the task realistic for a real-world application we should include the actual information that the parties had access to before the final judgement took place, but access to this information is very hard to get for most cases.

Ethics Statement

The primary objective of this research is to advance legal NLP and more specifically the use of LLMs as tools that assist–without replacing–legal professionals. A diverse set of communities can be benefited from our research: (a) the NLP community can challenge existing and future LLMs on an advanced legal reasoning dataset and even build new datasets for other courts, (b) legal practitioners can improve their understanding of the way these models make decisions and (c) the legal tech community can gain useful insights into LLM capabilities across different courts and legal systems, enabling them to design appropriate use cases and develop more accurate tools.

Most previous work in legal NLP, including both benchmarks and models, (Guha et al., 2023; Niklaus et al., 2023; Chalkidis et al., 2020), advocate that they do not aim to replace judges, but instead to assist them in reaching more informed decisions. However, most of them are trying to predict the outcome of legal decisions, without providing or evaluating legal reasoning explanations. In contrast, our work evaluates the ability of LLMs to identify the correct next statement in a judge's chain of legal arguments, which is closely linked to their capacity to produce valid legal reasoning.

When introducing a new legal NLP task, it is vital to consider the intended use cases for potential models designed for it (Medvedeva and Mcbride, 2023; Tsarapatsanis and Aletras, 2021). In our case, we advocate that such models be used solely as supporting tools to review the reasoning of legal professionals, rather than to produce their own legal reasoning (let alone predict the outcome of a case).

For example, we propose developing a legal verification tool, i.e. a tool that can verify the validity of the legal reasoning of an argument chain. This tool could be used by judges to validate the 'Law' section of the proceedings (after the final decision is taken) before publishing them. If a potential reasoning weakness is located by the model, then it could provide its own CoT explanation to pinpoint the root cause of the problem. The judges would then evaluate if they agree with the model or not, and if their reasoning requires revision. In this example ethical risks are almost completely mitigated, because the decision is already taken. This tool would help the judges prepare the proceedings faster and it could decrease oversights.

We recognize the ethical importance of data privacy and confidentiality. All data is obtained from publicly accessible online sources, without infringing any proprietary rights, and in accordance with the licenses under which they were released. The data from LAM:ECHR were released under the `'Apache 2.0'` license along with the respective software.[8] The data from ECtHR B were released under the 'Creative Commons Attribution-NonCommercial-ShareAlike 4.0' (`'CC BY-NC-SA 4.0'`) license.[9] In accordance to `'CC BY-NC-SA 4.0'`, we released our dataset under the same license as well.[10]

[8] https://github.com/trusthlt/mining-legal-arguments/blob/main/LICENSE

[9] https://huggingface.co/datasets/AUEB-NLP/ecthr_cases

[10] https://creativecommons.org/licenses/

Acknowledgments

This work has been partially supported by project MIS 5154714 of the National Recovery and Resilience Plan Greece 2.0 funded by the European Union under the NextGenerationEU Program. In addition, AWS resources were provided by the National Infrastructures for Research and Technology GRNET and funded by the EU Recovery and Resiliency Facility.

References

Nikolaos Aletras, Dimitrios Tsarapatsanis, Daniel Preotiuc-Pietro, and Vasileios Lampos. 2016. Predicting judicial decisions of the european court of human rights: a natural language processing perspective. *PeerJ Comput. Sci.*, 2:e93.

Dor Bernsohn, Gil Semo, Yaron Vazana, Gila Hayat, Ben Hagag, Joel Niklaus, Rohit Saha, and Kyryl Truskovskyi. 2024. LegalLens: Leveraging LLMs for legal violation identification in unstructured text. In *Proceedings of the 18th Conference of the European Chapter of the Association for Computational Linguistics (Volume 1: Long Papers)*, pages 2129–2145, St. Julian's, Malta. Association for Computational Linguistics.

Leonard Bongard, Lena Held, and Ivan Habernal. 2022. The legal argument reasoning task in civil procedure. In *Proceedings of the Natural Legal Language Processing Workshop 2022*, pages 194–207, Abu Dhabi, United Arab Emirates (Hybrid). Association for Computational Linguistics.

Ilias Chalkidis, Manos Fergadiotis, Prodromos Malakasiotis, Nikolaos Aletras, and Ion Androutsopoulos. 2020. LEGAL-BERT: The muppets straight out of law school. In *Findings of the Association for Computational Linguistics: EMNLP 2020*, pages 2898–2904, Online. Association for Computational Linguistics.

Ilias Chalkidis, Manos Fergadiotis, Dimitrios Tsarapatsanis, Nikolaos Aletras, Ion Androutsopoulos, and Prodromos Malakasiotis. 2021. Paragraph-level rationale extraction through regularization: A case study on European court of human rights cases. In *Proceedings of the 2021 Conference of the North American Chapter of the Association for Computational Linguistics: Human Language Technologies*, pages 226–241, Online. Association for Computational Linguistics.

Ilias Chalkidis, Abhik Jana, Dirk Hartung, Michael Bommarito, Ion Androutsopoulos, Daniel Katz, and Nikolaos Aletras. 2022. LexGLUE: A benchmark dataset for legal language understanding in English. In *Proceedings of the 60th Annual Meeting of the Association for Computational Linguistics (Volume 1: Long Papers)*, pages 4310–4330, Dublin, Ireland. Association for Computational Linguistics.

Peter Clark, Isaac Cowhey, Oren Etzioni, Tushar Khot, Ashish Sabharwal, Carissa Schoenick, and Oyvind Tafjord. 2018. Think you have solved question answering? try arc, the ai2 reasoning challenge. *Preprint*, arXiv:1803.05457.

Pierre Colombo, Telmo Pires, Malik Boudiaf, Rui Melo, Dominic Culver, Sofia Morgado, Etienne Malaboeuf, Gabriel Hautreux, Johanne Charpentier, and Michael Desa. 2024a. Saullm-54b & saullm-141b: Scaling up domain adaptation for the legal domain. *Preprint*, arXiv:2407.19584.

Pierre Colombo, Telmo Pessoa Pires, Malik Boudiaf, Dominic Culver, Rui Melo, Caio Corro, Andre F. T. Martins, Fabrizio Esposito, Vera Lúcia Raposo, Sofia Morgado, and Michael Desa. 2024b. Saullm-7b: A pioneering large language model for law. *Preprint*, arXiv:2403.03883.

Bhavana Dalvi, Peter Jansen, Oyvind Tafjord, Zhengnan Xie, Hannah Smith, Leighanna Pipatanangkura, and Peter Clark. 2021. Explaining answers with entailment trees. In *Proceedings of the 2021 Conference on Empirical Methods in Natural Language Processing*, pages 7358–7370, Online and Punta Cana, Dominican Republic. Association for Computational Linguistics.

Abhimanyu Dubey, Abhinav Jauhri, Abhinav Pandey, Abhishek Kadian, Ahmad Al-Dahle, Aiesha Letman, Akhil Mathur, Alan Schelten, Amy Yang, Angela Fan, Anirudh Goyal, Anthony Hartshorn, Aobo Yang, Archi Mitra, Archie Sravankumar, Artem Korenev, Arthur Hinsvark, Arun Rao, Aston Zhang, Aurelien Rodriguez, Austen Gregerson, et al. 2024. The llama 3 herd of models. *Preprint*, arXiv:2407.21783.

Zhiwei Fei, Xiaoyu Shen, Dawei Zhu, Fengzhe Zhou, Zhuo Han, Songyang Zhang, Kai Chen, Zongwen Shen, and Jidong Ge. 2023. Lawbench: Benchmarking legal knowledge of large language models. *arXiv preprint arXiv:2309.16289*.

Neel Guha, Julian Nyarko, Daniel E. Ho, Christopher Ré, Adam Chilton, Aditya Narayana, Alex Chohlas-Wood, Austin Peters, Brandon Waldon, Daniel N. Rockmore, Diego Zambrano, Dmitry Talisman, Enam Hoque, Faiz Surani, Frank Fagan, Galit Sarfaty, Gregory M. Dickinson, Haggai Porat, Jason Hegland, et al. 2023. Legalbench: A collaboratively built benchmark for measuring legal reasoning in large language models. *Preprint*, arXiv:2308.11462.

Ivan Habernal, Daniel Faber, Nicola Recchia, Sebastian Bretthauer, Iryna Gurevych, Indra Spiecker genannt Döhmann, and Christoph Burchard. 2024. Mining legal arguments in court decisions. *Artificial Intelligence and Law*, 32(3):1–38.

Dan Hendrycks, Collin Burns, Steven Basart, Andy Zou, Mantas Mazeika, Dawn Song, and Jacob Steinhardt. 2021. Measuring massive multitask language understanding. *Proceedings of the International Conference on Learning Representations (ICLR)*.

Albert Q. Jiang, Alexandre Sablayrolles, Antoine Roux, Arthur Mensch, Blanche Savary, Chris Bamford, Devendra Singh Chaplot, Diego de las Casas, Emma Bou Hanna, Florian Bressand, Gianna Lengyel, Guillaume Bour, Guillaume Lample, Lélio Renard Lavaud, Lucile Saulnier, Marie-Anne Lachaux, Pierre Stock, et al. 2024. Mixtral of experts. *Preprint*, arXiv:2401.04088.

Abhinav Joshi, Shounak Paul, Akshat Sharma, Pawan Goyal, Saptarshi Ghosh, and Ashutosh Modi. 2024. IL-TUR: Benchmark for Indian legal text understanding and reasoning. In *Proceedings of the 62nd Annual Meeting of the Association for Computational Linguistics (Volume 1: Long Papers)*, pages 11460–11499, Bangkok, Thailand. Association for Computational Linguistics.

Percy Liang, Rishi Bommasani, Tony Lee, Dimitris Tsipras, Dilara Soylu, Michihiro Yasunaga, Yian Zhang, Deepak Narayanan, Yuhuai Wu, Ananya Kumar, Benjamin Newman, Binhang Yuan, Bobby Yan, Ce Zhang, Christian Cosgrove, Christopher D. Manning, Christopher Ré, et al. 2023. Holistic evaluation of language models. *Preprint*, arXiv:2211.09110.

Varun Magesh, Faiz Surani, Matthew Dahl, Mirac Suzgun, Christopher D. Manning, and Daniel E. Ho. 2024. Hallucination-free? assessing the reliability of leading ai legal research tools. *Preprint*, arXiv:2405.20362.

Masha Medvedeva and Pauline Mcbride. 2023. Legal judgment prediction: If you are going to do it, do it right. In *Proceedings of the Natural Legal Language Processing Workshop 2023*, pages 73–84, Singapore. Association for Computational Linguistics.

Arvind Neelakantan, Tao Xu, Raul Puri, Alec Radford, Jesse Michael Han, Jerry Tworek, Qiming Yuan, Nikolas Tezak, Jong Wook Kim, Chris Hallacy, Johannes Heidecke, Pranav Shyam, Boris Power, Tyna Eloundou Nekoul, Girish Sastry, Gretchen Krueger, David Schnurr, Felipe Petroski Such, Kenny Hsu, and othes. 2022. Text and code embeddings by contrastive pre-training. *Preprint*, arXiv:2201.10005.

Joel Niklaus, Veton Matoshi, Pooja Rani, Andrea Galassi, Matthias Stürmer, and Ilias Chalkidis. 2023. LEXTREME: A multi-lingual and multi-task benchmark for the legal domain. In *Findings of the Association for Computational Linguistics: EMNLP 2023*, pages 3016–3054, Singapore. Association for Computational Linguistics.

OpenAI, Josh Achiam, Steven Adler, Sandhini Agarwal, Lama Ahmad, Ilge Akkaya, Florencia Leoni Aleman, Diogo Almeida, Janko Altenschmidt, Sam Altman, Shyamal Anadkat, Red Avila, Igor Babuschkin, Suchir Balaji, Valerie Balcom, Paul Baltescu, Haiming Bao, Mohammad Bavarian, Jeff Belgum, et al. 2024. Gpt-4 technical report. *Preprint*, arXiv:2303.08774.

Aarohi Srivastava, Abhinav Rastogi, Abhishek Rao, Abu Awal Md Shoeb, Abubakar Abid, Adam Fisch, Adam R. Brown, Adam Santoro, Aditya Gupta, Adrià Garriga-Alonso, Agnieszka Kluska, Aitor Lewkowycz, Akshat Agarwal, Alethea Power, Alex Ray, Alex Warstadt, Alexander W. Kocurek, Ali Safaya, , et al. 2023. Beyond the imitation game: Quantifying and extrapolating the capabilities of language models. *Preprint*, arXiv:2206.04615.

Dimitrios Tsarapatsanis and Nikolaos Aletras. 2021. On the ethical limits of natural language processing on legal text. In *Findings of the Association for Computational Linguistics: ACL-IJCNLP 2021*, pages 3590–3599, Online. Association for Computational Linguistics.

Santosh T.y.s.s., Rashid Haddad, and Matthias Grabmair. 2024. ECtHR-PCR: A dataset for precedent understanding and prior case retrieval in the European court of human rights. In *Proceedings of the 2024 Joint International Conference on Computational Linguistics, Language Resources and Evaluation (LREC-COLING 2024)*, pages 5473–5483, Torino, Italia. ELRA and ICCL.

Alex Wang, Yada Pruksachatkun, Nikita Nangia, Amanpreet Singh, Julian Michael, Felix Hill, Omer Levy, and Samuel Bowman. 2019. Superglue: A stickier benchmark for general-purpose language understanding systems. In *Advances in Neural Information Processing Systems*, volume 32. Curran Associates, Inc.

Alex Wang, Amanpreet Singh, Julian Michael, Felix Hill, Omer Levy, and Samuel Bowman. 2018. GLUE: A multi-task benchmark and analysis platform for natural language understanding. In *Proceedings of the 2018 EMNLP Workshop BlackboxNLP: Analyzing and Interpreting Neural Networks for NLP*, pages 353–355, Brussels, Belgium. Association for Computational Linguistics.

Jason Wei, Xuezhi Wang, Dale Schuurmans, Maarten Bosma, Brian Ichter, Fei Xia, Ed Chi, Quoc Le, and Denny Zhou. 2023. Chain-of-thought prompting elicits reasoning in large language models. *Preprint*, arXiv:2201.11903.

Rowan Zellers, Yonatan Bisk, Roy Schwartz, and Yejin Choi. 2018. SWAG: A large-scale adversarial dataset for grounded commonsense inference. In *Proceedings of the 2018 Conference on Empirical Methods in Natural Language Processing*, pages 93–104, Brussels, Belgium. Association for Computational Linguistics.

Rowan Zellers, Ari Holtzman, Yonatan Bisk, Ali Farhadi, and Yejin Choi. 2019. HellaSwag: Can a machine really finish your sentence? In *Proceedings of the 57th Annual Meeting of the Association for Computational Linguistics*, pages 4791–4800, Florence, Italy. Association for Computational Linguistics.

A Prompt

The following is the complete version of the prompt presented in Table 4, that we designed for LAR-ECHR.

```
You will be provided with the
introductory Facts in a European Court
of Human Rights (ECHR) case, an excerpt
of arguments of that case and several
possible continuations of these
arguments. Your task is to determine
which continuation accurately extends
the original argument from the case. To
complete this task successfully:

1. Thoroughly analyze each provided
option to identify its connection to the
 initial argument presented.
2. Choose the option that not only
maintains the theme and context of the
initial argument but also follows
logically and seamlessly from it.
3. After selecting the most appropriate
continuation, provide a detailed
rationale for your choice.
4. Clearly state your answer by
specifying the letter corresponding to
the correct option.

Output format:
- Analysis: Provide an in-depth
evaluation of how each option relates to
 the initial argument.
- Explanation: Articulate why your
chosen option is the correct
continuation.
- Answer: State the letter of your
selected answer.
```

B Complete Example

The following is the complete version of the instance presented in Table 1. The facts of the case are presented first, then the examples as they were given to the LLMs for evaluation. After the input of the example, the complete CoT response of GPT-4o follows to help the reader understand the reasoning of the LLM. The explanations should not be considered an accurate representation of the inner thinking of the LLM, but still can help us understand its reasoning and can help non-experts understand the legal terms.

Facts:

```
The applicant, born in 1979, married B
in April 2001, giving birth to a
daughter, C, shortly after. B, who
suffered from psychiatric disorders due
to his traumatic experiences during the
Homeland War, subjected the applicant to
 verbal and physical abuse between 2003
and 2005. He was arrested in November
2005 and indicted for violent behavior
but released in December 2005. The
applicant moved to a women's shelter
with C in January 2006 for safety. B
continued his abusive behavior, leading
to further legal proceedings, including
charges of making death threats against
the applicant and a police officer, for
which he was found guilty and sentenced
to imprisonment in 2006. A restraining
order was issued, and subsequent appeals
 by B and the State Attorney's Office
were dismissed in 2007, though the
sentence was not enforced. Multiple
other criminal and minor offenses cases
were initiated against B over the years
for domestic violence and threatening
behavior. Meanwhile, the marriage of the
 applicant and B was dissolved in
November 2006. The applicant faced
difficulties in securing safe
accommodation due to B's continued
harassment, including hiring a private
detective to locate her. The legal
proceedings against B were ongoing, with
 several hearings adjourned due to B's
absence, and no psychiatric treatment
had been ensured despite recommendations
. Overall, the applicant struggled with
legal enforcement and protective
measures against B's continued threat
and harassment, affecting her and her
daughter's safety and stability.
```

Arguments:

```
The Government argued that in Croatia
the protection of victims of domestic
violence was ensured through the
mechanisms of criminal law, and in
particular the Protection against
Domestic Violence Act. In the present
case the relevant authorities had
```

reacted to the incidents of violence against the applicant by B, had instituted several sets of both criminal and minor offences proceedings and had applied such criminal sanctions and protective measures against B as they had considered proper and suitable in the circumstances. The Government submitted that the prison term imposed on B for not paying in full the fine imposed in the decision of the Z. Minor Offences Court of 2 October 2006 had not been enforced because Z. Prison had been full to capacity. Likewise, the measure of compulsory psycho-social treatment imposed on B in the same decision had not been implemented owing to the lack of licensed individuals or agencies able to execute such a protective measure (see paragraphs 31 and 34 above).
In addition, the Government had adopted two national strategies for protection against domestic violence (the first one covering the period between 2005 and 2007 and the second covering the period between 2008 and 2010) which included, inter alia, the education of all those involved in cases of domestic violence and cooperation with the non-governmental organisations working in that field as well as financial and other support for them. Thus, in 2008 only sixteen new shelters with a total of 329 places for the victims of violence had been established, of which six were State-funded.
The Court takes note of B's repeated violent behaviour towards the applicant. The facts in issue concern frequent episodes of violence in the period between November 2003 and June 2006, amounting to some two years and seven months. The violence was both verbal, including serious death threats, and physical, including hitting and kicking the applicant in the head, face and body , causing her injuries. In view of the fact that all the incidents of domestic violence in the present case concerned the same perpetrator and occurred in a continual manner, the Court will examine them as a continuous situation.

Continuation options:

(A) The Court takes further note of the psychiatric reports concerning B which indicated that he suffered from several mental disorders, including a severe form of PTSD, emphasised his tendency towards violence and his reduced ability to control his impulses, and reiterated the recommendation for continuing compulsory psychiatric treatment (see paragraphs 6, 12 and 13 above).

(B) Insofar as the applicant's complaint under Article 5 - 1 of the Convention is concerned, his confinement in the mental hospital can be divided into two periods: between 9 and 20 December 2002, and after 20 December 2002, when the hospital became his guardian.

(C) The Court notes, and this is not in dispute, that in August and October 2009 the police collected information about the applicant's character from his neighbours and relatives, pursuant to the instruction of the President of the Krasnogvardiyskyy Court (see paragraphs 13-15 and 20 above). That information was apparently used by the psychiatric hospital's specialists in the context of the forensic psychiatric examination of the applicant.

(D) The applicant firstly complained that (i) the decisions to order her to undergo a psychiatric examination and to arrest her and (ii) her detention for a total period of eighty-three days were in breach of Article 8 of the Convention . However, the Court considers that these complaints do not raise any separate issue which is not covered by the finding of a violation of Article 5 - 1 of the Convention.

GPT-4o Response:

Analysis:
To find the correct continuation of the initial argument, we need to focus

on both the factual context and legal analysis provided.
- Option (A) aligns closely with the initial arguments by addressing the psychiatric reports about B, reinforcing the situation's consistency with his diagnosed mental disorders. It maintains the theme of continuous violence and the need for psychiatric treatment, linking back to the facts concerning B's mental health.
- Option (B) discusses periods of confinement in a mental hospital, but this appears unrelated to the specific facts of the case involving B's violent behavior toward the applicant and does not further the argument regarding domestic violence or its handling by Croatian authorities.
- Option (C) mentions the police collecting information about the applicant's character and a forensic psychiatric examination, which appears out of context, as there is no mention of such actions linked to either the applicant or B in the provided facts.
- Option (D) pertains to complaints about forced psychiatric evaluations and unrelated detention, diverging from the continuity of violence by B and responses by Croatian authorities, and thus, it does not logically follow the given argument.

Explanation:
Option (A) is the most logical continuation as it directly ties into and extends the argument concerning the failure of the Croatian authorities to implement appropriate protective measures and treatment for B despite his documented psychiatric issues and violent tendencies. This reflects the Court's approach of understanding the situation as a "continuous situation" of abuse, emphasizing the importance of ongoing psychiatric intervention, which was previously recommended and not enacted.

Answer: A ✔

Gaps or Hallucinations? Scrutinizing Machine-Generated Legal Analysis for Fine-grained Text Evaluations

Abe Bohan Hou ♣ **William Jurayj** ♣ **Nils Holzenberger** ♠
Andrew Blair-Stanek ♣ ◇ **Benjamin Van Durme** ♣
♣ Johns Hopkins University ◇ University of Maryland, Carey School of Law
♠Télécom Paris, Institut Polytechnique de Paris
bhou4@jhu.edu

Abstract

Large Language Models (LLMs) show promise as a writing aid for professionals performing legal analyses. However, LLMs can often hallucinate in this setting, in ways difficult to recognize by non-professionals and existing text evaluation metrics. In this work, we pose the question: **when can machine-generated legal analysis be evaluated as acceptable?** We introduce the neutral notion of *gaps* – as opposed to hallucinations in a strict erroneous sense – to refer to the difference between human-written and machine-generated legal analysis. Gaps do not always equate to invalid generation. Working with legal experts, we consider the CLERC generation task proposed in Hou et al. (2024b), leading to a taxonomy, a fine-grained detector for predicting gap categories, and an annotated dataset for automatic evaluation. Our best detector achieves 67% F_1 score and 80% precision on the test set. Employing this detector as an automated metric on legal analysis generated by SOTA LLMs, we find around 80% contain hallucinations of different kinds.[1]

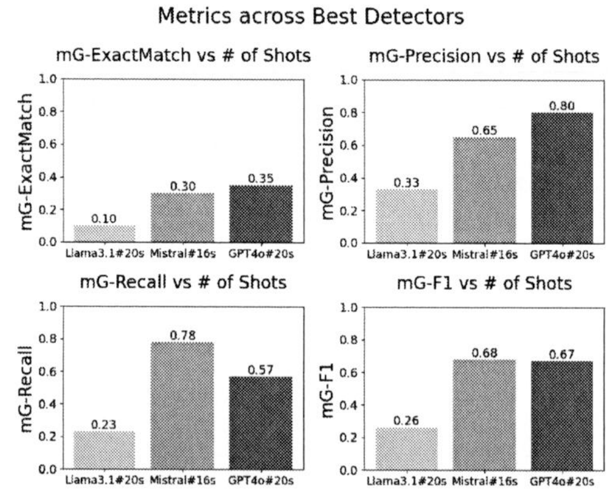

Figure 1: Detection results among the best detectors with different base models. $M\#ds$ means the best detector of base model M has d in-context demonstrations. **GPT-4o#20s achieves the highest $mGEM$ and mGP, while Mistral-Nemo-Instruct-2407#16s achieves the highest mGR and mGF_1.**

1 Introduction

Legal professionals write legal analysis to help precisely communicate a legal issue or persuade judges (Legal Information Institute, 2023). Despite recent work demonstrating that LLMs have the potential to generate realistic legal analyses to aid lawyers, they severely hallucinate (Hou et al., 2024b; Magesh et al., 2024). In order to drive improvements, it is important to develop insights on the nature, categories, and sources of these hallucinations.

Evaluating legal analysis generation is challenging because the generation may: (1) have **multiple ground truths**, as legal practitioners can write an acceptable piece of analysis in many ways, (2) have **implicit and complex criteria to be judged based on legal expertise**, which makes obtaining human annotation data costly, (3) process **long-context**, which creates difficulties for evaluating faithfulness to previous contexts, and (4) involve **retrieving cited sources** and might propagate retrieval inaccuracies to downstream generation. A similar task to this is the automatic generation of research ideas, which is also challenging and expensive to evaluate (Si et al., 2024; Lu et al., 2024). Evaluation of legal analysis is further complicated due to (5) **disagreement on the analysis and interpretation of law**, even between the most experienced legal professionals like Supreme Court judges. A law is interpreted both *objectively* according to varying theories of legal interpretations, and also *subjectively* according to the stance of the interpreter (Greenberg, 2021). This is exemplified by the range of concurring and dissenting opinions written in the U.S. Supreme Court's 2022 *Dobbs v. Jackson*

[1]We release the code and data at https://github.com/bohanhou14/GapHalu.

Proceedings of the Natural Legal Language Processing Workshop 2024, pages 280–302
November 16, 2024 ©2024 Association for Computational Linguistics

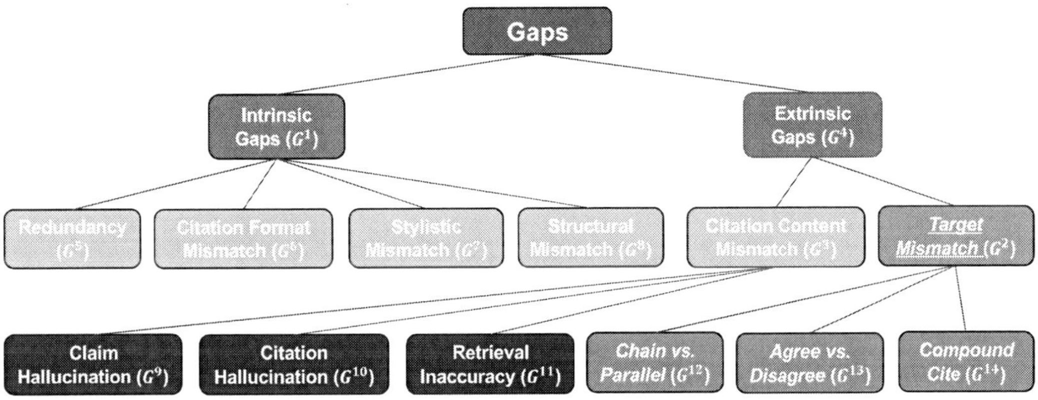

Figure 2: Our proposed taxonomy of gaps. Each category is discussed in depth in Section 3. We highlight *Target mismatch* (G^2) and its *child nodes* (G^{12}, G^{13}, G^{14}) as we show they do not indicate hallucinations as opposed to other gap categories (with examples in Appendix B). Meanwhile, **citation content mismatch** and **intrinsic gaps** are generally considered hallucination and both indicate invalidity of generation.

decision overturning *Roe v. Wade* (Kaveny, 2023).

Hou et al. (2024b) propose a legal analysis task, evaluating the capabilities of models in generating an analytical paragraph, compared with the human-written paragraph (*target*) from an original case using reference-based metrics such as ROUGE and BARTScore (Lin, 2004; Yuan et al., 2021). Following common practice in evaluating generation systems, this evaluation scheme assumes the target is the ground truth and scores paragraphs less similar to the target as having lower validity and quality. In contrast, here we argue that **dissimilarities between machine-generated and human-written legal analyses are not necessarily errors or hallucinations**. We denote such dissimilarities with a neutral term, *gaps*, inspired by the naming of Pillutla et al. (2021), to show that dissimilarities are not determinant for evaluating generated analyses.

We also note that the general notion of gaps is not specific to legal analysis generation, but applicable to any generation setting when multiple ground truths are possible. We focus on gaps in legal analysis generation as it is a domain especially suitable for this exploration. Unlike multiple translations or abstract summarizations which may have differences in syntax and word choice or the facts deemed essential to carry into a summary, valid legal analyses can illustrate significantly higher variability. Moreover, the creation of multiple references for legal analysis is cost prohibitive, as it requires legal experts to create an alternative writing that leads to the same result.

In this work, our contributions include:

1. A detailed taxonomy of gaps to enable more fine-grained evaluation of legal analysis.

2. A manually annotated detection dataset, obtained by working with legal experts.

3. LLM-based detectors with best performance of 67% F_1 and 80% precision on the test set.

4. Automated evaluation metrics for legal analysis, GAPSCORE and GAPHALU, which reveal that around 80% of CLERC generations using GPT-4o (Josh Achiam et al., 2024) and Llama-3-8B-Instruct (Team, 2024) contain hallucinations.

The rest of the work is laid out as follows: we provide background on legal analysis and hallucination in Section 2, then explain our proposed gap taxonomy in Section 3. We develop detectors for classifying gaps according to the taxonomy in Section 4 and apply these to evaluate legal analysis generations in Section 5. Lastly, we provide suggestions for mitigating legal hallucinations in Section 6 and discuss related work in Section 7.

2 Background

2.1 Legal Analysis Generation

We create our taxonomy based on the legal analysis generation task proposed in CLERC (Hou et al., 2024b), which is formulated as a retrieval-augmented next-paragraph prediction problem. Given a legal case document, which cites a set of other legal cases, R, to support its writing, an autoregressive language model (LM) is asked to generate the next paragraph based on its prefix and the cited external documents, formally as: $\hat{p}_t \sim P_{LM}(\cdot|p_1, \ldots, p_{t-1}, R)$, where $\hat{p}_t \sim P_{LM}(\cdot|p_1, \ldots, p_{t-1})$ is a paragraph-level notation we introduce to refer to the sampling of the next paragraph given previous paragraphs. Note that under this formulation, CLERC also assumes R is given, whereas in practice this is achieved via an imperfect legal document retrieval process that makes this task more challenging (Hou et al., 2024b; Mahari et al., 2023). The machine generation is evaluated by comparing $\hat{p}_t$ to p_t, the human-written target paragraph. Since each case document has thousands of words, CLERC instead selects the most salient paragraph within each cited document as the input, ensuring it can fit the context window of a LLM. CLERC also guarantees the target paragraphs to contain analysis via a heuristic selection process, for which we refer readers to Hou et al. (2024b) for details.

2.2 Hallucination

Numerous recent works have characterized hallucination (Ji et al., 2023; Mishra et al., 2024; Chen et al., 2024; Zhang et al., 2023), and our definition of hallucination also aligns with prior works. We define hallucination as a span of LM-generated natural language which is incoherent, unfaithful to the contexts, or contain inaccurate or irrelevant information. As discussed in Zhang et al. (2023), hallucinations can arise from three sources: conflicts with prompts to the language model, previous contexts, or facts. We adapt the notions of intrinsic and extrinsic hallucinations from Ji et al. (2023), classifying whether a hallucination is intrinsic or extrinsic based on the **sources of conflicts:** conflicts with the prompts and previous contexts cause **intrinsic hallucinations**, whereas conflicts with external sources and facts induce **extrinsic hallucinations**.

2.3 Hallucination in Legal Generation

While there are various works dedicated to the understanding and mitigation of hallucinations in general (Dhuliawala et al., 2023; Li et al., 2023; McKenna et al., 2023), few have studied hallucinations in the legal domain (Magesh et al., 2024; Dahl et al., 2024). Magesh et al. (2024) characterizes retrieval-augmented legal hallucinations based on two key criteria: **correctness**, which is whether the facts in the generation are correct and relevant to the prompt, and **groundedness**, which is whether the generation makes valid references to relevant legal documents. They also discuss a typology of retrieval-augmented generation errors consisting of four categories and analyze the contributing causes of the errors. In this work, we further breakdown the key criteria for determining hallucination, proposing a more fine-grained taxonomy consisting of 14 categories and introducing the notion of false positive hallucination (i.e. target mismatch). We also analyze the application of the taxonomy as automated evaluation metrics (GAPSCORE and GAPHALU) for legal analysis generation.

3 A Taxonomy of Gaps

As popular reference-based metrics such as ROUGE and BARTScore (Lin, 2004; Yuan et al., 2021) and factuality metrics like FActScore (Min et al., 2023) only partially indicate validity of legal analysis generation (Hou et al., 2024a,b), an automated metric for evaluating legal analysis generation is necessary. We first study the nature and typology of hallucinations, motivating a detailed taxonomy and error analysis, and then apply it to enable text evaluations (see Section 5).

We systematically review generation data from CLERC and propose a detailed taxonomy of gaps in Figure 2. We classify the gaps into two types, in line with Ji et al. (2023): *intrinsic*, which refer to gaps that derive from the internal inaccuracies of LLMs in following prompts and previous contexts; and *extrinsic*, which refer to gaps due to mismatches with cited sources and lacks of grounding on logical rules and existing facts. We attach examples in Figure 3 and Appendix A, and for each fine-grained gap category in Appendix B.

3.1 Intrinsic Gaps

We discover and discuss four types of intrinsic gaps. **Redundancy** is when the generation appears to make repetitive statements (such as exact n-gram matches) and does not add further information to the analysis. **Citation format mismatch** is when the generation appears not to match the standard styles of the uniform legal citation guide for US law, the Bluebook (Columbia Law Review, 2020), since CLERC is a US-specific legal dataset. Applying the taxonomy in international contexts, this gap can be adapted to the citation guides in other legal systems. **Stylistic mismatch** is when the generation uses an informal register or style of language that does not match with legalese. **Structural mis-**

Generation:
...In Butner v. United States, 440 U.S. 48, 55, the Supreme Court emphasized that property rights in the assets of a bankrupt's estate are determined by state law unless a federal interest dictates otherwise. In this case, we must determine the debtor's obligations under Puerto Rican law and assess the applicability of interest on the debt owed to Nelson Torres Ruiz.
Consistent with the principles outlined in 114 B.R. 326, the determination of whether the debtor has a legal or equitable interest in the obligation to return the $3,000 option money necessitates an analysis grounded in applicable nonbankruptcy state law. Article 1061 of the P.R. Civil Code, 31 Laws of P.R.Ann., Section 3025, establishes that where a debtor fails to perform an obligation, the creditor is entitled to interest as indemnification for damages and losses incurred.
Debtor's claim of impossibility of performance is addressed under Article 1138 of the Civil Code of Puerto Rico, but as established earlier, such a defense is unwarranted when the impossibility is not due to legal or physical barriers (31 Laws of P.R.Ann., Section 3193). Given the absence of such barriers, the return of the $3,000 is mandated.
Furthermore, in alignment with 117 B.R. 15, the initiation of bankruptcy proceedings does not alter the creditor's right to claim interest at the legal rate. Should the contract fail to specify an interest rate, Article 1061 defaults to a legal interest rate of 6% per annum.
Thus, Mr. Bonilla is obliged to reimburse the full amount of $3,000 plus the applicable legal interest rate of 6% from the expiration of the option contract until the filing of the bankruptcy petition.

citations needed to make: ['440 U.S. 48', '114 B.R. 326', '117 B.R. 15']

Target:
See generally, 3 Collier On Bankruptcy, (15th ed.) paragraph 502.02 (1990). See also, Butner v. U.S., 440 U.S. 48, 99 S.Ct. 914, 59 L.Ed.2d 136 (1979); In re MacDonald, 114 B.R. 326 (D.Mass. 1990); In re Milford Common J.V. Trust, 117 B.R. 15 (Bkrtcy.Mass., 1990).

Label: [2]

Explanation: The generated text provides detailed context and elaboration for each citation, whereas the target text chain cites them without additional detail. This indicates a target mismatch.

Figure 3: An example generated legal analysis from CLERC (Hou et al., 2024b), labeled with 2 (target mismatch) and given an explanation. See the full version of this example and prompts to LLM-based detectors in Figure 9, 20.

match is when the generation appears to generate the document from scratch or concludes the document prematurely, such as containing words like ORDER that typically appears at the beginning of case document, rather than predicting the next paragraph.

3.2 Extrinsic Gaps

We subdivide extrinsic gaps into two types. **Target mismatch** refers to when the generation is obviously dissimilar from the target paragraph, but it can still be considered as another form of acceptable analysis. **Citation content mismatch** refers to when the generation does not faithfully and factually reflect the content of the cited cases or hallucinate citations. We will discuss each subcategory in detail in this section.

3.2.1 Target Mismatch

We define three kinds of target mismatches, which are all caused by how the generation organizes the citations and their associated claims differently from the target. **Chain-versus-parallel** is when the target cites cases in a series (chain), all supporting the same claim, yet the generation elaborates every cited case and provides each with a claim. We also count the opposite scenario (i.e. the target does parallel and generation does chain) into this category. This gap is not necessarily unacceptable, as long as it does not make additional false claims, since it conveys the same overall meaning either in a concise or elaborate way. Similarly, **agree-versus-disagree** arises from mismatches on ways to characterize the relationship between multiple cited cases. The target might cite case A reversing the ruling in case B, whereas the generation might discuss case A and B respectively without highlighting the reversal relationship. **Compound cite** happens when the target combines the respective law from case A and B and makes a compound statement in a deductive manner, while the generation discusses them separately.

3.2.2 Citation Content Mismatch

We also discuss three kinds of citation content mismatches. **Claim hallucination** is when the claim supported by the citation is not truthful, not related to the context, or incoherent from cited paragraphs or the previous context. This was also discussed in Hou et al. (2024a) as the major hallucination scenario. Furthermore, we also have hallucinations caused by **retrieval inaccuracy**. Since the generated analysis needs to find external case documents as support, the retrieval process for documents can be inaccurate. To fit in the input context, the most salient chunk rather than the full text can be chosen, whose selection process might introduce additional inaccuracies. Lastly, **citation hallucination** refers to when the generated analysis contains non-existent citations, includes ones that were not supposed to appear, or omits citations that are supposed to be cited.

3.3 When Are Legal Analyses Unacceptable?

The presence of intrinsic gaps is generally considered intrinsic hallucinations, as they signal the failure of language models in understanding the task, following prompts and previous contexts, making coherent generations, and adapting linguistic styles appropriate to legal analyses. Among extrinsic gaps, citation content mismatch also qualifies as hallucination, for they all either introduce inaccurate information or contradict with the cited sources, in line with prior work on defining hallucinations (Mishra et al., 2024; Ji et al., 2023). On the other hand, we should not consider target mismatches as necessarily wrong since they mainly organize the information in a different way from the target paragraph (see examples in Figure 15, 16, 17). As legal analysis does not have a single definitive ground truth, the presence of target mismatch alone cannot indicate generation validity.

We observe that generated analysis tends to include more than one category of gaps. Since intrinsic gaps and citation content mismatch are considered hallucinations in a stricter sense, we categorize generations that include any of them as unacceptable. On the contrary, if a generation does not include any of the gaps or only includes target mismatch, we count it as acceptable.

4 Gap Detection

In this section, we build a detector to classify gap categories according to our proposed taxonomy.

4.1 Problem Formulation

Suppose we have m total gap categories, given a piece of generated legal analysis p_t which has gap categories $g_t = (G_t^1, \ldots, G_t^m)^\intercal$, we predict the gap categories from a detector $\hat{g}_t \sim f(\cdot|p_t)$, where $\hat{g}_t = (\hat{G}_t^1, \ldots, \hat{G}_t^m)^\intercal$. $f : D \to \mathbb{R}^m$ is a detector function returning a m-dimensional vector, where

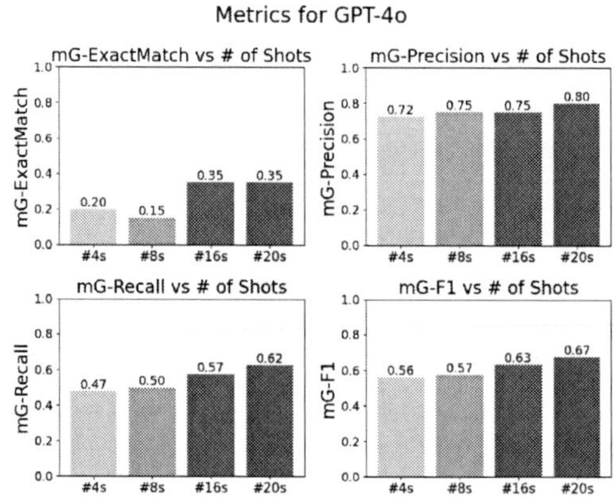

Figure 4: Detection results of the GPT-4o detector with different number of in-context demonstrations. **The full 20-shot detector yields the best overall detection accuracy**, while 16-shot has a marginal drop in accuracy.

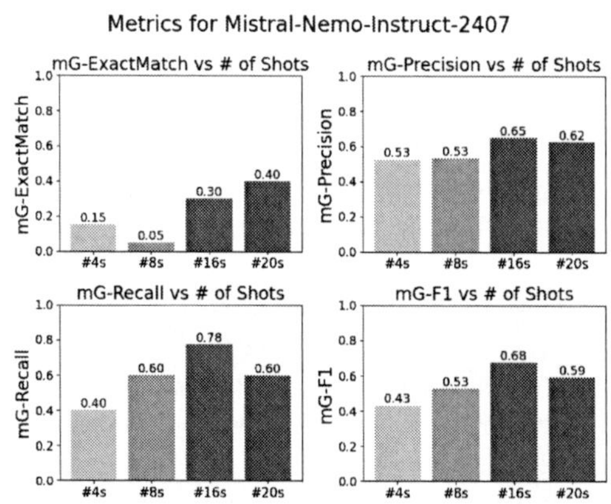

Figure 5: Detection results of the Mistral-Nemo detector with different number of in-context demonstrations. **The model achieves the maximal performance at 16 demonstrations and overfits at 20 demonstrations.**

Gap Name	Definition	Train Dist. (%)	Test Dist. (%)
Intrinsic gaps (1)	contradict with the instructions or context	13.79	18.18
Target mismatch (2)	organize info in a different way from the target	37.93	36.36
Citation content mismatch (3)	contradict with the cited sources	31.03	45.45
No gaps (0)	more or less equivalent with the target paragraph	17.24	0.00
Dataset Balance		**0.94**	**0.75**

Table 1: Detection dataset statistics. **Train/Test Dist.** refers to the distribution of labels in the train/test set. **Dataset Balance** is measured on a scale of [0-1], by the ratio of entropy of dataset labels over the entropy of perfectly balanced labels. A dataset is more balanced if the ratio is closer to 1, and **our dataset has a high balance.**

each entry corresponds to a gap category, and the k-th gap for t-th generation exists if $G_t^k = 1$ and 0 otherwise. We evaluate the detector on an arbitrary i-th piece of legal analysis with:

$$\text{GAP-EXACTMATCH}(GEM) = \mathbb{I}[\hat{g}_i = g_i]$$

$$\text{GAP-PRECISION}(GP) = \frac{\hat{g}_i \cdot g_i}{\|\hat{g}_i\|^2}$$

$$\text{GAP-RECALL}(GR) = \frac{\hat{g}_i \cdot g_i}{\|g_i\|^2}$$

$$\text{GAP-F1}(GF_1) = \frac{2GP \cdot GR}{GP + GR}$$

where $\mathbb{I}$ is the indicator function, g_i records gap categories of the i-th piece of legal analysis, and $\|\cdot\|$ is the norm of a vector. We calculate the mean of each metric over N examples (e. g. $mGEM = \frac{1}{N}\sum_{i=1}^{N} GEM_i$) to reflect the overall performance of the detector.

4.2 Experimental Setup

We obtain and prepare our dataset from CLERC test set generations[2]. Due to the extraordinary expenses in hiring enough legal professionals for classifying 10 most granular gap categories (see Figure 2) and having enough data for each category, we choose to work at the second level of granularity, labeling each example with one or more from {intrinsic gaps (G^1), target mismatch (G^2), citation content mismatch (G^3), no gaps (G^0)}. Although we do not label the most specific 10 categories (G^5 - G^{14}), we include and explain them in the instructions to annotators, which help clarify second-level gaps that are based on these bottom-level categories.

Working with legal experts[3], we manually label 40 example generations respectively by GPT-4o (Josh Achiam et al., 2024) and Llama-3-Instruct-8B (Team, 2024) (instructions in Appendix C). We select 20 examples with an equal ratio of both model generations as the train set of the detector and the remaining 20 examples as the test set. Our detection dataset statistics is in Table 1.

Our detector is based on prompting a long-context LLM with in-context demonstrations of examples labeled by humans (Brown et al., 2020; Lewis et al., 2020), then asking it to predict the labels of a new example (prompts in Appendix D). For the base model of our detector, we use GPT-4o (Josh Achiam et al., 2024), Llama-3.1-8B-instruct, and Mistral-Nemo-Instruct-2407 (Jiang et al., 2023). Our models are deployed with `vLLM` (Kwon et al., 2023) with 1 A100 for Llama-3.1-8B-instruct and 4 A100s for Mistral-Nemo-Instruct-2407 to support the 128K tokens context window.

We first label 20 examples along with brief explanations for the reasoning process behind our labeling. The prompt for our detector includes a summary of the instructions for human annotators and at most 20 labeled examples as in-context demonstrations. We also conduct an ablation study varying the number of demonstrations and present the results in Figure 4. To assess the detector accuracy, we prompt it to predict 20 unlabeled examples and then manually label them, evaluating the mean of metrics discussed in Section 4.1 respectively, namely $mGEM$, mGP, mGR, and mGF_1.

4.3 Detection Results

Figure 1 compares the performances of three best detectors for each base model and discover that GPT-4o achieves the maximum $mGEM$ and mGP with 20 demonstrations, while Mistral-Nemo-Instruct-2407 achieves the maximum mGR and also mGF_1 with 16 demonstrations, by a small margin over GPT-4o, with the Llama-3.1-8B-instruct detector with 20 demonstrations being the worst among the three. We select the best detector for each base model according to our ablation studies on the number of in-context demonstrations. We find that the optimal number of in-context demon-

[2] `https://huggingface.co/datasets/jhu-clsp/CLERC`

[3] A tenured law professor who also co-authors this paper.

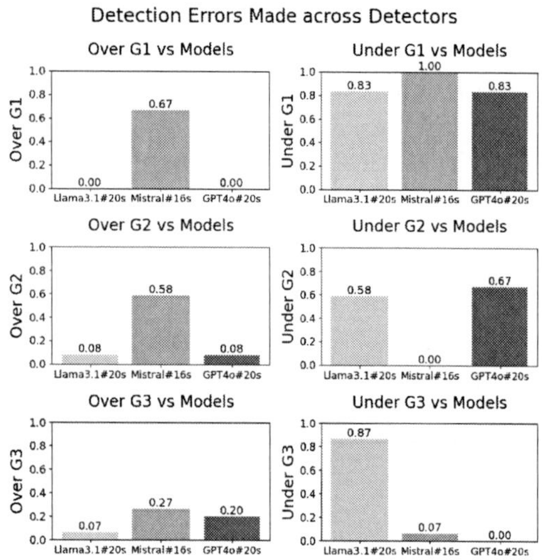

Figure 6: Error analysis of different detectors. **G1** refers to *intrinsic gaps*, **G2** refers to *target mismatch*, and **G3** refers to *citation content mismatch*. **Mistral-Nemo tends to over-predict the presence of gaps, whereas GPT-4o and Llama-3.1 tend to under-predict.**

strations is different for each model, with results presented in Figure 4, 5, 10.

To further understand the behavior and biases of detectors, we analyze the percentages of each label being over-predicted and under-predicted and present the results in Figure 6. The Mistral-Nemo detector tends to over-predict across all gap categories, which explains why it has a high recall but relatively low precision compared to the GPT-4o detector. On the other hand, the GPT-4o detector under-predicts G^1 and G^2 but overall maintains the highest precision and exact match. Llama-3.1-Instruct has the worst performance. The three detectors all tend to under-predict G^1, which can be caused due to a relative lack of G^1 training data, or that the detection of G^1 is challenging per se.

In sum, since G^2 generally does not indicate invalidity, **the GPT-4o detector is most useful to evaluate legal analysis generations as it is most accurate at identifying G^1 and G^3.**

5 Re-Evaluate Legal Analysis Generation

5.1 GapScore and GapHalu

In this section, we discuss an application of the detector in evaluating legal analysis generations. With a fine-grained detector, we can distinguish between generations with intrinsic gaps, target mismatches, and citation content mismatch, enabling the fine-grained evaluation of legal analysis genration. We propose the following metrics:

$$\text{GapScore} = \frac{1}{N}\sum_{i=1}^{N} m_1(G_i^1 + G_i^2 + G_i^3)$$

$$\text{GapHalu} = \frac{1}{N}\sum_{i=1}^{N} m_1(G_i^1 + G_i^3)$$

where G_i^k is a binary variable that returns 1 when the i-th example contains G^k and 0 otherwise. $m_1(\cdot)$ refers to $\min(\cdot, 1)$. GapScore measures the ratio of N examples having gaps, and GapHalu measures the ratio of hallucinations.

Metric (× 100)	GPT-4o	Llama-3-8B-Instruct
R1 ↑	**26.73**	24.88
R2 ↑	**10.13**	8.86
RL ↑	**24.83**	23.20
BF ↑	**-3.13**	-3.33
GapScore ↓	96.31	**95.46**
GapHalu ↓	**79.51**	82.05
G^1 ↓	**24.80**	25.20
G^2 ↓	**82.99**	84.96
G^3 ↓	61.48	**60.94**

Table 2: Evaluation of GPT-4o and Llama-3 CLERC generations with the Mistral-Nemo detector and F-Scores of ROUGE and BARTScore (BF). GPT-4o has higher GapScore while lower GapHalu than Llama-3, meaning that it has less hallucination. Over the fine-grained categories, GPT-4o has lower proportion of intrinsic gaps and target mismatches but higher percentage of citation content mismatch than Llama-3. **Both models generate legal analysis with severe hallucinations, as ∼ 80% (indicated by GapHalu) contain hallucinations.**

5.2 Experimental Setup

We sample 500 GPT-4o and Llama-3-8B-Instruct generations from CLERC respectively, and evaluate with the detector developed in Section 4. While GPT-4o detector has the highest accuracy at identifying hallucinations, we run the Mistral-Nemo detector due to significant expenses incurred in accessing the GPT-4o API. We also run ROUGE and BARTScore evaluations over the texts for a comparison with GapScore and GapHalu.

5.3 Re-Evaluation of Legal Analysis

Table 2 presents results of evaluating legal analysis generations with automated metrics. Our experimental results of ROUGE and BARTScore highly align with the results in Hou et al. (2024b).

We discover that GPT-4o generations have less hallucination compared to Llama-3-8B-Instruct, as indicated by a lower GAPHALU score. However, it has a slightly higher proportion of citation content mismatch (G^3). As our proposed taxonomy classifies citation hallucination as a type of citation content mismatch, this result is partially explained by the findings in Hou et al. (2024b) that GPT-4o tends to hallucinate more false positive citations than other models.

In addition, we find that Llama-3-8B-Instruct generations tend to have more target mismatch, which might explain why they score lower on ROUGE and BARTScore. Since target mismatch often features obvious dissimilarities (see examples in Figure 15, 16), having a higher proportion of target mismatch potentially causes a great lack of textual overlap and lowers reference-based metrics like ROUGE and BARTScore more significantly.

Overall, we discover that **around 80% of the generated legal analysis contain hallucinations like intrinsic gaps and citation content mismatch, which indicates the limitation of SOTA LLMs at generating legal analyses.** We estimate the actual percentage of legal hallucinations to be even higher, as we discuss in Section 4.3 that the Mistral-Nemo detector tends to under-predict the presence of intrinsic gaps.

6 Mitigation Suggestions

In this section, we discuss general strategies to mitigate legal hallucinations as well as specific suggestions related to each gap category.

6.1 General Strategies

Intrinsic gaps often arise from failures to follow prompts and previous contexts, lack of adaptation to the linguistic styles and citation formats of the legal domain. Target mismatches also reflect that LLMs struggle with finding patterns consistent with human preferences to organize information in legal writing. Therefore, we suggest continued pre-training of SOTA LLMs on the legal domain with similar approaches in Chalkidis et al. (2020); Niklaus et al. (2024); Gururangan et al. (2020) to address the model domain shift and improve its adaptation to legalese.

Furthermore, **decomposition of the reasoning structure in legal analysis** may critically improve generation quality and mitigate hallucinations, and even improve retrieval of cited sources. A legal case is usually structured with an introduction and summary of facts, an identification of the core dispute, and then breaks down the core dispute into subclaims to be analyzed with, until an eventual logical conclusion is formed. The reasoning is hierarchical, which enables extraction of an explicit structure. Such reasoning structure can be utilized to enhance downstream applications via combining with prompting or with a symbolic solver (Weir et al., 2024). LLMs would be able to parse missing points from the reasoning structure and generate the necessary information, and avoid claims already addressed. A complex legal reasoning task can be effectively decomposed into simpler sub-problems, enabling the generation of high-quality legal analysis through a divide-and-conquer strategy.

6.2 Intrinsic Gaps

Aside from the general strategies, intrinsic gaps also indicate that LLMs may struggle with using the correct citation formats in legal writing. We suggest incorporating domain-specific knowledge about legal citations through fine-tuning, RAG, or tool use (Team, 2024; Yang et al., 2023).

6.3 Extrinsic Gaps

Extrinsic hallucinations in retrieval-augmented legal analysis generation can be attributed to conflicts with the cited sources or the cited sources retrieved being irrelevant. Improving retrieval architecture, especially with long-context retrieval strategy with awareness of the latent logical structure, can be one critical direction to improve generation and mitigate hallucinations (Sarthi et al., 2024).

7 Related Work

7.1 Citation Ontology

Even before internet-scale citation graphs were tractable, bibliometric research focused on the social and cognitive implications of different citation schemata (Cronin, 1981). Peroni and Shotton (2012)'s popular framework categorizes citations based on the factual and rhetorical roles that the cited document plays in the citing paper. More recent work has used LLMs to generate or classify citations in scientific literature (Cohan et al., 2019; Xing et al., 2020; Luu et al., 2021).

7.2 Argument Analysis

Generating and analyzing persuasive arguments is another useful formulation for case-based legal writing. Some efforts have explored how various argument rating approaches can train models to persuade more effectively (Mouchel et al., 2024; Durmus et al., 2024). Saha et al. (2021) use human annotations to train a system that converts textual arguments into logical graphs. By searching over these graphs, LMs can generate deductive arguments to prove or disprove claims based on evidence from cited documents (Weir and Van Durme, 2022; Sanders et al., 2024).

7.3 Legal Reasoning

Legal reasoning is challenging even for the most powerful LMs (Blair-Stanek et al., 2023). Finetuning smaller LMs can result in higher performance over generic models (Niklaus et al., 2024; Chalkidis et al., 2020). An alternative appraoch is to integrate symbolic solvers during reasoning (Padhye, 2024; Holzenberger and Van Durme, 2023).

8 Conclusion and Future Work

To facilitate a fine-grained evaluation of generated legal analysis, we propose a taxonomy of gaps and develop detectors to analyze the sources of legal hallucinations, also experimenting with GAPSCORE and GAPHALU to assess the validity of generated legal analysis. For future work, we will extend our framework of analyzing gaps on the general text domain for fine-grained text evaluations.

Limitations

Our work builds up the foundation for legal hallucination evaluation metrics, but the detection of gaps can be imperfect, since the LLMs used as the base models of the detectors generally struggle on legal tasks and experience domain shifts (Blair-Stanek et al., 2023, 2024; Chalkidis et al., 2020). Moreover, the parsing of legal citations is still an open problem to the legal NLP community, and this imperfect process introduces minor inaccuracies that propagate to affect the robustness of our detectors.

Ethical Considerations

Our work concerns with U.S. historical law data, with cases dated earliest from the year of 1658 (CAP, 2024). The data might express outdated views and ideologies, such as racism and sexism, which are disturbing and considered unethical to the current academic community. It raises interesting questions and needs for further discussions on how we can strike the balance between generating safe and harmless speech, versus having to process controversial laws and historical legal facts to produce accurate analyses.

Acknowledgement

This work was supported in part by the U.S. National Science Foundation under grant 2204926. Opinions, findings, and conclusions or recommendations expressed in this article come from the authors and do not reflect the views of the National Science Foundation. We also thank JHU CLSP members Guanghui Qin and Orion Weller for their advice on data analysis and paper writing, Brian Lu for his feedback on the figure design, as well as Tianjian Li and Jingyu Zhang for suggestions on the paper organization.

References

Andrew Blair-Stanek, Nils Holzenberger, and Benjamin Van Durme. 2023. Can gpt-3 perform statutory reasoning? In *Proceedings of the Nineteenth International Conference on Artificial Intelligence and Law*, ICAIL '23, page 22–31, New York, NY, USA. Association for Computing Machinery.

Andrew Blair-Stanek, Nils Holzenberger, and Benjamin Van Durme. 2024. Blt: Can large language models handle basic legal text? *Preprint*, arXiv:2311.09693.

Tom B. Brown, Benjamin Mann, Nick Ryder, Melanie Subbiah, Jared Kaplan, Prafulla Dhariwal, Arvind Neelakantan, Pranav Shyam, Girish Sastry, Amanda Askell, Sandhini Agarwal, Ariel Herbert-Voss, Gretchen Krueger, Tom Henighan, Rewon Child, Aditya Ramesh, Daniel M. Ziegler, Jeffrey Wu, Clemens Winter, Christopher Hesse, Mark Chen, Eric Sigler, Mateusz Litwin, Scott Gray, Benjamin Chess, Jack Clark, Christopher Berner, Sam McCandlish, Alec Radford, Ilya Sutskever, and Dario Amodei. 2020. Language models are few-shot learners.

CAP. 2024. Caselaw access project.

Ilias Chalkidis, Manos Fergadiotis, Prodromos Malakasiotis, Nikolaos Aletras, and Ion Androutsopoulos. 2020. LEGAL-BERT: the muppets straight out of law school. *CoRR*, abs/2010.02559.

Xiang Chen, Chenxi Wang, Yida Xue, Ningyu Zhang, Xiaoyan Yang, Qian Li, Yue Shen, Lei Liang, Jinjie Gu, and Huajun Chen. 2024. Unified hallucination detection for multimodal large language models. *ArXiv*, abs/2402.03190.

Arman Cohan, Waleed Ammar, Madeleine van Zuylen, and Field Cady. 2019. Structural scaffolds for citation intent classification in scientific publications. In *Proceedings of the 2019 Conference of the North American Chapter of the Association for Computational Linguistics: Human Language Technologies,*

Volume 1 (Long and Short Papers), pages 3586–3596, Minneapolis, Minnesota. Association for Computational Linguistics.

Columbia Law Review. 2020. *The Bluebook: A Uniform System of Citation*. The Harvard LawReview Association Gannett House, 1511 Massachusetts Avenue Cambridge, Massachusetts 02138 U.S.A.

Blaise Cronin. 1981. The Need for a Theory of Citing. *Journal of Documentation*, 37(1):16–24. Publisher: MCB UP Ltd.

Matthew Dahl, Varun Magesh, Mirac Suzgun, and Daniel E. Ho. 2024. Large legal fictions: Profiling legal hallucinations in large language models. *ArXiv*, abs/2401.01301.

Shehzaad Dhuliawala, Mojtaba Komeili, Jing Xu, Roberta Raileanu, Xian Li, Asli Celikyilmaz, and Jason Weston. 2023. Chain-of-verification reduces hallucination in large language models. *ArXiv*, abs/2309.11495.

Esin Durmus, Liane Lovitt, Alex Tamkin, Stuart Ritchie, Jack Clark, and Deep Ganguli. 2024. Measuring the persuasiveness of language models.

Mark Greenberg. 2021. Legal Interpretation. In Edward N. Zalta, editor, *The Stanford Encyclopedia of Philosophy*, Fall 2021 edition. Metaphysics Research Lab, Stanford University.

Suchin Gururangan, Ana Marasović, Swabha Swayamdipta, Kyle Lo, Iz Beltagy, Doug Downey, and Noah A. Smith. 2020. Don't stop pretraining: Adapt language models to domains and tasks. *ArXiv*, abs/2004.10964.

Nils Holzenberger and Benjamin Van Durme. 2023. Connecting symbolic statutory reasoning with legal information extraction. *Proceedings of the Natural Legal Language Processing Workshop 2023*.

Abe Bohan Hou, Zhengping Jiang, Guanghui Qin, Orion Weller, Andrew Blair-Stanek, and Benjamin Van Durme. 2024a. L-tresco: Factual recall evaluation score for legal analysis generation. In *Proceedings of 2nd Generative AI + Law Workshop at International Conference on Machine Learning*.

Abe Bohan Hou, Orion Weller, Guanghui Qin, Eugene Yang, Dawn Lawrie, Nils Holzenberger, Andrew Blair-Stanek, and Benjamin Van Durme. 2024b. Clerc: A dataset for legal case retrieval and retrieval-augmented analysis generation. *ArXiv*.

Ziwei Ji, Nayeon Lee, Rita Frieske, Tiezheng Yu, Dan Su, Yan Xu, Etsuko Ishii, Ye Jin Bang, Andrea Madotto, and Pascale Fung. 2023. Survey of hallucination in natural language generation. *ACM Comput. Surv.*, 55(12).

Albert Qiaochu Jiang, Alexandre Sablayrolles, Arthur Mensch, Chris Bamford, Devendra Singh Chaplot, Diego de Las Casas, Florian Bressand, Gianna Lengyel, Guillaume Lample, Lucile Saulnier, L'elio Renard Lavaud, Marie-Anne Lachaux, Pierre Stock, Teven Le Scao, Thibaut Lavril, Thomas Wang, Timothée Lacroix, and William El Sayed. 2023. Mistral 7b. *ArXiv*, abs/2310.06825.

Josh Achiam, Steven Adler, Sandhini Agarwal, and et al. 2024. GPT-4 Technical Report.

M. Cathleen Kaveny. 2023. Abortion and the law in the united states: From roe to dobbs and beyond. *Theological Studies*, 84:134 – 156.

Woosuk Kwon, Zhuohan Li, Siyuan Zhuang, Ying Sheng, Lianmin Zheng, Cody Hao Yu, Joseph E. Gonzalez, Haotong Zhang, and Ion Stoica. 2023. Efficient memory management for large language model serving with pagedattention. *Proceedings of the 29th Symposium on Operating Systems Principles*.

Legal Information Institute. 2023. Legal writing.

Patrick Lewis, Ethan Perez, Aleksandra Piktus, Fabio Petroni, Vladimir Karpukhin, Naman Goyal, Heinrich Kuttler, Mike Lewis, Wen-tau Yih, Tim Rocktaschel, Sebastian Riedel, and Douwe Kiela. 2020. Retrieval-Augmented Generation for Knowledge-Intensive NLP Tasks. In *Proceedings of Conference on Neural Information Processing Systems (NeurIPS)*.

Junyi Li, Xiaoxue Cheng, Wayne Xin Zhao, Jianyun Nie, and Ji rong Wen. 2023. Halueval: A large-scale hallucination evaluation benchmark for large language models. *ArXiv*, abs/2305.11747.

Chin-Yew Lin. 2004. Rouge: A package for automatic evaluation of summaries. In *Annual Meeting of the Association for Computational Linguistics*.

Chris Lu, Cong Lu, Robert Tjarko Lange, Jakob N. Foerster, Jeff Clune, and David Ha. 2024. The ai scientist: Towards fully automated open-ended scientific discovery.

Kelvin Luu, Xinyi Wu, Rik Koncel-Kedziorski, Kyle Lo, Isabel Cachola, and Noah A. Smith. 2021. Explaining Relationships Between Scientific Documents. *arXiv preprint*. ArXiv:2002.00317 [cs].

Varun Magesh, Faiz Surani, Matthew Dahl, Mirac Suzgun, Christopher D. Manning, and Daniel E. Ho. 2024. Hallucination-free? assessing the reliability of leading ai legal research tools.

Robert Mahari, Dominik Stammbach, Elliott Ash, and Alex'Sandy' Pentland. 2023. Lepard: A large-scale dataset of judges citing precedents. *arXiv preprint*.

Nick McKenna, Tianyi Li, Liang Cheng, Mohammad Javad Hosseini, Mark Johnson, and Mark Steedman. 2023. Sources of hallucination by large language models on inference tasks. In *Conference on Empirical Methods in Natural Language Processing*.

Sewon Min, Kalpesh Krishna, Xinxi Lyu, Mike Lewis, Wen tau Yih, Pang Wei Koh, Mohit Iyyer, Luke Zettlemoyer, and Hannaneh Hajishirzi. 2023. Factscore: Fine-grained atomic evaluation of factual precision in long form text generation. *ArXiv*, abs/2305.14251.

Abhika Mishra, Akari Asai, Vidhisha Balachandran, Yizhong Wang, Graham Neubig, Yulia Tsvetkov, and Hannaneh Hajishirzi. 2024. Fine-grained hallucination detection and editing for language models. *ArXiv*, abs/2401.06855.

Luca Mouchel, Debjit Paul, Shaobo Cui, Robert West, Antoine Bosselut, and Boi Faltings. 2024. A logical fallacy-informed framework for argument generation. *Preprint*, arXiv:2408.03618.

Joel Niklaus, Lucia Zheng, Arya D. McCarthy, Christopher Hahn, Brian M. Rosen, Peter Henderson, Daniel E. Ho, Garrett Honke, Percy Liang, and Christopher D. Manning. 2024. Flawn-t5: An empirical examination of effective instruction-tuning data mixtures for legal reasoning. *ArXiv*, abs/2404.02127.

Rohan Padhye. 2024. Software engineering methods for ai-driven deductive legal reasoning.

Silvio Peroni and David Shotton. 2012. FaBiO and CiTO: Ontologies for describing bibliographic resources and citations. *Journal of Web Semantics*, 17:33–43.

Krishna Pillutla, Swabha Swayamdipta, Rowan Zellers, John Thickstun, Sean Welleck, Yejin Choi, and Zaid Harchaoui. 2021. Mauve: Measuring the gap between neural text and human text using divergence frontiers. In *NeurIPS*.

Swarnadeep Saha, Prateek Yadav, Lisa Bauer, and Mohit Bansal. 2021. ExplaGraphs: An explanation graph generation task for structured commonsense reasoning. In *Proceedings of the 2021 Conference on Empirical Methods in Natural Language Processing*, pages 7716–7740, Online and Punta Cana, Dominican Republic. Association for Computational Linguistics.

Kate Sanders, Nathaniel Weir, and Benjamin Van Durme. 2024. Tv-trees: Multimodal entailment trees for neuro-symbolic video reasoning. *ArXiv*, abs/2402.19467.

Parth Sarthi, Salman Abdullah, Aditi Tuli, Shubh Khanna, Anna Goldie, and Christopher D. Manning. 2024. Raptor: Recursive abstractive processing for tree-organized retrieval. In *International Conference on Learning Representations (ICLR)*.

Chenglei Si, Diyi Yang, and Tatsunori Hashimoto. 2024. Can llms generate novel research ideas? a large-scale human study with 100+ nlp researchers.

Llama3 Team. 2024. The llama 3 herd of models. *ArXiv*, abs/2407.21783.

Nathaniel Weir, Kate Sanders, Orion Weller, Shreya Sharma, Dongwei Jiang, Zhengping Jiang, Bhavana Dalvi Mishra, Oyvind Tafjord, Peter Jansen, Peter Clark, and Benjamin Van Durme. 2024. Enhancing systematic decompositional natural language inference using informal logic. *Preprint*, arXiv:2402.14798.

Nathaniel Weir and Benjamin Van Durme. 2022. Nellie: A neuro-symbolic inference engine for grounded, compositional, and explainable reasoning. *Proceedings of the Thirty-ThirdInternational Joint Conference on Artificial Intelligence*.

Xinyu Xing, Xiaosheng Fan, and Xiaojun Wan. 2020. Automatic Generation of Citation Texts in Scholarly Papers: A Pilot Study. In *Proceedings of the 58th Annual Meeting of the Association for Computational Linguistics*, pages 6181–6190, Online. Association for Computational Linguistics.

Rui Yang, Lin Song, Yanwei Li, Sijie Zhao, Yixiao Ge, Xiu Li, and Ying Shan. 2023. Gpt4tools: Teaching large language model to use tools via self-instruction. *ArXiv*, abs/2305.18752.

Weizhe Yuan, Graham Neubig, and Pengfei Liu. 2021. Bartscore: Evaluating generated text as text generation. *ArXiv*, abs/2106.11520.

Yue Zhang, Leyang Cui, Wei Bi, and Shuming Shi. 2023. Alleviating hallucinations of large language models through induced hallucinations. *ArXiv*, abs/2312.15710.

A A Full Example of Legal Analysis and Example Annotations

We present the full version of the example from Figure 3 in Figure 7, 8, and 9. An example annotation is included after the line break in Figure 9.

B Examples of Fine-grained Gap Categories

We present examples of the most fine-grained gap categories (G^5 - G^{14}) in Figure 11, 12 13, 14, and particularly, examples of target mismatches in Figure 15, 16, 17.

C Annotation Instruction

We present the annotation instruction for human annotators in Figure 18 and 19.

D Prompts to LLM Detectors

We present prompts to LLM detectors in Figure 20. The `variables` in {} are specific inputs to the prompt, and we vary k demonstrations for conducting the ablation studies.

Generation:
. . . In Butner v. United States, 440 U.S. 48, 55, the Supreme Court emphasized that property rights in the assets of a bankrupt's estate are determined by state law unless a federal interest dictates otherwise. In this case, we must determine the debtor's obligations under Puerto Rican law and assess the applicability of interest on the debt owed to Nelson Torres Ruiz.
Consistent with the principles outlined in 114 B.R. 326, the determination of whether the debtor has a legal or equitable interest in the obligation to return the $3,000 option money necessitates an analysis grounded in applicable nonbankruptcy state law. Article 1061 of the P.R. Civil Code, 31 Laws of P.R.Ann., Section 3025, establishes that where a debtor fails to perform an obligation, the creditor is entitled to interest as indemnification for damages and losses incurred.
Debtor's claim of impossibility of performance is addressed under Article 1138 of the Civil Code of Puerto Rico, but as established earlier, such a defense is unwarranted when the impossibility is not due to legal or physical barriers (31 Laws of P.R.Ann., Section 3193). Given the absence of such barriers, the return of the $3,000 is mandated.
Furthermore, in alignment with 117 B.R. 15, the initiation of bankruptcy proceedings does not alter the creditor's right to claim interest at the legal rate. Should the contract fail to specify an interest rate, Article 1061 defaults to a legal interest rate of 6% per annum.
Thus, Mr. Bonilla is obliged to reimburse the full amount of $3,000 plus the applicable legal interest rate of 6% from the expiration of the option contract until the filing of the bankruptcy petition.

citations needed to make: ['440 U.S. 48', '114 B.R. 326', '117 B.R. 15']

Target:
See generally, 3 Collier On Bankruptcy, (15th ed.) paragraph 502.02 (1990). See also, Butner v. U.S., 440 U.S. 48, 99 S.Ct. 914, 59 L.Ed.2d 136 (1979); In re MacDonald, 114 B.R. 326 (D.Mass. 1990); In re Milford Common J.V. Trust, 117 B.R. 15 (Bkrtcy.Mass., 1990).

reference_case_1: 440 U.S. 48
506 F. 2d 1242, 1243 (CA4 1974). See generally 4A W. Collier, Bankruptcy ¶ 70.16, pp. 157-165 (14th ed. 1975); Hill, The Erie Doctrine in Bankruptcy, 66 Harv. L. Rev. 1013 (1953). In some title States, the mortgagee's right to rents and profits may be exercised even prior to default, see Me. Rev. Stat. Ann., Tit. 33, § 502 (1964); in all events, the right at least attaches upon default, see Uvalda Naval Stores Co. v. Cullen, 165 Ga. 115, 117, 139 S. E. 810, 811 (1927). See generally R. Kratovil, Modern Mortgage Law and Practice § 294, p. 204 (1972); Comment, The Mortgagee's Right to Rents and Profits Following a Petition in Bankruptcy, 60 Iowa L. Rev. 1388, 1390-1391 (1975). North Carolina has been classified as a "title" State, Comment, The Mortgagee's Right to Rents After Default, 50 Yale L. J. 1424, 1425 n. 6 (1941), although it does not adhere to this theory in its purest form. Under its case law, a mortgagee is entitled to possession of the mortgaged property upon default, and need not await actual foreclosure. Such possession might be secured either with the consent of the mortgagor or by an action in ejectment. But so long as the mortgagor does remain in possession, even after default, he — not the mortgagee — appears to be entitled to the rents and profits. See Brannock v. Fletcher, 271 N. C. 65, 155 S. E. 2d 532 (1967); Gregg v. Williamson, 246 N. C. 356, 98 S.

reference_case_2: 114 B.R. 326
U.S.C. § 363(b)(1). "Property of the estate" includes "all legal or equitable interests of the debtor in property as of the commencement of the case." 11 U.S.C. § 541(a)(1). It is "necessary to look to nonbankruptcy law, usually state law, to determine whether the debtor has any legal or equitable interest in any particular item." 4 Collier on Bankruptcy, ¶ 541.02[1] at 541-13 (15th ed. 1989). Since "property interests are created and defined by state law," such interests are analyzed under state law in bankruptcy proceedings unless "some federal interest requires a different result." Butner v. United States, 440 U.S. 48, 55, 99 S.Ct. 914, 918, 59 L.Ed.2d 136 (1979). See also In re Prichard Plaza Associates Ltd. Partnership, 84 B.R. 289, 293 (Bankr.D.Mass.1988). This Court's resolution of the dispute over the debtor's interest in Spectrum Wire is grounded in state corporations law, and takes into account the equitable powers of the bankruptcy court. However, in light of the bankruptcy court decision under review, this Court's analysis of the appellants' ownership interest in the Spectrum Wire stock must begin with a discussion of the Massachusetts law of trusts. A. Stock as the Subject Matter of an Express Trust The bankruptcy court found that conduct and verbal agreements by the debtor's father "manifested an intention to hold in trust for the Debtor the shares of Spectrum stock standing in the father's name." In re MacDonald, 101 B.R. at 841. This conclusion, that an express trust was created by the debtor's father,

reference_case_3: 117 B.R. 15
order against the debtor. The automatic stay prevented any further action by the Bank, including service of the restraining order. The debtor has remained in physical possession and has continued to collect all of its rents. The Bank promptly filed with the bankruptcy court an emergency motion for relief from stay and for authority to continue with its possession and to collect the rents. The law was clarified by the United States Supreme Court in 1979 in the case of Butner v. United States, 440 U.S. 48, 99 S.Ct. 914, 59 L.Ed.2d 136, 4 B.C.D. 1259. The court held that: ... Congress has generally left the determination of property rights in the assets of a bankrupt's estate to state law. Property interests are created and defined by state law. Unless some federal interest requires a different result, there

(CONTINUED NEXT PAGE)

Figure 7: (1/3) A full example machine-generated legal analysis from (Hou et al., 2024b), with previous context and cited sources provided. Texts after the line break are added when prompting LLM-based detectors.

(CONTINUED FROM LAST PAGE)

is no reason why such interests should be analyzed differently simply because an interested party is involved in a bankruptcy proceeding. Looking to Massachusetts law, an assignment of rent gives the mortgagee a valid security interest which becomes effective upon a default and an overt act by the mortgagee to take actual or constructive possession. Bankruptcy does not change the assignee/mortgagee's right to the rent so long as possession was obtained pre-fil-ing, or a request is made to the bankruptcy-court for relief. The matter was further extensively analyzed by Bankruptcy Judge James F. Queenan, Jr. in the case of In re Prichard Plaza Associates Limited Partnership, 84 B.R. 289 (Bkrtcy.D.Mass.1988). For a

previous_text:

OPINION AND ORDER SARA E. de JESUS, Bankruptcy Judge. The matter pending before the Court is whether creditors Nelson and Elizabeth Torres are entitled to the payment of interest on Claim # 13, and the applicable interest rate. Pursuant to Debtor's request for a valuation of claim # 13, we held an evidentiary hearing. The parties have agreed to the following facts: "a. That on July 22, 1980, Nelson Torres Ruiz and Adrián Bonilla Montalvo signed an Option Contract for the purchase of a plot of land marked number twenty (20). b. The price of said plot of land was $7,250.00, of which at the signing of the Option Contract, Nelson Torres Ruiz paid Adrián Bonilla Montalvo the sum of $500.00 and later that same day paid him $2,500.00 for a total of $3,000.00. c. The Option Contract enumerated a period of two years from the date of signing within which the debtor, Adrián Bonilla Montalvo, was to execute the purchase deed or reimburse Nelson Torres Ruiz the sum of $3,000.00., d. That Mr. Nelson Torres Ruiz was single when he entered into an option agreement for certain lot of land on July 22, 1980. e. That Mr. Nelson Torres Ruiz gave Mr. Adrián Bonilla $3,000.00 as option money- f. That debtor according to clause # 6 of the option contract is obliged, and has accepted to do so, to return to this creditor the $3,000.00. g. That debtor has recognized the debt of $3,000.00 owed to Mr. Nelson Torres and has scheduled the same as $900.00 priority and $2,100.00 as general unsecured claim. h. Mrs. Elizabeth Hermida de Torres married Mr. Nelson Torres Ruiz after the option contract was signed. i. Mrs. Elizabeth Hermida de Torres was not a party to the option contract signed on July 22, 1980 by debtor and Mr. Nelson Torres. j. .That on January 12, 1984, Mrs. Elizabeth Hermida de Torres was deputy clerk of the Superior Court of Puerto Rico, Courtroom of Mayaguez. k. That Banco Comercial de Mayaguez filed suit number 81-1138 against debtor and his ex-wife on the Superior Court of Puerto Rico, Courtroom of Mayaguez. l. That on June 7, 1983 Attorney Jovino Martinez wrote a letter to debtor on behalf of Mr. Nelson Torres requesting the return of the option money given by him to debt- or. m. The plot of land where Mr. Nelson Torres had his option was sold after the filing for relief and with the authority of this Court." Two Joint Exhibits were also admitted: the Option contract executed by the Debtor and Nelson Torres on July 22, 1980; and a letter dated June 7, 1983 from Attorney Jovino Martinez Ramirez to Attorney Adrián Bonilla Montalvo requesting the return of the money paid by Mr. Torres plus legal interest. CONCLUSIONS OF LAW In bankruptcy, issues as to the validity and legality of a claim are determined pursuant to applicable state law. Thus, we must decide the question at hand by applying the pertinent Articles of the Civil Code of P.R. The option contract executed by Debtor and Nelson Torres Ruiz, called for the execution of the deed of sale within two years from July 22, 1980. However, the contractual terms also required Mr. Bonilla to return the total price for the option, if he could not obtain the permits required by the local government allowing him to segregate and sell the optioned plot, within this same two year period. The contract does not mention interest payments. The Debtor raises the defense of impossibility of compliance with the obligation in order to release himself from the obligation and/or any liability. Mr. Bonilla claims a legal and physical impossibility based on events which occured almost six years after the Option contract had expired, and, in any event, these events concern his fiscal or monetary problems. Article 1138 of the Civil Code of Puerto Rico, 31 Laws of P.R.Ann., Section 3193, provides that, "In obligations to do, the debtor shall also be released when the prestation appears to be legally or physically impossible." However, Debtor's reliance on this Article of the Civil Code is unwarranted inasmuch as the legal and physical impossibility contemplated by law are not present in this contested matter. Article 1061 of the P.R.Civil Code, 31 Laws of P.R.Ann., Section 3025, provides that when the obligation consists in the payment of a sum of money, and the person incurs in default, the creditor is entitled to be indemnified for damages and losses suffered, which will consist in the payment of interest. If the parties failed to agree upon the payment of interest and or the interest rate, then the interest to be paid will be the legal interest at the applicable rate. Furthermore, "Until another rate is fixed by the Government, interest at the rate of six percent per annum shall be considered as legal." Under these circumstances, Mr. Bonilla must reimburse the full amount of the option contract paid by Mr. Torres, plus interest at the legal rate of 6% per year, from the date the option contract expired to the date this petition was filed, pursuant to 11 U.S.C. Section 502(b)(2). . During the hearing, Nelson Torres Ruiz and his wife Elizabeth waived their claims for damages other than interest discussed herein. . 11 U.S.C. Section 502(c)(2). . It was also undisputed that Debtor was not able to secure the government permits needed to segregate and sell the plot to the

(CONTINUED NEXT PAGE)

Figure 8: (2/3) A full example machine-generated legal analysis from (Hou et al., 2024b), with previous context and cited sources provided texts after the line break are example annotations.

(CONTINUED FROM LAST PAGE)

Optionee, and the deed of sale was never executed. . The Court takes judicial notice that the petition for bankruptcy pursuant to Chapter 11 of the Code was entered on February 19, 1987; and that Nelson and Elizabeth Torres, filed proof of claim no. 13 in the amount of $25,-000.00. Attached thereto are the copies of the following documents: the option contract entered into by the debtor Adrián Bonilla Montal-vo and Nelson Torres Ruiz on July 22, 1980; the complaint filed by Mr. Torres Ruiz against the debtor before the Superior Court of Puerto Rico, Mayaguez Part, Civil No. CS-88-896, for collection of money and damages; and a copy of a sworn statement of Nelson Torres Ruiz dated June 22, 1988. .During the hearing the parties testified this suit was stayed by the filing of this petition.

Output a valid JSON object with the fields of "label": [(one or more integers from 0-3 indicating the gap categories, expressed in a list)], "explanation": a short explanation justifying the label.. Do not output anything else such as 'json' or newline characters or redundant spaces. Answer after output:
output:

Label: [2]

Explanation: The generated text provides detailed context and elaboration for each citation, whereas the target text chain cites them without additional detail. This indicates a target mismatch.

Figure 9: (3/3) A full example machine-generated legal analysis from (Hou et al., 2024b), with previous context and cited sources provided texts after the line break are example annotations.

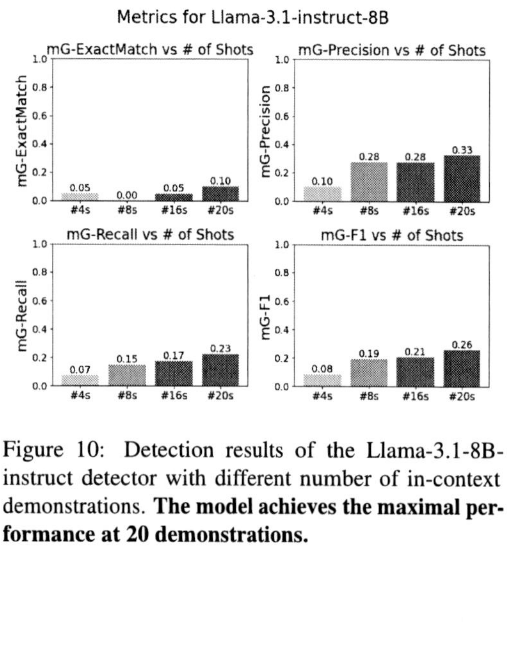

Figure 10: Detection results of the Llama-3.1-8B-instruct detector with different number of in-context demonstrations. **The model achieves the maximal performance at 20 demonstrations.**

Generation:
. . . The court's action was an error in law. In a recent case, the court held that Rule 25(a) (1) "is not designed to require a plaintiff to take affirmative action to locate the representative of the deceased party. Rather, it is designed to provide a mechanism for the court to manage the case in the event the deceased party has not been substituted." 359 F.2d 292, 294 (C.A. 4, 1966). In another case, the court held that the Rule "does not require a plaintiff to institute machinery in order to produce a representative of the estate ad litem, pending appointment of the representative contemplated by law of the domicile of the deceased." 379 F.2d 94, 96 (C.A. 7, 1967). In that case, the court noted that the "plaintiff's attorney did not know whether probate of the will might be contested, or who would be appointed representative of the estate." Id. at 96. The court held that the suggestion of death was ineffective to trigger the 90-day period under Rule 25(a) (1) where the suggestion did not identify a successor or representative of the deceased party. Id. at 96. See also, 4A Wright & Miller, Federal Practice and Procedure: Civil 2d, 2451 (1969). The court's action was an error in law. The judgment is reversed, and the case is remanded for further proceedings not inconsistent with this opinion. Reversed. (Emphasis added.)

citations needed to make: ['379 F.2d 94', '359 F.2d 292']

Target:
The amendment to Rule 25(a) (1) was intended to dispel unwarranted rigidity and allow more flexibility in substitution. "It was intended that liberal effect be given to the 1963 amendment." Roscoe v. Roscoe, 126 U.S.App.D.C. 317, 322, 379 F.2d 94, 99 (1967). "[T]he 90 day period was not intended to act as a bar to otherwise meritorious actions." Staggers v. Otto Gerdau Co., 359 F.2d 292, 296 (2d Cir. 1966).
reference_case_1: 379 F.2d 94
the proper parties. Unless the motion for substitution is made not later than 90 days after the death is suggested upon the record by service of a statement of the fact of the death as provided herein for the service of the motion, the action shall be dismissed as to the deceased party." Here not only had the 90-day period not expired when the court entered summary judgment, the appellant by her motion for reconsideration had specifically invoked the discretion of the court. Rule 6(b) provides pertinently that when "by these rules * * * an act is required or allowed to be done at or within a specified time, the court for cause shown may at any time in its discretion (1) with or without motion or notice order the period enlarged if request therefor is made before the expiration of the period originally prescribed * * Originally the Rule had precluded an extension of time for taking action under Rule 25(a) (1), but by purposeful amendment, it was sought to relieve against the hardship of the Court's holding in Anderson v. Yungkau, 329 U.S. 482, 67 S.Ct. 428, 91 L.Ed. 436 (1947). It was intended that liberal effect be given to the 1963 amendment. Graham v. Pennsylvania Railroad, 119 U.S.App.D.C. 335, 342 F.2d 914 (1964), cert. denied, 381 U.S. 904, 85 S.Ct. 1446, 14 L.Ed.2d 286 (1965). We are constrained to reverse for further proceedings not inconsistent with this opinion. Reversed. The only "party" then
reference_case_2: 359 F.2d 292
insertion of a "reasonable time" standard. In 1963, the Advisory Committee suggested the present rule and noted: "Present Rule 25(a) (1), together with present Rule 6(b), results in an inflexible requirement that an action be dismissed as to a deceased party if substitution is not carried out within a fixed period measured from the time of the death. The hardships and inequities of this unyielding requirement plainly appear from the cases. * * * The amended rulé establishes a time limit for the motion to substitute based not upon the time of the death, but rather upon the time information of the death is provided by means of a suggestion of death upon the record, i. e. service of a statement of the fact of the death." See Notes of Advisory Committee on the Civil Rules, 28 U.S.C. Rule 25 (1964). Rule 6(b) of the Federal Rules of Civil Procedure was also amended in 1963 and the prohibition against extending the time for taking action under Rule 25 was eliminated. The Advisory Committee on the Civil Rules noted: "It is intended that the court shall have discretion to enlarge that period." The amendments of Rules 6(b) and 25(a) (1) provided needed flexibility. It was assumed that discretionary extensions would be liberally granted. Movants under Rule 25 can ordinarily control when a death is "suggested upon the record" and appellants' attorney was under no obligation to file his affidavit of Staggers' death on the date he did. He could have filed
previous_text:
LEVENTHAL, Circuit Judge: The District Court held that Rule 25(a) (1) of the Federal Rules of Civil Procedure required dismissal of the plaintiffs' tort action because defendant's counsel had filed a suggestion of death of the defendant yet plaintiff had not made any substitution of parties within 90 days. We reverse on the ground that the suggestion of death, which was neither filed by nor identified a successor or representative of the deceased, such as an executor or administrator, was ineffective to trigger the running of the 90-day period provided by the Rule. Mr. and Mrs. John Rende filed an action in the District Court individually and on behalf of their infant son who had been struck and injured by Alfred S. Kay while driving his car. On August 27, 1967, defendant Kay died.
. . .
In our opinion the Rule, as amended, cannot fairly be construed, as the de fendant's attorney argues, to make his suggestion of death operative to trigger the 90-day period even though he was neither a successor nor representative of the deceased, and gave no indication of what person was available to be named in substitution as a representative of the deceased. Counsel's construction would open the door to a tactical maneuver to place upon the plaintiff the burden of locating the representative of the estate within 90 days. We can conceive of cases wherein even the lawyer retained to represent a defendant might know the defendant had died, yet not readily know where his estate would be administered.
(GAP CATEGORIES AND EXPLANATION INCLUDED NEXT PAGE)

Figure 11: (1/2) An example machine-generated legal analysis which contains *redundancy*, *structural mismatch*, *claim hallucination*, *citation hallucination*, and *retrieval inaccuracy*.

(CONTINUED FROM LAST PAGE)

In the present case, plaintiff's attorney did know the court of probate, but he did not know whether probate of the will might be contested, or who would be appointed representative of the estate. The tactic of the defendant's attorney would place on plaintiff the burden, where no conventional representative was appointed for the estate in probate court, of instituting machinery in order to produce some representative of the estate ad litem, pending appointment of the representative contemplated by law of the domicile of the deceased. **Gap Categories:** Redundancy (G^5), Structural Mismatch (G^8), Claim Hallucination (G^9), Citation Hallucination (G^{10}), and Retrieval Inaccuracy (G^{11}).

Explanation:
1. The generation has redundancy because it repeats "The court's action was an error in law" verbatim twice and also repeats "Reversed" multiple times. 2. The generation has structural mismatch because it prematurely concludes the case with "Reversed", which is structurally inappropriate. 3. It contains claim hallucination, as when it elaborates case 379 F.2d 94, it should focus on the aspects related to "It was intended that liberal effect be given to the 1963 amendment." as this is the relevant claim. However, it talks about "does not require a plaintiff to institute machinery in order to produce a representative of the estate ad litem, pending appointment of the representative contemplated by law of the domicile of the deceased", which is rather irrelevant. 4. The generation also suffers from retrieval inaccuracy. The generation should retrieve the salient chunk from case 359 F.2d 292 centering on "T]he 90 day period was not intended to act as a bar to otherwise meritorious actions.", yet the retrieved chunk is not so relevant.

Figure 12: (2/2) Explanation of the example in Figure 11.

Generation:
. . . This case presents the question whether an employee welfare benefits plan creates an entitlement to lifetime benefits or just to benefits that can be terminated by an amendment to the plan. The plan administrator, Motorola, amended the plan to place a two-year limit on benefits for disability resulting from certain mental conditions, including the plaintiff's condition. The plaintiff, Marrs, argues that the plan's provision stating that no amendment shall adversely affect the rights of any participant to receive benefits with respect to periods of disability prior to the adoption date of the amendment is violated. He interprets "periods of disability prior to the adoption date" to mean one or more periods of disability that began before the plan was amended but may not have ended before then. However, the plan administrator's interpretation is reasonable, and we are inclined to stop with that observation. The Supreme Court's decision in Glenn v. Metropolitan Life Ins. Co. (128 S.Ct. 2343, 171 L.Ed.2d 299 (2008)) is relevant in this case. The Court held that a conflict of interest by the plan administrator should be given weight in judicial review of the denial of benefits. However, the weight to be given to the conflict of interest depends on the circumstances of the case. In this case, the plan administrator had an incentive to resolve a close case in favor of a denial of benefits, but this incentive may be outweighed by other incentives, such as an employer's interest in maintaining a reputation among current and prospective employees for fair dealing. The employees who actually decide benefits claims at the plan- administrator level may not be acutely concerned with the financial implications of a benefits award for their employer. We conclude that the plan administrator's decision to deny benefits is reasonable and that the conflict of interest does not render the decision unreasonable. The judgment of the district court is Affirmed. References: 1. Glenn v. Metropolitan Life Ins. Co., 128 S.Ct. 2343, 171 L.Ed.2d 299 (2008) 2. Marrs v. Motorola, 908 F.2d 1385 (7th Cir. 1990) 3. Rogers v. Department of Health & Environmental Control, 174 F.3d 431, 435 (4th Cir. 1999) 4. Kahane v. UNUM Life Ins. Co., 563 F.3d 1210, 1212 (11th Cir.

citations needed to make: ['564 F.3d 856', '576 F.3d 240', '560 F.3d 620', '504 F.3d 665', '908 F.2d 1385', '855 F.2d 394']

Target:
There are two ways to read the majority opinion. One, which tracks its language and has been echoed in opinions in this and other circuits, e.g., Jenkins v. Price Waterhouse Long Term Disability Plan, 564 F.3d 856, 861-62 (7th Cir.2009); Holland v. Int'l Paper Co. Retirement Plan, 576 F.3d 240, 246-49 (5th Cir.2009), makes the existence of a conflict of interest one factor out of many in determining reasonableness. That sounds like a balancing test in which unweighted factors mysteriously are weighed. Such a test is not conducive to providing guidance to courts or plan administrators. "Multifactor tests with no weight assigned to any factor are bad enough from the standpoint of providing an objective basis for a judicial decision; multifactor tests when none of the factors is concrete are worse." Menard, Inc. v. Commissioner, 560 F.3d 620, 622-23 (7th Cir.2009) (citations omitted); see also Sullivan v. William A. Randolph, Inc., 504 F.3d 665, 671 (7th Cir.2007); Short v. Belleville Shoe Mfg. Co., 908 F.2d 1385, 1394 (7th Cir.1990) (concurring opin ion); Stevens v. Tillman, 855 F.2d 394, 399-400 (7th Cir.1988).

previous_text:
POSNER, Circuit Judge. This suit under ERISA for disability payments presents the recurring question whether an employee welfare benefits plan creates an entitlement to lifetime benefits rather than just to benefits that can be terminated by an amendment to the plan. In 1997 Michael Marrs, an employee of Motorola, ceased working because of a psychiatric condition and began drawing disability benefits under Motorola's Disability Income Plan. Six years later Motorola amended the plan to place a two-year limit on benefits for disability resulting from certain "Mental, Nervous, Alcohol, [or] Drug-Related" (MNAD) conditions, including Marrs's. Such limitations on MNAD conditions are common in employee disability plans.
Then too, the employees who actually decide benefits claims at the plan-administrator level may not be acutely concerned with the financial implications of a benefits award for their employer. Id. at 821; Perlman v. Swiss Bank Corp. Comprehen sive Disability Protection Plan, 195 F.3d 975, 981 (7th Cir.1999). But especially when a firm is struggling (which may or may not be the case here — there is nothing in the record bearing on the question), an opportunity for short-run economies may dominate decision making by benefits officers. In any event, a majority of the Supreme Court Justices consider the potential conflict of interest of a plan administrator (or its staff) serious enough to be given weight in judicial review of the denial of benefits. But how much weight should it be given? The nub of the Glenn opinion is the following passage: [W]hen judges review the lawfulness of benefit denials, they will often take account of several different considerations of which a conflict of interest is one. This kind of review is no stranger to the judicial system. Not only trust law, but also administrative law, can ask judges to determine lawfulness by taking account of several different, often case-specific, factors, reaching a result by weighing all together. In such instances, any one factor will act as a tiebreaker when the other factors are closely balanced, the degree of closeness necessary depending upon the tiebreaking factor's inherent or case-specific importance. The conflict of interest at issue here, for example, should prove more important (perhaps of great importance) where circumstances suggest a higher likelihood that it affected the benefits decision, including, but not limited to, cases where an insurance company administrator has a history of biased claims administration. It should prove less important (perhaps to the vanishing point) where the administrator has taken active steps to reduce potential bias and to promote accuracy, for example, by walling off claims administrators from those interested in firm finances, or by imposing management checks that penalize inaccurate decisionmaking irrespective of whom the inaccuracy benefits. 128 S.Ct.

(GAP CATEGORIES AND EXPLANATION ARE INCLUDED IN THE NEXT PAGE).

Figure 13: (1/2) An example machine-generated legal analysis that contains *citation format mismatch*, *structural mismatch*, *citation hallucination*, and *stylistic mismatch*.

(CONTINUED FROM LAST PAGE)

at 2351 (citations omitted). A dissent by Justice Scalia argued that a conflict of interest should prompt an inquiry only into the existence of improper motive that would render the plan administrator's decision unreasonable. If the decision is reasonable, he argued, in the sense in which "a reasonable decision is one over which reasonable minds seeking the 'best' or 'right' answer could disagree," the fact that the administrator had a conflict of interest is irrelevant, id. at 2360, "unless the conflict actually and improperly motivates the decision." Id. at 2357 (emphasis in original).

Gap Categories:

Citation Format Mismatch (G^6), Stylistic Mismatch (G^7), Structural Mismatch (G^8), and Citation Hallucination (G^{10}).

Explanation:

1. The generation has citation format mismatch because it includes inappropriate citation formats (underlined) to legal writing. 2. The generation has stylistic mismatch because it should not use language like "This case" when it should be continuing the generation, and using a third-person pronoun makes it appear like analyzing a separate piece of text rather than continuing it. 3. The generation has structural mismatch, since it "conclude(s)" the case, which is inappropriate structurally. 4. The generation contains citation hallucination as it fails to cite most of the citations needed to make.

Figure 14: (2/2) Explanation of the example in Figure 13.

Generation:

CONCLUSIONS OF LAW (continued) In Butner v. United States, 440 U.S. 48, 55, the Supreme Court emphasized that property rights in the assets of a bankrupt's estate are determined by state law unless a federal interest dictates otherwise. In this case, we must determine the debtor's obligations under Puerto Rican law and assess the applicability of interest on the debt owed to Nelson Torres Ruiz. Consistent with the principles outlined in 114 B.R. 326, the determination of whether the debtor has a legal or equitable interest in the obligation to return the $3,000 option money necessitates an analysis grounded in applicable nonbankruptcy state law. Article 1061 of the P.R. Civil Code, 31 Laws of P.R.Ann., Section 3025, establishes that where a debtor fails to perform an obligation, the creditor is entitled to interest as indemnification for damages and losses incurred. Debtor's claim of impossibility of performance is addressed under Article 1138 of the Civil Code of Puerto Rico, but as established earlier, such a defense is unwarranted when the impossibility is not due to legal or physical barriers (31 Laws of P.R.Ann., Section 3193). Given the absence of such barriers, the return of the $3,000 is mandated. Furthermore, in alignment with 117 B.R. 15, the initiation of bankruptcy proceedings does not alter the creditor's right to claim interest at the legal rate. Should the contract fail to specify an interest rate, Article 1061 defaults to a legal interest rate of 6% per annum. Thus, Mr. Bonilla is obliged to reimburse the full amount of $3,000 plus the applicable legal interest rate of 6% from the expiration of the option contract until the filing of the bankruptcy petition.

Target:

See generally, 3 Collier On Bankruptcy, (15th ed.) paragraph 502.02 (1990). See also, Butner v. U.S., 440 U.S. 48, 99 S.Ct. 914, 59 L.Ed.2d 136 (1979); In re MacDonald, 114 B.R. 326 (D.Mass. 1990); In re Milford Common J.V. Trust, 117 B.R. 15 (Bkrtcy.Mass., 1990).

Gap Categories:

Chain vs. Parallel (G^{12})

Explanation:

The target text does not elaborate any of the cases cited whereas the generation chooses to elaborate each citation.

Figure 15: An example machine-generated legal analysis which contains *chain vs. parallel*.

Generation:
In Reference case 47 M.J. 370, the court held that the automatic total-forfeiture rule and the 14-day provision of Article 57(a)(1) violate the Ex Post Facto Clause. Similarly, in Reference case 45 M.J. 567, the court found that the Article 57 amendment does not violate the ex post facto prohibition, as it does not increase the duration of the punishment.

Target:
Appellant's ex post facto arguments were resolved by the United States Court of Appeals for the Armed Forces in United States v. Gorsky 47 M.J. 370 (1997). We intend to apply that decision despite appellate government counsel's argument that we should ignore our superior Court's opinion and adhere to our decision in United States v. Pedrazoli, 45 M.J. 567(A.F.Ct.Crim.App.1997), **which Gorski essentially reversed**. See United States v. Plumb, 47 M.J. 771 (A.F.Ct.Crim. App.1997).

Gap Categories:
Agree vs. Disagree (G^{13}) and Citation Hallucination (G^{10})

Explanation:
In the target text, case 47 M.J. 370 reversed the ruling of case 45 M.J. 567 (highlighted in bold). However, the generation illustrates the two cases in a parallel manner, as shown by the conjuctive adverb "Similarly". Moreover, the generation also does not mention case 47 M.J. 771, which is cited in the target.

Figure 16: An example machine-generated legal analysis which contains *agree vs. disagree* and *citation hallucination*.

Generation:
This dismissal might be an error. According to established precedents, an action can be dismissed as frivolous under 28 U.S.C. § 1915(d) only if it is beyond doubt that the petitioner can prove no set of facts in support of his claim that would entitle him to relief (699 F.2d 434; 741 F.2d 209).

Target:
A district court may dismiss an action as frivolous only if it appears beyond a doubt that the plaintiff can prove no set of facts in support of his claim which would entitle him to relief. Smith v. Bacon, 699 F.2d 434, 436 (8th Cir.1983). A complaint which is good against a motion to dismiss for failure to state a claim may not be dismissed as frivolous under 28 U.S.C. § 1915(d). Horsey v. Asher, 741 F.2d 209, 212 (8th Cir.1984).

Gap Categories:
Compound Cite (G^{14})

Explanation:
The target text cites two cases to illustrate two claims ("A district court may dismiss an action as frivolous only if it appears beyond a doubt that the plaintiff can prove no set of facts in support of his claim which would entitle him to relief." and "A complaint which is good against a motion to dismiss for failure to state a claim may not be dismissed as frivolous under 28 U.S.C. § 1915(d).") However, the generation combines the two claims ("an action can be dismissed as frivolous under 28 U.S.C. § 1915(d) only if it is beyond doubt that the petitioner can prove no set of facts in support of his claim that would entitle him to relief ") and cites the two cases together.

Figure 17: An example machine-generated legal analysis which contains *compound cite*.

Instructions for annotators:

Task Overview
You are tasked to classify categories of gaps between machine-generated and human-written legal analysis.
Definitions:
generation: machine-generated legal analysis.
target: human-written legal analysis. Note that the target is only one form of acceptable legal analysis. There are other acceptable legal analysis. It is possible for a generation to not match with the target but still considered acceptable.
previous_context: we set the goal of LLM to generate a paragraph of legal analysis and feed in the previous context to this paragraph as the input.
cited_paragraphs: in addition to the previous context, we also feed in the other paragraphs that are supposed to be cited in this generation.
citation: citation refers to the special string which points to a legal case, with style and format specified by the Bluebook.
claim: the sentence which is supported by the citation, i.e. the case referred to. Claim usually appears in the vicinity of the citation.
Intrinsic Gaps: the presence of intrinsic gaps signals that the machine-generated legal analysis is an unacceptable form. We can tell intrinsic gaps exist by *only* looking at the previous context and the generation itself.
Extrinsic Gaps: extrinsic gaps, as its name suggests, can be discovered by comparing the generation with external texts, i.e. the cited paragraphs or the target paragraph that can be seen as the "answer". Extrinsic gaps contain two kinds: citation content mismatch and target mismatch. Target mismatch does not indicate that the generated legal analysis is necessarily wrong.

Annotation Instructions:
Receiving the following prompt, a language model will generate a paragraph of legal analysis, but often times they make different kinds of errors and mismatches.

```
User prompt:
Here are some reference articles for legal cases:
# Reference case {case_key_1}
{text of cited case 1}
# Reference case {case_key_2}
{text of cited case 2}
...
# Reference case {case_key_N}
{text of cited case N}

Here is the text I've written so far:
# Paragrah
{previous_text}

Continue to write it following the style of my writeup. Your answer contains 100 to
400 words. You must explicitly use the reference cases and mention their reference ids, i.e.
{case_key_1}, {case_key_2} . . . {case_key_N}. Wrap your answer with <answer></answer>. Make
your answer concise and avoid redundant languages.
```

The instructions for you to classify these errors and mismatches are as follows:

1. **Intrinsic gap**:
This category refers to generation that is unacceptable, due to the language model has fundamentally failed to follow the instruction, or make a lot of redundancy, or generate something that does not look like legal text (structural mismatch). More specificially, if it makes one or more of the following:

- Redundancy (sentence-level, appearing as neural degeneration): the generation appears to make repetitive statements that do not add more meaning to the analysis. For example, multiple occurences of an exact sentence or phrase.
- Citation Format Mismatch: the generation appears not matching with the citation format of the standard Bluebook.
  - Please be aware that, for example, 440 U.S. 48, 55' is a proper format. Although its full citation should be 'Butner v. United States, 440 U.S. 48, 55 (1979)', the format '440 U.S. 48, 55' is still acceptable as a concise form.
- Structural Mismatch: the generation appears to generate the document from scratch (like containing words such as "ORDER" which only appear in the beginning).
- Stylistic Mismatch: contain sentences that do not match the styles of legalese.

(CONTINUED IN NEXT PAGE)

Figure 18: (1/2) Annotation instructions for human annotators.

(CONTINUED FROM LAST PAGE)

If this type of gaps is present, add the label '1'. Continue to item 2.
Side note: You should be able to classify this purely based on the generation itself, without having to look at cited examples.

2.**Target mismatch**:
While language model's generated text may be obviously wrong and substantively different from the target (i.e. the original/target text from the case), the claims it makes are still logically and factually sound and can be seen as acceptable. This could be because

- Chain cite: the citations appear in a chain cite but the generation cites them parallely, or the other way around.
  - Clarification: "The rule that certain acts of a creditor in the course of a bankruptcy proceeding and during the statutory period for filing proof of claim, may give rise to something equivalent to a proof of claim and afford a sufficient basis for allowing an amendment after the statutory period for filing, was recognized and applied in many cases decided before the 1938 amendment of the Bankruptcy Act. See In re Atlantic Gulf & Pacific S. S. Corporation, D.C., 26 F.2d 751; In re Fant, D.C., 21 F.2d 182; Globe Indemnity Co. of Newark, N. J., v. Keeble, 4 Cir., 20 F.2d 84; In re Coleman & Titus Corporation, D.C., 286 F. 303; In re Roeber, 2 Cir., 127 F. 122." **would be a chain cite** because all of these citations support the previous claim "The rule that certain acts of a creditor in the course of a bankruptcy proceeding and during the statutory period for filing proof of claim, may give rise to something equivalent to a proof of claim and afford a sufficient basis for allowing an amendment after the statutory period for filing, was recognized and applied in many cases decided before the 1938 amendment of the Bankruptcy Act."
- Agree versus disagree: the citations reverse the ruling in each other but the generation cites them parallely, or the other way around.
- Compound cite: the citations of different cases are cited together, separated by semicolons, or the other way around.

Although it does not match with the target, it is still considered somewhat acceptable, but we should label it out.
If this type of mismatch is present add the label "2". Continue to item 3.

3. **Citation Mismatch**:
The language model's generated text does not align with the content of the citation it points to. This might be because one or more of the following:

- Claim Hallucination: the claim supported by the citation is not truthful or not related to the context or from cited paragraphs or the previous context. The generated text makes different and possibly (although not necessarily) contradictory claims about one or more citations, which you can check from comparing to the reference case. Or, the generated text attributes information from one citation to a different citation.
- Retrieval Inaccuracy: the claims supported by the citation is not relevant because the cited paragraph looks irrelevant compared to the target paragraph.
- Citation Hallucination: the citation is non-existent or pulled from a citation in the cited paragraphs or the previous context, or there misses a citation (the generated text fails to use one of the citations that were given to it).

If this type of mismatch is **present**, add the label "3" and move on to the next example. If none of the above errors are present, label "0".

Note that where an example falls into multiple categories, you should include both labels, separated by a comma.

Figure 19: (2/2) Annotation instructions for human annotators.

System Prompt:
You are a trained lawyer from Silicon Valley with a computer science background. Now, you are asked to annotate legal analysis generated by large language models and classify the errors and mismatch made by these models. To produce these legal analysis, a language model will receive the following prompt:

Here are some reference articles for legal cases:
Reference case
{case_key_1} {text of cited case 1}
Reference case
{case_key_2} {text of cited case 2}
...
Reference case
case_key_N {text of cited case N}

Here is the text I've written so far:
Paragraph {previous_text} Continue to write it following the style of my writeup. Your answer contains 100 to 400 words. You must explicitly use the reference cases and mention their reference ids, i.e. {case_key_1}, {case_key_2} . . . {case_key_N}. Wrap your answer with <answer></answer>. Make your answer concise and avoid redundant languages.
Receiving the prompt above, a language model will generate a paragraph of legal analysis, but often times they make different kinds of errors and mismatches.
The instructions for you to classify these errors and mismatches are as follows:
You should classify the LLM-generated legal analysis to these categories:
`{Summary of the gap categories, same from the instructions to human annotators.}`
Here are some examples for demonstration:
`{Example annotation 1}`
`{Example annotation 2}`
⋮
`{Example annotation k}`

–End Demonstration–
Now, we will give you more instances and have you annotate 1, 2, 3, or 0. Output a json object containing the label and explanation for each example. If you label a 3, please elaborate the explanation for it a bit more.

User Prompt:
Generation: `{generation}`

citations needed to make: `{[citation_1, . . . , citation_N]}`

Target:`{target}`

reference_case_1: `{case_key_1}`
`{reference_case_1}`
⋮
reference_case_N: `{case_key_N}`
`{reference_case_N}`

previous_text: `{previous_text}`

Output a valid JSON object with the fields of "label": [(one or more integers from 0-3 indicating the gap categories, expressed in a list)], "explanation": a short explanation justifying the label.. Do not output anything else such as 'json' or newline characters or redundant spaces. Answer after output:
output:

Figure 20: Prompts to LLM-based detectors. The number of k varies from {4, 8, 16, 20} in our ablation studies.

Classify First, and Then Extract: Prompt Chaining Technique for Information Extraction

Alice Saebom Kwak[1], **Clayton T. Morrison**[2],
Derek E. Bambauer[3], **Mihai Surdeanu**[4]

[1]Department of Linguistics, The University of Arizona
[2]College of Information Science, The University of Arizona
[3]Levin College of Law, The University of Florida
[4]Department of Computer Science, The University of Arizona
{[1]alicekwak, [2]claytonm, [4]msurdeanu}@arizona.edu
[3]bambauer@law.ufl.edu

Abstract

This work presents a new task-aware prompt design and example retrieval approach for information extraction (IE) using a prompt chaining technique. Our approach divides IE tasks into two steps: (1) text classification to understand what information (e.g., entity or event types) is contained in the underlying text and (2) information extraction for the identified types. Initially, we use a large language model (LLM) in a few-shot setting to classify the contained information. The classification output is used to select the relevant prompt and retrieve the examples relevant to the input text. Finally, we ask a LLM to do the information extraction with the generated prompt. By evaluating our approach on legal IE tasks with two different LLMs, we demonstrate that the prompt chaining technique improves the LLM's overall performance in a few-shot setting when compared to the baseline in which examples from all possible classes are included in the prompt. Our approach can be used in a low-resource setting as it does not require a large amount of training data. Also, it can be easily adapted to many different IE tasks by simply adjusting the prompts. Lastly, it provides a cost benefit by reducing the number of tokens in the prompt.

1 Introduction

This work introduces a new prompt chaining technique for information extraction (IE) in the in-context learning (ICL) setting. Since the large language model (LLM)'s capability of handling various tasks in a few-shot setting has been demonstrated (Brown et al., 2020), many researchers have investigated using LLMs in the ICL setting.

A key challenge in this research area is example retrieval. Retrieving *good* examples for the prompt improves the performance of LLMs in the ICL setting (Gao et al., 2021; Liu et al., 2022). Different approaches have been made to retrieve good examples, but they rely mostly on semantic similarity with the underlying text. However, semantic similarity-based example retrieval does not guarantee good example quality. As Wan et al. (2023) indicates, there are cases where task-aware example retrieval works better. For example, when working on a IE task from a domain-specific document in which many sentences share high semantic similarity yet contain different types of information, retrieving examples based on the information *type* contained in each sentence is a better option than using a semantic similarity-based approach. There are a few works that present task-aware example retrieval techniques (Wan et al., 2023; Huang et al., 2023). However, the techniques are not easily adaptable because they require training or fine-tuning a model. They also focus on addressing specific tasks rather than general IE tasks.

Our approach with the prompt chaining technique provides an alternative to these methods as it does not involve any training nor fine-tuning. Also, it can be easily adapted to various IE tasks by simply adjusting prompts. The main idea of our approach is to split the IE tasks into two steps: (1) text classification and (2) information extraction. In the text classification step, an input text is classified based on the information contained in it. We prompt a LLM to do the text classification in a few-shot setting. The output from this step is used to retrieve examples of the relevant type(s) that are relevant to the input text. With the retrieved examples, the prompt for the information extraction is generated. Lastly, we ask a LLM to do the information extraction using the generated prompt.

Proceedings of the Natural Legal Language Processing Workshop 2024, pages 303–317
November 16, 2024 ©2024 Association for Computational Linguistics

The main contributions of this work are:

- This work introduces a new task-aware example retrieval technique using prompt chaining. This approach does not require any model training nor fine-tuning. It can be applied in the low-resource setting as it does not require training data. Also, this approach can be easily adapted to many IE tasks by simply adjusting the prompts.

- We demonstrate that the prompt chaining technique improves LLM's performance on the IE tasks in a few-shot setting when compared to the baseline model in which examples from all possible classes are included in the prompt. GPT-4's results show that in the in-domain dataset, the prompt chaining approach improves the F1 score by 3.41 percentage points for entity extraction (76.40% vs. 72.99%) and 3.68 percentage points for event extraction (67.02% vs. 63.34%) compared to the baseline. In the out-of-domain dataset, it also outperforms the baseline for entity extraction (56.89% vs. 54.97%) and event extraction (39.44% vs. 38.08%). GPT-4o mini shows a similar trend, with the prompt chaining boosting entity extraction by 1.52 percentage points (77.05% vs. 75.53%) and event extraction by 2.37 percentage points (70.67% vs. 68.30%) in-domain. Out-of-domain, it improves entity extraction by 0.71 percentage points (58.82% vs. 58.11%) and event extraction by 7.09 percentage points (42.13% vs. 35.04%).

- Employing the technique provides cost benefits by reducing the number of tokens contained in a prompt. In our evaluation, the prompt chaining approach is 6.99 times cheaper in input processing compared to the baseline model.

2 Related Work

2.1 Prompt Engineering Focusing on Example Retrieval

Recently there has been considerable research on prompt engineering techniques, focused particulary on example retrieval. Earlier works focus on retrieving examples that are semantically similar to the query. Gao et al. (2021) and Liu et al. (2022) use a k-nearest neighbors (NN) algorithm to retrieve examples that are semantically similar to the query.

More recent works train example retrievers to find examples with higher relevance to the input query. Rubin et al. (2022), Luo et al. (2023) and Li et al. (2023b) train dense retriever using the LLM's training signal. Wang et al. (2024) presents a framework which can be used to train dense retrievers iteratively by employing a reward model trained on the LLM's training signal.

Another approach emphasizes the inclusion of a wide range of examples, rather than just those that are semantically similar or relevant to the query. Ye et al. (2023) and Polat et al. use a Maximal Marginal Relevance-based approach to select examples that are not only relevant to the given query, but also complementary to each other. Mo et al. (2024) uses k-NN algorithm and a self-consistency retrieval strategy to include both correct/semantically similar examples and wrong/negative examples in the prompt. He et al. (2023) and Guo et al. (2024) focus on constructing diverse demonstrations to handle document information extraction and unified information extraction, respectively.

There are a few works that concentrate on task-aware retrieval. Wan et al. (2023) proposes two task-aware retrieval methods for relation extraction tasks: (1) entity-prompted sentence embedding and (2) fine-tuned relation representations. Huang et al. (2023) presents a API Entity-Relation Joint Extraction framework, which consists of a dynamic prompt generator and a joint entity-relation extractor. The work employs a BERT-based classifier to identify the top-3 candidate relations from an input text, generating a prompt that includes only examples relevant to these candidate relations.

Our work also concentrates on task-aware retrieval, but it differs from previous efforts in two aspects. First, our work does not involve any model training or fine-tuning. Both Wan et al. (2023) and Huang et al. (2023) require training or fine-tuning a model. Our approach can be applied in a low-resource setting as it does not require a large amount of training data. Second, our approach can be adapted to various types of IE tasks. If the prompt is adjusted properly, our approach can handle a variety of IE tasks ranging from entity extraction to complex event extraction. In contrast, Wan et al. (2023) and Huang et al. (2023) focus on addressing specific tasks (relation extraction and API entity and relation extraction).

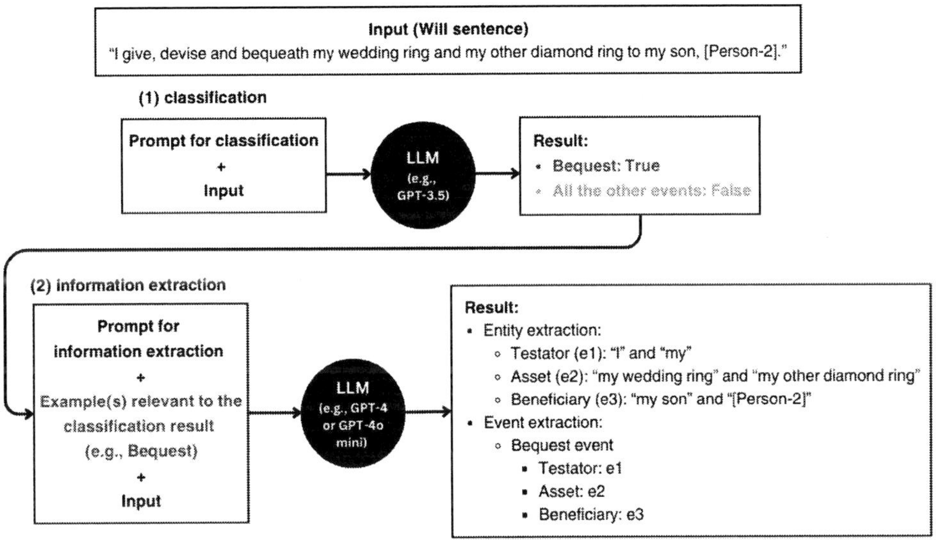

Figure 1: This figure shows an overview of our prompt chaining technique for information extraction. When an input text is given, it is first classified based on the information contained in it to understand which entities and events are likely to be present. We prompt an LLM (e.g., GPT-3.5 in this work) to do the text classification in a few-shot setting. Based on the text classification result, the examples for inclusion in the information extraction prompt are chosen. With the prompt completed with the chosen examples, we ask a second LLM (e.g., GPT-4 or GPT-4o mini in this work) to perform the information extraction task and produce the final result.

2.2 IE using LLMs with In-context Learning

With the rapid development of LLMs' capability in the ICL setting, many works investigate using LLMs in the ICL setting for various tasks, including information extraction. In particular, many works focus on named entity recognition (NER) and relation extraction (RE). For instance, Jimenez Gutierrez et al. (2022) evaluates GPT-3 on biomedical NER and RE in the ICL setting, while Kwak et al. (2023) examines GPT-4's performance in legal NER and RE. Additionally, Rajpoot and Parikh (2023) investigates LLMs for financial RE in the ICL setting. Wadhwa et al. (2023) evaluates GPT-3 and Flan-T5 on standard relation extraction tasks and reports that GPT-3 achieves near SOTA performance in the few-shot setting. Xu et al. (2023) experiments with GPT-3.5 to investigate if in-context learning and data generation enhance the model's performance on the few-shot RE. Li et al. (2023a) investigates the capabilities of LLMs on zero-shot RE. Wan et al. (2023) propose a new framework for RE using LLM in the ICL setting which utilizes task-aware example retrieval and incorporates gold label-induced reasoning logic into the demonstrations. Mo et al. (2024) presents a new example retrieval technique which utilizes both the correct/positive examples and the wrong/negative examples and evaluates it on NER and RE tasks.

There are a few works that address IE tasks other than NER or RE. He et al. (2023) proposes a new framework to perform IE from visually rich documents in the ICL setting. Peng et al. (2023) demonstrates how agricultural information, which includes entities, attributes, and descriptions, can be extracted from unstructured data using LLM in the zero-shot setting. Gao et al. (2023) assesses the LLM's generalizing capability to unseen information types and tasks in the ICL setting using the fine-grained IE benchmark dataset. Guo et al. (2024) proposes a framework for unified information extraction in the ICL setting utilizing diverse demonstrations.

Compared to NER and RE, event extraction in the ICL setting has been less investigated. Sun et al. (2024) evaluates the ChatGPT's capability of extracting pharmacovigilance events in the ICL setting and reports that it performs reasonably well when used with appropriate demonstration selection strategies. Further investigation is needed to confirm this finding, as the evaluation was conducted a specific task in a single domain (i.e., medical) using a single dataset. Our work addresses this gap by investigating event extraction in the ICL setting in a distinct domain (the legal one) using a different dataset.

3 Method

We introduce a new information extraction approach using prompt chaining. Prompt chaining is a concept introduced by Wu et al. (2022). It is a method that divides a complex task into multiple smaller steps and prompts an LLM in each step; the output from an earlier prompt becomes an input for the following prompt.

Huang et al. (2023) suggests that using a dynamic prompt containing the reduced number of examples relevant to each input text improves extraction accuracy. Their method for generating dynamic prompts involves training a BERT classifier. Unlike them, we investigate using the prompt chaining technique to generate a dynamic prompt without training or fine-tuning a model. We divide the IE task into two steps: (1) text classification, to understand which types are likely to be present in the underlying text, and (2) IE using prompts just for the likely types. Both steps are implemented using ICL and a vanilla LLM (i.e., not fine-tuned for the task). Figure 1 depicts our overall approach.

3.1 Few-shot Text Classification

We prompt a LLM to classify an input text based on the information that is contained in it, such as the types of entities or events that are mentioned. In this work, we perform text classification only based on the event types. This is because entities are included in the examples chosen based on the event types they participate in.[1]

Figure 2 shows the prompt for the text classification task (the first component of our method). The prompt consists of three parts: task instruction, format instruction, and example. The task instruction states the system's role and provides the full list of information types. The format instruction specifies the output format with a brief demonstration. The example demonstrates how the classification should be done using the chain-of-thought technique.

Text classification is implemented with GPT-3.5[2] in a three-shot setting. k value (for k-shot learning) was tuned on the development partition. The temperature is set to 0 and the maximum token size for the generation is set to 4096. The model's context size is 16,385 tokens.

Instruction (task)

Your task is to classify a will text based on the events contained in it.

Here's the list of events: WillCreation, Direction, Bequest, Nomination, SignWill, Attestation, Authorization, Revocation, Excuse.

Read the given will text carefully and evaluate if each event type is contained in the text.

Instruction (format)

You should produce the output in a python list format containing 0 and 1. If a will text contains an event type, then it's 1 and if it doesn't, then it's 0.

The order of the list should be [WillCreation, Direction, Bequest, Nomination, SignWill, Attestation, Authorization, Revocation, Excuse]. For example, if a will text contains a WillCreation event and a Revocation event, the expected output is [1, 0, 0, 0, 0, 0, 0, 1, 0].

Example

Let's consider a few example cases step by step.

%%

(1) Will text: I, [Person-1], domiciled in Ripley, Lauderdale County, Tennessee, do hereby make, publish, and declare this to be my Last Will and Testament, hereby revoking all wills and codicils heretofore made by me. (WillCreation, Revocation)

Expected output: [1, 0, 0, 0, 0, 0, 0, 1, 0]

Explanation: There's a phrase "make, publish, and declare this to be my Last Will and Testament". This suggests that the will text contains a WillCreation event. There's another phrase "revoking all wills and codicils". This shows that the will text contains a Revocation event.

%%

Instruction (task)

Following the instructions above, classify the will text below and give me the result in a python list (only the list).

Figure 2: The prompt for classification of events contained in text.

3.2 Few-Shot Information Extraction

We create a prompt for the information extraction task based on the text classification result. Depending on the information type that the text contains, the examples to be included in the prompt are decided. Suppose our task is to extract A, B, and C events from a given text. If the text classification output suggests that only an A event is present in the text, then we select k (1 or 5 in this work) examples that are relevant to the A event from an example pool. If there are more than k relevant examples available, we randomly select k from the set of relevant ones. The selected examples are added to the prompt for the information extraction task. An example sample in the actual output format can be found in Appendix A.

Once the prompt is completed with these exam-

[1]Texts containing the same event types typically feature similar types of entities.

[2]The model used in this work is `gpt-3.5-turbo-0125`. `https://platform.openai.com/docs/models/gpt-3-5-turbo`

Instruction (task)

Your task is to extract all instances of the following entities and events (including pronouns) from the will texts and output the extraction in JSON format.

%entities: Testator, Beneficiary, Witness, State, County, Asset, Bond, Executor, Date, Time, Trustee, Will, Codicil, Debt, Expense, Tax, Duty, Right, Condition, Guardian, Trust, Conservator, Affidavit, NotaryPublic, NonBeneficiary

%events: WillCreation, SignWill, Attestation, Revocation, Codicil, Bequest, Nomination, Disqualification, Renunciation, Death, Probate, Direction, Authorization, Excuse, Give, Notarization, NonProbateInstrumentCreation, Birth, Residual, Removal

Example & Format

Here's some examples of expected outputs in the desired format.

{Examples chosen based on the text classification result}

(e.g., If the classification result suggests that the input text contains Bequest event, the examples relevant to the Bequest event are added here)

Figure 3: The prompt for information extraction, containing only the examples of entities/events identified during the text classification step.

ples, we use it to ask a LLM to extract the information from the given text. Figure 3 shows the complete prompt. The prompt consists of instructions and examples. The instructions explain the task and provide the full list of information types to be extracted. The instructions are accompanied by examples chosen based on the classification output. The example demonstrates how the task should be completed while specifying the desired output format at the same time.

In this work, information extraction is done with GPT-4[3] and GPT-4o mini[4] in one-shot and five-shot settings. For both models, the temperature is set to 0, and the maximum token limit for generation is set to 4096. The context size for both models is 128,000 tokens.

4 Task and Evaluation

We evaluate our approach on the entity and event extraction tasks from the legal will dataset introduced by Kwak et al. (2023)[5]. We chose to do our evaluation on this legal task because wills contain highly diverse types of entities and events, and because the number of entity and event types is relatively large (see next subsection). Extracting many types of entities and events using the LLM in a standard few-shot setting can be challenging because the prompt should provide examples for all the entity and event types. These characteristics of the legal domain make it a good candidate for our approach, which focuses on (1) selecting examples with the same information type without depending on semantic similarity and (2) including only selected examples in the prompt.

4.1 Dataset and Task

We used the legal will dataset introduced by Kwak et al. (2023) for the evaluation. The dataset consists of wills from two US states: Tennessee and Idaho. The extractions from Tennessee wills are in-domain data while the ones from Idaho wills are out-of-domain (OOD) data. Tennessee and Idaho are considered different domains from the legal perspective since they have different probate codes (Kwak et al., 2023). The dataset contains 457 in-domain datapoints (will text segments, usually sentences) and 108 OOD datapoints. Among the 457 in-domain datapoints, 203 datapoints were used as an example pool and 145 datapoints were used as a development partition. The rest of the in-domain datapoints (109) and all of the OOD datapoints (108) were used as test partitions.

The dataset contains the annotations of 26 types of entities, 18 types of relations, and 20 types of events extracted from 45 wills. Our work focuses on extracting 25 types of entities (i.e., 26 entity types minus "Trigger") and 20 types of events.[6] In entity extraction, we identify key entities in wills, such as testator, beneficiary, executor, and asset. In event extraction, we capture key events in wills, which include will creation, signing will, bequest, nominations, and attestation. The full list of entities and events extracted in this work can be found in Appendix B. A detailed explanation of the entities and the events can be found in Kwak et al. (2023).

We prompt GPT-4 and GPT-4o mini to extract the entities and the events from given will text segments and output the result in JSON format. An example of entity and event extraction is shown as the Result in Figure 1. Although the prompt chaining technique improves example selection for

[3]The model used in this work is `gpt-4-1106-preview`. `https://platform.openai.com/docs/models/gpt-4-turbo-and-gpt-4`

[4]The model used in this work is `gpt-4o-mini-2024-07-18`. `https://platform.openai.com/docs/models/gpt-4o-mini`

[5]The dataset is licensed under CC BY-NC 4.0. Our use of the dataset is consistent with their intended use.

[6]Our primary interest lies in evaluating our approach on event extraction. Entity extraction is necessary for this purpose as entities function as arguments of events. We did not include relation extraction in our evaluation because it is less pertinent to our purpose.

Dataset	Setting	Model	Entity			Event		
			Precision	Recall	F1	Precision	Recall	F1
In domain	1-shot	Ceiling	*76.69 (0.98)*	*59.58 (1.85)*	*67.05 (1.36)*	*58.42 (0.14)*	*48.98 (0.72)*	*53.28 (0.36)*
		Prompt Chaining	76.85 (0.85)	60.08 (0.06)	67.44 (0.29)	55.06 (2.09)	45.80 (1.65)	50.00 (1.78)
		Full prompt	77.67 (0.39)	60.79 (0.92)	68.20 (0.67)	57.07 (2.34)	46.56 (2.55)	51.28 (2.48)
	5-shot	Ceiling	*84.38 (0.64)*	*70.92 (1.32)*	*77.06 (1.04)*	*73.05 (0.91)*	*65.14 (0.36)*	*68.87 (0.42)*
		Prompt Chaining	**83.49** (1.46)	**70.42** (1.71)	**76.40** (1.59)	**71.95** (1.51)	**62.72** (2.21)	**67.02** (1.88)
		Full prompt	82.09 (0.84)	65.71 (0.28)	72.99 (0.49)	70.51 (1.56)	57.51 (1.72)	63.34 (1.57)
OOD	1-shot	Ceiling	*65.43 (1.55)*	*47.12 (0.92)*	*54.78 (1.01)*	*45.40 (1.30)*	*32.72 (0.58)*	*38.02 (0.75)*
		Prompt Chaining	64.00 (0.58)	45.76 (0.66)	53.36 (0.64)	42.96 (0.88)	30.67 (0.88)	35.78 (0.88)
		Full prompt	67.58 (0.94)	49.35 (0.81)	57.04 (0.81)	45.42 (0.32)	31.08 (0.50)	36.90 (0.46)
	5-shot	Ceiling	*71.64 (0.08)*	*53.95 (0.56)*	*61.55 (0.39)*	*50.77 (2.13)*	*36.41 (0.77)*	*42.40 (1.17)*
		Prompt Chaining	**69.20** (1.28)	**52.59** (0.78)	**59.76** (0.93)	**50.53** (0.69)	**38.26** (0.95)	**43.55** (0.87)
		Full prompt	68.68 (1.02)	47.18 (0.98)	55.93 (0.86)	46.68 (0.77)	30.97 (0.63)	37.24 (0.69)

Table 1: GPT-4's results for the entity and event extraction tasks. The table shows the average scores from three-iteration experiments, with the standard deviation in parentheses. Overall, GPT-4 performs better in the 5-shot setting than a 1-shot setting. The model achieves the best F1 scores with the prompt chaining approach in both the in-domain dataset and the OOD dataset for both tasks. The results from the ceiling model (italicized) are given only to show the theoretical upper bound of our approach; they were not considered when determining the best scores because they were obtained from the ideal setting where the text classification is 100% correct.

a given input, our approach is still affected by the randomness within each example pool. To mitigate this, we run our experiment three times under the same settings and report the average scores from the three iterations, with standard deviations shown in parentheses.

4.2 Evaluator

We use an automatic scoring script that compares the LLM's outputs with the gold data. The automatic evaluator compares each entity and event in the LLM's output with the one in the gold data and finds matching pairs. Any entities or events that match more than 70% with the gold data are considered to be correct in this work. As several previous works have pointed out (Wadhwa et al., 2023; Polat et al.), the open-ended nature of outputs from LLMs makes it hard to evaluate them with the predefined standards. One solution to this is to manually review the outputs, but its cost would be too high. As an alternative, we have tested our automatic evaluator with varying thresholds (60–100%) for matching. The threshold is heuristically set at 70% as it best aligned with the human reviewer's judgments during manual evaluation. A more detailed explanation of the evaluation can be found in Appendix C.

4.3 Benchmark Models

We compare our approach against two models: a *ceiling* model and a strong baseline called *full prompt* model. The ceiling model presents the results from the ideal setting where the text classification result is 100% correct. In this case, the examples in the IE prompt were chosen based on the type of events present in the gold data. This model suggests a theoretical upper bound for our approach. The full prompt model shows the results from the setting where the prompt contains the examples for all the major event types.

5 Results

5.1 Text Classification Task

In the three-shot setting, the accuracy scores for the text classification task, the first component of our method, are 96.74 for the in-domain data and 93.21 for the OOD dataset respectively. The result from the text classification task suggests that GPT-3.5 performs the text classification task well in a few-shot setting.

5.2 Information Extraction Task

5.2.1 GPT-4

Table 1 presents GPT-4's results for the entity and event extraction tasks. This is the second component of our method, which produces the final output. The table shows the average scores from three-iteration experiments, with the standard deviation in parentheses. The scores suggest that GPT-4 performs better in the 5-shot setting than in the 1-shot setting for both the in-domain test dataset and the OOD dataset. Overall, the model shows the best performance with the prompt chaining approach as suggested by the highest F1 scores within each category. In the in-domain dataset, the

Dataset	Setting	Model	Entity			Event		
			Precision	Recall	F1	Precision	Recall	F1
In domain	1-shot	Ceiling	*80.71 (0.96)*	*60.48 (0.97)*	*69.14 (0.95)*	*65.30 (0.74)*	*52.16 (0.65)*	*57.99 (0.38)*
		Prompt Chaining	80.71 (1.34)	60.13 (1.32)	68.92 (1.32)	67.25 (1.96)	55.98 (2.52)	61.09 (2.28)
		Full prompt	80.62 (1.21)	62.56 (1.38)	70.45 (1.34)	71.49 (3.08)	53.82 (3.67)	61.40 (3.53)
	5-shot	Ceiling	*84.18 (0.57)*	*69.36 (0.48)*	*76.05 (0.52)*	*77.96 (3.02)*	*66.41 (2.04)*	*71.71 (2.29)*
		Prompt Chaining	**85.21** (0.41)	**70.31** (0.76)	**77.05** (0.57)	**77.42** (1.00)	**65.01** (1.30)	**70.67** (1.18)
		Full prompt	82.78 (0.52)	69.45 (1.01)	75.53 (0.73)	75.34 (1.90)	62.47 (0.95)	68.30 (1.17)
OOD	1-shot	Ceiling	*68.68 (2.06)*	*43.17 (1.28)*	*53.01 (1.57)*	*50.09 (0.12)*	*28.72 (0.52)*	*36.50 (0.45)*
		Prompt Chaining	68.37 (1.18)	40.74 (0.79)	51.06 (0.95)	48.17 (1.12)	27.38 (1.26)	34.91 (1.30)
		Full prompt	69.29 (1.82)	45.75 (1.01)	55.11 (1.31)	49.88 (2.08)	25.85 (1.40)	34.05 (1.70)
	5-shot	Ceiling	*74.28 (1.51)*	*50.46 (0.87)*	*60.08 (0.70)*	*58.23 (2.11)*	*33.44 (1.16)*	*42.48 (1.43)*
		Prompt Chaining	**72.69** (0.66)	49.40 (0.33)	**58.82** (0.16)	**57.23** (2.77)	**33.33** (1.63)	**42.13** (2.03)
		Full prompt	70.48 (1.73)	**49.43** (1.35)	58.11 (1.52)	49.70 (2.03)	27.08 (1.76)	35.04 (1.88)

Table 2: GPT-4o mini's results of the entity and event extraction tasks. The table shows the average scores from three-iteration experiments, with the standard deviation in parentheses. As with GPT-4, GPT-4o mini performs better in a 5-shot setting than the 1-shot setting. The model achieves the best F1 scores with the prompt chaining approach in both the in-domain dataset and the OOD dataset for both tasks. As mentioned earlier, results from the ceiling model (italicized) are given only to show the theoretical upper bound of our approach; they were not considered when determining the best scores because they were obtained from the ideal setting where the text classification is 100% correct.

F1 score from the prompt chaining approach is 3.41 percentage points higher than the one from the full prompt approach for the entity extraction (76.40% vs. 72.99%). For event extraction, the score difference is 3.68 percentage points (67.02% vs. 63.34%). The score difference is even larger in the OOD dataset (3.83 percentage points for the entity extraction and 6.31 percentage points for the event extraction). In both cases, the F1 scores achieved with the prompt chaining approach are higher than the ones achieved with the full prompt approach (59.76% vs. 55.93% for entity extraction and 43.55% vs. 37.24% for event extraction).

5.2.2 GPT-4o mini

Table 2 presents GPT-4o mini's results of the entity and event extraction tasks. As explained earlier, it shows the average scores from three-iteration experiments, with the standard deviation in parentheses. The scores indicate that GPT-4o mini performs better in the 5-shot setting than in the 1-shot setting for both the in-domain test dataset and the OOD dataset, similar to the trends observed for GPT-4. GPT-4o mini performed the best with the prompt chaining approach as suggested by the highest F1 scores within each category. In the in-domain dataset, the F1 score for entity extraction with prompt chaining is 1.52 percentage points higher than with the full prompt approach (77.05% vs. 75.53%), which aligns with the performance improvements seen for GPT-4. Similarly, for event extraction, the prompt chaining approach outperforms the full prompt method by 2.37 percentage points (70.67% vs. 68.30%). The OOD dataset shows a smaller score difference for entity extraction (0.71 percentage points) but a larger one for event extraction (7.09 percentage points). Overall, the F1 scores with the prompt chaining approach exceed those of the full prompt method, consistent with the findings for GPT-4, with scores of 58.82% vs. 58.11% for entity extraction and 42.13% vs. 35.04% for event extraction.

6 Discussion

6.1 Prompt Chaining vs. Full Prompt

As suggested by the higher F1 scores, both GPT-4 and GPT-4o mini perform better with the prompt chaining approach than in the full prompt approach in the 5-shot setting. However, in the OOD dataset, GPT-4o mini achieves a marginally higher recall score with the full prompt approach than it does with the prompt chaining approach for the entity extraction task (49.43% vs. 49.40%). It is also noticeable that for GPT-4, the difference in scores between the prompt chaining approach and the full prompt approach is smaller in precision compared to recall. Specifically, for entity extraction, the precision difference is 1.4 percentage points in the in-domain dataset and 0.52 percentage points in the out-of-domain dataset, while the recall difference is 4.71 percentage points in the in-domain dataset and 5.41 percentage points in the out-of-domain dataset. For event extraction, the precision difference is

1.44 percentage points in the in-domain dataset and 3.85 percentage points in the out-of-domain dataset, whereas the recall difference is 5.21 percentage points in the in-domain dataset and 7.28 percentage points in the out-of-domain dataset.

This tendency suggests that for GPT-4, the prompt chaining technique is more effective at reducing false negatives than reducing false positives. Providing examples specifically relevant to the input text helps the model focus on the targeted information, leading to fewer false negatives. In contrast, using a variety of example types (as in the full prompt approach) helps the model differentiate between relevant and irrelevant information, which reduces false positives. However, this pattern was not observed with GPT-4o mini, suggesting that this effect may be specific to the GPT-4 model.

Whether or not the tendency is present, the prompt chaining approach generally proves more effective than the full prompt approach when a sufficient number of examples is provided for each information type (e.g., in a 5-shot setting). This is supported by the fact that both GPT-4 and GPT-4o mini achieve higher F1 scores for entity and event extraction in both the in-domain and out-of-domain datasets when using the prompt chaining approach in the 5-shot setting.

6.2 1-Shot vs. 5-Shot

As previously noted, in the 1-shot setting, the models occasionally perform better with the full prompt approach compared to the prompt chaining approach. This is likely because the number of examples included in the prompt often becomes too small when using the prompt chaining approach in the 1-shot setting. On average, across the test and OOD datasets, the prompt chaining model includes 1.43 examples in the prompt, compared to 10 examples for the full prompt model. Considering the complexity of the task and the output format, 1.43 examples are not sufficient for the model to learn the details. The model occasionally makes formatting mistakes with the prompt-chaining approach in the 1-shot setting. This suggests that the model struggles to grasp the details of the output format from a few examples given.

In the 5-shot setting, at least 5 examples[7] are added to the prompt even in the prompt chaining scenario. As there are sufficient number of examples from which the model can learn the details of the task and the output format, the model does not show any formatting errors in the 5-shot setting.

Based on this observation, the prompt chaining approach should be used in the few-shot setting (e.g., 5-shot) rather than in the 1-shot setting to secure a sufficient number of examples, especially if the task and the output format are complex.

6.3 Ceiling vs. Prompt Chaining

The ceiling model offers the theoretical upper bound scores for the prompt chaining approach where the text classification is perfectly done. However, contrary to expectations, there are a few cases where the prompt chaining model *outperforms* the ceiling model. In the 5-shot setting, GPT-4 achieves a higher F1 score with the prompt chaining model compared to the ceiling model for event extraction in the OOD dataset (43.55% vs. 42.40%). Similarly in the 5-shot setting, GPT-4o mini obtains a higher F1 score with the prompt chaining model compared to the ceiling model for entity extraction in the test dataset (77.05% vs. 76.05%).

This can be explained by two factors: the high accuracy score for the text classification task in the test dataset (96.74%) and the randomness of the examples within the example pool for each information type. First, the accuracy of the text classification for the test dataset is very high: there are few cases where the classification results differ between the ceiling model and the prompt chaining model. This high accuracy likely stems from the formal language used in wills. This formality, aimed at ensuring clarity and legal precision, makes it easier for the model to classify these documents. Thus, the ceiling model offers little benefit over the prompt chaining model in the test dataset.

In addition, the randomness of examples within the example pool for each information type can contribute to the variability of the models' performance. The examples in the prompt are chosen based on the text classification result, but it does not guarantee consistent quality in the examples. To be precise, what is chosen is which information type's *example pool* is to be used, not the examples themselves. Once it is decided which information type's example pool is to be used, examples for the prompt are randomly selected from within the pool. The quality of each example varies within

[7]When there is no major event included in the given input, it is classified as containing the 'Etc.' event and the examples for the 'Etc.' event type (which also does not contain any major event) are added. This is to prevent cases where no example is added to the prompt.

the example pool. Some examples contain rich information while others do not. Therefore, it is possible that the examples' randomness can affect the models' performance. If the prompt chaining model is randomly given examples with rich information while the ceiling model is randomly given examples that contain less information, it is possible that the prompt chaining model could exceed the ceiling model.

6.4 Performance Decrease in Out-of-Domain

The performance of the LLMs (both GPT-4 and GPT-4o-mini) shows a marked decline on out-of-domain (OOD) data. For the entity extraction task, F1 scores in the in-domain setting range from 67.05 to 77.06, while in the OOD setting, they drop to a range of 51.06 to 61.55. Similarly, for the event extraction task, F1 scores range from 50.00 to 71.71 in-domain, but fall to 34.05 to 43.55 in the OOD scenario. This trend is consistent across all three models tested (ceiling, prompt-chaining, and full-prompt), with no approach showing a significantly larger drop in performance. This suggests that the performance degradation is more likely due to domain differences rather than any specific fault of the models themselves.

The error analysis of the OOD partition suggests that the performance decline is at least partially due to differences in formality between the two domains (i.e., Tennessee wills and Idaho wills). Idaho operates under a different probate code than Tennessee, and the template for drafting wills also varies. Idaho wills often include clauses that are uncommon in Tennessee wills. For example, declarations of marital status and/or children are frequently included at the beginning of Idaho wills, whereas such declarations rarely appear in Tennessee wills. Another example is the inclusion of no-contest clauses, which prevent beneficiaries from contesting the will. These clauses are common in Idaho wills but infrequent in Tennessee. This variation in formality leads to high error rates, as there are few relevant examples available for such cases.

6.5 Cost-Efficiency of Prompt Chaining

The prompt chaining approach not only improves the overall performance of the model, but also provides cost benefits. By using only examples that are relevant to information contained in the input text, it allows the prompt to have smaller tokens than with the full prompt approach has. As the API services for the LLM bill their clients based on token number, reducing the number of tokens in the prompt offers benefits in terms of lower cost.

For example, in our work, the average number of tokens per example is 468.89, and each input text contains an average of 1.43 information types. For the full prompt approach, we use the examples for the 10 major event types[8]. With a quick calculation, we conclude that the input for the prompt chaining approach contains 4018.39 ($468.89 \times 10 - 468.89 \times 1.43 = 4018.39$) fewer tokens compared to the full prompt approach, making the input processing cost 6.99 times cheaper (10/1.43 = 6.99) in our case. As demonstrated by this example, the prompt chaining approach offers cost benefits while also improving the model's overall performance on the task.

7 Conclusion

This work introduces a new prompt chaining technique for information extraction. The key idea of this approach is to split the information extraction into two steps: (1) text classification to understand which entity/event types are likely to be present, and (2) information extraction for the identified types. Both steps are implemented using an LLM with in-context learning. By classifying each input text based on the information type present in it first, we can complete the prompt for the information extraction task with the examples that are relevant to each input text. With the completed prompt, we ask a LLM to conduct the information extraction task. We evaluate this technique on entity and event extraction tasks in the legal domain. The evaluation results demonstrate that the prompt chaining technique improves the model's overall performance. The prompt chaining approach also provides cost benefits by reducing the number of tokens in the prompt. The code used in this work can be found at: `https://github.com/ml4ai/pc4wills/`

8 Limitations

The prompt chaining technique introduced in our work can be adapted to various IE tasks and used in different domains. However, we evaluated the technique with only a few models (i.e., GPT-4 and

[8]The 10 major event types include 9 event types listed in the text classification prompt plus the 'Etc.' event type. Any event type that either (1) does not occur independently of other event types (e.g., 'Death' event type does not occur on its own; it always accompanies other event type as it is used as a condition for another event.) or (2) has less than 50 occurrences across all the datasets falls under 'Etc.' category.

GPT-4o-mini) and a single dataset. Our findings need to be confirmed with further evaluation on different models and/or datasets. Even though the prompt chaining technique helps select better examples for the given input, our approach is still prone to the randomness of the examples within each example pool as discussed in the section 6.3. Using a semantic similarity-based technique for ICL example selection in conjunction with ours might mitigate this issue, as they are complementary to each other. Further investigation is needed to confirm this hypothesis.

Acknowledgments

We thank the reviewers for their thoughtful comments and suggestions. This work was partially supported by the National Science Foundation (NSF) under grant #2217215, and by University of Arizona's Provost Investment Fund. Mihai Surdeanu and Clayton Morrison declares a financial interest in lum.ai. This interest has been properly disclosed to the University of Arizona Institutional Review Committee and is managed in accordance with its conflict of interest policies.

References

Tom B. Brown, Benjamin Mann, Nick Ryder, Melanie Subbiah, Jared Kaplan, Prafulla Dhariwal, Arvind Neelakantan, Pranav Shyam, Girish Sastry, Amanda Askell, Sandhini Agarwal, Ariel Herbert-Voss, Gretchen Krueger, Tom Henighan, Rewon Child, Aditya Ramesh, Daniel M. Ziegler, Jeffrey Wu, Clemens Winter, Christopher Hesse, Mark Chen, Eric Sigler, Mateusz Litwin, Scott Gray, Benjamin Chess, Jack Clark, Christopher Berner, Sam McCandlish, Alec Radford, Ilya Sutskever, and Dario Amodei. 2020. Language models are few-shot learners. In *Proceedings of the 34th International Conference on Neural Information Processing Systems*, NIPS '20, Red Hook, NY, USA. Curran Associates Inc.

Jun Gao, Huan Zhao, Yice Zhang, Wei Wang, Changlong Yu, and Ruifeng Xu. 2023. Benchmarking large language models with augmented instructions for fine-grained information extraction. *Preprint*, arXiv:2310.05092.

Tianyu Gao, Adam Fisch, and Danqi Chen. 2021. Making pre-trained language models better few-shot learners. In *Proceedings of the 59th Annual Meeting of the Association for Computational Linguistics and the 11th International Joint Conference on Natural Language Processing (Volume 1: Long Papers)*, pages 3816–3830, Online. Association for Computational Linguistics.

Qian Guo, Yi Guo, and Jin Zhao. 2024. Diluie: Constructing diverse demonstrations of in-context learning with large language model for unified information extraction. *Neural Computing and Applications*.

Jiabang He, Lei Wang, Yingpeng Hu, Ning Liu, Hui juan Liu, Xingdong Xu, and Hengtao Shen. 2023. Icl-d3ie: In-context learning with diverse demonstrations updating for document information extraction. *2023 IEEE/CVF International Conference on Computer Vision (ICCV)*, pages 19428–19437.

Qing Huang, Yanbang Sun, Zhenchang Xing, Min Yu, Xiwei Xu, and Qinghua Lu. 2023. Api entity and relation joint extraction from text via dynamic prompt-tuned language model. *ACM Trans. Softw. Eng. Methodol.*, 33(1).

Bernal Jimenez Gutierrez, Nikolas McNeal, Clayton Washington, You Chen, Lang Li, Huan Sun, and Yu Su. 2022. Thinking about GPT-3 in-context learning for biomedical IE? think again. In *Findings of the Association for Computational Linguistics: EMNLP 2022*, pages 4497–4512, Abu Dhabi, United Arab Emirates. Association for Computational Linguistics.

Alice Kwak, Cheonkam Jeong, Gaetano Forte, Derek Bambauer, Clayton Morrison, and Mihai Surdeanu. 2023. Information extraction from legal wills: How well does GPT-4 do? In *Findings of the Association for Computational Linguistics: EMNLP 2023*, pages 4336–4353, Singapore. Association for Computational Linguistics.

Guozheng Li, Peng Wang, and Wenjun Ke. 2023a. Revisiting large language models as zero-shot relation extractors. In *Findings of the Association for Computational Linguistics: EMNLP 2023*, pages 6877–6892, Singapore. Association for Computational Linguistics.

Xiaonan Li, Kai Lv, Hang Yan, Tianyang Lin, Wei Zhu, Yuan Ni, Guotong Xie, Xiaoling Wang, and Xipeng Qiu. 2023b. Unified demonstration retriever for in-context learning. In *Proceedings of the 61st Annual Meeting of the Association for Computational Linguistics (Volume 1: Long Papers)*, pages 4644–4668, Toronto, Canada. Association for Computational Linguistics.

Jiachang Liu, Dinghan Shen, Yizhe Zhang, Bill Dolan, Lawrence Carin, and Weizhu Chen. 2022. What makes good in-context examples for GPT-3? In *Proceedings of Deep Learning Inside Out (DeeLIO 2022): The 3rd Workshop on Knowledge Extraction and Integration for Deep Learning Architectures*, pages 100–114, Dublin, Ireland and Online. Association for Computational Linguistics.

Man Luo, Xin Xu, Zhuyun Dai, Panupong Pasupat, Mehran Kazemi, Chitta Baral, Vaiva Imbrasaite, and Vincent Y Zhao. 2023. Dr.icl: Demonstration-retrieved in-context learning. *Preprint*, arXiv:2305.14128.

Ying Mo, Jian Yang, Jiahao Liu, Shun Zhang, Jingang Wang, and Zhoujun Li. 2024. C-icl: Contrastive in-context learning for information extraction. *Preprint*, arXiv:2402.11254.

Ruoling Peng, Kang Liu, Po Yang, Zhipeng Yuan, and Shunbao Li. 2023. Embedding-based retrieval with llm for effective agriculture information extracting from unstructured data. *Preprint*, arXiv:2308.03107.

Fina Polat, Ilaria Tiddi, and Paul Groth. Testing prompt engineering methods for knowledge extraction from text.

Pawan Rajpoot and Ankur Parikh. 2023. GPT-FinRE: In-context learning for financial relation extraction using large language models. In *Proceedings of the Sixth Workshop on Financial Technology and Natural Language Processing*, pages 42–45, Bali, Indonesia. Association for Computational Linguistics.

Ohad Rubin, Jonathan Herzig, and Jonathan Berant. 2022. Learning to retrieve prompts for in-context learning. In *Proceedings of the 2022 Conference of the North American Chapter of the Association for Computational Linguistics: Human Language Technologies*, pages 2655–2671, Seattle, United States. Association for Computational Linguistics.

Zhaoyue Sun, Gabriele Pergola, Byron Wallace, and Yulan He. 2024. Leveraging ChatGPT in pharmacovigilance event extraction: An empirical study. In *Proceedings of the 18th Conference of the European Chapter of the Association for Computational Linguistics (Volume 2: Short Papers)*, pages 344–357, St. Julian's, Malta. Association for Computational Linguistics.

Somin Wadhwa, Silvio Amir, and Byron Wallace. 2023. Revisiting relation extraction in the era of large language models. In *Proceedings of the 61st Annual Meeting of the Association for Computational Linguistics (Volume 1: Long Papers)*, pages 15566–15589, Toronto, Canada. Association for Computational Linguistics.

Zhen Wan, Fei Cheng, Zhuoyuan Mao, Qianying Liu, Haiyue Song, Jiwei Li, and Sadao Kurohashi. 2023. GPT-RE: In-context learning for relation extraction using large language models. In *Proceedings of the 2023 Conference on Empirical Methods in Natural Language Processing*, pages 3534–3547, Singapore. Association for Computational Linguistics.

Liang Wang, Nan Yang, and Furu Wei. 2024. Learning to retrieve in-context examples for large language models. In *Proceedings of the 18th Conference of the European Chapter of the Association for Computational Linguistics (Volume 1: Long Papers)*, pages 1752–1767, St. Julian's, Malta. Association for Computational Linguistics.

Tongshuang Wu, Michael Terry, and Carrie Jun Cai. 2022. Ai chains: Transparent and controllable human-ai interaction by chaining large language model prompts. In *Proceedings of the 2022 CHI Conference on Human Factors in Computing Systems*, CHI '22, New York, NY, USA. Association for Computing Machinery.

Xin Xu, Yuqi Zhu, Xiaohan Wang, and Ningyu Zhang. 2023. How to unleash the power of large language models for few-shot relation extraction? In *Proceedings of The Fourth Workshop on Simple and Efficient Natural Language Processing (SustaiNLP)*, pages 190–200, Toronto, Canada (Hybrid). Association for Computational Linguistics.

Xi Ye, Srinivasan Iyer, Asli Celikyilmaz, Veselin Stoyanov, Greg Durrett, and Ramakanth Pasunuru. 2023. Complementary explanations for effective in-context learning. In *Findings of the Association for Computational Linguistics: ACL 2023*, pages 4469–4484, Toronto, Canada. Association for Computational Linguistics.

A Example for the Information Extraction Task


```
{
    "text": "II (A) I give, devise and
        bequeath all my property, real,
        personal and mixed, of whatever
        kind and nature and wheresoever
        situated, to my wife, [Person
        -2], if she survives me.",
    "entities": [
        {
            "id": "e1",
            "texts": [
                "all my property, real,
                    personal and mixed,
                    of whatever kind and
                     nature and
                    wheresoever situated
                    "
            ],
            "type": "Asset"
        },
        {
            "id": "e2",
            "texts": [
                "if she survives me"
            ],
            "type": "Condition"
        },
        {
            "id": "e3",
            "texts": [
                "my",
                "I",
                "me"
            ],
            "type": "Testator"
        },
        {
            "id": "e4",
            "texts": [
                "my wife",
                "[Person-2]",
                "she"
            ],
            "type": "Beneficiary"
        }
    ],
    "events": [
        {
            "id": "v1",
            "type": "Bequest",
            "Asset": [
                "e1"
            ],
            "Condition": [
                "e2"
            ],
            "Testator": [
                "e3"
            ],
            "Beneficiary": [
                "e4"
            ]
        }
    ]
}
```


B Data Taxonomy

Below is a list of the entities and events extracted during our task. Each entity is accompanied by a description, while each event includes both a description and its associated arguments. The descriptions in this list were sourced from Kwak et al. (2023).

- Entities
    - *Testator*: a person who makes a will
    - *Beneficiary*: a person or an entity (e.g., organization) that receives something from a will
    - *Executor*: a person who executes a will (=personal representative)
    - *Witness*: a person witnessing a will
    - *Trustee*: a person who manages a trust
    - *Guardian*: a person who has a legal right and responsibility of taking care of someone who cannot takes care of themselves (usually a minor or an legally incompetent person)
    - *Conservator*: a person who handles the financial and personal affairs who cannot handles such affairs by themselves (usually a minor or an legally incompetent person)
    - *Notary Public*: a person who is authorized by state government to witness the signing of important documents and administer oaths
    - *Non-Beneficiary*: a person who is excluded from being beneficiary
    - *State*: any US state names
    - *County*: any US county names
    - *Date*: any dates
    - *Time*: any expression denoting a particular point in time
    - *Condition*: a condition under which an event (e.g., will execution, bequest, etc.) occurs
    - *Asset*: any money, personal property, or real estate owned by a testator
    - *Bond*: any bonds (usually probate bonds, which is a type of bond ordered and required by a court before they will appoint a person or entity as the personal representative of an estate)
    - *Debt*: any debts

- *Expense*: any expenses
- *Tax*: any taxes
- *Trust*: a fiduciary arrangement that allows a trustee to hold assets on behalf of a beneficiary
- *Duty*: any duty directed by a testator to fiduciaries (e.g., executors, trustees, guardians, or conservators)
- *Right*: any rights authorized by a testator to fiduciaries (e.g., executors, trustees, guardians, or conservators)
- *Will*: a legal document containing a person's wishes regarding the disposal of one's asset after death
- *Codicil*: a testamentary or supplementary document that modifies or revokes a will or part of a will
- *Affidavit*: a legal statement sworn and signed by a testator and witnesses to confirm the validity of a will (usually attached to a will)

• Events

- *Will Creation*: an event in which a testator creates a will
  * Testator
  * Will
  * Condition
- *Sign Will*: an event in which a testator or a witness signs a will
  * Testator
  * Will
  * Date
  * Condition
- *Attestation*: an event in which a witness attests the validity of a will
  * Witness
  * Attested events (e.g., Sign Will)
- *Revocation*: an event in which a testator revokes a will or a codicil
  * Testator
  * Will
  * Codicil
- *Codicil*: an event in which a codicil is made
  * Testator
  * Codicil
  * Time
- *Bequest*: an event in which a testator bequeath asset to a beneficiary
  * Testator
  * Asset
  * Beneficiary
  * Condition
- *Nomination*: an event in which a testator nominates a fiduciary
  * Testator
  * Executor
  * Trustee
  * Guardian
  * Conservator
  * Condition
- *Disqualification*: an event in which a beneficiary or a fiduciary is disqualified
  * Executor
  * Beneficiary
- *Renunciation*: an event in which a fiduciary renounces
  * Executor
- *Death*: an event in which any entity (e.g., testator, beneficiary, executor, etc.) dies
  * Testator
  * Beneficiary
  * Executor
- *Probate*: an event in which a will or any part of the will is probated
  * Will
  * Debt
  * Expense
  * Tax
  * Expense
  * Condition
  * Time
- *Direction*: an event in which a testator gives direction to someone (usually a fiduciary)
  * Testator
  * Executor
  * Duty
  * Directed events (e.g., Excuse)
- *Authorization*: an event in which a testator authorizes a fiduciary to a right
  * Testator
  * Executor
  * Right
  * Condition

- *Excuse*: an event in which a testator excuses a fiduciary from a duty
  * Testator
  * Executor
  * Duty
  * Bond
- *Give*: an event in which a testator gives a compensation to a fiduciary
  * Testator
  * Executor
  * Asset
  * Time
  * Condition
- *Notarization*: an event in which an affidavit is notarized by a notary public
  * Notary Public
  * Date
- *Non Probate Instrument Creation*: an event in which a non probate instrument (e.g., trust) is created
  * Testator
  * Asset
  * Trust
  * Condition
- *Birth*: an event in which a beneficiary is born
  * Beneficiary
  * Date
- *Residual*: an event in which asset becomes residuary estate
  * Asset
  * Condition
- *Removal*: an event in which a beneficiary is removed from a will
  * Beneficiary
  * Condition

C Description of Evaluation

The evaluator compares LLM's outputs against gold data, utilizing advanced similarity metrics for both entities and events. It comprises several key components:

1. Optimal matching: It is essential to match predicted entities and events with those in the gold data, as data contains multiple entities and events. The evaluator implements a greedy approach to identify optimal pairings between the predicted and the gold data. It operates at both the list level (for entity matching) and the dictionary level (for event matching).

2. Similarity Computation: The evaluator implements two distinct approaches: a) For entities: A weighted combination of type matching and text similarity. b) For events: A set-based comparison of key-value pairs, excluding the 'id' field. Similarity is calculated as the ratio of common values to total unique values across both dictionaries. True positives (TP), false positives (FP), and false negatives (FN) for both entities and events are calculated based on similarity thresholds.

3. Metrics Calculation: The evaluator computes precision, recall, and F1 score based on the TP, FP, and FN counts calculated earlier.

The evaluator employs a similarity threshold to determine whether the predicted output matches the gold data. The threshold in this work is heuristically set at 70% as it best aligned with the human reviewer's judgments. Below are the examples that received a similarity score of over 70%:

- Entity:
  - Gold data: my will (type: Will)
  - Predicted output: this my will (type: Will)
  - Similarity score: 73.68%
- Event:
  - Gold data:
    {'id': 'v1',
    'type': 'Authorization',
    'Condition': ['e1'],
    'Executor': ['e2'],
    'Testator': ['e3'],
    'Right': ['e4']}
  - Predicted output:
    {'id': 'v1',
    'type': 'Authorization',
    'Right': ['e1', 'e4'],
    'Executor': ['e2'],
    'Testator': ['e3']}
  - Similarity score: 75%

In both cases, the difference between the gold data and the predicted output is not significant. For the entity, the only variation is the addition of "this" before "my will", which is not necessarily incorrect. In the case of the event, the predicted output categorized one entity (e1) differently, but this distinction does not significantly impact the overall results.

The examples below are the ones that received a similarity score of less than 70%:

- Entity:
  - Gold data: Idaho (type: County)
  - Predicted output: Buhl, Idaho (type: County)
  - Similarity score: 62.5%
- Event:
  - Gold data:
    {'id': 'v4',
    'type': 'Probate',
    'Tax': ['e2'],
    'Expense': ['e3', 'e14'],
    'Debt': ['e12'],
    'Condition': ['e10']}
  - Predicted output:
    {'id': 'v2',
    'type': 'Probate',
    'Expense': ['e3', 'e14'],
    'Debt': ['e12'],
    'Condition': ['e4']}
  - Similarity score: 66.67%

The difference between the gold data and the predicted output is more prominent in these cases. For example, it is evident that "Buhl, Idaho" is an incorrect extraction for county. It is also clear that the event from the predicted output misses a key argument ('Tax') and incorrectly identifies a condition ('e4' instead of 'e10').

The code and additional details can be found at: `https://github.com/ml4ai/pc4wills/`

Augmenting Legal Decision Support Systems with LLM-based NLI for Analyzing Social Media Evidence

Ram Mohan Rao Kadiyala *
University of Maryland
rkadiyal@umd.edu

Siddartha Pullakhandam *
University of Wisconsin
pullakh2@uwm.edu

Kanwal Mehreen
Traversaal.ai
kanwal@traversaal.ai

Subhasya Tippareddy
University of South Florida
subhasyat@usf.edu

Ashay Srivastava
University of Maryland
ashays06@umd.edu

Abstract

This paper presents our system description and error analysis of our entry for NLLP 2024 shared task on Legal Natural Language Inference (L-NLI) (Hagag et al., 2024). The task required classifying these relationships as entailed, contradicted, or neutral, indicating any association between the review and the complaint. Our system emerged as the winning submission, significantly outperforming other entries with a substantial margin and demonstrating the effectiveness of our approach in legal text analysis. We provide a detailed analysis of the strengths and limitations of each model and approach tested, along with a thorough error analysis and suggestions for future improvements. This paper aims to contribute to the growing field of legal NLP by offering insights into advanced techniques for natural language inference in legal contexts, making it accessible to both experts and newcomers in the field.

1 Introduction

In today's digital age, vast amounts of information circulate online, creating an overwhelming stream of text that spans news articles, social media, and user-generated content. Within this unstructured data, legal violations often remain hidden, blending into the surrounding noise. Legal violations frequently leave behind data traces. To identify these traces and detect violations, prior research in Legal NLI (Koreeda and Manning, 2021) has typically utilized specialized models designed for particular domain applications (Silva et al., 2020) (Yu et al., 2020). Uncovering these violations is not only crucial for upholding individual rights and ethical standards, but also for maintaining societal justice in an increasingly digital world. Addressing this challenge requires more than traditional methods. While existing models have proven effective within their specialized domains, they lack the flexibility needed to tackle the complex and varied nature of legal violations found in diverse online contexts. Our work seeks to bridge this gap by leveraging advanced language models for the nuanced task of Legal Natural Language Inference (L-NLI), as part of the NLLP 2024 shared task. The aim was to classify relationships between legal complaints and reviews as either entailed, contradicted, or neutral. In this study, we implemented a range of techniques, including multi-layered fine-tuning and alignment strategies, to enhance text classification. We experimented with several LLMs, such as Gemma (Team, 2024), Phi3 (Abdin, 2024), Zephyr (Tunstall et al., 2023), LLaMA (Dubey et al., 2024), Mistral (Jiang et al., 2023), OpenHermes (Teknium, 2023) and Qwen (Yang et al., 2024) refining each model for optimal performance. These approaches proved highly effective, with our system outperforming other entries by a large margin. Beyond technical achievements, we present a thorough error analysis, highlighting where the models excelled / struggled. Through our findings, we aim to advance the field of legal NLP, making complex legal analysis accessible to a wider audience, while pushing the boundaries of NLI in legal domain. The code and models used in the official submission and the later found best model can be found here. [1] [2]

* equal contribution

[1] https://github.com/1-800-SHARED-TASKS/EMNLP-2024-NLLP

[2] https://huggingface.co/collections/1-800-SHARED-TASKS/

Proceedings of the Natural Legal Language Processing Workshop 2024, pages 318–325
November 16, 2024 ©2024 Association for Computational Linguistics

2 Dataset

The dataset for the NLI task consists of a legal premise (a summary of resolved class-action cases) and a corresponding hypothesis (an online media text). The training and test splits of the dataset consist of 312 and 84 samples. For the initial fine-tuning, the test and validation subsets of the SNLI dataset (Bowman et al., 2015) were used consisting of 20000 samples. The distributions of each of the training sets and the test set can be seen in Table 1. The original dataset (Bernsohn et al., 2024) used had just 312 rows, the aggregation of datasets is explained in detail in Appendix. The length of the texts are both mostly 4-7 sentences long in both the premise and hypothesis.

	Train-1	Train-2	Test
Entailed	34.0%	32.7%	47.6%
Neutral	33.1%	33.9%	34.5%
Contradict	32.9%	33.3%	17.9%

Table 1: Distributions of each class in each data split
* Train-1 is a subset of SNLI dataset , Train-2 is the NLLP dataset

3 System Description

Various LLMs were tested with and without additional training data or additional training stages. They were also tested with various alignment approaches in various configurations. The metrics obtained on the test set with each of these approaches/models can be seen in Table 2. The official metric used was Macro F1 score [F1]. Additionally accuracy [A], precision [P] and recall [R] were also reported.

3.1 Multi-stage Learning

Given the small size of the existing training dataset (312 samples), we have additionally tested multi-stage learning by first fine-tuning over a subset of 20000 rows from the SNLI dataset to first let the models adapt to generic NLI tasks with a lower learning rate and then further fine-tuned the resultant models on the NLLP training samples with a higher learning rate. Additionally we have tested using additional training data from previous works (more in Appendix). Both of these approaches did result in better performance. An overview of the process can be seen in Figure 1.

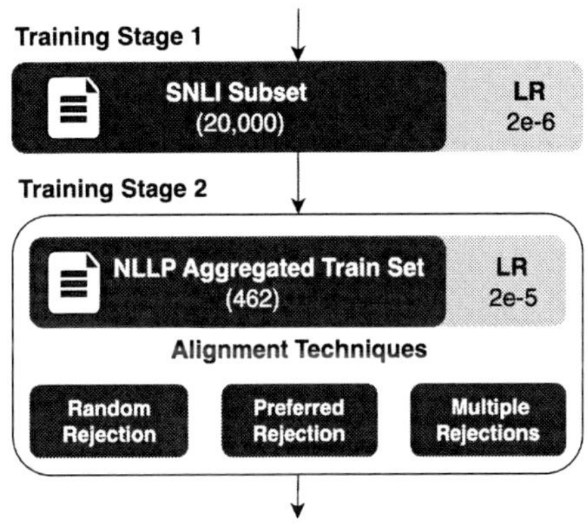

Figure 1: Multi-stage Training Overview

3.2 Alignment approaches used

We have tested using ORPO (Hong et al., 2024) during fine-tuning using various LLMs in 3 different configurations i.e the rejected sample being a) random, b) preferred and c) multiple rejected samples. The usage of ORPO did improve the performance over all of the domains in any of the configurations.

3.2.1 Random Rejection

In this approach, the actual label being the accepted response would lead to the rejected response being a random class form the remaining two. The results did improve compared to not using ORPO but by a very slight margin.

3.2.2 Preferred Rejection

In cases where the actual label is Neutral, a random label is chosen as the rejected sample among the other two. We chose 'Neutral' as the rejected response when the actual label is either Entailed or Contradict. The reason being all of the errors being one of the other two classes being labelled as 'Neutral or vice versa. This did improve the performance significantly by reducing the mis-classified samples between Neutral and the other classes.

3.2.3 Multiple Rejections

In this approach, while the label class would be the accepted class, both the other two classes were added as the rejected samples. Although this was computationally expensive, the results were close to those from preferred rejection approach.

4 Error Analysis

We were able to completely avoid Type-1 errors i.e classification of 'Entailed' as 'Contradict' and

emnlp-2024-nllp-66e7af534b7e708a36db02df

LLM Used	Trained on	Alignment approach	A	P	R	F1
GEMMA-2-27B	NLLP*	None	0.857	0.871	0.894	0.871
GEMMA-2-27B	NLLP	None	0.857	0.859	0.891	0.865
Mistral-8x7B	NLLP*	None	**0.869**	0.877	**0.902**	0.881
QWEN-2-7B	NLLP*	None	0.833	0.828	0.868	0.839
QWEN-2-7B	NLLP	None	0.821	0.852	0.869	0.842
Phi-3-Medium	NLLP*	None	0.821	0.853	0.813	0.820
OpenHermes-13B	NLLP*	None	0.774	0.820	0.832	0.803
GEMMA-2-27B	SNLI, NLLP*	None	**0.869**	0.866	0.899	0.874
GEMMA-2-27B	SNLI, NLLP	None	0.821	0.828	0.862	0.831
GEMMA-2-27B	SNLI, NLLP*	ORPO Random	0.845	0.852	0.882	0.855
GEMMA-2-27B	NLLP*	ORPO Multiple	0.833	0.842	0.860	0.840
GEMMA-2-27B	SNLI, NLLP*	ORPO Preferred	**0.869**	**0.885**	**0.902**	**0.887**
Mistral-NEMO	NLLP*	ORPO Multiple	**0.869**	0.867	0.890	0.877
Phi-3-Medium	NLLP*	ORPO Multiple	0.845	0.872	0.833	0.838
Zephyr-7B	NLLP*	ORPO Multiple	0.810	0.838	0.858	0.832
Phi-3-Medium‘	NLLP‘	ORPO Multiple‘	*0.845‘*	*0.884‘*	*0.844‘*	*0.853‘*
baseline	-	-	-	-	-	0.807

Table 2: Metrics on the test set with some of the approaches/models tested
* Indicated aggregated train set of NLLP (more in appendix)
‘ indicates official submission

vice versa, limiting the error cases to Type-2 errors i.e classification of 'Neutral' as another and vice versa. Confusion matrix of our models' predictions on the test set can be seen in Figure 2 and Figure 3.

It can be observed from both Figure 2 and Figure 3 that most common case of errors was those being mis-classified among Neutral and Entailed. We found these to be cases where the hypothesis consisted of multiple sentences which entail the premise followed by a vague / unrelated statement, while some are to be labelled as 'Entailed' and rest as 'Neutral' based on the perceived tone/feeling of the user, it would be likely that there might not be consensus among human annotators as well in many such cases. It is worth looking into the performance of models trained on not just the labels, but also the reasoning of the annotators on why a certain label was chosen, as it might help the model learn better.

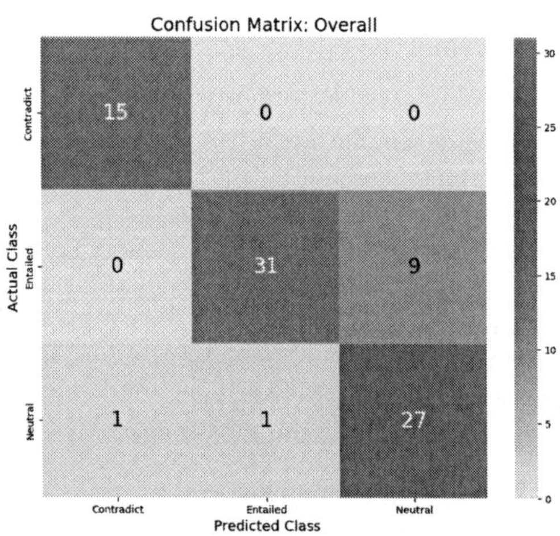

Figure 2: Confusion Matrix : Our system's (best) predictions over the test set

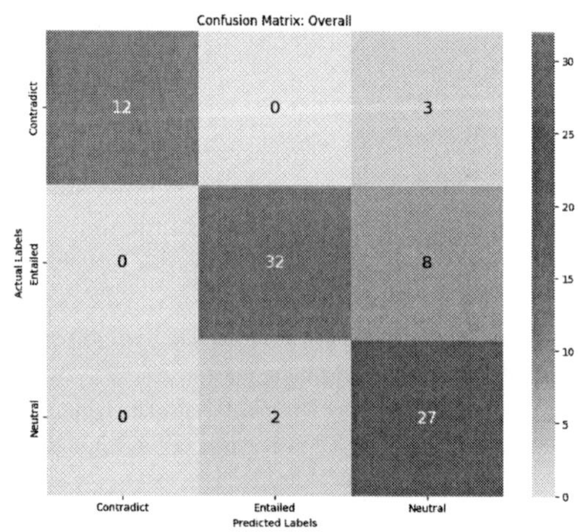

Figure 3: Confusion Matrix : Our system's (submission) predictions over the test set

Legal act	in Train set	Domain	in Test set	A	P	R	F1
Privacy	229	BIPA	22	0.73	0.80	0.86	0.77
		Data-Breach	20	0.95	0.96	0.95	0.95
		VPPA	6	1.00	1.00	1.00	1.00
TCPA	111	TCPA	9	0.89	0.89	0.93	0.90
Consumer	102	Consumer	8	0.88	0.92	0.92	0.90
WAGE	20	WAGE	19	0.89	0.80	0.92	0.83
Overall(best)	-	-	-	**0.87**	**0.89**	**0.90**	**0.89**
Overall(submission)	-	-	-	**0.85**	**0.89**	**0.84**	**0.85**

Table 3: Performance of our models on the test set : Domain wise

4.1 Performance on each Domain

The performance of our system on each domain in the test set can be seen in Table 3. The metrics obtained on most of the domains were significantly higher than that of the baseline. The system worked well on all domains, however comparatively weaker on BIPA which was imbalanced in the training set.

5 Scope For Improvement

As seen in Table 3 the performance across each domain varied by a significant margin. However, the domains over which some models underperformed, some other performed well. It is likely that using ensembles can improve the performance by a considerable margin.

5.1 Low training data

Some cases did get misclassified too often especially those whose domain data was less represented in the training dataset. From what was observed from comparison of performance over original and aggregated datasets and the models with and without SNLI fine-tuning step involved, It can be determined that more training data would improve the performance considerably especially the domains with less data.

5.2 Individual Annotations availability

In models built using Preferred Rejection, cases with Neutral as the label had used a random label from the other two as the rejected sample. However availability of individual annotations might provide more info on what choice of rejected label might lead to better results compared to choosing a rejected label at random.

6 Conclusion

Compared to the well known SNLI dataset which consist of premise and hypothesis pair which are usually one or two sentences long, the current dataset has texts (both premise and hypothesis) which are roughly four times longer leading to more complexity. Since, the SNLI dataset has a 98% consensus and 58% unanimous annotation among 5 annotators, it can be expected that a human annotation on the current dataset can lead to even less proportion of texts where a consensus or unanimous vote can be reached. Yet, our models were able to provide a reliable performance completely avoiding Type-1 errors, performing better than human annotations expected from those with domain knowledge, hinting at a potential of practical applicability.

Limitations

Due to computational resource limitations, the base models of LLMs were initially loaded in 4-bit precision, It is likely that a larger model used in full-precision might perform better. Since the test dataset used in the task is relatively small, the LLMs/approaches that might perform better in practical scenarios may vary from those found to be better on the current dataset.

Ethics Statement

Automating the identification of legal violations may inadvertently generate false positives or negatives, potentially impacting individual rights and the integrity of the legal system. Therefore, we emphasize that our models are intended to complement, not replace, legal professionals. It is critical that any use of our models is approached with caution, recognizing the inherent limitations and biases that automated systems may present.

References

et al. Abdin, Marah. 2024. Phi-3 technical report: A highly capable language model locally on your phone.

Dor Bernsohn, Gil Semo, Yaron Vazana, Gila Hayat, Ben Hagag, Joel Niklaus, Rohit Saha, and Kyryl Truskovskyi. 2024. Legallens: Leveraging llms for legal violation identification in unstructured text.

Samuel R. Bowman, Gabor Angeli, Christopher Potts, and Christopher D. Manning. 2015. A large annotated corpus for learning natural language inference.

William Bruno and Dan Roth. 2022. Lawngnli: A long-premise benchmark for in-domain generalization from short to long contexts and for implication-based retrieval.

Alexis Conneau, Douwe Kiela, Holger Schwenk, Loic Barrault, and Antoine Bordes. 2018. Supervised learning of universal sentence representations from natural language inference data.

Abhimanyu Dubey, Abhinav Jauhri, Abhinav Pandey, Abhishek Kadian, Ahmad Al-Dahle, Aiesha Letman, Akhil Mathur, Alan Schelten, Amy Yang, Angela Fan, et al. 2024. The llama 3 herd of models. *arXiv preprint arXiv:2407.21783*.

Neel Guha, Julian Nyarko, Daniel Ho, Christopher Ré, Adam Chilton, Aditya K, Alex Chohlas-Wood, Austin Peters, Brandon Waldon, Daniel Rockmore, Diego Zambrano, Dmitry Talisman, Enam Hoque, Faiz Surani, Frank Fagan, Galit Sarfaty, Gregory Dickinson, Haggai Porat, Jason Hegland, Jessica Wu, Joe Nudell, Joel Niklaus, John Nay, Jonathan Choi, Kevin Tobia, Margaret Hagan, Megan Ma, Michael Livermore, Nikon Rasumov-Rahe, Nils Holzenberger, Noam Kolt, Peter Henderson, Sean Rehaag, Sharad Goel, Shang Gao, Spencer Williams, Sunny Gandhi, Tom Zur, Varun Iyer, and Zehua Li. 2023. Legalbench: A collaboratively built benchmark for measuring legal reasoning in large language models. In *Advances in Neural Information Processing Systems*, volume 36, pages 44123–44279. Curran Associates, Inc.

Ben Hagag, Liav Harpaz, Gil Semo, Dor Bernsohn, Rohit Saha, Pashootan Vaezipoor, Kyryl Truskovskyi, and Gerasimos Spanakis. 2024. Legallens shared task 2024: Legal violation identification in unstructured text.

Jiwoo Hong, Noah Lee, and James Thorne. 2024. Orpo: Monolithic preference optimization without reference model.

John Hudzina, Kanika Madan, Dhivya Chinnappa, Jinane Harmouche, Hiroko Bretz, Andrew Vold, and Frank Schilder. 2020. Information extraction/entailment of common law and civil code. In *JSAI International Symposium on Artificial Intelligence*, pages 254–268. Springer.

Albert Q Jiang, Alexandre Sablayrolles, Arthur Mensch, Chris Bamford, Devendra Singh Chaplot, Diego de las Casas, Florian Bressand, Gianna Lengyel, Guillaume Lample, Lucile Saulnier, et al. 2023. Mistral 7b. *arXiv preprint arXiv:2310.06825*.

Daniel Martin Katz, Dirk Hartung, Lauritz Gerlach, Abhik Jana, and Michael J. Bommarito II au2. 2023. Natural language processing in the legal domain.

Yuta Koreeda and Christopher D. Manning. 2021. Contractnli: A dataset for document-level natural language inference for contracts.

Alice Kwak, Gaetano Forte, Derek E Bambauer, and Mihai Surdeanu. 2023. Transferring legal natural language inference model from a us state to another: What makes it so hard? In *Proceedings of the Natural Legal Language Processing Workshop*.

Alice Saebom Kwak, Jacob O. Israelsen, Clayton T. Morrison, Derek E. Bambauer, and Mihai Surdeanu. 2022. Validity assessment of legal will statements as natural language inference.

Paulo Silva, Carolina Gonçalves, Carolina Godinho, Nuno Antunes, and Marilia Curado. 2020. Using nlp and machine learning to detect data privacy violations. In *IEEE INFOCOM 2020 - IEEE Conference on Computer Communications Workshops (INFOCOM WKSHPS)*, pages 972–977.

Joe Stacey, Pasquale Minervini, Haim Dubossarsky, and Marek Rei. 2022. Logical reasoning with span-level predictions for interpretable and robust nli models.

et al. Team, Gemma. 2024. Gemma 2: Improving open language models at a practical size.

Teknium. 2023. Openhermes-13b.

Lewis Tunstall, Edward Beeching, Nathan Lambert, Nazneen Rajani, Kashif Rasul, Younes Belkada, Shengyi Huang, Leandro von Werra, Clémentine Fourrier, Nathan Habib, Nathan Sarrazin, Omar Sanseviero, Alexander M. Rush, and Thomas Wolf. 2023. Zephyr: Direct distillation of lm alignment.

An Yang, Baosong Yang, Binyuan Hui, Bo Zheng, Bowen Yu, Chang Zhou, Chengpeng Li, Chengyuan Li, Dayiheng Liu, Fei Huang, et al. 2024. Qwen2 technical report. *arXiv preprint arXiv:2407.10671*.

Zhanye Yang. 2022. Legalnli: natural language inference for legal compliance inspection. In *International Conference on Advanced Algorithms and Neural Networks (AANN 2022)*, volume 12285, pages 144–150. SPIE.

Yaoquan Yu, Yuefeng Guo, Zhiyuan Zhang, Mengshi Li, Tianyao Ji, Wenhu Tang, and Qinghua Wu. 2020. Intelligent classification and automatic annotation of violations based on neural network language model. In *2020 International Joint Conference on Neural Networks (IJCNN)*, pages 1–7.

A Training Data Aggregation

Due to training dataset provided being not large enough, we have used additional training data which include the dataset from the LegalLens paper. The aggregated training dataset used is what was obtained by merging both the datasets, upon removal of duplicates.

- Current Dataset huggingface.co/datasets/darrow-ai/LegalLensNLI-SharedTask : 312 training samples
- Additional Dataset huggingface.co/datasets/darrow-ai/LegalLensNLI : 312 training samples
- Aggregated Dataset huggingface.co/datasets/1-800-SHARED-TASKS/EMNLP-2024-NLLP : 462 training samples

B System Replication

We have used each of the LLMs tested by loading them in 4bit precision before fine-tuning on each dataset in both the training stages using LoRA. The hyper parameters used in each of the training stages can be seen in Table 4. The hyper parameters not specified below were used with their default values in both stages. The code used can be found here : github.com/1-800-SHARED-TASKS/EMNLP-2024-NLLP.

parameter	Stage-1 (SNLI)	Stage-2 (NLLP)
Learning Rate	2e-6	2e-5
Max Length (tokens)	1024	2048
LoRA alpha	32	16
LoRA dropout	0	0
beta	0.1	0.1
random state	1024	1024
number of epochs	1	3
loaded prev. model as	fp4	fp32

Table 4: Hyperparameters used in each training stage

C Models used / SNLI version of LLMs

The models used in the paper including the best performing model and the one used in the official submission can be found here :

- Best performing model : huggingface.co/1-800-SHARED-TASKS/EMNLP-NLLP-NLI-GEMMA2-27B-withSNLI-withORPO
- Model used for submission : huggingface.co/1-800-SHARED-TASKS/EMNLP-NLLP-NLI-PHI3-medium-withoutSNLI-withORPO

Additionally the models obtained after fine-tuning LLMs used on the SNLI dataset can be found here :

- GEMMA NLI : huggingface.co/1-800-SHARED-TASKS/GEMMA2-27B-NLI-16bit
- PHI3 NLI : huggingface.co/1-800-SHARED-TASKS/PHI3-Medium-NLI-16bit

D Performance of both models : domain wise

The performance of our best performing model (GEMMA-2-27B-SNLI) can be seen below followed by those from our submission model (PHI-3-SNLI).

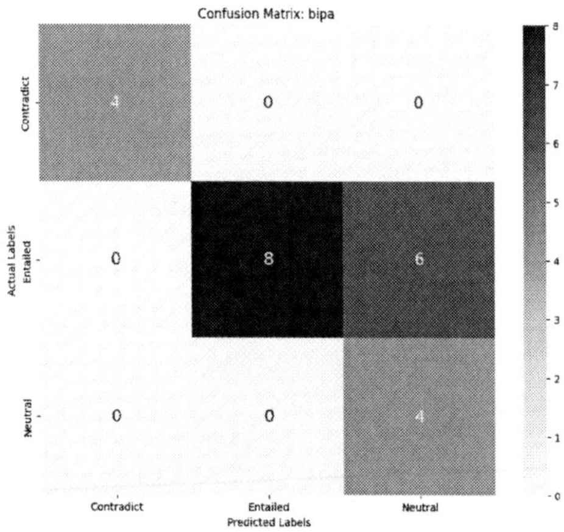

Figure 4: performance on test set : GEMMA2-SNLI : BIPA

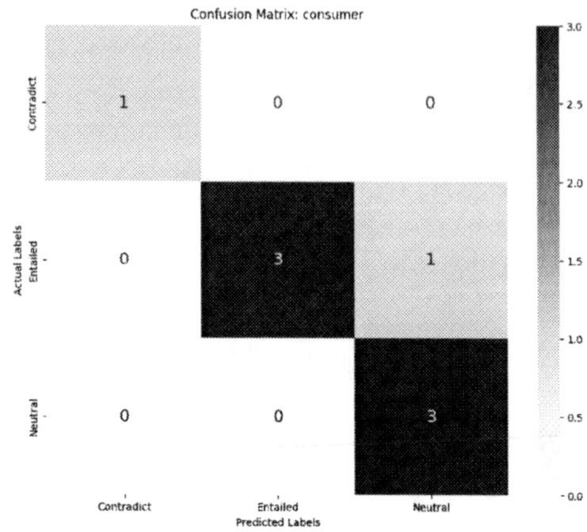

Figure 5: performance on test set : GEMMA2-SNLI : Consumer

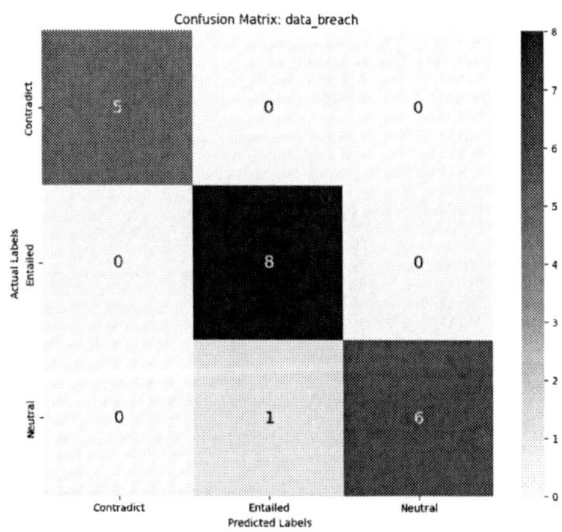

Figure 6: performance on test set : GEMMA2-SNLI : Data Breach

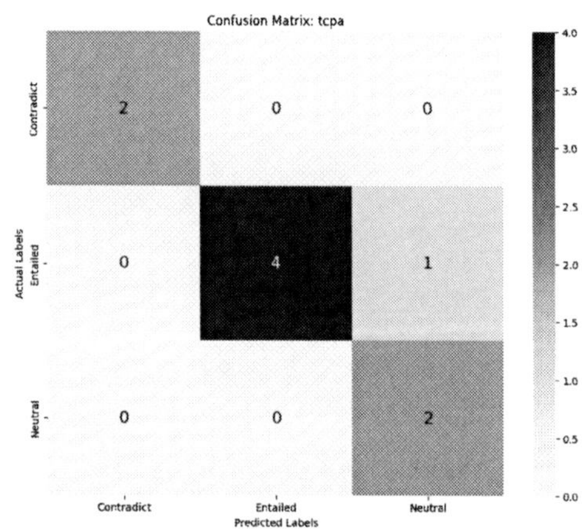

Figure 7: performance on test set : GEMMA2-SNLI : TCPA

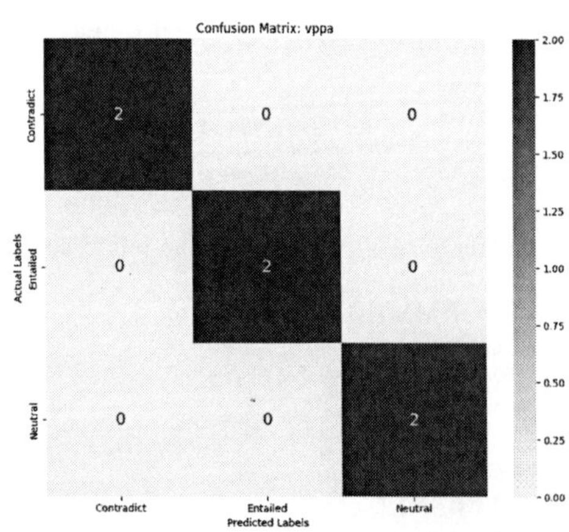

Figure 8: performance on test set : GEMMA2-SNLI : VPPA

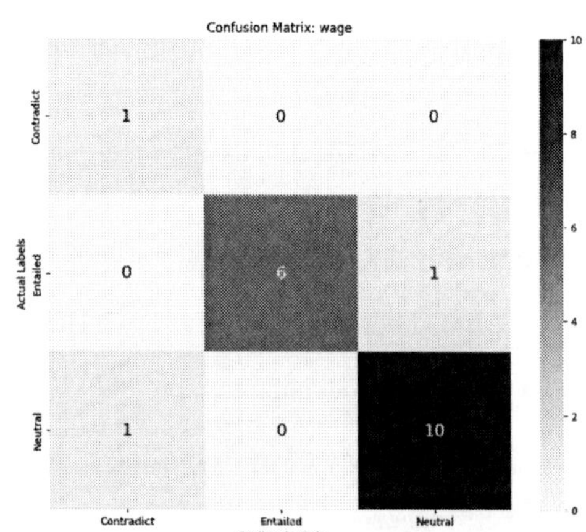

Figure 9: performance on test set : GEMMA2-SNLI : WAGE

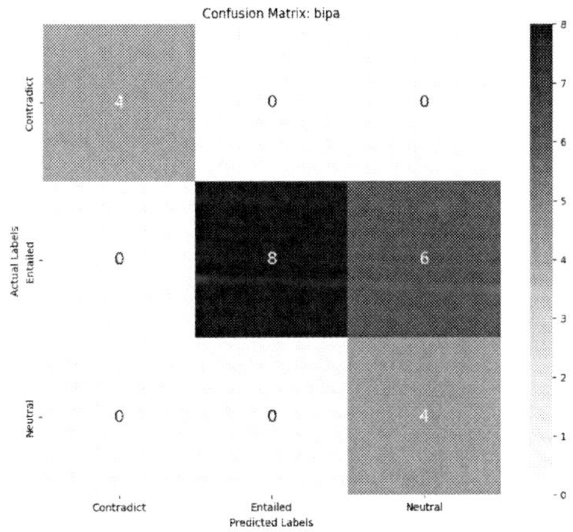

Figure 10: performance on test set : PHI3-SNLI : BIPA

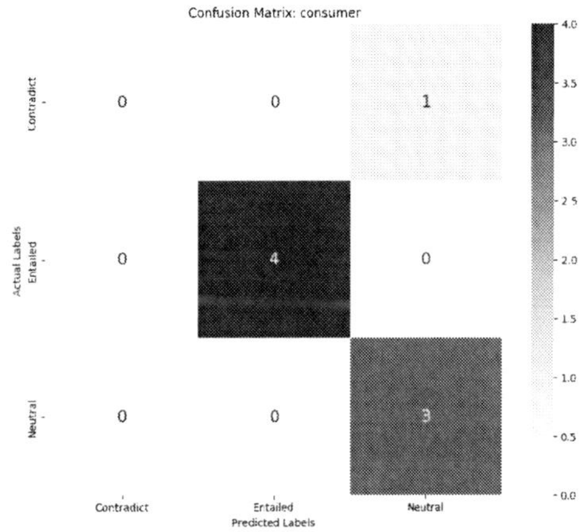

Figure 11: performance on test set : PHI3-SNLI : Consumer

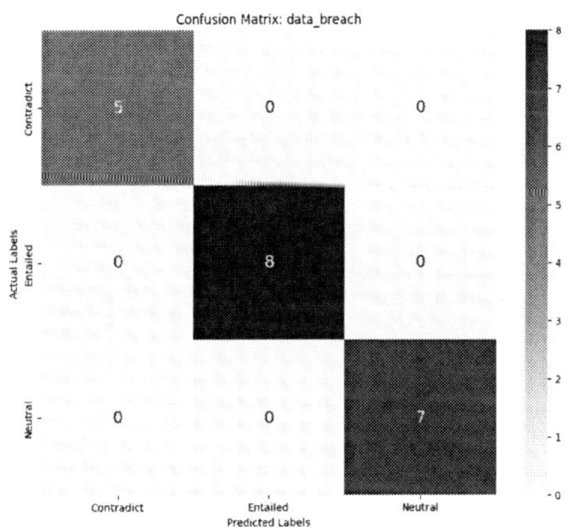

Figure 12: performance on test set : PHI3-SNLI : Data Breach

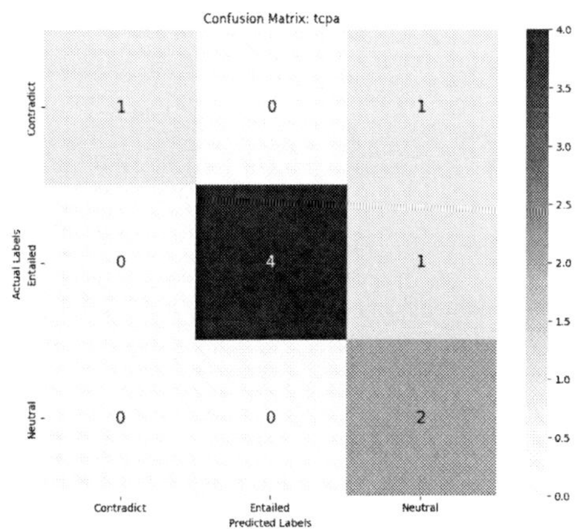

Figure 13: performance on test set : PHI3-SNLI : TCPA

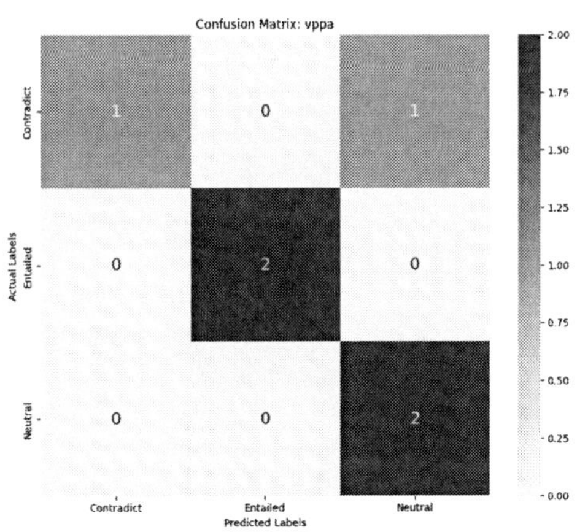

Figure 14: performance on test set : PHI3-SNLI : VPPA

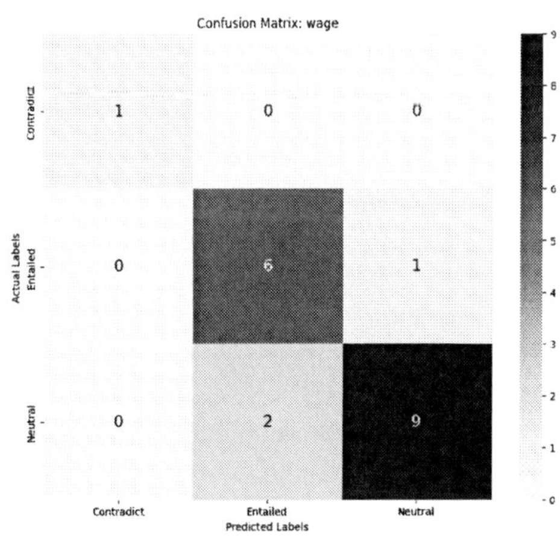

Figure 15: performance on test set : PHI3-SNLI : WAGE

Empowering Air Travelers: A Chatbot for Canadian Air Passenger Rights

Maksym Taranukhin[1] **Sahithya Ravi**[2,3] **Gábor Lukács**[4]
Evangelos Milios[1] **Vered Shwartz**[2,3]
[1] Faculty of Computer Science, Dalhousie University
[2] Department of Computer Science, University of British Columbia
[3] Vector Institute for AI [4] Air Passenger Rights
{m.t,eem}@cs.dal.ca, {sahiravi,vshwartz}@cs.ubc.ca,
lukacs@airpassengerrights.ca

Abstract

The Canadian air travel sector has seen a significant increase in flight delays, cancellations, and other issues concerning passenger rights. Recognizing this demand, we present a chatbot to assist passengers and educate them about their rights. Our system breaks a complex user input into simple queries which are used to retrieve information from a collection of documents detailing air travel regulations. The most relevant passages from these documents are presented along with links to the original documents and the generated queries, enabling users to dissect and leverage the information for their unique circumstances. The system successfully overcomes two predominant challenges: understanding complex user inputs, and delivering accurate answers, free of hallucinations, that passengers can rely on for making informed decisions. A user study comparing the chatbot to a Google search demonstrated the chatbot's usefulness and ease of use. Beyond the primary goal of providing accurate and timely information to air passengers regarding their rights, we hope that this system will also enable further research exploring the tradeoff between the user-friendly conversational interface of chatbots and the accuracy of retrieval systems.[1]

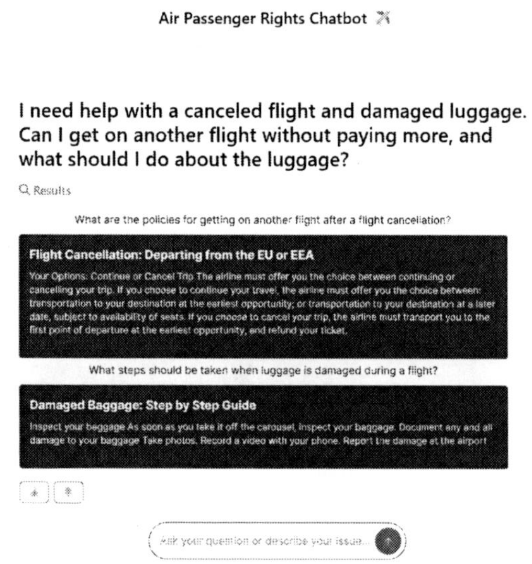

Figure 1: User interface of the Air Passenger Rights chatbot.

1 Introduction

Air travel in Canada has seen many challenges when it comes to passenger rights. Canada's deficient regulations lag behind the standards adopted by other Western countries such as members of the European Union (Air Passenger Rights, 2022). Canada also lacks meaningful enforcement of passengers' existing rights by the federal regulator, whose cozy relationship with the airline industry and impartiality has been questioned by a Parliamentary committee (Badawey, 2021) and by the judiciary (Federal Court of Appeal, 2021). This situation has led to a high number of questions from passengers trying to understand their rights and find solutions. A group of dedicated volunteers[2] is handling these questions, providing information on the rights and options available to affected passengers. However, the growing number of inquiries calls for a more efficient, automated solution to ensure quick and accurate responses.

To address this issue, we propose a chatbot (Figure 1) that can adeptly understand narratives detailing air travel concerns and extract pertinent information from relevant sources. Our goal is to streamline the process of informing and educating passengers about their rights and options, ultimately empowering them to make informed decisions. This will reduce the workload of the human volunteers, allowing them to focus on the more

[1]The code is available at https://github.com/maksym-taranukhin/apr_chatbot

[2]https://airpassengerrights.ca

Proceedings of the Natural Legal Language Processing Workshop 2024, pages 326–335
November 16, 2024

complex questions from users.

Crucially, this application has a very low tolerance for errors and hallucinations, which may cost passengers time and money. Tellingly, in a recent incident, a chatbot developed by Air Canada provided incorrect information, leading to negative consequences for both the passenger and the airline.[3] Our chatbot is designed to mitigate such risks via retrieval from a reliable collection of documents.

Our approach simplifies complex questions, ensures systematic coverage of different aspects, and enhances search efficiency. Furthermore, to prevent hallucinations, we do not generate a response to the user based on the extracted information, as in the traditional RAG approach. Instead, we present the generated queries and the relevant passages from the source documents to the user. This method allows users to directly view the authoritative information that is relevant to their input, which they can then apply to their specific circumstances.

We conducted an extensive user study to evaluate the chatbot's performance across several dimensions: usefulness, user satisfaction, ease of use, and ease of learning. The results indicated that the chatbot was highly effective at providing pertinent information quickly and efficiently. The participants also reported that the chatbot's interface was more convenient than a manual Google search. Also, we compared our system to a standard RAG-based system and found that the latter had a hallucination rate of 27.5%, which exceeds the acceptable threshold. In contrast, our chatbot produced zero hallucinations, highlighting its reliability in delivering accurate information.

In terms of the application itself, the proposed chatbot is first a prototype. Given the users' preference for the chatbot over a Google search, we are encouraged to develop future versions of the chatbot that are more conversational and that further contextualize the answers, while maintaining a strict zero-hallucination policy. The importance of this research goes beyond assisting air passengers; it introduces a way of using recent advances in NLP to provide legal information with greater accessibility and accuracy, especially in areas with complex regulations such as law and medicine.[4]

[3]`https://bc.ctvnews.ca/air-canada-s-chatbot-gave-a-b-c-man-the-wrong-information-now-the-airline-has-to-pay-for-the-mistake-1.6769454`

[4]Video demo is available here.

2 Chatbot Architecture

Our chatbot architecture, which is depicted in Figure 2, is composed of 2 main components. The *query understanding* component (Sec 2.1) is responsible for interpreting the user input and generating a series of simpler queries. These queries go into the *document retrieval* component (Sec 2.2) which is tasked with extracting relevant information from the knowledge base. Finally, the extracted information is formatted and the answer is presented to the user (Sec 2.3).

2.1 Input Understanding

The query understanding component is specifically designed to handle complex and multi-part questions that require a nuanced understanding of context, intent, and the relationships between different pieces of information. In our chatbot, this component is built upon the GPT-4 model (OpenAI, 2023) and in-context learning to perform the following two key tasks.

Decontextualization. Given a dialogue history and the current user input, the contextual query isolation component rephrases the current user input into a standalone text. For example, if the user input contains coreferences, such as referring to the previously mentioned airline using the pronoun "they", the contextual query isolation component will resolve these coreferences by replacing "they" with "the airline". This task can be considered a form of decontextualization in a dialogue context (Choi et al., 2021) and is crucial for ensuring that the user input can be understood and processed independently of its preceding conversation. See Appendix A for the prompt.

Decompositional Query Generation. Once isolated, the user input undergoes decompositional query generation where the goal is to dissect the standalone complex query into simpler, more manageable sub-questions. Consider the example in Figure 2, where the user asks a question related to two distinct issues, namely, flight cancellation and damaged luggage. Decompositional query generation would parse this complex question into two simpler sub-questions focusing on each of the issues separately. Therefore, such division into discrete, more precise inquiries targets specific aspects of the original query, allowing for a more focused and efficient information retrieval process (Perez et al., 2020). See Appendix A for the prompt.

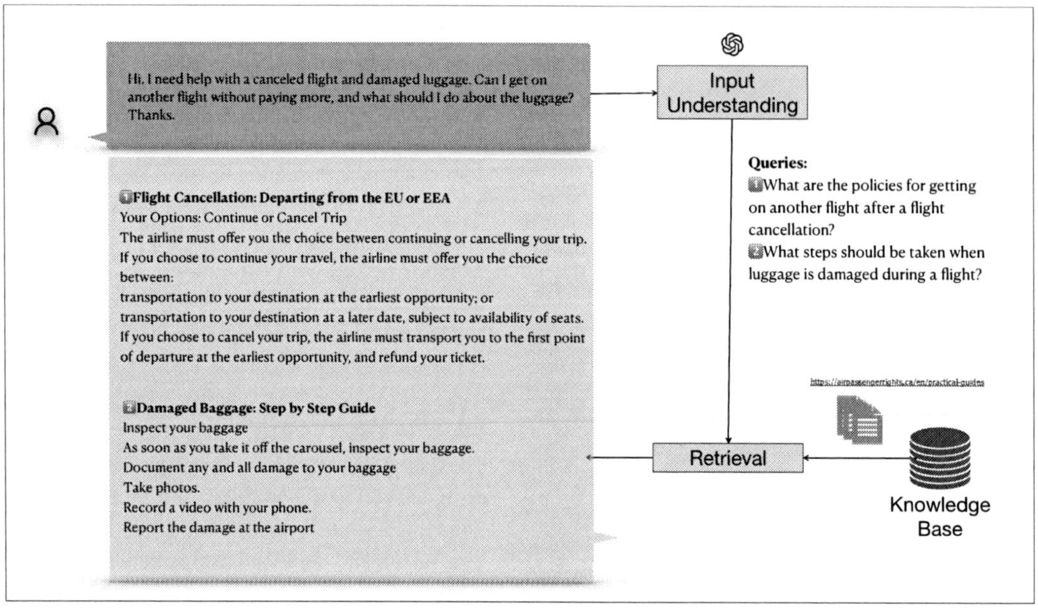

Figure 2: Overall Architecture of the Air Passenger Chatbot exemplified on an input query from the user: We use a LLM to decontextualize and decompose a given query, and provide a response by retrieving the relevant passages to answer the simplified queries.

2.2 Document Retrieval

The document retrieval component is responsible for extracting relevant information from the knowledge base using the queries generated by the complex query understanding component. The document retrieval component employs a dense retrieval approach (Karpukhin et al., 2020) to find the most relevant passages from the knowledge base for each generated query. Our dense retrieval approach uses OpenAI embeddings to encode both the queries and the documents into a high-dimensional space, and then uses cosine similarity to identify the top 5 relevant documents with scores greater than 0.7 for each query. We remove queries from the results if no relevant documents are found for them.

2.3 Answer Presentation

Once the relevant information is retrieved, the chatbot presents the information to the user in a structured manner as shown in Figure 1. For each generated query, the chatbot provides the query and the corresponding passages from the source documents. This approach allows users to view the authoritative information that is relevant to their query, which they can then apply to their specific circumstances. By presenting the information in this way, the chatbot ensures that users receive accurate and reliable information, reducing the risk of model hallucinations that could occur if the system were to generate synthesized responses as in the traditional RAG architecture.

3 Implementation Details

3.1 Data Collection

Our chatbot utilizes a specialized knowledge base (KB), tailored specifically for addressing a variety of passenger issues in the Canadian air travel sector. This KB consists of domain-specific documents that extensively cover air travel regulations, with an emphasis on practical solutions for common problems such as flight delays, baggage mishandling, and boarding difficulties.

To construct this KB, we collected data from 88 web pages with regulatory details, step-by-step guidelines for resolving travel issues, a glossary of legal terminology, and other pertinent information. The documents were sourced primarily from two sections: the Practical Guides on the Air Passenger Rights website[5] and the Know Your Rights section from the Canadian Air Passenger Protection website.[6] We split all the documents (except step-by-step guides) by HTML headers to improve the

[5] https://airpassengerrights.ca/en/practical-guides

[6] https://rppa-appr.ca/eng/know-your-rights

precision of the retriever and to reduce information overload when the document is presented to the user.

3.2 Web Application

The chatbot is implemented as a web application with a backend built using Python and FastAPI, and a dynamic frontend created with Next.js, a popular React framework for developing web-based user interfaces.

Backend. The backend is responsible for the core functionalities of the chatbot, including processing user queries, extracting relevant information, and generating responses. The backend of our system leverages the GPT-4 model and OpenAI embeddings, accessed via the OpenAI API for the user input understanding and document retrieval components.[7] We set the generation temperature to 0 and the maximum sequence length to 300 tokens for GPT-4. The orchestration of all the backend components is managed using the LangChain library.[8]

Frontend. The frontend is a web based interface that can be accessed from any device with an internet connection (Figure 1). It is designed to be intuitive and user-friendly, allowing passengers to interact with the system easily. The interface includes a chat window where the user can type their queries and view the chatbot's responses. Each response from the chatbot contains the query text, relevant passages from the KB, and links to the source documents for users who want to explore the information in more detail.

4 Evaluation

Usability dimension	Chatbot	Google Search
Usefulness	**1.75**	1.46
Ease of use	1.06	**1.23**
Ease of learning	2.18	**2.27**
Satisfaction	**2.46**	1.51

Table 1: Usability test results. **Takeaways:** Users rated the chatbot as more useful and satisfying, while its ease of use and learnability were on par with Google Search.

4.1 User Study

To evaluate the chatbot, we conducted a comparative usability study against a manual web search using Google. The test aimed to assess the chatbot's usefulness, user satisfaction as well as its ease of use and learning.

Methodology. We recruited 15 participants who had no prior experience or familiarity with NLP technologies to ensure that the study outcomes were not influenced by the participants' technical background. Each participant was asked to find information about 4 air travel-related issues randomly sampled from a pool of 40 issues covering a range of common passenger concerns, such as flight delays, cancellations, baggage issues and others. Each participant was asked to answer two questions using the chatbot and two others using Google search, with a random order of system used to control for any order effects.

Each session lasted approximately 30 minutes, during which participants interacted with each system to find answers for the assigned scenarios. To understand the user experience with each system, participants were asked to fill out a post-interaction survey immediately after using each system. The survey included both 7-point Likert scale questions (ranging from -3 for *totally disagree* to +3 for *totally agree*) measuring 4 usability dimensions based on the USE Questionnaire (Lund, 2001), as well as open-ended questions to collect free-form feedback such as opinions and suggestions. The questionnaire is available in Appendix B.

Quantitative Results. Table 1 shows the average score for each usability dimension and each system. The chatbot scored notably high in terms of user satisfaction and usefulness. Out of a maximum of 3 points, the chatbot received an average score of 1.75 points for usefulness and 2.46 points for user satisfaction, with substantial gaps from the respective scores for Google search, especially for satisfaction. These findings suggest that the chatbot was more adept at providing targeted information quickly and effectively, leading to a more positive user experience. The chatbot scored close to Google search in terms of ease of use (-0.17 points difference) and ease of learning (-0.09 points difference). Given that participants are likely very well accustomed to searching Google, this suggests that the chatbot was intuitive to use.

Qualitative Results. The participants' free-form feedback revealed that they appreciated the chatbot's conversational interface, which allowed for a more natural interaction. Some participants re-

[7]https://platform.openai.com/docs/api-reference

[8]https://python.langchain.com

User Input	Chatbot	Google Search
My flight was cancelled and they lost my bag. What are my compensation options?	**Query:** *What are the compensation policies for flight cancellation?* **Docs:** 1. "Compensation for flight delays and cancellations" 2. "Flight Cancellation General Principles"	**Query:** *flight cancellations compensation* **Docs:** 1. "Compensation for flight delays and cancellations" (5th place in search results)
	Query: *What are the compensation policies for lost luggage?* **Docs:** 1. "Lost, damaged or delayed baggage" 2. "Delayed Baggage: FAQ"	**Query:** *lost luggage compensation* **Docs:** 1. "Delayed or Damaged Baggage (Air Canada)" (4th place in search results)
Is there a time limit on filing a luggage claim?	**Query:** *Is there a deadline for filing a claim for lost luggage with an airline?* **Docs:** 1. "Filing a baggage claim with the airline" 2. "Lost Baggage I General Principles"	**Query:** *lost luggage claim deadline* **Docs:** 1. "Lost, damaged or delayed baggage" (2th place in search results)

Table 2: Comparative case study: Chatbot vs. Google Search for a compound travel issue. The retrieved documents are represented by their titles.

	P@5	R@5	F1@5	MAP@5
Chatbot	0.78	0.83	0.8	0.88

Table 3: Chatbot retrieval performance at top 5 documents.

ported that they found the chatbot's direct answers to be more convenient than sifting through multiple search results on Google. On the downside, a few participants mentioned that the chatbot sometimes did not understand their queries or provided generic responses, which required rephrasing queries or formulating follow-up queries to get the desired information.

4.2 Hallucination Analysis: Chatbot vs. RAG Approach

Recent studies have shown that LLMs, such as GPT-4, are prone to generating responses that are inconsistent with legal facts in at least 58% of cases for certain NLP tasks (Dahl et al., 2024). To assess how effectively the chatbot approach mitigates this issue, we conducted a quantitative comparison between the chatbot and the traditional RAG approach, focusing on answer hallucination. To this end, we manually evaluated the accuracy of the RAG system's response generation component using 40 examples from the user study, along with their corresponding ground truth documents, excluding the document retrieval component to avoid confounding factors. We measured the hallucination rate, defined as the percentage of responses containing information either not supported by the retrieved documents or factually incorrect.

The results showed that the RAG approach had a hallucination rate of 27.5% (11 examples). Of these, 10% (4 examples) were factually incorrect, while 22.5% (9 examples) included information not present in the documents. These findings align with other studies in legal nlp, which reported hallucination rates between 17% and 33% for RAG-based systems (Magesh et al., 2024). In contrast, the chatbot produces zero hallucinations, as it does not generate responses but instead presents the relevant passages from the source documents to the user.

Hallucinations can have serious consequences, particularly in high-stakes contexts where users rely on accurate information to make critical decisions. In the context of air travel regulations, even a minor hallucination could lead to a traveler misunderstanding the rules and facing delays or penalties. Hallucinations in the RAG approach can severely undermine user trust and lead to poor decision-making. Unlike the RAG approach, the chatbot's ability to completely avoid hallucinations makes it a more reliable tool for providing accurate information to users.

4.3 Case Study

We present a detailed case study to demonstrate the capability of the chatbot in handling complex air travel-related queries in comparison with manual Google searches, focusing on document relevance, interactivity, and efficiency. In Table 2, the dialogue showcases a scenario where a user seeks information on compensation for both a cancelled flight and lost luggage, followed by an inquiry about the time limit for filing a lost luggage claim.

Document Retrieval. The example highlights the chatbot's ability to directly retrieve top documents relevant to the user's queries. In contrast, the first relevant document for both flight cancellations and lost luggage appeared lower in Google search results (5th and 4th place, respectively). This highlights the chatbot's efficiency in swiftly providing relevant information to the user. Additionally, Table 3 provides quantitative results of the chatbot's performance in document retrieval at the top 5 documents as evaluated on 40 examples used in user-study, further confirming the chatbot's ability to prioritize the most relevant documents effectively.

Interactivity. The chatbot demonstrated superior interactivity by correctly interpreting a "luggage claim" as a claim for *lost* luggage in the user's second turn. This ability to parse and respond to complex and context-dependent, multifaceted questions conversationally is a key advantage of dialogue systems over traditional search engines, which require users to input precise queries for each specific concern.

The effectiveness of the chatbot was evident in its ability to reduce the time and effort required from the user to obtain actionable information. Instead of navigating through multiple search results and possibly encountering irrelevant information (e.g., laws from other countries, news), the user received a tailored response that directly addressed their concerns.

5 Related Work

In recent years, research has focused on AI systems designed to aid individuals, especially those without legal expertise, in navigating complex legal procedures, bridging the gap between legal information and laypeople. The proposed chatbot operates within the domain of document-grounded dialogue systems (DGDS) that enable more trustworthy and informed user interactions. In this section, we overview the evolution of access to justice tools alongside the datasets and methods relevant to DGDS.

5.1 Access to Justice Systems

A variety of AI-driven systems have been developed to assist individuals without legal training in navigating legal processes, with a strong focus on addressing access to justice. Early systems used rule-based approaches to help litigants understand procedural requirements for specific legal domains, such as protection orders or housing issues (Branting, 2001; Paquin et al., 1991). Later systems expanded this by leveraging web-based, expert-guided platforms that further provided customized legal advice in areas like family law and consumer disputes (Thompson, 2015; Bickel et al., 2015). More recent efforts have concentrated on hybrid systems that integrate rule-based reasoning with case-based analysis, enabling users to receive guidance based on both codified law and prior legal decisions (Westermann and Benyekhlef, 2023; Westermann et al., 2019). Recent advancements in LLMs allow legal systems to scale across different domains without requiring extensive model training on vast amounts of data (Tan et al., 2023). However, these models are prone to hallucination, generating plausible but factually incorrect legal advice, which could mislead users. To address this, we introduce a novel system that presents an answer to a user consisting of a set of extracted legal passages from a legal corpus, rather than generating a single response therefore improving the reliability of legal information and eliminating the risk of hallucination.

5.2 Datasets for DGDS

Incorporating documents into dialogue systems gained momentum with the rise of deep neural networks and large-scale datasets. One prominent dataset is the MultiWOZ (Budzianowski et al., 2018), which comprises dialogues from a restaurant-search domain where the dialogue state is grounded in a set of documents containing information about hotels, restaurants, and other entities. Similarly, Zhou et al. (2018) created a dataset with conversations based on Wikipedia articles about popular movies. In information-seeking DGDS, Doc2dial (Feng et al., 2020) and Multidoc2Dial (Feng et al., 2021) serve as realistic benchmarks to model goal-oriented information-seeking dialogues that are grounded on single or multiple documents. An interesting data collection paradigm was investigated in QuAC (Choi et al., 2018), a Question Answering in Context dataset containing, 14000 information-seeking QA dialogues. The collection involved two crowd workers: one acting as to learn as much as possible about a hidden Wikipedia text, and one posing as a teacher who answers the questions by providing short excerpts from the text.

5.3 Approaches for DGDS

In terms of approaches to DGDS, different methods for incorporation of external knowledge have been exhaustively explored to improve dialogue generation (Lowe et al., 2015; Liu et al., 2018; Chen et al., 2019; Sun et al., 2020; Yu et al., 2020). A particular focus has been directed at knowledge selection, the process of choosing relevant contextual information (Kim et al., 2020; Yang et al., 2022; Sun et al., 2023). Some methods focus on the reasoning aspects of document-oriented dialogue, such as building an interpretable reasoning path to the evidence in the documents (Huang et al., 2019), decomposing complex questions (Min et al., 2019), and performing multi-hop reasoning (Tu et al., 2019). More recently, (Lai et al., 2023), introduce a new architecture for DGDS that includes a dense passage retriever, a re-ranker, and a response generation model. With the rise of LLMs as zero and few-shot learners, Braunschweiler et al. (2023) perform a human evaluation as opposed to automatic evaluation of ChatGPT on document-grounded dialogue MultiDoc2Dial. In the context of the faithfulness of knowledge, Razumovskaia et al. (2023) explore behavioral tuning to improve the faithfulness to the knowledge source in document-oriented dialogue.

6 Conclusion

We developed a chatbot that provides accurate and timely information about Canadian air travel regulations and passenger rights, supporting the manual process currently handled by a group of volunteers.

The chatbot utilizes retrieval augmented generation and in-context learning to interpret complex user inputs and extract relevant information from a comprehensive knowledge base. Instead of generating a synthesized response, it provides users with a direct presentation of the formulated queries and corresponding passages from the source documents, reducing the risk of hallucination.

A user study comparing the chatbot to a Google search demonstrated its ability to accurately interpret and respond to user queries and successfully inform passengers of their rights. In future work, we plan to improve the chatbot's usefulness by contextualizing the answer for the user query, and reasoning over multiple extracted passages to synthesize an answer. We will explore how to achieve these properties without compromising the answers' accuracy.

7 Limitations

While our chatbot has shown promise in enhancing the accessibility of legal information regarding passenger rights, we recognize several limitations in the current iteration of the system that we plan to address in future work.

First, the chatbot's effectiveness is limited by its knowledge base's comprehensiveness. Missing information, like recent regulatory changes, can prevent it from providing complete answers. Therefore, it is crucial to continually expand and update the knowledge base to mitigate this limitation in a real system.

Secondly, the chatbot's current design does not facilitate an interactive dialogue which can be crucial for resolving uncertainties in user queries. For instance, if a user does not specify the origin and destination of their flight, the chatbot might not discern the applicable laws, as they can vary significantly from region to region—such as between Canada, Europe, and the United States. We plan to explore methods that allow the chatbot to ask follow-up questions to clarify such ambiguities.

Lastly, we've assumed users can understand and apply the legal information given, which might not hold true for everyone. Recognizing this, we intend to introduce simplified summaries and practical advice to enhance accessibility for users with varying levels of legal knowledge.

8 Ethics Statement

User Study. Our user study scenarios are based on posts from the Air Passenger Rights (Canada) Facebook group.[9] To protect user privacy, we anonymized the posts and used GPT-4 to generate variations covering a broad range of air travel issues, that we manually reviewed. We did not collect any personal information from the user study participants and we compensated participants CAD20 for a 30-minute session, which is well above the CAD16.75 hourly minimum wage in British Columbia, Canada.

User Privacy. We used the paid API for GPT-4, which does not store user interactions, to respect user privacy and confidentiality. In future versions, we will consider switching to open-source locally-hosted LLMs instead.

[9] `https://www.facebook.com/groups/441903102682254`

System Output. Since our application has very little tolerance for providing users with the wrong information, we opted instead for a retrieval-based output. Thus, it is not subject to outputting offensive, dangerous, or factually incorrect text as do generative LLM-based models.

Acknowledgements

We would like to express our sincere gratitude to the Digital Research Alliance of Canada for providing the computational resources that were instrumental in conducting the experiments and analysis presented in this paper.

Furthermore, we would like to acknowledge the invaluable contributions of Air Passenger Rights. The unique insights gained from this partnership greatly enriched the quality and impact of our research. Also, Vered's and Sahithya's research is supported by the Vector Institute for AI. Additionally Vered's research is supported by the CIFAR AI Chair program, and the Natural Sciences and Engineering Research Council of Canada. Evangelos' research is supported by the Natural Sciences and Engineering Research Council of Canada.

Finally, this research project has benefitted from the Microsoft Accelerate Foundation Models Research (AFMR) grant program.

References

Air Passenger Rights, 2022. 2022. From the Grounds Up: Revamp Canada's Air Passenger Protection Regime. Accessed: October 24, 2023.

Vance Badawey. 2021. Emerging from the Crisis: A Study of the Impact of the COVID-19 Pandemic on the Air Transport Sector. Report, Standing Committee on Transport, Infrastructure and Communities, House of Commons of Canada. Accessed: 2023-11-19.

Esmée A Bickel, Maria Anna Jozefa van Dijk, and Ellen Giebels. 2015. *Online legal advice and conflict support: A Dutch experience*. University of Twente.

L. Karl Branting. 2001. Advisory systems for pro se litigants. In *Proceedings of the 8th International Conference on Artificial Intelligence and Law*, ICAIL '01, page 139–146, New York, NY, USA. Association for Computing Machinery.

Norbert Braunschweiler, Rama Sanand Doddipatla, Simon Keizer, and Svetlana Stoyanchev. 2023. Evaluating large language models for document-grounded response generation in information-seeking dialogues. *ArXiv*, abs/2309.11838.

Paweł Budzianowski, Tsung-Hsien Wen, Bo-Hsiang Tseng, Iñigo Casanueva, Stefan Ultes, Osman Ramadan, and Milica Gašić. 2018. MultiWOZ - a large-scale multi-domain Wizard-of-Oz dataset for task-oriented dialogue modelling. In *Proceedings of the 2018 Conference on Empirical Methods in Natural Language Processing*, pages 5016–5026, Brussels, Belgium. Association for Computational Linguistics.

Xiuyi Chen, Jiaming Xu, and Bo Xu. 2019. A working memory model for task-oriented dialog response generation. In *Annual Meeting of the Association for Computational Linguistics*.

Eunsol Choi, He He, Mohit Iyyer, Mark Yatskar, Wen-tau Yih, Yejin Choi, Percy Liang, and Luke Zettlemoyer. 2018. QuAC: Question answering in context. In *Proceedings of the 2018 Conference on Empirical Methods in Natural Language Processing*, pages 2174–2184, Brussels, Belgium. Association for Computational Linguistics.

Eunsol Choi, Jennimaria Palomaki, Matthew Lamm, Tom Kwiatkowski, Dipanjan Das, and Michael Collins. 2021. Decontextualization: Making sentences stand-alone. *Transactions of the Association for Computational Linguistics*, 9:447–461.

Matthew Dahl, Varun Magesh, Mirac Suzgun, and Daniel E Ho. 2024. Large Legal Fictions: Profiling Legal Hallucinations in Large Language Models. *Journal of Legal Analysis*, 16(1):64–93.

Federal Court of Appeal, 2021. 2021. *Air Passenger Rights v. Canada (Attorney General)*, 2021 fca 201 at paras. 5-6. Federal Court of Appeal. 2021 FCA 201.

Song Feng, Siva Sankalp Patel, Hui Wan, and Sachindra Joshi. 2021. MultiDoc2Dial: Modeling dialogues grounded in multiple documents. In *Proceedings of the 2021 Conference on Empirical Methods in Natural Language Processing*, pages 6162–6176, Online and Punta Cana, Dominican Republic. Association for Computational Linguistics.

Song Feng, Hui Wan, Chulaka Gunasekara, Siva Patel, Sachindra Joshi, and Luis Lastras. 2020. doc2dial: A goal-oriented document-grounded dialogue dataset. In *Proceedings of the 2020 Conference on Empirical Methods in Natural Language Processing (EMNLP)*, pages 8118–8128, Online. Association for Computational Linguistics.

Hsin-Yuan Huang, Eunsol Choi, and Wen tau Yih. 2019. FlowQA: Grasping flow in history for conversational machine comprehension. In *International Conference on Learning Representations*.

Vladimir Karpukhin, Barlas Oguz, Sewon Min, Patrick Lewis, Ledell Wu, Sergey Edunov, Danqi Chen, and Wen-tau Yih. 2020. Dense passage retrieval for open-domain question answering. In *Proceedings of the 2020 Conference on Empirical Methods in Natural Language Processing (EMNLP)*, pages 6769–6781, Online. Association for Computational Linguistics.

Byeongchang Kim, Jaewoo Ahn, and Gunhee Kim. 2020. Sequential latent knowledge selection for knowledge-grounded dialogue. *ArXiv*, abs/2002.07510.

Tuan M. Lai, Giuseppe Castellucci, Saar Kuzi, Heng Ji, and Oleg Rokhlenko. 2023. External knowledge acquisition for end-to-end document-oriented dialog systems. In *Proceedings of the 17th Conference of the European Chapter of the Association for Computational Linguistics*, pages 3633–3647, Dubrovnik, Croatia. Association for Computational Linguistics.

Shuman Liu, Hongshen Chen, Zhaochun Ren, Yang Feng, Qun Liu, and Dawei Yin. 2018. Knowledge diffusion for neural dialogue generation. In *Proceedings of the 56th Annual Meeting of the Association for Computational Linguistics (Volume 1: Long Papers)*, pages 1489–1498, Melbourne, Australia. Association for Computational Linguistics.

Ryan Thomas Lowe, Nissan Pow, Laurent Charlin, and Joelle Pineau. 2015. Incorporating unstructured textual knowledge sources into neural dialogue systems. In *Neural Information Processing Systems Workshop on Machine Learning for Spoken Language Understanding*.

Arnold M Lund. 2001. Measuring usability with the use questionnaire. *Usability interface*, 8(2):3–6.

Varun Magesh, Faiz Surani, Matthew Dahl, Mirac Suzgun, Christopher D. Manning, and Daniel E. Ho. 2024. Hallucination-Free? Assessing the Reliability of Leading AI Legal Research Tools.

Sewon Min, Victor Zhong, Luke Zettlemoyer, and Hannaneh Hajishirzi. 2019. Multi-hop reading comprehension through question decomposition and rescoring. In *Proceedings of the 57th Annual Meeting of the Association for Computational Linguistics*, pages 6097–6109, Florence, Italy. Association for Computational Linguistics.

OpenAI. 2023. Gpt-4 technical report.

Louis-Claude Paquin, François Blanchard, and Claude Thomasset. 1991. Loge–expert: from a legal expert system to an information system for non-lawyers. In *Proceedings of the 3rd International Conference on Artificial Intelligence and Law*, ICAIL '91, page 254–259, New York, NY, USA. Association for Computing Machinery.

Ethan Perez, Patrick Lewis, Wen-tau Yih, Kyunghyun Cho, and Douwe Kiela. 2020. Unsupervised question decomposition for question answering. In *Proceedings of the 2020 Conference on Empirical Methods in Natural Language Processing (EMNLP)*, pages 8864–8880, Online. Association for Computational Linguistics.

Evgeniia Razumovskaia, Ivan Vulic, Pavle Markovic, Tomasz Cichy, Qian Zheng, Tsung-Hsien Wen, and Pawel Budzianowski. 2023. Dial beinfo for faithfulness: Improving factuality of information-seeking dialogue via behavioural fine-tuning. *CoRR, abs/2311.09800*.

Weiwei Sun, Pengjie Ren, and Zhaochun Ren. 2023. Generative knowledge selection for knowledge-grounded dialogues. In *Findings*.

Yajing Sun, Yue Hu, Luxi Xing, J. Yu, and Yuqiang Xie. 2020. History-adaption knowledge incorporation mechanism for multi-turn dialogue system. In *AAAI Conference on Artificial Intelligence*.

Jinzhe Tan, Hannes Westermann, and Karim Benyekhlef. 2023. Chatgpt as an artificial lawyer? In *Artificial Intelligence for Access to Justice (AI4AJ 2023)*.

Darin Thompson. 2015. Creating new pathways to justice using simple artificial intelligence and online dispute resolution. *IJODR*, 2:4.

Ming Tu, Kevin Huang, Guangtao Wang, Jing Huang, Xiaodong He, and Bowen Zhou. 2019. Select, answer and explain: Interpretable multi-hop reading comprehension over multiple documents. In *AAAI Conference on Artificial Intelligence*.

Hannes Westermann and Karim Benyekhlef. 2023. Justicebot: A methodology for building augmented intelligence tools for laypeople to increase access to justice. In *Proceedings of the Nineteenth International Conference on Artificial Intelligence and Law*, ICAIL '23, page 351–360, New York, NY, USA. Association for Computing Machinery.

Hannes Westermann, Vern R. Walker, Kevin D. Ashley, and Karim Benyekhlef. 2019. Using factors to predict and analyze landlord-tenant decisions to increase access to justice. In *Proceedings of the Seventeenth International Conference on Artificial Intelligence and Law*, ICAIL '19, page 133–142, New York, NY, USA. Association for Computing Machinery.

Chenxu Yang, Zheng Lin, JiangNan Li, Fandong Meng, Weiping Wang, Lan Wang, and Jie Zhou. 2022. Take: Topic-shift aware knowledge selection for dialogue generation. In *International Conference on Computational Linguistics*.

W. Yu, Wenhao Yu, Chenguang Zhu, Zaitang Li, Zhiting Hu, Qingyun Wang, Heng Ji, and Meng Jiang. 2020. A survey of knowledge-enhanced text generation. *ACM Computing Surveys*, 54:1 – 38.

Kangyan Zhou, Shrimai Prabhumoye, and Alan W Black. 2018. A dataset for document grounded conversations. In *Proceedings of the 2018 Conference on Empirical Methods in Natural Language Processing*, pages 708–713, Brussels, Belgium. Association for Computational Linguistics.

A Prompts

A.1 Contextual Query Isolation Prompt

```
Given the following conversation and
the follow-up input, rephrase the
follow-up input into a standalone
text that is not dependent on the
conversation history. Make it as
concise as possible, including only
the necessary information.

Chat History:
{chat_history}

Follow Up Input:
{question}

Text:
```

A.2 Decompositional Query Generation Prompt

```
Identify the information needed to
respond to the following input.
Provide your answer as a numbered
list of questions, with each question
focusing on a single, answerable
aspect of the input. Limit the list
to a maximum of 3 questions.

Input: {query}

Questions:
```

B USE Questionnaire

The questionnaires were constructed as seven-point Likert rating scales, ranging from -3 (totally disagree) to +3 (totally agree)

1. Usefulness
   (a) It helps me be more effective.
   (b) It helps me be more productive.
   (c) It is useful.
   (d) It gives me more control over the activities in my life.
   (e) It makes the things I want to accomplish easier to get done.
   (f) It saves me time when I use it.
   (g) It meets my needs.
   (h) It does everything I would expect it to do.
2. Ease of Use
   (a) It is easy to use.
   (b) It is simple to use.
   (c) It is user friendly.
   (d) It requires the fewest steps possible to accomplish what I want to do with it.
   (e) It is flexible.
   (f) Using it is effortless.
   (g) I can use it without written instructions.
   (h) I don't notice any inconsistencies as I use it.
   (i) Both occasional and regular users would like it.
   (j) I can recover from mistakes quickly and easily.
   (k) I can use it successfully every time.
3. Ease of Learning
   (a) I learned to use it quickly.
   (b) I easily remember how to use it.
   (c) It is easy to learn to use it.
   (d) I quickly became skillful with it.
4. Satisfaction
   (a) I am satisfied with it.
   (b) I would recommend it to a friend.
   (c) It is fun to use.
   (d) It works the way I want it to work.
   (e) It is wonderful.
   (f) I feel I need to have it.
   (g) It is pleasant to use.

Enhancing Legal Violation Identification with LLMs and Deep Learning Techniques: Achievements in the LegalLens 2024 Competition

Tan-Minh Nguyen[1], **Ngoc-Duy Mai**[1], **Xuan-Bach Le**[1], **Huu-Dung Nguyen**[1]
Cong-Minh Pham[1], **Ha-Thanh Nguyen**[2] and **Thi-Hai-Yen Vuong**[1,*]
[1]VNU University of Engineering and Technology, Hanoi, Vietnam,
[2]National Institute of Informatics, Tokyo, Japan,
[1]{20020081,21020512,22024506,22028076,22028239}@vnu.edu.vn
[2]nguyenhathanh@nii.ac.jp
[*] **Correspondence:** yenvth@vnu.edu.vn

Abstract

LegalLens is a competition organized to encourage advancements in automatically detecting legal violations. This paper presents our solutions for two tasks Legal Named Entity Recognition (L-NER) and Legal Natural Language Inference (L-NLI). Our approach involves fine-tuning BERT-based models, designing methods based on data characteristics, and a novel prompting template for data augmentation using LLMs. As a result, we secured first place in L-NER and third place in L-NLI among thirty-six participants. We also perform error analysis to provide valuable insights and pave the way for future enhancements in legal NLP. Our implementation is available at https://github.com/lxbach10012004/legal-lens/tree/main.

1 Introduction

A violation of law refers to the actions of breaking rules or regulations set by the legal system and authority. These violations harm individuals, organizations, and the principles of fairness and justice, particularly in the digital age. Therefore, developing intelligent systems to detect violations and assist legal experts is essential. Thanks to the exploration of advanced techniques in NLP, prior studies developed specialized models to address the problems of detecting violations automatically (Silva et al., 2020; Yu et al., 2020; Breve et al., 2023). This year, LegalLens (Hagag et al., 2024) is first held with the aim of detecting and monitoring violations in various domains including commercial, privacy, environmental law, and consumer protection. The competition contains two tasks: violation detection via named entity recognition (L-NER) and predicting potential victims of the violation using natural language inference (L-NLI). The L-NER task requires a model to determine four types of entities (law, violation, violated by, violated on) given a passage. The L-NLI task identifies whether the relationship between a complaint (premise) and a review (hypothesis) is entailed, contradicted, or neutral.

The paper reports the work of NOWJ team in both tasks. For the first task, L-NER, independent classification is limited because there are strong dependencies in the output sequence (e.g. B-LAW cannot follow I-LAW, details in Section 3.1). Therefore, we address the problem by following sequence labeling with an architecture of BERT and conditional random field (CRF) to compute output probability jointly. Regarding the second task, one of the main challenges is the lack of a high-quality labeled dataset, whereas general NLI data has been highly developed on large datasets. Thus, we propose a novel prompt for data augmentation using recent LLMs to overcome the shortage of labeled data. State-of-the-art language models are then fine-tuned on augmented training data to develop consistent models for the legal domain.

The following sections of the paper are organized as follows: Section 2 presents prior studies addressing named entity recognition and natural language inference tasks, especially in the legal domain. We describe details of our methodology for two tasks in Sections 3 and 4. Section 5 concludes the paper and points out some future work.

2 Related Work

Legal Named Entity Recognition: NER has been one of the most important tasks in NLP, with various applications in special domains such as biomedicine (Kundeti et al., 2016; Hofer et al., 2018), law (Leitner et al., 2019a; Kalamkar et al., 2022; Au et al., 2022) or cross-domain (Jia et al., 2019). Previously, various classical machine learning methods have been developed to address NER in legal texts such as logistic regression, Support Vector Machines, Naive Bayes, and heuristic-based approaches to extract elements or entities from le-

Proceedings of the Natural Legal Language Processing Workshop 2024, pages 336–345
November 16, 2024

gal documents (Chalkidis et al., 2017; Cardellino et al., 2017; Glaser et al., 2018). Another approach addresses NER as a sequence-to-sequence problem and trains a pointer generator network to overcome the absence of noisy training data (Skylaki et al., 2021). Many studies have investigated the performance of transformer-based models, domain-specific embeddings, and neural components (i.e., LSTM, BiLSTM, CNN) combined with CRF (Leitner et al., 2019b; Kalamkar et al., 2022; Keshavarz et al., 2022; Çetindağ et al., 2023), inspired by (Lample et al., 2016). The impacts of CRF, word embeddings, and domain-specific knowledge have proven effective in NER.

Legal Natural Language Inference: NLI, also known as textual entailment recognition has gained interest from researchers in recent years. There are a few law-related resources in NLI, including ContractNLI (Koreeda and Manning, 2021), LawngNLI (Bruno and Roth, 2022), LegalNLI (Yang, 2022), and an annual competition COLIEE (Goebel et al., 2024). However, the cost of constructing high-quality datasets in the legal domain is expensive due to expert-effort requirements in data annotation. Thus, prior studies (Aoki et al., 2022) focused on data augmentation to overcome the limited dataset. Aoki et al. (2022) proposed a data augmentation process based on logical structures of original statutory articles to enrich the training set automatically. Recently, LLMs have shown their state-of-the-art in various NLP tasks, including legal NLP. Nguyen et al. (2024), the winner of the legal statute entailment task in COLIEE 2024, leveraged the powers of LLMs for data augmentation and explore the hidden relations between the premise and hypothesis. Particularly, they summarized the legal article (premise) as complementary information and experimented with various prompting techniques on FlanT5-XXL, an open-source model.

3 Legal Named Entity Recognition

3.1 Problem statement

Given a sequence of tokens $\mathbf{x} = \{x_1, x_2, ..., x_n\}$, the task is to assign a corresponding sequence of labels $\mathbf{y} = \{y_1, y_2, ..., y_n\}$ from a predefined label set $\mathcal{C}$. Our objective is to determine the most likely sequence of labels by maximizing the conditional probability:

$$\hat{y} = \arg\max_{y} P(y \mid x)$$

where $P(y \mid x)$ represents the probability of each label y_i given the token x_i. For the L-NER task, the label set $\mathcal{C}$ utilizes the B-I-O (begin, inside, and outside) tagging scheme and includes 4 entities: *law, violation, violated by,* and *violated on.*

3.2 Data Analysis

We identified two versions of the L-NER datasets. The older version[1] consists of 1327 samples, including a training set with 710 samples and a test set with 617 samples. The newer version[2] contains only a training set with 975 samples. However, we found that the new training set appears in the old data. Therefore, we employ 352 samples of the old data that do not intersect the new data as the validation set. Figure 1 depicts the data sets used for this task.

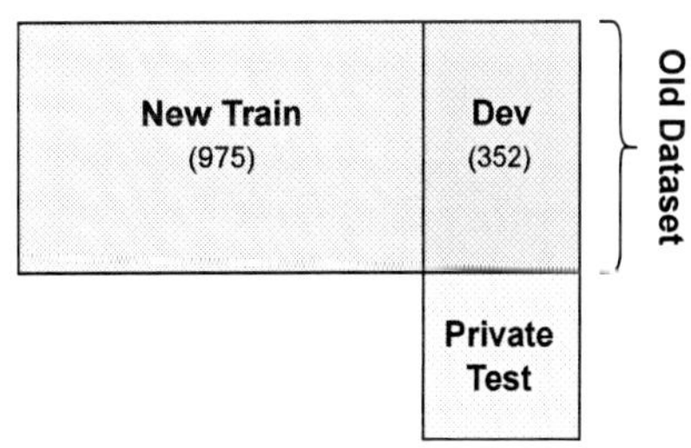

Figure 1: An illustration of our training and validation sets in L-NER.

Table 1 presents the statistics of the training and validation sets in the L-NER task. Further analysis reveals that only 20% samples contain four entities within the sequence. The others include only the *violation* entity type. Additionally, no entity type appears more than once per input sequence. Thus, there is a great imbalance between entities in the dataset. Table 2 shows the statistics of the private test set. The test set contains 380 samples, which is approximately equal to our validation set. Further analysis reveals that the distribution of the private test is quite different from the public data. Firstly, compared to the training and validation sets, the entity distribution is more balanced in the test set. Secondly, the number of *violation* entities in the private test is greater than the number of samples in the test set. While one sequence in the public data only contains as much one time of an entity, a sample in the test set could contain multiple appear-

[1]https://huggingface.co/datasets/darrow-ai/LegalLensNER

[2]https://huggingface.co/datasets/darrow-ai/LegalLensNER-SharedTask

ances of each entity. Finally, the average lengths of entities in the private test set are longer than those in the public set. These differences could pose challenges for models in handling unseen data.

	Training		Validation	
	# Samples	Mean # tokens	# Samples	Mean # tokens
Law	210	3.98	82	4.52
Violation	975	12.30	352	12.57
Violated By	210	2.91	82	3.10
Violated On	210	3.25	82	3.18

Table 1: Statistics of the training and validation sets in L-NER.

	Private Test	
	# Samples	Mean # tokens
Law	246	4.30
Violation	446	16.59
Violated By	399	3.21
Violated On	342	3.66

Table 2: Statistics of the L-NER private test set.

3.3 Methodology

For the L-NER task, we use pre-trained language models combined with a Linear-Chain CRF on top to leverage contextual word embeddings and jointly compute the output probabilities. The architecture is designed to identify and classify named entities within input sequences, as depicted in Figure 2. The vector representation of the input sequence produced by encoders is fed into a linear transformation to map these vectors into a label space. After that, the CRF layer is employed to model the dependencies using these vectors as inputs.

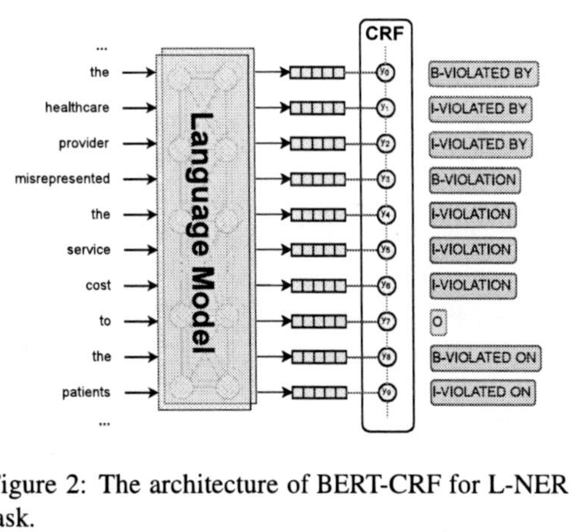

Figure 2: The architecture of BERT-CRF for L-NER task.

3.3.1 Pre-processing

We employ WordPiece (Wu et al., 2016), a subword tokenization technique specifically designed for BERT-based language models. This technique breaks down complex or uncommon words into smaller subword units, enhancing the model's ability to generalize across various word forms. For example, the word "misrepresent" is tokenized into <mis>, <##re>, <##pres>, and <##ent>. After tokenization, the original word labels are realigned with the subword tokens. The first subword retains the original label, while subsequent tokens are assigned a placeholder label (*X*) to ensure label consistency.

3.3.2 Language Model Backbone

Pre-trained language models are utilized to produce contextual embeddings for given input tokens, effectively capturing dependency within the sequence. A linear transformation is then applied to map these embeddings into a label space, with each dimension representing a potential NER tag. This transformation can be represented as follows:

$$\mathbf{H} = Enc(\mathbf{x}) \tag{1}$$

$$\mathbf{P} = \mathbf{H} * \mathbf{W}^\top + \mathbf{b} \tag{2}$$

where $\mathbf{H} \in \mathbb{R}^{n \times d}$ is the matrix of hidden states for the token sequence produced by language models, with n being the sequence length and d is the encoder's dimension. $\mathbf{W} \in \mathbb{R}^{k \times d}$ is the weight matrix mapping the hidden dimension d to the number of labels k. $\mathbf{b} \in \mathbb{R}^k$ is the bias vector for each label. Finally, $\mathbf{P} \in \mathbb{R}^{n \times k}$ is the emission score matrix, where each row represents a token, and each column represents a label. This sequence of token-level score matrix is then passed to the CRF layer to capture dependencies between labels.

3.3.3 Conditional Random Field

The Linear-Chain CRF is used to model the dependencies between labels in the output sequence. Particularly, CRF assigns a score to each sequence of labels, ensuring that the predicted sequence is globally optimal.

Scoring Algorithm: The score for a sequence of labels $\mathbf{y} = \{y_1, y_2, \dots, y_n\}$ given a sequence of input tokens $\mathbf{x} = \{x_1, x_2, \dots, x_n\}$ is computed as follows:

$$\text{Score}(\mathbf{x}, \mathbf{y}) = \sum_{t=1}^{n} \left(P_{t,y_t} + A_{y_t,y_{t-1}}\right) \quad (3)$$

where P_{t,y_t} is the emission score for the label y_t at position t, and $A_{y_t,y_{t-1}}$ is the transition score from label y_{t-1} to y_t.

3.3.4 Model Training and Inference

During training, the model parameters are optimized by minimizing the negative log-likelihood loss through backpropagation. Both the LM and CRF layers are trained jointly to maximize the likelihood of the correct label sequences.

Alpha Recursion: The model computes the partition function (normalizing factor) over all possible label sequences. This is expressed as follows:

$$Z(\mathbf{x}) = \sum_{\mathbf{y}'} \exp(\text{Score}(\mathbf{x}, \mathbf{y}')) \quad (4)$$

where the sum is taken over all possible label sequences $\mathbf{y}'$.

Training Objective: The model is trained using the negative log-likelihood (NLL) of the correct label sequence. The NLL loss is given by:

$$\mathcal{L}(\mathbf{x}, \mathbf{y}) = -\log \frac{\exp(\text{Score}(\mathbf{x}, \mathbf{y}))}{Z(\mathbf{x})} \quad (5)$$

The objective is to minimize this loss, which drives the model to assign higher scores to the correct label sequences.

Viterbi Decoding: During inference, the Viterbi algorithm is applied to decode the most probable sequence of labels for a given input sequence. The decoded labels are then output as the predicted NER tags:

$$\hat{\mathbf{y}} = \arg\max_{\mathbf{y}'} \text{Score}(\mathbf{x}, \mathbf{y}') \quad (6)$$

3.3.5 Post-processing

For pre-existing subwords in the data, which are predicted as *X*, we align them with the label of the preceding token. Only if the preceding token is predicted with a beginning tag (*B-*. . .), the *X* label is converted into an inside tag (*I-*. . .) of the same entity type.

For example, consider the following tokenized sequence and its predicted tags: *[<committed> / O, <against> / O, <mr> / B-VIOLATED ON,* $<.>$ */***X**, *<ciesniewski,> / I-VIOLATED ON].* During post-processing, the **X** tag for the token $<.>$ is aligned with the preceding *B-VIOLATED ON* tag for $< mr >$ and converted to *I-VIOLATED ON*. This ensures that punctuation or subwords with *X* tags are correctly aligned with the preceding entity labels.

3.4 Experiments and Results

To address the L-NER task, we implement our proposed architecture with different backbone models. This design enables the model to capture both contextual word embeddings from language models and sequential dependencies from the CRF effectively. Following the architecture design, we fine-tune several BERT-based models, including BERT (Devlin et al., 2018), RoBERTa (Liu et al., 2019), and Longformer (Beltagy et al., 2020), and compared the performance with their legal-domain counterparts such as LegalBERT (Chalkidis et al., 2020), LegalRoBERTa (Chalkidis* et al., 2023), and LegalLongformer (Chalkidis* et al., 2023). Additionally, we evaluate the BERT-NER[3] model which is a fine-tuned version of BERT for NER tasks. Each model is trained for 30 epochs using the Adam optimizer (Kingma and Ba, 2017), with an initial learning rate of $5e-5$ for the backbone model and $8e-5$ for the CRF layer. All the experiments are carried out on P100 GPU 16GB via the Kaggle platform. We select the best checkpoint on the validation set for each model based on performance metrics. The official evaluation metric for the L-NER task in LegalLens 2024 is the Macro-F1 score, and the results obtained for these models are presented below:

Model	Precision	Recall	F1
BERT-base	0.8675	0.8904	0.8780
Longformer-base	0.8938	0.8861	0.8891
BERT-base NER	0.8876	0.8925	0.8895
LegalBERT-base	0.8946	0.8907	0.8920
RoBERTa-base	0.8943	0.9002	0.8968
LegalRoBERTa-base	0.9254	0.8939	0.9089
LegalLongformer-base	**0.9264**	**0.9217**	**0.9238**

Table 3: Performances of different backbone models on the validation set.

Table 3 presents the performances of backbone models on the validation set. The model that uses LegalLongformer as the backbone achieves the best scores in all three metrics. There is a slight difference in the performances of the three models BERT, Longformer, RoBERTa. Notably, domain-specific models consistently surpass the general

[3] https://huggingface.co/dslim/bert-base-NER

models by 3.1%pt (i.e. percentage point) to 3.6%pt in precision. This leads to superior performances of three models LegalBERT, LegalRoBERTa, and LegalLongformer in the leaderboard. Our experiments prove the contribution of pre-training language models in specific domains, especially when high-quality data is limited.

According to reports on the validation set, we use the best checkpoint of LegalLongformer-CRF as the submission. The final results of the private test set are presented in Table 4.

Team	F1 Score
NOWJ	**0.416**
Flawless Lawgic	0.402
UOttawa	0.402
Baseline	0.381
Masala-chai	0.380
UMLaw & TechLab	0.321
Bonafide	0.305

Table 4: Final leaderboard of L-NER. The top-six teams among thirty-six participants are reported.

Table 4 presents the ranking of the top-six teams on the private test of L-NER. We secured first place in the L-NER task with an F1 score of 0.416, which increases the baseline by 9.1% pt. This result shows the effectiveness of combining CRF and pre-trained language models on the specific-domain NER task. A noteworthy point is the final result is significantly different from the validation result. The baseline method also achieves fourth place in the leaderboard. Indeed, these indicate the challenges of NER in the legal domain. There is room for improving our models' performance and robustness to handle real-world scenarios.

3.5 Error Analysis

Tag	Precision	Recall	F1
B-LAW	0.8870	0.6707	0.7639
I-LAW	0.9299	0.6868	0.7901
B-VIOLATION	0.8138	0.7152	0.7613
I-VIOLATION	0.9021	0.7520	0.8202
B-VIOLATED BY	0.0894	0.0401	0.0553
I-VIOLATED BY	0.1145	0.0572	0.0763
B-VIOLATED ON	0.5106	0.2807	0.3623
I-VIOLATED ON	0.6206	0.2855	0.3911
Macro Average	0.6085	0.4360	0.5027

Table 5: Performance of our model on distinct tags in the L-NER Test Set.

Table 5 shows the performance of our model on different tags in the test set. Overall, our model shows promising results on the *LAW* and *VIOLATION* tags, which capture the violated actions and related law's content. In contrast, identifying two remaining tags is limited, especially with tag *VIOLATED BY*. These two tags capture the entities or organizations in the sequence, one causes the violation, and one is the patient. Further analysis reveals that our model often mistakes the preposition in the tag label. The model also tends to recognize the second occurrence of these entities (person or organizer), while the ground truth labels often pertain to the first occurrence. Furthermore, the length of *VIOLATED ON* tag is relatively short (averaging 3.66 tokens), this pattern negatively impacts the overall performance.

4 Legal Natural Language Inference

4.1 Problem statement

Given an input text pair *(premise, hypothesis)*, the NLI task is to determine the relationship between these texts, whether they are *entailed*, *contradicted*, or *neutral*. This can be framed as a multi-class classification problem, where the goal is to predict the correct category by maximizing the conditional probability of the following:

$$\hat{y} = \arg\max_{y} P(y \mid p, h)$$

Here, p and h denote the premise and hypothesis, respectively. $\hat{y}$ denotes the predicted class, obtained by choosing the class $y \in \{Entailed, Contradict, Neutral\}$ with the highest conditional probability.

4.2 Data Analysis

There are two versions of datasets provided. The older version[4] and newer version[5] both contain 312 samples. After some pre-processing steps, we found that there are 152 samples that both appear in two sets. Therefore, we construct new data consisting of 472 samples, including two public sets, except the intersection part. The train/validation sets are divided with a ratio of 6/4. The statistics of our dataset for the L-NLI are shown in Table 6. The distribution of labels is uniform, whereas there is no dominant label in the public dataset.

[4] https://huggingface.co/datasets/darrow-ai/LegalLensNLI

[5] https://huggingface.co/datasets/darrow-ai/LegalLensNLI-SharedTask

Label	Samples	Mean # Hypo tokens	Mean # Premise tokens
Contradict	154	71.93	162.14
Entailed	160	75.11	159.87
Neutral	158	62.46	160.99

Table 6: Statistics of the L-NLI public set.

Table 7 presents the statistics of the L-NLI private test set. This test set contains only 84 samples, which is less than five times the size of the public dataset. The private test set exhibits an imbalance, with the *Entailed* label accounting for approximately 50% of the dataset. These differences in the data distribution between the private test and the public sets could negatively impact the model's generalization and consistency.

Label	Samples	Mean # Hypo tokens	Mean # Premise tokens
Contradict	15	43.80	169.46
Entailed	40	59.27	171.05
Neutral	29	40.96	164.62

Table 7: Statistics of L-NLI private test set.

4.3 Methodology

The main difficulty of the L-NLI task is the limited dataset, which consists of 472 samples. Indeed, this would lead to poor generalization and potentially biased outcomes, as the models reflect the narrow perspectives in the datasets. Therefore, we introduce a novel prompt for data augmentation using LLMs. We then fine-tune pre-trained language models on the enriched data to secure stable performances across multiple iterations.

4.3.1 Data Augmentation

To improve the performance and robustness of our models, we employ data augmentation to improve the diversity and variability of the training set. GPT-4o-mini is utilized via the API of OpenAI to generate new data using a novel prompt.

Particularly, we instruct LLMs to paraphrase a hypothesis-premise pair following two styles: one reflecting an IELTS score of 6.5 and the other an 8.5. This approach introduces linguistic diversity in sentence structures, vocabulary, and phrasing while maintaining the core semantic meaning. Figure 3 presents the prompt we used to generate new data. Special symbols {hypothesis} and {premise} are replaced with the content of two paragraphs accordingly. The new training set contains 665 samples including original and augmented data, while the validation set remains the same. New data generated by two levels of IELTS is illustrated in Table 8. Table 9 reports the statistics of the new training set for the L-NLI task.

"I am doing a Natural Language Inference task and I need you to help me augment my training data for a richer dataset.
Here is the hypothesis {hypothesis} and here is the premise {premise}.
Given a legal pair of hypothesis and premise. I need you to paraphrase them, both the hypothesis and premise each have 2 versions.
One version is as if you have the English level of a person with IELTS 8.5.
One version is as if you have the English level of a person with IELTS 6.5.
Please read and paraphrase carefully so that it does not lose meaning."

Figure 3: A novel prompt to generate new data following two styles.

4.3.2 Pre-trained Language Models

We conduct experiments using various language models, including encoder-only and encoder-decoder models.

- **BERT** (Devlin et al., 2018), a widely regarded model, utilizes a multi-layer bidirectional Transformer with an encoder-only architecture. Rather than employing the original base model released by Google, we opted for a domain-specific variant, LEGAL-BERT (Chalkidis et al., 2020), pre-trained on an extensive corpus tailored to the legal domain.

- **T5** (Raffel et al., 2020), on the other hand, employs a full encoder-decoder architecture. This model generates predictions by outputting one of three textual labels: *Entailed*, *Neutral*, or *Contradict*.

- **DeBERTa** (He et al., 2021), while belonging to the BERT family, extends BERT's capabilities by incorporating a novel attention mechanism known as Disentangled Attention, which introduces additional projection matrices to capture relative positional information, integrating them into the attention score computation.

While T5 is fine-tuned following the text generation task, LegalBERT and DeBERTa are fine-tuned

Original data	Been punching in and out with this hand scanner thingy at Superior Health Linens for a while now. You know, the usual 9 to 5 grind. Felt like something out of a sci-fi movie every time I clocked in, but hey, it's the 21st century, right? Technology and all that jazz.
IELTS 6.5	I've been using this hand scanner to clock in and out at Superior Health Linens for a while. It feels like a scene from a sci-fi movie every time I check in, but I guess that's just how things are in the 21st century with all this technology.
IELTS 8.5	I have been clocking in and out with this hand scanner at Superior Health Linens for some time now. Each time I log in, it feels reminiscent of a futuristic film, yet I suppose this is simply the reality of the 21st century, given the prevalence of technology.

Table 8: An example of paraphrasing a hypothesis following different styles.

Label	Samples	Mean # Hypo tokens	Mean # Premise tokens
Contradict	226	66.86	158.08
Entailed	231	72.91	155.81
Neutral	208	58.60	161.53

Table 9: Statistics of the new training set for task L-NLI.

following the sequence classification task. The vector representation of the special token [CLS] is fed into a classification head as follows:

$$H_{cls} = Enc(p, h) \quad (7)$$

$$\mathbf{y} = softmax(H_{cls} * W^{\top} + b) \quad (8)$$

where $H_{cls} \in \mathbb{R}^d$ is the vector representation of the token [CLS], produced by pre-trained language models, d is the model's hidden size, $W \in \mathbb{R}^{k \times d}$, $b \in \mathbb{R}^k$ are trainable parameters. The output $\mathbf{y} \in \mathbb{R}^k$ represents the predicted probabilities for each class, where $\sum y_i = 1$, k is the number of labels.

4.4 Experiments and Results

Each model is trained for 10 epochs using Adam optimizer (Kingma and Ba, 2017) with an initial learning rate of $5e-6$. The training process is repeated five times to compute the average scores. All the experiments are carried out on P100 GPU 16GB via the Kaggle platform. The official metric for the L-NLI task is the macro F1 score. We experiment with five language models, with and without data augmentation, presented in Table 10 and Table 11. We find that DeBERTa-large outperforms other models in both training cases. Furthermore, DeBERTa models demonstrate stable performance across multiple iterations. The number of parameters also contributes to the results, whereas large models consistently surpass base models. Notably, training models on augmented data could improve the results in all metrics. Particularly, the F1 score saw a rise of 2.9%pt to 5.5%pt on the validation set. Indeed, these results highlight the contribution of data augmentation in handling legal downstream tasks. We select the DeBERTa-large checkpoint with the highest performance on the validation set as the final submission.

Model	Precision	Recall	F1
LegalBERT-base	0.8378	0.8401	0.8342
T5-base	0.8421	0.8676	0.8502
T5-large	0.8685	0.8645	0.8717
DeBERTa-base	**0.8943**	0.8788	0.8831
DeBERTa-large	0.8895	**0.8917**	**0.8848**

Table 10: Average performances of models on the validation set. Before data augmentation.

Model	Precision	Recall	F1
LegalBERT-base	0.8801	0.8813	0.8722
T5-base	0.8882	0.9016	0.8977
T5-large	0.9058	0.9063	0.9043
DeBERTa-base	0.9126	0.9052	0.9089
DeBERTa-large	**0.9210**	**0.9220**	**0.9204**

Table 11: Average performances of models on the validation set. After data augmentation.

Table 12 presents the results of the top six teams in the competition. Our model achieves the F1-macro score of 0.746 on the private test set, placing third place among thirty-six participants. Even though our model could achieve impressive performance on the validation set, it is limited on the private test set. In addition, only the winning team could surpass the baseline in the L-NLI task. Indeed, these results emphasize the challenge of legal downstream tasks.

Team	F1 Score
1-800-Shared-Tasks	0.853
Baseline	*0.807*
Semantists	0.785
NOWJ	**0.746**
UOttawa	0.724
bonafide	0.653
masala-chai	0.525

Table 12: The final leaderboard of the L-NLI task.

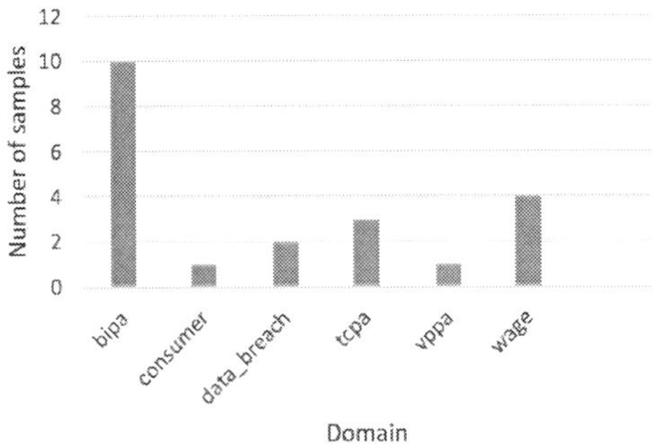

Figure 4: Statistics of wrong prediction's domain.

4.5 Error Analysis

Table 13 presents the error analysis of our model on the L-NLI test set. The proposed method achieves a promising performance on the neutral label, where the precision and recall scores are balanced. In contrast, there is a trade of pattern between results of labels contradict and entailed. While the recall score of the contradict label is 1.0, the model gets a 0.9615 precision score on the entailed label. This result suggests that our model is heavily biased toward the contradict label if there is a relationship between two texts. Another noteworthy point is that approximately 50% of the wrong predictions belong to the Biometric Information Privacy Act (BIPA) domain as shown in Figure 4. This could be attributed to the lack of BIPA area in the training set. Future work could focus on exploiting logical knowledge to reinforce the model's reasoning and inference abilities, which would help to better distinguish the contradict and entailed relations.

	Precision	Recall	F1-score
Contradict	0.5556	1.0000	0.7143
Entailed	0.9615	0.6250	0.7576
Neutral	0.7419	0.7931	0.7667
Macro Average	0.7530	0.8060	0.7462

Table 13: Error analysis of our model on L-NLI test set.

5 Conclusion

This paper presents our work in the LegalLens competition. For the L-NER task, we leverage the contextual embeddings of BERT-based models and compute sequence dependency using a Linear-Chain CRF layer. For the L-NLI tasks, we propose a novel prompt to generate synthesis data using LLMs. The experiments highlight the effectiveness of data augmentation in improving language models' performance. Consequently, we secured first place in L-NER and third place in L-NLI. We also perform error analysis to offer valuable insights and groundwork for future advancements in legal NLP. Future work would focus on improving the robustness and performance of models by exploiting the integration of logical knowledge and LLMs.

Limitations

We outline the following limitations in this work: (1) one of the main challenges is the shortage of datasets. Even though we employed data augmentation with LLMs in task 2, the dataset remained limited, affecting the diversity and generalization of our model. Therefore, there is a decline in the performance of our method on the private test set compared to the validation set. Furthermore, the data augmentation using LLMs should be further discussed and studied, to ensure the quality of enriched data. (2) Although domain-specific models are utilized in this work to address legal downstream tasks, the legal logic reasoning is not yet considered explicitly. Indeed, this approach should be studied throughout to enhance the reliability and accuracy of deep learning models in the legal domain. (3) The use of closed-source models like GPT4 is limited by many constraints, which may pose difficulty in reproducing our experiments. Well acknowledging the problem, we would make our code and implementation publicly accessible in the future. Nonetheless, the discussions and insights in this work demonstrate the promising benefits of leveraging LLMs and deep learning techniques for legal violation identification.

Acknowledgments

This work was supported by AIP challenge funding in relation with JST, AIP Trilateral AI Research, Grant Number JPMJCR20G4, by JSPS KAKENHI

Grant Numbers, JP22H00543, JST, AIP Trilateral AI Research, Grant Number JPMJCR20G4 and the MEXT "R&D Hub Aimed at Ensuring Transparency and Reliability of Generative AI Models" project.

References

Yasuhiro Aoki, Masaharu Yoshioka, and Youta Suzuki. 2022. Data-augmentation method for bert-based legal textual entailment systems in coliee statute law task. *The Review of Socionetwork Strategies*, 16(1):175–196.

Ting Wai Terence Au, Vasileios Lampos, and Ingemar Cox. 2022. E-NER — an annotated named entity recognition corpus of legal text. In *Proceedings of the Natural Legal Language Processing Workshop 2022*, pages 246–255, Abu Dhabi, United Arab Emirates (Hybrid). Association for Computational Linguistics.

Iz Beltagy, Matthew E. Peters, and Arman Cohan. 2020. Longformer: The long-document transformer. *arXiv:2004.05150*.

Bernardo Breve, Gaetano Cimino, and Vincenzo Deufemia. 2023. Identifying security and privacy violation rules in trigger-action iot platforms with nlp models. *IEEE Internet of Things Journal*, 10(6):5607–5622.

William Bruno and Dan Roth. 2022. LawngNLI: A long-premise benchmark for in-domain generalization from short to long contexts and for implication-based retrieval. In *Findings of the Association for Computational Linguistics: EMNLP 2022*, pages 5019–5043, Abu Dhabi, United Arab Emirates. Association for Computational Linguistics.

Cristian Cardellino, Milagro Teruel, Laura Alonso Alemany, and Serena Villata. 2017. A low-cost, high-coverage legal named entity recognizer, classifier and linker. In *Proceedings of the 16th Edition of the International Conference on Articial Intelligence and Law*, ICAIL '17, page 9–18, New York, NY, USA. Association for Computing Machinery.

Ilias Chalkidis, Ion Androutsopoulos, and Achilleas Michos. 2017. Extracting contract elements. In *Proceedings of the 16th Edition of the International Conference on Articial Intelligence and Law*, ICAIL '17, page 19–28, New York, NY, USA. Association for Computing Machinery.

Ilias Chalkidis, Manos Fergadiotis, Prodromos Malakasiotis, Nikolaos Aletras, and Ion Androutsopoulos. 2020. LEGAL-BERT: The muppets straight out of law school. In *Findings of the Association for Computational Linguistics: EMNLP 2020*, pages 2898–2904, Online. Association for Computational Linguistics.

Ilias Chalkidis*, Nicolas Garneau*, Catalina Goanta, Daniel Martin Katz, and Anders Søgaard. 2023. LeXFiles and LegalLAMA: Facilitating English Multinational Legal Language Model Development. In *Proceedings of the 61st Annual Meeting of the Association for Computational Linguistics*, Toronto, Canada. Association for Computational Linguistics.

Jacob Devlin, Ming-Wei Chang, Kenton Lee, and Kristina Toutanova. 2018. BERT: pre-training of deep bidirectional transformers for language understanding. *CoRR*, abs/1810.04805.

Ingo Glaser, Bernhard Waltl, and Florian Matthes. 2018. Named entity recognition, extraction, and linking in german legal contracts. In *IRIS: Internationales Rechtsinformatik Symposium*, pages 325–334.

Randy Goebel, Yoshinobu Kano, Mi-Young Kim, Juliano Rabelo, Ken Satoh, and Masaharu Yoshioka. 2024. Overview of benchmark datasets and methods for the legal information extraction/entailment competition (coliee) 2024. In *New Frontiers in Artificial Intelligence*, pages 109–124, Singapore. Springer Nature Singapore.

Ben Hagag, Liav Harpaz, Gil Semo, Dor Bernsohn, Rohit Saha, Pashootan Vaezipoor, Kyryl Truskovskyi, and Gerasimos Spanakis. 2024. Legallens shared task 2024: Legal violation identification in unstructured text. *Preprint*, arXiv:2410.12064.

Pengcheng He, Xiaodong Liu, Jianfeng Gao, and Weizhu Chen. 2021. {DEBERTA}: {DECODING}-{enhanced} {bert} {with} {disentangled} {attention}. In *International Conference on Learning Representations*.

Maximilian Hofer, Andrey Kormilitzin, Paul Goldberg, and Alejo Nevado-Holgado. 2018. Few-shot learning for named entity recognition in medical text. *arXiv preprint arXiv:1811.05468*.

Chen Jia, Xiaobo Liang, and Yue Zhang. 2019. Cross-domain NER using cross-domain language modeling. In *Proceedings of the 57th Annual Meeting of the Association for Computational Linguistics*, pages 2464–2474, Florence, Italy. Association for Computational Linguistics.

Prathamesh Kalamkar, Astha Agarwal, Aman Tiwari, Smita Gupta, Saurabh Karn, and Vivek Raghavan. 2022. Named entity recognition in Indian court judgments. In *Proceedings of the Natural Legal Language Processing Workshop 2022*, pages 184–193, Abu Dhabi, United Arab Emirates (Hybrid). Association for Computational Linguistics.

Hossein Keshavarz, Zografoula Vagena, Pigi Kouki, Ilias Fountalis, Mehdi Mabrouki, Aziz Belaweid, and Nikolaos Vasiloglou. 2022. Named entity recognition in long documents: An end-to-end case study in the legal domain. In *2022 IEEE International Conference on Big Data (Big Data)*, pages 2024–2033.

Diederik P. Kingma and Jimmy Ba. 2017. Adam: A method for stochastic optimization. *Preprint*, arXiv:1412.6980.

Yuta Koreeda and Christopher Manning. 2021. ContractNLI: A dataset for document-level natural language inference for contracts. In *Findings of the Association for Computational Linguistics: EMNLP 2021*, pages 1907–1919, Punta Cana, Dominican Republic. Association for Computational Linguistics.

Srinivasa Rao Kundeti, J Vijayananda, Srikanth Mujjiga, and M Kalyan. 2016. Clinical named entity recognition: Challenges and opportunities. In *2016 IEEE International Conference on Big Data (Big Data)*, pages 1937–1945.

Guillaume Lample, Miguel Ballesteros, Sandeep Subramanian, Kazuya Kawakami, and Chris Dyer. 2016. Neural architectures for named entity recognition. In *Proceedings of the 2016 Conference of the North American Chapter of the Association for Computational Linguistics: Human Language Technologies*, pages 260–270, San Diego, California. Association for Computational Linguistics.

Elena Leitner, Georg Rehm, and Julian Moreno-Schneider. 2019a. Fine-grained Named Entity Recognition in Legal Documents. In *Semantic Systems. The Power of AI and Knowledge Graphs. Proceedings of the 15th International Conference (SEMANTiCS 2019)*, number 11702 in Lecture Notes in Computer Science, pages 272–287, Karlsruhe, Germany. Springer. 10/11 September 2019.

Elena Leitner, Georg Rehm, and Julian Moreno-Schneider. 2019b. Fine-grained named entity recognition in legal documents. In *Semantic Systems. The Power of AI and Knowledge Graphs*, pages 272–287, Cham. Springer International Publishing.

Yinhan Liu, Myle Ott, Naman Goyal, Jingfei Du, Mandar Joshi, Danqi Chen, Omer Levy, Mike Lewis, Luke Zettlemoyer, and Veselin Stoyanov. 2019. Roberta: A robustly optimized BERT pretraining approach. *CoRR*, abs/1907.11692.

Phuong Nguyen, Cong Nguyen, Hiep Nguyen, Minh Nguyen, An Trieu, Dat Nguyen, and Le-Minh Nguyen. 2024. Captain at coliee 2024: Large language model for legal text retrieval and entailment. In *New Frontiers in Artificial Intelligence*, pages 125–139, Singapore. Springer Nature Singapore.

Colin Raffel, Noam Shazeer, Adam Roberts, Katherine Lee, Sharan Narang, Michael Matena, Yanqi Zhou, Wei Li, and Peter J Liu. 2020. Exploring the limits of transfer learning with a unified text-to-text transformer. *Journal of machine learning research*, 21(140):1–67.

Paulo Silva, Carolina Gonçalves, Carolina Godinho, Nuno Antunes, and Marilia Curado. 2020. Using nlp and machine learning to detect data privacy violations. In *IEEE INFOCOM 2020 - IEEE Conference on Computer Communications Workshops (INFOCOM WKSHPS)*, pages 972–977.

Stavroula Skylaki, Ali Oskooei, Omar Bari, Nadja Herger, and Zac Kriegman. 2021. Legal entity extraction using a pointer generator network. In *2021 International Conference on Data Mining Workshops (ICDMW)*, pages 653–658.

Yonghui Wu, Mike Schuster, Zhifeng Chen, Quoc V. Le, Mohammad Norouzi, Wolfgang Macherey, Maxim Krikun, Yuan Cao, Qin Gao, Klaus Macherey, Jeff Klingner, Apurva Shah, Melvin Johnson, Xiaobing Liu, Łukasz Kaiser, Stephan Gouws, Yoshikiyo Kato, Taku Kudo, Hideto Kazawa, Keith Stevens, George Kurian, Nishant Patil, Wei Wang, Cliff Young, Jason Smith, Jason Riesa, Alex Rudnick, Oriol Vinyals, Greg Corrado, Macduff Hughes, and Jeffrey Dean. 2016. Google's neural machine translation system: Bridging the gap between human and machine translation. *CoRR*, abs/1609.08144.

Zhanye Yang. 2022. Legalnli: natural language inference for legal compliance inspection. In *International Conference on Advanced Algorithms and Neural Networks (AANN 2022)*, volume 12285, pages 144–150. SPIE.

Yaoquan Yu, Yuefeng Guo, Zhiyuan Zhang, Mengshi Li, Tianyao Ji, Wenhu Tang, and Qinghua Wu. 2020. Intelligent classification and automatic annotation of violations based on neural network language model. In *2020 International Joint Conference on Neural Networks (IJCNN)*, pages 1–7.

Can Çetindağ, Berkay Yazıcıoğlu, and Aykut Koç. 2023. Named-entity recognition in turkish legal texts. *Natural Language Engineering*, 29(3):615–642.

LegalLens 2024 Shared Task: Masala-chai Group Submission

Khalid Rajan[*]
Georgian
khalidrajan14@gmail.com

Royal Sequiera[*]
Georgian
royal@georgian.io

Abstract

In this paper, we describe masala-chai team's participation in the LegalLens 2024 shared task, and outline our approach to predicting legal entities and performing natural language inference in the legal domain. We experimented with several transformer-based models including BERT, RoBERTa, Llama 3.1, and GPT-4o. Our experiments indicated that state-of-art models such as GPT-4o do not work well for NER and NLI tasks despite using techniques such as bootstrapping and prompt optimization. Our best evaluations on the NER task (F1 macro: 0.380) was obtained using a finetuned RoBERTa model and NLI (accuracy: 0.825, F1 macro: 0.833) using a finetuned Llama 3.1 8B model. However, RoBERTa, despite having a fraction of Llama 3.1 8B's parameters, delivered comparable results. Key findings and insights from our experiments are discussed in detail. We make our results and code available for reproducibility and further analysis at https://github.com/rosequ/masala-chai.

1 Introduction

Information extraction tasks, such as Named Entity Recognition (NER) have been predominantly limited to identifying common entities such as `Person`, `Location`, and `Organization`. As an extension, previous studies using benchmark datasets, such as CoNLL 2003 (Sang and De Meulder, 2003), have achieved high metrics for effectiveness. For example, finetuned BERT Base model achieved an F1 macro of 92.4 on ConLL 2003 dataset (Devlin et al., 2018). However, applying NER to specialized domains, such as legal and medical texts, presents challenges due to their complex terminology, domain-specific language, and limited availability of annotated training data.

The LegalLens 2024 shared task aims to push the research in the areas of legal NLP by inviting participants to work on two tasks: Legal Named Entity Recognition (L-NER), and Legal Natural Language Inference (L-NLI) (Hagag et al., 2024). The first subtask involves identifying violation indicators by extracting legal entities such as `Law`, `Violation`, `Violated By`, and `Violated On`. Similarly, the motivation behind Legal Natural Language Inference is to understand the relationship between a pair of legal texts (hypothesis and premise) as contradiction, entailment, and neutral.

In this paper, we present our team—masala-chai's—submission to the LegalLens shared task. We explore the performance of various transformer models, both open-source and commercial, on NER and NLI tasks in the legal domain. While we suggest enhancing performance with DSPy and TextGrad, the results still fall short compared to fine-tuning smaller models like RoBERTa.

Our experiments revealed that while models like GPT-4o struggled with legal tasks, even when using advanced techniques like prompt optimization, smaller models like RoBERTa performed competitively, achieving an F1 macro score of 0.701 for NER and 0.833 for NLI. This highlights that fine-tuning smaller, more efficient models can deliver results comparable to larger language models. We present our findings, discuss the nuances of using LLMs, and share our code to support reproducibility and further exploration.

2 Tasks

2.1 Named Entity Recognition (NER)

Named Entity Recognition (NER) is the task of identifying and classifying entities in a given text into predefined categories. Formally, let S be a sentence with a sequence of tokens $S = \{t_1, t_2, \ldots, t_n\}$, where t_i represents the i-th token in the sentence. The goal of NER is to assign a label y_i from a set of predefined labels $\mathcal{Y}$ to each token t_i, such that $\mathbf{y} = \{y_1, y_2, \ldots, y_n\}$, where

[*]Equal contribution

Proceedings of the Natural Legal Language Processing Workshop 2024, pages 346–354
November 16, 2024 ©2024 Association for Computational Linguistics

$y_i \in \mathcal{Y}$.

The label set $\mathcal{Y}$ for our task includes the entity types LAW (legal statutes or regulations), VIOLATION (specific violations), VIOLATED BY (responsible entities), VIOLATED ON (victim or affected party), as well as a non-entity label O (Outside any named entity).

2.2 Natural Language Inference (NLI)

In the legal domain, natural language inference is important for automating legal reasoning; therefore, understanding the relationships between statements is a necessary step. The aim of the NLI task is to determine the relationship between a pair of sentences—a *premise* and a *hypothesis*. If a hypothesis can be logically inferred from the premise (entailment), the hypothesis contradicts the premise (contradiction), or the hypothesis is neither entailed by nor contradicts the premise (neutral).

3 System Description

Our approaches for the Named Entity Recognition (NER) and Natural Language Inference (NLI) tasks involved i) fine-tuning pre-trained language models, and ii) utilizing prompt engineering techniques. We experimented with pre-trained transformer models, including BERT (both uncased and cased versions) (Devlin et al., 2018), DistilBERT (Sanh, 2019), RoBERTa (Liu, 2019), FLAN T5 (Chung et al., 2024), Llama 3.1 (Dubey et al., 2024), and GPT-4o (OpenAI et al., 2024). Each model was fine-tuned on the train split.

3.1 NER

For the NER task, we began by finetuning BERT, DistilBERT, FLAN T5, and RoBERTa. We also used GPT-4o in four different settings for NER, by running GPT-4o as it is (GPT-4o raw), using bootstrapping and Chain of Thought (CoT) reasoning via DSPy (Khattab et al., 2023), prompt optimization on top of GPT-4o raw by using TextGrad (Yuksekgonul et al., 2024), and by finetuning GPT-4o for NER task.

For both the DSPy and TextGrad implementation, we had to reformulate the original sequence tagging problem to an entity extraction problem so that it was easier for the frameworks to predict entities. The DSPy signature corresponding to this reformulation is shown in Appendix A. The original prompt for TextGrad can be found in Appendix B.

Since our preliminary analysis showed that finetuning RoBERTa yielded the best results, we attached a Conditional Random Field (CRF) head to the RoBERTa model and finetuned that model as well. The rationale behind appending a CRF layer is to model dependencies between labels in the entire sequence thereby maximizing the probability of a complete list of BIO tags given a list of tokens.

All NER models were finetuned on an Apple M2 Pro, 12-core CPU, and 32GB memory.

3.2 NLI

For our experiments with NLI, we picked best set of transformer models from Bernsohn et al.: Falcon 7B and RoBERTa. Additionally, we employed GPT-4o with few-shot setting, finetuned GPT-4o, and Llam 3.1 8B.

We used the 4-bit quantized version of the Llama 3.1 model with 8B parameters. This model was optimized for memory and computational efficiency. Specifically, we enabled 4-bit precision loading, employed single quantization, and used the Non-Ferroelectric Four-level (NF4) quantization type. The model was instantiated with a causal language modeling head, using 16-bit floating-point computation.

We fine-tuned the Llama 3.1 8B model on Amazon Web Services (AWS) SageMaker, using the p4d.24xlarge instance, which features 8 Nvidia A100 GPUs and 96 vCPUs. To ensure determinism, we set a data seed in the Hugging Face training arguments. The utility `transformers.enable_full_determinism(seed=42)` was needed to ensure reproducible results in distributed training.

3.3 Pre-processing

For both tasks, we divided the dataset into a 70% training set and a 30% validation set. All models were finetuned on the training set, and results were evaluated on the validation set. The datasets were tokenized using Hugging Face AutoTokenizer. During inference, input prompts were tokenized with truncation enabled.

3.4 Training Procedure

For brevity, in this subsection, we only describe the hyperparameters for the best performing models.

Hyperparameters: For the NER task, the RoBERTa + CRF model was fine-tuned with a learning rate of 2×10^{-5} over 10 epochs. We

Model	Size	Method	Dev Accuracy	Dev F1	Test Accuracy	Test F1
BERT Uncased	66M	Fine-tune	0.948	0.871	0.804	0.685
BERT Cased	108M	Fine-tune	0.946	0.864	0.802	0.675
DistilBERT Cased	66M	Fine-tune	0.943	0.853	0.799	0.666
FLAN T5 Base	110M	Fine-tune	0.928	0.800	0.796	0.627
RoBERTa	125M	Fine-tune	**0.956**	0.891	**0.811**	0.696
RoBERTa + CRF	125M	Fine-tune	0.955	**0.892**	0.806	**0.701**
GPT-4o raw*	-	zero-shot	0.711	0.160	0.562	0.236
GPT-4o finetuned*	-	Fine-tune	0.923	0.779	0.822	0.635
GPT-4o raw + DSPy*	-	Few-shot	0.863	0.644	0.794	0.612
GPT-4o raw + TextGrad	-	prompt-optimization	0.824	0.200	0.823	0.214

Table 1: NER Task Results with Size and Method. *Note: GPT-4o implementation numbers have been calculated only using samples where the length of the list of predicted BIO tags was equivalent to the length of the list of input tokens. Note that we consider the `O` tag for our evaluations.

Model	Size	Method	Dev Accuracy	Dev F1 Macro	Test Accuracy	Test F1 Macro
Falcon	7B	QLoRA	0.734	0.710	0.750	0.766
RoBERTa	125M	Fine-tune	0.830	0.840	**0.833**	0.816
GPT-4o + DSPy	-	Few-shot	0.780	0.770	0.798	0.772
GPT-4o	-	Fine-tune	0.340	0.140	0.800	0.780
Llama 3.1	8B	QLoRA	**0.861**	**0.858**	0.825	**0.833**

Table 2: NLI Task Results with Size and Method

employed 500 warmup steps to stabilize the learning rate during training. A weight decay of 0.01 was applied to regularize the model and prevent overfitting.

For the NLI task, Llama 3.1 was finetuned with a per-device batch size of 1, with a gradient accumulation set to 4, effectively increasing the batch size to 4. The learning rate was set to 2×10^{-4}, and the model was trained for 30 epochs. Mixed precision training was used, and the Paged AdamW (Loshchilov and Hutter, 2019) optimizer was employed in 32-bit mode. A constant learning rate schedule was applied, and the maximum gradient norm was set to 0.3. Additionally, a warmup ratio of 3% was used to stabilize training.

Parameter-Efficient Fine-Tuning (PEFT): For Llama 3.1, the PEFT configuration was applied with a `LoRA Alpha` of 32, a rank (`r`) of 16, and a dropout rate of 0.05. The task type was set to be causal language modeling.

Training Prompt: Llama 3.1 was fine-tuned using the `SFTTrainer`, configured with the aforementioned training arguments and PEFT settings. The maximum sequence length was set to 512 tokens, and text packing was enabled during dataset processing.

3.5 Inference

During inference for the NLI task, generation was performed using a sampling strategy with a top-p of 0.95 and a temperature of 0.01 to control the randomness of predictions.

4 Results

4.1 NER

The results for NER are shown in Table 1. Our results are consistent with Bernsohn et al., where we see that BERT-based models perform better than commercially available LLMs such as GPT-4o.

Finetuning GPT-4o and utilizing bootstrapping and CoT did produce improved results compared to GPT-4o raw, but the issue of mismatch between the length of input and output sequences persisted. With all GPT-4o configurations, we were only able to evaluate using less than 10% of samples in the test set, where the length of input tokens was equivalent to the length of the NER tags.

The results of the NER task indicate that RoBERTa achieved the highest effective measures on the held-out validation set prompting us to submit the model predictions to the shared task.

While most of the BERT based models also performed well, GPT-4o showed lower performance, suggesting that it may require different approaches to handle legal language effectively. In the submission we made for the shared task, the finetuned RoBERTa model achieved an F1 score of 0.689.

4.2 NLI

The NLI results are shown in Table 2. While the fine-tuned Llama 3.1 8B model performed well on the dev set during the testing phase, these results did not carry over to the evaluation phase of the shared task. After the shared task ended, we discovered that Llama 3.1 exhibited non-deterministic behavior, producing inconsistent results even when trained on the same dataset with identical hyperparameters, including a fixed random seed. This inconsistency led to a significantly lower F1 macro score of 0.525 during the shared task evaluation. However, after resolving the non-deterministic issue, Llama 3.1 consistently achieved an F1 macro of 0.833 on the test set.

It is worth noting that the finetuned version of RoBERTa model also performed competitively in the NLI task. The NLI results similarly reflected the challenges of the NER task, with transformer models performing well but still struggling with the complexities of legal reasoning.

5 Discussion

While finetuning GPT-4o for NER, we noticed the primary reason GPT-4o achieves inferior performance is due to i) its difficulty tagging long sequences of text, and ii) hallucination of entities.

We notice that for a given sequence of tokens, once the model predicts entities such as `B-VIOLATION`, it goes on to predict `I-VIOLATION` entities until the end of the sequence. As for the hallucinatory nature of LLMs, we notice that there are entities that are outside the label set $\mathcal{Y}$ are being predicted (entities such as `B-L-I` are hallucinated). Observing the loss plots corresponding to GPT-4o finetuning from Figure 1 also shows that there tends to be high variance during finetuning.

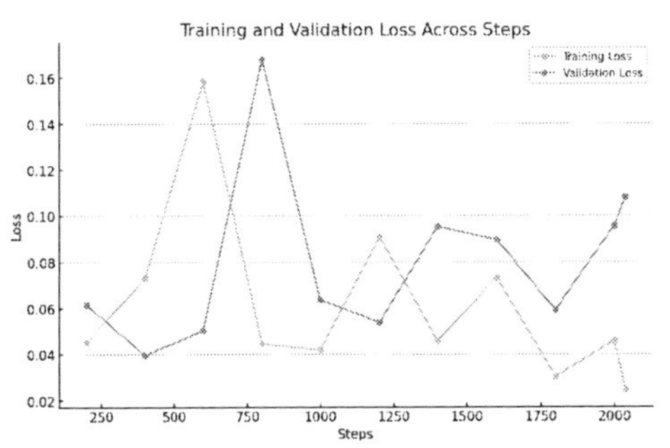

Figure 1: Training vs validation for GPT-4o finetuning

The LLMs also fail to output a sequence consistently of BIO tags that are the same length as the input sequence of tokens. This presents challenges for evaluating performance, as the truth label sequences are supposed to be of equivalent length to the input sequence. While running inference with GPT-4o configurations, we noticed a mismatch in the length of the list of input tokens and output tags in both validation and test sets. Specifically, we saw a mismatch of 92.9% samples in the test set when running inference with GPT-4o raw, 92.1% of samples in the test set when running inference with a finetuned GPT-4o model, and 91.8% of samples in the test set when running inference with GPT-4o + DSPy, making GPT-4o unsuitable for legal NER.

In the case of NLI, while Llama 3.1 delivers the best performance, RoBERTa comes close, despite having only 1.5% of Llama 3.1's 8B parameters. We anticipate that further research into smaller language models, through methods like continued pretraining, could eventually achieve performance parity if not superior results—a direction we reserve for future exploration. Additionally, methods for fine-tuning Llama 3.1 8B including full fine-tuning with a larger legal corpus can also be explored to for further improvements.

6 Conclusion

In this report, we outlined our approach to tackling Named Entity Recognition (NER) and Natural Language Inference (NLI) tasks in the legal domain as part of the LegalLens shared task. Our experiments highlighted the strengths of fine-tuning transformer-based models such as RoBERTa and Llama 3.1, particularly for handling complex legal text. Despite the strong performance of these models, especially RoBERTa for NER, we observed limitations in commercially available large language models like GPT-4o, which struggled with sequence length mismatches and hallucinations during NER tasks.

Additionally, while Llama 3.1 achieved the best NLI results, RoBERTa demonstrated competitive performance despite having significantly fewer parameters. This suggests that smaller models, when fine-tuned effectively, can rival much larger models in legal NLP tasks. Our results indicate that there is still room for improvement in entity extraction and reasoning in the legal domain.

7 Ethics Statement

To the best of our knowledge, the framework presented in this paper is not intended for any unethical applications. Our goal is to contribute to advancing research in legal Natural Language Processing by contributing to tasks such as Named Entity Recognition and Natural Language Inference. We hope this work will support the responsible and ethical development of legal AI systems.

Acknowledgments

We thank the organizers of the LegalLens 2024 shared task for their constant support throughout the competition.

References

Dor Bernsohn, Gil Semo, Yaron Vazana, Gila Hayat, Ben Hagag, Joel Niklaus, Rohit Saha, and Kyryl Truskovskyi. 2024. Legallens: Leveraging llms for legal violation identification in unstructured text. *Preprint*, arXiv:2402.04335.

Hyung Won Chung, Le Hou, Shayne Longpre, Barret Zoph, Yi Tay, William Fedus, Yunxuan Li, Xuezhi Wang, Mostafa Dehghani, Siddhartha Brahma, et al. 2024. Scaling instruction-finetuned language models. *Journal of Machine Learning Research*, 25(70):1–53.

Jacob Devlin, Ming-Wei Chang, Kenton Lee, and Kristina Toutanova. 2018. Bert: Pre-training of deep bidirectional transformers for language understanding. *arXiv preprint arXiv:1810.04805*.

Abhimanyu Dubey, Abhinav Jauhri, Abhinav Pandey, Abhishek Kadian, Ahmad Al-Dahle, Aiesha Letman, Akhil Mathur, Alan Schelten, Amy Yang, Angela Fan, et al. 2024. The llama 3 herd of models. *arXiv preprint arXiv:2407.21783*.

Ben Hagag, Liav Harpaz, Gil Semo, Dor Bernsohn, Rohit Saha, Pashootan Vaezipoor, Kyryl Truskovskyi, and Gerasimos Spanakis. 2024. Legallens shared task 2024: Legal violation identification in unstructured text. *Preprint*, arXiv:2410.12064.

Omar Khattab, Arnav Singhvi, Paridhi Maheshwari, Zhiyuan Zhang, Keshav Santhanam, Sri Vardhamanan, Saiful Haq, Ashutosh Sharma, Thomas T Joshi, Hanna Moazam, et al. 2023. Dspy: Compiling declarative language model calls into self-improving pipelines. *arXiv preprint arXiv:2310.03714*.

Yinhan Liu. 2019. Roberta: A robustly optimized bert pretraining approach. *arXiv preprint arXiv:1907.11692*.

Ilya Loshchilov and Frank Hutter. 2019. Decoupled weight decay regularization. *Preprint*, arXiv:1711.05101.

OpenAI, Josh Achiam, Steven Adler, Sandhini Agarwal, Lama Ahmad, Ilge Akkaya, Florencia Leoni Aleman, Diogo Almeida, Janko Altenschmidt, Sam Altman, Shyamal Anadkat, Red Avila, Igor Babuschkin, Suchir Balaji, Valerie Balcom, Paul Baltescu, Haiming Bao, Mohammad Bavarian, Jeff Belgum, Irwan Bello, Jake Berdine, Gabriel Bernadett-Shapiro, Christopher Berner, Lenny Bogdonoff, Oleg Boiko, Madelaine Boyd, Anna-Luisa Brakman, Greg Brockman, Tim Brooks, Miles Brundage, Kevin Button, Trevor Cai, Rosie Campbell, Andrew Cann, Brittany Carey, Chelsea Carlson, Rory Carmichael, Brooke Chan, Che Chang, Fotis Chantzis, Derek Chen, Sully Chen, Ruby Chen, Jason Chen, Mark Chen, Ben Chess, Chester Cho, Casey Chu, Hyung Won Chung, Dave Cummings, Jeremiah Currier, Yunxing Dai, Cory Decareaux, Thomas Degry, Noah Deutsch, Damien Deville, Arka Dhar, David Dohan, Steve Dowling, Sheila Dunning, Adrien Ecoffet, Atty Eleti, Tyna Eloundou, David Farhi, Liam Fedus, Niko Felix, Simón Posada Fishman, Juston Forte, Isabella Fulford, Leo Gao, Elie Georges, Christian Gibson, Vik Goel, Tarun Gogineni, Gabriel Goh, Rapha Gontijo-Lopes, Jonathan Gordon, Morgan Grafstein, Scott Gray, Ryan Greene, Joshua Gross, Shixiang Shane Gu, Yufei Guo, Chris Hallacy, Jesse Han, Jeff Harris, Yuchen He, Mike Heaton, Johannes Heidecke, Chris Hesse, Alan Hickey, Wade Hickey, Peter Hoeschele, Brandon Houghton, Kenny Hsu, Shengli Hu, Xin Hu, Joost Huizinga, Shantanu Jain, Shawn Jain, Joanne Jang, Angela Jiang, Roger Jiang, Haozhun Jin, Denny Jin, Shino Jomoto, Billie Jonn, Heewoo Jun, Tomer Kaftan, Łukasz Kaiser, Ali Kamali, Ingmar Kanitscheider, Nitish Shirish Keskar, Tabarak Khan, Logan Kilpatrick, Jong Wook Kim, Christina Kim, Yongjik Kim, Jan Hendrik Kirchner, Jamie Kiros, Matt Knight, Daniel Kokotajlo, Łukasz Kondraciuk, Andrew Kondrich, Aris Konstantinidis, Kyle Kosic, Gretchen Krueger, Vishal Kuo, Michael Lampe, Ikai Lan, Teddy Lee, Jan Leike, Jade Leung, Daniel Levy, Chak Ming Li, Rachel Lim, Molly Lin, Stephanie Lin, Mateusz Litwin, Theresa Lopez, Ryan Lowe, Patricia Lue, Anna Makanju, Kim Malfacini, Sam Manning, Todor Markov, Yaniv Markovski, Bianca Martin, Katie Mayer, Andrew Mayne, Bob McGrew, Scott Mayer McKinney, Christine McLeavey, Paul McMillan, Jake McNeil, David Medina, Aalok Mehta, Jacob Menick, Luke Metz, Andrey Mishchenko, Pamela Mishkin, Vinnie Monaco, Evan Morikawa, Daniel Mossing, Tong Mu, Mira Murati, Oleg Murk, David Mély, Ashvin Nair, Reiichiro Nakano, Rajeev Nayak, Arvind Neelakantan, Richard Ngo, Hyeonwoo Noh, Long Ouyang, Cullen O'Keefe, Jakub Pachocki, Alex Paino, Joe Palermo, Ashley Pantuliano, Giambattista Parascandolo, Joel Parish, Emy Parparita, Alex Passos, Mikhail Pavlov, Andrew Peng, Adam Perelman, Filipe de Avila Belbute Peres, Michael Petrov, Henrique Ponde de Oliveira Pinto, Michael, Pokorny, Michelle Pokrass, Vitchyr H. Pong, Tolly Powell, Alethea Power, Boris Power, Elizabeth Proehl, Raul Puri, Alec Radford, Jack Rae, Aditya Ramesh, Cameron Raymond, Francis Real, Kendra Rimbach, Carl Ross, Bob Rotsted, Henri Roussez, Nick Ryder, Mario Saltarelli, Ted Sanders, Shibani Santurkar, Girish Sastry, Heather Schmidt, David Schnurr, John Schulman, Daniel Selsam, Kyla Sheppard, Toki Sherbakov, Jessica Shieh, Sarah Shoker, Pranav

Shyam, Szymon Sidor, Eric Sigler, Maddie Simens, Jordan Sitkin, Katarina Slama, Ian Sohl, Benjamin Sokolowsky, Yang Song, Natalie Staudacher, Felipe Petroski Such, Natalie Summers, Ilya Sutskever, Jie Tang, Nikolas Tezak, Madeleine B. Thompson, Phil Tillet, Amin Tootoonchian, Elizabeth Tseng, Preston Tuggle, Nick Turley, Jerry Tworek, Juan Felipe Cerón Uribe, Andrea Vallone, Arun Vijayvergiya, Chelsea Voss, Carroll Wainwright, Justin Jay Wang, Alvin Wang, Ben Wang, Jonathan Ward, Jason Wei, CJ Weinmann, Akila Welihinda, Peter Welinder, Jiayi Weng, Lilian Weng, Matt Wiethoff, Dave Willner, Clemens Winter, Samuel Wolrich, Hannah Wong, Lauren Workman, Sherwin Wu, Jeff Wu, Michael Wu, Kai Xiao, Tao Xu, Sarah Yoo, Kevin Yu, Qiming Yuan, Wojciech Zaremba, Rowan Zellers, Chong Zhang, Marvin Zhang, Shengjia Zhao, Tianhao Zheng, Juntang Zhuang, William Zhuk, and Barret Zoph. 2024. Gpt-4 technical report. *Preprint*, arXiv:2303.08774.

Erik F Sang and Fien De Meulder. 2003. Introduction to the conll-2003 shared task: Language-independent named entity recognition. *arXiv preprint cs/0306050*.

V Sanh. 2019. Distilbert, a distilled version of bert: Smaller, faster, cheaper and lighter. *arXiv preprint arXiv:1910.01108*.

Mert Yuksekgonul, Federico Bianchi, Joseph Boen, Sheng Liu, Zhi Huang, Carlos Guestrin, and James Zou. 2024. Textgrad: Automatic" differentiation" via text. *arXiv preprint arXiv:2406.07496*.

A DSPy Signature

```
class NERTag(Enum):
    """Docstring for MyEnum."""
    beginning_violated_by = 'B-VIOLATED BY'
    outside = 'O'
    inside_violation = 'I-VIOLATION'
    inside_violated_by = 'I-VIOLATED BY'
    beginning_law = 'B-LAW'
    inside_violated_on = 'I-VIOLATED ON'
    inside_law = 'I-LAW'
    beginning_violated_on = 'B-VIOLATED ON'
    beginning_violation = 'B-VIOLATION'

class NerTagTuple(pydantic.BaseModel):
    token: str
    ner_tag: NERTag

class Output(pydantic.BaseModel):
    ner_tags: list[NerTagTuple]

class ExtractLegalViolationEntities(dspy.Signature):
    """
    You are a legal expert who has been asked to extract legal entities from a given text. Please extract the following entities from the text, and return a list of Beginning Outside Inside (BIO) tags.
    The possible tags you could return are:
        - 'B-VIOLATED BY'
        - 'O'
        - 'I-VIOLATION'
        - 'I-VIOLATED BY'
        - 'B-LAW'
        - 'I-VIOLATED ON'
        - 'I-LAW'
        - 'B-VIOLATED ON'
        - 'B-VIOLATION'

    Do not return any other tags.
    """

    tokens: str = dspy.InputField(desc="input text")
    ner_tags: Output = dspy.OutputField(desc="list of NER tags")
```

B Prompts

Original system prompt for the NER task

You are a legal expert who answers questions about legal entities in a given text. You will extract the exact text from the text without ever adding any additional information.
The questions will be in the following order. If there are mutiple answers for a question, separate them with a comma. - LAW: What existing law or regulation does the violation pertain to? For example, GDPR, HIPAA, etc. - VIOLATION: What specific violation of the law occurred? Use the exact phrase from the input text. - VIOLATED BY: Exact individual, organization, company, etc. be specific, who violated the law, don't be generic - VIOLATED ON: Who was affected by the violation, for example, a person, users, customers, etc. be specific.
If there are multiple entities of the same type, separate them with a comma. Pick None if the entity is not present.

Examples: 1. text: "i'm writing this review to express my disappointment with a certain movie production company. they've been found spreading false and misleading information about their box office earnings and royalty payments . initially , they admitted to some issues with their royalty payments and promised to disclose more after an internal audit . but then , they submitted a document to the sec saying their previously reported earnings were unreliable and they were considering filing for bankruptcy . this caused a huge drop in their stock price and trading volume . its a real shame ."
LAW: None,
VIOLATION: [spreading false and misleading information about their box office earnings and royalty payments]
VIOLATED BY: [a certain movie production company]
VIOLATED ON: None
2. text: "Cant believe what happened recently . some company got busted for breaking the can-spam act . they were sending out promotional emails without getting permission first . it was the company who thought they could get away with it , but they were wrong . they were doing this to regular folks like you and me . not cool .",
LAW: ["can-spam act"]
VIOLATION: ["sending out promotional emails without getting permission first"]
VIOLATED BY: ["the company"]
VIOLATED ON: ["to regular folks like you and me"]
3. text: "anyone else notice that petcoke stuff being sold ? its a waste byproduct from an oil refinery with high levels of dangerous heavy metals and sulfur . instead of getting rid of it safely , its being marketed and distributed . its a total disregard for the environment . not cool ."
""VIOLATION": ["a waste byproduct from an oil refinery with high levels of dangerous heavy metals and sulfur"]
4. text: "caught wind of some dodgy dealings . these folks are manipulating the prices of cash wheat and wheat futures contracts for their own financial gain . its a disgrace to the entire industry !"
LAW: None
VIOLATION: ["manipulating the prices of cash wheat and wheat futures contracts"]
VIOLATED BY: None
VIOLATED ON: None

Extract the entities from the following text: "prompt". Think step by step.

Optimized system prompt for the NER task–Part 1

You are a legal expert who answers questions about legal entities in a given text. You will extract only the exact phrases directly related to the questions asked, without adding any additional information or context. Ensure that the terminology used in your responses matches the terminology found in the input text as closely as possible. Follow the exact structure of the ground truth answer, including the order and presence of keys. If an entity is not present, explicitly state 'None'. Be as specific as possible when identifying entities, avoiding generic terms.
The questions will be in the following order. If there are multiple answers for a question, separate them with a comma. - LAW: What existing law or regulation does the violation pertain to? For example, GDPR, HIPAA, etc. - VIOLATION: What specific violation of the law occurred? Use the exact phrase from the input text. - VIOLATED BY: Exact individual, organization, company, etc. Be specific, who violated the law, don't be generic. - VIOLATED ON: Who was affected by the violation, for example, a person, users, customers, etc. Be specific.
If there are multiple entities of the same type, separate them with a comma. Pick None if the entity is not present.

Examples: 1. text: "im writing this review to express my disappointment with a certain movie production company . theyve been found spreading false and misleading information about their box office earnings and royalty payments . initially , they admitted to some issues with their royalty payments and promised to disclose more after an internal audit . but then , they submitted a document to the sec saying their previously reported earnings were unreliable and they were considering filing for bankruptcy . this caused a huge drop in their stock price and trading volume . its a real shame ."
LAW: None,
VIOLATION: [spreading false and misleading information about their box office earnings and royalty payments]
VIOLATED BY: [a certain movie production company]
VIOLATED ON: None
2. text: "Cant believe what happened recently . some company got busted for breaking the can-spam act . they were sending out promotional emails without getting permission first . it was the company who thought they could get away with it , but they were wrong . they were doing this to regular folks like you and me . not cool .",
LAW: ["can-spam act"]
VIOLATION: ["sending out promotional emails without getting permission first"]
VIOLATED BY: ["the company"]
VIOLATED ON: ["to regular folks like you and me"]
3. text: "anyone else notice that petcoke stuff being sold ? its a waste byproduct from an oil refinery with high levels of dangerous heavy metals and sulfur . instead of getting rid of it safely , its being marketed and distributed . its a total disregard for the environment . not cool ."
LAW: None
VIOLATION: ["a waste byproduct from an oil refinery with high levels of dangerous heavy metals and sulfur"]
VIOLATED BY: None
VIOLATED ON: None
4. text: "caught wind of some dodgy dealings . these folks are manipulating the prices of cash wheat and wheat futures contracts for their own financial gain . its a disgrace to the entire industry !"
LAW: None
VIOLATION: ["manipulating the prices of cash wheat and wheat futures contracts"]
VIOLATED BY: None
VIOLATED ON: None

Optimized system prompt for the NER task–Part 2

Think step by step: First, identify the relevant law or regulation by looking for specific mentions of legal terms. Next, extract the specific violation by finding the exact phrase that describes the unlawful action. Then, identify who violated the law by looking for specific mentions of individuals or organizations. Finally, determine who was affected by the violation by identifying mentions of people or groups impacted. Pay special attention to key phrases that are central to the context of the violation, and ensure they are included in your response. Avoid ambiguous phrases and clarify any potentially ambiguous statements to match the ground truth more closely. Ensure that your responses match the ground truth exactly, without adding or omitting any information. If an entity is not explicitly mentioned in the text, use 'None' for that field. Avoid using ellipsis ('...') in your responses. Provide complete and clear phrases. Be concise and precise in your responses. Do not add any information that is not explicitly stated in the text.
Additional Guidelines: 1. **Exact Matching**: Your output must match the ground truth exactly, including the use of "None" where applicable. 2. **Handling Ambiguities**: If the text does not clearly identify the violator or the affected party, default to "None". 3. **Avoid Over-Specification**: Do not infer or add any information that is not explicitly stated in the text, even if it seems relevant. 4. **Ellipses and Exact Phrasing**: Ensure that any ellipses (...) in the violation description are used exactly as they appear in the ground truth. Match the wording precisely, including any placeholders or specific phrases. 5. **Combining Violations**: Combine related violations into a single string, separated by 'and' if necessary. 6. **Entity Recognition**: Look for specific terms like "charges," "billing," "unauthorized," and "complaints" when identifying violations. 7. **Post-Processing**: Re-evaluate the input text if the initial output is "None" to ensure no violations were missed.
Examples with Detailed Annotations: 1. text: "im writing this review to express my disappointment with a certain movie production company. they've been found spreading false and misleading information about their box office earnings and royalty payments. initially, they admitted to some issues with their royalty payments and promised to disclose more after an internal audit. but then , they submitted a document to the sec saying their previously reported earnings were unreliable and they were considering filing for bankruptcy. this caused a huge drop in their stock price and trading volume. its a real shame." LAW: None, VIOLATION: [spreading false and misleading information about their box office earnings and royalty payments] VIOLATED BY: [a certain movie production company] VIOLATED ON: None
2. text: "Cant believe what happened recently. some company got busted for breaking the can-spam act. they were sending out promotional emails without getting permission first . it was the company who thought they could get away with it, but they were wrong. they were doing this to regular folks like you and me. not cool.", LAW: ["can-spam act"] VIOLATION: ["sending out promotional emails without getting permission first"] VIOLATED BY: ["the company"] VIOLATED ON: ["to regular folks like you and me"] 3. text: "anyone else notice that petcoke stuff being sold? its a waste byproduct from an oil refinery with high levels of dangerous heavy metals and sulfur. instead of getting rid of it safely, its being marketed and distributed. its a total disregard for the environment. not cool." LAW: None VIOLATION: ["a waste byproduct from an oil refinery with high levels of dangerous heavy metals and sulfur"] VIOLATED BY: None VIOLATED ON: None
4. text: "caught wind of some dodgy dealings. these folks are manipulating the prices of cash wheat and wheat futures contracts for their own financial gain. its a disgrace to the entire industry!" LAW: None VIOLATION: ["manipulating the prices of cash wheat and wheat futures contracts"] VIOLATED BY: None VIOLATED ON: None
Reinforce Key Directives: - Ensure that your responses match the ground truth exactly, without adding or omitting any information. - If an entity is not explicitly mentioned in the text, use 'None' for that field. - Avoid using ellipsis ('...') in your responses. Provide complete and clear phrases. - Be concise and precise in your responses. - Do not add any information that is not explicitly stated in the text.

Semantists at LegalLens-2024: Data-efficient Training of LLM's for Legal Violation Identification

Rajaraman Kanagasabai
Institute for Infocomm Research,
Agency for Science, Technology and Research
1 Fusionopolis Way
Singapore 138632,
kanagasa@i2r.a-star.edu.sg

Hariram Veeramani
University of California,
Los Angeles,
USA.
hariram@ucla.edu

Abstract

In this paper, we describe our system for LegalLens-2024 Shared Task on automatically identifying legal violations from unstructured text sources. We participate in Subtask B, called Legal Natural Language Inference (L-NLI), that aims to predict the relationship between a given premise summarizing a class action complaint and a hypothesis from an online media text, indicating any association between the review and the complaint. This task is challenging as it provides only limited labelled data. In our work, we adopt LLM based methods and explore various data-efficient learning approaches for maximizing performance. In the end, our best model employed an ensemble of LLM's fine-tuned on the task-specific data, and achieved a Macro F1 score of 78.5% on test data, and ranked 2nd among all teams submissions.

1 Introduction

Legal violation identification is an important problem that aims to automatically uncover legal violations from unstructured text sources and assign potential victims to these violations. In the past, several works have addressed this but often relied on specialized models tailored for specific domain applications (Chalkidis et al., 2020; Yang, 2022). These models, while effective in their specific domains, lack the versatility needed to address the wide array of legal violations that can occur across different contexts.

The LegalLens Shared Task (Hagag et al., 2024) proposes to address the legal violation identification task using named entity recognition (NER), and the other for associating these violations with potentially affected individuals using natural language inference (NLI). In this paper, we report our system for addressing the NLI task (Sub-Task B).

Broadly, our approach is to adopt LLM based methods and explore various data-efficient learning approaches for maximizing performance on the NLI task. Our best model employed an ensemble of LLM's fine-tuned on the task-specific data. Our final system achieved a Macro F1 score of 78.5 and ranked 2nd among all teams submissions. Surprisingly, the classical Falcon LLM's outperformed many other SOTA LLM's. Also, our benchmark results highlight the challenge of these tasks and indicate there is ample room for model improvement. We demonstrate the limitation of the general LLM based methods and discuss possible future work.

2 Task and Dataset Description

The LegalLens challenge (Hagag et al., 2024) proposes two shared sub-tasks:

- Sub-Task A. Legal Named Entity Recognition (L-NER)
- Sub-Task B. Legal Natural Language Inference (L-NLI)

Participants can choose either of the two sub-task or both. We participate in Sub-Task B, defined as below.

2.1 Subtask B

Legal Natural Language Inference (L-NLI) Given a premise summarizing a class action complaint and a hypothesis from an online media text, the task is to determine if the relationship is entailed, contradicted, or neutral, indicating any association between the review and the complaint.

In contrast to NER which can help in detecting legal violations within unstructured textual data, the NLI task assists in associating these violations with potentially affected individuals.

2.2 Dataset

To facilitate the L-NLI task, the participants are provided with a dateset constructed based on previous class action cases and legal news. The latter is done by first summarizing the news to create the

Proceedings of the Natural Legal Language Processing Workshop 2024, pages 355–360
November 16, 2024

Domain	Labels #E/#C/#N	#Samples
Consumer Protection	16/17/29	62
Privacy	56/54/53	163
TCPA	26/27/21	74
Wage	6/3/4	13
Total	104/101/107	312

Table 1: Distribution of L-NLI Task Training Data, including the number of samples (column 3) and the class distribution (column 2) under each legal domain, where the classes 'Entailed' (E), 'Contradicted' (C), and 'Neutral' (N) are denoted using their first letters respectively.

premise, and generating a hypothesis using GPT-4 (Achiam et al., 2023) and subsequently validated by domain experts.

The data covers 4 legal domains namely Consumer Protection, Privacy, TCPA and Wage. In total, the data comprises 312 labeled samples (See Table 1). This is clearly small in size which makes the task quite challenging due to the risk of overfitting and limited generalization.

3 Our Approach

Natural language inference (NLI) is the task of detecting inferential relationships between a premise text and a hypothesis text (Dagan et al., 2010; Romanov and Shivade, 2018; Storks et al., 2019), which is considered fundamental in natural language understanding (NLU) research (Bowman et al., 2015). In L-NLI task, the premise is a summary of a class action complaint and the hypothesis an online media text, and the objective is to determine if the relationship is 'entailed', 'contradicted', or 'neutral'.

Several NLI systems have been proposed in the literature (Bowman et al., 2015; Storks et al., 2019), and can be adapted for the L-NLI task. (Bernsohn et al., 2024) investigated this by fine-tuning popular Small language models, such as BERT and RoBERTa, and reported that the models struggled with the task. Also, using their legal counterparts, like Legal-BERT (Chalkidis et al., 2020), Legal- RoBERTa (Chalkidis et al., 2023), and Legal- English-RoBERTa (Niklaus et al., 2023) models also did not lead to much improvements. This can be attributed to the small data, as most of the models typically assume sufficiently large number of labelled data. This is particularly true for NLI which is essentially a 3-way sentence pair classification problem.

In comparison, LLMs are reported to learn relatively better in low data situations and generalize well to out-of-distribution (OOD) test data sets (Brown et al., 2020). This is in part due to their pre-training on variety of datasets, eg. SNLI and MNLI, as supported by the preliminary results of (Bernsohn et al., 2024) using fine-tuned Falcon (Almazrouei et al., 2023) and Llama (Touvron et al., 2023) models.

In our work, we perform a more extensive study by considering more LLM's and explore various LLM based strategies and techniques, beyond prompt engineering, for maximizing performance in the given task.

3.1 Vanilla Fine-tuning of LLM's

We consider several popular LLM's and fine-tune the models using the task-specific labeled data. This helps in adjusting the parameters of a pre-trained large language models to the L-NLI task. However, as the training data is too sparse, we do not use full fine-tuning but instead resort to Parameter Efficient Fine-Tuning (PEFT) (Houlsby et al., 2019). PEFT is a technique used to improve the performance of pre-trained LLMs on specific downstream tasks while minimizing the number of trainable parameters. It offers a more efficient approach by updating only a minor fraction of the model parameters during fine-tuning. PEFT technique selectively modifies only a small subset of the LLM's parameters, typically by adding new layers or modifying existing ones in a task-specific manner. This approach significantly reduces the computational and storage requirements while maintaining comparable performance to full fine-tuning. We adopt QLoRA (Dettmers et al., 2024), which applies a low-rank approximation to the weight update matrix and also quantizes the weights of the LoRA (Hu et al., 2021) adapters resulting in reduced memory footprint and storage requirements.

3.2 Data Augmentation

Data augmentation involves the adoption of new methods aimed at improving model efficacy by enriching training data diversity without necessitating further data collection efforts. Data augmentation using LLMs has heralded innovative learning paradigms, marking a significant departure from traditional methods (Ding et al., 2024). In our case, we employ data augmentation to address the challenging categories such as 'Wage' which has only 13 samples in total. We explore various strategies including 1. Data creation which leverages the few-shot learning ability of LLMs to create a large synthetic dataset; 2. Data labeling which uses the LLM to label existing datasets; 3. Data reformation which transforms existing data to produce new data.

3.3 LLM Ensembleing

Open-source LLMs exhibit diverse strengths and weaknesses due to variations in data, architectures and hyperparameters, making them complementary. Often there does not exist one LLM that dominates the competition for all examples. Thus, it is attractive to ensemble the output of the best LLMs (based on input, task and domain) to give consistently superior performance across examples. By combining their unique contributions; the biases, errors and uncertainties in individual LLMs can be alleviated, resulting in outputs aligned with human preferences (Rajamanickam and Rajaraman, 2023, Yang et al., 2023).

In our experiments, we pool multiple LLM's and explore ensembling their individual predictions using voting strategies to improve overall robustness and accuracy.

Our experiments and results are described in detail in the following section.

4 Experiments & Results

In the L-NLI challenge dataset, there are 312 instances distributed across 4 legal domains (See Table 1). For training the models, we randomly split the instances into 80% training and 20% validation, repeat the experiments five times and report the average performance. The results are presented below, where performance metrics are quoted in % for easier interpretation, unless stated otherwise.

The experiments were executed on NVIDIA-GeForce RTX 2080 series with eight cores of GPU machines with 8*12 GB of memory for all our experiments. Also, to train T5 large models, we have used NVIDIA-GeForce Tesla V100 series SXM2-32GB with 5 cores of GPU machines. Models were trained for 3-5 hours for training and reasoning. The pretrained weights for the transformers prior to fine-tuning were from the HuggingFace NLP Library.

Model	Val (Macro F1)
T5-base	81.4
Falcon-7b	88.4
Llama2-7b	86.6
Gemma-7b	84.5
Data Augmentation	84.5
LLM Ensembling	**89.4**

Table 2: Comparison of performance of the models explored in our experiments.

4.1 Approach 1: (Vanilla Fine-tuning of LLM's) :

We first evaluated a basic fine-tuning approach. We considered SOTA LLM's such as Llama2-7b (Touvron et al., 2023), Gemma-7b (Team et al., 2024). Additionally, we included Falcon-7b (Almazrouei et al., 2023) as it had good reported performance (Bernsohn et al., 2024). Also included was T5 (Raffel et al., 2020) to serve as a baseline.

We adopted QLoRA fine-tuning, which applies a low-rank approximation to the weight update matrix and also quantizes the weights (Dettmers et al., 2024). For parameter settings, we use a QLoRA rank of 64, alpha of 32, and trained the models for 20 epochs with an initial learning rate of 2e-4, and a dropout rate of 0.25.

We observed that Falcon-7b performed surprisingly better than SOTA models like Llama and Gemma, and achieved 88.4% on validation data. Hence we decided to adopt it for further studies.

4.2 Approach 2: (Data Augmentation) :

We considered Falcon-7b, and employed data augmentation specifically to address the challenging category 'Wage' which has only 13 samples in total. In particular, we adopted data creation, labeling and reformation strategies to augment the training data, as below.

Using GPT-4 (Achiam et al., 2023), we created additional data using prompt engineering by first leveraging the few-shot learning ability to create synthetic samples and labels. Then, for each source sample, say 'Entailed', transform existing sample to produce samples for 'Contradict' and 'Neutral'. Thus we triple the labeled data and use random sampling to create train/val sets.

However, fine-tuning with the augmented data resulted in F1 score below that of unaugmented data, and so we abandoned it.

Domain	Labels #E/#C/#N	#Samples
BIPA	14/4/4	22
Consumer	4/1/3	8
Data Breach	8/5/7	20
TCPA	5/2/2	9
VPPA	2/2/2	6
Wage	7/1/11	19
Total	40/15/29	84

Table 3: Distribution of L-NLI Test Data, including the number of samples (column 3) and the class distribution (column 2) under each legal domain, where the classes 'Entailed' (E), 'Contradicted' (C), and 'Neutral' (N) are denoted using their first letters respectively.

4.3 Approach 3: (LLM Ensembling) :

Ensembling aims to combine the outputs of multiple LLMs (based on input, task and domain) so as to achieve better accuracy and robustness across all samples. Towards this, we trained 3 instances of Falcon-7b, each with a different set of randomly split (80-20) training data. (Ideally a partitioned data is preferred but due to small size we decided against it.) We ran inference individually on the 3 models, and aggregated the predictions using majority voting. This ensemble approach achieved the best score (See Table 2), making it as our final submission.

We planned to perform extensive ensembling experiments using different LLM's, data sizes, etc. but could not complete them due to resource limitations. This deserves further study.

4.4 Analysis of Test Results

The test results and the data with target labels were announced soon after submission deadline. Our system achieved a Macro F1 score of 78.5% on test data, and ranked 2nd among all teams submissions.

Table 3 provides details about test data statistics. We note that the test data is from 6 domains, compared to 4 domains in training data. This clearly requires OOD performance, and possibly the reason for the significant drop in F1 from validation score.

As further investigation, we performed error analysis using two types of classification errors (Bernsohn et al., 2024): first-class errors, which involve confusions between "Contradict" and "Entailed", and second-class errors, which are misclassifications of "Contradict" or "Entailed" as "Neutral". Our final model had 21 Class-2 errors, and no Class-1 errors, which implies that the model has difficulty in identifying edge cases whether there is violation or not.

Domain	#Correctly Classified	#Misclassified
BIPA	13	9
Consumer	7	1
Data Breach	18	2
TCPA	8	1
VPPA	4	2
Wage	13	6
Total	63	21

Table 4: Performance of our final model on the Test Data, across the 6 domains included in the data

We present a distribution of errors across the domains in Table 4. The model performed well on Consumer, Data Breach and TCPA which had similar ones in training set. In contrast, the proportion of errors in the unseen domains BIPA and VPPA were significantly larger. Similar performance degradation was also observed for 'Wage' which can be recalled as one that had too few training samples.

In summary, we conclude that our LLM ensemble model performed fairly well for identifying legal violations, though there is scope for further improvements in tackling small data and OOD situations.

5 Discussion and Conclusion

This paper described our system for LegalLens-2024 Shared Task that aims to automatically uncover legal violations from unstructured text sources and assign potential victims to these violations. We participate in Subtask B, called Legal Natural Language Inference (L-NLI), that aims to predict the relationship between a given premise summarizing a class action complaint and a hypothesis from an online media text, indicating any association between the review and the complaint.

This task is challenging in view of the limited labelled data, and hence we explored various approaches for data-efficient learning with LLM's, such as PEFT fine-tuning, Data Augmentation and LLM Ensembling. In the end, our ensemble approach performed the best and achieved a Macro F1 score of 78.5%, and ranked 2nd among all teams submissions. The key findings are:

- LLM Fine-tuning improves zero-shot and few-shot performance. This possibly implies that specific domains can benefit from task specific training data even if smallish in size.

- The performance of various LLM's overall are somewhat close. Though Falcon emerged as the winner, the margins were not huge, and our T5 baseline was not far behind.

- Simple data augmentation may not be enough to guarantee improved performance. More careful data generation and possibly some human involvement is required.

- Ensemble approach has strong promise to achieve robust performance across all examples.

In summary, our research highlight the challenge of legal violation identification in real-life, and the limitations of SOTA LLM's. This further suggests that there is ample room for model improvement and scope for possible future work, especially under limited data settings.

Limitations

Our work explored various LLM strategies for identifying legal violations under small data settings, but is clearly preliminary. We were limited by resource constraints and so could not do explore fine-tuning very large models (11b or bigger) or try other data augmentation experiments, along with extensive hyperparameter optimization. A more rigorous experimentation may be required to further validate the findings of the paper.

Acknowledgments

This work was supported by fundings from A*STAR Epidemic Preparedness Horizontal Coordinating Office (EP HTCO) FY22_CF_HTCO SEED_EP_IDLabs_C22714020

References

Josh Achiam, Steven Adler, Sandhini Agarwal, Lama Ahmad, Ilge Akkaya, Florencia Leoni Aleman, Diogo Almeida, Janko Altenschmidt, Sam Altman, Shyamal Anadkat, et al. 2023. Gpt-4 technical report. *arXiv preprint arXiv:2303.08774*.

Ebtesam Almazrouei, Hamza Alobeidli, Abdulaziz Alshamsi, Alessandro Cappelli, Ruxandra Cojocaru, Mérouane Debbah, Étienne Goffinet, Daniel Hesslow, Julien Launay, Quentin Malartic, et al. 2023. The falcon series of open language models. *arXiv preprint arXiv:2311.16867*.

Dor Bernsohn, Gil Semo, Yaron Vazana, Gila Hayat, Ben Hagag, Joel Niklaus, Rohit Saha, and Kyryl Truskovskyi. 2024. Legallens: Leveraging llms for legal violation identification in unstructured text. *arXiv preprint arXiv:2402.04335*.

Samuel R Bowman, Gabor Angeli, Christopher Potts, and Christopher D Manning. 2015. A large annotated corpus for learning natural language inference. In *Proceedings of the 2015 Conference on Empirical Methods in Natural Language Processing*. Association for Computational Linguistics.

Tom B Brown, Benjamin Mann, Nick Ryder, Melanie Subbiah, Jared Kaplan, Prafulla Dhariwal, Arvind Neelakantan, Pranav Shyam, Girish Sastry, Amanda Askell, et al. 2020. Language models are few-shot learners. In *Proceedings of the 34th International Conference on Neural Information Processing Systems*, pages 1877–1901.

Ilias Chalkidis, Manos Fergadiotis, Prodromos Malakasiotis, Nikolaos Aletras, and Ion Androutsopoulos. 2020. Legal-bert: The muppets straight out of law school. *arXiv preprint arXiv:2010.02559*.

Ilias Chalkidis, Nicolas Garneau, Catalina Goanta, Daniel Katz, and Anders Søgaard. 2023. Lexfiles and legallama: Facilitating english multinational legal language model development. In *The 61st Annual Meeting Of The Association For Computational Linguistics*.

Ido Dagan, Bill Dolan, Bernardo Magnini, and Dan Roth. 2010. Recognizing textual entailment: Rational, evaluation and approaches–erratum. *Natural Language Engineering*, 16(1):105–105.

Tim Dettmers, Artidoro Pagnoni, Ari Holtzman, and Luke Zettlemoyer. 2024. Qlora: Efficient finetuning of quantized llms. *Advances in Neural Information Processing Systems*, 36.

Bosheng Ding, Chengwei Qin, Ruochen Zhao, Tianze Luo, Xinze Li, Guizhen Chen, Wenhan Xia, Junjie Hu, Anh Tuan Luu, and Shafiq Joty. 2024. Data augmentation using large language models: Data perspectives, learning paradigms and challenges.

Ben Hagag, Liav Harpaz, Gil Semo, Dor Bernsohn, Rohit Saha, Pashootan Vaezipoor, Kyryl Truskovskyi, and Gerasimos Spanakis. 2024. Legallens shared task 2024: Legal violation identification in unstructured text.

Neil Houlsby, Andrei Giurgiu, Stanislaw Jastrzebski, Bruna Morrone, Quentin De Laroussilhe, Andrea Gesmundo, Mona Attariyan, and Sylvain Gelly. 2019. Parameter-efficient transfer learning for nlp. In *International conference on machine learning*, pages 2790–2799. PMLR.

Edward J Hu, Yelong Shen, Phillip Wallis, Zeyuan Allen-Zhu, Yuanzhi Li, Shean Wang, Lu Wang, and Weizhu Chen. 2021. Lora: Low-rank adaptation of large language models. *arXiv preprint arXiv:2106.09685*.

Joel Niklaus, Veton Matoshi, Matthias Stürmer, Ilias Chalkidis, and Daniel E Ho. 2023. Multilegalpile: A 689gb multilingual legal corpus. *arXiv preprint arXiv:2306.02069*.

Colin Raffel, Noam Shazeer, Adam Roberts, Katherine Lee, Sharan Narang, Michael Matena, Yanqi Zhou, Wei Li, and Peter J Liu. 2020. Exploring the limits of transfer learning with a unified text-to-text transformer. *Journal of machine learning research*, 21(140):1–67.

Saravanan Rajamanickam and Kanagasabai Rajaraman. 2023. I2r at semeval-2023 task 7: Explanations-driven ensemble approach for natural language inference over clinical trial data. In *Proceedings of the 17th International Workshop on Semantic Evaluation (SemEval-2023)*, pages 1630–1635.

Alexey Romanov and Chaitanya Shivade. 2018. Lessons from natural language inference in the clinical domain. In *Conference on Empirical Methods in Natural Language Processing*. Association for Computational Linguistics.

Shane Storks, Qiaozi Gao, and Joyce Y Chai. 2019. Recent advances in natural language inference: A survey of benchmarks, resources, and approaches. *arXiv preprint arXiv:1904.01172*.

Gemma Team, Thomas Mesnard, Cassidy Hardin, Robert Dadashi, Surya Bhupatiraju, Shreya Pathak, Laurent Sifre, Morgane Rivière, Mihir Sanjay Kale, Juliette Love, et al. 2024. Gemma: Open models based on gemini research and technology. *arXiv preprint arXiv:2403.08295*.

Hugo Touvron, Thibaut Lavril, Gautier Izacard, Xavier Martinet, Marie-Anne Lachaux, Timothée Lacroix, Baptiste Rozière, Naman Goyal, Eric Hambro, Faisal Azhar, et al. 2023. Llama: Open and efficient foundation language models. *arXiv preprint arXiv:2302.13971*.

Han Yang, Mingchen Li, Huixue Zhou, Yongkang Xiao, Qian Fang, and Rui Zhang. 2023. One llm is not enough: Harnessing the power of ensemble learning for medical question answering. *medRxiv*.

Zhanye Yang. 2022. Legalnli: natural language inference for legal compliance inspection. In *International Conference on Advanced Algorithms and Neural Networks (AANN 2022)*, volume 12285, pages 144–150. SPIE.

LegalLens Shared Task 2024: Legal Violation Identification in Unstructured Text

Ben Hagag[⋆] **Liav Harpaz**[⋆] **Gil Semo**[⋆] **Dor Bernsohn**[⋆] **Rohit Saha**[†]
Pashootan Vaezipoor[†] **Kyryl Truskovskyi**[‡] **Gerasimos Spanakis**[◇]

[⋆]Darrow AI Ltd., Tel Aviv, Israel {firstname.lastname}@darrow.ai
[†]Georgian.io, Toronto, Canada {firstname}@georgian.io
[‡]Scoreinforce, Toronto, Canada {firstname}@Scoreinforce.com
[◇]Maastricht University, Maastricht, Netherlands jerry.spanakis@maastrichtuniversity.nl

Abstract

This paper presents the results of the LegalLens Shared Task, focusing on detecting legal violations within text in the wild across two sub-tasks: LegalLens-NER for identifying legal violation entities and LegalLens-NLI for associating these violations with relevant legal contexts and affected individuals. Using an enhanced LegalLens dataset covering labor, privacy, and consumer protection domains, 38 teams participated in the task. Our analysis reveals that while a mix of approaches was used, the top-performing teams in both tasks consistently relied on fine-tuning pretrained language models, outperforming legal-specific models and few-shot methods. The top-performing team achieved a 7.11% improvement in NER over the baseline, while NLI saw a more marginal improvement of 5.7%. Despite these gains, the complexity of legal texts leaves room for further advancements.

1 Introduction

Legal violations are everywhere, but often go unnoticed. In many areas such as privacy, consumer protection, environmental law, and labor regulations, traces of these violations, indicating wrongdoing, are frequently lost in the vast amounts of digital information. As the world becomes increasingly digital, it is inevitable that traces of these legal violations can be found online. This concept is the foundation of the LegalLens project (Bernsohn et al., 2024). These violations pose significant risks to individuals and institutions, undermining legal and ethical standards in our increasingly digital society. Therefore, developing advanced methods to detect and address these violations is crucial.

Identifying legal violations on the open web presents two primary challenges: first, determining where to search, and second, accurately interpreting whether the information indicates a legal violation. The first challenge involves going through massive amounts of online content, selecting sources that are likely to yield relevant information while accounting for varying levels of credibility and relevance. The second challenge lies in applying legal knowledge and to determine the legal grounds for these potential violations, and identify victims who may be entitled to compensation.

To advance this field, and to address these challenges, LegalLens tasks were presented in (Bernsohn et al., 2024). The underlying assumption of LegalLens is that Legal violations often leave digital traces, which can be uncovered through careful analysis. LegalLens presented a two-step approach to tackle these challenges: The first is LegalLens-NER (Named Entity Recognition) to extract legal violation entities from online data. The task involves detection and categorization of specific legal violation entities such as laws, violations, violators, and victims within unstructured text. Simple NER methods do not focus on these types of entities and fail to capture the ambiguity of legal language. Figure 3 shows an example of the NER task.

The second step is the LegalLens-NLI (Natural Language Inference) to associate identified violations with relevant legal cases or statutes. More specifically, the task given a premise (allegation summary of a legal case) determine the relationship to a hypothesis (a potential detected violation) and classify their relationship as entailment, contradiction, or neutrality. Figure 2 shows an example of the NLI task.

The datasets for these two sub-tasks were built upon proprietary data by Darrow.ai[1], designed to be as realistic as possible and to capture the nuances and variability of real-world cases. The data was generated in utilizing GPT-4o (OpenAI, 2023) and domain experts, ensuring both realism and com-

[1]https://www.darrow.ai/

Proceedings of the Natural Legal Language Processing Workshop 2024, pages 361–370
November 16, 2024 ©2024 Association for Computational Linguistics

plexity.

The 1st Shared Task on `LegalLens` was organized to encourage new research at the intersection of natural language processing and legal studies and to stimulate interest in legal violation detection within the NLP community.

In this paper, we present the results of the Shared Task, offering a detailed description of the evaluation data and the systems developed by participants. We analyze the performance of the participating systems, evaluating their capabilities in processing legal language and identifying legal violations. The top-performing systems for NER showed a substantial improvement over the baseline, with a 7.11% increase in F1 score for the best team. The NLI task saw more marginal progress, with only one team outperforming the baseline by 5.7%. While these improvements highlight progress in legal violation detection, particularly in entity recognition, there remains significant room for further advancements in handling the complexities of natural legal language inference.

As a result, this shared task holds value not just for experts in Machine Learning and NLP, but also for legal professionals, sociologists, and policymakers. This initiative has the potential to foster interdisciplinary collaborations and contribute to advancements in detecting legal violations in the digital era. We are happy to see interdisciplinary teams with participants from CS and NLP alongside legal practitioners, students and social science.

The remainder of this paper is structured as follows: In Section 2, we provide an overview of the `LegalLens` tasks. Section 3 describes our data collection process, while Section 4 presents the systems and results. Section 5 delves into the details of the three winning teams, and Section 6 offers an overview of the current research landscape.

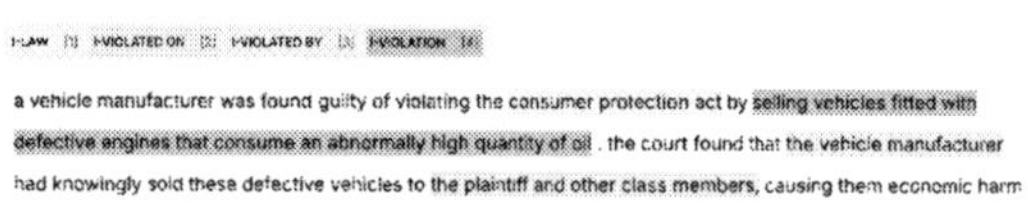

Figure 1: NER sub-task example showing highlighted legal violation entities, including Law, Violation, Violation By, and Violation On.

2 What is `LegalLens`

To efficiently detect legal violations across various domains in the online digital data, a system must be developed that can scan large datasets, isolate relevant information, and accurately map it to appropriate legal grounds. This involves scanning large amount of online data, contextualizing the findings by linking them to specific legal grounds, and clearly explaining potential violations. Additionally, the system must identify the affected individuals or entities who may be entitled to legal recourse, thereby enabling effective enforcement and remediation.

`LegalLens` is designed to address these challenges by providing a structured approach to detecting legal violations in digital data. It achieves this by breaking down the task into two key components: `LegalLens-NER` to identify relevant legal entities and `LegalLens-NLI` to determine the relationship between data points and legal grounds. In the following section, we will delve deeper into each of these sub-tasks, explaining how they con-

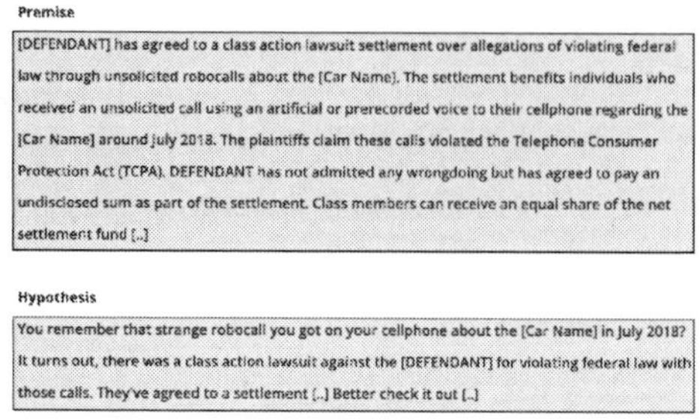

Figure 2: An example of the LegalLens NLI task, where the model assesses whether the provided hypothesis (a potential legal violation) is supported, contradicted, or unrelated to the premise (an allegation summary).

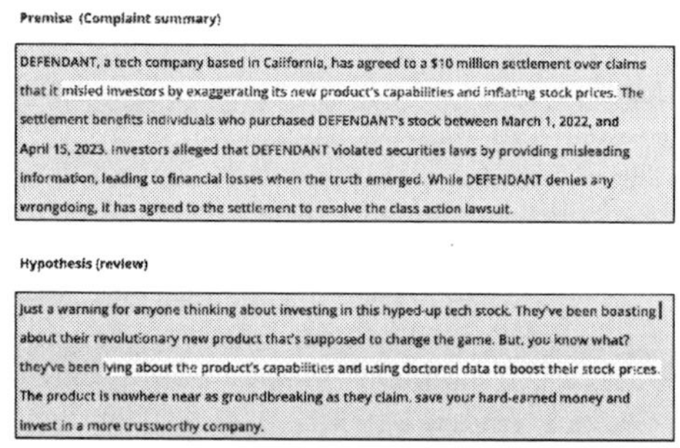

Figure 3: Example of the NLI sub-task showing how premises like court-filed complaints or articles are used to identify individuals harmed by violations. Both the premise and hypothesis were selected due to matching violation entities identified by the LegalLens-NER model, illustrating the system's ability to link legal grounds to personal experiences and recognize potential victims.

tribute to the overall goal of efficiently detecting and contextualizing legal violations. For the full description of both tasks please refer to the original `LegalLens` work (Bernsohn et al., 2024).

2.1 LegalLens-NER

The `LegalLens-NER` task in the `LegalLens` framework aims to identify key legal entities relevant to detecting violations in unstructured text. The `LegalLens-NER` model classifies tokens into predefined categories: *Law* (the specific law violated), *Violation* (the nature of the infraction), *Violated By* (the responsible entity), and *Violated On* (the affected party).

Given the sheer volume of data and the challenge of identifying relevant information, the `LegalLens-NER` task acts as an initial filter, extracting critical entities like laws and violations while discarding irrelevant or non-essential information. This process ensures that only the most pertinent data is selected for further analysis and association with legal grounds in subsequent tasks (`LegalLens-NLI`). The primary goal is to highlight relevant data points for deeper legal examination, making the subsequent steps more efficient and focused.

The dataset for the `LegalLens-NER` task was curated from class action complaints, with the key violation sections extracted and then summarized and refined using GPT-4. The generated text was formatted as articles, reviews, and social media posts. Human experts validated the realism of the output and annotated the entities. Two prompting strategies were used: explicit, focusing on multiple entities with specific structure, and implicit, centering on a single entity, particularly the violation content. Additional parameters like cause of action and industry were also included to tailor the content to various and real-world scenarios.

2.2 LegalLens-NLI

The NLI task in the `LegalLens` framework is designed to map identified legal violations to the most relevant Cause of Action (CoA) or legal statute. By proceeding the `LegalLens-NER` model, this model aligns the relevant data with specific legal frameworks, such as laws or precedents, and provides a justification or reasoning for the connection between the identified violations and the applicable legal grounds.

As we worked on this task, we understood that `LegalLens-NLI` can serve another important purpose: identifying individuals who may have been harmed by the violation. By using descriptions of violations—such as court-filed complaints, articles, or other texts—as premises, the NLI task can analyze relevant online content, like reviews or posts, where people describe their personal experiences. This allows the system to link the identified legal violations to specific individuals who have suffered harm, thus expanding its capability to both identify legal grounds and recognize victims of these violations.

This combined approach strengthens the process of tracing violations back to real-world consequences, making it possible to identify affected individuals with greater precision and relevance.

The dataset is derived from curated legal news articles, with the key violation sections summarized and refined using LLM. The premise for each sample consists of these curated and summarized violation descriptions. The hypotheses were generated using different LLM setups to simulate various scenarios and complaints to reflect real-world situations.

The dataset is labeled with three categories: *Entailment* where the violation is directly supported by the legal grounds; *Contradiction*, where the violation contradicts the legal grounds; and *Neutral*, where the relationship between the violation and the legal grounds is ambiguous or irrelevant.

Human experts validated the correctness and completeness of the premises and hypotheses, and annotated the NLI labels accordingly.

3 Dataset Curation for LegalLens Shared Task

Building upon the original `LegalLens` dataset and addressing its limitations, we have created a more comprehensive and challenging benchmark for `LegalLens` sub-tasks.

Our goal was to create a dataset that not only mimics real-world scenarios but also presents a challenging benchmark for state-of-the-art NLP models in the legal domain.

The resulting dataset for the shared task maintains the dual-task structure of the original `LegalLens`, focusing on NER for violation identification and NLI for matching violations with known cases. With improved prompt practices, better annotators guidelines, human expert practices, and following feedback from the original paper(Bernsohn et al., 2024), we improve the generation process and the resulting annotations, yielding more realistic content, improve data quality and reduce bias.

Our enhancement process consisted of three primary steps: The first was to clean the dataset from duplicated or almost duplicates examples. In some cases we have found that similar patterns appears in the dataset too often that is not making sense. We have tried to detect these patterns and exclude instances that repeat them. Also, to prevent potential biases and ensure broader applicability, we masked all company names within the dataset, including Defendants and Plaintiff names in the NLI dataset. We found that models were prone to overfitting if this masking process was not applied.

Additionally, we have implemented an improved three-step validation where legal experts conducted a multi-stage validation process, including a review for factual accuracy and legal relevance, cross-validation of NER annotations, and examination of premise-hypothesis pairs for logical consistency, completeness and correctness in the NLI task. All annotation conducted via Argilla (Daniel and Francisco, 2023) available under an Apache-2.0 license.

Table 1 shows the datasets tokens distribution. Also, table 2 shows the distribution of labeled samples across various legal domains for the NLI task, formatted as Contradiction/Entailment/Neutral.

Entity	Description	# Labeled Samples
LAW	Specific law or regulation breached.	373
VIOLATION	Content describing the violation.	1665
VIOLATED BY	Entity committing the violation.	373
VIOLATED ON	Victim or affected party.	373

Table 1: Distribution of NER entities generated through the combined dataset from the original paper and the updated process, excluding duplicates.

Entity	Description	Labels	# Labeled Samples
Consumer Protection	Deceptive advertising, fraud and unfair business practices.	28/47/32	107
Privacy	Unauthorized collection, use, or disclosure of personal data.	80/72/82	234
TCPA	Unauthorized telemarketing calls, faxes and text messages.	38/34/39	111
Wage	Illegal underpayment and unfair compensation practices by employers.	9/7/5	21

Table 2: Distribution of labeled samples across various legal domains for the NLI task, formatted as Contradiction/Entailment/Neutral. This dataset combines samples from the original paper and the updated process, excluding duplicates.

4 System Descriptions and Performance

The competition was hosted on CodaBench[2] (Xu et al., 2022). During the evaluation phase, the leaderboard was hidden, meaning participants did not receive feedback on their submission scores until the phase concluded. Each team was allowed one submission per sub-task.

Both sub-tasks were evaluated as in the original paper: the `LegalLens-NER` sub-task was assessed using the weighted F1 score, to account for class imbalance, with each class's F1 score weighted by the number of true instances. Evaluation was conducted using the seqeval(Nakayama, 2018) method, which requires exact matches between predicted and true entity spans—both the boundaries and the entity type must match precisely. We followed the IBO format (Inside, Beginning, Outside), where a correct match requires both the boundaries and tags to be accurate. The `LegalLens-NLI` sub-task used the standard macro F1 score. Participants received the hidden test set only two days before the submission deadline, after submitting the source code of their best architecture. Changes to the model were not permitted after the release of the hidden test set. During the evaluation phase, organizers verified that the predictions could be reproduced using the submitted source code.

4.1 Baseline Systems

As a baseline for the each sub-task, we use the best models from the original LegalLens paper (Bernsohn et al., 2024). We trained and evaluated the best models on the new datasets generated for the shared task, as described above. That is to make sure our baseline is up-to-date and performance improvement by participants is by better models, not just by our new dataset. For `LegalLens-NER` the best model is RoBERTa-base which was fine tuned on the `LegalLens-NER` dataset. The macro F1-Score for this model is 38.1%. For `LegalLens-NLI`: the best model is Falcon-7B (Almazrouei et al., 2023) which achieved the highest score of 80.7% macro F1 on average across domains.

[2]LegalLens shared task website: https://www.codabench.org/competitions/3052/

4.2 Participating teams

A total of 87 individual users grouped in 38 teams participated in the shared task, out of which the highest seven teams elected to write a system description paper. Most of the teams participated in both sub-tasks. Table 3 presents the results for the top six teams in the `LegalLens-NER` sub-task, Table 4 shows the results for the `LegalLens-NLI` sub-task, and Table 5 shows an entity level performance for the `LegalLens-NER` sub-task. Most teams achieved better results than our baseline. Another point worth noting is that success in one sub-task does not necessarily translate to success in the other. Out of the 38 teams, only the NowJ team made it to the top three systems in both tasks. This highlights that the challenges posed by the `LegalLens-NER` and `LegalLens-NLI` sub-tasks are distinct, requiring different approaches and strengths.

Lastly, we note that there is a ceiling in terms of performances in the NER task. The top 4 teams achieve score around 70% F1 score, which seems to be the plateau. suggesting that there is room for improvement.

We present the leaderboard for both NER and NLI tasks, showcasing the top six teams and their F1 scores. The next section delves into the leading approaches in each task.

Team Name	Test F1 Score
Nowj	0.416
Flawless Lawgic	0.402
UOttawa	0.402
Baseline	0.381
Masala-chai	0.380
UMLaw&TechLab	0.321
Bonafide	0.305

Table 3: Top six teams for the `LegalLens-NER` sub-task,with performance measured by weighted F1 scores on a hidden test set.

In the NLI task, the leading team employed a Mixture-of-Experts approach(Jiang et al., 2024), which significantly outperformed the subsequent teams.

All submitted models are available in Darrow.ai's Hugging Face Space[3].

[3]https://huggingface.co/darrow-ai

Team Name	Test F1 Score
1-800-Shared-Tasks	0.853
Baseline	0.807
Semantists	0.785
Nowj	0.746
UOttawa	0.724
bonafide	0.653
masala-chai	0.525

Table 4: Top six teams for the `LegalLens-NLI` sub-task,with performance measured by Macro F1 scores on a hidden test set.

Team	Law	Violation	V-By	V-On
Nowj	0.7310	0.630	0.041	0.337
Flawless Lawgic	0.711	0.582	0.081	0.310
UOttawa	0.701	0.626	0.045	0.299
Baseline	0.668	0.499	0.087	0.353
Masala-chai	0.636	0.589	0.042	0.308
UMLaw&TechLab	0.596	0.573	0.047	0.104
Bonafide	0.750	0.230	0.152	0.264

Table 5: Entity-specific performance for each team in the `LegalLens-NER` sub-task, showing F1 scores for the identification of Law, Violation, Violated-By, and Violated-On entities.

5 Deeper Analysis

In this section, we describe the key methodologies and innovative techniques employed by the top-performing teams in the LegalLens Shared Task.

5.1 `LegalLens-NER` Methodologies Overview

The NowJ team, which achieved the highest score in the `LegalLens-NER` sub-task, with 0.416 weighted F1 score, adopted a methodical approach that involved data utilization, preprocessing, and model fine-tuning. They have leveraged both LegalLens-NER datasets, the one from the original paper, and the one introduced for the shared task. The former consisted of 710 training samples and 617 test samples, totaling 1,327 samples. The latter contained 976 samples. To optimize training, the team selected the 976 samples from the `LegalLensNER-SharedTask` as the training set, with the remaining 351 samples (that are not included in the original dataset) from the `LegalLensNER` dataset used as the validation set. The model architecture combined a pre-trained language model with a Conditional Random Field (CRF) layer. Pre-trained Language Model - the team used the `Legal Longformer` (`lexlms/legal-longformer-base`)(Chalkidis* et al., 2023), a transformer-based model specialized for legal text. This model produced contextualized word embeddings, which was used for capturing the semantic nuances of the input text. Conditional Random Field (CRF) Layer modeled dependencies between labels, to ensure valid label sequences by optimizing the Maximum Likelihood Estimate (MLE). The team implemented the forward(Blunsom, 2004) and Viterbi(Forney, 1973) algorithms during training and inference to calculate the probabilities of label sequences and decode the most likely sequence, respectively. Training setting includes: LM: Legal lexlms/legal-longformer-base(Chalkidis* et al., 2023), Max Sequence Length: 256, Initial Learning Rate: 5e-5, Learning Rate for CRF and Fully Connected Layer: 8e-5, Weight Decay (Fine-Tuning): 1e-5, Weight Decay (CRF and Fully Connected Layer): 5e-6, Batch Size: 16, Total Training Epochs: 30 (Best epoch: 18th), Warmup Proportion: 0.1.

To address the issue of subword tokens in the datasets, where subwords were predicted with the 'X' label, the team implemented a post-processing step. This involved replacing any 'X' label with the label of the preceding token. If the preceding token was a 'B-' (beginning) label, the 'X' label was converted to the corresponding 'I-' (inside) label, ensuring the sequence followed the correct labeling structure.

The uOttawa team, which achieved the third-best score in the `LegalLens-NER` sub-task, with a 0.402 weighted F1 score, developed their model using the SpaCy library(Honnibal and Montani, 2017). The team implemented preprocessing steps to clean and remove null values and to ensure each token had a corresponding NER tag. The team treated the tokens as features, a transformer model, `microsoft/deberta-v3-base` for contextual embedding, and a custom NER component via `Tok2Vec(Honnibal et al., 2020)` layer, to represent tokens in a high-dimensional vector space to capture semantic similarities between words. The model's performance was evaluated after each epoch on a validation set to monitor over-fitting.

5.2 `LegalLens-NLI` Methodologies Overview

The Bonafide team, which achieved the fifth highest score in the `LegalLens-NLI` subtask, developed a methodology involving data augmentation and model fine-tuning. They used Mixtral 8x7b-instruct-v0.1-hf model (Jiang et al., 2024) to generate paraphrases for both premises and hypotheses across the original 312 rows of data. The model was prompted to produce realistic rephrasings that retained all the details of the original text, resulting in a final dataset of 936 rows. For model training, the Bonafide team utilized the `sileod/deberta-v3-small-tasksource-nli` (Sileo, 2023) encoder, which is based on the DeBERTa-v3-small architecture. This encoder, fine-tuned on tasksource for 250,000 steps and oversampled for long NLI tasks, was further fine-tuned on the augmented dataset. The training dataset was tailored to each legal domain, comprising only synthetic data relevant to that domain, while the test dataset remained unaltered. The hyperparameters used for training included a batch size of 8, a learning rate of 2e-5, and a linear learning rate scheduler. The models were trained for 10 epochs with early stopping to optimize performance. Final predictions on the test dataset were derived by aggregating outcomes from four domain-specific models. The most confident label was selected by calculating the argmax on the confidence levels of all four models.

The 1-800-Shared-Tasks team, which achieved the highest score in the `LegalLens-NLI` sub-task, with 0.853 macro f1 score, implemented a method involving the use of the `FastLanguageModel` from the Unsloth library[4]. Their approach focused on fine-tuning the `PHI3-Medium-NLI-16bit` model, with specific configurations to optimize performance on the NLI task. The model was loaded with a maximum sequence length of 2048 and configured to operate in 4-bit precision to manage computational efficiency. They further enhanced the model using LoRA (Low-Rank Adaptation) adapters (Hu et al., 2021), allowing for the fine-tuning of only 1% to 10% of the model's parameters.

The **NowJ** team, which achieved the third-best score in the `LegalLens-NLI` sub-task, utilized two datasets provided by the competition organizers on HuggingFace: `darrow-ai/LegalLensNLI` and `darrow-ai/LegalLensNLI-SharedTask`. Both datasets contained only a training split with 312 samples. Upon preprocessing, which included converting text to lowercase, removing punctuation, and eliminating extra spaces, they identified approximately 160 differing samples between the two datasets. To maximize data utilization, the participants created a unified dataset comprising the original 312, and the new 160

[4]https://github.com/unslothai/unsloth

samples. The combined dataset was then split into training and validation sets, with a test size of 0.4, resulting in 283 examples for training (`train_raw`) and 189 examples for validation. Additionally, augmented versions of the examples from the first dataset were appended to create an expanded training set: 665 examples for training set and 189 examples for validation set. The data augmentation implemented using LangChain (Chase, 2022) and the GPT-4o-mini (Achiam et al., 2023) model via API. The goal was to paraphrase both the hypotheses and premises to simulate varying levels of English language proficiency, specifically targeting IELTS[5] levels 6.5 and 8.5[6]. The dataset was expanded with columns to track original and augmented examples, distinguishing versions by IELTS levels. A Pydantic model ensured data consistency, while the GPT-4o-mini model was guided by structured prompts to generate paraphrases. A custom Paraphraser class managed the process, maintaining the integrity of the original meaning. The NowJ team conducted a thorough evaluation of state-of-the-art pre-trained models, including LegalBERT (Chalkidis et al., 2020), T5(Raffel et al., 2020), and DeBERTa, to identify the optimal architecture for the NLI subtask. DeBERTa (`MoritzLaurer/DeBERTa-v3-large-mnli-fever-anli-ling-wanli`) emerged as the best-performing model due to its stability and high F1-macro scores across multiple training iterations.

Performance across teams varied significantly by legal domain. The 1-800-Shared-Tasks team for instance, performed exceptionally well in structured domains like Privacy (1.0 F1) and TCPA, yet underperformed in complex domains like Wage, likely due to its smaller dataset size and implicit nature of violations. Similarly, NowJ and UOttawa also struggled in domains like Wage, but Semantists fared better due to a more balanced approach across legal domains, highlighting differences in generalization capability across teams. Models fine-tuned on larger datasets showed better overall performance, but those specializing in domain-specific tasks demonstrated marginal improvements, revealing a gap in domain adaptation.

[5]https://ielts.org/

[6]https://ielts.org/take-a-test/preparation-resources/understanding-your-score

6 Related Work

In recent years, there has been increased interest at the intersection of NLP and the Legal domain, with work spanning legal judgment prediction (Chalkidis et al., 2019; Semo et al., 2022; Medvedeva and Mcbride, 2023) to Information Extraction(Holzenberger and Van Durme, 2023; Bommarito II et al., 2021) to Document analysis (Song et al., 2022; Mamakas et al., 2022) to Text Generation agarwal-etal-2022-extractive.

In the Information Extraction field, specifically in Named Entity Recognition (NER), (Amaral et al., 2023) have focused on evaluating data agreements for compliance with European privacy laws using NLP techniques. In another study, (Smădu et al., 2022) employed multi-task domain adaptation for NER within the legal domain, showing modest improvements in recall across Romanian and German languages. The work by (Barale et al., 2023) asked language models to detect legal entity types. Additionally, NER has seen increased usage in the legal domain, including efforts to extract entities from court judgment documents in various jurisdictions (Kalamkar et al., 2022). Additionally, (Au et al., 2022) presented E-NER; an Annotated Named Entity Recognition Corpus of Legal Text. However, these entity types, even in legal domain NER tasks, aren't specifically tailored for detecting legal violations and lack the complexity needed for this challenging task. Despite these advancements, existing research typically focuses on a standard set of entity types such as *plaintiff* and *defendant*, with limited exploration of more diverse or nuanced entities relevant to legal violations. Furthermore, these studies are limited in scope, often focusing on specific legal domains or industries.

NLI in the legal domain has gained significant attention in recent years. (Koreeda and Manning, 2021) explored NLI at the document level for contracts, while (Bruno and Roth, 2022) introduced LawngNLI from US legal opinions. (Mathur et al., 2022) presented CaseHoldNLI and a document-level NLI model using optimal evidence selection. (Kwak et al., 2022) introduced a legal NLI dataset for the validity assessment of legal will statements and (Kwak et al., 2023) evaluated the validity of legal will statements across states, using three inputs—statement, condition, and law—to classify the relationship as *support*, *refute*, or *unrelated*. Despite the increased interest, (Bernsohn et al., 2024) is the first to introduce legal violation detection as a general NLI task across multiple domains.

Prior work has focused on domain-specific use cases, such as privacy protection (Amaral et al., 2023; Silva et al., 2020; Nyffenegger et al., 2023), but these models lack the versatility needed to address the broad spectrum of legal violations across different contexts. LegalLens was the first to establish a cross-domain approach for detecting legal violations.

7 Conclusion and Future work

The LegalLens Shared Task demonstrated the potential of leveraging NLP techniques to address the challenge of legal violation detection across diverse domains. Despite the task's rapid timeline—less than two months from launch to completion—the significant participation of 87 individuals, organized into 38 teams, and the promising results underscore the community's interest and the relevance of this problem.

We call on the broader research community, particularly those in interdisciplinary fields, to contribute resources, methodologies, and diverse perspectives. Collecting and consolidating these perspectives will deepen our understanding of the complexities within this field. As we refine and build upon the LegalLens framework, we encourage diverse perspectives and innovative approaches that can address the challenges of this important task. Collaboration across disciplines will be crucial in advancing the state of the art in this important area.

The top models achieved a 0.416 F1 score in LegalLens-NER (microsoft/deberta-v3-base) and 0.853 F1 score in LegalLens-NLI (phi3). However, a significant drop was observed in identifying the "Violated By" and "Violated On" entities, indicating room for improvement. This gap suggests the potential for integrating other information extraction techniques, even possibly from outside the legal domain.

Key questions remain unresolved: How will the techniques scale with larger language models and adapt to less-resourced languages? Can we enhance the granularity of legal entity interactions, particularly in more implicit scenarios? Additionally, how will these approaches generalize across broader legal domains and real-world applications?

Limitations

A challenge of identifying cases of legal violation in the open web is information sparsity. In other words, these cases do not present themselves in entirety, and in one place. Often times, the salient details of a case are spread across multiple sources on the web, and individually do not offer much insight into the case. It is only when these individual details are stitched together, do they afford themselves to a holistic understanding of the full story, and subsequent evaluation of the case.

Ethics Statement

We strive to adhere to the ACL Code of Ethics.

Bias and fairness in machine learning have been subjects of long-standing research. As we aim to develop more complex and impactful solutions to address the evolving media and world knowledge, we understand that this goes beyond merely developing or implementing ML algorithms. Inherent biases arise from datasets, task definitions, culture, and even researchers' beliefs and motivations. Addressing these biases effectively requires collaboration across disciplines. Our technology is designed to supplement, not replace, legal professionals, with responsible application and awareness of potential limitations and biases in automated systems. All data used in this research have been anonymized and stripped of personally identifiable information in compliance with relevant data protection regulations. The data utilized in this study are sourced from publicly available online platforms and do not infringe on any proprietary rights of individuals or entities.

Acknowledgements

We would like to extend our gratitude to Darrow.ai for providing the dataset, computational resources, and domain expertise that made this research possible. Our thanks also go to the NLLP workshop for facilitating and helping to organize this shared task.

References

Josh Achiam, Steven Adler, Sandhini Agarwal, Lama Ahmad, Ilge Akkaya, Florencia Leoni Aleman, Diogo Almeida, Janko Altenschmidt, Sam Altman, Shyamal Anadkat, et al. 2023. Gpt-4 technical report. *arXiv preprint arXiv:2303.08774*.

Ebtesam Almazrouei, Hamza Alobeidli, Abdulaziz Alshamsi, Alessandro Cappelli, Ruxandra Cojocaru, Merouane Debbah, Etienne Goffinet, Daniel Heslow, Julien Launay, Quentin Malartic, Badreddine

Noune, Baptiste Pannier, and Guilherme Penedo. 2023. Falcon-40B: an open large language model with state-of-the-art performance.

Orlando Amaral, Muhammad Ilyas Azeem, Sallam Abualhaija, and Lionel C Briand. 2023. Nlp-based automated compliance checking of data processing agreements against gdpr. *IEEE Transactions on Software Engineering*.

Ting Wai Terence Au, Ingemar J Cox, and Vasileios Lampos. 2022. E-ner–an annotated named entity recognition corpus of legal text. *arXiv preprint arXiv:2212.09306*.

Claire Barale, Michael Rovatsos, and Nehal Bhuta. 2023. Do language models learn about legal entity types during pretraining? *arXiv preprint arXiv:2310.13092*.

Dor Bernsohn, Gil Semo, Yaron Vazana, Gila Hayat, Ben Hagag, Joel Niklaus, Rohit Saha, and Kyryl Truskovskyi. 2024. Legallens: Leveraging llms for legal violation identification in unstructured text. In *Proceedings of the 18th Conference of the European Chapter of the Association for Computational Linguistics (Volume 1: Long Papers)*, pages 2129–2145.

Phil Blunsom. 2004. Hidden markov models. *Lecture notes, August*, 15(18-19):48.

Michael J Bommarito II, Daniel Martin Katz, and Eric M Detterman. 2021. Lexnlp: Natural language processing and information extraction for legal and regulatory texts. In *Research handbook on big data law*, pages 216–227. Edward Elgar Publishing.

William Bruno and Dan Roth. 2022. Lawngnli: A long-premise benchmark for in-domain generalization from short to long contexts and for implication-based retrieval. *arXiv preprint arXiv:2212.03222*.

Ilias Chalkidis, Ion Androutsopoulos, and Nikolaos Aletras. 2019. Neural legal judgment prediction in English. In *Proceedings of the 57th Annual Meeting of the Association for Computational Linguistics*, pages 4317–4323, Florence, Italy. Association for Computational Linguistics.

Ilias Chalkidis, Manos Fergadiotis, Prodromos Malakasiotis, Nikolaos Aletras, and Ion Androutsopoulos. 2020. LEGAL-BERT: The muppets straight out of law school. In *Findings of the Association for Computational Linguistics: EMNLP 2020*, Online. Association for Computational Linguistics.

Ilias Chalkidis*, Nicolas Garneau*, Catalina Goanta, Daniel Martin Katz, and Anders Søgaard. 2023. LeXFiles and LegalLAMA: Facilitating English Multinational Legal Language Model Development. In *Proceedings of the 61st Annual Meeting of the Association for Computational Linguistics*, Toronto, Canada. Association for Computational Linguistics.

Harrison Chase. 2022. LangChain.

Vila-Suero Daniel and Aranda Francisco. 2023. Argilla - Open-source framework for data-centric NLP.

G David Forney. 1973. The viterbi algorithm. *Proceedings of the IEEE*, 61(3):268–278.

Nils Holzenberger and Benjamin Van Durme. 2023. Connecting symbolic statutory reasoning with legal information extraction. In *Proceedings of the Natural Legal Language Processing Workshop 2023*, pages 113–131. Association for Computational Linguistics.

Matthew Honnibal and Ines Montani. 2017. spaCy 2: Natural language understanding with Bloom embeddings, convolutional neural networks and incremental parsing. To appear.

Matthew Honnibal, Ines Montani, Sofie Van Landeghem, and Adriane Boyd. 2020. spaCy: Industrial-strength Natural Language Processing in Python.

Edward J Hu, Yelong Shen, Phillip Wallis, Zeyuan Allen-Zhu, Yuanzhi Li, Shean Wang, Lu Wang, and Weizhu Chen. 2021. Lora: Low-rank adaptation of large language models. *arXiv preprint arXiv:2106.09685*.

Albert Q Jiang, Alexandre Sablayrolles, Antoine Roux, Arthur Mensch, Blanche Savary, Chris Bamford, Devendra Singh Chaplot, Diego de las Casas, Emma Bou Hanna, Florian Bressand, et al. 2024. Mixtral of experts. *arXiv preprint arXiv:2401.04088*.

Prathamesh Kalamkar, Astha Agarwal, Aman Tiwari, Smita Gupta, Saurabh Karn, and Vivek Raghavan. 2022. Named entity recognition in Indian court judgments. In *Proceedings of the Natural Legal Language Processing Workshop 2022*, pages 184–193, Abu Dhabi, United Arab Emirates (Hybrid). Association for Computational Linguistics.

Yuta Koreeda and Christopher D Manning. 2021. Contractnli: A dataset for document-level natural language inference for contracts. *arXiv preprint arXiv:2110.01799*.

Alice Kwak, Gaetano Forte, Derek E Bambauer, and Mihai Surdeanu. 2023. Transferring legal natural language inference model from a us state to another: What makes it so hard? In *Proceedings of the Natural Legal Language Processing Workshop*.

Alice Kwak, Jacob Israelsen, Clayton Morrison, Derek Bambauer, and Mihai Surdeanu. 2022. Validity assessment of legal will statements as natural language inference. In *Findings of the Association for Computational Linguistics: EMNLP 2022*, pages 6047–6056.

Dimitris Mamakas, Petros Tsotsi, Ion Androutsopoulos, and Ilias Chalkidis. 2022. Processing long legal documents with pre-trained transformers: Modding legalbert and longformer.

Puneet Mathur, Gautam Kunapuli, Riyaz Bhat, Manish Shrivastava, Dinesh Manocha, and Maneesh Singh. 2022. Docinfer: Document-level natural language inference using optimal evidence selection. In *Proceedings of the 2022 Conference on Empirical Methods in Natural Language Processing*, pages 809–824.

Masha Medvedeva and Pauline Mcbride. 2023. Legal judgment prediction: If you are going to do it, do it right. In *Proceedings of the Natural Legal Language Processing Workshop 2023*, pages 73–84.

Hiroki Nakayama. 2018. seqeval: A python framework for sequence labeling evaluation. Software available from https://github.com/chakki-works/seqeval.

Alex Nyffenegger, Matthias Stürmer, and Joel Niklaus. 2023. Anonymity at risk? assessing re-identification capabilities of large language models.

OpenAI. 2023. Gpt-4 technical report.

Colin Raffel, Noam Shazeer, Adam Roberts, Katherine Lee, Sharan Narang, Michael Matena, Yanqi Zhou, Wei Li, and Peter J Liu. 2020. Exploring the limits of transfer learning with a unified text-to-text transformer. *Journal of machine learning research*, 21(140):1–67.

Gil Semo, Dor Bernsohn, Ben Hagag, Gila Hayat, and Joel Niklaus. 2022. ClassActionPrediction: A challenging benchmark for legal judgment prediction of class action cases in the US. In *Proceedings of the Natural Legal Language Processing Workshop 2022*, pages 31–46, Abu Dhabi, United Arab Emirates (Hybrid). Association for Computational Linguistics.

Damien Sileo. 2023. tasksource: Structured dataset preprocessing annotations for frictionless extreme multi-task learning and evaluation. *arXiv preprint arXiv:2301.05948*.

Paulo Silva, Carolina Gonçalves, Carolina Godinho, Nuno Antunes, and Marilia Curado. 2020. Using nlp and machine learning to detect data privacy violations. In *IEEE INFOCOM 2020 - IEEE Conference on Computer Communications Workshops (INFOCOM WKSHPS)*, pages 972–977.

Răzvan-Alexandru Smădu, Ion-Robert Dinică, Andrei-Marius Avram, Dumitru-Clementin Cercel, Florin Pop, and Mihaela-Claudia Cercel. 2022. Legal named entity recognition with multi-task domain adaptation. In *Proceedings of the Natural Legal Language Processing Workshop 2022*, pages 305–321, Abu Dhabi, United Arab Emirates (Hybrid). Association for Computational Linguistics.

Dezhao Song, Andrew Vold, Kanika Madan, and Frank Schilder. 2022. Multi-label legal document classification: A deep learning-based approach with label-attention and domain-specific pre-training. *Information Systems*, 106:101718.

Zhen Xu, Sergio Escalera, Adrien Pavão, Magali Richard, Wei-Wei Tu, Quanming Yao, Huan Zhao, and Isabelle Guyon. 2022. Codabench: Flexible, easy-to-use, and reproducible meta-benchmark platform. *Patterns*, 3(7):100543.

DeBERTa Beats Behemoths: A Comparative Analysis of Fine-Tuning, Prompting, and PEFT Approaches on LegalLensNER

Hanh Thi Hong Tran*[1,2,3], Nishan Chatterjee*[1,2,3], Senja Pollak[2], Antoine Doucet[1]
[1] La Rochelle University, France
[2] Jožef Stefan Institute, Slovenia
[3] Jožef Stefan International Postgraduate School, Slovenia
*Equal contribution
Correspondence: thi.tran, nchatter@univ-lr.fr

Abstract

This paper summarizes the participation of our team (Flawless Lawgic) in the legal named entity recognition (L-NER) task at *LegalLens 2024: Detecting Legal Violations*. Given possible unstructured texts (e.g., online media texts), we aim to identify legal violations by extracting legal entities such as "*violation*", "*violation by*", "*violation on*", and "*law*". This system-description paper discusses our approaches to address the task, empirically highlighting the performances of fine-tuning models from the Transformers family (e.g., `RoBERTa` and `DeBERTa`) against open-sourced LLMs (e.g., `Llama`, `Mistral`) with different tuning settings (e.g., `LoRA`, Supervised Fine-Tuning (`SFT`) and prompting strategies). Our best results, with a weighted F1 of 0.705 on the test set, show a 30 percentage points increase in F1 compared to the baseline and rank 2 on the leaderboard, leaving a marginal gap of only 0.4 percentage points lower than the top solution. Our solutions are available at @honghanhh/lner.

1 Introduction

The internet has revolutionized how we share and interact with information. Every day, we generate an enormous quantity of digital textual data in the form of news articles, blogs, and social media posts. The information we consume and produce, not to mention the platforms we interact on contain a multitude of legal claims, and violations are no exceptions. It is undeniable that these violations pose potential risks to individuals and organizations as well as go against the fabric of legal and ethical standards, including individual rights, societal norms, and the principles of justice.

Previous studies often trace the legal violations from their data trails by using specialized models tailored for specific domain applications (Silva et al., 2020; Yu et al., 2020). While these models can be effective in their narrow domains, they often lack the necessary versatility to address the wide array of legal violations across contexts. To address this, Bernsohn et al. (2024) formulate a new task of automatically identifying legal violations from unstructured text sources in the form of legal named entity recognition (L-NER). While baseline methods have been created to address this task, there remains a gap in developing more advanced methods to sort through this online noise and identify these breaches.

Inspired by the work of Bernsohn et al. (2024) on *LegalLens* consisting of a novel textual dataset for legal violation identification using large-scale language models (LLMs), we address a comparative analysis of different approaches on this dataset through the *LegalLens 2024: Detecting Legal Violations* shared task (Hagag et al., 2024). The contributions of this paper are two-fold:

- We propose a comparative evaluation of different techniques, including the adaptation of various language models (e.g., `RoBERTa` (Liu et al., 2019), `DeBERTa` (He et al., 2021)) as fined-tuning token classifiers against open-sourced LLMs with token classification and supervised fine-tuning using `LoRA`, and zero-shot prompt engineering approaches, gaining valuable insights into their applicability and limitations in the context of legal NLP.
- Our code is publicly available as an open-sourced repository on GitHub and our models are accessible via HuggingFace, making our work more transparent and reproducible.

The paper is organized as below. Section 2 summarizes the previous works for the L-NER task. Section 3 describes the architecture, dataset, and evaluation metrics for the comparative analysis. In Section 4, we report the performances of our methods on the development set. We also compare our best classifier on the development set with the test set against the baseline. Finally, we propose error

Proceedings of the Natural Legal Language Processing Workshop 2024, pages 371–380
November 16, 2024 ©2024 Association for Computational Linguistics

analysis in Section 5, followed by the conclusion with future works in Section 6.

2 Related Works

The primary works for legal violation identification were mostly on domain-specific topics such as data agreements for compliance (Amaral et al., 2023), data privacy breaches (Silva et al., 2020), and industry-specific regulations (Nyffenegger et al., 2024; Yu et al., 2020). Despite their potential, these studies suffered from the limitation of specific types of legal domains or particular sectors.

One of the most popular directions for legal violation identification was to consider the task as a named entity recognition (Hanh et al., 2021; Ivačič et al., 2023; González-Gallardo et al., 2024) task, or so-called L-NER. In non-neural approaches, Dozier et al. (2010) extracted the named entities (NEs) in the US case law and many other legal documents by implementing list lookups, contextual rules, and statistical models. In neural ones, Leitner et al. (2019) suggested a biLSTM-CRF model for their novel manually annotated datasets about German court decisions with 19 NEs while others proposed LSTM-CRF for LeNER-Br[1] legal documents in Brazilian. Chalkidis et al. (2020) presented LEGAL-BERT[2] with different BERT-based model fine-tuned on 12 GB of English legal texts. Further works (Vardhan et al., 2021) elaborated the neural architecture for legal identification via NER task by convolutional neural networks (CNN) and multi-layer perceptions (MLP). Several other language models (e.g., BERT, DistilBERT, RoBERTa) were also fine-tuned to enhance the performance of legal violation identification (Bernsohn et al., 2024) in the same LegalLens[3] corpora.

With the advent of large-scale language models (LLMs), numerous works have been done to take advantage of LLMs to [1] explain legal terms present in legislative documents (Nyffenegger et al., 2024), [2] analyze the legal textual data (e.g., court decision analysis, rivalling seasoned law students) in depth (Savelka et al., 2023), [3] generate synthetic data in legal domains (Oliveira et al., 2024; Bernsohn et al., 2024), or [4] fine-tune a specialized classifier (e.g., `Llama-2`) for the downstream task (Bernsohn et al., 2024), to mention a few.

[1] https://github.com/peluz/lener-br

[2] https://github.com/nonameemnlp2020/legalBERT

[3] https://github.com/darrow-labs/LegalLens

3 Methods

In this section, we explore three different setups to tackle the challenge of the L-NER task, including: [1] We evaluate Transformers variants (e.g., `RoBERTa` (Liu et al., 2019), `DeBERTa` (He et al., 2021), and `DeBERTa-LSTM`) through the process of fine-tuning; [2] We explore prompting LLMs in zero-shot settings (Li, 2023) with different fine-tuned checkpoints (e.g., `Mistral` (Jiang et al., 2023), `Llama-2` (Touvron et al., 2023a), `Llama-3.1` (Dubey et al., 2024)); and [3] We perform parameter-efficient fine-tuning (`PEFT`) using low-rank adaptation (`LoRA`) with LLMs.

3.1 Architecture

Fine-tuning on the Transformers family: We evaluate the effectiveness of transformer-based language models by fine-tuning `RoBERTa`[4] (as a baseline) and `DeBERTa`[5] with and without an additional `LSTM` layer (Hochreiter and Schmidhuber, 1997) following the success of Bernsohn et al. (2024). We train the models using the AutoModel classes from the HuggingFace Transformers library. Each model was trained for 10 epochs with an initial learning rate of $2e-5$, batch size of 16, warm-up steps of 500, weight decay of 0.01, random seed of 42, and a max sequence length of 512 tokens. For the additional layers incorporating `DeBERTa`, we set the dropout rate to 0.3. Early stopping was applied to prevent overfitting.

Prompting LLMs in Zero-Shot Settings: We evaluate several open-sourced instruction-tuned LLMs to test their ability on this task. In zero-shot settings, we treat the L-NER task as a slot-filling problem, where each slot corresponds to a class label. We use three different prompts, where: [1] Prompt 1 is similar to the implicit prompt Bernsohn et al. (2024) used for their few-shot classification setting; [2] Prompt 2 is what Bernsohn et al. (2024) used to create their dataset using GPT-4 (OpenAI et al., 2024) before human annotation; and [3] Prompt 3 is based on rephrasing the prompt explicitly as a slot-filling problem instead of a NER task. The prompts can be seen in Figure 2. We use the JSONFormer[6] to constrain the outputs into a structured format. The top experiment's results

[4] https://huggingface.co/FacebookAI/roberta-base

[5] https://huggingface.co/microsoft/deberta-v3-base

[6] https://github.com/1rgs/JSONFormer

have been listed in Table 1, while the complete list can be found in Table 6 in the Appendix B. This helps us understand whether fine-tuning is necessary for tackling this task and identify potential candidates for fine-tuning.

LoRA with Open-Sourced LLMs: We experiment using different open-sourced LLM families, including Qwen2 (Yang et al., 2024), Mistral (Jiang et al., 2023), Llama-2 (Touvron et al., 2023b), and Llama-3x (Dubey et al., 2024). We consider the same data sizes of 7-8 billion parametric versions for all the tested LLMs. Following the success of PEFT for fine-tuning LLMs as a token classifier, we leverage LoRA (Hu et al.), a fine-tuning technique that adds a small, low-rank matrix to the pre-trained model weights, allowing for efficient adaptation to new tasks with fewer trainable parameters. LoRA works by keeping the majority of the model's weights frozen and only training a small number of parameters specific to the task, drastically reducing the computational cost while maintaining high performance. Each model was trained for the same 10 epochs with a batch size of LoRA r of 12, LoRA alpha of 32, and LoRA dropout of 0.1. We use Li et al. (2023)'s LlamaForTokenClassification and MistralForTokenClassification, which use Label Supervision (LS) to constrain the output predictions. In addition, we perform Supervised Fine-tuning (SFT) using LoRA on Llama3.1-8b (Dubey et al., 2024) using the Llama-3 instruction format to produce JSONFormer-like JSON outputs. We use the same LoRA configurations as before for training and JSONFormer for testing.

3.2 Datasets

We use the training and development sets from LegalLens (Bernsohn et al., 2024) designed for the L-NER task to identify violations with four distinct classes: "*violation*", "*violation by*", "*violation on*", and "*law*". The class description, the number of instances per class, and their average phrase length are presented in Table 4 in Section A.

3.3 Evaluation Metrics

The L-NER task's performance is assessed using Precision, Recall, and weighted F1-score.

4 Results

Table 1 presents the performance of different models given three settings: [1] Fine-tuning (e.g., RoBERTa, DeBERTa); [2] Prompting (e.g., Mistral, Llama); and [3] LoRA (e.g., Qwen2, Mistral, Llama). In general, all the fine-tuned BERT-based language models outperform LLMs for both LoRA and instruction-tuning settings by a significant margin. Across all models, DeBERTa attains the best performances, achieving an F1 of 64.8% and a Precision of 63.3% on the development set.

Table 1: Comparison of different methodologies for L-NER on the development set. The table showcases various models, their sizes, the methods employed, and their performance metrics, where P is Precision, R is Recall, and F1 is the F1-score. Both Prompting and SFT use Prompt 2 as the instruction (see Figure 2).

Models	Size	Methods	P	R	F1
RoBERTa	125M	Fine-tune	0.568	0.674	0.616
DeBERTa-v3	250M	Fine-tune	**0.633**	0.664	**0.648**
DeBERTa-v3+LSTM	250M	Fine-tune	0.577	**0.688**	0.627
Mistral-v0.3	7B	Prompting	0.246	0.258	0.252
Llama-2-hf	7B	Prompting	0.122	0.173	0.143
Dolphin-2.9-Llama-3	8b	Prompting	0.425	0.509	0.463
Meta-Llama3.1	8B	Prompting	0.456	0.282	0.348
Qwen2	7B	LS-LoRA	0.228	0.333	0.270
Mistral-v0.3	7B	LS-LoRA	0.160	0.272	0.202
Llama-2	7B	LS-LoRA	0.372	0.536	0.439
Dolphin-2.9-Llama-3	8B	LS-LoRA	0.228	0.370	0.282
Llama-3.1	8B	LS-LoRA	0.448	0.637	0.526
Llama-3.1	8B	SFT-LoRA	0.015	0.110	0.027

Given the best performance on the development set of DeBERTa as a fine-tuned token classifier, we reported the results in weighted F1 of our classifier on the hidden test set in comparison with other competitors and the baseline from the *LegalLens 2024: Detecting Legal Violations* task in Table 2.

Table 2: Results on the test set in the leaderboard.

Teams	F1
Nowj	0.416
Flawless Lawgic (Ours)	**0.402**
UOttawa	0.402
Masala-chai	0.380
UMLaw & TechLab	0.321
Bonafide	0.305
Baseline	0.381

For the LegalLens NER part of the shared task (Hagag et al., 2024), all competitors performed higher than the baseline, where our team obtained second place with only a marginal gap of 4 percentage points from the winning solution on the test set.

5 Error Analysis

Entity Type Errors: Figure 1 visualizes the comparison in F1 performance for each class among different models reported in Table 1.

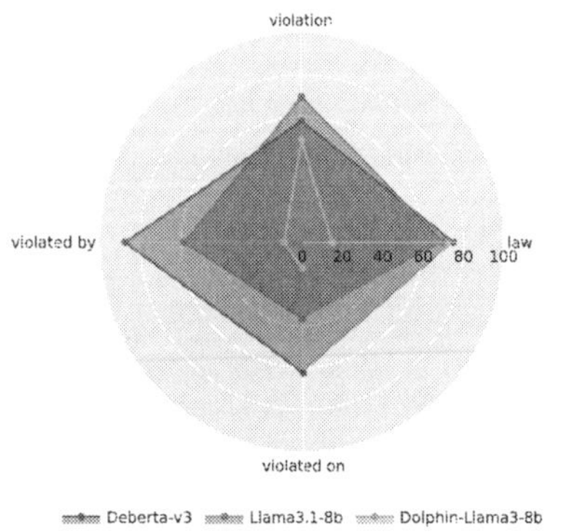

Figure 1: Comparing performance in F1 of models from Table 1 on the development set for each class.

Of all classes, the entity type "*violation*" had the lowest F1 despite its richness in training examples, especially for longer and more complex entities, followed by "*violated on*". DeBERTA showed the most competitive performance for all classes, especially in identifying the entity types "*violated on*" and "*violated by*" by a large margin. The performance of our best classifier on the development set is reported in Table 3. This indicates that training separate models for each class, or certain classes grouped together might be an interesting avenue to explore.

Additionally, the three datasets exhibit significant variability, as illustrated by the distinct class coverage of models in Figure 3 in Appendix B, which provides insights into the data distribution. This variability may explain why models trained on the training set may not generalize well to the development and test sets. Moreover, analyzing the named entities present in each slot and examining how various models perform about these, could yield additional valuable findings.

Table 3: Results per class on the development set using DeBERTA token classifier.

Classes	Precision	Recall	F1-score
LAW	0.928	0.853	0.888
VIOLATED BY	0.969	0.840	0.900
VIOLATED ON	0.608	0.600	0.604
VIOLATION	0.574	0.627	0.599

The Disparity in Performance: Although DeBERTa outperformed other masked language models of smaller size (e.g., RoBERTa), a larger model size does not always lead to better performance, especially when LoRA fine-tuning is used, which can sometimes lead to poorer results. This is consistent with the results of Li et al. (2023), which highlighted the difficulties in fine-tuning the LLMs compared to the smaller masked language models (e.g., BERT), especially when the amount of training data is limited.

Furthermore, we acknowledged the difference in objective functions between DeBERTa as a fine-tuned token classifier and other LLMs (e.g., Llama-3.1) as a SFT-LoRA classifier. While DeBERTa employed the per-token cross-entropy objective function, LLMs fine-tuned via causal language modelling, wherein the task is to learn the joint probability distribution of all tokens by maximizing the likelihood of the data. As a result, DeBERTa provided a more fine-grained and stronger gradient signal that well constrained the class space by the number of possible entities in our dataset. This highlights the gap between masked and casual language models in token classification tasks for specific domains like L-NER. Additionally, as shown in the findings of Li et al. (2023), LS LoRA provided significant improvement over SFT-LoRA. However, there is still room for improvement when compared to DeBERTa.

Practical Use of LLMs for Legal Domain: Despite not surpassing the performance of fine-tuned and LoRA methods, prompt-based methods are still a promising tool for finding the potential violation for legal documents, especially when working with limited data of the same domain or when no annotated data is available for a given domain. While it may not be as good as models trained on dedicated annotated data (fully supervised ones), it can significantly speed up the process by suggesting the violation types later reviewed and refined by human experts.

Additionally, tools like JSONFormer, which enforce structured output constraints, can help significantly in automating these tasks. By ensuring that model outputs conform to predefined formats (e.g., JSON), these tools simplify post-processing workflows, making the outputs easier to analyze and validate using non-LLM methods, as structured formats facilitate clearer interpretation and error-checking mechanisms (Liu et al., 2024).

In-Domain Fine-Tuning: We evaluated the performance of fine-tuned DeBERTa checkpoints on several NER datasets relevant to this task [7]. Surprisingly, no significant improvement was observed compared to the base DeBERTa model. However, based on our analysis of the zero-shot performance capabilities of LLMs (see Figure 3), there appears to be greater overlap between the dataset styles of the training set and the hidden test set than between the training and development sets. This suggests that having better distributions of train-dev-test splits can help with improving upon this task. Additionally, domain-specific fine-tuning where similar patterns are reflected could also potentially enhance the performance of LLMs, although further experimentation is required to validate this hypothesis. Therefore, future work could explore fine-tuning an LLM on a legal domain corpus, which may yield better results for this and similar tasks (Jiang et al., 2024).

6 Conclusion

In this study, we presented a comparative analysis of three different approaches to identify the legal violations via the L-NER task at *LegalLens 2024: Detecting Legal Violations*, including [1] fine-tuning masked language models as token classifier; [2] zero-shot prompt engineering with LLMs; [3] fine-tuning LLMs with LoRA as token classifier. Overall, the first approach using DeBERTa as the backbone outperformed other settings, demonstrating the gap in performance between masked language models and other causal LLMs in token classification tasks, especially when the amount of training data is limited. As a result, when a complete training dataset is accessible, opting for a fully-supervised fine-tuned system remains the optimal choice. However, instruction-tuning LLMs with well-defined prompting is still a potential technique with competitive results when no annotated data is available.

Acknowledgments

The authors acknowledge the financial support from the Slovenian Research and Innovation Agency through the core research programme, Knowledge Technologies (P2-0103), the research project, Linguistic Accessibility of Social Assistance Rights in Slovenia (J5-50169), the project, Cross-lingual and cross-domain methods for Terminology Extraction and Alignment, and a bilateral project funded by the program, PROTEUS, under the grant number BI-FR/23-24-PROTEUS006. This work has also been supported by the TERMITRAD (2020-2019-8510010) project funded by the Nouvelle-Aquitaine Region, France.

[7]For example, CONLL 2003 (Tjong Kim Sang and De Meulder, 2003), OntoNotes 5.0 (Pradhan et al., 2013), and WikiANN (Rahimi et al., 2019)

References

Orlando Amaral, Sallam Abualhaija, and Lionel Briand. 2023. Ml-based compliance verification of data processing agreements against gdpr. In *2023 IEEE 31st international requirements engineering conference (RE)*, pages 53–64. IEEE.

Dor Bernsohn, Gil Semo, Yaron Vazana, Gila Hayat, Ben Hagag, Joel Niklaus, Rohit Saha, and Kyryl Truskovskyi. 2024. Legallens: Leveraging llms for legal violation identification in unstructured text. In *Proceedings of the 18th Conference of the European Chapter of the Association for Computational Linguistics (Volume 1: Long Papers)*, pages 2129–2145.

Ilias Chalkidis, Manos Fergadiotis, Prodromos Malakasiotis, Nikolaos Aletras, and Ion Androutsopoulos. 2020. Legal-bert: The muppets straight out of law school. *arXiv preprint arXiv:2010.02559*.

Christopher Dozier, Ravikumar Kondadadi, Marc Light, Arun Vachher, Sriharsha Veeramachaneni, and Ramdev Wudali. 2010. *Named entity recognition and resolution in legal text*. Springer.

Abhimanyu Dubey, Abhinav Jauhri, Abhinav Pandey, Abhishek Kadian, Ahmad Al-Dahle, Aiesha Letman, Akhil Mathur, Alan Schelten, Amy Yang, Angela Fan, Anirudh Goyal, Anthony Hartshorn, Aobo Yang, Archi Mitra, Archie Sravankumar, Artem Korenev, Arthur Hinsvark, Arun Rao, Aston Zhang, Aurelien Rodriguez, Austen Gregerson, Ava Spataru, Baptiste Roziere, Bethany Biron, Binh Tang, Bobbie Chern, Charlotte Caucheteux, Chaya Nayak, Chloe Bi, Chris Marra, Chris McConnell, Christian Keller, Christophe Touret, Chunyang Wu, Corinne Wong, Cristian Canton Ferrer, Cyrus Nikolaidis, Damien Allonsius, Daniel Song, Danielle Pintz, Danny Livshits, David Esiobu, Dhruv Choudhary, Dhruv Mahajan, Diego Garcia-Olano, Diego Perino, Dieuwke Hupkes, Egor Lakomkin, Ehab AlBadawy, Elina Lobanova, Emily Dinan, Eric Michael Smith, Filip Radenovic, Frank Zhang, Gabriel Synnaeve, Gabrielle Lee, Georgia Lewis Anderson, Graeme Nail, Gregoire Mialon, Guan Pang, Guillem Cucurell, Hailey Nguyen, Hannah Korevaar, Hu Xu, Hugo Touvron, Iliyan Zarov, Imanol Arrieta Ibarra, Isabel Kloumann, Ishan Misra, Ivan Evtimov, Jade Copet, Jaewon Lee, Jan Geffert, Jana Vranes, Jason Park, Jay Mahadeokar, Jeet Shah, Jelmer van der Linde, Jennifer Billock, Jenny Hong, Jenya Lee, Jeremy Fu, Jianfeng Chi, Jianyu Huang, Jiawen Liu, Jie Wang, Jiecao Yu, Joanna Bitton, Joe Spisak, Jongsoo Park, Joseph

Rocca, Joshua Johnstun, Joshua Saxe, Junteng Jia, Kalyan Vasuden Alwala, Kartikeya Upasani, Kate Plawiak, Ke Li, Kenneth Heafield, Kevin Stone, Khalid El-Arini, Krithika Iyer, Kshitiz Malik, Kuenley Chiu, Kunal Bhalla, Lauren Rantala-Yeary, Laurens van der Maaten, Lawrence Chen, Liang Tan, Liz Jenkins, Louis Martin, Lovish Madaan, Lubo Malo, Lukas Blecher, Lukas Landzaat, Luke de Oliveira, Madeline Muzzi, Mahesh Pasupuleti, Mannat Singh, Manohar Paluri, Marcin Kardas, Mathew Oldham, Mathieu Rita, Maya Pavlova, Melanie Kambadur, Mike Lewis, Min Si, Mitesh Kumar Singh, Mona Hassan, Naman Goyal, Narjes Torabi, Nikolay Bashlykov, Nikolay Bogoychev, Niladri Chatterji, Olivier Duchenne, Onur Çelebi, Patrick Alrassy, Pengchuan Zhang, Pengwei Li, Petar Vasic, Peter Weng, Prajjwal Bhargava, Pratik Dubal, Praveen Krishnan, Punit Singh Koura, Puxin Xu, Qing He, Qingxiao Dong, Ragavan Srinivasan, Raj Ganapathy, Ramon Calderer, Ricardo Silveira Cabral, Robert Stojnic, Roberta Raileanu, Rohit Girdhar, Rohit Patel, Romain Sauvestre, Ronnie Polidoro, Roshan Sumbaly, Ross Taylor, Ruan Silva, Rui Hou, Rui Wang, Saghar Hosseini, Sahana Chennabasappa, Sanjay Singh, Sean Bell, Seohyun Sonia Kim, Sergey Edunov, Shaoliang Nie, Sharan Narang, Sharath Raparthy, Sheng Shen, Shengye Wan, Shruti Bhosale, Shun Zhang, Simon Vandenhende, Soumya Batra, Spencer Whitman, Sten Sootla, Stephane Collot, Suchin Gururangan, Sydney Borodinsky, Tamar Herman, Tara Fowler, Tarek Sheasha, Thomas Georgiou, Thomas Scialom, Tobias Speckbacher, Todor Mihaylov, Tong Xiao, Ujjwal Karn, Vedanuj Goswami, Vibhor Gupta, Vignesh Ramanathan, Viktor Kerkez, Vincent Gonguet, Virginie Do, Vish Vogeti, Vladan Petrovic, Weiwei Chu, Wenhan Xiong, Wenyin Fu, Whitney Meers, Xavier Martinet, Xiaodong Wang, Xiaoqing Ellen Tan, Xinfeng Xie, Xuchao Jia, Xuewei Wang, Yaelle Goldschlag, Yashesh Gaur, Yasmine Babaei, Yi Wen, Yiwen Song, Yuchen Zhang, Yue Li, Yuning Mao, Zacharie Delpierre Coudert, Zheng Yan, Zhengxing Chen, Zoe Papakipos, Aaditya Singh, Aaron Grattafiori, Abha Jain, Adam Kelsey, Adam Shajnfeld, Adithya Gangidi, Adolfo Victoria, Ahuva Goldstand, Ajay Menon, Ajay Sharma, Alex Boesenberg, Alex Vaughan, Alexei Baevski, Allie Feinstein, Amanda Kallet, Amit Sangani, Anam Yunus, Andrei Lupu, Andres Alvarado, Andrew Caples, Andrew Gu, Andrew Ho, Andrew Poulton, Andrew Ryan, Ankit Ramchandani, Annie Franco, Aparajita Saraf, Arkabandhu Chowdhury, Ashley Gabriel, Ashwin Bharambe, Assaf Eisenman, Azadeh Yazdan, Beau James, Ben Maurer, Benjamin Leonhardi, Bernie Huang, Beth Loyd, Beto De Paola, Bhargavi Paranjape, Bing Liu, Bo Wu, Boyu Ni, Braden Hancock, Bram Wasti, Brandon Spence, Brani Stojkovic, Brian Gamido, Britt Montalvo, Carl Parker, Carly Burton, Catalina Mejia, Changhan Wang, Changkyu Kim, Chao Zhou, Chester Hu, Ching-Hsiang Chu, Chris Cai, Chris Tindal, Christoph Feichtenhofer, Damon Civin, Dana Beaty, Daniel Kreymer, Daniel Li, Danny Wyatt, David Adkins, David Xu, Davide Testuggine, Delia David, Devi Parikh, Diana Liskovich, Didem Foss, Dingkang Wang, Duc Le, Dustin Holland, Edward Dowling, Eissa Jamil, Elaine Montgomery, Eleonora Presani, Emily Hahn, Emily Wood, Erik Brinkman, Esteban Arcaute, Evan Dunbar, Evan Smothers, Fei Sun, Felix Kreuk, Feng Tian, Firat Ozgenel, Francesco Caggioni, Francisco Guzmán, Frank Kanayet, Frank Seide, Gabriela Medina Florez, Gabriella Schwarz, Gada Badeer, Georgia Swee, Gil Halpern, Govind Thattai, Grant Herman, Grigory Sizov, Guangyi, Zhang, Guna Lakshminarayanan, Hamid Shojanazeri, Han Zou, Hannah Wang, Hanwen Zha, Haroun Habeeb, Harrison Rudolph, Helen Suk, Henry Aspegren, Hunter Goldman, Ibrahim Damlaj, Igor Molybog, Igor Tufanov, Irina-Elena Veliche, Itai Gat, Jake Weissman, James Geboski, James Kohli, Japhet Asher, Jean-Baptiste Gaya, Jeff Marcus, Jeff Tang, Jennifer Chan, Jenny Zhen, Jeremy Reizenstein, Jeremy Teboul, Jessica Zhong, Jian Jin, Jingyi Yang, Joe Cummings, Jon Carvill, Jon Shepard, Jonathan McPhie, Jonathan Torres, Josh Ginsburg, Junjie Wang, Kai Wu, Kam Hou U, Karan Saxena, Karthik Prasad, Kartikay Khandelwal, Katayoun Zand, Kathy Matosich, Kaushik Veeraraghavan, Kelly Michelena, Keqian Li, Kun Huang, Kunal Chawla, Kushal Lakhotia, Kyle Huang, Lailin Chen, Lakshya Garg, Lavender A, Leandro Silva, Lee Bell, Lei Zhang, Liangpeng Guo, Licheng Yu, Liron Moshkovich, Luca Wehrstedt, Madian Khabsa, Manav Avalani, Manish Bhatt, Maria Tsimpoukelli, Martynas Mankus, Matan Hasson, Matthew Lennie, Matthias Reso, Maxim Groshev, Maxim Naumov, Maya Lathi, Meghan Keneally, Michael L. Seltzer, Michal Valko, Michelle Restrepo, Mihir Patel, Mik Vyatskov, Mikayel Samvelyan, Mike Clark, Mike Macey, Mike Wang, Miquel Jubert Hermoso, Mo Metanat, Mohammad Rastegari, Munish Bansal, Nandhini Santhanam, Natascha Parks, Natasha White, Navyata Bawa, Nayan Singhal, Nick Egebo, Nicolas Usunier, Nikolay Pavlovich Laptev, Ning Dong, Ning Zhang, Norman Cheng, Oleg Chernoguz, Olivia Hart, Omkar Salpekar, Ozlem Kalinli, Parkin Kent, Parth Parekh, Paul Saab, Pavan Balaji, Pedro Rittner, Philip Bontrager, Pierre Roux, Piotr Dollar, Polina Zvyagina, Prashant Ratanchandani, Pritish Yuvraj, Qian Liang, Rachad Alao, Rachel Rodriguez, Rafi Ayub, Raghotham Murthy, Raghu Nayani, Rahul Mitra, Raymond Li, Rebekkah Hogan, Robin Battey, Rocky Wang, Rohan Maheswari, Russ Howes, Ruty Rinott, Sai Jayesh Bondu, Samyak Datta, Sara Chugh, Sara Hunt, Sargun Dhillon, Sasha Sidorov, Satadru Pan, Saurabh Verma, Seiji Yamamoto, Sharadh Ramaswamy, Shaun Lindsay, Shaun Lindsay, Sheng Feng, Shenghao Lin, Shengxin Cindy Zha, Shiva Shankar, Shuqiang Zhang, Shuqiang Zhang, Sinong Wang, Sneha Agarwal, Soji Sajuyigbe, Soumith Chintala, Stephanie Max, Stephen Chen, Steve Kehoe, Steve Satterfield, Sudarshan Govindaprasad, Sumit Gupta, Sungmin Cho, Sunny Virk, Suraj Subramanian, Sy Choudhury, Sydney Goldman, Tal Remez, Tamar Glaser, Tamara Best, Thilo Kohler, Thomas Robinson, Tianhe Li, Tianjun Zhang, Tim Matthews, Timothy Chou, Tzook Shaked, Varun Vontimitta, Victoria Ajayi, Victoria Montanez, Vijai Mohan, Vinay Satish Kumar, Vishal Mangla, Vítor Albiero, Vlad Ionescu, Vlad Poenaru,

Vlad Tiberiu Mihailescu, Vladimir Ivanov, Wei Li, Wenchen Wang, Wenwen Jiang, Wes Bouaziz, Will Constable, Xiaocheng Tang, Xiaofang Wang, Xiaojian Wu, Xiaolan Wang, Xide Xia, Xilun Wu, Xinbo Gao, Yanjun Chen, Ye Hu, Ye Jia, Ye Qi, Yenda Li, Yilin Zhang, Ying Zhang, Yossi Adi, Youngjin Nam, Yu, Wang, Yuchen Hao, Yundi Qian, Yuzi He, Zach Rait, Zachary DeVito, Zef Rosnbrick, Zhaoduo Wen, Zhenyu Yang, and Zhiwei Zhao. 2024. The llama 3 herd of models. *Preprint*, arXiv:2407.21783.

Carlos-Emiliano González-Gallardo, Tran Thi Hong Hanh, Ahmed Hamdi, and Antoine Doucet. 2024. Leveraging open large language models for historical named entity recognition. In *The 28th International Conference on Theory and Practice of Digital Libraries*.

Ben Hagag, Liav Harpaz, Gil Semo, Dor Bernsohn, Rohit Saha, Pashootan Vaezipoor, Kyryl Truskovskyi, and Gerasimos Spanakis. 2024. Legallens shared task 2024: Legal violation identification in unstructured text. *Preprint*, arXiv:2410.12064.

Tran Thi Hong Hanh, Antoine Doucet, Nicolas Sidere, Jose G Moreno, and Senja Pollak. 2021. Named entity recognition architecture combining contextual and global features. In *International Conference on Asian Digital Libraries*, pages 264–276. Springer.

Pengcheng He, Xiaodong Liu, Jianfeng Gao, and Weizhu Chen. 2021. Deberta: Decoding-enhanced bert with disentangled attention. *Preprint*, arXiv:2006.03654.

Sepp Hochreiter and Jürgen Schmidhuber. 1997. Long short-term memory. *Neural Computation*, 9(8):1735–1780.

Edward J Hu, Phillip Wallis, Zeyuan Allen-Zhu, Yuanzhi Li, Shean Wang, Lu Wang, Weizhu Chen, et al. Lora: Low-rank adaptation of large language models. In *International Conference on Learning Representations*.

Nikola Ivačič, Thi Hong Hanh Tran, Boshko Koloski, Senja Pollak, and Matthew Purver. 2023. Analysis of transfer learning for named entity recognition in south-slavic languages. In *Proceedings of the 9th Workshop on Slavic Natural Language Processing 2023 (SlavicNLP 2023)*, pages 106–112.

Albert Q. Jiang, Alexandre Sablayrolles, Arthur Mensch, Chris Bamford, Devendra Singh Chaplot, Diego de las Casas, Florian Bressand, Gianna Lengyel, Guillaume Lample, Lucile Saulnier, Lélio Renard Lavaud, Marie-Anne Lachaux, Pierre Stock, Teven Le Scao, Thibaut Lavril, Thomas Wang, Timothée Lacroix, and William El Sayed. 2023. Mistral 7b. *Preprint*, arXiv:2310.06825.

Ting Jiang, Shaohan Huang, Shengyue Luo, Zihan Zhang, Haizhen Huang, Furu Wei, Weiwei Deng, Feng Sun, Qi Zhang, Deqing Wang, and Fuzhen Zhuang. 2024. Improving domain adaptation through extended-text reading comprehension. *Preprint*, arXiv:2401.07284.

Elena Leitner, Georg Rehm, and Julian Moreno-Schneider. 2019. Fine-grained named entity recognition in legal documents. In *International conference on semantic systems*, pages 272–287. Springer.

Yinheng Li. 2023. A practical survey on zero-shot prompt design for in-context learning. In *Proceedings of the Conference Recent Advances in Natural Language Processing - Large Language Models for Natural Language Processings*, RANLP, page 641–647. INCOMA Ltd., Shoumen, BULGARIA.

Zongxi Li, Xianming Li, Yuzhang Liu, Haoran Xie, Jing Li, Fu-lee Wang, Qing Li, and Xiaoqin Zhong. 2023. Label supervised llama finetuning. *arXiv preprint arXiv:2310.01208*.

Yong Lin, Hangyu Lin, Wei Xiong, Shizhe Diao, Jianmeng Liu, Jipeng Zhang, Rui Pan, Haoxiang Wang, Wenbin Hu, Hanning Zhang, Hanze Dong, Renjie Pi, Han Zhao, Nan Jiang, Heng Ji, Yuan Yao, and Tong Zhang. 2024. Mitigating the alignment tax of rlhf. *Preprint*, arXiv:2309.06256.

Michael Xieyang Liu, Frederick Liu, Alexander J. Fiannaca, Terry Koo, Lucas Dixon, Michael Terry, and Carrie J. Cai. 2024. "we need structured output": Towards user-centered constraints on large language model output. In *Extended Abstracts of the CHI Conference on Human Factors in Computing Systems*, CHI '24, page 1–9. ACM.

Xiao Liu, Yanan Zheng, Zhengxiao Du, Ming Ding, Yujie Qian, Zhilin Yang, and Jie Tang. 2023. Gpt understands, too. *Preprint*, arXiv:2103.10385.

Yinhan Liu, Myle Ott, Naman Goyal, Jingfei Du, Mandar Joshi, Danqi Chen, Omer Levy, Mike Lewis, Luke Zettlemoyer, and Veselin Stoyanov. 2019. Roberta: A robustly optimized BERT pretraining approach. *CoRR*, abs/1907.11692.

Alex Nyffenegger, Matthias Stürmer, and Joel Niklaus. 2024. Anonymity at risk? assessing re-identification capabilities of large language models in court decisions. In *Findings of the Association for Computational Linguistics: NAACL 2024*, pages 2433–2462.

Vitor Oliveira, Gabriel Nogueira, Thiago Faleiros, and Ricardo Marcacini. 2024. Combining prompt-based language models and weak supervision for labeling named entity recognition on legal documents. *Artificial Intelligence and Law*, pages 1–21.

OpenAI, Josh Achiam, Steven Adler, Sandhini Agarwal, Lama Ahmad, Ilge Akkaya, Florencia Leoni Aleman, Diogo Almeida, Janko Altenschmidt, Sam Altman, Shyamal Anadkat, Red Avila, Igor Babuschkin, Suchir Balaji, Valerie Balcom, Paul Baltescu, Haiming Bao, Mohammad Bavarian, Jeff Belgum, Irwan Bello, Jake Berdine, Gabriel Bernadett-Shapiro, Christopher Berner, Lenny Bogdonoff, Oleg Boiko, Madelaine Boyd, Anna-Luisa Brakman, Greg Brockman, Tim Brooks, Miles Brundage, Kevin Button, Trevor Cai, Rosie Campbell, Andrew Cann, Brittany Carey, Chelsea Carlson, Rory Carmichael, Brooke

Chan, Che Chang, Fotis Chantzis, Derek Chen, Sully Chen, Ruby Chen, Jason Chen, Mark Chen, Ben Chess, Chester Cho, Casey Chu, Hyung Won Chung, Dave Cummings, Jeremiah Currier, Yunxing Dai, Cory Decareaux, Thomas Degry, Noah Deutsch, Damien Deville, Arka Dhar, David Dohan, Steve Dowling, Sheila Dunning, Adrien Ecoffet, Atty Eleti, Tyna Eloundou, David Farhi, Liam Fedus, Niko Felix, Simón Posada Fishman, Juston Forte, Isabella Fulford, Leo Gao, Elie Georges, Christian Gibson, Vik Goel, Tarun Gogineni, Gabriel Goh, Rapha Gontijo-Lopes, Jonathan Gordon, Morgan Grafstein, Scott Gray, Ryan Greene, Joshua Gross, Shixiang Shane Gu, Yufei Guo, Chris Hallacy, Jesse Han, Jeff Harris, Yuchen He, Mike Heaton, Johannes Heidecke, Chris Hesse, Alan Hickey, Wade Hickey, Peter Hoeschele, Brandon Houghton, Kenny Hsu, Shengli Hu, Xin Hu, Joost Huizinga, Shantanu Jain, Shawn Jain, Joanne Jang, Angela Jiang, Roger Jiang, Haozhun Jin, Denny Jin, Shino Jomoto, Billie Jonn, Heewoo Jun, Tomer Kaftan, Łukasz Kaiser, Ali Kamali, Ingmar Kanitscheider, Nitish Shirish Keskar, Tabarak Khan, Logan Kilpatrick, Jong Wook Kim, Christina Kim, Yongjik Kim, Jan Hendrik Kirchner, Jamie Kiros, Matt Knight, Daniel Kokotajlo, Łukasz Kondraciuk, Andrew Kondrich, Aris Konstantinidis, Kyle Kosic, Gretchen Krueger, Vishal Kuo, Michael Lampe, Ikai Lan, Teddy Lee, Jan Leike, Jade Leung, Daniel Levy, Chak Ming Li, Rachel Lim, Molly Lin, Stephanie Lin, Mateusz Litwin, Theresa Lopez, Ryan Lowe, Patricia Lue, Anna Makanju, Kim Malfacini, Sam Manning, Todor Markov, Yaniv Markovski, Bianca Martin, Katie Mayer, Andrew Mayne, Bob McGrew, Scott Mayer McKinney, Christine McLeavey, Paul McMillan, Jake McNeil, David Medina, Aalok Mehta, Jacob Menick, Luke Metz, Andrey Mishchenko, Pamela Mishkin, Vinnie Monaco, Evan Morikawa, Daniel Mossing, Tong Mu, Mira Murati, Oleg Murk, David Mély, Ashvin Nair, Reiichiro Nakano, Rajeev Nayak, Arvind Neelakantan, Richard Ngo, Hyeonwoo Noh, Long Ouyang, Cullen O'Keefe, Jakub Pachocki, Alex Paino, Joe Palermo, Ashley Pantuliano, Giambattista Parascandolo, Joel Parish, Emy Parparita, Alex Passos, Mikhail Pavlov, Andrew Peng, Adam Perelman, Filipe de Avila Belbute Peres, Michael Petrov, Henrique Ponde de Oliveira Pinto, Michael, Pokorny, Michelle Pokrass, Vitchyr H. Pong, Tolly Powell, Alethea Power, Boris Power, Elizabeth Proehl, Raul Puri, Alec Radford, Jack Rae, Aditya Ramesh, Cameron Raymond, Francis Real, Kendra Rimbach, Carl Ross, Bob Rotsted, Henri Roussez, Nick Ryder, Mario Saltarelli, Ted Sanders, Shibani Santurkar, Girish Sastry, Heather Schmidt, David Schnurr, John Schulman, Daniel Selsam, Kyla Sheppard, Toki Sherbakov, Jessica Shieh, Sarah Shoker, Pranav Shyam, Szymon Sidor, Eric Sigler, Maddie Simens, Jordan Sitkin, Katarina Slama, Ian Sohl, Benjamin Sokolowsky, Yang Song, Natalie Staudacher, Felipe Petroski Such, Natalie Summers, Ilya Sutskever, Jie Tang, Nikolas Tezak, Madeleine B. Thompson, Phil Tillet, Amin Tootoonchian, Elizabeth Tseng, Preston Tuggle, Nick Turley, Jerry Tworek, Juan Felipe Cerón Uribe, Andrea Vallone, Arun Vijayvergiya, Chelsea Voss, Carroll Wainwright, Justin Jay Wang, Alvin Wang, Ben Wang, Jonathan Ward, Jason Wei, CJ Weinmann, Akila Welihinda, Peter Welinder, Jiayi Weng, Lilian Weng, Matt Wiethoff, Dave Willner, Clemens Winter, Samuel Wolrich, Hannah Wong, Lauren Workman, Sherwin Wu, Jeff Wu, Michael Wu, Kai Xiao, Tao Xu, Sarah Yoo, Kevin Yu, Qiming Yuan, Wojciech Zaremba, Rowan Zellers, Chong Zhang, Marvin Zhang, Shengjia Zhao, Tianhao Zheng, Juntang Zhuang, William Zhuk, and Barret Zoph. 2024. Gpt-4 technical report. *Preprint*, arXiv:2303.08774.

Sameer Pradhan, Alessandro Moschitti, Nianwen Xue, Hwee Tou Ng, Anders Björkelund, Olga Uryupina, Yuchen Zhang, and Zhi Zhong. 2013. Towards robust linguistic analysis using OntoNotes. In *Proceedings of the Seventeenth Conference on Computational Natural Language Learning*, pages 143–152, Sofia, Bulgaria. Association for Computational Linguistics.

Afshin Rahimi, Yuan Li, and Trevor Cohn. 2019. Massively multilingual transfer for NER. In *Proceedings of the 57th Annual Meeting of the Association for Computational Linguistics*, pages 151–164, Florence, Italy. Association for Computational Linguistics.

Jaromir Savelka, Kevin D Ashley, Morgan A Gray, Hannes Westermann, and Huihui Xu. 2023. Can gpt-4 support analysis of textual data in tasks requiring highly specialized domain expertise? *arXiv preprint arXiv:2306.13906*.

Paulo Silva, Carolina Gonçalves, Carolina Godinho, Nuno Antunes, and Marilia Curado. 2020. Using nlp and machine learning to detect data privacy violations. In *IEEE INFOCOM 2020-IEEE conference on computer communications workshops (INFOCOM WKSHPS)*, pages 972–977. IEEE.

Erik F. Tjong Kim Sang and Fien De Meulder. 2003. Introduction to the CoNLL-2003 shared task: Language-independent named entity recognition. In *Proceedings of the Seventh Conference on Natural Language Learning at HLT-NAACL 2003*, pages 142–147.

Hugo Touvron, Thibaut Lavril, Gautier Izacard, Xavier Martinet, Marie-Anne Lachaux, Timothée Lacroix, Baptiste Rozière, Naman Goyal, Eric Hambro, Faisal Azhar, Aurelien Rodriguez, Armand Joulin, Edouard Grave, and Guillaume Lample. 2023a. Llama: Open and efficient foundation language models. *Preprint*, arXiv:2302.13971.

Hugo Touvron, Louis Martin, Kevin Stone, Peter Albert, Amjad Almahairi, Yasmine Babaei, Nikolay Bashlykov, Soumya Batra, Prajjwal Bhargava, Shruti Bhosale, Dan Bikel, Lukas Blecher, Cristian Canton Ferrer, Moya Chen, Guillem Cucurull, David Esiobu, Jude Fernandes, Jeremy Fu, Wenyin Fu, Brian Fuller, Cynthia Gao, Vedanuj Goswami, Naman Goyal, Anthony Hartshorn, Saghar Hosseini, Rui Hou, Hakan Inan, Marcin Kardas, Viktor Kerkez, Madian Khabsa, Isabel Kloumann, Artem Korenev, Punit Singh Koura,

Marie-Anne Lachaux, Thibaut Lavril, Jenya Lee, Diana Liskovich, Yinghai Lu, Yuning Mao, Xavier Martinet, Todor Mihaylov, Pushkar Mishra, Igor Molybog, Yixin Nie, Andrew Poulton, Jeremy Reizenstein, Rashi Rungta, Kalyan Saladi, Alan Schelten, Ruan Silva, Eric Michael Smith, Ranjan Subramanian, Xiaoqing Ellen Tan, Binh Tang, Ross Taylor, Adina Williams, Jian Xiang Kuan, Puxin Xu, Zheng Yan, Iliyan Zarov, Yuchen Zhang, Angela Fan, Melanie Kambadur, Sharan Narang, Aurelien Rodriguez, Robert Stojnic, Sergey Edunov, and Thomas Scialom. 2023b. Llama 2: Open foundation and fine-tuned chat models. *Preprint*, arXiv:2307.09288.

Harsh Vardhan, Nitish Surana, and BK Tripathy. 2021. Named-entity recognition for legal documents. In *Advanced Machine Learning Technologies and Applications: Proceedings of AMLTA 2020*, pages 469–479. Springer.

An Yang, Baosong Yang, Binyuan Hui, Bo Zheng, Bowen Yu, Chang Zhou, Chengpeng Li, Chengyuan Li, Dayiheng Liu, Fei Huang, et al. 2024. Qwen2 technical report. *arXiv preprint arXiv:2407.10671*.

Yaoquan Yu, Yuefeng Guo, Zhiyuan Zhang, Mengshi Li, Tianyao Ji, Wenhu Tang, and Qinghua Wu. 2020. Intelligent classification and automatic annotation of violations based on neural network language model. In *2020 International Joint Conference on Neural Networks (IJCNN)*, pages 1–7. IEEE.

A Dataset Statistics

We provide additional statistics and descriptions to help understand the data distribution as shown in Figure 4. The most interesting part is the distribution of data in each split: The train split has a data distribution of roughly 3:1 for VIOLATION to the other classes, whereas this becomes 8:1 for the development set. However, the test set has almost a 1:1 ratio. Additionally, if we look at the tokens per class, then the train and development set have comparable distributions, whereas the test set has more tokens per class.

Table 4: Entity distribution and the average length of L-NER entities in LegalLens.

Entities	# Examples			Average Length		
	Train	Dev	Test	Train	Dev	Test
LAW	217	75	246	8.38	3.04	19.27
VIOLATION	710	616	371	88.02	80.45	139.81
VIOLATED BY	217	75	379	5.94	2.39	16.65
VIOLATED ON	217	75	333	5.68	2.38	21.72

The entities include: LAW (specific law or regulation breached), VIOLATION (content describing the violation), VIOLATED BY (entity committing the violation), and VIOLATED ON (victim or affected party).

B Empirical studies on zero-shot instruction tuning

To elaborate on the potential of instruction-tuning using LLMs without the need for adequate annotated data and computation resources, we provided an ablation study on zero-shot performances to identify legal violations given 3 prompt designs where the first two prompts (P1 and P2) were inspired by the work of Bernsohn et al. (2024) and the last prompt (P3) considers the task as a slot-filling problem instead of token classification task (see the prompt examples in Figure 2).

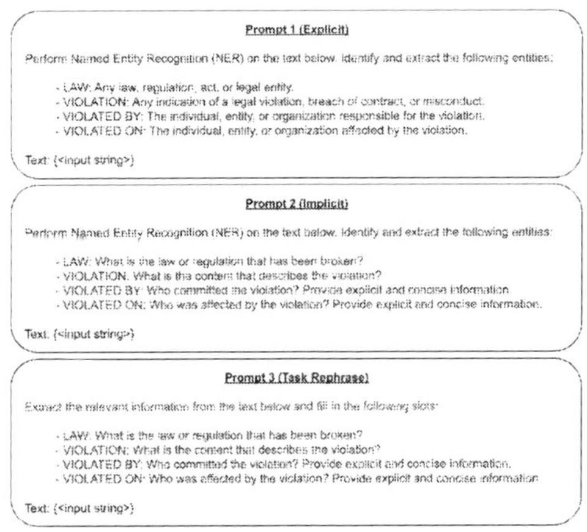

Figure 2: The three prompts we experimented with for the zero-shot setting. The color changes highlight the differences between each prompt.

Table 6 reports the zero-shot performances of three different prompt designs on the training, development, and test sets of the LegalLens dataset. Four groups of LLMs have been investigated, including [1] Llama variants (e.g., Meta-Llama2-7b, Meta-Llama3-8b, Dolphin-Llama3-8b, Meta-Llama3.1-8b); [2] Mistral variants (e.g., Sauf-7b, Mistral-7b, Dolphin Mistral-7b); [3] Gemma (e.g., Gemma2-2b); and [4] Phi (e.g., Phi-3-mini, Phi-3.5-mini). Overall, the P2 prompt structure consistently yielded better results than the other two prompts for all the tested LLMs. We suspect P2 is better because this is the style used to create the examples in the first place using GPT-4 (Bernsohn et al., 2024). Additionally, when the explicit prompts (P1) specify which items to look for, whereas P2 implicitly formulates the question.

However, using a T-test (see Table 5), we find that none of the p-values are below the common threshold of 0.05. This means there's no statistically significant difference in F1 among the three prompts. In other words, based on this test, no single prompt stands out as significantly better than the others in terms of performance. Therefore, p-tuning (Liu et al., 2023) might be an interesting dimension to explore in the future.

Table 5: T-test results for prompt comparison.

Comparison	t-statistic	p-value	Significant ($p < 0.05$)
P1 vs P2	-1.352	0.194	No
P1 vs P3	-0.366	0.718	No
P2 vs P3	1.028	0.318	No

Table 6: Zero-shot performances on the training, development, and test sets. The bold scores perform best, while the highlighted scores are models that reach over 0.4 in F1.

Model	Prompt	Train F1	Dev F1	Test F1
Saul-7b	1	0.114	0.063	0.157
	2	0.316	0.259	0.318
	3	0.259	0.171	0.266
Meta-Llama2-7b	1	0.149	0.120	0.198
	2	0.175	0.143	0.215
	3	0.152	0.110	0.177
Meta-Llama3-8b	1	0.255	0.180	0.290
	2	0.327	0.247	0.347
	3	0.294	0.195	0.322
Dolphin-Llama3-8b	1	0.406	0.334	0.422
	2	**0.463**	0.360	**0.474**
	3	0.438	**0.363**	0.451
Meta-Llama3.1-8b	1	0.254	0.195	0.305
	2	0.319	0.253	0.348
	3	0.271	0.203	0.310
Mistral-7b	1	0.166	0.082	0.262
	2	0.354	0.252	0.400
	3	0.348	0.211	0.383
Dolphin Mistral-7b	1	0.330	0.270	0.390
	2	0.424	0.356	0.419
	3	0.381	0.301	0.416
Gemma2-2b	1	0.232	0.192	0.237
	2	0.292	0.217	0.318
	3	0.182	0.146	0.199
Phi-3-mini	1	0.386	0.308	0.430
	2	0.398	0.338	0.416
	3	0.305	0.225	0.374
Phi-3.5-mini	1	0.417	0.342	0.467
	2	0.420	0.338	0.470
	3	0.377	0.287	0.425

The graph highlights significant variability across the three datasets, as evidenced by the three distinct regions, which offers valuable insights into the data distribution from a qualitative standpoint (see Figure 3). This, along with the token distribution variability as discussed in Section A helps us understand why models trained on the training set struggle to generalize effectively to the development and test sets. To further explore this, it would be beneficial to evaluate the model coverage on the other solutions across the three dataset splits.

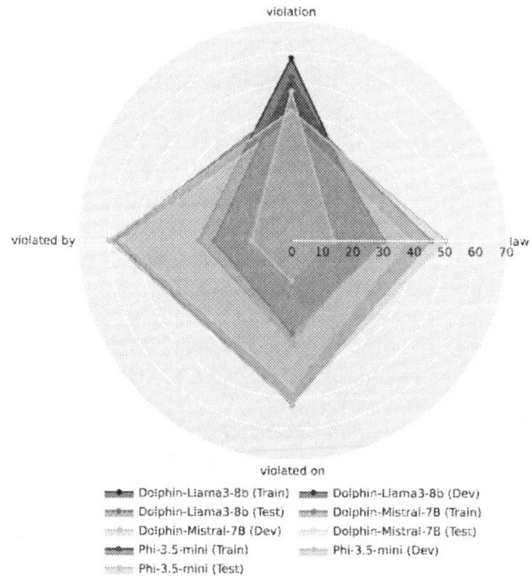

Figure 3: Per-class performance of the three models (based on overall F1) for the training, development, and test sets using zero-shot prompting. We use Prompt 2 for all since it consistently worked better than the other two across all models. Fine-grained values have been mentioned in Table 6.

It should be noted that given the token distribution, smaller LLM (up to 8b parameters as we tested) could come with the limitation of not being able to reproduce longer phrases (especially for "*violation*") which could be improved by scaling up the model sizes, especially given that the original dataset was curated using GPT-4 (Bernsohn et al., 2024).

We also find that Dolphin, the uncensored checkpoints of both `Llama-3-8b` and `Mistral-7b`, significantly outperform their aligned counterparts in the zero-shot classification task. This could be due to the alignment tax (Lin et al., 2024). However, additional qualitative investigation into the data is required before this can be confirmed.

LexSumm and LexT5: Benchmarking and Modeling Legal Summarization Tasks in English

Santosh T.Y.S.S, Cornelius Weiss, Matthias Grabmair
School of Computation, Information, and Technology;
Technical University of Munich, Germany

Abstract

In the evolving NLP landscape, benchmarks serve as yardsticks for gauging progress. However, existing Legal NLP benchmarks only focus on predictive tasks, overlooking generative tasks. This work curates LexSumm, a benchmark designed for evaluating legal summarization tasks in English. It comprises eight English legal summarization datasets, from diverse jurisdictions, such as the US, UK, EU and India. Additionally, we release LexT5, legal oriented sequence-to-sequence model, addressing the limitation of the existing BERT-style encoder-only models in the legal domain. We assess its capabilities through zero-shot probing on LegalLAMA and fine-tuning on LexSumm. Our analysis reveals abstraction and faithfulness errors even in summaries generated by zero-shot LLMs, indicating opportunities for further improvements. LexSumm benchmark and LexT5 model are available at `https://github.com/TUMLegalTech/LexSumm-LexT5`.

1 Introduction

Language serves as the bedrock of the legal domain, facilitating precise communication in this complex field. Legal systems globally engage in the production, consumption and interpretation of massive volumes of text. Legal professionals, comprising lawyers, judges and regulators, continually author a diverse array of complex legal documents, such as briefs, memos, statutes, regulations, contracts, patents and judicial decisions (Coupette et al., 2021). In their routines, these professionals not only craft these documents but also immerse themselves in extensive volumes of text, refining their comprehension of the law for effective human behavior management. Beyond the realms of consumption and production, the practice of law and the art of lawyering hinge on the analysis and interpretation of textual content (Chalkidis et al., 2022a), often perceived by laypersons as legalese or legal gobbledygook (Katz et al., 2023).

Recent advancements in NLP stand poised to revolutionize legal tasks and significantly benefit stakeholders within the legal domain (Zhong et al., 2020b). By automating labor-intensive processes, such as document analysis (Wang et al., 2023; Koreeda and Manning, 2021; Lippi et al., 2019; Graham et al., 2023; Sancheti et al., 2023), information extraction (Luz de Araujo et al., 2018; Chen et al., 2020; Hendrycks et al., 2021; Chalkidis et al., 2017), question answering (Ravichander and Alan, 2019; Kien et al., 2020; Zhong et al., 2020a,c; Chen et al., 2023; Louis et al., 2023; Zheng et al., 2021), text classification (Chalkidis et al., 2019, 2021; Tuggener et al., 2020; Santosh et al., 2024d), information retrieval (Louis and Spanakis, 2022; Ma et al., 2021; Shao et al., 2020; Santosh et al., 2024a,b) and summarization (Shukla et al., 2022; Bhattacharya et al., 2019, 2021; Schraagen et al., 2022; Elaraby and Litman, 2022; Elaraby et al., 2023; Zhong et al., 2019; Xu et al., 2021; Xu and Ashley, 2023; Santosh et al., 2024c; Tyss et al., 2024), NLP with its ability to understand and interpret complex legal language can enhance efficiency and accelerate decision-making. NLP can act as a force multiplier by not only streamlining tasks but also amplifiying the capabilities of legal professionals, leading to increased productivity of legal stakeholders (Katz et al., 2023).

To enable a systematic comparison of approaches, legal evaluation benchmarks like LexGLUE (Chalkidis et al., 2022a) and LEXTREME (Niklaus et al., 2023a) have been proposed, focusing on predictive tasks. However, there is an absence of a dedicated benchmark designed for assessing legal generation capabilities. Moreover, resources on Legal Natural Language Generation (NLG) are sporadic and scattered. In response to this, we introduce LexSumm, a new benchmark curated for training and evaluating legal English

Proceedings of the Natural Legal Language Processing Workshop 2024, pages 381–403
November 16, 2024

summarization models. It includes eight English legal summarization datasets from various jurisdictions, such as the US, UK, EU, and India, for training task-specific models—distinguishing it from LegalBench (Guha et al., 2023) and LawBench (Fei et al., 2023), oriented towards zero/few-shot LLM evaluation.

LexSumm represents the distinctive characteristic of legal documents, marked by their long length, posing a challenge for pre-trained models like BART (Lewis et al., 2020) and T5 (Raffel et al., 2020). In our benchmarking efforts, we evaluate LexSumm using long-context models such as LED (Beltagy et al., 2020), LongT5 (Guo et al., 2022), and PRIMERA (Xiao et al., 2022). We also explore contemporary approaches of adopting short-range pre-trained models like T5 (Raffel et al., 2020) with fusion-in-decoder techniques as in SLED (Ivgi et al., 2023) and integration of retrieval techniques, as demonstrated in Unlimiformer (Bertsch et al., 2023), to adopt them for longer documents. Additionally, we compare recent long-context zero-shot LLMs like GPT-3.5 and Claude on LexSumm.

Pre-trained language models such as BERT (Devlin, 2018), RoBERTa (Liu et al., 2019) have significantly transformed the NLP landscape, showcasing remarkable efficacy in general-domain text. However, their performance diminishes when applied to domain-specific tasks, leading to concept of continued pre-training with domain-specific unlabeled data (Gururangan et al., 2020). This resulted in the development of legal-specific pretrained models like LegalBERT (Chalkidis et al., 2020; Zheng et al., 2021; Henderson et al., 2022; Chalkidis et al., 2023). To the best of our knowledge, there has been a lack of sequence-to-sequence model tailored for the legal domain. To address this gap, we introduce LexT5, an English legal-oriented sequence-to-sequence model pre-trained on the LeXFiles corpus (Chalkidis et al., 2023), from six English-speaking legal systems (EU, European Council, Canada, US, UK, India). To evaluate the legal knowledge acquired by LexT5, we compare its to T5 on LegalLAMA (Chalkidis et al., 2023), a zero-shot legal probing suite. We also assess LexT5's performance on LexSumm by incorporating into SLED and Unlimiformer frameworks to accommodate longer inputs.

Our quantitative and qualitative analysis reveal that LexSumm presents a substantial challenge for existing models including zero-shot LLMs such as GPT-3.5, leaving much room for the research community to improve upon. To streamline future model evaluations, we will release our benchmark and our pre-trained LexT5 model on the Hugging Face Hub, contributing to the advancement of legal NLP research.

2 Related Work

NLG benchmarks Liu et al. 2021 introduced GLGE, a benchmark focusing on English NLG with eight datasets across four tasks. For Chinese, there are CUGE (Yao et al., 2021) and LOT (Guan et al., 2022), with both language understanding and generation tasks. BanglaNLG (Bhattacharjee et al., 2023) serves as a generation benchmark for Bangla with seven datasets across six tasks. Dolphin (Elmadany et al., 2023) offers a comprehensive benchmark for Arabic NLG, covering 13 different tasks. GEMv1 (Gehrmann et al., 2021) is a multilingual NLG benchmark spanning 18 languages and 13 datasets. It has been extended with GEMv2 (Gehrmann et al., 2022), encompassing 51 languages. IndoNLG (Cahyawijaya et al., 2021) focuses on 3 Indonesian languages, while IndicNLG (Kumar et al., 2022) covers 11 Indic languages. MTG (Chen et al., 2022) spans 5 languages.

Turning to specific domains, MedEval (He et al., 2023) and M3 (Otmakhova et al., 2022) are benchmarks tailored for the medical domain, with classification and generation tasks. In line with these efforts, this work introduces LexSumm, a legal domain-specific summarization benchmark with eight datasets.

Benchmarks for Legal Domain LexGLUE (Chalkidis et al., 2022a) stands out as the pioneering benchmark in the legal domain, evaluating NLP models on tasks related to legal language understanding. It encompasses seven classification tasks derived from six English legal NLP datasets, spanning jurisdictions such as the US, EU, and the Council of Europe. LEXTREME (Niklaus et al., 2023a) is a multilingual benchmark for the legal domain, comprising 11 relevant NLU datasets covering 24 languages from two language families (Indo- European and Uralic). FairLex (Chalkidis et al., 2022b), another legal benchmark focuses on assessing fairness across five attributes—gender, age, region, language, and legal area—across legal NLP tasks. FairLex covers four jurisdictions (European Council, USA, Switzerland, and China), supports five languages (English, German, French,

Italian, and Chinese). LBOX (Hwang et al., 2022) benchmarks Korean legal tasks, consisting of two classification tasks, two legal judgment prediction tasks, and one summarization task. LegalBench (Guha et al., 2023) is construced to assess legal reasoning consisting of 162 tasks covering six different types of legal reasoning, designed for benchmarking zero/few-shot LLM paradigm for English language primarily based on American laws. Similarly, LawBench (Fei et al., 2023) is LLM oriented benchmark designed for assessing chinese civil-law system, containing 20 diverse tasks covering 5 task types: single-label, multi-label classification, regression, extraction and generation.

In this work, we curate LexSumm benchmark, focusing on eight legal summarization datasets in English, facilitating fine-tuning of task-specific models, an important setting for numerous applications. LexSumm Benchmark, with generative tasks, complements the LexGLUE benchmark (Chalkidis et al., 2022a) for legal text understanding in English.

Legal Pre-trained models Gururangan et al. (2020) demonstrated continuing pre-trained models on domain-specific text improves performance on domain tasks. Subsequently, there have been efforts to continue pre-training on diverse English legal text like legislation, court cases, and contracts, spanning US, EU, and UK jurisdictions resulting in the creation of LegalBERT (Chalkidis et al., 2020). In a similar vein, CaseLawBERT (Zheng et al., 2021) is another law-specific BERT model trained using the Harvard Law case corpus from US federal and state courts. Henderson et al. (2022) compiled an extensive corpus known as Pile of Law, incorporating documents from the US, Canada, and EU and trained BERT-large on this corpus, giving rise to the PoLBERT. Paul et al. 2023 extended pre-training on the Indian legal corpora, culminating in InLegalBERT. Recently, Chalkidis et al. 2023 introduced LexLMs, pre-trained on LeXFiles, a diverse multinational English legal corpus from six primarily English-speaking legal systems.

While the aforementioned models focus on English legal corpora, parallel endeavors have emerged to develop legal pre-trained models other languages. French legal model, JuriBERT (Douka et al., 2021) is trained using corpora from the Court of Cassation, France's highest court. Similar initiatives include JurBERT for Romanian (Masala et al., 2021), LamBERTa, ItalianLegalBERT for Italian (Tagarelli and Simeri, 2022; Licari and Comandè, 2022), RoBERTalex for Spanish (Gutiérrez-Fandiño et al., 2021), Lawformer for Chinese (Xiao et al., 2021), AraLegalBERT for Arabic (Al-qurishi et al., 2022), LCUBE for Korean (Hwang et al., 2022), and LegalBERT-pt, BERTBR for Portuguese (Ciurlino, 2021). Recently, Niklaus et al. (2023b) introduced LegalXLM, a multilingual model pre-trained on the MultiLegalPile, a diverse legal corpus comprising 24 languages from 17 jurisdictions.

It is noteworthy that the aforementioned legal domain-specific pre-trained language models predominantly adhere to the BERT-style encoder-only architecture and currently, there is a lack of sequence-to-sequence models specifically adapted for legal text. Addressing this gap, we present LexT5, legal-oriented sequence-to-sequence model pre-trained on the LexFiles corpus for English.

3 LexSumm Benchmark

LexSumm Benchmark is a collection of eight legal NLG datasets in English language spanning across US, EU, UK and India jurisdictions. In this section, we describe these datasets and their characteristics.

BillSum (Kornilova and Eidelman, 2019) is a summarization dataset of US Congressional bills, sourced from the Govinfo service by the US Government Publishing Office along with human-written summary from the Congressional Research Service. It consists of 22218 document-summary pairs split into training (16664), validation (2222) and test (3322) sets.

EurLexSum (Aumiller et al., 2022) EUR-Lex platform provides access to various legal documents published by various European Union organs. This dataset focuses on the enforced EU legislation along with their summaries, available across all 24 european languages. We restrict to English version of the dataset spanning 1504 document-summary pairs, split into 1128/151/225 for training, validation and testing respectively.

GovReport (Huang et al., 2021) contains 19,465 national policy reports published by U.S. Government Accountability Office An expert-written summary is provided along with each report and it is split into 14598, 2919, 1946 for training, validation and test sets respectively.

MultiLexSum-Tiny/Short/Long (Shen et al., 2022) consists of 9280 expert-written summaries for 4500 documents from U.S. federal civil rights lawsuits. It has summaries at three different granularities for the same source: (a) Long (L) summaries contain multiple paragraphs, covering the case background, parties involved, major case events and proceedings. (b) Short (S) summaries have only one paragraph with a shorter description of the background, parties involved and the outcome of the case. (c) Tiny (T) summaries have one sentence intended to appear on Twitter. Input spans across multiple sources such as first complaint, last amended complaint, settlement agreements, opinions, orders etc. Three different summarization tasks at each granularity are proposed emulating real-world tasks at the Civil Rights Litigation Clearinghouse. Long, Short and Tiny versions have a total of 4539, 3138 and 1603 document-summary pairs respectively which are split into (3404/454/681), (2340/312/486) and (1207/145/251) for train, validation and test.

InAbs (Shukla et al., 2022) consists of Indian Supreme Court judgements collected from the website of Legal Information Institute of India . It provides summaries (also called 'headnotes') for some of the cases resulting in total of 7150 case document-summary pairs, which are split into training (5346), validation (713) and test (1069) sets.

UKAbs (Shukla et al., 2022) dataset is collected from the UK Supreme court website which provides all judgements that were ruled since 2009. For most of the cases, along with the judgements, it also provides the official press summary of the cases. It consists of 793 document-summary pairs which are split into 595, 79, 119 for training, validation and test respectively.

3.1 Dataset Characteristics

We report the following characteristics on the eight datasets of LexSumm in Table 1.
(a) Average number of words in the input text and the summary. We also plot the token length distribution for the input and summary in Fig. 1 and 2. (b) Compression Ratio (Grusky et al., 2018) indicates the token ratio between the input to the summary. (c) Coverage@n (Grusky et al., 2018) quantifies the extent to which a summary is derivative of a input text. It indicates the ratio of n-grams in the summary that are part of an extractive fragment within the input. (d) Density@n (Grusky et al., 2018) quantifies how well the n-gram sequence of a summary can be described as a series of extractions. It is defined as the average length of the extractive fragment to which each n-gram in the summary belongs. For instance, a summary might contain many individual n-grams from the input indicating a high coverage. However, if dispersed across the input (less density), these n-grams of the summary could still be used in abstractive sense and not merely extractive from the article. (e) Fusion score (Shaham et al., 2022) measures how the summary sentences are synthesized from multiple sentences or compressed from a single sentence in the input. We plot the distribution of fusion score in Fig. 1 and 2, by computing fusion spread score for each instance as the standard deviation between the locations of output bigrams in the input (if exists).

We observe that LexSumm encompasses datasets with a diverse range of input-output lengths, leading to varying compression ratios. MultiLexSumm, with its three different granularities, exhibits higher compression ratios, indicating the need to precisely capture the critical aspects of the input text, highlighting its challenging nature. Although the coverage@1 scores for all datasets exceed 0.8, indicating fewer novel terms introduced into the summary (less paraphrasing involved), hinting at the extractive nature. However, the bi-gram coverage is lower, indicating that these extractive tokens are dispersed across the input, resulting in less density and larger fusion spread in Fig. 1 and 2. INAbs emerges as the most extractive dataset with a smaller compression ratio and higher coverage and density values, followed by UKAbs and GovReport. Conversely, MultiLexSumm, with its higher compression ratio, lower coverage and density values, emerges as the most abstractive dataset.

4 LexT5

We build LexT5, a legal-specific seq2seq pre-trained model. T5 is an encoder-decoder model initially pre-trained in an unsupervised manner on the C4 corpus (Raffel et al., 2020), using span denoising objective which involves replacing 15% of the tokens with sentinel tokens along with consecutive tokens marked for removal being replaced by a single sentinel token. The resulting corrupted text serves as input to the model to predict the masked-out span. Then the model is further fine-tuned using supervised training on various downstream tasks, including those from the GLUE and SuperGLUE (Wang et al., 2018, 2019) benchmarks, casting them into text-to-text format for training.

	BillSum	EurLexSum	GovReport	MLS-Long	MLS-Short	MLS-Tiny	INAbs	UKAbs
Input Len	1665.14	16390.28	8765.03	75255.36	99460.62	118347.65	4839.76	15911.07
Summary Len	204.09	960.46	556.31	639.18	128.63	25.19	941.58	1240.75
Comp. Ratio	13.21	17.29	17.83	98.82	874.18	5681.723	5.97	12.65
Coverage@1	0.89	0.87	0.94	0.93	0.95	0.92	0.94	0.96
Coverage@2	0.58	0.53	0.67	0.61	0.65	0.51	0.76	0.67
Density@1	3.89	6.11	9.27	4.07	3.33	2.26	13.99	9.91
Density@2	2.61	4.89	8.09	2.93	2.21	1.18	12.67	8.66

Table 1: Characteristics of eight datasets in LexSumm. MLS, Len denote MultiLexSumm and length respectively.

We initialize the model with T5-base checkpoint of Raffel et al. (2020) and continue pre-training using the span denoising objective on the train split of LeXFiles (Chalkidis et al., 2023). LeXFiles is a diverse legal corpus across 6 primarily English-speaking legal systems (EU, European Court of Human Rights, Canada, US, UK, India) covering various legal documents such as legislation, case law and contracts. It comprises approx. 6 million documents totalling up to approx. 19 billion tokens. We employ a sentence sampling rate from each sub-corpora proportional to number of tokens with exponential smoothing factor of 0.5 (Liu et al., 2020). Implementation details in App B.

4.1 Probing Legal Knowledge

To assess legal knowledge acquired by the model during pre-training phase, we use LegalLAMA (Chalkidis et al., 2023), a legal concept probing benchmark suite similar to LAnguage Models Analysis (LAMA) probing suite (Petroni et al., 2019). The zero-shot probing task is defined as follows: Given a sentence with a masked span [mask], the model must predict the gold masked span. Unlike encoder-only models like BERT, which require multiple masks to predict multi-token targets, T5's pre-training strategy replaces consecutive masked tokens with a single mask token resulting in a more robust evaluation for the probing task. Note that LegalLAMA instances are derived from the test subset of LexFiles to prevent contamination from pre-training corpus.

LegalLAMA consists of 8 tasks: (i) Articles (ECHR): The model predicts the masked article number in paragraphs from ECtHR decisions. (ii) Contractual Section Titles (US): Predicting the masked section titles in US contracts. (iii) Contract Types (US): Predicting the masked contract type in introductory paragraphs of US contracts. (iv) Crime Charges (US): Predicting masked criminal charges in paragraphs from US court judgments. (v) Legal Terminology (US): Predicting masked legal terms based on vocabularies from the Legal Information Institute in paragraphs from US court judgments. (vi) Legal Terminology (EU): Predicting masked legal terms based on subject matters from the CURIA database in paragraphs from CJEU judgments. (vii) Legal Terminology (ECHR): Predicting masked legal terms or issues based on keywords from the HUDOC database in paragraphs from ECHR case documents. (viii) Criminal Code Sections (Canada): Predicting masked sections of the Criminal Code of Canada in paragraphs from Criminal Court of Canada decisions.

Statistics about the test instances count, average input token count, target spans count and average tokens per target span for the eight tasks are presented in Table 2. We calculate token-normalized negative log-likelihood (NLL) loss across the golden target span for each instance and report average across all instances. Lower NLL signifies a better aquisition of legal knowledge by the model. We also compute Mean Reciprocal Rank (MRR) (Voorhees et al., 1999) for each instance based on the ranking list over the set of candidate target spans and report the average across all instances. The ranking list is based on the increasing order of token-normalized NLL values. Higher MRR indicates a superior acquisition of legal knowledge, with an ideal value of 1.0.

We present the NLL and MRR values for both the T5 and LexT5 models in Table 2. Across all tasks, we observe that LexT5 achieves lower NLL and higher MRR values compared to T5, indicating acquisition of legal knowledge through pre-training on the LeXFiles corpus. Notably, Crime Charges (US) and Contractual Section Titles (US) exhibit the smallest increase, with a marginal 0.07 MRR points, despite US being the dominant in LexFiles ($\approx 70\%$). Surprisingly, we do not find a correlation between the target spans count and the average token count in target span with performance improvements, contradicting findings of (Chalkidis et al.,

Tasks	#Inp	#Tok/ Inp	#Tgt	#Tok/ Tgt	T5		LexT5	
					NLL ↓	MRR ↑	NLL ↓	MRR ↑
Articles (ECHR)	5063	147.67	13	1	1.77	0.45	0.31	0.93
Contractual Sec. Titles (US)	1527	224.58	20	2.5	1.97	0.64	1.44	0.71
Contract Types (US)	1062	149.34	15	1.4	4.63	0.38	2.87	0.68
Crime Charges (US)	4518	276.99	116	3.28	1.9	0.49	1.67	0.56
Legal Terminology (US)	5806	286.04	145	3.13	2.58	0.53	1.74	0.74
Legal Terminology (EU)	2127	160.92	53	3.49	2.38	0.55	0.91	0.83
Legal Terminology (ECHR)	6273	166.49	143	3.36	2.24	0.55	0.78	0.88
Criminal Code Sec. (Canada)	321	148.56	195	3.42	2.2	0.33	0.91	0.7

Table 2: Data Characterstics of LegalLAMA probing suite and NLL, MRR values for T5 and LexT5 models. #Inp, #Tok/Inp, #Tgt, #Tok/Tgt indicate number of test instances, average number of tokens per input, the number of target spans and the average number of tokens per target respectively.

2023), which observed an increase in performance negatively correlated with the average tokens count of target spans. We attribute this discrepancy to the probing design bias in encoder-only models, where the number of masks already encode a signal for the token count of the target span. In contrast, our setup ensures a more reliable approach by not leaking the number of tokens in the target span, as we only have one mask for the whole span.

5 Benchmarking Experiments

We benchmark 8 LexSumm tasks using the following seq2seq models, designed to handle longer inputs. Implementation details are in App. C.

LED (Beltagy et al., 2020) is based on Longformer, an efficient transformer model with linear complexity relative to input length. It features encoder and decoder components, employing efficient local+global attention in the encoder and full quadratic attention in the decoder. LED is initialized from pre-trained BART (Lewis et al., 2020), with the position embedding matrix initialized by duplicating BART's 1K position embeddings 16 times to handle 16k input tokens.

PRIMERA (Xiao et al., 2022) is initialized with the LED model and pre-trained with a novel summarization-specific masking objective based on the entity pyramid evaluation method, inspired by the Gap Sentence Generation objective of Pegasus (Zhang et al., 2020). It can handle 4096 tokens.

LongT5 (Guo et al., 2022) employs transient global attention, inspired by local+global attention from ETC (Ainslie et al., 2020) and integrates summarization-specific pre-training from PEGASUS into the T5 model to handle longer sequences. We use LongT5-base which can handle flexible lengths (unless constrained by memory) due to relative positional embeddings, unlike BART architecture with absolute position embeddings.

SLED (Ivgi et al., 2023) processes long sequences by partitioning them into overlapping chunks and encoding each chunk with a short-range pre-trained encoder. Information across chunks is fused by the decoder by attending to all input tokens, akin to fusion-in-decoder (Izacard and Grave, 2021). SLED can be applied on top of any short-range model, resulting in SLED-T5 and SLED-LexT5 derived from their respective base models. While it can handle any input length, it is ultimately memory-bound.

Unlimiformer (Bertsch et al., 2023) utilizes a retrieval-based approach to enable short-range pre-trained models to process inputs of unbounded length. It adopts a strategy akin to SLED but focuses solely on the top-k tokens retrieved from a k-nearest-neighbor index constructed over the hidden states of all input tokens at each standard cross-attention head in every decoder layer. This distinguishes Unlimiformer from SLED which is limited by memory when attending to all input tokens in the decoder. We derive Unlimiformer-T5 and Unlimiformer-LexT5 from their base models.

Evaluation Metrics: We use ROUGE-1/2/L (Lin, 2004) and BERTScore (Zhang et al., 2019) to measure the lexical and semantic overlap between the model generated output and the reference summary.

5.1 Results

We report the results across eight LexSumm tasks in Table 3. Notably, the LED consistently outperforms PRIMERA, a difference largely attributed to the contrasting input lengths (16k vs. 4k), particularly evident in R-L scores of datasets with longer inputs like EurLexSumm and UKAbs. Despite PRIMERA's initialization with LED and continued pre-training using the Entity Pyramid mask-

	R-1 / 2 / L / BS	R-1 / 2 / L / BS	R-1 / 2 / L / BS	R-1 / 2 / L / BS
	BillSum	**EurLexSumm**	**GovReport**	**MLS-Long**
LED	**38.7** / 22.1 / 36.0 / 64.1	36.8 / 18.8 / 33.7 / 67.3	38.6 / 19.3 / 35.9 / 66.4	40.1 / 20.4 / 37.0 / 68.3
PRIMERA	37.0 / 21.7 / 35.5 / 63.6	32.7 / 16.8 / 30.8 / 64.8	37.8 / 19.0 / 35.1 / 65.5	38.2 / 19.0 / 35.4 / 67.6
LongT5	38.6 / 22.9 / 36.1 / 65.6	34.7 / 17.6 / 30.8 / 66.6	38.3 / 19.8 / 35.5 / 66.4	39.1 / 20.2 / 36.2 / 67.7
SLED-T5	36.8 / 22.9 / 35.2 / 64.8	36.5 / 18.7 / 33.2 / 67.0	38.4 / 19.7 / 35.4 / 66.1	38.6 / 19.5 / 35.5 / 66.2
Unlim.- T5	36.9 / 23.2 / 35.4 / 65.1	35.5 / 18.6 / 33.5 / 67.1	38.2 / 19.5 / 35.9 / 65.7	38.7 / 20.0 / 36.2 / 66.9
SLED-LexT5	38.2 / 24.5 / 36.1 / 66.0	37.4 / **19.3** / **34.3** / **67.6**	39.4 / 20.7 / 36.4 / **66.8**	40.4 / 19.8 / 36.5 / 68.4
Unlim.-LexT5	38.4 / **24.7** / **36.4** / **66.1**	**37.9** / 19.1 / 34.1 / 67.5	**40.2** / **21.2** / **36.9** / 66.6	**41.6** / **20.8** / **37.6** / **68.8**
	MLS-Short	**MLS-Tiny**	**INAbs**	**UKAbs**
LED	37.5 / 18.4 / 34.4 / 65.1	24.9 / 11.1 / 22.6 / 56.8	**42.8** / 23.8 / 39.2 / 67.9	**38.8** / 18.2 / 35.4 / 67.5
PRIMERA	36.4 / 18.2 / 33.5 / 64.0	24.5 / 10.8 / 22.5 / 56.9	39.2 / 21.0 / 36.1 / 66.1	36.4 / 16.6 / 33.1 / 65.1
LongT5	37.7 / 18.0 / 34.6 / **65.6**	24.4 / 10.3 / 22.0 / 56.5	40.6 / 21.4 / 36.8 / 66.6	36.1 / 17.3 / 33.4 / 66.1
SLED-T5	36.8 / 17.8 / 34.2 / 64.7	24.4 / 11.0 / 22.2 / 56.6	39.5 / 22.3 / 36.7 / 67.1	36.5 / 18.3 / 34.3 / 66.7
Unlim.- T5	36.3 / 17.6 / 34.1 / 64.4	25.2 / 11.1 / 23.7 / 56.7	40.0 / 22.7 / 37.1 / 67.2	37.5 / 18.2 / 34.2 / 66.9
SLED-LexT5	38.4 / 18.7 / **35.6** / **65.6**	26.3 / 12.2 / 23.7 / 56.8	41.1 / 24.3 / 39.5 / 68.2	**38.8** / 18.8 / 35.5 / **68.0**
Unlim.-LexT5	**38.8** / **19.1** / **35.6** / 65.3	**27.5** / **12.4** / **24.7** / **57.3**	42.2 / **24.5** / **39.7** / **68.4**	38.2 / **18.9** / **35.9** / 67.9

Table 3: Evaluation results of various models across eight datasets of LexSumm. Best and second best value under each metrics is bolded and underlined respectively.

ing strategy, we can also attribute its decline to PRIMERA's entity-centric masking strategy which turns out to be less suitable for legal corpora. This underscores the need for domain-specific masking strategies to facilitate effective transfer. LongT5 demonstrates superior performance compared to PRIMERA and comparable/lower performance to LED, benefiting from its end-to-end pre-training for longer sequences using the Gap Sentence Selection masking. This emphasizes the critical role of longer length pre-training unlike LED which is not explicitly pre-trained for longer sequences.

SLED-T5 and Unlimiformer-T5 exhibit comparable performance to long-range pre-trained models like LED and LongT5, even surpassing PRIMERA in most datasets. This suggests that leveraging off-the-shelf short-range pre-trained language models and integrating them into frameworks for longer context tasks can yield competitive results. Our LexT5 models, pre-trained on legal corpora using random span masking strategies without specific long-range or summarization pre-training, when plugged into SLED and Unlimiformer consistently outperform all others across all datasets, particularly excelling in more challenging higher n-gram metrics (R-2, R-L). This underscores the importance of domain-specific training and thanks to the flexibility of these frameworks that allow easy integration of any pre-trained short-range language models without the need for expensive long-sequence pre-training. Furthermore, Unlimiformer-LexT5 outperforms SLED-LexT5 in 7 out of 8 datasets, indicating that attending only to the top-k input keys can be an accurate approximation of full attention, motivating design of effective retrieval methods to handle long context processing.

Zero-shot evaluation with LLMs: We use stratified sampling to select 50 instances from each of test split of the LexSumm dataset, across diverse input lengths. We always include the most 10 longest inputs from test set and sampled 10, 15, 15 from the three buckets derived from rest of the test set based on their input lengths. We evaluate two long-context based LLM models - Claude-Instant-1.2 and GPT-3.5-Turbo with hierarchical merging strategy for summarization following Chang et al. (2023) where in the input is divided it into smaller chunks to summarize individually and then partial summaries are repeatedly merged to form final summary. Detailed illustration and prompts are in App. D. We reported the performance of these models in Table 4. We observe that Claude model performing better than GPT-3.5-Turbo across all the datasets consistently. On comparing with fine-tuned variant of Unlimiformer-LexT5, we observe fine-tuned variant performing better compared to them, in most challenging ROUGE-2 and -L scores.

Qualitative Analysis: We examine outputs from PRIMERA and LED on the In-Abs case in E.1. PRIMERA's summary completely misrepresents the case by incorrectly stating that the issue concerns the validity of dismissal orders under "r. 149 of the Code of Civil Procedure," whereas it should refer to Rules 148(3) and 149(3) of the Indian Railway Establishment Code, focusing on whether they violate articles 14 and 311(2) of the Constitution of India. The summary's focus omits details about the Supreme Court's decision. Although the phrase "code of civil procedure" is mentioned in the in-

	R-1 / 2 / L / BS	R-1 / 2 / L / BS	R-1 / 2 / L / BS	R-1 / 2 / L / BS
	BillSum	**EurLexSumm**	**GovReport**	**MLS-Long**
GPT-3.5-Turbo	31.0 / 13.3 / 27.9 / 61.9	22.1 / 6.9 / 19.4 / 62.0	24.4 / 8.1 / 22.0 / 60.2	24.2 / 8.7 / 21.8 / 59.9
Claude Instant	31.5 / 13.5 / 28.5 / 61.5	24.0 / 8.2 / 21.9 / 61.9	28.5 / 8.8 / 26.1 / 61.4	29.1 / 10.8 / 26.6 / 61.2
Unlim-LexT5	37.1 / 21.8 / 33.9 / 65.8	34.8 / 17.7 / 30.1 / 66.6	37.2 / 17.3 / 34.4 / 64.9	37.9 / 17.2 / 34.8 / 67.1
	MLS-Short	**MLS-Tiny**	**INAbs**	**UKAbs**
GPT-3.5-Turbo	21.8 / 7.95 / 19.5 / 56.9	15.3 / 3.3 / 12.8 / 49.3	20.8 / 6.6 / 18.3 / 58.1	24.2 / 7.8 / 21.6 / 59.0
Claude Instant	27.7 / 10.3 / 25.6 / 57.8	16.5 / 3.4 / 13.5 / 50.2	23.9 / 7.8 / 21.8 / 60.3	29.0 / 9.6 / 26.6 / 61.9
Unlim-LexT5	35.2 / 17.8 / 33.4/ 64.8	26.6 / 11.8 / 22.6 / 56.2	36.5 / 16.6 / 32.1 / 63.1	34.8 / 14.2 / 31.3 / 64.3

Table 4: Evaluation results of LLM models across eight subsampled test datasets of LexSumm.

put, it is unrelated to the context in the summary. PRIMERA's summary emphasizes procedural details, while the original text primarily discusses procedural fairness under article 311(2). This discrepancy in understanding the case's context and focus of the summary is attributed to the limited input context of PRIMERA. While the 16k-based LED attempts to produce a more faithful summary, it reduces a multi-applicant case to a single one and incorrectly mentions "under Rule 148" instead of the specific Rules 148(3) and 149(3), resulting in misrepresentation. LED still struggles to accurately capture the final outcome presented towards the end of the 39k-token input. To analyze the impact of legal pre-training, we compare Unlimiformer-T5 with LexT5 using GovReport input on climate change in App. E.2. While the T5 introduces Government Accountability Office (GAO) in summary, not even mentioned in the input, LexT5 avoids such entity-level hallucinations but emphasizes only on certain portions such as the U.S. climate policy landscape, leaving discussion on pitfalls.

We analyze outputs from the MLS-Tiny dataset, tackling a needle-in-the-haystack problem to distill crucial case details into a single tweet-like sentence. Reference summary and various model generations are presented in App E.3. The document outlines a legal complaint by the American-Arab Anti-Discrimination Committee against U.S. Customs and Border Protection, alleging wrongful withholding of records. These records pertain to Arab and Muslim American residents being unfairly removed from the Global Entry program. The conclusion indicates a consensus that previously secret records will be disclosed. PRIMERA captures the essence but omits the legal basis (FOIA) mentioned in the reference summary. Its resemblance to a full sentence rather than a Twitter post style can be attributed to its pre-training objective of gap sentence generation, making it less adaptable to switch to a Twitter style. LED summary highlights the action succinctly but generalizes it to a travel ban. LongT5 misses and misrepresents main information, being partially unfaithful. SLED and Unlimiformer summaries partially present the lawsuit but omit resolution details, indicating the challenge of fusing information across chunks. Lex summaries provide additional details but struggle to synthesize final outcome into the summary.

We present the zero-shot outputs from GPT-3.5 and Claude on the IN-Abs in App. E.4. Both summaries offer a high-level abstraction of the case details, focusing on the main legal issue under scrutiny and the court's findings. Despite differing from the reference summary style, both summaries effectively highlight key document aspects, ensuring easy understanding, albeit with some pertinent details omitted. Claude provides more complete and grounded summary than GPT-3.5 by elaborating on crucial elements like Article 311(2) of the Constitution. Future work should assess the quality of these generations on large scale with diverse legal experts given the subjective nature of quality.

6 Conclusion

In this work, we curate LexSumm benchmark for training and evaluating legal summarization tasks in English. LexSumm can serve as an evaluation platform to foster development of approaches dealing with long legal text using efficient transformer architectures or retrieval-based methods adopted for longer context, legal-oriented pre-training or masking schemes, faithful decoding strategies. We pre-train LexT5, a legal seq2seq model and evaluate on LegalLAMA probing task and LexSumm downstream benchmark. We compare LexT5 wrapped in long-range adaptation frameworks such as SLED and Unlimiformer with T5 model in long-range adaptation, other long-range pre-trained models, and even zero-shot LLMs. We release LexT5 to the community, hoping it will serve as a backbone model for various legal generative tasks. Additionally, we envision LexSumm evolving into a dynamic benchmark, expanding with new datasets over time.

Limitations

An important limitation of our benchmark is its reliance on English-only evaluation, which limits the generalizability of our findings to legal systems operating in languages other than English. Given the global nature of legal systems, each conducting proceedings in their official languages, there is a clear need for multilingual legal generative models. However, our ability to develop such models is hindered by the scarcity of multilingual legal generative task data, except for Chinese datasets. Furthermore, our dataset predominantly consists of data from English-speaking nations, where data availability is more accessible, thereby constraining the diversity and inclusivity of our study. Overcoming this limitation poses additional challenges, including bureaucratic hurdles in accessing court records, dependence on outdated technology for managing legal documents and privacy concerns related to contracts. Additionally, obtaining annotated data for downstream tasks proves to be expensive due to the need for specialized legal expertise.

Our LexSumm evaluation primarily relies on established summarization metrics such as ROUGE and BERTScore. While these metrics have been used in many prior works on legal document summarization and are known to provide a quantitative measure of summarization quality, they may not fully capture the nuanced legal content, context and intricacies essential for legal professionals. A potential avenue for further research could be developing additional legal domain-specific evaluation metrics. Another significant limitation of our study is the absence of direct participation or validation by legal experts in the assessment of summarization outputs, which we could not perform due to lack of access to legal experts.

Although LexT5 has primarily been evaluated on summarization tasks within LexSumm, we intend to broaden its evaluation scope to include Legal NLU and other generation tasks such as simplification or translation. Evaluating seq2seq models on Legal NLU datasets like LexGLUE (Chalkidis et al., 2022a) poses a challenge due to the multi-label nature of tasks. This complexity necessitates additional modifications to enable seq2seq models for multi-label tasks (Kementchedjhieva and Chalkidis, 2023).

Ethics Statement

All datasets incorporated into LexSumm are openly accessible and have been previously published, with citations provided to the original sources. We strongly encourage users of LexSumm to acknowledge these sources, suggesting referencing this work alongside citing the original sources when utilizing multiple LexSumm datasets and employing the LexSumm evaluation framework. Otherwise, citation of only the original sources is appropriate.

The aim of LexSumm is to introduce a unified legal NLP benchmark to expedite the development of legal models and assess various technical approaches in handling legal tasks. By offering a comprehensive benchmark spanning multiple jurisdictions, this initiative aims to provide guidance to system developers on best practices, serve as a crucial yardstick for measuring progress and guide research efforts, ultimately aiding practitioners in creating supportive technology tailored for legal professionals and laypersons alike.

While datasets in LexSumm such as EurLexSumm, BillSum, and GovReport primarily consist of legislation or policy material and are unlikely to contain personal data, other datasets like MultiLexSum, UKAbs, and InAbs contain personal data of the parties and individuals involved in legal proceedings. However, these datasets are published by respective courts in accordance with data protection laws. We do not anticipate any harm resulting from our experiments beyond the disclosure of this information.

We train and release the LexT5 model using historical legal data sourced from prior work on LeXFiles (Chalkidis et al., 2023). These historical corpora inherently encode biases and inequities present within the legal domain, which might be inherited by these models. Deploying LexT5 without robust scrutiny and mitigation strategies could perpetuate and amplify these biases, potentially leading to unjust outcomes in legal decision-making processes. Furthermore, the widespread adoption of LexT5 in legal applications could exacerbate disparities in access to justice, as marginalized communities may be disproportionately affected by biased model predictions. To address these ethical concerns, it is imperative to conduct thorough bias audits, implement mitigation techniques, ensure transparency and accountability in model deployment, and continuously monitor and evaluate the model's performance in real-world settings.

Moreover, fine-tuned models developed for each specific task of LexSumm may exhibit performance variations across different partitions within the same legal domain. For instance, as highlighted in Agarwal et al. 2022. in contexts like the Board of Veterans' Appeals, cases involving rarely occurring disabilities or specialized legal and military situations may lead to suboptimal summaries due to sparsity in the training data. This variability could disproportionately impact groups that should be treated equally if their characteristics coincide with these less frequent legal configurations. Engaging domain experts to curate datasets with better representation across different types of injuries and legal phenomena can be a proactive step in enhancing the model's understanding of uncommon or group-related legal contexts, potentially mitigating disparities in performance.

References

Abhishek Agarwal, Shanshan Xu, and Matthias Grabmair. 2022. Extractive summarization of legal decisions using multi-task learning and maximal marginal relevance. *arXiv preprint arXiv:2210.12437*.

Joshua Ainslie, Santiago Ontanon, Chris Alberti, Vaclav Cvicek, Zachary Fisher, Philip Pham, Anirudh Ravula, Sumit Sanghai, Qifan Wang, and Li Yang. 2020. Etc: Encoding long and structured inputs in transformers. In *Proceedings of the 2020 Conference on Empirical Methods in Natural Language Processing (EMNLP)*, pages 268–284.

Muhammad Al-qurishi, Sarah Alqaseemi, and Riad Souissi. 2022. Aralegal-bert: A pretrained language model for arabic legal text. In *Proceedings of the Natural Legal Language Processing Workshop 2022*, pages 338–344.

Dennis Aumiller, Ashish Chouhan, and Michael Gertz. 2022. EUR-lex-sum: A multi- and cross-lingual dataset for long-form summarization in the legal domain. In *Proceedings of the 2022 Conference on Empirical Methods in Natural Language Processing*, pages 7626–7639, Abu Dhabi, United Arab Emirates. Association for Computational Linguistics.

Iz Beltagy, Matthew E Peters, and Arman Cohan. 2020. Longformer: The long-document transformer. *arXiv preprint arXiv:2004.05150*.

Amanda Bertsch, Uri Alon, Graham Neubig, and Matthew R Gormley. 2023. Unlimiformer: Long-range transformers with unlimited length input. *arXiv preprint arXiv:2305.01625*.

Abhik Bhattacharjee, Tahmid Hasan, Wasi Ahmad, and Rifat Shahriyar. 2023. Banglanlg and banglat5: Benchmarks and resources for evaluating low-resource natural language generation in bangla. In *Findings of the Association for Computational Linguistics: EACL 2023*, pages 714–723.

Paheli Bhattacharya, Kaustubh Hiware, Subham Rajgaria, Nilay Pochhi, Kripabandhu Ghosh, and Saptarshi Ghosh. 2019. A comparative study of summarization algorithms applied to legal case judgments. In *Advances in Information Retrieval: 41st European Conference on IR Research, ECIR 2019, Cologne, Germany, April 14–18, 2019, Proceedings, Part I 41*, pages 413–428. Springer.

Paheli Bhattacharya, Soham Poddar, Koustav Rudra, Kripabandhu Ghosh, and Saptarshi Ghosh. 2021. Incorporating domain knowledge for extractive summarization of legal case documents. In *Proceedings of the eighteenth international conference on artificial intelligence and law*, pages 22–31.

Samuel Cahyawijaya, Genta Indra Winata, Bryan Wilie, Karissa Vincentio, Xiaohong Li, Adhiguna Kuncoro, Sebastian Ruder, Zhi Yuan Lim, Syafri Bahar, Masayu Khodra, et al. 2021. Indonlg: Benchmark and resources for evaluating indonesian natural language generation. In *Proceedings of the 2021 Conference on Empirical Methods in Natural Language Processing*, pages 8875–8898.

Ilias Chalkidis, Ion Androutsopoulos, and Achilleas Michos. 2017. Extracting contract elements. In *Proceedings of the 16th edition of the International Conference on Articial Intelligence and Law*, pages 19–28.

Ilias Chalkidis, Emmanouil Fergadiotis, Prodromos Malakasiotis, and Ion Androutsopoulos. 2019. Large-scale multi-label text classification on eu legislation. In *Proceedings of the 57th Annual Meeting of the Association for Computational Linguistics*, pages 6314–6322.

Ilias Chalkidis, Manos Fergadiotis, and Ion Androutsopoulos. 2021. Multieurlex-a multi-lingual and multi-label legal document classification dataset for zero-shot cross-lingual transfer. In *Proceedings of the 2021 Conference on Empirical Methods in Natural Language Processing*, pages 6974–6996.

Ilias Chalkidis, Manos Fergadiotis, Prodromos Malakasiotis, Nikolaos Aletras, and Ion Androutsopoulos. 2020. Legal-bert: The muppets straight out of law school. In *Findings of the Association for Computational Linguistics: EMNLP 2020*, pages 2898–2904.

Ilias Chalkidis, Nicolas Garneau, Catalina Goanta, Daniel Katz, and Anders Søgaard. 2023. LeXFiles and LegalLAMA: Facilitating English multinational legal language model development. In *Proceedings of the 61st Annual Meeting of the Association for Computational Linguistics (Volume 1: Long Papers)*, pages 15513–15535, Toronto, Canada. Association for Computational Linguistics.

Ilias Chalkidis, Abhik Jana, Dirk Hartung, Michael Bommarito, Ion Androutsopoulos, Daniel Katz, and Nikolaos Aletras. 2022a. Lexglue: A benchmark dataset for legal language understanding in english. In *Proceedings of the 60th Annual Meeting of the Association for Computational Linguistics (Volume 1: Long Papers)*, pages 4310–4330.

Ilias Chalkidis, Tommaso Pasini, Sheng Zhang, Letizia Tomada, Sebastian Schwemer, and Anders Søgaard. 2022b. Fairlex: A multilingual benchmark for evaluating fairness in legal text processing. In *Proceedings of the 60th Annual Meeting of the Association for Computational Linguistics (Volume 1: Long Papers)*, pages 4389–4406.

Yapei Chang, Kyle Lo, Tanya Goyal, and Mohit Iyyer. 2023. Booookscore: A systematic exploration of book-length summarization in the era of llms. In *The Twelfth International Conference on Learning Representations*.

Andong Chen, Feng Yao, Xinyan Zhao, Yating Zhang, Changlong Sun, Yun Liu, and Weixing Shen. 2023. Equals: A real-world dataset for legal question answering via reading chinese laws. In *Proceedings of the Nineteenth International Conference on Artificial Intelligence and Law*, pages 71–80.

Yanguang Chen, Yuanyuan Sun, Zhihao Yang, and Hongfei Lin. 2020. Joint entity and relation extraction for legal documents with legal feature enhancement. In *Proceedings of the 28th International Conference on Computational Linguistics*, pages 1561–1571.

Yiran Chen, Zhenqiao Song, Xianze Wu, Danqing Wang, Jingjing Xu, Jiaze Chen, Hao Zhou, and Lei Li. 2022. Mtg: A benchmark suite for multilingual text generation. In *Findings of the Association for Computational Linguistics: NAACL 2022*, pages 2508–2527.

Victor Hugo Ciurlino. 2021. Bertbr: a pretrained language model for law texts.

Corinna Coupette, Janis Beckedorf, Dirk Hartung, Michael Bommarito, and Daniel Martin Katz. 2021. Measuring law over time: A network analytical framework with an application to statutes and regulations in the united states and germany. *Frontiers in Physics*, 9:658463.

Jacob Devlin. 2018. Bert: Pre-training of deep bidirectional transformers for language understanding. *arXiv preprint arXiv:1810.04805*.

Stella Douka, Hadi Abdine, Michalis Vazirgiannis, Rajaa El Hamdani, and David Restrepo Amariles. 2021. Juribert: A masked-language model adaptation for french legal text. In *Proceedings of the Natural Legal Language Processing Workshop 2021*, pages 95–101.

Mohamed Elaraby and Diane Litman. 2022. Arglegalsumm: Improving abstractive summarization of legal documents with argument mining. *arXiv preprint arXiv:2209.01650*.

Mohamed Elaraby, Yang Zhong, and Diane Litman. 2023. Towards argument-aware abstractive summarization of long legal opinions with summary reranking. *arXiv preprint arXiv:2306.00672*.

Abdelrahim Elmadany, Ahmed El-Shangiti, Muhammad Abdul-Mageed, et al. 2023. Dolphin: A challenging and diverse benchmark for arabic nlg. In *Findings of the Association for Computational Linguistics: EMNLP 2023*, pages 1404–1422.

Zhiwei Fei, Xiaoyu Shen, Dawei Zhu, Fengzhe Zhou, Zhuo Han, Songyang Zhang, Kai Chen, Zongwen Shen, and Jidong Ge. 2023. Lawbench: Benchmarking legal knowledge of large language models. *arXiv preprint arXiv:2309.16289*.

Sebastian Gehrmann, Tosin Adewumi, Karmanya Aggarwal, Pawan Sasanka Ammanamanchi, Anuoluwapo Aremu, Antoine Bosselut, Khyathi Raghavi Chandu, Miruna Clinciu, Dipanjan Das, Kaustubh Dhole, et al. 2021. The gem benchmark: Natural language generation, its evaluation and metrics. In *Proceedings of the 1st Workshop on Natural Language Generation, Evaluation, and Metrics (GEM 2021)*, pages 96–120.

Sebastian Gehrmann, Abhik Bhattacharjee, Abinaya Mahendiran, Alex Wang, Alexandros Papangelis, Aman Madaan, Angelina Mcmillan-major, Anna Shvets, Ashish Upadhyay, and Bernd Bohnet. 2022. Gemv2: Multilingual nlg benchmarking in a single line of code. In *Proceedings of the The 2022 Conference on Empirical Methods in Natural Language Processing: System Demonstrations*, pages 266–281.

S Georgette Graham, Hamidreza Soltani, and Olufemi Isiaq. 2023. Natural language processing for legal document review: categorising deontic modalities in contracts. *Artificial Intelligence and Law*, pages 1–22.

Max Grusky, Mor Naaman, and Yoav Artzi. 2018. Newsroom: A dataset of 1.3 million summaries with diverse extractive strategies. In *Proceedings of the 2018 Conference of the North American Chapter of the Association for Computational Linguistics: Human Language Technologies, Volume 1 (Long Papers)*, pages 708–719.

Jian Guan, Zhuoer Feng, Yamei Chen, Ruilin He, Xiaoxi Mao, Changjie Fan, and Minlie Huang. 2022. Lot: A story-centric benchmark for evaluating chinese long text understanding and generation. *Transactions of the Association for Computational Linguistics*, 10:434–451.

Neel Guha, Julian Nyarko, Daniel E Ho, Christopher Re, Adam Chilton, Aditya Narayana, Alex Chohlas-Wood, Austin Peters, Brandon Waldon, Daniel Rockmore, et al. 2023. Legalbench: A collaboratively built benchmark for measuring legal reasoning in large language models. In *Thirty-seventh Conference on Neural Information Processing Systems Datasets and Benchmarks Track*.

Mandy Guo, Joshua Ainslie, David C Uthus, Santiago Ontanon, Jianmo Ni, Yun-Hsuan Sung, and Yinfei Yang. 2022. Longt5: Efficient text-to-text transformer for long sequences. In *Findings of the Association for Computational Linguistics: NAACL 2022*, pages 724–736.

Suchin Gururangan, Ana Marasović, Swabha Swayamdipta, Kyle Lo, Iz Beltagy, Doug Downey, and Noah A Smith. 2020. Don't stop pretraining: Adapt language models to domains and tasks. In *Proceedings of the 58th Annual Meeting of the Association for Computational Linguistics*, pages 8342–8360.

Asier Gutiérrez-Fandiño, Jordi Armengol-Estapé, Aitor Gonzalez-Agirre, and Marta Villegas. 2021. Spanish legalese language model and corpora. *arXiv preprint arXiv:2110.12201*.

Zexue He, Yu Wang, An Yan, Yao Liu, Eric Chang, Amilcare Gentili, Julian McAuley, and Chun-nan Hsu. 2023. Medeval: A multi-level, multi-task, and multi-domain medical benchmark for language model evaluation. In *Proceedings of the 2023 Conference on Empirical Methods in Natural Language Processing*, pages 8725–8744.

Peter Henderson, Mark Krass, Lucia Zheng, Neel Guha, Christopher D Manning, Dan Jurafsky, and Daniel Ho. 2022. Pile of law: Learning responsible data filtering from the law and a 256gb open-source legal dataset. *Advances in Neural Information Processing Systems*, 35:29217–29234.

Dan Hendrycks, Collin Burns, Anya Chen, and Spencer Ball. 2021. Cuad: An expert-annotated nlp dataset for legal contract review. In *Thirty-fifth Conference on Neural Information Processing Systems Datasets and Benchmarks Track (Round 1)*.

Luyang Huang, Shuyang Cao, Nikolaus Parulian, Heng Ji, and Lu Wang. 2021. Efficient attentions for long document summarization. In *Proceedings of the 2021 Conference of the North American Chapter of the Association for Computational Linguistics: Human Language Technologies*, pages 1419–1436.

Wonseok Hwang, Dongjun Lee, Kyoungyeon Cho, Hanuhl Lee, and Minjoon Seo. 2022. A multi-task benchmark for korean legal language understanding and judgement prediction. *Advances in Neural Information Processing Systems*, 35:32537–32551.

Maor Ivgi, Uri Shaham, and Jonathan Berant. 2023. Efficient long-text understanding with short-text models. *Transactions of the Association for Computational Linguistics*, 11:284–299.

Gautier Izacard and Édouard Grave. 2021. Leveraging passage retrieval with generative models for open domain question answering. In *Proceedings of the 16th Conference of the European Chapter of the Association for Computational Linguistics: Main Volume*, pages 874–880.

Daniel Martin Katz, Dirk Hartung, Lauritz Gerlach, Abhik Jana, and Michael James Bommarito. 2023. Natural language processing in the legal domain. *Available at SSRN 4336224*.

Yova Kementchedjhieva and Ilias Chalkidis. 2023. An exploration of encoder-decoder approaches to multilabel classification for legal and biomedical text. In *The 61st Annual Meeting Of The Association For Computational Linguistics*.

Phi Manh Kien, Ha-Thanh Nguyen, Ngo Xuan Bach, Vu Tran, Minh Le Nguyen, and Tu Minh Phuong. 2020. Answering legal questions by learning neural attentive text representation. In *Proceedings of the 28th International Conference on Computational Linguistics*, pages 988–998.

Yuta Koreeda and Christopher D Manning. 2021. Contractnli: A dataset for document-level natural language inference for contracts. In *Findings of the Association for Computational Linguistics: EMNLP 2021*, pages 1907–1919.

Anastassia Kornilova and Vladimir Eidelman. 2019. Billsum: A corpus for automatic summarization of us legislation. In *Proceedings of the 2nd Workshop on New Frontiers in Summarization*, pages 48–56.

Aman Kumar, Himani Shrotriya, Prachi Sahu, Amogh Mishra, Raj Dabre, Ratish Puduppully, Anoop Kunchukuttan, Mitesh M Khapra, and Pratyush Kumar. 2022. Indicnlg benchmark: Multilingual datasets for diverse nlg tasks in indic languages. In *Proceedings of the 2022 Conference on Empirical Methods in Natural Language Processing*, pages 5363–5394.

Mike Lewis, Yinhan Liu, Naman Goyal, Marjan Ghazvininejad, Abdelrahman Mohamed, Omer Levy, Veselin Stoyanov, and Luke Zettlemoyer. 2020. Bart: Denoising sequence-to-sequence pre-training for natural language generation, translation, and comprehension. In *Proceedings of the 58th Annual Meeting of the Association for Computational Linguistics*, pages 7871–7880.

Daniele Licari and Giovanni Comandè. 2022. Italian-legal-bert: A pre-trained transformer language model for italian law. In *CEUR Workshop Proceedings (Ed.), The Knowledge Management for Law Workshop (KM4LAW)*.

Chin-Yew Lin. 2004. Rouge: A package for automatic evaluation of summaries. In *Text summarization branches out*, pages 74–81.

Marco Lippi, Przemysław Pałka, Giuseppe Contissa, Francesca Lagioia, Hans-Wolfgang Micklitz, Giovanni Sartor, and Paolo Torroni. 2019. Claudette: an automated detector of potentially unfair clauses in online terms of service. *Artificial Intelligence and Law*, 27:117–139.

Dayiheng Liu, Yu Yan, Yeyun Gong, Weizhen Qi, Hang Zhang, Jian Jiao, Weizhu Chen, Jie Fu, Linjun Shou, Ming Gong, et al. 2021. Glge: A new general language generation evaluation benchmark. In *Findings of the Association for Computational Linguistics: ACL-IJCNLP 2021*, pages 408–420.

Yinhan Liu, Jiatao Gu, Naman Goyal, Xian Li, Sergey Edunov, Marjan Ghazvininejad, Mike Lewis, and Luke Zettlemoyer. 2020. Multilingual denoising pretraining for neural machine translation. *Transactions of the Association for Computational Linguistics*, 8:726–742.

Yinhan Liu, Myle Ott, Naman Goyal, Jingfei Du, Mandar Joshi, Danqi Chen, Omer Levy, Mike Lewis, Luke Zettlemoyer, and Veselin Stoyanov. 2019. Roberta: A robustly optimized bert pretraining approach. *arXiv preprint arXiv:1907.11692*.

Ilya Loshchilov and Frank Hutter. 2018. Decoupled weight decay regularization. In *International Conference on Learning Representations*.

Antoine Louis and Gerasimos Spanakis. 2022. A statutory article retrieval dataset in french. In *Proceedings of the 60th Annual Meeting of the Association for Computational Linguistics (Volume 1: Long Papers)*, pages 6789–6803.

Antoine Louis, Gijs van Dijck, and Gerasimos Spanakis. 2023. Interpretable long-form legal question answering with retrieval-augmented large language models. *arXiv preprint arXiv:2309.17050*.

Pedro Henrique Luz de Araujo, Teófilo E de Campos, Renato RR de Oliveira, Matheus Stauffer, Samuel Couto, and Paulo Bermejo. 2018. Lener-br: a dataset for named entity recognition in brazilian legal text. In *Computational Processing of the Portuguese Language: 13th International Conference, PROPOR 2018, Canela, Brazil, September 24–26, 2018, Proceedings 13*, pages 313–323. Springer.

Yixiao Ma, Yunqiu Shao, Yueyue Wu, Yiqun Liu, Ruizhe Zhang, Min Zhang, and Shaoping Ma. 2021. Lecard: a legal case retrieval dataset for chinese law system. In *Proceedings of the 44th international ACM SIGIR conference on research and development in information retrieval*, pages 2342–2348.

Mihai Masala, Radu Cristian Alexandru Iacob, Ana Sabina Uban, Marina Cidota, Horia Velicu, Traian Rebedea, and Marius Popescu. 2021. jurbert: A romanian bert model for legal judgement prediction. In *Proceedings of the Natural Legal Language Processing Workshop 2021*, pages 86–94.

Joel Niklaus, Veton Matoshi, Pooja Rani, Andrea Galassi, Matthias Stürmer, and Ilias Chalkidis. 2023a. Lextreme: A multi-lingual and multi-task benchmark for the legal domain. *arXiv preprint arXiv:2301.13126*.

Joel Niklaus, Veton Matoshi, Matthias Stürmer, Ilias Chalkidis, and Daniel E Ho. 2023b. Multilegalpile: A 689gb multilingual legal corpus. *arXiv preprint arXiv:2306.02069*.

Julia Otmakhova, Karin Verspoor, Timothy Baldwin, Antonio Jimeno Yepes, and Jey Han Lau. 2022. M3: Multi-level dataset for multi-document summarisation of medical studies. In *Findings of the Association for Computational Linguistics: EMNLP 2022*, pages 3887–3901.

Shounak Paul, Arpan Mandal, Pawan Goyal, and Saptarshi Ghosh. 2023. Pre-trained language models for the legal domain: a case study on indian law. In *Proceedings of the Nineteenth International Conference on Artificial Intelligence and Law*, pages 187–196.

Fabio Petroni, Tim Rocktäschel, Sebastian Riedel, Patrick Lewis, Anton Bakhtin, Yuxiang Wu, and Alexander Miller. 2019. Language models as knowledge bases? In *Proceedings of the 2019 Conference on Empirical Methods in Natural Language Processing and the 9th International Joint Conference on Natural Language Processing (EMNLP-IJCNLP)*, pages 2463–2473.

Colin Raffel, Noam Shazeer, Adam Roberts, Katherine Lee, Sharan Narang, Michael Matena, Yanqi Zhou, Wei Li, and Peter J Liu. 2020. Exploring the limits of transfer learning with a unified text-to-text transformer. *The Journal of Machine Learning Research*, 21(1):5485–5551.

Abhilasha Ravichander and W Alan. 2019. Question answering for privacy policies: Combining computational and legal perspectives. In *Empirical Methods in Natural Language Processing*.

Abhilasha Sancheti, Aparna Garimella, Balaji Srinivasan, and Rachel Rudinger. 2023. What to read in a contract? party-specific summarization of legal obligations, entitlements, and prohibitions. In *Proceedings of the 2023 Conference on Empirical Methods in Natural Language Processing*, pages 14708–14725.

TYS Santosh, Rashid Gustav Haddad, and Matthias Grabmair. 2024a. Ecthr-pcr: A dataset for precedent understanding and prior case retrieval in the european court of human rights. *arXiv preprint arXiv:2404.00596*.

TYS Santosh, Elvin Quero Hernandez, and Matthias Grabmair. 2024b. Query-driven relevant paragraph extraction from legal judgments. *arXiv preprint arXiv:2404.00595*.

TYS Santosh, Vatsal Venkatkrishna, Saptarshi Ghosh, and Matthias Grabmair. 2024c. Beyond borders: Investigating cross-jurisdiction transfer in legal case summarization. *arXiv preprint arXiv:2403.19317*.

TYS Santosh, Tuan-Quang Vuong, and Matthias Grabmair. 2024d. Chronoslex: Time-aware incremental training for temporal generalization of legal classification tasks. *arXiv preprint arXiv:2405.14211*.

Marijn Schraagen, Floris Bex, Nick Van De Luijtgaarden, and Daniël Prijs. 2022. Abstractive summarization of dutch court verdicts using sequence-to-sequence models. In *Proceedings of the Natural Legal Language Processing Workshop 2022*, pages 76–87.

Uri Shaham, Elad Segal, Maor Ivgi, Avia Efrat, Ori Yoran, Adi Haviv, Ankit Gupta, Wenhan Xiong, Mor Geva, Jonathan Berant, et al. 2022. Scrolls: Standardized comparison over long language sequences. In *Proceedings of the 2022 Conference on Empirical Methods in Natural Language Processing*, pages 12007–12021.

Yunqiu Shao, Jiaxin Mao, Yiqun Liu, Weizhi Ma, Ken Satoh, Min Zhang, and Shaoping Ma. 2020. Bert-pli: Modeling paragraph-level interactions for legal case retrieval. In *IJCAI*, pages 3501–3507.

Noam Shazeer and Mitchell Stern. 2018. Adafactor: Adaptive learning rates with sublinear memory cost. In *International Conference on Machine Learning*, pages 4596–4604. PMLR.

Zejiang Shen, Kyle Lo, Lauren Yu, Nathan Dahlberg, Margo Schlanger, and Doug Downey. 2022. Multi-lexsum: Real-world summaries of civil rights lawsuits at multiple granularities. *Advances in Neural Information Processing Systems*, 35:13158–13173.

Abhay Shukla, Paheli Bhattacharya, Soham Poddar, Rajdeep Mukherjee, Kripabandhu Ghosh, Pawan Goyal, and Saptarshi Ghosh. 2022. Legal case document summarization: Extractive and abstractive methods and their evaluation. In *Proceedings of the 2nd Conference of the Asia-Pacific Chapter of the Association for Computational Linguistics and the 12th International Joint Conference on Natural Language Processing*, pages 1048–1064.

Andrea Tagarelli and Andrea Simeri. 2022. Lamberta: Law article mining based on bert architecture for the italian civil code. In *Proc. 18th Italian Research Conference on Digital Libraries*, volume 3160.

Don Tuggener, Pius Von Däniken, Thomas Peetz, and Mark Cieliebak. 2020. Ledgar: A large-scale multi-label corpus for text classification of legal provisions in contracts. In *Proceedings of the Twelfth Language Resources and Evaluation Conference*, pages 1235–1241.

Santosh Tyss, Mahmoud Aly, and Matthias Grabmair. 2024. Lexabsumm: Aspect-based summarization of legal decisions. In *Proceedings of the 2024 Joint International Conference on Computational Linguistics, Language Resources and Evaluation (LREC-COLING 2024)*, pages 10422–10431.

Ellen M Voorhees, Dawn M Tice, et al. 1999. The trec-8 question answering track evaluation. In *TREC*, volume 1999, page 82.

Alex Wang, Yada Pruksachatkun, Nikita Nangia, Amanpreet Singh, Julian Michael, Felix Hill, Omer Levy, and Samuel Bowman. 2019. Superglue: A stickier benchmark for general-purpose language understanding systems. *Advances in neural information processing systems*, 32.

Alex Wang, Amanpreet Singh, Julian Michael, Felix Hill, Omer Levy, and Samuel Bowman. 2018. Glue: A multi-task benchmark and analysis platform for natural language understanding. In *Proceedings of the 2018 EMNLP Workshop BlackboxNLP: Analyzing and Interpreting Neural Networks for NLP*, pages 353–355.

Steven H Wang, Antoine Scardigli, Leonard Tang, Wei Chen, Dimitry Levkin, Anya Chen, Spencer Ball, Thomas Woodside, Oliver Zhang, and Dan Hendrycks. 2023. Maud: An expert-annotated legal nlp dataset for merger agreement understanding. *arXiv preprint arXiv:2301.00876*.

Chaojun Xiao, Xueyu Hu, Zhiyuan Liu, Cunchao Tu, and Maosong Sun. 2021. Lawformer: A pre-trained language model for chinese legal long documents. *AI Open*, 2:79–84.

Wen Xiao, Iz Beltagy, Giuseppe Carenini, and Arman Cohan. 2022. Primera: Pyramid-based masked sentence pre-training for multi-document summarization. In *Proceedings of the 60th Annual Meeting of the Association for Computational Linguistics (Volume 1: Long Papers)*, pages 5245–5263.

Huihui Xu and Kevin Ashley. 2023. Argumentative segmentation enhancement for legal summarization. *arXiv preprint arXiv:2307.05081*.

Huihui Xu, Jaromir Savelka, and Kevin D Ashley. 2021. Toward summarizing case decisions via extracting argument issues, reasons, and conclusions. In *Proceedings of the eighteenth international conference on artificial intelligence and law*, pages 250–254.

Yuan Yao, Qingxiu Dong, Jian Guan, Boxi Cao, Zhengyan Zhang, Chaojun Xiao, Xiaozhi Wang, Fanchao Qi, Junwei Bao, Jinran Nie, et al. 2021. Cuge: A chinese language understanding and generation evaluation benchmark. *arXiv preprint arXiv:2112.13610*.

Jingqing Zhang, Yao Zhao, Mohammad Saleh, and Peter Liu. 2020. Pegasus: Pre-training with extracted gap-sentences for abstractive summarization. In *International Conference on Machine Learning*, pages 11328–11339. PMLR.

Tianyi Zhang, Varsha Kishore, Felix Wu, Kilian Q Weinberger, and Yoav Artzi. 2019. Bertscore: Evaluating text generation with bert. *arXiv preprint arXiv:1904.09675*.

Lucia Zheng, Neel Guha, Brandon R Anderson, Peter Henderson, and Daniel E Ho. 2021. When does pretraining help? assessing self-supervised learning for law and the casehold dataset of 53,000+ legal holdings. In *Proceedings of the eighteenth international conference on artificial intelligence and law*, pages 159–168.

Haoxi Zhong, Yuzhong Wang, Cunchao Tu, Tianyang Zhang, Zhiyuan Liu, and Maosong Sun. 2020a. Iteratively questioning and answering for interpretable legal judgment prediction. In *Proceedings of the AAAI Conference on Artificial Intelligence*, volume 34, pages 1250–1257.

Haoxi Zhong, Chaojun Xiao, Cunchao Tu, Tianyang Zhang, Zhiyuan Liu, and Maosong Sun. 2020b. How does nlp benefit legal system: A summary of legal artificial intelligence. In *Proceedings of the 58th Annual Meeting of the Association for Computational Linguistics*, pages 5218–5230.

Haoxi Zhong, Chaojun Xiao, Cunchao Tu, Tianyang Zhang, Zhiyuan Liu, and Maosong Sun. 2020c. Jec-qa: a legal-domain question answering dataset. In *Proceedings of the AAAI Conference on Artificial Intelligence*, volume 34, pages 9701–9708.

Linwu Zhong, Ziyi Zhong, Zinian Zhao, Siyuan Wang, Kevin D Ashley, and Matthias Grabmair. 2019. Automatic summarization of legal decisions using iterative masking of predictive sentences. In *Proceedings of the seventeenth international conference on artificial intelligence and law*, pages 163–172.

A Data Characteristics

Fig. 1 and 2 display the input text length, summary text length and fusion score distribution for each of the dataset in LexSumm benchmark.

B Implementation Details for LexT5

We use a learning rate of 0.005, linear warmup of 2.5k steps, inverse square root learning rate decay, maximum sequence length of 512 and is pre-trained for 250k steps. We employ a batch size of 65536 tokens and is optimized end-to-end using Adafactor optimizer (Shazeer and Stern, 2018) with a corrupted token ratio of 15% with the mean noise span length of 3. Pre-training is carried out using Google Cloud TPU with 8 cores (v3.8).

C Implementation Details for downstream tasks

We fine-tune each of our models on individual datasets using the AdamW optimizer (Loshchilov and Hutter, 2018) with hyperparameters $\beta = (0.9, 0.98)$ and $\epsilon = 1e-6$, alongside mixed precision (fp16) and gradient checkpointing techniques. For consistency, we set the maximum target sequence length to 512 across all models, while the input sequence length is set to 16384 for all models except PRIMERA and LongT5, which support 4096 and 8192 tokens, respectively, during training. We train LongT5, PRIMERA, and LongT5 with a learning rate of 2e-5, while Unlimiformer and SLED are trained with a learning rate of 1e-4 for 15 epochs. To control the learning rate, we employ a scheduler that warms up from zero during the first 10% of the steps and then linearly decays back to zero for the remaining steps. For models utilizing chunking, we set the chunk overlap ratio to 0.5. During inference, we set the minimum length to 16 for datasets with shorter outputs such as BillSum, MultiLexSumm-Tiny, and MultiLexSumm-Short, and to 128 for the remaining datasets. The maximum length is set to 16384 to ensure the model generates text without abruptly ending. Additionally, we utilize four beams for datasets with longer outputs and seven beams for datasets with shorter outputs. We apply a length penalty of 0.8 and 2 for datasets with shorter and longer outputs, respectively. Early stopping is disabled for datasets with longer outputs and enabled for datasets with shorter outputs.

D Zero-shot Summarization

An illustration of hierarchical merging strategy for long input summarization can be visualized in Fig. 3. Hierarchical merging strategy requires three prompts as follows:

(i) Summarizing an input chunk:

```
Below is a part of a legal
document:
--
{input}
--
We are creating one comprehensive
summary for the legal document by
recursively merging summaries of
its chunks. Now, write a summary
for the excerpt provided above,
making sure to include vital
information related to legal
arguments, backgrounds, legal
settings, key figures, their
objectives, and motivations. If
a legal norm or code is cited,
it must be correct and include
the right number. Summarize all
key events and everything that
is relevant to the case. Be
```

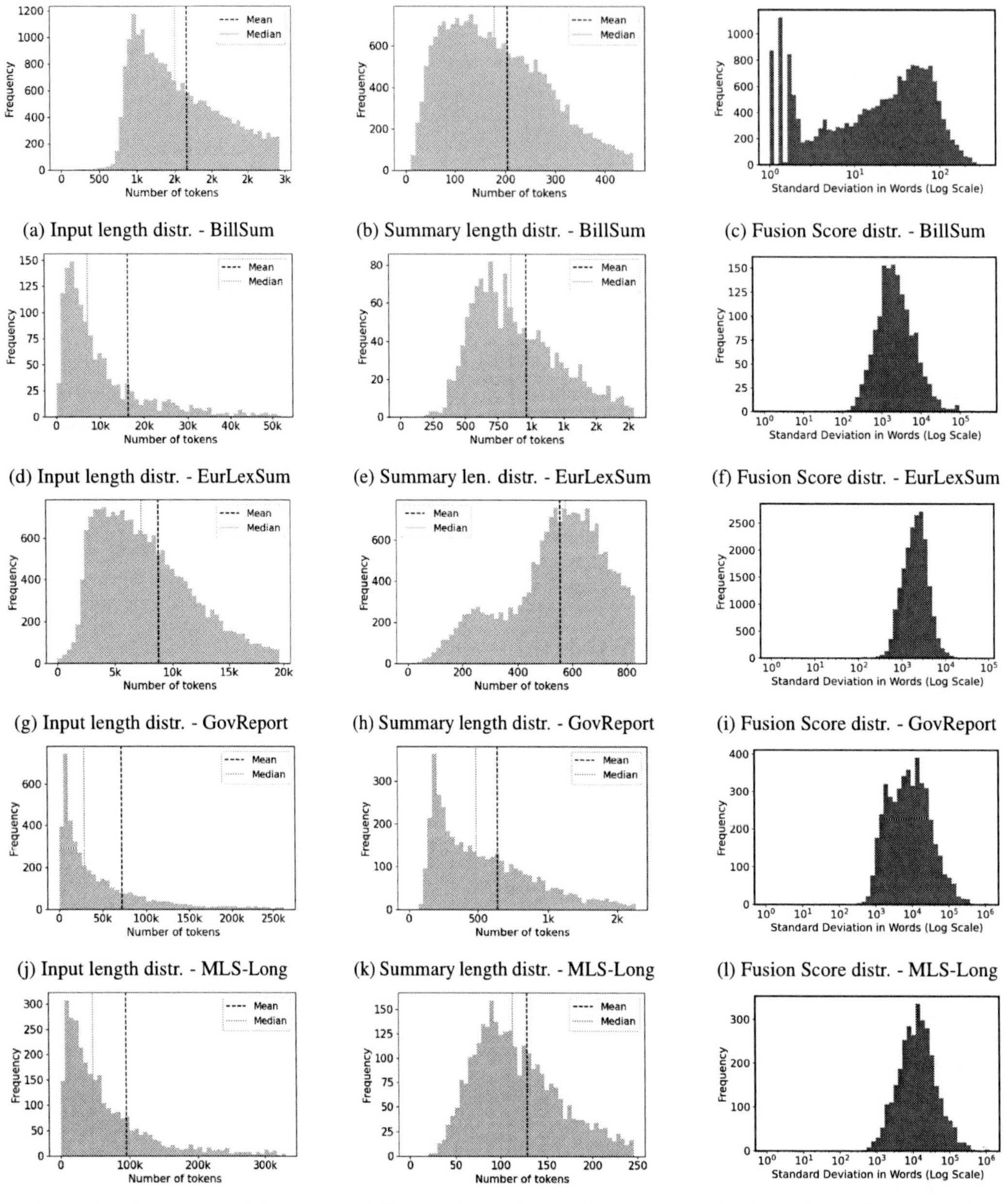

(a) Input length distr. - BillSum (b) Summary length distr. - BillSum (c) Fusion Score distr. - BillSum

(d) Input length distr. - EurLexSum (e) Summary len. distr. - EurLexSum (f) Fusion Score distr. - EurLexSum

(g) Input length distr. - GovReport (h) Summary length distr. - GovReport (i) Fusion Score distr. - GovReport

(j) Input length distr. - MLS-Long (k) Summary length distr. - MLS-Long (l) Fusion Score distr. - MLS-Long

(m) Input length distr. - MLS-Short (n) Summary length distr. - MLS-Short (o) Fusion Score distr. - MLS-Short

Figure 1: Distribution of input length, summary length and fusion scores for LexSumm datasets.

```
concise and use legal notation
and language. The summary must
be within {words} and could
include multiple paragraphs.
```

(ii) Merging two chunk-level summaries:

```
Below are several summaries of
consecutive parts of a legal
document:
--
{input}
--
We are creating one comprehensive
summary for the legal document
by recursively merging summaries
of its chunks. Now, merge the
given summaries into one single
```

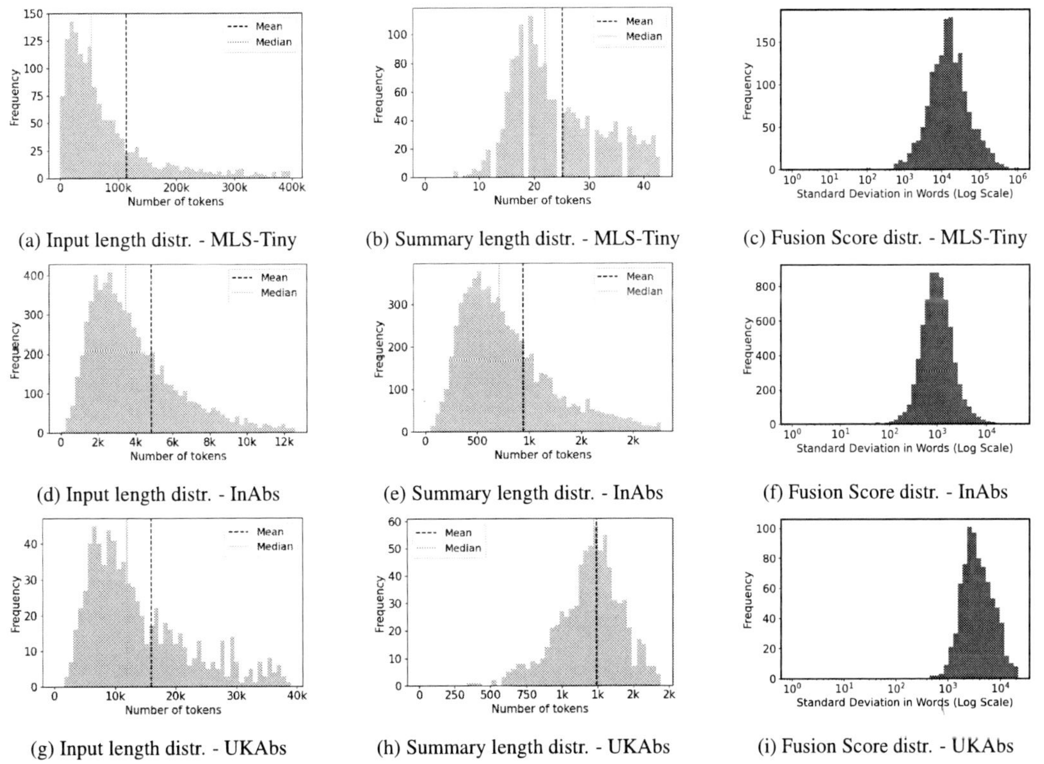

(a) Input length distr. - MLS-Tiny (b) Summary length distr. - MLS-Tiny (c) Fusion Score distr. - MLS-Tiny

(d) Input length distr. - InAbs (e) Summary length distr. - InAbs (f) Fusion Score distr. - InAbs

(g) Input length distr. - UKAbs (h) Summary length distr. - UKAbs (i) Fusion Score distr. - UKAbs

Figure 2: Distribution of input length, summary length and fusion scores for LexSumm datasets.

```
summary, making sure to include
vital information related to
legal arguments, backgrounds,
legal settings, key figures,
their objectives, and motivations.
The summary must be within words
and could include multiple
paragraphs.
```

(iii) Merging two summaries with added context from previously-generated merged summaries

```
Below is a summary of the context
preceding some parts of a legal
document:
--
{context}
--
Below are several summaries of
consecutive parts of a legal
document:
--
{input}
--
We are creating one comprehensive
summary for the legal document by
recursively merging summaries
of its chunks.  Now, merge
the preceding context and
the summaries into one single
summary, making sure to include
vital information related to
legal arguments, backgrounds,
legal settings, key figures,
their objectives, and motivations.
The summary must be within words
and could include multiple
paragraphs.
```

The prompts above have been used for all datasets in the LexSummZero benchmark, except MLS - Tiny dataset, where the output is a single-sentence Twitter post and the following prompts are used for that dataset.

(i) Summarizing an input chunk:

```
Below is a part of a legal
document:
--
```

```
{input}
--
We are creating one comprehensive
summary for the legal document,
stylized as a single-sentence
Twitter post.  This summary
should encapsulate the most
relevant information:  who is
involved, when did it happen,
to whom it concerns, on what
legal basis, and the location
(as a shortened reference).
Ensure to capture key legal
arguments, backgrounds, legal
settings, key figures, their
objectives, and motivations.
If a legal norm or code is
cited, include the correct
number succinctly.  Despite the
complexity of legal arguments,
references to precedent cases,
or switches between different
legal viewpoints, the summary
must present a coherent argument
in one concise sentence.
```

(ii) Merging two chunk-level summaries:

```
Below are several summaries of
consecutive parts of a legal
document:
--
{input}
--
We are merging these summaries
into a single, comprehensive
summary, stylized as a
single-sentence Twitter post.
This summary should include who
is involved, when it happened,
to whom it concerns, on what
legal basis, and include a
location reference.  Ensure
to merge vital information
related to legal arguments,
backgrounds, legal settings, key
figures, their objectives, and
motivations.  Introduce legal
concepts, statutes, and other
elements briefly if mentioned
for the first time.  If a legal
norm or code is cited, include
the correct number succinctly.
Organize the summary to present a
consistent and coherent argument,
all within one concise sentence.
```

(iii) Merging two summaries with added context from previously-generated merged summaries

```
Below is a summary of the context
preceding some parts of a legal
document:

--

{context}

--

Below are several summaries of
consecutive parts of a legal
document:

--

{input}

--

We are merging the preceding
context and the summaries into
one comprehensive summary, styled
as a single-sentence Twitter post.
This summary should include who
is involved, when it happened, to
whom it concerns, on what legal
basis, and a location reference.
Ensure to incorporate vital
information related to legal
arguments, backgrounds, legal
settings, key figures, their
objectives, and motivations.
Briefly introduce legal concepts,
statutes, and other elements if
they are mentioned for the first
time.  If a legal norm or code
is cited, include the correct
number succinctly.  Despite the
complexity, the summary must
present a coherent argument in
one concise sentence.
```

We set the size of each chunk to 3300, IZE is set to 3300, maximum input and output length are set to 4096 and 512. We specified summary length based on average output size of benchmark.

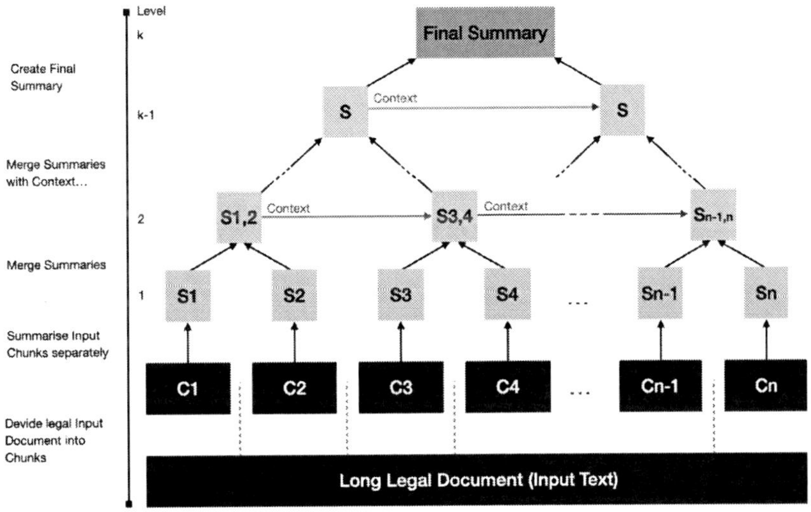

Figure 3: Visualization of Hierarchical merging strategy for summarization of Long Inputs: "S" represents the summary, "C" denotes the chunk, "n" is the total number of chunks, and "k" indicates the maximum number of levels

E Qualitative Analysis

E.1 Impact of length

E.1.1 PRIMERA summary

The appellants challenged the validity of the orders of dismissal passed by the General Manager, North East Frontier Railway, against the three respondents, under r. 149 of the Code of Civil Procedure, on the ground that they were invalid. The High Court dismissed the writ petitions. On appeal by special leave, Held, that the orders were invalid and the appellants were entitled to the appeal. Rule 148(3) provided that the services of other railway servants shall be liable to termination on notice on either side for the periods shown below. Such notice is not however, required in cases of dismissal or removal as a disciplinary measure after compliance with the provisions of clause (2) of Article 311 of the Constitution, retirement on attaining the age of superannuation, and termination of service due to mental or physical incapacity. By this new sub section, protection was given to the civil servant by providing that he shall not be dismissed or reduced in rank until he had been given a reasonable opportunity of showing cause against the action proposed to be taken in regard to him. There was, however, a saving clause contained in section 130 of the said Act which preserved the earlier tenures of servants and continued the rules and regulations applicable to them. Section 3 conferred on the Secretary of State all powers which had till then vested in the Court of Directors, while section 4 provided for the exercise of the President's powers and the Governor's power to make rules for regulating the classification of the Civil Services in India, the method of recruitment, the conditions of service, pay and allowances and discipline and conduct while sub section (4) declared that all service rules then in force had been duly made and confirmed the same. In 1935, the Government of India Act 1935 was passed and section 96B(1) was reproduced in sub sections (1) and (3) of section 240, and a new Sub section was added as sections (3). The doctrine of pleasure is thus embodied by article 310(1). It deals with the termination of services of a permanent railway servant after giving them notice for the specified period. It also provides that no person in that service may be dismissed by any authority subordinate to that by which he was appointed. Under r. 148(4), the appointing authorities are empowered to reduce or waive, at their discretion, the stipulated period of notice to be given by an employee, but the reason justifying their action should be recorded. This power cannot be re delegated. Though r

E.1.2 LED summary

The appellant was a peon employed by the North Eastern Railway, Gorakhpur. His services were terminated by the respondent General Manager of the said Railway. The appellant moved the Allahabad High Court under article 226 of the Constitution and challenged the validity of the order terminating his services on the ground that Rule 148 of the Indian Railway Establishment Code was invalid. This plea was rejected by the High Court and his writ petition to quash the said order was dismissed by the Punjab High Court. In appeal to this Court it was contended on behalf of the appellant that: (i) the termination of the services of a permanent railway servant under Rule 148(3) or Rule 149(3), which had superseded it, amounted to his removal under article 311(2) of the Constitu tion; (ii) the impugned Rules contravened the Constitutional safeguard guaranteed to civil servants by article 311 (2); (iii) the employment in civil service could be terminated only after complying with article 311 and any rule which violated the guarantee provided by the said Article would be invalid; (iv) the rule of compulsory retirement did not amount to removal or dismissal within the meaning of article 311; (v) the pleasure of the President was controlled by the proviso to article 309; and (vi) the rules of superannuation which were based on considerations of life expectation, mental capacity of the civil servant, and other relevant conditions of service prescribed by the rules, could not be exercised in accordance with the pleasure exercised by the President or the Governor in exercise of his pleasure. HELD: (1) It is well settled that articles 310 and 311 must be read together. If there are any other provisions in the Constitution which impinge upon the Constitution, the provisions of article 310(1) must, therefore, be read subject to them. [699 B C] (2) The President's pleasure has to be exercised subject to the limitations prescribed by article 31 1. There can be no doubt that the pleasure contemplated by article 310 (I) must be exercised, subject to such limitations as are specified in article 31 I. (3) Articles 309 and 310 have to be read separately. Therefore, the pleasure which has been so controlled would be lost on all the parties and it would still be relevant to all cases of termination of services of permanent civil servants under the rules framed under article 309. It is significant that article 311 has not been read in a very general and wide sense but it has

E.2 Impact of legal pre-training

E.2.1 Unlimiformer-T5 summary

The United States is the world's largest emitter of greenhouse gases (GHG). The United Nations Framework Convention on Climate Change (UNFCCC) requires the United States to commit to reducing its GHG emissions below 1990 levels by 2050. The 112th Congress has enacted a number of bills that would have established comprehensive climate change policy, including a cap on emissions of GHG and a ̆cap-and-trade ̆system. The Energy Policy Act of 2005 (P.L. 109-58), the Clean Air Act (CAA), and the Clean Energy Standard (CES) have been introduced in recent Congresses. This report examines (1) what is known about the extent to which the U.S. climate system is changing, (2) what are the challenges to setting and implementing policies to address climate change, and (3) what tools, if any, could be used to facilitate the transition to a low-GHG economy. To address these objectives, GAO analyzed relevant literature, interviewed federal, state, and local scientists, and others. GAO also analyzed studies on the effects of climate change on human health, welfare, and the environment, and analyzed data from the Environmental Protection Agency (EPA) and the Department of the Interior (Interior). GAO's work on climate change has been a long-standing topic of interest to Congress. In recent years, Congress has engaged in a variety of policy tools, including regulatory, financial, and technical assistance programs, such as the Energy Star program, which claims savings in the utility bills of consumers assisted by the program in 2010. Many of these tools are already in use in the public and private sectors (e.g., the Departments of Agriculture and Energy and the Interior), but they are relatively undeveloped. For example, some of the tools have been proposed by the Obama Administration, as well as by Senators Jeff Bingaman and Lisa Murkowski. Some of these instruments are used in the private sector, and some of them are already used by the public sector. Others are used by private firms to promote the development of new technologies and to promote technological development. In addition, many of these programs are aimed at reducing greenhouse gas emissions, but they have not been implemented in the 111th Congress. Among the tools available to Congress are the following: (1) science-based analysis, (2) market facilitation, (3) financial incentives, (4) technical assistance.

E.2.2 Unlimiformer-LexT5 summary

The U.S. economy is changing. Changes are exhibited in observations of average temperatures over land and in the oceans, melting glaciers and ice caps, shifting growing seasons, shifting distributions of plants and animals, and a variety of additional observations. Over time, the consequences of climate change for the United States and the globe will be influenced by choices made or left to others by the United Nations Framework Convention on Climate Change (UNFCCC), as well as for protecting human health and general welfare. Over the past three decades, some federal programs have sought to slow greenhouse gas (GHG)-induced climate change through regulatory, voluntary, and financial efforts to abate emissions. Many such proposals remain controversial and few have been enacted. The United States has been a federal program to improve understanding of climate changes (past and predicted) and their implications. This report outlines (1) conceptual approaches to setting goals for policies, (2) science-based goals, (3) economics-based policies, (4) incrementalism or adaptive management. For several decades, policymakers have been aware of the large range of projections of GHG concentrations of gas concentrations in the atmosphere at a level that would prevent dangerous anthropogenic interference with the climate system, and predictions of climate-related risks. Some of those in Congress consider such programs to take actions when they perceive that the benefits of the action exceed their costs. Some have expressed the likelihood that research may continue to continue to rise indefinitely a given level of risk reductions in order to avoid any particular level of risks. For example, the science-centric approach assumes that science alone can provide an objective standard of a šafeör ïolerablelevel or rate for climate change. Some experts have argued that science could not provide a mathematical basis for determining the cost-benefit analysis (CBA), but they have expressed their views of which the costs and benefits may be considered too much. For some, some researchers have suggested that a science-dynamic approach would be framed as a practical basis for allocating responsibilities to the sources of emissions, but they may not clearly reflect the many complex dimensions of climate science, such as changes in local temperature extremes, a deciduous forest, storm severity, or sea levels, or enforcing that might be considered to be considered more monetary considerations, but some may have framed in a more complete framework.

E.3 MLS-Tiny: Needle in the haystack

E.3.1 Reference Summary

D.C. District Court enforces FOIA request against Customs and Border Protection. (D.D.C.)

E.3.2 PRIMERA summary

A D.C. District Court judge issued a preliminary injunction requiring the U.S. Customs and Border Protection to disclose its policies and practices regarding events like the Muslim Ban.

E.3.3 LED Summary

D.C. District Court enjoins Customs and Border Protection from releasing agency records re the Muslim travel ban.

E.3.4 LongT5 summary

American-Arab Anti-Discrimination Council sued U.S. Customs and Border Protection for revoked, suspended, or terminated participation in the Global Entry System (D.D.C.)

E.3.5 SLED-T5 summary

Arab Americans and Arab Americans sue Customs and Border Protection for wrongful withholding of records relating to CBP's global entry program (D.D.C.)

E.3.6 Unlimiformer-T5 summary

@AmericanAntiDiscrimination Council (ADC) sued @CBP in 2017 for wrongful withholding of agency records in violation of FOIA (D.D.C.)

E.3.7 SLED-LexT5 summary

The American-Arab Anti-Discrimination Committee sued the Customs and Border Protection (D.D.C.)

E.3.8 Unlimiformer-LexT5 summary

Arab American Anti-Discrimination Council (ADC) sued Customs and Border Protection (CBP) in 2017 for withholding records in violation of FOIA (D.D.C.)

E.4 Summaries generated by zero-shot models

E.4.1 GPT-3.5 generated summary

The legal document under scrutiny delves into the critical issue of providing security to permanent civil servants, particularly within the realm of railway services, to uphold their independence and efficiency. It meticulously examines the implications of Rules 148(3) and 149(3) within the Indian Railway Establishment Code, stressing the potential insecurity and broad powers wielded by authorities under these rules. The document ardently argues that the termination of services pursuant to these rules essentially equates to removal, significantly infringing upon the fundamental right of employees to serve until attaining the superannuation age.
Central to the document are multiple appeals challenging the Constitutional validity of Rules 148(3) and 149(3), with various railway employees contesting the termination of their services under these contentious rules in diverse High Courts. The crux of the matter revolves around whether the actions taken under Rule 148(3) or Rule 149(3) can be categorized as řemovaläs defined in Article 311(2) of the Constitution. The core contention lies in whether these impugned Rules run afoul of the Constitutional protection accorded to civil servants under Article 311(2).
Representing the appellants, who encompass a spectrum of aggrieved railway employees, the document underscores the argument that Rules 148(3) and 149(3) contravene the safeguards enshrined in Article 311(2). It challenges the validity of these rules, contending that they are incompatible with the constitutional provisions safeguarding the interests of civil servants. Moreover, the document meticulously explores the premise that railway employees who entered service with knowledge of these rules should not be precluded from challenging their validity, emphasizing the paramount nature of the constitutional guarantee enshrined in Article 311(2).

In a broader legal context, the document meticulously dissects the intricacies of Article 311(2) of the Constitution, which serves as a bulwark protecting civil servants from arbitrary removal or dismissal without a proper inquiry. It underscores the significance of ensuring due process and procedural fairness in matters concerning the termination of civil servants, particularly within the specialized domain of railway services. The document meticulously weaves together legal arguments, precedents, and constitutional provisions to construct a robust case against the impugned Rules, aiming to secure the rights and protections of railway employees ensnared in the web of uncertainty and potential injustice created by Rules 148(3) and 149(3) of the Indian Railway Establishment Code.

E.4.2 Claude generated summary

The document discusses the validity of Rules 148(3) and 149(3) of the Indian Railway Establishment Code under Articles 311(2) and 14 of the Constitution of India. Rules 148(3) and 149(3) relate to the termination of services of Group 'C' and Group 'D' railway employees. Rule 148(3) deals with the termination of services of Group 'C' railway employees on the ground of "inefficiency or misbehavior." It lays down that no such employee shall be terminated from service unless he has been given at least one month's notice or one month's pay in lieu of notice. Rule 149(3) contains similar provisions for termination of services of Group 'D' railway employees.
Article 311(2) of the Constitution guarantees equal treatment in matters of appointment and promotion to civil servants. It states that no civil servant shall be "dismissed or removed by an authority subordinate to the one which appointed him." Article 14 guarantees equality before the law and equal protection of laws to all persons. It prohibits the State from denying any person equality before the law or equal protection of laws within the territory of India.
The document analyzes whether Rules 148(3) and 149(3) violate the principles of equal opportunity and are discriminatory under Article 14 of the Constitution. It discusses key legal arguments regarding the validity of these Rules. On one hand, it can be argued that Rules 148(3) and 149(3) violate Article 14 by denying equal treatment to railway employees in matters of termination. On the other hand, it may be argued that the Rules satisfy the test of reasonableness and are not arbitrary or discriminatory.

The objective of the document appears to be to synthesize information on the constitutional validity of Rules 148(3) and 149(3) by outlining relevant facts, key legal arguments on both sides, and the aims of Articles 311(2) and 14 without making inferences beyond the supplied context. The summary encompasses the essence of the context and subsequent segments within the 512-word limit as instructed.

Towards Supporting Legal Argumentation with NLP: Is More Data Really All You Need?

Santosh T.Y.S.S.[1], **Kevin D. Ashley** [2], **Katie Atkinson**[3], **Matthias Grabmair**[1]
[1]Technical University of Munich, Germany
[2]University of Pittsburgh, USA
[3]University of Liverpool, UK

Abstract

Modeling legal reasoning and argumentation justifying decisions in cases has always been central to AI & Law, yet contemporary developments in legal NLP have increasingly focused on statistically classifying legal conclusions from text. While conceptually "simpler", these approaches often fall short in providing usable justifications connecting to appropriate legal concepts. This paper reviews both traditional symbolic works in AI & Law and recent advances in legal NLP, and distills possibilities of integrating expert-informed knowledge to strike a balance between scalability and explanation in symbolic vs. data-driven approaches. We identify open challenges and discuss the potential of modern NLP models and methods that integrate conceptual legal knowledge.

1 Introduction

Law has been an attractive domain for AI in both symbolic knowledge representation and statistical NLP. Both strands share the common goal of supporting legal practice through enhancing legal research, document analysis, drafting, and decision making. A focal question distinguishing them remains whether, and how, the process of legal reasoning [1] underlying all textual data shall be explicitly represented or left to opaque components, such as generative language models or neural classifiers.

In principle, legal reasoning resembles IF-THEN-like inference. Legal rules are established from sources (statutes, regulations, precedent, custom, etc.) and mandate that certain consequences follow if factual requirements are met in a specific situation. In reality, however, such logic-like inferences are interwoven with areas of ambiguity, vagueness, and human discretion (Urbina, 2002). At the same time, legal orders evolve over time, continuously refining and adjusting to a dynamic world. In knowledge engineering communities, legal reasoning is characterized as 'defeasible' (Carlos, 2001) rather than monotonic. Rules that are applicable on their face can be trumped by special exceptions, conflicting superior rules, or by distinguishing the precedent from which the rule derives. Thus legal decisions are subject to change, as they can be overturned on appeal. The evolving nature of law to align with shifting social values leads to different legal conclusions. When two parties are in conflict and desire two different resolutions, their argument will combine law and facts in a way that is beneficial to their respective goals - through adversarial discourse (Khairoulline, 2007). Legal argumentation can be seen as an exercise in competitive theory formation in front of an arbitrator, with each side constructing arguments supported by evidence, written law, cases and other authority to favor their desired conclusions while addressing pitfalls of opposing theories (Rissland et al., 2003).

AI & Law as a field started started in the 1970s, when Buchanan and Headrick (1970) suggested that computer modeling of legal reasoning would be a promising area for research to better understand legal reasoning and argumentation. Many approaches have been proposed over the past three decades capturing several types of reasoning by means of symbolic representations. Some 50 years after the field's beginnings, the legal profession is experiencing considerable disruption by NLP technology, most prominently large language models (LLMs). In this paper, we provide a review of AI & Law work offering faithful modeling of legal reasoning but also requiring expensive legal expertise. We contrast this to modern, largely non-explainable, data-driven methods, which predict

[1]By 'legal reasoning', we refer to the wide range of activities involving interpreting, arguing, and applying legal principles to reach conclusions. Legal reasoning is not a single task but a collection of related tasks around the main theme of legal decision making as the interrelation of more of less well-defined rules and societal values with the facts of a specific case towards an outcome. Given the limited space available, we use 'legal reasoning' as an umbrella term to cover the diverse contributions on this topic in the literature.

Proceedings of the Natural Legal Language Processing Workshop 2024, pages 404–421
November 16, 2024 ©2024 Association for Computational Linguistics

legal conclusions directly without engaging in any explicit legal reasoning.

Our main contributions are as follows:

- An introduction to legal systems to sensitize readers to assumptions made in technical work
- Surveys of (1) landmark AI & Law work and its lessons learned, and (2) data-driven approaches to legal AI and legal NLP
- A detailed discussion of perspectives to unify both strands to meet future challenges.

Our discussion makes the following arguments:

- Future work on legal AI must strive to integrate legal expertise with data-derived models.
- Conveniently available legal NLP datasets come with structural assumptions, noise, and biases, which must be accounted for.
- Change of legal systems over time remains an under-explored aspect in NLP works.
- LLMs help alleviate knowledge acquisition bottleneck for domain model construction.
- There is value in NLP that produces and assesses arguments about legal conclusions in an explainable way with domain knowledge representation.
- Qualified evaluation in legal NLP is underdeveloped given the often non-well-defined nature of legal practice support tasks, resulting in exaggerated attention on convenient but uninformative benchmark metrics.

While prior surveys of Katz et al. (2023b) and Zhong et al. (2020b) focus on cataloging various use cases, tasks, and NLP techniques in legal AI, our paper critically examines the historical integration of expert knowledge into legal systems and advocates for its revival and synthesis with data-driven methods. We emphasize the unique value of expert-informed knowledge in ensuring legal reasoning aligns with established principles, which is not the primary focus of the aforementioned reviews. In contrast to Mahari et al. (2023), which highlights the disconnect between the tasks that are pursued in legal NLP research and the actual needs of legal practitioners, our work emphasizes the critical importance of integrating expert-informed knowledge to avoid this gap. We also present directions for synthesizing expert knowledge with current technological advancements, thereby overcoming traditional bottlenecks in knowledge acquisition and enhancing the efficacy of structured argumentation models.

Most importantly, we contribute a comprehensive distillation of the conceptual ideas developed and researched by the AI & Law community prior to the recently surging interest in law as an application domain for mainstream NLP. In part, our motivation is to connect these communities. Much legal NLP work does not build on formal models of legal knowledge and reasoning but characterizes it mostly as precursor work to modern statistical methods. Our position is that this view does not do justice to the insights gained and legal authenticity captured in this body of research. Symbolic AI & Law has thought about how to incorporate legal expertise in models more deeply than most current NLP works, and hence the fields should merge and learn from one another. We strive to drive home the necessity of a paradigm shift in legal NLP, one that values and integrates the profound expertise of domain specialists with the capabilities of data-driven technologies.

2 Legal Systems in a Nutshell

Legal systems revolve around legal subjects, institutions and actors, and sources of law. While there is variation across settings, the most relevant sources typically comprise a national constitution, primary legislation (often referred to as 'statutes', etc.), secondary 'executive' regulation, precedents decided by courts, and other auxiliary sources. A major division exists with regard to the role of precedents relative to written law, as well as the methodology of arguing with them. Legal systems primarily influenced by continental Europe follow the 'civil law' approach, where important decisions are mostly condensed into context-free interpretive rules to codified law that are compiled in secondary literature (e.g., so-called 'commentaries'). In parts of the world with primarily English legal influence, so-called 'common law' systems, precedents are regularly applied by means of analogizing and distinguishing arguments that take into account the facts of the case in much greater extent than civil-law-type reasoning will. International courts (e.g., the European Court of Justice, the European Court of Human Rights) usually follow hybrid methodologies that are specific to the legal regime they govern. Despite some recent diversification, virtually all AI & Law research comes from either civil or common law backgrounds and makes corresponding assumptions, which is why we include this introduction. It is important to note that this coarse systematization is a great simplification of the world's diverse legal systems and cultures, and only intended to supplement our survey.

Written law generally consists of primary (i.e., parliamentary) legislation and secondary (i.e., executive) regulation. While enacted by two different branches of government, they are structurally similar in that they encode rules that can be formalized in IF-THEN relations. They also contain ambiguous and vague formulations in need of interpretation, for which special methods exist that are beyond the scope of this work. It is typically up to the judiciary (i.e., the courts) to settle open questions through landmark cases, often after arguments being developed in academic literature. These decisions then become part of the discourse accordingly in the applicable methodology. This transition from rule-based to case-based reasoning (in the common law) has intuitively been termed "when the rules run out" by (Gardner, 1987).

When arguing a case relative to a precedent, it is a fundamental principle of justice that similar cases should be treated alike. In common law jurisdictions, this principle is formalised in the doctrine of *stare decisis*, which obliges decisions of the appropriate status to be followed when deciding a new case. Civil law legal orders also recognize a binding effect of high court precedent, but argue with them differently. While higher court decisions bind lower courts, cases move in the opposite direction. They are first filed in, for example, district or trial courts, where evidence is heard and first decisions are made. Decisions can then be appealed to the Appeals Courts, and eventually to Supreme Courts. At some point in this progression, arguments on evidence will be considered settled and only purely legal errors will be permissible grounds for further escalation. In a legal system, such 'appeals tracks' exist for various jurisdictions (civil, criminal, administrative, etc.) and can be spread across geographic entities (e.g., federal vs state courts).

It is worthwhile to acknowledge that legal systems are inherently human-centric, involving complex decision-making processes where persuasion, interpretation, and subjective judgment play critical roles. Legal decisions are not solely about determining which side should win as a matter of justice, but about who can present the most convincing argument within the framework of established laws, principles, and precedents. The main vision of AI & Law is that state and private actors in all aspects of the legal system can benefit from supporting software that seamlessly connects to the concepts and concerns they have been trained for and work with. Notably, legal reasoning not only happens in courts, but also in public administration and law enforcement (i.e., the executive branch), where law needs to be applied to specific situations (e.g., permits, taxes, public safety, etc.). Human accountability is paramount for the trust in the overall workings of a democratically governed society. Hence, this vision is one of AI supporting human decision makers and not replacing or unduly influencing it.

3 Knowledge-based Approaches

AI & Law research started with modeling of legal reasoning by means of knowledge representation.

Rule-based Approaches Early landmark work demonstrated how British immigration law could be represented in Prolog (Sergot et al., 1986) and outlined challenges faced in this process, including the law's rule-exception pattern, negation-as-failure (i.e., failure to prove true) vs. classical negation (logical, certain falseness), and counterfactual reasoning. Waterman and Peterson (1980) developed a specialized language for rule-based legal inference. Rules establish conclusions from antecedents in a forward/backward chaining manner, thereby spanning open a derivation tree of a case outcome. They justify a position and explain how a conclusion can be reached, but they do not capture the dialectical aspects associated with argumentation, since no conflicting arguments are generated and no indeterminacy is accounted for. Gardner (1987) extended by using augmented transition networks to model contract formation over time given agent actions with a basic form of uncertainty - If a condition was a 'hard question' and could not be decided, the network would fork into two alternative ways to legally treat the facts. Overall, early rule-based systems were still predominantly derivations rather than argumentation models, although they correspond well to how lawyers analyze cases.

Case-based Approaches The adversarial nature of law naturally demands to represent arguments for both dispute sides. The precedent-focused nature of US common law was a suitable domain for the development of what became known as 'legal case based reasoning' systems. In the prominent TAXMAN system, McCarty (1976) modeled the majority's and minority's theories and arguments in the famous tax law case of *Eisner v Macomber,*

252 U.S. 189 (1920) (Eisner v. Macomber), surveying the intricacies one must account for, if resolved to capture all decision-relevant concerns in depth. The HYPO system (Ashley, 1991) modeled parts of US Trade Secrets Law by means of dimensions. These are typical fact patterns that favor different sides of the dispute, and can be used to analogize and distinguish cases argumentatively by means of set comparison. The focal concept here is a 'three-ply argument': A proponent cites the most-on-point precedent with the greatest factor overlap. The opponent distinguishes by pointing to a disfavorable factor in the precedent but not in the new case, or a favorable factor in the current case but not in the precedent, and cites a counterexample precedent. Finally, the proponent offers a rebuttal by distinguishing the counterexample. This was built upon in the CATO system (Aleven, 1997), which arranged 'factors' into a hierarchy, on the basis of which more sophisticated argumentation was possible (e.g., using hierarchy parent factors).

Hybrid & Extended Systems CABARET (Rissland and Skalak, 1991) first combined rule-based reasoning with HYPO-style case based reasoning around ill-defined terms contained in the rules. The integration is performed via a collection of control heuristics that interleave arguments of both kinds to support a particular conclusion. GREBE (Branting, 1991) further extends this hybrid architecture with formalized domain knowledge and a semantic network representation to retrieve and compare cases. BankXX (Rissland et al., 1996, 1997) embeds HYPO-style factor-based reasoning with a domain model into a 'legal theory space' that can be searched for plausible arguments.

Integration with Prediction CATO had been developed as a tutoring system and did not predict case outcomes. Issue-Based Prediction (IBP) (Bruninghaus and Ashley, 2003) extended the factor-based representation with a model of legal 'issues', each of which could be predicted via case-based reasoning. Ashley and Brüninghaus (2009) even proposed SMILE + IBP, classifying the presence of factors in cases by means of NLP, whereas prior factor-based systems had all relied on manual factor coding of cases. It pioneered data-driven approaches for ascribing factors to be used in conjunction with a domain model without circumventing the reasoning process entirely.

Values, Time, and Procedure: Berman & Hafner explored deeper aspects of representing cases, many of which remain challenging to this day. Berman and Hafner 1993 proposed to supplement each factor with "legal purpose(s) which it affects, and each legal purpose in turn specifies whether it favours the plaintiff or defendant". Parties may offer competing arguments based on factor-based case analogies. *Teleological* knowledge allows a model to go beyond factual similarities to include broader jurisprudential concepts. This was highly influential in subsequent work (Greenwood et al., 2003; Chorley and Bench-Capon, 2005b; Wyner et al., 2007; Grabmair and Ashley, 2011; Muthuri et al., 2017; Grabmair, 2017; Maranhao et al., 2021), which converged towards speaking of "values" rather than purposes.

Berman and Hafner (1995) contributed a pioneering model of the temporal dynamics of case-based legal reasoning: "legal precedents are embedded in a temporal context of evolving legal doctrine, which can result in a strong precedent becoming weaker over time, to the point where a skillful attorney could reasonably predict that it will no longer be followed." This temporal dimension has also received attention in other works (Rissland and Xu, 2011; Henderson and Bench-Capon, 2019; Prakken and Sartor, 1998; Branting, 1993).

Berman and Hafner 1991 observe that the support of a precedent decision for a case to be argued is linked to its respective procedural setting. They distinguish the pleading, pre-verdict, and verdict stage. A further difference exists between decisions on procedural matters and decisions on matters of fact and/or law. A decision in favour of the defendant party based on a procedural matter (e.g., lack of evidence) may not support the same decision in a new case which shares the factual features of the precedent but is to be decided on its merits. The question of decision context has received limited attention in subsequent works (e.g., Wyner and Bench-Capon 2009; Verheij 2016). Even in the recent works on NLP-based legal judgment prediction, case outcomes are often greatly simplified, up to the point of an impoverished binary variable of whether a party won the case or not.

Theory Construction Approach: As McCarty 1995 pointed out, "[T]he task for a lawyer or a judge in a hard case is to construct a theory of the disputed rules that produces the desired legal result, and then to persuade the relevant audience that this theory is preferable to any theories offered by an opponent". Bench-Capon and Sartor (2000,

2003, 2001) model a 'theory' as a set of factor-based rules and preferences among them derived from value preferences. Different theories can be compared with reference to the number of cases whose outcome they explain. The rules and preference relations form tradeoffs between sets of values raised by factors in the cases. These establish preferences among rules, which in turn predict case outcomes. The CATE system (Chorley and Bench-Capon, 2004) enabled manual creation and testing of theories as prolog programs. The AGATHA system (Chorley and Bench-Capon, 2005a) constructed theories autonomously using A* search.

Computational Argumentation: Producing an argument by using a rule-driven strategy implemented with case-driven argument moves remains a central way of justifying conclusions in cases. In the 90s this was mainly pursued using dialogue games which were designed to allow an adversarial discussion between the two parties, one represented by the computer and one by the user. Examples include Gordon 1993; Hage et al. 1993; Prakken and Sartor 1997, 1998; Loui and Norman 1995. While many of the systems referenced thus far model argumentation ad hoc, the AI & Law field interacted considerably with its neighboring discipline of general computational models of argumentation. Of particular interest in this context is the concept of 'argument schemes' as well as the connection to models of so-called 'abstract argumentation'.

Argument Schemes: An argument scheme is a stereotypical pattern of reasoning primarily constituting a claim, a set of positive premises, and, optionally, a set of negative exceptions. Argument schemes have a long history, as laid out in (Macagno et al., 2017). In modern times, schemes were used by Perelman and Olbrechts-Tyteca 1969 and Toulmin 1958. In AI & Law, the Toulmin argument model had been historically popular. It recognizes different roles of statements in an argument: Claim, Qualifier/Strength, Data/Premises, Warrant/Inference, Backing, and Rebuttal. This is suitable for legal reasoning by incorporating authority for the warrant and by including a rebuttal component in recognition of the defeasible nature of legal reasoning. Walton (1996) introduced a variety of schemes into AI & Law (e.g., from Expert Opinion, from Negative Consequences, from Rules, etc). Verheij (2001); Gordon and Walton (2009) supplemented them further (e.g., from position to know, from ontology, from cases, from testimonial evidence). Schemes have become central in AI & Law research, being used in reasoning with evidence (Bex et al., 2003; Bex, 2011), reasoning with cases (Prakken et al., 2015), e-democracy (Atkinson et al., 2006), statutory interpretation (Araszkiewicz, 2021), and value-based argumentation (Grabmair, 2016; Greenwood et al., 2003).

Abstract Argumentation Framework: In seminal work, Dung (1995) defined *abstract argumentation frameworks* (AAFs), which were introduced to AI & Law by Prakken 1995. An abstract argumentation framework comprises a set of arguments and set of attack relations between them. The justified arguments are then evaluated based on subsets of arguments ('extensions') defined under a range of semantics. The abstract nature of Dung's theory says nothing about the structure of arguments, the nature of attack or defeat, or use of preferences. This opacity, and the coupling with argument schemes, motivated the development of structured argument models. For example, ASPIC (Caminada and Amgoud, 2007) adopts an intermediate level of abstraction by making some minimal assumptions on the nature of the logical language and the inference rules, and then providing abstract accounts of the structure of arguments, the nature of attack, and the use of preferences. Prakken 2010; Modgil 2009 generalised the ASPIC framework to develop ASPIC+, which can capture a broader range of systems with various assumption-based argumentation and systems using argument schemes. ASPIC+ has been applied to study legal reasoning in the works of Prakken 2012; Prakken et al. 2015.

Abstract Dialectical Frameworks (ADFs) (Brewka et al., 2013) generalize the AAF representation to node-and-directed-relations form with a set of local acceptance conditions. This allows both attack and support influence, resulting in an abstract yet intuitive model for legal reasoning. For example, the ANGELIC method (Al-Abdulkarim et al., 2016b) uses ADFs for representing case law in an explainable inference model on the basis of a hierarchical factor representation. The maintainability of such a representation is discussed in (Al-Abdulkarim et al., 2016a). Atkinson et al. (2019) extended to reasoning about factors with magnitude, thereby going beyond purely boolean proposition representations of cases.

Overall, the advantages of knowledge-based approaches are that they explicitly model legal reasoning and provide explanations of inferences.

4 Data-driven Approaches

Relationship to Political Science Research: Data originating in the legal system has been the subject of extensive analytical study in the field of *empirical legal studies*, including court and judge decision/voting behavior (e.g., Segal 1984; Kort 1957; Nagel 1963; Ruger et al. 2004). As most of them neither model legal reasoning nor apply NLP techniques, we do not include them in our survey.

Early AI & Law: Knowledge-centered approaches can achieve high degrees of faithfulness in their representation and explainability in their inferences, but face the 'knowledge acquisition bottleneck', as they require large amounts of expertise and modeling effort. This is in contrast to data-driven models with less hand-crafted expertise. Early works by Mackaay and Robillard (1974) used nearest-neighbor methods for outcome classification. In the 1990's, Pannu 1995; Bochereau et al. 1991; Philipps 1989; Bench-Capon 1993 trained neural networks to predict outcomes and derive input feature weights. Unsurprisingly, such early applications of ML attracted criticism (Aikenhead, 1996; Hunter, 1994). Obtaining substantial amounts of processable data was challenging and extensive feature engineering was necessary. These works focused on the application of neural networks to identify how influential certain information is for the decision and did not engage in comparative benchmarking.

Towards Modern Legal NLP: Recent years saw a resurging interest in case prediction through the use of data-driven methods learning from the large datasets now available from different jurisdictions, such as the ECtHR (Chalkidis et al., 2019, 2022a, 2021; Aletras et al., 2016; Medvedeva et al., 2021; SAYS, 2020; Tyss et al., 2023b,a; Santosh et al., 2024c; Liu and Chen, 2017; Medvedeva et al., 2020; SAYS, 2020) Chinese Criminal Courts (Luo et al., 2017; Yue et al., 2021; Zhong et al., 2020a, 2018; Yang et al., 2019), , US Supreme Court (Katz et al., 2017; Kaufman et al., 2019), Indian Courts (Malik et al., 2021; Shaikh et al., 2020) French court of Cassation (Şulea et al., 2017b,a; Bertalan and Ruiz, 2020) Supreme Court of Switzerland (Niklaus et al., 2021), Turkish Constitutional court (Sert et al., 2021), UK courts (Strickson and De La Iglesia, 2020), German courts (Waltl et al., 2017), Brazilian courts (Lage-Freitas et al., 2022) and Philippine courts (Virtucio et al., 2018).

Earlier works employed bag-of-words features (Aletras et al., 2016; Şulea et al., 2017a,b; Virtucio et al., 2018; Shaikh et al., 2020; Medvedeva et al., 2020). More recent approaches use deep learning techniques (Zhong et al., 2018, 2020a; Yang et al., 2019) involving convolutional or recurrent networks followed by adoption of pre-trained transformer models (Chalkidis et al., 2019; Niklaus et al., 2021), including legal-domain specific pre-trained variants (Zheng et al., 2021; Chalkidis et al., 2020, 2023; Douka et al., 2021; Masala et al., 2021; Xiao et al., 2021; Hwang et al., 2022; Niklaus et al., 2023). Classification tasks on legal text interrelate, and so other words have leveraged dependencies between tasks for improving models (Santosh et al., 2023a; Yue et al., 2021; Valvoda et al., 2023; Zhong et al., 2018; Feng et al., 2022; Ma et al., 2021; Dong and Niu, 2021; Yang et al., 2019; Huang et al., 2021; Hu et al., 2018) and added additional loss constraints (such as contrastive learning exploiting label information), (Tyss et al., 2023b; Zhang et al., 2023; Gan et al., 2022; Liu et al., 2022) and injected legal knowledge (Liu et al., 2023; Santosh et al., 2023b, 2024c; Gan et al., 2021; Zhong et al., 2020a; Feng et al., 2022)

Overall, one can observe a trend towards applying NLP models to legal text with little to no architectural bias or explicit domain representation. These are then compared along quantitative metrics, typically with regard to high level classification/prediction goals (e.g., case outcome variables and document-level keywords) at the cost of interpretability. As Berman & Hafner have observed in the 1990s, however, case outcomes are highly contextual in time, procedure, and socio-legal purpose. Classification benchmarks risk decoupling a sense of technical progress towards a notion of model 'understanding' from supporting a realistic task (e.g., legal argumentation) by focusing on a highly reductive representation of its outcome. For instance, case outcome predictions are often treated as binary targets based on the majority opinion, even though judges on the same bench frequently have conflicting reasoning, leading to dissenting or concurrent opinions (Xu et al., 2024). This reductive approach overlooks the nuanced legal argumentation underpinning each decision, focusing on a single outcome instead of capturing the depth of legal reasoning and debate.

Limits of Classification Benchmarks: The working assumption of these approaches is that by getting better at the benchmark, models encode more legal knowledge which can be extracted as explanations for predictions. To the best of our understanding, however, this promise has not been fulfilled. Initial works on data from the EtCHR, Aletras et al. 2016; Chalkidis et al. 2019 listed words based on feature importance or highlighted text based on attention scores. In later works, Chalkidis et al. (2021) used regularization techniques to identify paragraphs that support a finding of a violation of ECtHR. The extracted rationales did not correspond well to the annotation by a single legal expert. Santosh et al. (2022); Malik et al. (2021) continued the trend of computing paragraph level importance using interpretability techniques such as Integrated Gradient and tried to assess them against expert-annotated important paragraphs, also with only moderate success. In the ECtHR context, Santosh et al. (2022) discovered evidence that BERT-based classifiers rely on shallow predictors. This can be mitigated using adversarial training, but alignment still remains low. Recently, Xu et al. (2023) assessed rationale alignment at the more difficult, fine-grained word level. The experiment uncovered inconsistencies in the court metadata and illustrated how even annotations by two legal experts may not align well. To add to the challenge, a pilot study by Branting et al. (2021) discovered that human performance in a prediction task does not improve if users are given access to a saliency map derived from a prediction model. Recent work by Mumford et al. (2023b) reported that human performance on the judgment prediction task closely resembled randomness and was unaffected by domain knowledge. These results all cast doubt on the assumption that, at least for classifiers models, benchmark performance correlates with better explanations. The data may be noisy, the labeling too simplified, the predictors too shallow, the expert disagreement low, and the utility of a salience map limited. It should also be noted that the potential leakage of benchmark test data into training corpora remains under-discussed and unmeasured.

Other body of works on outcome classification of ECtHR cases predict the decision from a textual description of the case facts alone. By contrast, what lawyers actually need is the explanation why the resolution of a case is the proper application of the law and in line with what traditional AI & Law work would call a 'theory' of ECtHR jurisprudence. The outcome must be based on a justification which presents equitable arguments, can be reviewed on appeal, and hold up under public scrutiny.

Shift to Generative Models: LLMs have also been evaluated against case outcome classification as a benchmark. Chalkidis (2023); Vats et al. (2023); Trautmann et al. (2022); Shui et al. (2023) tested various early models and found them to score relatively low in quantitative metrics, which stands in contrast to their scores on some bar exams (Katz et al., 2023a; Freitas and Gomes, 2023). They report on experiments with several models and prompting techniques, including zero/few-shot prompting, prompt ensembling, chain-of-thought, and activation fine-tuning. Yu et al. (2022, 2023) employ prompts that are derived from legal reasoning methods (such as the common law IRAC (Issue, Rule, Application, Conclusion). Trautmann (2023) uses prompt chaining with an initial summarization step to deal with lengthy legal documents. Jiang and Yang (2023); Deng et al. (2023) develop syllogism prompting providing the three deductive reasoning steps for major premise (article/law retrieval), minor premise (element extraction from facts) and conclusion (judgement).

LegalBench (Guha et al., 2023) recently presented the first aggregated benchmark beyond classification-like evaluation to test the reasoning abilities of generative models. Kang et al. (2023) applies the IRAC methodology comprehensively to LegalBench subtasks. While ancillary challenges remain (e.g., the need to manually assess model performance non certain tasks), this development is in line with our arguments in this paper.

5 Challenges & Future Directions

Combining Knowledge and Data: The pressing question is how best to integrate legal knowledge and ML so that a system can learn from data and still seamlessly interface to a lawyer's understanding of the domain by means of a conceptual representation. A number of such hybrid systems can be found outside of NLP: *Split Up* (Stranieri et al., 1999) combined expert-crafted rules and neural networks trained from data in a factor-based model of Australian family law to predict divorce asset division. In the CATO line of work, both AGATHA (Chorley and Bench-Capon, 2005a) and VJAP (Grabmair, 2017) leveraged structured legal argumentation for prediction with signals derived from a case base. Moving to NLP, one intuitive combination is to ascribe factors from cases using text processing and proceed with formalized legal inference. This was employed in SCALE (Branting et al., 2021) to enable a logic model to predict WIPO domain name disputes, and in the ECtHR domain by inference using an ADF representation Mumford et al. (2022, 2023a). Gray et al. (2023) automatically identified factors in Fourth Amendment auto stop cases, demonstrated their predictive value, and used ML techniques to explain case outcomes in terms legal professionals can understand. Holzenberger and Van Durme (2021) apply neural models to identify argument slots in legal provisions and find suitable filling elements from fact descriptions, thereby enabling rule-based inference. Similarly, Holzenberger and Van Durme (2023) automates the translation of cases into a knowledge base by posing it as an information extraction task.

Data Utilized: Ideally, outcome prediction systems in the legal domain should rely on the information available before proceedings start and legal conclusion are determined (e.g., argumentative memoranda from the parties). Most case outcome classification research is conducted based on fact descriptions that are taken from judgments. These are often highly selective summaries tailored to align with the decision (Tippett et al., 2021). Although they may not explicitly contain outcomes, this can introduce confounding effects as demonstrated in Santosh et al. (2022). To illustrate the effect of proxy data on performance, Medvedeva et al. (2021) utilized data from ECtHR 'communicated cases', court-prepared summary data derived from applicant submissions, published before trial and observed a decline compared to facts statements from judgments, highlighting the need to select appropriate data for this task to draw reliable conclusions (Medvedeva et al., 2023; Medvedeva and Mcbride, 2023). Such work may also be subject to data selection bias related to which cases reach which court, and with regard to how they are published. For example, a higher court will receive a different distribution of cases (i.e., such with grounds for appeal) than a district court, and only a subset of them may be published. Finally, many cases are settled before or during trial, further skewing the dataset (Osbeck and Gilliland, 2018).

Temporal Dynamics Current legal NLP methods often operate under the implicit assumption that past training data is homogeneous and neglect its sequential nature. In reality, attitudes and case law change over time, with later cases altering and superseding the roles of older ones. All shifts in jurisprudence confront the model with a cold start problem of little training data for a new legal rule and copious training data for outdated ones. These dynamics can in principle be modeled. For instance, overruling detection can identify where previous legal precedents have been overturned, and trigger techniques such as model unlearning (see Nguyen et al. 2022) or selective forgetting. One can also strive to detect updates in beliefs/knowledge expressed in decisions over time, and modify such beliefs within the model (Hase et al., 2021). Santosh et al. (2024b) accounts for the temporally evolving nature of classification tasks on legal data using continual learning approaches.Overall, however, the temporal dynamics of legal corpora remain largely unaddressed in recent works.

Domain Model Construction Rule-based models of the law are powerful tools to develop software that supports legal practice, but constructing them demands considerable legal expertise. Modern LLMs put us into a position to create these structures in a (semi-) automated fashion. Savelka et al. (2023) shows constructive evidence of this, but it remains an open questions whether LLMs can systematize large complexes of legal source material into well-formed, legally correct representations. Ascribing factors from facts text in unseen cases by means of developing classifiers requires training data relative to an exhaustively defined list of factors. The more likely scenario is that generative models can be prompted with specific facts to subsume them under a factor pattern description. For example, Gray et al. (2024) applied generative AI automatically to identify factors in Fourth Amendment auto stop cases.

From Argument Mining to Generation: The task of constructing abstract argumentation models closely dovetails with the field of argument mining (i.e., the detection of argumentative text segments and their interlinking). Traditionally, argument mining mainly encompasses four sub-tasks as formalized by seminal work in Palau and Moens 2009: text segmentation, argument span detection, classification (e.g., conclusion, premise), and prediction of graph relations between spans. Follow up work by Wyner et al. 2010; Grabmair et al. 2015; Poudyal et al. 2020; Habernal et al. 2023; Ali et al. 2022, 2023; Grundler et al. 2022 focused on the first three subtasks, with fewer models engaging in graph construction. Modeling the relationships and comparative strength between conflicting arguments is a crucial piece to connect these extractive argumentative mining efforts to structured argumentation, largely unaddressed by existing works.

Even with powerful LLMs available, optimal argumentation support systems for legal practitioners benefit from structured representations of legal information and argumentation. While argumentative text can now be generated by current models, it remains a challenging cognitive task to systematize and assess arguments strategically. A productive support system should produce arguments in a transparent manner, and offer the user an intuitive way of resolving multiple complex arguments towards a justification of a decision. Naturally, this also entails questions around mindful interface design and organizational processes to facilitate accountable human decision making where capable text generation systems are accessible.

Role of Evaluation: The true value in NLP for legal applications lies in producing, structuring, and assessing arguments about legal conclusions in an explainable way so that they may maximally support human experts. This human-centric nature of legal systems introduces a level of complexity that purely data-driven systems often struggle to capture when classifying variables from close-to-raw data. By the same token, LLMs may generate text that may seem lawyer-like, but integrating them in processes of legal practice regularly involves interfacing them with symbolic data structures on both input and output ends, as well as maximizing consistency and correctness of generated text in ways that is defined by the legal concepts of the application context. This may include obfuscating cumbersome and error-prone model prompting behind traditional user interfaces composed of elements that map to symbols in the domain (e.g., types of contract clauses, factor-like aspects of cases, information elements of interest to draft process memoranda, etc.). The complexity of human legal decision-making highlights the inadequacy of current evaluation metrics. Legal NLP works should, ideally, tangibly indicate progress towards optimal argumentation support systems for legal practitioners, yet frequently convenient evaluations are prioritized over informative ones. This is, of course, due to the nuanced and often ill-defined characteristic of legal practice tasks. Still, legal databases are more than large repositories of text for autoregressive pre-training, but resources for tackling these use cases, including, for example, using prior decisions in constructing and responding to arguments. Legal NLP's efforts should be evaluated - and reviewed - in terms of how well models provide such functionality (Ashley, 2022). Many legal NLP works specify use cases, yet few account for them in their evaluative framework by conducting studies with legal experts, or benchmark their automatic metrics against human evaluations. Research on evaluation criteria that better capture the practical utility of legal NLP systems in real-world settings should be among our top priorities.

Examples of human evaluations in specified use cases include the following: In Elaraby et al. (2024) human experts evaluated the legal argument coverage in generated summaries. In Mullick et al. (2022) and Salaün et al. (2022), humans assessed legal summaries' relevance, readability, fluency, or adequacy. In Xu and Ashley (2022) expert evaluators assessed the information quality of legal summaries in terms of generated question-answer pairs. Experts evaluated the legal importance of automatically identified paragraphs in Santosh et al. (2022) but achieving expert annotation agreements is challenging, especially given noisy metadata (Xu et al., 2023). Evaluations benchmarked human classification of case verdicts under ECHR Article 6 in Mumford et al. (2023b) and compared expert annotations to automatically generated explanations in Malik et al. (2021) and to automatically identified factor sentences in Gray et al. (2023).

6 Conclusions

We believe that knowledge-based approaches to building legal argument support systems deserve the attention of the modern NLP community, as they embody a culture and method of capturing intricacies of legal systems and argumentation that are often simplified away in the increasingly easier application of large mainstream models to legal data. The prominent role of benchmarks compounds this by drawing attention towards quantitative progress instead of real, empirical investigations of downstream benefit to practitioners. At the same time, LLMs widen the knowledge acquisition bottleneck for structured models considerably, opening up new opportunities. We believe there is great value in combining knowledge- and data-driven systems rather than continuing the assumption that deep expertise will reliably emerge given large enough amounts of data and computation.

Limitations

This paper focuses on legal NLP as applied to tasks that involve the application of legal source material to case facts, analysis of case texts, and legal argumentation in general. Other subfields of NLP in the legal domain do not focus on argumentation about the legal significance of case facts, such as technology-assisted review in e-Discovery, contract analysis, and patent search. Similarly, legal question answering, automatic summarization of judgments, legal information retrieval, and models supporting regulatory compliance, although important, are in focus for our argumentation-related narrative. We strive to synthesize a very broad notion of the important role of expert legal knowledge to facilitate better NLP systems that will be of high utility to the stakeholders involved in the ecosystem. In our way, the way forward requires input from diverse perspectives and collaboration across multiple disciplines, including law, computer science, linguistics, and ethics to achieve a comprehensive understanding of the challenges and opportunities. We hope that the insights provided in this paper will stimulate an open discussion within the legal NLP community and beyond.

Ethics Statement

It is important to acknowledge that utilizing historical data to train data-driven models may inadvertently introduce biases into the system. For example, Chalkidis et al. (2022b) investigated disparities in classification performance based on factors such as gender, age, and respondent state in human rights litigation. Similar efforts to scrutinize for fairness and bias have been undertaken by Wang et al. (2021); Santosh et al. (2024a), Li et al. (2022). Moreover, recent pre-trained models can inherit biases encoded within their pre-training data. Therefore, any data-driven legal NLP system intended for practical deployment must undergo rigorous scrutiny to ensure compliance with applicable equal treatment and transparency imperatives. This should encompass their performance, behavior, and intended application.

We reiterate the pioneering work in AI & Law by Buchanan and Headrick 1970, which suggested that the computer modeling of legal reasoning would be a fruitful area for research, so as to foster better understanding of legal reasoning and legal argument formation. While we do not advocate for the direct application of predictive systems within courts, the contributions of this paper are intended to facilitate research in this area to enhance transparency, accountability, and explainability. Our goal is to align NLP systems supporting legal practitioners as closely as possible with legal expertise, and to contribute to the discussion around their ethical use.

References

Michael Aikenhead. 1996. Uses and abuses of neural networks in law, the. *Santa Clara Computer & High Tech. LJ*, 12:31.

Latifa Al-Abdulkarim, Katie Atkinson, and Trevor Bench-Capon. 2016a. Accommodating change. *Artificial Intelligence and Law*, 24:409–427.

Latifa Al-Abdulkarim, Katie Atkinson, and Trevor Bench-Capon. 2016b. A methodology for designing systems to reason with legal cases using abstract dialectical frameworks. *Artificial Intelligence and Law*, 24:1–49.

Nikolaos Aletras, Dimitrios Tsarapatsanis, Daniel Preoţiuc-Pietro, and Vasileios Lampos. 2016. Predicting judicial decisions of the european court of human rights: A natural language processing perspective. *PeerJ computer science*, 2:e93.

Vincent AWMM Aleven. 1997. *Teaching case-based argumentation through a model and examples*. Citeseer.

Basit Ali, Sachin Pawar, Girish Palshikar, Anindita Sinha Banerjee, and Dhirendra Singh. 2023. Legal argument extraction from court judgements using integer linear programming. In *Proceedings of the 10th Workshop on Argument Mining*, pages 52–63.

Basit Ali, Sachin Pawar, Girish Palshikar, and Rituraj Singh. 2022. Constructing a dataset of support and attack relations in legal arguments in court judgements using linguistic rules. In *Proceedings of the Thirteenth Language Resources and Evaluation Conference*, pages 491–500.

Michal Araszkiewicz. 2021. Critical questions to argumentation schemes in statutory interpretation. *FLAP*, 8(1):291–320.

Kevin D Ashley. 1991. Reasoning with cases and hypotheticals in hypo. *International journal of man-machine studies*, 34(6):753–796.

Kevin D Ashley. 2022. Prospects for legal analytics: some approaches to extracting more meaning from legal texts. *University of Cincinnati Law Review*, 90(4):5.

Kevin D Ashley and Stefanie Brüninghaus. 2009. Automatically classifying case texts and predicting outcomes. *Artificial Intelligence and Law*, 17:125–165.

Katie Atkinson, Trevor Bench-Capon, and Peter McBurney. 2006. Parmenides: facilitating deliberation in democracies. *Artificial Intelligence and Law*, 14:261–275.

Katie Atkinson, Trevor Bench-Capon, Tom Routen, Alejandro Sánchez, Stuart Whittle, Rob Williams, Catriona Wolfenden, and LLP Weightmans. 2019. Implementing angelic designs using logiak. Technical report, Technical Report ULCS-19-002, University of Liverpool.

Trevor Bench-Capon. 1993. Neural networks and open texture. In *Proceedings of the 4th international conference on Artificial intelligence and law*, pages 292–297.

Trevor Bench-Capon and Giovanni Sartor. 2001. Theory based explanation of case law domains: 38. In *Proceedings of the 8th international conference on artificial intelligence and law*, pages 12–21.

Trevor Bench-Capon and Giovanni Sartor. 2003. A model of legal reasoning with cases incorporating theories and values. *Artificial Intelligence*, 150(1-2):97–143.

Trevor JM Bench-Capon and Giovanni Sartor. 2000. Using values and theories to resolve disagreement in law. *Legal knowledge and information systems: Jurix*, pages 73–84.

Donald H Berman and Carole D Hafner. 1991. Incorporating procedural context into a model of case-based legal reasoning. In *Proceedings of the 3rd international conference on Artificial intelligence and law*, pages 12–20.

Donald H Berman and Carole D Hafner. 1993. Representing teleological structure in case-based legal reasoning: the missing link. In *Proceedings of the 4th international conference on Artificial intelligence and law*, pages 50–59.

Donald H Berman and Carole D Hafner. 1995. Understanding precedents in a temporal context of evolving legal doctrine. In *Proceedings of the 5th international conference on Artificial intelligence and law*, pages 42–51.

Vithor Gomes Ferreira Bertalan and Evandro Eduardo Seron Ruiz. 2020. Predicting judicial outcomes in the brazilian legal system using textual features. In *DHandNLP@ PROPOR*, pages 22–32.

Floris Bex. 2011. *Arguments, stories and criminal evidence: A formal hybrid theory*, volume 92. Springer Science & Business Media.

Floris Bex, Henry Prakken, Chris Reed, and Douglas Walton. 2003. Towards a formal account of reasoning about evidence: argumentation schemes and generalisations. *Artificial Intelligence and Law*, 11:125–165.

Laurent Bochereau, Danièle Bourcier, and Paul Bourgine. 1991. Extracting legal knowledge by means of a multilayer neural network application to municipal jurisprudence. In *Proceedings of the 3rd international conference on Artificial intelligence and law*, pages 288–296.

L Karl Branting. 1991. Building explanations from rules and structured cases. *International journal of man-machine studies*, 34(6):797–837.

L Karl Branting. 1993. A computational model of ratio decidendi. *Artificial intelligence and law*, 2:1–31.

L Karl Branting, Craig Pfeifer, Bradford Brown, Lisa Ferro, John Aberdeen, Brandy Weiss, Mark Pfaff, and Bill Liao. 2021. Scalable and explainable legal prediction. *Artificial Intelligence and Law*, 29:213–238.

Gerhard Brewka, Stefan Ellmauthaler, Hannes Strass, Johannes Peter Wallner, and Stefan Woltran. 2013. Abstract dialectical frameworks revisited. In *Proceedings of the Twenty-Third international joint conference on Artificial Intelligence*, pages 803–809.

Stefanie Bruninghaus and Kevin D Ashley. 2003. Predicting outcomes of case based legal arguments. In *Proceedings of the 9th international conference on Artificial intelligence and law*, pages 233–242.

Bruce G Buchanan and Thomas E Headrick. 1970. Some speculation about artificial intelligence and legal reasoning. *Stan. L. Rev.*, 23:40.

Martin Caminada and Leila Amgoud. 2007. On the evaluation of argumentation formalisms. *Artificial Intelligence*, 171(5-6):286–310.

Juan Bayón Carlos. 2001. Why is legal reasoning defeasible? In *Pluralism and law*, pages 327–346. Springer.

Ilias Chalkidis. 2023. Chatgpt may pass the bar exam soon, but has a long way to go for the lexglue benchmark. *arXiv preprint arXiv:2304.12202*.

Ilias Chalkidis, Ion Androutsopoulos, and Nikolaos Aletras. 2019. Neural legal judgment prediction in english. In *Proceedings of the 57th Annual Meeting of the Association for Computational Linguistics*, pages 4317–4323.

Ilias Chalkidis, Manos Fergadiotis, Prodromos Malakasiotis, Nikolaos Aletras, and Ion Androutsopoulos. 2020. Legal-bert: The muppets straight out of law school. In *Findings of the Association for Computational Linguistics: EMNLP 2020*, pages 2898–2904.

Ilias Chalkidis, Manos Fergadiotis, Dimitrios Tsarapatsanis, Nikolaos Aletras, Ion Androutsopoulos, and Prodromos Malakasiotis. 2021. Paragraph-level rationale extraction through regularization: A case study on european court of human rights cases. *arXiv preprint arXiv:2103.13084*.

Ilias Chalkidis, Nicolas Garneau, Catalina Goanta, Daniel Martin Katz, and Anders Søgaard. 2023. Lex-files and legallama: Facilitating english multinational legal language model development. *arXiv preprint arXiv:2305.07507*.

Ilias Chalkidis, Abhik Jana, Dirk Hartung, Michael Bommarito, Ion Androutsopoulos, Daniel Katz, and Nikolaos Aletras. 2022a. Lexglue: A benchmark dataset for legal language understanding in english. In *Proceedings of the 60th Annual Meeting of the Association for Computational Linguistics (Volume 1: Long Papers)*, pages 4310–4330.

Ilias Chalkidis, Tommaso Pasini, Sheng Zhang, Letizia Tomada, Sebastian Felix Schwemer, and Anders Søgaard. 2022b. Fairlex: A multilingual benchmark for evaluating fairness in legal text processing. *arXiv preprint arXiv:2203.07228*.

Alison Chorley and Trevor Bench-Capon. 2004. Support for constructing theories in case law domains. In *International Conference on Database and Expert Systems Applications*, pages 508–517. Springer.

Alison Chorley and Trevor Bench-Capon. 2005a. Agatha: Using heuristic search to automate the construction of case law theories. *Artificial Intelligence and Law*, 13:9–51.

Alison Chorley and Trevor Bench-Capon. 2005b. An empirical investigation of reasoning with legal cases through theory construction and application. *Artificial Intelligence and Law*, 13:323–371.

Wentao Deng, Jiahuan Pei, Keyi Kong, Zhe Chen, Furu Wei, Yujun Li, Zhaochun Ren, Zhumin Chen, and Pengjie Ren. 2023. Syllogistic reasoning for legal judgment analysis. In *Proceedings of the 2023 Conference on Empirical Methods in Natural Language Processing*, pages 13997–14009.

Qian Dong and Shuzi Niu. 2021. Legal judgment prediction via relational learning. In *Proceedings of the 44th International ACM SIGIR Conference on Research and Development in Information Retrieval*, pages 983–992.

Stella Douka, Hadi Abdine, Michalis Vazirgiannis, Rajaa El Hamdani, and David Restrepo Amariles. 2021. Juribert: A masked-language model adaptation for french legal text. In *Proceedings of the Natural Legal Language Processing Workshop 2021*, pages 95–101.

Phan Minh Dung. 1995. On the acceptability of arguments and its fundamental role in nonmonotonic reasoning, logic programming and n-person games. *Artificial intelligence*, 77(2):321–357.

Eisner v. Macomber. 252 U.S. 189, 207, 40 S.Ct. 189, 64 L.Ed. 521 (1920).

Mohamed Elaraby, Huihui Xu, Morgan Gray, Kevin D Ashley, and Diane Litman. 2024. Adding argumentation into human evaluation of long document abstractive summarization: A case study on legal opinions. In *Proceedings of the Fourth Workshop on Human Evaluation of NLP Systems (HumEval)@ LREC-COLING 2024*, pages 28–35.

Yi Feng, Chuanyi Li, and Vincent Ng. 2022. Legal judgment prediction via event extraction with constraints. In *Proceedings of the 60th Annual Meeting of the Association for Computational Linguistics (Volume 1: Long Papers)*, pages 648–664.

Pedro Miguel Freitas and Luís Mendes Gomes. 2023. Does chatgpt pass the brazilian bar exam? In *EPIA Conference on Artificial Intelligence*, pages 131–141. Springer.

Leilei Gan, Kun Kuang, Yi Yang, and Fei Wu. 2021. Judgment prediction via injecting legal knowledge into neural networks. In *Proceedings of the AAAI Conference on Artificial Intelligence*, volume 35, pages 12866–12874.

Leilei Gan, Baokui Li, Kun Kuang, Yi Yang, and Fei Wu. 2022. Exploiting contrastive learning and numerical evidence for improving confusing legal judgment prediction. *arXiv preprint arXiv:2211.08238*.

Anne von der Lieth Gardner. 1987. *An artificial intelligence approach to legal reasoning*. MIT press.

Thomas F Gordon. 1993. The pleadings game: An exercise in computational dialectics. *Artificial Intelligence and Law*, 2:239–292.

Thomas F Gordon and Douglas Walton. 2009. Legal reasoning with argumentation schemes. In *Proceedings of the 12th international conference on artificial intelligence and law*, pages 137–146.

Matthias Grabmair. 2016. *Modeling purposive legal argumentation and case outcome prediction using argument schemes in the value judgment formalism*. Ph.D. thesis, University of Pittsburgh.

Matthias Grabmair. 2017. Predicting trade secret case outcomes using argument schemes and learned quantitative value effect tradeoffs. In *Proceedings of the 16th edition of the International Conference on Artificial Intelligence and Law*, pages 89–98.

Matthias Grabmair and Kevin D Ashley. 2011. Facilitating case comparison using value judgments and intermediate legal concepts. In *Proceedings of the 13th international conference on Artificial intelligence and law*, pages 161–170.

Matthias Grabmair, Kevin D Ashley, Ran Chen, Preethi Sureshkumar, Chen Wang, Eric Nyberg, and Vern R Walker. 2015. Introducing luima: an experiment in legal conceptual retrieval of vaccine injury decisions using a uima type system and tools. In *Proceedings of the 15th international conference on artificial intelligence and law*, pages 69–78.

Morgan Gray, Jaromir Savelka, Wesley Oliver, and Kevin Ashley. 2023. Automatic identification and empirical analysis of legally relevant factors. In *Proceedings of the Nineteenth International Conference on Artificial Intelligence and Law*, pages 101–110.

Morgan A Gray, Jaromir Savelka, Wesley M Oliver, and Kevin D Ashley. 2024. Empirical legal analysis simplified: reducing complexity through automatic identification and evaluation of legally relevant factors. *Philosophical Transactions of the Royal Society A*, 382(2270):20230155.

Katie Greenwood, Trevor Bench Capon, and Peter McBurney. 2003. Towards a computational account of persuasion in law. In *Proceedings of the 9th international conference on artificial intelligence and law*, pages 22–31.

Giulia Grundler, Piera Santin, Andrea Galassi, Federico Galli, Francesco Godano, Francesca Lagioia, Elena Palmieri, Federico Ruggeri, Giovanni Sartor, and Paolo Torroni. 2022. Detecting arguments in cjeu decisions on fiscal state aid. In *Proceedings of the 9th Workshop on Argument Mining*, pages 143–157.

Neel Guha, Julian Nyarko, Daniel E Ho, Christopher Ré, Adam Chilton, Aditya Narayana, Alex Chohlas-Wood, Austin Peters, Brandon Waldon, Daniel N Rockmore, et al. 2023. Legalbench: A collaboratively built benchmark for measuring legal reasoning in large language models. *arXiv preprint arXiv:2308.11462*.

Ivan Habernal, Daniel Faber, Nicola Recchia, Sebastian Bretthauer, Iryna Gurevych, Indra Spiecker genannt Döhmann, and Christoph Burchard. 2023. Mining legal arguments in court decisions. *Artificial Intelligence and Law*, pages 1–38.

Jaap C Hage, Ronald Leenes, and Arno R Lodder. 1993. Hard cases: a procedural approach. *Artificial intelligence and law*, 2:113–167.

Peter Hase, Mona Diab, Asli Celikyilmaz, Xian Li, Zornitsa Kozareva, Veselin Stoyanov, Mohit Bansal, and Srinivasan Iyer. 2021. Do language models have beliefs? methods for detecting, updating, and visualizing model beliefs. *arXiv preprint arXiv:2111.13654*.

John Henderson and Trevor Bench-Capon. 2019. Describing the development of case law. In *Proceedings of the seventeenth international conference on artificial intelligence and law*, pages 32–41.

Nils Holzenberger and Benjamin Van Durme. 2021. Factoring statutory reasoning as language understanding challenges. In *Proceedings of the 59th Annual Meeting of the Association for Computational Linguistics and the 11th International Joint Conference on Natural Language Processing (Volume 1: Long Papers)*, pages 2742–2758.

Nils Holzenberger and Benjamin Van Durme. 2023. Connecting symbolic statutory reasoning with legal information extraction. In *Proceedings of the Natural Legal Language Processing Workshop 2023*, pages 113–131.

Zikun Hu, Xiang Li, Cunchao Tu, Zhiyuan Liu, and Maosong Sun. 2018. Few-shot charge prediction with discriminative legal attributes. In *Proceedings of the 27th International Conference on Computational Linguistics*, pages 487–498.

Yunyun Huang, Xiaoyu Shen, Chuanyi Li, Jidong Ge, and Bin Luo. 2021. Dependency learning for legal judgment prediction with a unified text-to-text transformer. *arXiv preprint arXiv:2112.06370*.

Dan Hunter. 1994. Looking for law in all the wrong places: Legal theory and legal neural networks. *Legal knowledge based systems: The relation with legal theory*, pages 55–64.

Wonseok Hwang, Dongjun Lee, Kyoungyeon Cho, Hanuhl Lee, and Minjoon Seo. 2022. A multi-task benchmark for korean legal language understanding and judgement prediction. *Advances in Neural Information Processing Systems*, 35:32537–32551.

Cong Jiang and Xiaolei Yang. 2023. Legal syllogism prompting: Teaching large language models for legal judgment prediction. In *Proceedings of the Nineteenth International Conference on Artificial Intelligence and Law*, pages 417–421.

Xiaoxi Kang, Lizhen Qu, Lay-Ki Soon, Adnan Trakic, Terry Yue Zhuo, Patrick Charles Emerton, and Genevieve Grant. 2023. Can chatgpt perform reasoning using the irac method in analyzing legal scenarios like a lawyer? In *The 2023 Conference on Empirical Methods in Natural Language Processing*.

Daniel Martin Katz, Michael J Bommarito, and Josh Blackman. 2017. A general approach for predicting the behavior of the supreme court of the united states. *PloS one*, 12(4):e0174698.

Daniel Martin Katz, Michael James Bommarito, Shang Gao, and Pablo Arredondo. 2023a. Gpt-4 passes the bar exam. *Available at SSRN 4389233*.

Daniel Martin Katz, Dirk Hartung, Lauritz Gerlach, Abhik Jana, and Michael J Bommarito II. 2023b. Natural language processing in the legal domain. *arXiv preprint arXiv:2302.12039*.

Aaron Russell Kaufman, Peter Kraft, and Maya Sen. 2019. Improving supreme court forecasting using boosted decision trees. *Political Analysis*, 27(3):381–387.

Vladimir Khairoulline. 2007. The discourse of court interpreting: Discourse practices of the law, the witness and the interpreter.

Fred Kort. 1957. Predicting supreme court decisions mathematically: A quantitative analysis of the "right to counsel" cases. *American Political Science Review*, 51(1):1–12.

André Lage-Freitas, Héctor Allende-Cid, Orivaldo Santana, and Lívia Oliveira-Lage. 2022. Predicting brazilian court decisions. *PeerJ Computer Science*, 8:e904.

Yanjun Li, Huan Huang, Qiang Geng, Xinwei Guo, and Yuyu Yuan. 2022. Fairness measures of machine learning models in judicial penalty prediction. *Journal of Internet Technology*, 23(5):1109–1116.

Dugang Liu, Weihao Du, Lei Li, Weike Pan, and Zhong Ming. 2022. Augmenting legal judgment prediction with contrastive case relations. In *Proceedings of the 29th International Conference on Computational Linguistics*, pages 2658–2667.

Yifei Liu, Yiquan Wu, Yating Zhang, Changlong Sun, Weiming Lu, Fei Wu, and Kun Kuang. 2023. Ml-ljp: Multi-law aware legal judgment prediction. In *Proceedings of the 46th International ACM SIGIR Conference on Research and Development in Information Retrieval*, pages 1023–1034.

Zhenyu Liu and Huanhuan Chen. 2017. A predictive performance comparison of machine learning models for judicial cases. In *2017 IEEE Symposium series on computational intelligence (SSCI)*, pages 1–6. IEEE.

Ronald Prescott Loui and Jeff Norman. 1995. Rationales and argument moves. *Artificial Intelligence and Law*, 3:159–189.

Bingfeng Luo, Yansong Feng, Jianbo Xu, Xiang Zhang, and Dongyan Zhao. 2017. Learning to predict charges for criminal cases with legal basis. In *Proceedings of the 2017 Conference on Empirical Methods in Natural Language Processing*, pages 2727–2736.

Luyao Ma, Yating Zhang, Tianyi Wang, Xiaozhong Liu, Wei Ye, Changlong Sun, and Shikun Zhang. 2021. Legal judgment prediction with multi-stage case representation learning in the real court setting. In *Proceedings of the 44th International ACM SIGIR Conference on Research and Development in Information Retrieval*, pages 993–1002.

Fabrizio Macagno, Douglas Walton, and Chris Reed. 2017. Argumentation schemes. history, classifications, and computational applications. *History, Classifications, and Computational Applications (December 23, 2017). Macagno, F., Walton, D. & Reed, C*, pages 2493–2556.

Ejan Mackaay and Pierre Robillard. 1974. *Predicting judicial decisions: The nearest neighbour rule and visual representation of case patterns.*

Robert Mahari, Dominik Stammbach, Elliott Ash, and Alex'Sandy' Pentland. 2023. The law and nlp: Bridging disciplinary disconnects. *arXiv preprint arXiv:2310.14346*.

Vijit Malik, Rishabh Sanjay, Shubham Kumar Nigam, Kripabandhu Ghosh, Shouvik Kumar Guha, Arnab Bhattacharya, and Ashutosh Modi. 2021. Ildc for cjpe: Indian legal documents corpus for court judgment prediction and explanation. In *Proceedings of the 59th Annual Meeting of the Association for Computational Linguistics and the 11th International Joint Conference on Natural Language Processing (Volume 1: Long Papers)*, pages 4046–4062.

Juliano Maranhao, Edelcio G de Souza, and Giovanni Sartor. 2021. A dynamic model for balancing values. In *Proceedings of the Eighteenth International Conference on Artificial Intelligence and Law*, pages 89–98.

Mihai Masala, Radu Cristian Alexandru Iacob, Ana Sabina Uban, Marina Cidota, Horia Velicu, Traian Rebedea, and Marius Popescu. 2021. jurbert: A romanian bert model for legal judgement prediction. In *Proceedings of the Natural Legal Language Processing Workshop 2021*, pages 86–94.

L Thorne McCarty. 1976. Reflections on taxman: An experiment in artificial intelligence and legal reasoning. *Harvard Law Review*, 90:837.

L Thorne McCarty. 1995. An implementation of eisner v. macomber. In *Proceedings of the 5th international conference on Artificial intelligence and law*, pages 276–286.

Masha Medvedeva and Pauline Mcbride. 2023. Legal judgment prediction: If you are going to do it, do it right. In *Proceedings of the Natural Legal Language Processing Workshop 2023*, pages 73–84.

Masha Medvedeva, Ahmet Üstün, Xiao Xu, Michel Vols, and Martijn Wieling. 2021. Automatic judgement forecasting for pending applications of the european court of human rights. In *ASAIL/LegalAIIA @ ICAIL*, pages 12–23.

Masha Medvedeva, Michel Vols, and Martijn Wieling. 2020. Using machine learning to predict decisions of the european court of human rights. *Artificial Intelligence and Law*, 28(2):237–266.

Masha Medvedeva, Martijn Wieling, and Michel Vols. 2023. Rethinking the field of automatic prediction of court decisions. *Artificial Intelligence and Law*, 31(1):195–212.

Sanjay Modgil. 2009. Reasoning about preferences in argumentation frameworks. *Artificial intelligence*, 173(9-10):901–934.

Ankan Mullick, Abhilash Nandy, Manav Nitin Kapadnis, Sohan Patnaik, R Raghav, and Roshni Kar. 2022. An evaluation framework for legal document summarization. *arXiv preprint arXiv:2205.08478*.

Jack Mumford, Katie Atkinson, and Trevor Bench-Capon. 2022. Reasoning with legal cases: A hybrid adf-ml approach. In *Legal Knowledge and Information Systems*, pages 93–102. IOS Press.

Jack Mumford, Katie Atkinson, and Trevor Bench-Capon. 2023a. Combining a legal knowledge model with machine learning for reasoning with legal cases. In *Proceedings of the Nineteenth International Conference on Artificial Intelligence and Law*, pages 167–176.

Jack Mumford, Katie Atkinson, and Trevor Bench-Capon. 2023b. Human performance on the ai legal case verdict classification task. *Frontiers in Artificial Intelligence and Applications*, 379:359–364.

Robert Muthuri, Guido Boella, Joris Hulstijn, Sara Capecchi, and Llio Humphreys. 2017. Compliance patterns: harnessing value modeling and legal interpretation to manage regulatory conversations. In *Proceedings of the 16th edition of the International Conference on Articial Intelligence and Law*, pages 139–148.

Stuart S Nagel. 1963. Applying correlation analysis to case prediction. *Tex. L. Rev.*, 42:1006.

Thanh Tam Nguyen, Thanh Trung Huynh, Phi Le Nguyen, Alan Wee-Chung Liew, Hongzhi Yin, and Quoc Viet Hung Nguyen. 2022. A survey of machine unlearning. *arXiv preprint arXiv:2209.02299*.

Joel Niklaus, Ilias Chalkidis, and Matthias Stürmer. 2021. Swiss-judgment-prediction: A multilingual legal judgment prediction benchmark. In *Proceedings of the Natural Legal Language Processing Workshop 2021*, pages 19–35.

Joel Niklaus, Veton Matoshi, Matthias Stürmer, Ilias Chalkidis, and Daniel E Ho. 2023. Multilegalpile: A 689gb multilingual legal corpus. *arXiv preprint arXiv:2306.02069*.

Mark K Osbeck and Michael Gilliland. 2018. Outcome prediction in the practice of law. *Foresight: The International Journal of Applied Forecasting*, (50):42–48.

Raquel Mochales Palau and Marie-Francine Moens. 2009. Argumentation mining: the detection, classification and structure of arguments in text. In *Proceedings of the 12th international conference on artificial intelligence and law*, pages 98–107.

Anandeep S Pannu. 1995. Using genetic algorithms to inductively reason with cases in the legal domain. In *Proceedings of the 5th international conference on Artificial intelligence and law*, pages 175–184.

Chaim Perelman and Lucie Olbrechts-Tyteca. 1969. The new rhetoric: a treatise on argumentation, trans. *John Wilkinson and Purcell Weaver (Notre Dame, IN: University of Notre Dame Press, 1969)*, 19.

Lothar Philipps. 1989. A neural network to identify legal precedents. In *Proceedings of the 9th Symposium on Legal Data Processing in Europe. Council of Europes*, pages 99–106.

Prakash Poudyal, Jaromír Šavelka, Aagje Ieven, Marie Francine Moens, Teresa Goncalves, and Paulo Quaresma. 2020. Echr: Legal corpus for argument mining. In *Proceedings of the 7th Workshop on Argument Mining*, pages 67–75.

Henry Prakken. 1995. From logic to dialectics in legal argument. In *Proceedings of the 5th international conference on artificial intelligence and law*, pages 165–174.

Henry Prakken. 2010. An abstract framework for argumentation with structured arguments. *Argument & Computation*, 1(2):93–124.

Henry Prakken. 2012. Reconstructing popov v. hayashi in a framework for argumentation with structured arguments and dungean semantics. *Artificial Intelligence and law*, 20:57–82.

Henry Prakken and Giovanni Sartor. 1997. A dialectical model of assessing conflicting arguments in legal reasoning. *Logical models of legal argumentation*, pages 175–211.

Henry Prakken and Giovanni Sartor. 1998. Modelling reasoning with precedents in a formal dialogue game. *Judicial applications of artificial intelligence*, pages 127–183.

Henry Prakken, Adam Wyner, Trevor Bench-Capon, and Katie Atkinson. 2015. A formalization of argumentation schemes for legal case-based reasoning in aspic+. *Journal of Logic and Computation*, 25(5):1141–1166.

Edwina L Rissland, Kevin D Ashley, and Ronald Prescott Loui. 2003. Ai and law: A fruitful synergy. *Artificial Intelligence*, 150(1-2):1–15.

Edwina L Rissland and David B Skalak. 1991. Cabaret: rule interpretation in a hybrid architecture. *International journal of man-machine studies*, 34(6):839–887.

Edwina L Rissland, David B Skalak, and M Timur Friedman. 1996. Bankxx: Supporting legal arguments through heuristic retrieval. *Artificial Intelligence and Law*, 4(1):1–71.

Edwina L Rissland, David B Skalak, and M Timur Friedman. 1997. Evaluating a legal argument program: The bankxx experiments. *Artificial Intelligence and Law*, 5:1–74.

Edwina L Rissland and Xiaoxi Xu. 2011. Catching gray cygnets: an initial exploration. In *Proceedings of the 13th international conference on artificial intelligence and law*, pages 151–160.

Theodore W Ruger, Pauline T Kim, Andrew D Martin, and Kevin M Quinn. 2004. The supreme court forecasting project: Legal and political science approaches to predicting supreme court decisionmaking. *Colum. L. Rev.*, 104:1150.

Olivier Salaün, Aurore Troussel, Sylvain Longhais, Hannes Westermann, Philippe Langlais, and Karim Benyekhlef. 2022. Conditional abstractive summarization of court decisions for laymen and insights from human evaluation. In *Legal Knowledge and Information Systems*, pages 123–132. IOS Press.

Santosh, Nina T.Y.S.S, Baumgartner, Matthias Stürmer, Matthias Grabmair, Joel Niklaus, et al. 2024a. Towards explainability and fairness in swiss judgement predicti on: Benchmarking on a multilingual dataset. *arXiv preprint arXiv:2402.17013*.

TYS Santosh, Marcel Perez San Blas, Phillip Kemper, and Matthias Grabmair. 2023a. Leveraging task dependency and contrastive learning for case outcome classification on european court of human rights cases. *arXiv preprint arXiv:2302.00768*.

TYS Santosh, Oana Ichim, and Matthias Grabmair. 2023b. Zero-shot transfer of article-aware legal outcome classification for european court of human rights cases. *arXiv preprint arXiv:2302.00609*.

TYS Santosh, Tuan-Quang Vuong, and Matthias Grabmair. 2024b. Chronoslex: Time-aware incremental training for temporal generalization of legal classification tasks. *arXiv preprint arXiv:2405.14211*.

TYSS Santosh, Mohamed Hesham Elganayni, Stanisław Sójka, and Matthias Grabmair. 2024c. Incorporating precedents for legal judgement prediction on european court of human rights cases. *arXiv preprint arXiv:2409.18644*.

Tyss Santosh, Shanshan Xu, Oana Ichim, and Matthias Grabmair. 2022. Deconfounding legal judgment prediction for european court of human rights cases towards better alignment with experts. In *Proceedings of the 2022 Conference on Empirical Methods in Natural Language Processing*, pages 1120–1138.

Jaromir Savelka, Kevin D Ashley, Morgan A Gray, Hannes Westermann, and Huihui Xu. 2023. Can gpt-4 support analysis of textual data in tasks requiring highly specialized domain expertise? *arXiv preprint arXiv:2306.13906*.

JURI SAYS. 2020. Prediction system for the european court of human rights. In *Legal Knowledge and Information Systems: JURIX 2020: The Thirty-third Annual Conference, Brno, Czech Republic, December 9-11, 2020*, volume 334, page 277. IOS Press.

Jeffrey A Segal. 1984. Predicting supreme court cases probabilistically: The search and seizure cases, 1962-1981. *American Political Science Review*, 78(4):891–900.

Marek J. Sergot, Fariba Sadri, Robert A. Kowalski, Frank Kriwaczek, Peter Hammond, and H Terese Cory. 1986. The british nationality act as a logic program. *Communications of the ACM*, 29(5):370–386.

Mehmet Fatih Sert, Engin Yıldırım, and İrfan Haşlak. 2021. Using artificial intelligence to predict decisions of the turkish constitutional court. *Social Science Computer Review*, page 08944393211010398.

Rafe Athar Shaikh, Tirath Prasad Sahu, and Veena Anand. 2020. Predicting outcomes of legal cases based on legal factors using classifiers. *Procedia Computer Science*, 167:2393–2402.

Ruihao Shui, Yixin Cao, Xiang Wang, and Tat-Seng Chua. 2023. A comprehensive evaluation of large language models on legal judgment prediction. In *Findings of the Association for Computational Linguistics: EMNLP 2023*, pages 7337–7348.

Andrew Stranieri, John Zeleznikow, Mark Gawler, and Bryn Lewis. 1999. A hybrid rule–neural approach for the automation of legal reasoning in the discretionary domain of family law in australia. *Artificial intelligence and law*, 7(2-3):153–183.

Benjamin Strickson and Beatriz De La Iglesia. 2020. Legal judgement prediction for uk courts. In *Proceedings of the 3rd International Conference on Information Science and Systems*, pages 204–209.

Octavia-Maria Şulea, Marcos Zampieri, Shervin Malmasi, Mihaela Vela, Liviu P Dinu, and Josef van Genabith. 2017a. Exploring the use of text classification in the legal domain.

Octavia-Maria Şulea, Marcos Zampieri, Mihaela Vela, and Josef van Genabith. 2017b. Predicting the law area and decisions of french supreme court cases. In *Proceedings of the International Conference Recent Advances in Natural Language Processing, RANLP 2017*, pages 716–722.

Elizabeth C Tippett, Charlotte S Alexander, Karl Branting, Paul Morawski, Carlos Balhana, Craig Pfeifer, and Sam Bayer. 2021. Does lawyering matter? predicting judicial decisions from legal briefs, and what that means for access to justice. *Tex. L. Rev.*, 100:1157.

Stephen Edelston Toulmin. 1958. The uses of argument.

Dietrich Trautmann. 2023. Large language model prompt chaining for long legal document classification. *arXiv preprint arXiv:2308.04138*.

Dietrich Trautmann, Alina Petrova, and Frank Schilder. 2022. Legal prompt engineering for multilingual legal judgement prediction. *arXiv preprint arXiv:2212.02199*.

Santosh Tyss, Oana Ichim, and Matthias Grabmair. 2023a. Zero-shot transfer of article-aware legal outcome classification for european court of human rights cases. In *Findings of the Association for Computational Linguistics: EACL 2023*, pages 593–605.

Santosh Tyss, Marcel Perez San Blas, Phillip Kemper, and Matthias Grabmair. 2023b. Leveraging task dependency and contrastive learning for case outcome classification on european court of human rights cases. In *Proceedings of the 17th Conference of the European Chapter of the Association for Computational Linguistics*, pages 1103–1103.

Sebastian Urbina. 2002. *Legal method and the rule of law*, volume 59. Springer Science & Business Media.

Josef Valvoda, Ryan Cotterell, and Simone Teufel. 2023. On the role of negative precedent in legal outcome prediction. *Transactions of the Association for Computational Linguistics*, 11:34–48.

Shaurya Vats, Atharva Zope, Somsubhra De, Anurag Sharma, Upal Bhattacharya, Shubham Nigam, Shouvik Guha, Koustav Rudra, and Kripabandhu Ghosh. 2023. Llms–the good, the bad or the indispensable?: A use case on legal statute prediction and legal judgment prediction on indian court cases. In *Findings of the Association for Computational Linguistics: EMNLP 2023*, pages 12451–12474.

Bart Verheij. 2001. Legal decision making as dialectical theory construction with argumentation schemes. In *proceedings of the 8th International Conference on Artificial Intelligence and Law*, pages 225–226.

Bart Verheij. 2016. Formalizing value-guided argumentation for ethical systems design. *Artificial Intelligence and Law*, 24:387–407.

Michael Benedict L Virtucio, Jeffrey A Aborot, John Kevin C Abonita, Roxanne S Avinante, Rother Jay B Copino, Michelle P Neverida, Vanesa O Osiana, Elmer C Peramo, Joanna G Syjuco, and Glenn Brian A Tan. 2018. Predicting decisions of the philippine supreme court using natural language processing and machine learning. In *2018 IEEE 42nd annual computer software and applications conference (COMPSAC)*, volume 2, pages 130–135. IEEE.

Bernhard Waltl, Georg Bonczek, Elena Scepankova, Jörg Landthaler, and Florian Matthes. 2017. Predicting the outcome of appeal decisions in germany's tax law. In *International conference on electronic participation*, pages 89–99. Springer.

Douglas N Walton. 1996. Argumentation schemes for presumptive reasoning.

Yuzhong Wang, Chaojun Xiao, Shirong Ma, Haoxi Zhong, Cunchao Tu, Tianyang Zhang, Zhiyuan Liu, and Maosong Sun. 2021. Equality before the law: Legal judgment consistency analysis for fairness. *arXiv preprint arXiv:2103.13868*.

Donald A Waterman and Mark Peterson. 1980. Rule-based models of legal expertise. In *AAAI*, volume 1, pages 272–275.

Adam Wyner and Trevor Bench-Capon. 2009. Modelling judicial context in argumentation frameworks. *Journal of Logic and Computation*, 19(6):941–968.

Adam Wyner, Raquel Mochales-Palau, Marie-Francine Moens, and David Milward. 2010. *Approaches to text mining arguments from legal cases*. Springer.

Adam Zachary Wyner, Trevor J. M. Bench-Capon, and Katie Atkinson. 2007. Arguments, values and baseballs: Representation of popov v. hayashi. In *Legal Knowledge and Information Systems - JURIX 2007: The Twentieth Annual Conference on Legal Knowledge and Information Systems, Leiden, The Netherlands, 12-15 December 2007*, volume 165 of *Frontiers in Artificial Intelligence and Applications*, pages 151–160. IOS Press.

Chaojun Xiao, Xueyu Hu, Zhiyuan Liu, Cunchao Tu, and Maosong Sun. 2021. Lawformer: A pre-trained language model for chinese legal long documents. *AI Open*, 2:79–84.

Huihui Xu and Kevin D. Ashley. 2022. Multi-granularity argument mining in legal texts. In *International Conference on Legal Knowledge and Information Systems*.

Shanshan Xu, Oana Ichim, Isabella Risini, Barbara Plank, Matthias Grabmair, et al. 2023. From dissonance to insights: Dissecting disagreements in rationale construction for case outcome classification. *arXiv preprint arXiv:2310.11878*.

Shanshan Xu, TYS Santosh, Oana Ichim, Barbara Plank, and Matthias Grabmair. 2024. Through the lens of split vote: Exploring disagreement, difficulty and calibration in legal case outcome classification. *arXiv preprint arXiv:2402.07214*.

Wenmian Yang, Weijia Jia, Xiaojie Zhou, and Yutao Luo. 2019. Legal judgment prediction via multi-perspective bi-feedback network. In *Proceedings of the 28th International Joint Conference on Artificial Intelligence*, pages 4085–4091.

Fangyi Yu, Lee Quartey, and Frank Schilder. 2022. Legal prompting: Teaching a language model to think like a lawyer. *arXiv preprint arXiv:2212.01326*.

Fangyi Yu, Lee Quartey, and Frank Schilder. 2023. Exploring the effectiveness of prompt engineering for legal reasoning tasks. In *Findings of the Association for Computational Linguistics: ACL 2023*, pages 13582–13596.

Linan Yue, Qi Liu, Binbin Jin, Han Wu, Kai Zhang, Yanqing An, Mingyue Cheng, Biao Yin, and Dayong Wu. 2021. Neurjudge: A circumstance-aware neural framework for legal judgment prediction. In *Proceedings of the 44th International ACM SIGIR Conference on Research and Development in Information Retrieval*, pages 973–982.

Han Zhang, Zhicheng Dou, Yutao Zhu, and Ji-Rong Wen. 2023. Contrastive learning for legal judgment prediction. *ACM Transactions on Information Systems*, 41(4):1–25.

Lucia Zheng, Neel Guha, Brandon R Anderson, Peter Henderson, and Daniel E Ho. 2021. When does pretraining help? assessing self-supervised learning for law and the casehold dataset of 53,000+ legal holdings. In *Proceedings of the eighteenth international conference on artificial intelligence and law*, pages 159–168.

Haoxi Zhong, Zhipeng Guo, Cunchao Tu, Chaojun Xiao, Zhiyuan Liu, and Maosong Sun. 2018. Legal judgment prediction via topological learning. In *Proceedings of the 2018 conference on empirical methods in natural language processing*, pages 3540–3549.

Haoxi Zhong, Yuzhong Wang, Cunchao Tu, Tianyang Zhang, Zhiyuan Liu, and Maosong Sun. 2020a. Iteratively questioning and answering for interpretable legal judgment prediction. In *Proceedings of the AAAI Conference on Artificial Intelligence*, volume 34, pages 1250–1257.

Haoxi Zhong, Chaojun Xiao, Cunchao Tu, Tianyang Zhang, Zhiyuan Liu, and Maosong Sun. 2020b. How does nlp benefit legal system: A summary of legal artificial intelligence. *arXiv preprint arXiv:2004.12158*.

Author Index

Androutsopoulos, Ion, 267
Ashley, Kevin, 404
Aspromonte, Marco, 205
Atkinson, Katie, 404
Attali, Hugo, 187

Bambauer, Derek, 303
Barale, Claire, 97
Beauchemin, David, 48
Beek, Ruby, 18
Bernsohn, Dor, 361
Bhattacharya, Arnab, 61
Blair-Stanek, Andrew, 216, 280
Bonifazi, Guglielmo, 176
Bordia, Shikha, 259
Bots, Michiel, 18
Brinkkemper, Sjaak, 18

C R, Chaitra, 1
Carter, Christine, 81
Chakraborty, Dipanjan, 1
Chatterjee, Nishan, 371
Chavallard, Pauline, 166
Cheniki, Nasredine, 233
Chlapanis, Odysseas, 267
Chowdhury, Saurav, 194
Cong Minh, Pham, 336
Contissa, Giuseppe, 205

Daudaravicius, Vidas, 233
De Boer, Maaike, 154
De Faria, Joana, 81
Deroy, Aniket, 61
Dey, Lipika, 194
Doucet, Antoine, 371

Etcheverry, Matias, 166

Feliachi, Abdelfettah, 233
Ferraris, Andrea, 205

Gagnon, Zachary, 48
Gajek, Martin, 176
Galanis, Dimitris, 267
Galli, Federico, 205
Gao, Shang, 176
Gatt, Albert, 18
Gil Semo, Gil, 361
Grabmair, Matthias, 381, 404
Grail, Quentin, 129, 176

Hagag, Ben, 361
Hardy, Didier, 233
Harpaz, Liav, 361
Hautli-Janisz, Annette, 115
Holzenberger, Nils, 216, 280
Hou, Abe, 280
Huu Dung, Nguyen, 336

Inkpen, Diana, 42
Itani, Abed, 115

Joshi, Suyog, 194
Jurayj, William, 280

Kadiyala, Ram Mohan Rao, 318
Khoury, Richard, 48
Kulkarni, Sankalp, 1
Kwak, Alice, 303
Küster, Marc Wilhelm, 233

Liu, Zhihao, 33
Lu, Mengyuan, 33
Lukacs, Gabor, 326

Maity, Subhankar, 61
Mali, Drish, 97
Mali, Rubash, 97
Meghdadi, Nima, 42
Mehreen, Kanwal, 318
Milios, Evangelos, 326
Morrison, Clayton, 303

Narendra, Savinay, 143
Ngoc Mai, Duy, 336
Nguyen, Ha Thanh, 336
Nigam, Shubham Kumar, 61

Ostapuk, Natalia, 176

Pandey, Shashank, 1
Pol, Adrian, 176
Pollak, Senja, 371
Pullakhandam, Siddartha, 318

Quartey, Lee, 129

Rajan, Khalid, 346
Rajaraman, Kanagasabai, 355
Ratnaparkhi, Adwait, 143
Ravi, Sahithya, 326
Real-del-Sarte, Thibaud, 166
Redelaar, Felicia, 154
Rutherford, Jonathan, 81

Sagi, Sai Rama Akash Varma, 1
Saha, Rohit, 361
Satoh, Ken, 243
Sequiera, Royal, 346
Shetty, Kaushal, 143
Shwartz, Vered, 326
Sie, Mika, 18
Siskou, Wassiliki, 115
Spanakis, Gerasimos, 361
Srivastava, Ashay, 318
Staliunaite, Ieva, 243
Steffek, Felix, 81
Surdeanu, Mihai, 303

T.Y.S.S, Santosh, 381, 404
Tan Minh, Nguyen, 336
Tan, Shao Min, 129
Taranukhin, Maksym, 326
Tippareddy, Subhasya, 318
Tomeh, Nadi, 187
Tran, Hanh Thi Hong, 371
Trautmann, Dietrich, 176
Truskovskyi, Kyryl, 361

Upadhyay, Prajna Devi, 1

Vaezipoor, Pashootan, 361
Valvoda, Josef, 243
Van Drie, Romy, 154
Van Durme, Benjamin, 216, 280
Veeramani, Hariram, 355
Verberne, Suzan, 154
Vuong, Thi Hai Yen, 336

Weiss, Cornelius, 381

Xie, Huiyuan, 81
Xuan Bach, Le, 336

Yalavarthy, Rohit, 1

Zhu, Yanzhen, 33

Association for Computational Linguistics
209 N. Eighth Street
Stroudsburg, Pennsylvania 18360

ISBN 979-8-3313-0849-0

CURRAN ASSOCIATES INC.
proceedings.com